BECOMING ATTACHED

ALSO BY ROBERT KAREN

When the Shooting Stops
Top Dog/Bottom Dog

BECOMING ATTACHED

&

*First Relationships and
How They Shape
Our Capacity to Love*

ROBERT KAREN

Oxford University Press
New York   Oxford
1998

Oxford University Press

Oxford   New York

Athens   Auckland   Bangkok   Bogotá   Bombay   Buenos Aires
Calcutta   Cape Town   Dar es Salaam   Delhi   Florence
Hong Kong   Istanbul   Karachi   Kuala Lumpur   Madras   Madrid
Melbourne   Mexico City   Nairobi   Paris   Singapore   Taipei
Tokyo   Toronto   Warsaw

and associated companies in

Berlin   Ibadan

Grateful acknowledgment is given to quote from the following:

The Continuum Concept © 1977 by Jean Liedloff. Reprinted by permission of Addison-Wesley Publishing Company, Inc.

Hospitals and Children: A Parent's eye View by James Robertson. Copyright © 1962 by the Tavistock Institute of Human Relations. Reprinted by permission of International Universities Press, Madison, CT, and by Victor Gollanz, London.

Infancy in Uganda by Mary Ainsworth. Used by permission of The Johns Hopkins University Press.

The Interpersonal World of the Infant by Daniel Stern © 1987 by BasicBooks, Inc. Reprinted by permission of BasicBooks, a division of HarperCollins Publishers, Inc.

Maternal Care and Mental Health (1951) by John Bowlby (WHO Monograph Series No. 2). Reprinted by permission of the World Health Organization, Geneva.

The Nature of the Child by Jerome Kagan. Copyright © 1984 by BasicBooks, Inc. Reprinted by permission of BasicBooks, a division of HarperCollins Publishers, Inc.

Your Child Is a Person by Stella Chess, Alexander Thomas and Herbert Birch. Copyright © 1965 by Dr. Stella Chess, Dr. Alexander Thomas, and Dr. Herbert G. Birch. Used by permission of Viking Penguin, a division of Penguin Books USA Inc.

Excerpts from J. Bowlby's *The Making and Breaking of Affectional Bonds*, which appear on pages 48–49, 50–51, and 363–364, were originally published in Sutherland, J.D. (Ed.). (1958). *Psychoanalysis and Contemporary Thought*. London: Hogarth Press.

Library of Congress Cataloging-in-Publication Data
Karen, Robert.
    Becoming attached: first relationships and how they shape our capacity to love / Robert Karen.
        p.   cm.
    Originally published: Warner Books, 1994.
    Includes bibliographical references and index.
    ISBN 0-19-511501-5 (pbk.)
        1. Mother and infant.   2. Attachment behavior.   3. Mother and child.   I. Title.
    [BF720.M68K37   1997]
    306.874'3—dc21   97-24822

9 8 7 6 5 4 3 2

Printed in the United States of America
on acid-free paper

For Rafie.

CONTENTS

BECOMING ATTACHED

INTRODUCTION

How Do We Become
Who We Are?

Love is the good we all search for, and yet we have different conceptions (and misconceptions) about what it is, ambivalence about how close we want to get to it, doubts about whether we can achieve it or even deserve it. Some of us repeat futile patterns with intimates, mates, and children to the point where we may question whether we are capable of close, satisfying relationships at all. At times it feels as if the shadow of our parents hangs over us like a fate we cannot elude. And we wonder: How much do our childhoods, and especially the quality of our first loving bonds, determine whether we can get love right as adults?

When my son was two and a half, I saw a slightly older boy, perhaps three, fall off a slide in the playground and bloody his lip. He stood, threw his arms in the air, and started wailing, but he made no effort to approach or attract or even look toward his mother who was sitting nearby on the bench. She promptly retrieved him, though, and sat him on her lap. The little fellow continued to wail miserably, his body stiffly unengaged with hers such that one might have thought he was being held by a stranger. The mother, meanwhile, rummaged through her bag looking for a tissue, all the while lecturing in a nonstop, mechanical, somewhat irritable way that seemed strangely disconnected from the boy struggling in her arms.

The child's cut was eventually attended to, but plainly his emotional needs were not. His mother held him with his lower body dangling awkwardly, and she never paused to respond to his cries with a cuddle or a kiss or a loving gaze. Rather she kept up her strange stream of muttered comments parallel to his ceaseless cries. I have heard people in therapy say, "The only way my mother could show love is when I was hurt or sick." But this mother seemed unable to show love in the case of injury. And I felt sure that the pain of not being heard and responded to was greater for this little boy than the pain of his cut lip.

What causes a parent and child to interact this way? What impact does the mother's emotional coldness have on her boy? Did his panicky response to his wound and his failure to approach his mother or even look at her throughout his ordeal reflect his expectation, based on previous experience, that she would not be available emotionally? If what I witnessed in the playground—the mother, in effect, rebuffing her son at a moment when his need for emotional comfort was high—is typical of her parenting style, how much of it is influenced by her son's temperament, which may be unusually demanding or irritable? How much by the quality of her relationship with her husband (assuming she has one), which may be distant and unsupportive? How much by the responsibilities that press on her and the backing she does or does not get from others? Could her response have been predicted by the quality of parenting she herself received?

Finally, to return to the issue raised above, what is this boy going to be like in the future? Assuming, again, that what I saw with his mother is typical, does it necessarily mean that his emotional development will be compromised? That his intimate relationships will be poisoned? That he will be clingy or isolated? Depressed when alone? Unable, despite a thousand efforts, to feel good about himself? That he will be a remote or sadistic father? Or will he manage to leave his early experience with his mother behind, take nourishment from other sources, and become whole in the process? What will determine which path predominates and can he—or someone who loves him—do anything to alter it?

These are some of the paramount questions facing psychologists today. They are part of a many-pronged debate about what children need and how to provide it, a debate about parenting style, day care, adoption, and basic psychology that roars through the halls of academia and out into the legislatures, the press, and the streets. It is a debate that effects not only our children but our hopes for ourselves, spilling over into sometimes bitter disputes about how people change and whether psychotherapy should attempt to deal with early experience and inner dynamics or just chemistry and behavior. The concept of "attachment," born in British psychoanalysis some forty years ago and nurtured to near maturity in the developmental psychology departments of American universities, spins at the center of these scientific and social whirlwinds. It encompasses both the quality and strength of the parent-child bond, the ways in which it forms and develops, how it can be damaged and repaired, and the long-term impact of separations, losses, wounds, and deprivations. Beyond that, it is a theory of love and its central place in human life.

The struggle to understand the parent-child bond touches us deeply because we intuitively sense that our first relationships hold many clues to how we've become who we are. We suspect that what happens between the little boy in the playground and his mother matters a great deal. And the terrible certainty some of us have that we will re-enact the worst aspects of our upbringing with our own children is not only widespread but seems distressingly well-founded. A disproportional number of child abusers were abused children, and clinical evidence suggests that many lesser miseries are passed on as well. What mother hasn't had the chilling experience of making what she assumes will be a legitimate disciplinary statement to her child only to hear some hated aspect of her own mother's voice leap from her throat?

There is no shortage of theories to explain this unwanted inheritance. But empirically verifiable explanations have been elusive. Indeed, until the last two decades, nothing could be said with scientific authority about almost any dimension of the parent-child bond, let alone how aspects of relatedness, good and bad, are transmitted. What early experiences enable a child to feel that the world of people is a positive place and that he has value? How does he become equipped with enough confidence to explore, to develop healthy peer relations, to rebound from adversity? Which of us are at risk of being parents who will raise insecure children, and what can be done to support or change us? Today, with mothers spending less time in the home, and with families falling apart and being reconstituted in new shapes and combinations, understanding all this seems more urgent than ever.

Much begins in infancy, a time when certain fundamental themes of personality and relatedness originate. We have to move beyond our need to be at the center of the universe, to be constantly adored and ministered to. We need to learn to manage our rage, which in the infant is like a cataclysm that seems to destroy everything in its wake. We need to learn that forgiveness and repair are possible. We need to develop the faith that we can nourish and be nourished by others. And yet because our own early experiences are shrouded in amnesia, and because babies cannot give reliable reports on what's going on inside them, infants are strangely alien beings about whose inner processes we can only speculate. Who they really are, whether they're truly "human," how they traverse the developmental stages that psychologists have bequeathed to them, and what their parents really mean to them have always been matters of guesswork, romance, and fantasy, some of it of the most absurd kind. The primitive level of discourse is evident if we recall the starkness of the nature-nurture debate as it existed as recently as fifty years ago.

One strain of thought, represented by the eugenics movement, saw the infant as essentially a genetic construction and believed that the human race could be perfected if substandard seedlings—those with bad health, low intelligence, or poor moral character—could be weeded out. Behaviorally or emotionally disturbed children, like mentally retarded children, were seen as unfortunate products of heredity who should not be allowed to propagate. The genetic view achieved its greatest respectability in Arnold Gesell, the eminent American pediatrician and pioneer in developmental psychology, who first brought attention to the child's inborn maturational timetables. Although Gesell believed that children should be treated kindly, he was convinced that children will pretty much be what they will be regardless of how they are raised: "The inborn tendency toward optimum development," he wrote, "is so inveterate that [the child] benefits liberally from what is good in our practice, and suffers less than he logically should from our unenlightenment."[1]

At the opposite end of the spectrum was behaviorist John B. Watson, a psychologist who believed that children were entirely products of their environment, pieces of clay—or blank slates, as John Locke had written two centuries earlier—that parents and other social forces mold into the final shape. He held that a mother's affection was potentially dangerous to the child's character, that picking up a child when it cried or feeding it on demand were pernicious forms of coddling. In his famous 1928 book on child rearing (published the same year as Gesell's book quoted above), Watson wrote:

Treat them as though they were young adults. Dress them, bathe them with care and circumspection. Let your behavior always be objective and kindly firm. Never hug and kiss them, never let them sit on your lap. If you must, kiss them once on the forehead when they say goodnight. Shake hands with them in the morning. Give them a pat on the head if they have made an extraordinary good job of a difficult task.[2]

Yet a third position was taken by psychoanalysts. Although certain aspects of psychoanalytic thinking stressed the hereditary makeup of the child—in particular the strength of his sexual and aggressive drives and his ease or difficulty in handling them—many analysts saw the infant-mother relationship as important to healthy emotional development. They, too, were environmentalists; but, unlike Watson, they expected the environment to be manifestly loving. Of this latter group, the late John Bowlby was among the most important. Bowlby, the founder of attachment theory, believed that it is in our first relationship, usually with our mother,* that much of our future well-being is determined. In sharp contrast to both Watson and Gesell, he believed that the infant needs and actively seeks affectionate relationships. He wrote:

> When a baby is born he cannot tell one person from another and indeed can hardly tell person from thing. Yet, by his first birthday he is likely to have become a connoisseur of people. Not only does he come quickly to distinguish familiars from strangers but amongst his familiars he chooses one or more favorites. They are greeted with delight; they are followed when they depart; and they are sought when absent. Their loss causes anxiety and distress; their recovery, relief and a sense of security. On this foundation, it seems, the rest of his emotional life is built—without this foundation there is risk for his future happiness and health.[3]

*For simplicity's sake, I will usually refer to the child's primary caregiver as the mother, as Bowlby and many others have done, but it should be understood that a father or a nonrelated adult can also play this role. Similarly, I will usually refer to the child as "he." This convention, which has become controversial lately, is still, I think, the most convenient for the reader, especially in sentences where mother and child are being discussed and using a second female pronoun would cause confusion. But whether the child is called "he," "she," or "it," I am almost always referring to children of both sexes.

Bowlby was part of a broad midcentury trend in philosophy and psychoanalysis that was moving away from seeing people as isolated energy systems and toward seeing them as embedded in relationships. Unlike other analysts, however, Bowlby was also a research scientist who borrowed from animal studies, systems theory, cognitive psychology, and behaviorism in a huge intellectual effort to bring Freud's early theories of motivation up to date. His work was controversial and rejected by most of his peers.

But in the early 1960s Mary Ainsworth, a Canadian psychologist who had worked with Bowlby and shared his views, began conducting research on babies at Johns Hopkins University that seemed to verify much of what Bowlby had been claiming. In a technique that was extremely unusual at the time, Ainsworth and her colleagues closely observed mothers and children in their homes, paying careful attention to the mother's style of responding to the infant in a number of fundamental areas: feeding, crying, cuddling, eye contact, smiling. At twelve months the infant and mother were taken to the lab and observed in what Ainsworth called a "strange situation." What she discovered there would have repercussions throughout psychology, psychiatry, and psychoanalysis, making the paired names "Bowlby and Ainsworth" a cause for reverence and rebuke to the present day.

Ainsworth was able to demonstrate that something she called "secure attachment" between infant and mother was of crucial importance to the child's psychological development and that a certain style of mothering —warm, sensitive, responsive, and dependable—was the key ingredient in bringing this about. Secure attachment was seen as a source of emotional health, giving a child the confidence that someone will be there for him and thus the capacity to form satisfying relationships with others. Insecure (or "anxious") attachment, on the other hand, could reverberate through the child's life in the form of lowered self-esteem, impaired relationships, inability to seek help or to seek it in an effective way, and distorted character development. Subsequent research suggested that close to a third of the children in middle-class American homes suffer from insecure attachment and that it tends to be transmitted from one generation to the next. In poor, unstable homes the percentage is higher.

Attachment research aroused great excitement in the field, partly because it finally offered empirical evidence for the origins of some of our psychological problems, but also because questions about child rearing that had only been speculated about could now be answered with greater authority. For years, to cite an obvious example, mothers had been warned against picking up their babies when they cried. It seemed contrary to nature and intuition, but behaviorist theory asserted that picking up the kid reinforced the crying, and if you did it enough you'd have a monstrous crybaby on your hands. Attachment research seems to have disproved this, at least as a general principle.

Indeed, the great promise of attachment theory has been the prospect of finally answering some of the fundamental questions of human emotional life: How do we learn what to expect from others? How do we come to feel the way we do about ourselves in the context of an intimate relationship? How do we come to use certain futile strategies in a vain effort to get the love we (often unconsciously) feel was denied us as children? How do we pass on our own parenting style to our kids? Attachment researchers have examined the fantasies that accompany insecure attachment. They have attempted to show how different types of insecurity get played out in various childhood disturbances—including excessive aggressiveness, withdrawal, clinginess, and inability to attend to schoolwork. Perhaps its most startling and controversial claim is that insecure attachment, which shows up at twelve months, is predictive of behavior not only at three, five, seven, or fourteen years of age—which has been well established in research—but also at twenty, thirty, and seventy, as people make romantic choices, parent their own children, get into marital squabbles, and face the loneliness of old age. Equally important, attachment researchers have attempted to show how insecure patterns of attachment can change, whether in childhood, as adjustments are made in the family, or later, as the adult attempts to work through his early experiences.

The debate over all this has been heated and at times filled with antipathy, as science took a back seat to politics and personal feelings. Not only have established theories been challenged, but styles of child raising, too; and psychologists, like others, have children, not always raised according to the Bowlby-Ainsworth precepts. The day-care issue has been most explosive. Attachment workers tend to see full-time day care in the first year as a risk, especially for certain children, and Jay Belsky, an attachment researcher at Pennsylvania State University, voiced the concern that if you put your baby in substitute care for more than twenty hours a week, you are invoking a serious risk of his becoming anxiously attached—which could skew all his subsequent efforts to relate with the outside world. Such assertions, needless to say, have drawn tremendous fire and bristle with political implications.

Attachment theory has also been faulted by feminists and working mothers for its nearly exclusive emphasis on the child's relationship with the mother. This has been a problem throughout developmental psychology, partly because mothers are usually the primary caregivers and partly because they are, therefore, more accessible to study. The emphasis on the primary caregiver and on infant experience is important, because so much gets established in that first relationship, so many psychological forces are set in motion. As important as it is, however, observing it in a vacuum leaves out a lot: the father's relationship with the child, which can have a potent effect, especially, in many families, as the child gets older and the father takes a more active role; the parents' relationship with each other, which may be warm, hostile, supportive, or undermining; sibling relationships and sibling order; general family dynamics, which may include other important figures, like grandparents who live in the home; not to mention community and cultural values. When these influences are not included, mothers often feel that the full weight of the child's psychological well-being rests on their shoulders. Most attachment theorists do not believe this—but there has been an evangelical enthusiasm for its findings which, as it spread into the popular realm, included an eagerness for mother improvement and mother blaming.

Classical analysts, behaviorists, and those who emphasize biology and heredity have raised numerous objections as well. Opponents question attachment theory's Darwinian claim that the newborn is "prewired" to seek a relationship with the mother. They reject attachment's explanation of how infants understand, retain, and incorporate experience. Perhaps most important, they dismiss the idea that the vast complexity of the infant-mother experience can be reduced to three or four attachment styles. They are perturbed by attachment theory's failure to pay adequate tribute to inborn temperament, which, some say, may be the real culprit in the tenacity of the patterns that attachment research has described. Indeed, in recent years, with the study of identical twins separated at birth, many of whom show remarkable psychological similarities despite having been raised in different environments, and the study of adoptive versus biological children in the same family, the genetic view has had its own renaissance, which can neither be ignored nor underestimated.

Although fur still flies, the debates provoked by attachment theory and research have caused all sides to make refinements in their thinking, so that now more than any time before, the nature-nurture question has the potential to go beyond its simplistic extremes and toward a synthesis that brings us closer to true understanding.

But I am getting ahead of my story, which is about the discoveries and intellectual battles of the last fifty years that brought us from knowing precious little about the infant-mother bond and parent-child relationships in general—indeed, about whether family ties mattered to the child at all—to the current flowering of knowledge. The story is told through the work of John Bowlby, Mary Ainsworth, and their followers, but at every step of the way their work has been enriched by others, including opponents, and I've tried to give a sense of the many tributaries that have flowed into and helped form this large river of understanding. I expect that for many readers this will be not just a voyage of discovery in child emotional development and its pertinence to adult life but a voyage of personal discovery as well, for it is almost impossible to read about this material without reflecting on one's own life as a child, a parent, and an intimate partner in love or marriage.

It often happens in science—for example, in brain studies, where the destruction of a particular organ or structure has proved to be the breakthrough in understanding its function—that advances in knowledge come in the wake of traumatic circumstances. In the case of the infant-mother bond, the trauma was maternal deprivation—children who'd been separated from their mothers at a very early age or who had no mother at all. In the history of the attachment idea, their plight might be considered the starting point.

Part I

What Do Children Need?

MOTHER-LOVE:
WORST-CASE SCENARIOS

In 1937 New York psychoanalyst David Levy reported the case of an eight-year-old girl I'll refer to as Anna whom he'd observed at the Institute for Child Guidance in New York City. Anna had been adopted at six and a half after an illegitimate birth and years of having been shifted around in foster care. The new parents apparently found her to be an appealing and responsive child. But they were nonplussed by the fact that when she was first shown her new home and her room, Anna had no apparent emotional reaction. Her adoptive mother soon had further cause for concern. While she continued to find Anna "affectionate on the surface," after a few weeks she complained that the child seemed incapable of real affection. She "would kiss you but it would mean nothing." Her husband assured her that there was nothing wrong with the child, that she only needed time; but after a few months he felt the same way. In fact, during this period, he had come to view Anna as deceitful and evasive. Levy said he felt particularly confident that these were loving parents. He noted that their natural child, four years older than Anna, was affectionate and well adjusted.

The parents tried to correct Anna's deceitful behavior, but nothing they did seemed to have an impact. A psychoanalyst was consulted. He recommended that all disciplinary action cease and that the parents substitute greater amounts of warmth. After a while, they felt that this, too, was ineffective. Anna's teacher complained that although she had good intelligence and did well in her subjects, she was inattentive and lacked pride in her work. A year and a half after adoption, none of Anna's iciness seemed to have thawed. "You can't get to her," the father told Levy. The mother said, "I have no more idea today what's going on in that child's mind than I knew the day she came."[1]

In perhaps the most upsetting sentence of his report, Levy said that cases like this were "familiar to everyone who works with children." But, in fact, no one had ever reported them before. Levy, one of the leaders of the child guidance movement in the United States, whose purpose was to effect social reforms in order to prevent emotional damage to children, would go on to great prominence in psychiatry. He was one of a handful of pioneers, a surprising number of them working in New York City at around the same time, who first brought attention to such deeply disturbed children and to a problem that would soon be an international cause: "maternal deprivation."

One senses intuitively that for the tiny child, mother-love, whether it comes from the biological mother or someone who has taken her place, promotes well-being. In the sunshine of her love, we grow and develop, take an interest in things and people, learn, acquire skills, become a proud member of the family. We babble in response to her, smile with her and at her, play special games with her in which we learn to take joy in interaction, check back earnestly to make sure she's still there when we're old enough to crawl away. We feel in a sense a part of her, her wonderfulness making us wonderful, too. Later, as we become aware of our separateness, we feel known by her in a way that helps us know ourselves and that warms us, making us feel loved and secure. These very early years would seem to represent an age when, for many infants, all the corny things ever recited about mother-love seem to glow with a truth untarnished by the ironies, failings, and complexities of later years.

This, despite the fact that, from the baby's point of view, mother-love is not always shining. There are times when mother does not come, when mother is insensitive, when mother does not please us because she doesn't respond or is too stimulating or because we are beyond soothing. Terrible hatreds boil up inside us and the earth darkens. We become filled with murderous wishes. We wail inconsolably, until our blood vessels seem ready to burst. Hell, pure hell, is everywhere. Mother is hell. Baby is hell. But then the sun comes out and the steaming toxins evaporate. Mother-love, pure and unclouded, shines again.

Of course, for many babies, even from their earliest days, mother-love is compromised in fundamental ways. Mother is cold and unresponsive much of the time; mother is unable to meet the needs of a very demanding or temperamental infant; mother is too preoccupied with herself and her feelings of deprivation to give of herself fully; mother is bitter and angry, and her rage boils over in fits. And yet even a troubled, incompetent, or neglectful mother is present in important ways. She feeds, she changes diapers, she takes baby for a walk, she rocks him to sleep. Through all her failings, failings that may haunt her child into his adulthood and old age, rays of mother-love shine through, and the baby has a place where he knows he belongs.

But what is it like for infants who lack mother-love entirely or have it taken away prematurely? Should we follow the analogy all the way, and assume that without it they are as perishable as a plant without sunshine? Do such infants lack the essential template on which to develop the ability to love and to relate to others? What if a child had its basic physiological needs met—food, shelter, a clean and comfortable environment—but lacked the loving relationship? What if he had to wait a while for a mother, till he was a year or two old? Would he be able to recover lost time and become like other children? What if he was shifted around in his early years, posted like a parcel from one mother figure to another, as often happens in foster care or when an extended family cares for a baby after his mother's death? Would a series of mothers be as good as one? What if the child was finally adopted, like Anna, at six or eight? Could normal life commence then? It was in the examination of such extreme questions that our understanding of the infant-mother bond began.

In 1760 a Spanish bishop wrote in his diary, "In the foundling home the child becomes sad and many of them die from sadness."[2] But to many physicians and scientists of the next two centuries, observations such as this seemed needlessly sentimental and even anthropomorphizing: These little creatures were not yet people and could not have real human feelings. They didn't become sad or lonely. If they deteriorated, there were other reasons: They were not hardy; they were broken by disease. But they certainly did not need others in any emotional or psychological way.

Even with the romance of motherhood and maternal bliss that accompanied the industrial revolution—when fathers and their work were removed from the home environment and the home of popular imagination became a feminine haven, free of the competitive harshness of the male workplace—this detached professional attitude toward maternally deprived infants did not appreciably change. Orphaned children or those who had been given up by their parents were still typically raised in institutions in their early years rather than placed immediately into foster care or an adoptive family. Eugenics proponents opposed early adoption on the grounds that it was better to let the child grow a bit and see if it was defective in any way. Prospective parents were encouraged to put off adopting until the child was old enough to match his characteristics with theirs—would the blue eyes stay blue? What color would the hair be when it came in? Was the intelligence quotient high enough?

The preoccupations with antisepsis had meanwhile led to sterile emotional conditions wherever children were cared for, with minimal handling or stimulation. Hospital policy typically forbade parental visits when a child was ill, and it was not uncommon for infants and young children to be in the hospital for over a year without ever seeing their mother. Across a broad front, maternal care and its substitutes placed second to other concerns, and few questioned whether anything was lost in the process.

But as child psychiatry came into being in the 1930s, as the first hospitals began to set aside psychiatric wards for children, and as research attention was focused on children who were brought into the child guidance centers that had sprung up around the nation, a number of disturbing trends were noticed among children raised without a stable mother figure, trends that, if taken together, constituted a silent plague.

David Levy encountered children like the affectionless Anna somewhat accidentally. He was studying another problem, "maternal overprotection"—that is, the emotional impact of mothers who are anxious, overly cautious, and generally infantilizing of their young. As part of his study, he had set up a control group of children who had lacked maternal care in their early years and had failed to make bonds with adoptive parents later on. This control group soon seized his attention. Other cases were as disturbing as Anna's. One concerned the illegitimate son of a woman of high status. The infant had been placed with an agency shortly after birth, put in an orphanage at the beginning of his second year, transferred to a boarding home at twenty-seven months, and finally adopted four months before his third birthday. The adoptive mother complained that the child did not respond to affection, rejected fondling, was unmanageable. By the time the boy was brought to the Child Guidance Center, Levy said, "The mother felt she had been taking punishment for a year and could stand it no longer."[3]

Levy's cases shared many similar features: children shifted around, adopted after several years, often pleasant and affectionate on the surface, indeed indiscriminately affectionate, but seemingly indifferent underneath; lacking pride; and displaying incorrigible behavior problems that often included sexual aggressiveness, fantastic lying, stealing, temper tantrums, immature or infantile demands, and failure to make meaningful friendships. And then there were the parents: pained, frustrated, at wit's end. None of the children seemed able to respond to psychotherapy. In one extraordinary case, a child who had shown no progress in therapy was sent by her adoptive parents to Vienna, where she lived with an Adlerian psychiatrist who treated her for three years. The child returned home with the same emotional flatness and more alarming aggressive symptoms.

Levy concluded that the children he'd observed were suffering from a form of emotional starvation he called "primary affect hunger." By this he did not simply mean hunger for affection, but rather for the full spectrum of human feelings, even including hostility, that arise from daily interaction with a mother. "Is it possible," he asked of these maternally deprived children, "that there results a deficiency disease of the emotional life, comparable to a deficiency of vital nutritional elements within the developing organism?"[4] Levy's paper on this subject, published in the *American Journal of Psychiatry*, made little stir and was quickly forgotten. But unbeknownst to Levy, his question was being asked by other researchers as well.

One of them was Loretta Bender, who headed the new child psychiatry service at New York's Bellevue Hospital. Many of the children on Bender's unit had debilitating organic psychiatric syndromes, like postencephalitic syndrome or autism. Others had no known organic deficits but were nevertheless severely behaviorally disturbed. The majority of them came from two major adoption agencies.

The children from the Jewish Foundling Homes were given excellent pediatric care and were physically healthy. But they had had few social contacts and almost nothing to play with. Bender believed that this accounted for their delayed speech and retarded behavior. After living in these conditions for three or three and a half years, she wrote, "they are placed in a foster home, to which they often cannot adjust, and are subsequently tried in five or six homes, each time becoming more of a problem."[5]

Stella Chess, who worked on Bender's unit at the time, recalls that these children had numerous problems, from inadequate toilet training, to ignorance of how the world worked, to superficial and indiscriminate affectionateness. "They were affectionate to everybody," she says. "The foster parents would find that they would call somebody Daddy who they saw for the first time in the street. One mother got new linoleum, which was the height of luxury in those days, and the kid the next day was pounding holes all through it—he was imitating the guy who put it in. These children had no experience whatsoever, no experience with what was good or bad, so pretty soon they'd be moving to another foster home. And pretty soon they were unplaceable. And at the age of five or six, they'd come onto our unit."[6]

The second organization, the Angel Guardian Home, a Catholic run institution, made "no effort to make the child feel secure." Like many such institutions of the day, the home believed it was wrong for a child to form an attachment to a person who wasn't going to be a permanent parent. They therefore moved the children from one home to the next every six months. By the time the children were five years old, they not only lacked attachments, they appeared to lack any feeling for others at all.[7]

> They have no play pattern [Bender wrote], cannot enter into group play but abuse other children, and cling to adults and exhibit a temper tantrum when cooperation is expected. They are hyperkinetic and distractible; they are completely confused about human relationships, and . . . lose themselves in a destructive fantasy life directed both against the world and themselves.[8]

She classified them as psychopathic personalities and attributed their condition to emotional deprivation during their formative years.

In the pediatric ward at Bellevue, as on all pediatric wards, there was great concern for sterility. Infections had been known to spread virulently wherever children lived in groups, and since Pasteur's discovery of germs in the mid-nineteenth century, there was a constant search for ways to make the infant environment as antiseptic as possible. In Bellevue, for instance, a single white coat was used by each staff member who handled a particular baby. The coat was then hung on a hook inside out, until the next person attending to that child put his arms through it. Signs admonished staff members on the need for sterility, and handling a baby was considered dangerous to its health. Babies in many institutions, like the Angel Guardian Home, were typically prop-fed, the bottle propped up for them so that they wouldn't have to be held during feeding. This was considered ideally antiseptic, and it was labor-saving as well.

That infants in such circumstances did not do well was no secret. It had been reported, for instance, in 1915 that infants admitted to ten asylums in the eastern United States had mortality rates of from 31.7 percent to 75 percent by the end of their second year. In 1920 a German medical journal reported that in one of the great foundling homes of Germany seven of ten infants died in their first year. Although conditions had greatly improved, particularly in the realm of hygiene and nutrition, there was still a 10 percent mortality rate in the best European and American institutions. The condition leading to death was sometimes called hospitalism, or failure to thrive, and seemed to be accompanied by what looked like depression and lost hope. From 1912 to 1922 malnutrition was the most frequent diagnosis of children in Bellevue's infant wards, for which a high death rate was reported. As nutrition improved, the new diagnosis used to account for the sickliness of the ward infants was infection, and those babies that withered away were assumed to be suffering from chronic infections.

In 1942 pediatrician Harry Bakwin, in a paper poignantly titled "Loneliness in Infants," reported:

> To lessen the danger of cross infections, the large open ward of the past has been replaced by small, cubicled rooms in which masked, hooded and scrubbed nurses and physicians move about cautiously so as not to stir up bacteria. Visiting parents are strictly excluded, and the infants receive a minimum of handling by the staff. Within recent years attempts at isolation have been intensified, and a short time ago there was

devised a box equipped with inlet and outlet valves and sleeve arrangements for the attendants. The infant is placed in this box and can be taken care of almost untouched by human hands.[9]

Why, asked Bakwin, do infants in hospitals fail to gain weight when given a diet they would thrive on at home? Why do they sleep less, smile rarely, hardly babble? Why don't they respond to a smile or a coo? Why do they seem so listless and unhappy? Why don't they seem to take any pleasure in eating? Why do infections that last a day or two at home persist for months on end on the ward?

When Bakwin took over the pediatric unit at Bellevue in 1931, he changed the routines. He took down the old signs emphasizing antisepsis ("Wash your hands twice before entering this ward"), and put up new ones: "Do not enter this nursery without picking up a baby." Nurses were instructed to fondle babies periodically and to sit them on their laps. Infection rates went down.[10]

In Bellevue child psychiatry a similar change was occurring. "I still remember," Stella Chess says, "one skin-and-bones infant, a failure to thrive, who landed on the psychiatric unit. This was a kid who was placed in a group home for infants, and he was starving. Loretta Bender put a single nurse in charge of him, and he gradually began to eat more and more. I never knew what happened to him in the end, but I watched him fill out. The nurse on the unit got terribly attached to this kid and the kid to her—you could see it. She'd change his diaper and the poor little thing, who had hardly the energy to move, would try to lift his butt up so that she could slip the diaper underneath."[11]

Bakwin similarly found that the symptoms of hospitalism began to disappear when the baby was placed in a good home, often with a rapidity that he described as "amazing." He wrote that "the baby promptly becomes more animated and responsive; fever, if present in the hospital, disappears in twenty-four to seventy-two hours; there is a gain in weight and an improvement in the color."[12]

Even intelligence was found to suffer in the institutional environment. Another researcher, Bill Goldfarb, a psychologist (and later a physician and psychoanalyst) who worked with Jewish Family Services, compared children raised in institutions with those raised in foster homes. In a remarkable series of studies, he found that institutionalized children at almost three years of age not only suffered from major deficits in their ability to form relationships and function maturely, but had a mean IQ of 68, which is mildly retarded, while the mean IQ of a matched group of children in foster care was 96, which is average. Bender had come to similar conclusions regarding the pernicious effect of institutionalization on intelligence.

The issue of intelligence and retardation was a controversial one, which affected adoption policies. Arnold Gesell, the great Yale psychologist, was among those who opposed early adoption because only time would tell which institutionalized infants were retarded and therefore undesirable to prospective parents. The pioneering child psychiatrist Milton Senn, also at Yale, argued that Gesell's practice of diagnosing institutionalized infants as suffering from "minimal brain damage" was itself mistaken and that it only served to stigmatize the children and prevent their adoption. In a revolutionary move, Senn favored early adoption, which he believed would prevent retardation, a policy that was sharply criticized by Gesell and others.[13]

The debate might have been settled by Harold Skeels and his colleagues at the Iowa Child Research Welfare Station, if their work during the 1930s had not been dismissed and forgotten after being scathingly attacked for lack of scientific rigor.[14] Skeels, who was the first to note the language deficits of deprived children, began with a study of children in severely depriving homes. Observing that older children in such homes had IQs that were consistently lower than their younger siblings, Skeels concluded that, over time, a severe lack of adequate loving attention took its toll on intellectual functioning. In his next study Skeels took a group of preschool children in a sterile orphanage and gave them an ongoing nursery-school experience. Their IQs, which averaged 82, remained stable during this period, while those of a control group from the same orphanage declined. Might they improve even more if they had something approaching real maternal care?

This question led to Skeels' most original and daring study. He placed thirteen institutionalized children, all under the age of two and a half, in a home for older feeble-minded girls. The children were each "adopted" by one of the older girls (or in some cases by an attendant), who took over many typical mothering functions. The touching simplicity of this study lay in the fact that the retarded but affectionate girls proved in these circumstances to be adequate surrogate mothers for children this age. Over a mean span of nineteen months the average IQs of the maternally deprived toddlers in their care rose from 64 to 92. Seven of the thirteen were later adopted by outside families, where they maintained their intellectual functioning.[15] Some thirty years later, when Skeels received the Joseph P. Kennedy Award in belated recognition of his work with disturbed and retarded children, he was introduced by a well-spoken, tuxedoed young man with a master's degree. He reported that he had been one of those children, depressed, withdrawn, deteriorating, "who sat in the corner rocking." As part of Skeels' study, he had been given over to a retarded girl for care and later adopted.[16]

Despite the evidence from the emerging fields of child psychology and psychiatry and from the work of a few radical pediatricians like Harry Bakwin, few people in or out of the medical profession had any idea of the suffering that infants endured when they did not get the routine flow of affectionate care that normal parents cannot help but give. The inertia of old views and old ways of doing things combined with a resistance to painful truths had quietly smothered the evidence. The preliminary medical and scientific views also helped people to distance themselves from children's suffering. It was temporary. It was hereditary. It wasn't really so bad. And the studies that suggested otherwise were flawed and should thus be dismissed. The resistance to seeing the pain of deprived, neglected, or abused children has a long history. Indeed, there has been some resistance to recognizing that children suffer at all. Many psychiatrists long denied that children were capable of experiencing depression. And, as we know, only recently has our society recognized the prevalence of child abuse, which was until the last decade thought to be so rare as not to be worth considering.

Regardless of what theories people adhered to in order to maintain this emotional distance, it seems plain now that the distance was needed because the suffering of children, especially when it is great, is terrible to witness. Even to see a little baby not have his spontaneous gestures responded to is heartrending; and the decline that follows is much worse. People who work with suffering children are sometimes the most hardened. To have to experience for forty hours a week the agony of a child who is too depressed to eat is a great deal to endure. Some way must be found to defend oneself from empathizing with such pain or life will not seem livable.

Also, in the case of institutionalized children, budgets and routines would be threatened with disruption by any effort to give each child individualized care. How would such a thing be paid for? To allow parents to visit their hospitalized children would disturb the nurse's smooth routines, especially since it was known that children who had furiously protested their parents' departure and had, at some length, finally settled down to a state of relative calm became upset and unmanageable after a parental visit. To change adoption policies such that children would be given away at birth, before they suffered institutionalized deprivation, would require a reeducation of numerous bureaucracies, public and private, not to mention the parents they deal with.

But then, in 1947, an unusual film, which would eventually be seen by thousands upon thousands of health care workers and student trainees, was shown to a group of physicians and psychoanalysts at the New York Academy of Medicine. It had been made by René Spitz, a psychoanalyst and a European émigré who was said to have been analyzed by Freud.[17] He was something of an original, considered eccentric by some of his peers, not least of all because he often carried with him a camera, either 16mm or still. He also had an unusual interest in observing infants and children. He had studied with two prominent Viennese psychologists, Charlotte Bühler and Lotte Schenk-Danziger, in the early 1930s, and he was trained to administer baby tests. Once in America, he began his own research, much of it supported by the fees earned from wealthy analytic patients. Spitz had already published a paper on which the film he was showing this night was based, but, like those written by Levy, Bender, Bakwin, and Goldfarb, it had caused little interest.

The film was called *Grief: A Peril in Infancy*. It was silent, crude, black-and-white, with occasional title cards to explain what was being seen. We are in an unnamed institution. In grainy, flickering images, we are shown Jane, a little black baby, just after her mother had been forced to leave her for what would turn out to be a three-month period. She's a happy, approachable baby, smiling and giggling as an adult observer plays with her. We are then shown Jane one week later. It is painful to recognize that this is the same child—depressed, eyes searching, completely unresponsive except, finally, for a tremendous, hopeless, frowning wail. A kindly male observer (actually Spitz himself) cannot soothe the child. She kicks and sobs in terrible agony. A title card tells us that the despairing expression, the tears, and the moaning are unusual at this age and that they lasted the entire three months her mother was gone. Looking at this child, we feel we are experiencing sadness at its ultimate depth, the most profound grief imaginable.

We are now shown a seven-month-old white baby with a happy,

delightful face and inquisitive eyes—an engaging, irresistibly sweet child, playing with Spitz, shaking hands, allowing herself to be picked up, exploring his face. She, too, is a new arrival. The scene changes to a few weeks later. The baby now looks fretful and sad, has bags under her eyes. She is not interested in playing and doesn't respond to a little bell. She looks as if she's been through an unspeakable ordeal. She allows herself to be picked up by Spitz, but her crying does not stop. She seems to be in a state of terror.

Another child, lying dejected on a cot. She does not respond to an observer's efforts to engage her. She refuses to make eye contact. After raising her head briefly and without much interest, she puts it back down on the cot. She is reminiscent of hospitalized mental patients who are so depressed they don't want to get out of bed. The camera lingers on the little girl's blank, dazed face. At last her mouth forms a wide, hollow cry.

The babies we are viewing are in a Mexican foundling home where they receive excellent nutritional, medical, and hygienic attention, but where there is only one head nurse and five assistant nurses for forty-five babies.

A title card explains that if the mother returns in less than three months, the recovery is rapid. But if the separation lasts much longer, the baby continues to display "a frozen, passive, apathetic attitude." Such children, we are told, no longer weep, just wail thinly. They cannot sit or stand. They cannot be engaged. They do not explore. We are now presented with the evidence.

The next baby looks like a concentration camp victim. It is eight months old, but appears to be only three. It seems almost nonhuman.

Now a baby of nine and a half months. Can he really be that old? His shaking is pitiful, his little fist up against his head. A title card explains that his motions are bizarre and "reminiscent of psychiatric disturbances." His despair seems beyond the ability of language to convey.

A ten-and-a-half-month baby. She is emaciated and looks strangely disturbed. She's a beautiful baby, with big, dark eyes, but in another world.

Now a fifteen-month-old who is the size of a three-month-old. She seems to have a skin disease. She smiles at Spitz's approach and then becomes fretful. She just lies there now, as if sick, crying and gnawing her hand.

Title card: "The cure: Give mother back to baby."

It's Jane again, the very first baby, who had seemed lost in inconsolable grief within a week of her mother's absence. Now, three months later, her mother has returned. Jane is playing with a female observer, clapping and laughing and allowing herself to be held. Her world seems once again a place of happiness and sunshine.

In his paper, Spitz had compared these babies to another set of infants that were being raised at a prison nursery in upstate New York. They were the children of delinquent women who were pregnant when sentenced. Unlike the founding home babies, the babies in the prison nursery had regular access to their mothers. They thrived.

The prison babies are shown in the film, exploring, climbing, toddling and flopping about, a stark contrast to the broken babies we've just seen. A healthy and determined little boy is climbing over his crib wall into another baby's crib, head first, legs in the air. The end.

The effect of the film on the audience was emotionally catastrophic. Nothing like it had been seen before. When it was over, one prominent New York analyst approached Spitz with tears in his eyes. "How could you do this to us?" he said.[18]

Spitz, whose reputation as a leading analyst and developmentalist would grow steadily over the next two decades and whose book, *The First Year of Life,* would be read by professionals worldwide, was soon the chief spokesman in the United States on the dangers of maternal deprivation, and he continued his assault on the issue for many years. The impact of the film was not immediate, and the acceptance of its basic tenets was hardly widespread. Its conclusions were hotly debated for a long time. As late as 1981, a textbook in developmental psychology disputed them.[19] But a spark had been ignited. Another maternal-deprivation researcher, a self-confident young Englishman named John Bowlby, would fan it into a fire.

2

ENTER BOWLBY:
THE SEARCH FOR
A THEORY OF RELATEDNESS

In a long-forgotten paper read before the British Psycho-Analytic Society in 1939 and published the following year, John Bowlby, then thirty-
three, outlined his views on the sorts of early childhood experiences that
lead to psychological disorders. He noted that analytic literature had
given only meager attention to this subject and politely suggested that
the reason might be that most analysts, because their time is spent sitting
with adult patients, had little opportunity to investigate what goes on
with children in their early lives. He insisted, nonetheless, that it was
important for psychoanalysts to make a scientific study of childhood
experience and relationships, as important as it is for "the nurseryman to
make a scientific study of soil and atmosphere."[1]

No one, perhaps, had done more than Freud to spread the view that
the child is the father to the man. By this time much of the educated
world thought of psychoanalysis not only as the promoter of the idea of
unconscious motivation but also of the notion that a good deal of what
we are is a result of what our parents did or did not do to us when we
were young. Who had not heard that an overly strict or punitive toilet
training, to cite one obvious example, could lead to such things as fastid-

iousness, compulsiveness, or anxiety about dirt in adult life? Even more widely known perhaps was the idea of early traumatic experience by which Freud had once explained the origin of devastating neurotic conditions. At Bellevue Harry Bakwin had the habit of telling distressed mothers that "there are no behavior-disturbed children, just behavior-disturbed parents"[2] (hardly a comforting idea for parents whose children were organically damaged), and this pronouncement, too, was considered very psychoanalytic.

But, in fact, although psychoanalysis stood firmly for the idea that the roots of our emotional life are found in infancy and childhood, it had expended little effort in working out the effects of upbringing on character development; and the trauma theory, although never forgotten by the public, had been largely abandoned by Freud and his followers. Although informally concerned with the quality of parenting and with the things parents could do to make it easier for their children during the difficult early years, psychoanalysts generally did not view such matters as a serious aspect of their work, and little was written about them in their professional journals. What really interested them now was the developing child's psychic structures and fantasy life, and instead of theorizing about why certain family conditions caused certain children to become disturbed, they sought the bigger picture: the internal conflicts that bedeviled all children as a result of the universal conditions of infancy and early childhood.

Nevertheless, a concern for the child's home life continued to grow markedly in the early decades of the century. Freud's trauma theory had struck a chord, as did the ideas of Adolph Meyer, the great Swiss-born psychiatrist who immigrated in 1892 to the United States. Meyer helped promote both the mental hygiene movement and the development of child psychiatry.[3] Both would come to see the child's early environment as critical in determining later mental health.

But despite the growing concern about the child's home life among child health care workers, no one really knew for certain what aspects of his home life mattered. Certain obvious things were focused on when a child was brought into a guidance center with behavior problems: Did he come from a broken home? Was the house well kept? Was there enough to eat? Were either of the parents drinkers? Did they establish a proper moral environment? Etc. As far as John Bowlby was concerned, however, such questions were almost entirely irrelevant, often reflecting no more than the prejudices of the day. Bowlby argued that in concerning themselves with such issues, child care workers overlooked critical factors of psychological importance. Their reports frequently concluded, "The environment appears satisfactory," when, from Bowlby's point of view, it was not satisfactory at all. "It is surprising what vital facts can be overlooked in a perfunctory interview," he wrote, "the mother being in a T.B. sanatorium for six months when the child was two, the grandmother dying in tragic circumstances in the child's home, the fact that a child was illegitimate and attempts had been made to abort the pregnancy...."[4] Intentionally or not, he said, parents often conceal such unhappy experiences and an interviewer must probe for them.

What mattered, Bowlby said, was not the physical or religious but the emotional quality of the home. And not just the emotional quality at the moment when the child was brought in for treatment, but going back to birth and even before. He pointed to a recent study of criminals in which the authors found in one case that delinquency had "no relationship to early or later unsatisfactory environment,"[5] when, in fact, the child was illegitimate and had been born in a Salvation Army home, facts that begged for further investigation.

While Bowlby believed that heredity could play a role in emotional disturbance, he doubted that hereditary difficulties would lead to neurosis unless the environment had somehow exacerbated them. And having worked in a child guidance clinic for several years, he found it rare that a child brought in for treatment had had an even average psychological environment.

Two environmental factors were paramount in early childhood, Bowlby said. The first was the death of the mother or a prolonged separation from her. To buttress this point, he offered examples of children who had had lengthy separations from their mothers when very young and who subsequently became cunning, unfeeling, thieving, and deceptive — qualities that were similar to what Levy, unbeknownst to Bowlby, had reported in the United States two years earlier.

The second factor was the mother's emotional attitude toward the child, an attitude that becomes apparent in how she handles feeding, weaning, toilet training, and the other mundane aspects of maternal care. One group of mothers demonstrates an unconscious hostility toward the child, Bowlby said, which often shows up in "minor pin-pricks and signs of dislike." Such mothers often compensate for their hostility with an overprotecting attitude — "being afraid to let the child out of their sight, fussing over minor illness, worrying lest something terrible should happen to their darlings. . . ."[6] The underlying hostility emerges, however, "in unnecessary deprivations and frustrations, in impatience over naughtiness, in odd words of bad temper, in a lack of the sympathy and understanding which the usually loving mother intuitively has." Another group of mothers is neurotically guilty and cannot withstand a child's hostility or criticism. "Such mothers will go to endless lengths to wheedle affection from their children and to rebuke in a pained way any show of what they call ingratitude."[7] In either case, the results for the child are lasting emotional damage.

This briefly summarizes the themes of Bowlby's first professional paper. The twin concepts presented there—of maternal separation and negative maternal attitude—would prove rich quarries for Bowlby and those who would eventually follow him. In formulating these ideas, he laid out a point of view to which he would adhere implacably for the next fifty years of his life.

When I met Bowlby in January of 1989, he was a soft-featured man of eighty-two with bushy white eyebrows, thinning white hair, and a proper, somewhat detached, upper-class bearing. He had what Victoria Hamilton, who worked with him for many years, described as "penetrating but responsive eyes beneath raised eyebrows which to me expressed both interest and a slight air of surprise and expectation."[8] He still had an office at the Tavistock Clinic, where he'd worked since shortly after the Second World War, and he lived in an old rambling house opposite Hampstead Heath that he'd acquired around the same time. One of his four children, Richard Bowlby, lived next door with his family.

When Bowlby died nearly two years later, an outpouring of reminiscences paid tribute to the affection, loyalty, and respect he'd engendered. There was some mention, too, of qualities like headstrongness, which might help explain how a young man so new to his chosen field could take positions of such strength despite the opposition of top people. He was often considered aloof and emotionally distant—a quality some attributed to shyness or awkwardness,[9] others to a protective shell that made it difficult for him to express his feelings.[10] Indeed, he rarely spoke of his feelings, was "completely inarticulate" when he tried, and seemed almost without curiosity about himself.[11] One longtime colleague noted that "he was perfectly able to 'take turns,' the essential ingredient of conversation"; but it seemed oddly touching that she should have felt it relevant to state that.[12] Those who came to work under him at the Tavistock

Clinic in later years, having learned in advance of his haughtiness and stubborn, sometimes pugnacious, adherence to his views, were often surprised by his gentle availability and deep fund of affection.

Intellectually, Bowlby was efficient, focused, and formidable—"the most formidable man I ever met," his wife Ursula would later say.[13] At some point in his life, he seems to have become the sort of person who never wastes a minute, never suffers through down time, never fails to understand and integrate everything he's read or studied. Ursula Bowlby thought of his mind as a "smoothly functioning Rolls-Royce."[14] But it was a Rolls Royce with artillery. His aggression showed plainly at times, as when he barked "Bowlby!" into the phone when disturbed by an unwanted call;[15] but he could also manage it masterfully, as when he fielded questions from unfriendly members of an audience with shrewdly pointed replies. In old age Bowlby admitted to having been "a rather arrogant young man," to which Ursula Bowlby adds, "He was also an arrogant middle-aged man and an arrogant old man (he knew he was right, in fact)."[16] Yet he was also very direct, admirably, almost touchingly, incapable of being devious, and possessed, according to his wife and others, of an unshakable integrity. He was also very well-mannered and had an unusual ability to maintain relations with those who held opposing views. He was in almost every respect an old-fashioned English gentleman.

This, then, was the upstart who emerged on the psychoanalytic scene in the late 1930s. Bowlby was brilliant, confident, impatient, decidedly off-putting at times, with a tremendous sense of purpose and not at all inclined to worship existing theories or their makers. In the coming years he would get under a lot of people's skin.

Many of the early child psychiatrists came to the field via pediatrics. That was not the case with Bowlby. Born in 1907, the son of a prominent baronet and surgeon to the king,[17] Edward John Mostyn Bowlby was the fourth child in a family of three girls and three boys. "Mine was a very stable background," he once announced with typical British finality.[18] But whatever Bowlby may have been trying to convey, "stability" here should not be taken to mean warm, secure, emotionally responsive or any of the other qualities that Bowlby believed were so important to a developing child. His parents were conventional upper-class people of their day, with a belief in intellectual rigor and a stiff-upper-lip approach to all things emotional. Although Bowlby never discussed the matter and seems to have put it out of his mind, he did not have happy relations with either of them. His mother was a sharp, hard, self-centered woman who never praised the children and seemed oblivious to their emotional lives; his father, although rarely present, something of an inflated bully.[19] Both parents set themselves utterly apart from their children, handing over their care to nannies and a governess. The children ate separately until each one reached the age of twelve, when, if the child still lived at home, he or she was permitted to join the parents for dessert. The nannydom consisted of a head nanny, herself a somewhat cold creature and the only stable figure in the children's lives, and an assortment of undernannies, mainly young girls who did not stay very long. Bowlby was apparently very attached to one of these young nannies and pained when she left.[20] On the other hand, he and his brother Tony were his mother's favorites, taken on many outings from which the others were excluded. This may have contributed to his uncommon self-confidence.[21]

At eight, Bowlby was sent away to boarding school where he joined Tony, only thirteen months older, with whom he shared a close and fiercely competitive relationship. Bowlby, who would never criticize his parents, later said he'd been sent away because the family was concerned that the German zeppelins would drop bombs on London. But since the other children remained behind, it is more likely that this is simply what upper-class English families did. In any case, he was unhappy, and he later told his wife, in a rare moment of candor, that he wouldn't send a dog to boarding school at that age. Although he never said as much and was probably unaware of it, almost everything he wrote in later years about the needs of young children could be seen as an indictment of the type of upbringing to which he'd been subjected and to the culture that had fostered it.

Bowlby studied at the Dartmouth Royal Naval College and Trinity College, Cambridge. When he enrolled at Cambridge, he was not especially interested in taking up his father's calling but "didn't know quite what else to do" and so studied medicine. He read psychology during his third year, however, was intrigued, and "decided to take it up—whatever that meant!"[22]

In the summer of 1928, Bowlby found himself drawn to the phenomenon of "progressive education"—a radical alternative to the philosophy by which he himself had been raised and educated. The British progressive schools, first started about ten years earlier, were essentially residential schools for maladjusted children and were considered quite beyond the fringe by mainstream educators. The most famous was Summerhill, founded and run by A. S. Neill, who argued that a disciplinary regime was exactly the opposite of what children needed, that it quashed their natural inquisitiveness and stunted their individuality. Instead, children at his school were pretty much allowed to do as they pleased, as long as they didn't impinge on others; and teachers were given special training so that they could be gently available rather than figures of fear and authority. This amalgam of anarchism, utopian socialism, and Freudianism must have struck the proper young Bowlby as quite a good mix, for it remained a cornerstone of his own views for the rest of his life. Almost thirty years later, in a lecture on child care, he would say:

> An immense amount of friction and anger in small children and loss of temper on the part of their parents can be avoided by such simple procedures as presenting a legitimate plaything before we intervene to remove his mother's best china, or coaxing him to bed by tactful humouring instead of demanding prompt obedience, or permitting him to select his own diet and to eat it in his own way, including, if he likes it, having a feeding bottle until he is two years of age or over. The amount of fuss and irritation which comes from expecting small children to conform to our own ideas of what, how, and when they should eat is ridiculous and tragic—the more so now that we have so many careful studies demonstrating the efficiency with which babies and young children can regulate their own diets and the convenience to ourselves when we adopt these methods.[23]

So attracted was Bowlby to the progressive philosophy that he abandoned his medical education and worked as a volunteer at two Neill-like institutions for the next year. Bowlby had little to say about the first school except that it was run by an "inspired manic-depressive" (and veterinary surgeon) named Theodore Faithfull.[24] At the second, a small school in Norfolk, he met John Alford, a troubled war veteran (and later an art teacher in Toronto) who had himself been through analysis and who took the young Bowlby under his wing, turning his attention to all those issues that would become central to the Bowlby canon. Most important, Alford explained the connections between the disturbed behavior that Bowlby was observing at the school and the unfortunate early histories of the children involved. Bowlby joined the staff without pay, receiving board and lodging for six months. He apparently connected well with some of the children, one of whom followed him everywhere and was known as his shadow.[25] He would later say that "everything has stemmed from that six months."[26]

In the fall of 1929, at Alford's urging, Bowlby, then aged twenty-two, enrolled at University College Hospital Medical School and began analytic training, which included his own analysis. Four years later, after completing his degree, he went on to train in psychiatry, while continuing his training in psychoanalysis.

His analyst was Joan Riviere, a close friend and follower of Melanie Klein, whose views were causing a sensation in British psychoanalysis at the time. Bowlby and Riviere were apparently not a good match. She no doubt found him a tough nut to crack, and she complained about Bowlby's critical, questioning attitude toward analytic theory—as if, she said prophetically, he was "trying to think everything out from scratch."[27] She was also known to be something of a bully[28] which could not have sat well with this patient. Their sessions must at times have seemed like polite wrestling matches.

Riviere no doubt saw Bowbly's persistent intellectual protests as resistance to the treatment, which they may well have been. Indeed, although Bowlby was over seven years in analysis with Riviere, seeing her almost daily, she was never satisfied with his progress; while he never gave any indication that she had the slightest impact on his life.[29] It was only with Riviere's reluctant approval—probably arrived at after considerable pressure from her determined young patient—that he qualified for associate membership in the British Psycho-Analytic Society in 1937.[30] When his new wife told him, in partial jest, that she couldn't see how he could "afford both a wife and to continue an analysis which had already lasted seven years (and used up most of his capital)," Bowlby apparently took this as just cause for putting an end to the treatment. (Characteristically, Bowlby spoke little of Riviere afterward. "The only thing he told [me] about her," Ursula Bowlby later said, "was that she was a lady, i.e. out of the top drawer like him."[31])

Meanwhile, in 1936 Bowlby had gone to work half-time at the London Child Guidance Clinic at Canonbury. The child guidance movement had been more or less exported to England through financial grants by the Commonwealth Fund, which supported the movement in the United States. Bowlby was one of the first British psychiatrists to become involved in child guidance, and he found that it provided him

with a singularly compatible home.[32] His three years at Canonbury represented a return to all the things Alford had taught him regarding the
impact of early parent-child relationship. His social work colleagues,
Molly Lowden and Nance Fairbairn, who had had some analytic training
themselves, were taking psychoanalysis in a practical direction that was
uniquely suited to a family mental health center. They would ultimately
have a greater impact on Bowlby's thinking than any of his teachers or
supervisors in analytic and psychiatric training.[33]

Lowden and Fairbairn introduced Bowlby to the idea that unresolved
conflicts from the parents' own childhoods were responsible for the hostile and deficient ways in which they sometimes treated their children.
As a result, the social workers gave therapeutic attention to the mothers
as well as the children, a process that struck Bowlby as immensely sensible. Later he would recall two examples from that period.

> In one a father was deeply concerned about his 8-year-old
> son's masturbation and in reply to my inquiries explained how,
> whenever he caught him with his hand on his genitals, he put
> him under a cold tap. This led me to ask father whether he
> himself had ever had any worry about masturbation, and he
> launched into a long and pathetic tale of how he had battled
> with the problem all his life. In another case a mother's puni-
> tive treatment of her 3-year-old's jealousy of the new baby was
> as quickly traced to the problem she had always had with her
> own jealousy of a younger brother.[34]

But, according to Bowlby, this approach was not mainstream, neither in
child guidance, child psychiatry, nor psychoanalysis, where, indeed, it
was looked down upon by his analytic superiors and caused him troubling
professional conflicts.

Psychoanalysis had certainly played an important part in sensitizing the
public to the dangers of early wounds. In the United States analysts and
analytically oriented workers were frequently among those who insisted
that a child's behavior is a reflection of his home life. A. S. Neill (a
friend and supporter of analyst Wilhelm Reich) and John Alford were
both solidly in the psychoanalytic camp, and almost all of those who did
the pioneering work on maternal deprivation were analysts, as Bowlby

himself would soon discover. But, for the most part, analysts tended to limit their focus to the impact of problems around feeding, toilet training, and exposure of the infant or young child to sexual intercourse between its parents. They were not interested in making a serious science of the way parents treated a child or of the quality of relationships in the family.

Freud had originally argued that neurosis was caused by early trauma. His female patients who suffered from hysteria—which included such symptoms as dizziness, delirium, fainting spells, paralysis of some part of the body—had apparently all recalled having been sexually molested when they were small children, often by their fathers, and Freud determined that that was the cause of their condition. But in a famous about-face, which has in recent years become the source of immense controversy, Freud announced, in 1897, that he had gotten it wrong the first time. He said that the unconscious is unable to distinguish between real memories and fantasies, and, finding it impossible to believe that so many of his patients had been seduced by their upstanding bourgeois fathers— and apparently distressed by the thought that his own father might be among the offenders—he concluded that the memory of seduction was actually the memory of a wish that had been played out in his patients' imagination. Young children, he argued, have a potent erotic drive that naturally causes them to want to have sexual love with their opposite-sex parent and to do away with the same sex parent. Here was born Freud's theory of infantile sexuality and of the Oedipus complex, with the guilty feelings and neurotic tensions that are often left in its wake. Although Freud always acknowledged the possibility of real seduction and real trauma, he never seriously considered the parenting factor again, and he seemed to have little sense of the intricate connections that could exist between the parent's emotional problems and the child's.[35]

It is now impossible, of course, to know whether Freud's hysterical patients were indeed seduced or molested by their fathers or anyone else. But even if they were and Freud made a grave error (as Bowlby and others came to believe), the alternative view he put forth did not inherently contradict the first one and could easily have lived alongside it: Some people become disturbed because they have been sexually abused or suffered other traumatic blows that their young minds were unable to assimilate at the time; but most others who develop neurotic conflicts have not experienced such overt traumas. Many considered the new view to be a victory for common sense. It was, as Charles Rycroft, hardly a

Freudian apologist, says, "the beginning of a new era, one in which it became possible to elucidate the way in which fantasies can distort memory and in which infantile sexual wishes and parental attitudes combine to generate what we now call the Oedipus complex."[36] But although "parental attitudes" may have been an implicit part of the new equation, with the abandonment of the trauma theory, orthodox analysts became disenchanted with almost all environmental issues.

The Oedipus complex, nevertheless, proved to be a gold mine for Freud, because rather than dealing exclusively with the traumatized few it spoke to the human condition and the conflicts inherent in emotional life. In the near-universal triangle of mother, father, and child, love, hatred, and jealousies arise that generate considerable inner conflict, the only difference between the mentally healthy person and the neurotic being one of degree, neurotics exhibiting "on a magnified scale feelings of love and hatred to their parents which occur less obviously and less intensely in the minds of most children."[37] The new view was not only more universally applicable, it was more revolutionary and, in a sense, more humane, for it narrowed the distance between neurotic and ordinary experience, between "us" (doctors, normals, upstanding citizens) and "them" (women, weaklings, defectives).

For children, the oedipal period (about three to five years of age in the standard view) is often a critical point of passage, and for many adults unresolved oedipal feelings are disturbing and frequently distorting of their lives. As a boy grows into a man, his relationships with women and with other men and his attitude toward himself as a man, including whether he is anxious about surpassing his father, are inevitably affected by how he worked through the competitive feelings that arose in the oedipal triangle.

One of the paradoxes of the debate over whether neurosis was caused by the child's own fantasies or actual molestation was the unspoken agreement by both camps that the oedipal theory somehow absolves parents. The assumption is that if a little girl, naturally in love with her father because of her own erotic drives, is haunted in later life by irrational guilt and the need to make unnecessary reparations, the fault for such an unhappy development lies in her. The reason why she, but not another girl with the same natural drives, ends up with neurotic symptoms in later life is that she must have had a constitutional disposition (perhaps her erotic drive was too strong) that made it impossible for her to resolve her Oedipus complex and move on up the developmental lad-

der. But, in fact, such a conclusion is usually unwarranted and t(
least, few analysts would hold to it.

True, neurotic conflicts can arise in the most caring environment.
Although parental behavior almost always contributes to them in some
way, it need not be behavior that we would consider seductive, manipulative, or rejecting. Achieving a completely untroubled adulthood is a
rare, if not impossible, accomplishment in any environment. But it is
also true that if a child has oedipal problems and grows up to be a troubled adult with irrational guilt, disturbing fantasies, and neurotic symptoms, something was probably amiss in the parenting. Clearly, some
parents handle oedipal issues in a way that helps the child develop his
own strength and personhood while maintaining a strong connection to
each of them. Others compete for the child's affections or use him as a
pawn in their struggles. A mother may be dependent on her son's affections and subtly seduce him emotionally, so that he remains caught in
her web rather than free to be his own person and to seek new relationships. She may allow her son to observe her humiliating his father,
thereby not only damaging his sense of maleness but leaving him with
guilty feelings over vanquishing his father. A father may be so dictatorial
with his son as to force him into an unhealthy alliance with his mother.
And so on, ad infinitum, with parallel problems for girls. The fact that
the child's fantasy life may be filled with all sorts of distortions of fact—
that his father hates him, for instance, or that he has injured his father in
some way—in no way alters the fact that parental behavior has left him
in a stew.

Freud's shift to an oedipal and away from a trauma view of the etiology
of neurosis does not, therefore, have to be seen as blaming children or
letting parents off the hook. Unfortunately, psychoanalysis—with much
of psychiatry in its tow—became so taken with the problems of the
child's fantasy life that real-life events were considered fundamentally
less important. Analysts became fascinated by how our unconscious
sexual and aggressive drives get bent, twisted, sublimated into healthy
channels; how they get hidden by reaction formations (compulsive help-
fulness masking hostility) or allowed their pleasures through compromise
activities (verbal aggression making do where physical aggression is desired). Relationships and life experiences were inevitably assumed to play
a part in this process, but that was an afterthought. The main focus was
on the individual and the workings of his unconscious.

In those days, Bowlby later wrote, "it was regarded as almost outside the proper interest of an analyst to give systematic attention to a person's real experiences." The standard view was that "anyone who places emphasis on what a child's *real experiences* may have been . . . was regarded as pitifully naive. Almost by definition it was assumed that anyone interested in the external world could not be interested in the internal world, indeed was almost certainly running away from it."[38]

It was an odd situation, since, in fact, many analysts were well aware that early relationships had an impact, often a deleterious one, and many were sensitive to this issue in their individual practices. Their published case studies attested to this. But important theory making was reserved for the unfolding of the internal world in what analyst Heinz Hartmann would call "the average expectable environment," and to leave aside issues of variation in upbringing. In the writings of leading classical analysts, the nature of a patient's relationships, past or present, often seemed like an incidental matter.

This gap in mainstream analytic thinking brought to the fore new schools of thought. Some Freudian loyalists, like Erik Erikson, attempted to adjust Freud's developmental stages by making them more attuned to social issues. Thus, in Erikson's hands, for instance, the oral stage (when the mouth is the center of the child's biological drives) retains all the Freudian contours but also becomes the time when one does or does not learn basic trust, according to the type of parenting one receives. Other thinkers insisted on more substantial revisions. Object relations theorists (in psychoanalysis the unfortunate word "object" usually means "person") like Melanie Klein, Ronald Fairbairn, Michael Balint, and Donald Winnicott in England, interpersonal and social theorists like Karen Horney, Harry Stack Sullivan, and Erich Fromm in the U.S., and later on family systems theorists, who were mainly nonpsychoanalytic, were all struggling over the relational ground left uncharted by the classical Freudian model. They argued that people are motivated by more than the desire to satisfy instinctual impulses, like hunger and sex; that they also have a primary need to be meaningfully connected to others.

Bowlby's years of analytic training coincided with the early development of object relations thinking among psychoanalysts in Britain, and it was to the development of this theory that he hoped to make a contribution. The object relations movement, begun by Melanie Klein, reflected not only a concern with neglected relationships, but a desire to move beyond neurotic symptoms, like irrational guilt, which was

believed to derive from oedipal conflicts, to the more fundamental problem of character.

This was also a time when analysts first began to see a new type
of patient, less sure of himself and what he should be than the well-to-
do bourgeois whom Freud usually treated. The new patients often felt
empty, didn't know who they were or how they should live, projected
what Winnicott called "false selves," and were assumed to be suffering
from personality distortions that began in infancy, before the oedipal
triangle became an issue. Their arrival in analytic offices demanded a
greater understanding of early relationships and their impact on personality.

Ronald Fairbairn's theory was probably the most compatible with
Bowlby's thinking and must have influenced him. In a bold move,
Fairbairn was in the process of abandoning Freud's drive theory, which
saw people as being motivated mainly by unconscious forces, like sexuality and aggression, which build up inside us and emerge in various ways,
many of them quite disguised. In Freud's theory, the id was the repository
of these powerful amoral forces; it only knew desire, pleasure, and the
urge for immediate gratification. The ego struggled to tame these forces
and find a way to live in the real world, where gratification often has to
be delayed and impulses controlled, and to accomplish this without vio-
lating the strictures of the superego. Fairbairn was the first to argue that
what Freud had underestimated in all this was the need for other people.
He argued that the libido, or sexual energy, was not pleasure-seeking, as
the classical theory held, but person-seeking and that psychopathology
originated in disturbances in early relationships.

But Fairbairn, up in Edinburgh, was not a major player in the Psycho-
Analytic Society of London. His theoretical revisions were considered
impudent and his analytic training substandard. With little more fore-
thought than the toss of a coin, Bowlby threw his lot in with Klein.

3

BOWLBY AND KLEIN:
FANTASY VS. REALITY

Melanie Klein was a brilliant Vienna-born analyst and originator of psychoanalytic play therapy who many believe to be the most important and original contributor to psychoanalysis after Freud. Klein perceived that children in their play communicate a great deal about their inner lives, their relationships, their anxieties—that, in effect, they free-associate through play—and that the analyst, by engaging in and reflecting aloud on their play, could have a profound therapeutic impact. This huge and original contribution was enough to earn her a place in the analytic pantheon, but it was only the beginning of a much larger body of insights that strongly influenced and divided the analytic world.

Freud had observed that people were troubled by conflicting wishes and feelings toward others, and even those who are very close to them are often loved and despised at the same time. He argued that in childhood such conflicts and unwelcome feelings are the rule not the exception, and Bowlby himself would later emphasize this point by speaking of "the stark nakedness and simplicity of the conflict with which humanity is oppressed—that of getting angry with and wishing to hurt the very person who is most loved."[1] The oedipal theory became the focal point of Freud's insights about such ambivalence and inner conflict. Melanie Klein took them much further.

Klein's work with children led her to develop new theories about early mental processes, how they develop, how they are reflected in later life, both normal and abnormal, and how they manifest themselves in the adult analytic situation. It also caused her to see the child's relationship with its mother in a new light. She believed that the child's early relationship with its mother lives within the child and that it becomes a template for future relationships.

Klein began discussing the infant's inner life in unheard of ways. She was one of the few Freudians to take Freud's death instinct seriously and, in so doing, energized his ideas about the links between love and hate and the feelings of ambivalence that haunt every relationship. Klein did away with the idea of the blissful innocent infant and spoke instead of infant rage, paranoia, and agony. She believed that the infant's first relationship is with the breast and that it projected onto the breast all its innate capacities for hatred and love. Indeed, she argued that projection and the distorting power of fantasy are such pervasive forces that the "mother" who lives in the child's fantasy world is considerably different and far more important in many ways than the real mother and that what the real mother does or doesn't do may be completely uncorrelated with the child's later emotional condition.

Because Anna Freud, the other pioneer in child analysis (who a decade later would also emigrate to London), took a sharply different view of theory and technique, the British Psycho-Analytic Society held a symposium in 1927 in which adherents of both sides had a chance to express their views. Joan Riviere, Bowlby's analyst, succinctly summarized the Kleinian position on the distorting power of childhood fantasy: "The boy wishes to be immensely big, powerful, rich, sadistic, as in his imagination his father appears to be. The girl wishes to be radiantly beautiful and adored, possessed of unlimited jewels, finery, children, and so on. Every day we see how little these phantasies tally with what the parents really were and really did and had."[2]

The very young infant is unable to grasp the idea of a person. Even though modern research reveals that newborn babies know the scent of their own mothers and prefer her to others, the baby's neurologic organization is apparently not advanced enough to make sense of individual people. The world is still composed of smaller parcels—breasts, faces, hands—to which the baby responds with pleasure, anger, fear, and whatever other emotions it is capable. Only in the second half of the first year, according to the analytic view, do whole people come into view. It takes much longer yet for the child to integrate good and bad feelings about its mother or anything else in its world: Mother is good when she is satisfying the child, bad when she is not, but never, at this early stage, a whole person comprised of good and bad traits. Drawing on this theoretical knowledge and on the evidence gained from play therapy, Klein assumed that during early infancy the most fundamental "being" in the infant's world is mother's breast and that the infant has a love-hate relationship with it, much as he will later have with mother.

There are moments in his relationship with the breast when what we think of as mother-love is shining brightly. The breast is available, the milk is flowing and sweet, mother is in a relaxed and cooperative mood, and the baby is not overtired, congested, or being pricked by a pin. Now the breast is good. There are other moments, according to Klein, when the relationship sours and the baby not only pushes the breast away but actively hates the breast and feels unloved and rejected by it.

The moments of bliss and misery that the baby experiences at the breast—and what breast-feeding mother hasn't seen both?—are not simply matters of physiological satisfaction or pain, according to Klein. They are relationship moments as well, in which the baby feels cared for and loved or deprived and persecuted. Klein argued, however, that, like many severely disturbed adults, the infant cannot tolerate the idea that its beloved and all-important breast, the giver of sustenance and satisfaction, is sometimes evil, that there are times when the child wants to destroy the very breast it loves and totally depends on. That would generate impossible levels of anxiety. And so, in the baby's immature mind, a necessary split takes place. It imagines two breasts, not left and right, but good and bad, one to love and one to hate. The good breast of the infant's fantasy is all-loving and giving; and this positive image reflects the infant's own capacity for love. In its relationship with the good breast, life itself seems good. The bad breast, on the other hand, is hostile and persecutory, reflecting the infant's innate capacity for envy, hatred, and aggression.

That a tiny infant, unable yet to grasp the idea of a whole person, might have a love affair with the breast seems inherently plausible. But hating the breast and seeing it as a persecutor seems odd. To get a better sense of Klein's vision it helps to imagine what is going on in the child's mind when its needs are not being met, when it feels irritable, when it is screaming itself blue and cannot be comforted. Would this not be a time to hate whatever it was that one held responsible for the conditions of one's life? To feel deprived and persecuted by it? Klein believed that "the young infant, without being able to grasp it intellectually, feels every discomfort as though it were inflicted by hostile forces."[3] And in the early months, before whole persons exist for the child, the breast is felt to be omnipotent and the cause for all that's good and bad in the baby's world. In short order, mommy herself will be seen to have this power and be similarly divided in the infant's mind.

Seeing small children acting out fantasies of mutilating, poisoning, and setting fire to their parents in play therapy gave Klein a new vision of the frustrated infant's violent inner life when the primitive capacities for love and hate rule in a pure and unevolved form, when good and evil are entirely separate, not yet softened by the ambiguities of real life:

> Although psychology and pedagogy [she wrote] have always maintained the belief that a child is a happy being without any conflicts, and have assumed that the sufferings of adults are the results of the burdens and hardships of reality, it must be asserted that *just the opposite is true*. What we learn about the child and the adult through psychoanalysis shows that all the sufferings of later life are for the most part repetitions of these earlier ones, and that every child in the first years of life goes through an immeasurable degree of suffering.[4]

Much of the child's psychic suffering—arising from its own innate, oral-sadistic impulses projected onto the environment—consists of fears "of being devoured, or cut up, or torn to pieces, or its terror of being surrounded and pursued by menacing figures." Of these terrors, Klein wrote: "I have no doubt from my own analytic observations that the identities behind these imaginary, terrifying figures are the child's own parents, and that those dreadful shapes in some way or other reflect the features of its father and mother, however distorted and fantastic the resemblance may be. . . ."[5]

In 1935 Klein enunciated her theory of the "depressive position," which described psychic pain that the child suffers when it dawns on him that the hated mother he wants to destroy is also the beloved mother who cares for him. Whereas before the child had been frightened of being destroyed by hostile forces, it now dreads its own aggression and fears that it will destroy what it loves. Because he still has difficulty distinguishing reality from fantasy, his destructive wishes bring on feelings of "guilt, irretrievable loss, and mourning."[6] This depressive position remains a part of the child and can be activated in later life, especially at times of loss. For some people it forms a prominent part of their adult psychology.

This, briefly and inadequately, is what Klein was beginning to make of the child's internal world based on her analytic work and her own creative leaps, as well as the inclinations of her own personality. Klein's description of infant fantasy life—seething with envy and aggression and filled with "part objects," like breasts and penises, and also excrement—were seen by many as profound forays into the infantile mind, as well as a way to account for some of the mental processes that had been observed in severely distressed or disturbed adults.

But others saw her theories as incredible, even repulsive, and they were soon a source of intense controversy. Could little babies have such fantasies? Could they experience such hatreds and malice? Were they born with such destructive inclinations? Klein had become the adoptive parent of Freud's disturbing and largely ignored death instinct, which pleased Freud to some extent but alienated those who were relieved that Freud had never made too much of it. Her personality was also a matter of controversy. She was an eccentric and difficult person who tended to ensnare and enmesh those around her. She encircled herself with disciples and, unable to tolerate opposition, sometimes organized attacks against those who disagreed with her.[7] She was estranged from her daughter, whom she had analyzed as a child, an act of therapeutic incest that later attracted much criticism. (The daughter, Melitta Schmideberg, herself a British analyst, became an implacable foe of Klein and an early friend and supporter of Bowlby. She later abandoned psychoanalysis altogether.) Some, including Klein's biographer, Phyllis Grosskurth, questioned whether her theories about the instinctive hostility, destructiveness, and (most strangely) envy of infants might not be her way of evading her own shortcomings, apparently quite severe, as a mother.[8] To this day she is remembered by many for being devious and nasty—"a frightfully vain old woman who manipulated people"[9] was John Bowlby's final assessment.

Klein's interests were almost totally opposite to Bowlby's and could in a sense be seen as complementary, although neither of them viewed it that way. Although she acknowledged "that a good relation to its mother and to the external world helps the baby to overcome its early paranoid anxieties,"[10] she certainly did not see those deathly anxieties as originating in reaction to the mother's behavior. Indeed, the mother's behavior was of little consequence to her. She did not really care too much about the child's environment or how its parents treated it. Psychic reality was more important to her than material reality; it was her passion, it was all she really wanted to explore, and she had a genius for it. Riviere echoed this Kleinian disposition when she issued, in the same symposium mentioned earlier, these uncompromising lines:

> Psycho-analysis is . . . not concerned with the real world, nor with the child's or the adult's adaptation to the real world [a direct slap at Anna Freud and her followers, who were concerned with just this adaptation], nor with sickness or health, nor virtue or vice. It is concerned simply and solely with the imaginings of the childish mind, the phantasied pleasures and the dreaded retributions.[11]

By the time Klein came to London in 1926 at the age of forty-four, such views had already made her well known there among analysts, who were excited by her brilliance, creativity, and uncanny ability to find in infant experience antecedents for so much of what they themselves had seen in extremely disturbed adults. Having received the unqualified support of Ernest Jones, who headed the British society, she soon had a major following. It was thus a great honor when Bowlby was informed in the spring of 1938 that Melanie Klein herself would supervise him.

The very first case set the tone. "I was seeing a small hyperactive boy, five days a week," Bowlby recalled. "He was anxious, in and out of the room, all over the place. His mother used to bring him, and her job was to sit in the waiting room and take him home again. She was an extremely anxious, distressed woman, who was wringing her hands, in a very tense, unhappy state." In the child guidance clinic, where Bowlby had now been working for three years, it was customary in such cases to meet with parents and to deal, as far as possible, with their emotional problems, as Bowlby did with the father who was distressed about his son's masturbation and the mother who was anxious about her first child's jealousy of the newborn. "But," Bowlby said, "I was forbidden by Melanie Klein to talk to this poor woman. It was just something that wasn't done, mustn't be done. Well, I found this a rather painful situation really."[12]

Klein took this extreme stance because the child's relationship with the mother did not concern her as much as how it had become internalized in the boy. Besides, she did not much believe in the efficacy of work-ing with neurotic parents, since giving them advice on how to care for their children would probably only increase their guilt and anxiety and make their attitude toward their child worse. "I do not, in the light of my own experiences, put much faith in the possibility of affecting the child's environment," she wrote. "It is better to rely upon the results achieved in the child itself."[13]

To Bowlby, who felt he had seen good results not so much advising parents—which he agreed was useless—but in treating them therapeuti-cally and helping them understand the roots of their own feelings, her rigidity was infuriating and unforgivable. "I held the view that real-life events—the way parents treat a child—is of key importance in deter-mining development, and Melanie Klein would have none of it. The object relations she was talking about were entirely internal relation-ships"—that is, fantasy. "The notion that internal relationships reflect external relationships was totally missing from her thinking.

"After three months the news reached me that the mother had been taken to a mental hospital—she had a state of anxiety or depression or both, which didn't surprise me. And when I came to report this to Melanie Klein, her response was, 'What a nuisance, we shall have to find another case'"—since there was no one to bring the child to treatment anymore. "The fact that this poor woman had had a breakdown was of no clinical interest to her whatever; it might have been the man in the moon who was bringing this boy. So this horrified me, to be quite frank. And from that point onwards my mission in life was to demonstrate that real-life experiences have a very important effect on development."[14]

A few months later all of Britain was mobilized and Bowlby was in the army, washing his hands of Klein (as shortly before he'd done with Riviere) and happily avoiding a confrontation for which he did not feel prepared. He and Klein were poles apart, each taking for granted, and in a sense, dismissing the very things that the other thought most necessary to explore. But despite Bowlby's distaste for Klein, he had been influ-enced by her. He resonated with her belief in the infant's capacity to form early relationships and he was affected not only by her emphasis on the powerful engine of childhood fantasy and its ambivalent swings toward love and hate, but her focus on loss, mourning, and depression as well. Meanwhile, his determination to create a science of the early envi-ronment and its effects on the developing child had been given a potent impetus by her imperious opposition.

4

PSYCHOPATHS IN THE MAKING: FORTY-FOUR JUVENILE THIEVES

When a child cries, "I hate you!" to his mother, the outburst is likely to induce a storm of inner conflict. Will his venomous hatred destroy the person that he loves and depends on? Will he himself be destroyed for his wickedness? The child's conflict will be different at various stages of his emotional growth—depending, for instance, on how developed his moral sense is—but the conflict will be powerful nonetheless and monopolize a great deal of psychic energy. What is he to do with his feelings of hatred? What is he to do with his murderous wishes? How can he hate and love and desperately want to be cared for by the same person? To one degree or another, every child has these feelings of ambivalence toward his parents and the internal struggle that goes with it. By the time he becomes an adult, the inner conflict he experiences over love and hate, the anxiety it produces, and his peculiar way of handling it will have helped define his character.

> If he follows a favourable course [Bowlby said], he will grow up not only aware of the existence within himself of contradictory impulses but able to direct and control them, and the

anxiety and guilt which they engender will be bearable. If his
progress is less favourable, he will be beset by impulses over
which he feels he has inadequate or even no control; as a
result, he will suffer acute anxiety regarding the safety of the
persons he loves and be afraid, too, of the retribution which
he believes will fall on his own head. This way lies danger. . . .[1]

The danger Bowlby perceived was the development of what was
known in psychoanalysis as "primitive defenses." Defenses help wall unwanted feelings out of consciousness. A mother who wants to strangle a
screaming infant may not be able to acknowledge to herself the extent of
her murderous wishes. But if she sweetly sings "Rock-a-Bye Baby," aware
that the lyrics reflect her own desire to see the impossible child crash
down from the treetops, she is managing her anger in a healthy way. She
allows herself to remain at least partly conscious of her feelings, she is
able to handle them in a way that neither harms the child nor divorces
her from her true self, and she perhaps fends off the intensity of her
wrath with humor, which is considered a mature defense.

Like humor, sublimation (hitting a tennis ball instead of the baby) is
considered one of the hallmarks of mature functioning. Other defenses,
like repression ("I'm not aware of ever having wanted to strangle him")
and reaction formation ("I only have the most loving, caring impulses
toward my child at all times"), are seen as neurotic, but are common
nevertheless in many well-functioning people. More primitive defenses,
like passive-aggressiveness ("Gee, I guess I just didn't hear him cry") or
acting out ("I must have pinched him too hard"), while likely to show up
in almost anyone, are typical of immature or adolescent personalities.
The most primitive defenses, like delusional projection ("That baby
wants to harm me") or the outright denial of reality ("We had a lovely
afternoon"), are often seen in people with psychotic tendencies.[2]

In the child's case, if he finds his conflicted feelings toward his mother
or father too terrible to vocalize or even to admit into consciousness, he
may resort to one of the more primitive defense mechanisms to keep
those feelings at bay. In many cases it is not just the hatred that is disavowed in this way but the love as well.

What exactly does the child do? Unable to tolerate his hateful wishes
toward his parent, he may displace these feelings onto a sibling or a pet
and torment them with sadistic behavior. He may dissociate from his
feelings in such a way that he is strangely bland when talking about

things that would normally be upsetting. He may go through a psychic convolution which enables him to believe that he is innocent of aggressive wishes and that they originate in the minds of others, who wish to persecute and destroy him. Or, as we shall see, he may act out his aggression in symbolic ways, like theft, which may simultaneously enact his wish for love. But under no condition must he become aware of his true feelings or the nature of his conflict. As such primitive defensive styles get worked into his developing character, the child becomes a disturbed personality with marked inhibitions, troubling symptoms, and a distorted view of himself and the world.

To Bowlby, of course, the key question in all this was: What conditions in the child's home life might make a favorable adjustment more or less likely? And, virtually alone among analysts, he now went about trying to define these conditions. One problem that he had already identified was the old-fashioned, very British style of parenting, which was impatient with the child's emotional demands, which held that the greatest sin was to spoil children by showing too much concern for their outbursts, protests, or plaints, which was insensitive to the harm done by separating the child from its primary caregiver, and which held that strict discipline was the surest route to maturity. All this he vehemently opposed, advocating in its stead a warmer, more tolerant household, whose hallmark is the ability of the parents to accept the expression of negative emotions:

> Nothing helps a child more than being able to express hostile and jealous feelings candidly, directly, and spontaneously [he said], and there is no parental task more valuable, I believe, than being able to accept with equanimity such expressions of filial piety as, 'I hate you, mummy,' or 'Daddy you're a beast.' By putting up with these outbursts we show our children that we are not afraid of hatred and that we are confident it can be controlled; moreover, we provide for the child the tolerant atmosphere in which self-control can grow.[3]

What many parents do, however, is just the opposite. Believing that feelings like hatred and jealousy are dangerous and must be stamped out, they either punish any expression of it or demonstrate their disapproval by shaming the child and exploiting his guilt. How can he be such an ingrate? How can he cause so much pain to his devoted parents? The effect is to drive the unacceptable feelings underground, creating a guilty and fearful child. What's more, both methods, Bowlby argued, "tend to create difficult personalities, the first—punishment—promoting rebels and, if very severe, delinquents; the second—shame—guilty and anxiety-ridden neurotics."[4]

As Bowlby's views about the impact of parental behavior on children evolved, he was aware that they were considered highly speculative by other analysts, especially his Kleinian colleagues, who steadfastly held that the child's fantasies correlated poorly with reality. He, therefore, sought some means to prove his point. He had hardly begun working at the Child Guidance Center when an opportunity arose.

Years earlier, while still at the Norfolk school with John Alford, Bowlby had encountered an intelligent boy who was dour and remote and who'd been expelled from one of the better schools for stealing. The assumption of Bowlby's colleagues had been, of course, that this boy's thievery was a product of his early experience, which included a rigid nurse and no real mother figure. Now, at the Child Guidance Center, Bowlby began to encounter other young thieves, with similar personalities, and this seemed fortuitous: Could he find something fundamentally similar in their backgrounds?

"I remember one particular small boy who was in constant trouble and seemed impervious to praise or blame. He was very delinquent, and he'd had a disastrous early life. He'd been for nine months in a hospital without any visiting between the age of eighteen months and two years three months, and he had never made any emotional relationship with his parents since. And then another child turned up—a little girl—with a very similar condition and a very similar story." Bowlby believed he saw a cause-and-effect relationship between the early deprivations and the criminal character, an idea, that, he said, "was regarded as mad at the time."[5] While at the clinic, from 1936 to 1939, he collected forty-four such cases aged six to sixteen. Some of the thieving children were depressed, some hyperactive, and some displayed the same detached quality that Levy and Bender were discovering in New York. Bowlby called these detached children "affectionless."

When social workers at the clinic examined the parents of the forty-four young thieves, they found attitudes and behaviors that were more drastically disturbed than the misguided notions of many otherwise normal British families. Claud's mother was "immoral, violent, and nagging." Clifford's mother "extremely anxious, fussing, critical, and hypochondriacal." Lily's mother was "drunken and cruel" and "did not want the child." Fred's mother "shouts and terrifies the children." Kathleen's mother was "extremely unstable and jealous," "had curious sexual ideas about the children and had been seen thrashing dogs in a sadistic way." Leo's mother "alternates between violent domination and sentimentality."

Several of the children had been blamed for a sibling's death. Cyril's mother "openly stated that she wished he had died instead of the baby." Fathers' attitudes were also problematic in a number of cases. Winnie's father "often beat her" and openly favored her younger sister. Reginald's father was "a morose man, who hated the child, shouted at him and gave him neither affection nor presents." Other fathers took no interest in their kids, and some made it plain they hadn't wanted them. Still, the mothers were obviously the primary problem, since they spent the most time with the children. All told seventeen of the twenty-seven children in this group had disturbed mothers.[6]

In trying to understand these children, Bowlby did not make a simple equation between bad mothering and bad behavior. Rather, he wanted to show, in modified Kleinian fashion, how mistreatment was filtered through the child's inevitable fantasies and distortions to produce the unhappy behavioral outcome. He argued that when a mother is irritable, nagging, and critical, when she unnecessarily interferes and frustrates the child, he will become not only angry and aggressive but greedy both for affection and for the things that represent affection to him, like sweets. In such aggression and greed lie the roots of theft. The child's hostility and avarice will at first be directed at the frustrating mother, which will make her all the more irritable, nagging, and critical. And thus a vicious cycle is established that will be incorporated into the child's view of the world and later relationships.

Having disturbed and emotionally abusive parents was not, however, unique to the young thieves. Indeed, there was very little difference in this respect between the thieves and the forty-four nonthieving disturbed children who also attended the clinic and constituted the control group for the study. Bowlby was thus unable to say anything conclusive about the etiology of thievery based on parental behavior. But he was relatively certain that if he were to look at a third set of forty-four normal children, he would not find these gross parental failings. In these prob-

lem parents he felt he had located a clear, if general, source of child emotional disturbance. But he didn't have a third set of children and so even
this aspect of his analysis remained speculative.

Bowlby sensed that such a study was beyond his reach in any case.
While it is easy enough to get anecdotal evidence of parental neglect and
abuse, making a comparison that has any claim to scientific validity is
difficult. How do you rate neglect, mistreatment, unkindness, unrespon-
siveness, abuse, not to mention subtler or more manipulative forms of
bad parenting? How can you be sure that the people who do the ratings
are looking at the same things in the same way? What's more, in interviews, some parents are more forthcoming, some more concealed; and
observing parents in the home over a long period of time is a costly
proposition, which can also be skewed by deception and efforts to stay on
good behavior. In this respect Bowlby's entire goal of creating a developmental psychopathology based on a scientific evaluation of the environment seemed doomed from the start.

But Bowlby found one environmental factor that was easy to document and not open to misinterpretation—namely, prolonged early separations of child and mother, and this was where he turned his attention.

Six-year-old Derek B. was the first young thief Bowlby met at the clinic.
He had been referred for persistent thieving, truancy, and staying out
late. He appeared to come from a normal, happy family, with sensible,
affectionate parents and an older brother who seemed perfectly well
adjusted. Derek's infancy was unremarkable. But at eighteen months he
contracted diphtheria and was sent to the hospital. He remained hospitalized for nine months without ever seeing his parents, which was the
standard procedure at the time. The hospital staff adored him, but when
he came home, he seemed a stranger. He called his mother "nurse" and
he showed no affection. "It seemed like looking after someone else's
baby,"[7] his mother said. Derek so stubbornly refused to eat that he was
finally allowed to starve for a time. After a year and a half, he seemed to
settle down, but he remained strangely detached, unmoved by either
affection or punishment. His mother described him as hard-boiled.

This was not the first impression he gave to Bowlby, who found Derek
to be sociable and engageable, "a genial, attractive little rogue."[8] But his
play was often violent and destructive, and he frequently stole the toys.
In fact, far from being genial, Derek seemed to care for no one, except
perhaps his brother. He preferred to play alone, fought frequently with

other children, destroyed his and their toys, lied to his teachers, and stole from everyone. He spent the money he stole on sweets, which he shared with his brother and other children. He was repeatedly beaten, by both his parents and school authorities, but such punishment seemed to have no impact, except to make him cry for a few moments.

Bowlby diagnosed Derek as an "affectionless character," but he might just as easily have used Loretta Bender's diagnosis of psychopathic personality disorder. Fourteen of his forty-four thieves fell into this affectionless category. Of those fourteen, fully twelve had, like Derek, suffered prolonged, early separations. This struck Bowlby as a stunning finding. Only five of the remaining thirty young thieves, who were not affectionless, had experienced such separations, and only two of the forty-four controls. This discovery—this association between prolonged early separation and affectionless character—would determine the future course of Bowlby's career, placing him in the forefront of the small group of mental health workers who were attempting to warn their peers about the dangers of maternal deprivation.

Derek's history was no more poignant than the other affectionless thieves, the main difference being that he appeared to have come from a less troubled home, most of the others having been illegitimate, unwanted, and generally suffering from the same neglect and mistreatment typical of the families in the study. Betty was seven months old when her pregnant mother discovered that her husband was married to another woman. She threw him out and soon married someone else, but meanwhile she put Betty in foster care. Betty went through a succession of foster homes and a year in a convent school before returning home at age five to her mother, step-father, and two new babies. Raymond's mother died of diphtheria when he was fifteen months old. He lived with his aunt for nine months, then a teenage sister whose care of him was described as "extremely casual"[9] and who would often go out and lock him up alone in the house without food. Norman's mother had tuberculosis and spent much of the time when he was two to five in the hospital. He was looked after by a variety of people during that period. And so on.

Except for their weird detachment, the surface personalities of the affectionless thieves were quite varied. Some gave the impression that they might easily develop into desperate and dangerous criminals; some were apathetic loners, some energetic and active, and some of the latter aggressive and bullying. Only one was overtly cruel. Kenneth, "although full of hard luck stories, was alert and resourceful."[10] A few seemed unnaturally eager to please. Charles washed himself frequently and was very concerned about his appearance.

Some of the affectionless children, if separated from their mothers early enough, when they were still only a few weeks old, did very well with a mother substitute thereafter. These children were traumatized only later when they were ripped out of their second home, sometimes in order to be returned to their first. In contrasting the various impacts of different separations, Bowlby noted that for the separation to be a cause of affectionless character, the child must be old enough—usually six months—to have established a firm emotional tie with his mother figure before being sent away.

There was much variety among the individual cases—the separations occurring at different ages, for different reasons, from families with different emotional climates, and ending in different ways. But each of them had what Bowlby called a "remarkable lack of warmth or feeling for anyone."[11] They were markedly different from almost all the other children in this respect. They tended to be solitary and unresponsive, impervious to punishment, indifferent to kindness. Foster parents typically complained that they could not reach these children—"We never seem to get near her" was a typical lament. The children wandered away from home, as if the very concept of home did not matter much to them. (Kenneth stayed away for a week once, sleeping in empty houses, after a mild altercation.) They were frequently truant from school. Many lied brazenly and had no real friendships. In a short interview they often made a good impression. But Bowlby quickly learned that their amiability was superficial and signified no authentic openness. He believed they formed the hard core of repeat offenders in the criminal population. (He need only have looked as far as John Dillinger, America's most famous desperado of that era, to have found an example of a hard-boiled career criminal whose childhood was very similar to that of the youngsters he observed.) But beneath the antisocial attitudes Bowlby saw a profound and unreachable depression, as if, when they lost their loving universe, a switch turned off in them that could not be turned back on. "Behind the mask of indifference," he wrote, "is bottomless misery and behind the apparent callousness despair."[12]

The attitudes of these haunted children toward material things gave uncanny voice to their inner torments, and Bowlby now turned his attention to the symbolic meaning of their behavior. In doing so, he would attempt to show that although the children's fantasies were full of distortions, the distortions were nevertheless stimulated by real experiences that were beyond their capacity to work through.

Although all stole repeatedly and compulsively, the thefts were often pointless, and two of the boys would destroy any presents given to them. Albert stole a bicycle despite having one of his own. Charles stole "a tin of baking powder, his father's razors, army discharge badge, and a bullet."[13] Roy stole toys from shops and rabbits, which he killed. Nansi stole money from her teacher's bag, from the landlady's pocket, from a Salvation Army box, which she pried open with a knife. Several of them robbed the psychiatrist during play, making off with one or more of the toys, even if they had already been given one. None of them seemed to have any sense of the meaning of what they had done. They could not say why they stole, and they seemed impervious to the wrong they had done to others.

A child who's been separated from his mother, Bowlby argued, not only craves her love but also the symbols of her love. And so, typically, the young thieves stole milk, food, or money to buy food. These are the things they naturally associate with gratification. Often they stole from their mothers, like Norman K., who broke into his mother's money box —a tragically perfect symbolic act, suggesting envy of what the mother has and is refusing to bestow on him, that Klein would have loved. Such wild and pathetic cravings and their ability to endure into adult life was epitomized for Bowlby by an adult patient he had at the time who took her morning tea from a baby bottle. He predicted that such longings, incorporated into the personalities of the affectionless children, would eventually be acted out sexually as well, and that many of the affectionless girls would become prostitutes, a supposition he supported with figures drawn from a League of Nations survey showing that a high proportion of prostitutes suffered severe early separations.

All children are subject to cravings and hostilities directed at their parents. But usually such impulses are checked as the young child develops a superego, a watchful inner monitor of right and wrong that some analysts believe first comes into being as the child realizes that the hated mother is the same person as the loved mother and wants to protect her from his rage and hostility. Bowlby suggested that the affectionless thieves lacked superego controls because their loving feelings had either never had the opportunity to develop or had been swamped by rage. Some children were removed from their mother at a time when their love for her was only beginning to coalesce (typically in the second half of the first year). Others, having established loving ties, were ripped out of their homes and somehow "expected to settle down cheerfully with strangers." Such children not only hated their foster mothers but hated their real mothers as well, and would typically have nothing to do with them if they visited and icily avoided them for long periods when and if they returned home.

To hate one's mother, Bowlby said (echoing Klein), is to conjure up a picture of her that is hateful and malicious. "Phantasy, born of rage," he said, "distorts the picture of the real mother. A kindly mother who has to put her child in hospital, a frustrating yet well-meaning mother and a really unkind mother can, by this process, alike come to be regarded as malicious and hostile figures."

> Normally [he wrote], when such phantasies arise in children, they are soon corrected to some degree by contact with the real mother, who, whatever her shortcomings, is never so bad as the bad mother which the child pictures to himself when he is in a rage. . . . But where a child does not see his mother for many months there is no opportunity for this correction of phantasy by reality-testing to operate. Extravagant phantasies of the kind described then become so entrenched that, when the child returns to the real situation, he can see it in no terms but those of his phantasies.[14]

People who grow up hating their parents invariably hate themselves as well. If we see them as malicious beings, how can we ourselves, who are so identified with them, be any better? What's more, to have such hateful feelings toward someone we feel we should love makes us feel all the more despicable. Thus, little Leo, who sported a devil-may-care attitude, also suffered pangs of suicidal depression. "I know I'm a wicked boy," he told his mother on one occasion. "You had better murder me, then I will be out of your life."[15]

The adults who tried to work with these children were repeatedly frustrated and infuriated by their hard-boiledness—a quality that Bowlby attributed to their determination never to be hurt again. Sometimes the indifference to others was only skin-deep. But they all presented themselves as utterly uninterested in affection or hostility, thereby disarming everyone they met of the power to affect them.

By this process Bowlby believed the affectionless thieves had become locked in a painful isolation that would imprison them forever, their hunger for love and their rage at its absence only showing itself in eruptions of meaningless sex, theft, and aggression. Were they utterly beyond reach? Not necessarily. But the task of establishing the love and trust necessary for a healing connection had become woefully complicated and perhaps beyond the capacity of the average parent to cope with.

Bowlby saw the tragic internal prison in which these children were trapped as an extreme manifestation of what other children suffer on a smaller scale. But in these extreme cases and in the separations that seemed to contribute so profoundly to their cause, he had the wedge he was seeking to open the debate on the impact of parenting and early experience on emotional development.

Written mainly in 1940, Bowlby's paper "Forty-four Juvenile Thieves: Their Characters and Home-Life," was finally published in the *International Journal of Psycho-Analysis* in 1944, after he came out of the army. The paper, Bowlby believed, benefited considerably from the influence of a group of army psychologists who had helped turn him into a research scientist during the war. In 1946 it was republished as a monograph, which gave it a second life and a wider readership.

The paper shows all the trademarks that characterize his later writing. It is beautifully and simply written. Aside from a few technical terms, virtually any intelligent person could read and understand it and be moved by it. His prose is clear and direct. He uses metaphors, many of them drawn from medicine, that forcefully drive home his themes. Thus: "Theft, like rheumatic fever, is a disease of childhood and adolescence, and, as in rheumatic fever, attacks in later life are frequently in the nature of recurrences."[16] He shows an unusual concern with matters outside the realm of psychiatry—in particular, with social problems and social policy; and he clearly believes that his work can be of service to more than psychiatric patients. In dealing with the contributions of others, he does not stir up fights or waste the reader's time with lengthy refutations of established views—no attacks, no bitterness, no pointed statements, no attempt to aggrandize himself in any way. He just states the facts as he sees them and keeps his feelings to himself regarding whatever inadequacies may exist in the theories he's building upon or implicitly disputing. When disagreeing, he does so plainly and quickly, without rancor or innuendo, and then moves on to an elaboration of his own view. His adaptation of Melanie Klein's material on child fantasy shows what will be a characteristic Bowlby trademark—an unhesitant acceptance of whatever he finds useful, regardless of its source, and a willingness to generously credit even those whom he dislikes or who have denounced his views. His voice is upstanding, sensible, and authoritative.

Further research would eventually establish that separations, even long separations, do not in themselves cause a child to become a psychopathic personality. It's the *depriving* separation that's so calamitous, where the child never has a chance to develop a true attachment; where there's no alternative mother figure to take up where the first mother left off and perhaps to keep her memory alive; or where there are, early on, a series of short-term mother figures and thus repeated losses, all of which cause a bitterness and mistrust to develop and the shutting down in the child of his natural tendency to reach out for love and connection. In all this, Bowlby's thinking would be largely validated; although his failure to make the distinction between types of separation would cause some enduring misunderstandings.[17] Later research would also find that where delinquency is a factor, separation is not the only cause; it is often preceded by distortions in the parent-child relationship, often with the father.[18] Meanwhile Bowlby's broad point, about the danger of early depriving separations, not only in terms of the suffering it causes but in its disturbing impact on character formation, had been made in a powerful way. His study would help inspire a revolution in child psychiatry, especially after it came to the attention of an important official at the newly founded United Nations.

5

CALL TO ARMS:
THE WORLD HEALTH REPORT

In 1948 the Social Commission of the United Nations decided to commission a study of the problems and needs of homeless children, a major concern in postwar Europe. Ronald Hargreaves, chief of the Mental Health Section of the World Health Organization in Geneva, was eager to get the WHO involved by reporting on the psychiatric aspects of the issue. Hargreaves, who'd met Bowlby in the army during the war, had been impressed with his monograph on the young thieves. Indeed, he had already proposed that Bowlby do a report for the WHO on juvenile delinquency, which Bowlby rejected. He now approached Bowlby again, this time suggesting a psychiatric report on homeless children. Bowlby promptly agreed. In 1950 he moved to Geneva for six months to investigate and write a report that would have ramifications in psychiatry, adoption procedures, and ordinary home life around the world.

Bowlby spent six weeks gathering data on the Continent—in France, Sweden, Switzerland, Holland—and then five weeks in the United States, using the opportunity to communicate with social workers and child psychiatrists (including David Levy, William Goldfarb, Milton Senn, and René Spitz) and to become acquainted with the literature. He found an unexpected gold mine: Levy writing about adopted children who were deceitful and eerily detached; Bender reporting on psycho-pathic-like children who had been in a series of foster care and adoptive homes; Bakwin, Goldfarb, and Spitz warning about the psychiatric dam-age done to institutionalized babies; and a number of European clinicians with similar, if less conclusive, findings. Bowlby quickly assimilated this and a related mass of material and six months later produced *Maternal Care and Mental Health* which finally united and gave a single voice—clear, eloquent, commanding—to the solitary figures who had been urg-ing modern society to see the suffering of its children.

Bowlby began by emphasizing the similarity of findings. Mainly un-aware of one another's work, they unanimously found the same symp-toms in children who'd been deprived of their mothers—the superficial relationships, the poverty of feeling for others, the inaccessibility, the lack of emotional response, the often pointless deceitfulness and theft, and the inability to concentrate in school. "So similar are the observa-tions and the conclusions—even the very words—that each might have written the others' papers."[1]

Beyond the startling consistency was the fact that the researchers had approached the problem with different methods, which proved comple-mentary to one another. Bakwin and Spitz directly observed the suffering of infants separated from their mothers. Bender's and Bowlby's studies had been retrospective, examining children who were already quite dis-turbed and attempting to discover what experiences they shared in com-mon. The problem with such studies, however, is that they are in a sense playing with loaded dice—they examine only disturbed children and say nothing about other children who may have had identical misfortunes yet remained undamaged. This shortcoming, however, was made up for by Goldfarb, who followed the development of a group of normal infants who had been given up in infancy by their mothers. One group was raised in an institution until approximately three and a half, when they were placed in foster care. Babies in the other group were placed in foster homes as soon as their mothers gave them up. On each test of develop-ment—general intelligence, visual memory, concept formation, language ability, school adjustment—the figures revealed the damage done to institutionalized children and the benefits of foster care. Most dramatic was the impact on the capacity to form relationships, with thirteen of the fifteen institutionalized children incapable of forming deep or lasting connections, a problem that did not exist for the children in foster care.

Wartime experience in England rounded out the picture. In Hampstead Dorothy Burlingham and Anna Freud ran a residential nursery for children whose parents' lives had been disrupted by the war, some of the mothers living in shelters because their homes had been bombed out in the blitz. The two analysts found that only infants in the first months of life adjusted easily to such an environment. They struggled to make the separation for the other young children in their care easier by doing it in slow stages, but while this process worked for children over three or four years of age, for children between one and a half to two and a half years, it proved a catastrophe. A typical case was Bobby, a twenty-four-month-old boy who, despite being looked after by a mother substitute and visited daily by his mother during the first week, started deteriorating when her visits tapered off, becoming listless, incontinent, aggressive, and unwilling to eat. Another little boy, named Reggie, who had been in the nurseries almost continuously since he was five months old, formed

> passionate relationships to two young nurses who took care of him at different periods. The second attachment was suddenly broken at two years and eight months when his "own" nurse married. He was completely lost and desperate after her departure, and refused to look at her when she visited him a fortnight later. He turned his head to the other side when she spoke to him, but stared at the door, which had closed behind her, after she had left the room. In the evening in bed he sat up and said: "My very own Mary-Ann! But I don't like her."[2]

Other stories were equally poignant. Three-year-old Patrick, whose mother was working in a munitions factory, kept himself from crying because his mother said she would not visit if he cried. In place of crying, he began a ritual that consisted of nodding his head whenever anyone looked at him and repeating that his mother would soon come for him, that she would dress him and take him home. If the listener accepted his story he seemed fine, but if he was contradicted he burst into tears. Within a few days the ritual became more monotonous and compulsive, Patrick constantly attempting to reassure himself with his story. As he continued, it became more elaborated: His mother would come for him, she would put on his coat and leggings, she would zip up the zipper, she would put on his pixie hat. When someone asked him whether he could stop repeating this again and again, he tried to be a good boy and cooperate. But now, instead of speaking the words, he mouthed them and simultaneously began enacting the ritual by putting on the imaginary clothes. Within a few days this was further streamlined and reduced to something of a tic. "While the other children were mostly busy with their toys, playing games, making music, etc., Patrick, totally uninterested, would stand somewhere in a corner, moving his hands and lips with an absolutely tragic expression on his face."[3]

In this case we see the way in which the mother's psychological problems—her unwillingness to tolerate Patrick's crying—complicated what would in any case have been a difficult grief reaction and pushed his behavior into a symptom, a chronic and compulsive tic that was dissociated from his feelings and from the situation in which those feelings originated.

Other children who seemed to have adapted well to the nursery fell apart when they left, often becoming hostile toward their mothers, demanding and jealous, throwing temper tantrums and developing a strange emotional detachment, sometimes accompanied by a monotonous rocking of the body and in extreme cases by head banging.[4]

Once again language function was singled out as suffering in the absence of a mother figure, and Burlingham and Freud found that "when children are home on visits ... they sometimes gain in speech in one or two weeks what they would have taken three months to gain in the nursery."[5] Only when the children had a substitute mother in the nursery did they seem to open up again to learning.[6]

After reading the reports of the wartime nursery, Bowlby spoke to Anna Freud about the experience. She said that nothing they did could prevent the severe deterioration of the very young children placed in their care. She and Burlingham felt the problems inherent in the situation were so grave and would take so many workers to correct that they concluded, "It would be preferred to arrange for each helper to take a couple of children home with her and close the nursery."[7]

All this proved an opportunity for Bowlby to argue that the mother-infant relationship is an extremely important one, that it was not a pleasant amenity for the child but an absolute necessity, and that significant early separations are perilous to the child and ultimately to society as well. Many professionals were resistant to accepting these findings. But Bowlby forcefully argued that they and their policies must change. He insisted that families, especially poor families, needed greater assistance if they were to stay intact. He advocated that large numbers of people be trained in marriage and child guidance and in work with parents of the very young. He said the large outlays of funds required would be far less than the later costs of institutional care and delinquency.

While noting that certain researchers were hopeful that, given extra-ordinary care, maternally deprived youngsters were capable of being rehabilitated, Bowlby warned that others had found such children damaged beyond repair.[8] He also acknowledged that some children do seem to escape the ravages of early separation. But, in a typical Bowlby flourish, he added, "the same is true of the consumption of tubercular-infected milk or exposure to the virus of infantile paralysis. In both these cases a sufficient proportion of children is so severely damaged that no one would dream of intentionally exposing a child to such hazards."[9]

At this time social workers in many countries typically separated children from their mothers because of unsatisfactory home conditions—which often meant untidiness or material want—or because the mother was unwed. To Bowlby this was madness. He argued that those responsible for child welfare had been so preoccupied with physical health and, often, physical appearance, that they had at times taken expensive steps "to convert a physically neglected but psychologically well-provided child into a physically well-provided but emotionally starved one."[10] He believed that, unless a mother (or a foster mother) was cruel or abusive, an untidy, disorganized, and unwed mother was often better equipped to emotionally care for a child than a tidy and well-run institution. In one of the many moving portions of the report, informed no doubt by his recent experiences as a father, he wrote:

> The mothering of a child is not something which can be arranged by roster; it is a live human relationship which alters the characters of both partners. The provision of a proper diet calls for more than calories and vitamins: we need to enjoy our food if it is to do us good. In the same way the provision of mothering cannot be considered in terms of hours per day but only in terms of the enjoyment of each other's company which mother and child obtain.
>
> Such enjoyment and close identification of feeling is only possible for either party if the relationship is continuous.... Just as the baby needs to feel that he belongs to his mother,

the mother needs to feel that she belongs to her child and it is only when she has the satisfaction of this feeling that it is easy for her to devote herself to him. . . .

It is for these reasons that the mother-love which a young child needs is so easily provided within the family, and is so very very difficult to provide outside it. The services which mothers and fathers habitually render their children are so taken for granted that their magnitude is forgotten. In no other relationship do human beings place themselves so unreservedly and so continuously at the disposal of others. This holds true even of bad parents—a fact far too easily forgotten by their critics, especially critics who have never had the care of children of their own. It must never be forgotten that even the bad parent who neglects her child is none the less providing much for him. Except in the worst cases, she is giving him food and shelter, comforting him in distress, teaching him simple skills, and above all is providing him with that continuity of human care on which his sense of security rests. He may be ill-fed and ill-sheltered, he may be very dirty and suffering from disease, he may be ill-treated, but, unless his parents have wholly rejected him, he is secure in the knowledge that there is *someone* to whom he is of value and who will strive, even though inadequately, to provide for him until such time as he can fend for himself.[11]

Bowlby admonished governments, social agencies, and the public for their failure to appreciate the central value of maternal care, as important for mental health in infancy and childhood "as are vitamins and proteins for physical health."[12] (This analogy, originally Levy's, would be associated with Bowlby's name for decades.) He warned that mothers should neither be sentimentalized nor punished. "At one time the punitive attitude took the form of removing the baby from his mother as a punishment for her sins. Nowadays this punitive attitude seems to lead in the opposite direction and to insist that she should take the responsibility for caring for what she has so irresponsibly produced, thereby foreclosing the chance for a happy adoption."[13]

Reporting data, synthesizing meanings, raising critical questions, Bowlby left barely a stone unturned. In emergencies, he said, children are ideally left with relatives, and he urged that funds be provided so that poor families could accomplish this when a relative lived far away. He reviewed the care of maladjusted and sick children, the proper way to run residential nurseries when there was no other recourse but to institutionalize a child, the causes of family failure in Western societies and how it could be reversed.

He warned that when children are neglected, "as happens in every country of the Western world today, they grow up to reproduce themselves." Again he used a medical metaphor: "Deprived children . . . are a source of social infection as real and serious as are carriers of diphtheria and typhoid."[14] Although it would be decades before research would prove his point, Bowlby declared that the psychopathic parent who was often found to be the cause of child neglect is usually the grown-up maternally deprived affectionless child.

In numerous areas—from adoption policy to the impact of short-term separations—Bowlby cited the lack of adequate research and suggested where it might proceed. Given his concerns and the directions they would eventually take, one recommendation stands out with special resonance to anyone reading his report more than forty years later: "The partial forms of maternal deprivation, due sometimes to ignorance but more often to unconscious hostility on the part of the mother deriving from experiences in her own childhood, could well form the subject of another report."[15]

The impact of the World Health report can barely be overstated. Most immediate was the effect on public policy, particularly adoption, social work, and hospital practices worldwide. It heightened interest in Spitz's work, helping to spread his film, which also had great impact. It caused new thinking about the causes and prevention of delinquency and the training of young women for motherhood. It stimulated an extraordinary flood of research, including experimental work with animals. It aroused new thinking about the nature of the infant-mother bond. And it made Bowlby a household name in Britain and a champion of child care workers in many parts of the globe. It also placed him at the center of a huge and stormy debate that in one form or another would swirl around him for the remainder of his life. The idea that early experiences have serious consequences for intellectual and psychosocial development was, amazingly, controversial in itself, but the controversy was only heightened by the fact that many of Bowlby's claims were exaggerated by others and quoted out of context.

The WHO report was followed two years later by the publication of a paperback abridgment. The paperback was the inspiration of Margery Fry, an educator, a juvenile court magistrate, and a member of the esteemed Fry family (Roger Fry, the painter, was her brother). Called *Child Care and the Growth of Love*, the book quickly became an international best-seller, ultimately reaching a half a million in sales.[16] The book led to a worldwide change in outlook toward the needs of small children and widespread improvement in institutional care, its impact compared to the exposure by Elizabeth Fry (an earlier member of the Fry clan) of the horrendous conditions in early-nineteenth century prisons.[17] The issue of mother-love and maternal deprivation had arrived in a big way, and so had Bowlby.

6

FIRST BATTLEFIELD:
"A TWO-YEAR-OLD
GOES TO HOSPITAL"

"My little boy was just 10 months old when he had gastroenteritis and was taken to hospital. . . . I accompanied him there but on entry he was firmly taken from me without even time for a goodbye kiss (this being explained as the best course of action, as long drawn out partings only made matters worse). . . ."

Thus wrote a British mother as recently as 1964. She continued:

> He fretted terribly and missed being played with, and every time we visited him he was crying, and even before he saw me coming down the corridor. I was allowed to give him his supper in the 1 hr. nightly visit and to change his nappy if necessary.
>
> I visited him thinking I could be natural with him but found myself upset too, especially at the leaving time when the bell went. He would stand at the end of his cot, tears streaming down his face and wouldn't even wave bye-bye. I knew they were doing all they could but how I wondered all evening if he had settled down to sleep or play and if he cried

all day. This lasted the whole of the two weeks he was there and on coming home with him he was very mistrustful of me leaving him even to go into the next room.[1]

When children are hospitalized today, parents are generally accorded unlimited visiting privileges. Fifty years ago they were often not allowed to visit at all, and later, in the 1950s and much of the 1960s, visiting hours were typically restricted to one hour a week. The children's wards in a hospital were tight little ships in which the intrusion of parents was unwelcome and, indeed, deemed unhealthy. The "happy children's ward" was part of the mythology of the era that hospital staff sought eagerly to promote. In the case of older children, the myth and the reality did not always clash. But for the very young, hospital visits, even short ones, were an emotional catastrophe. In the early fifties, the BBC's Christmas programming invariably included a visit to hospitalized children. When the microphone was brought to older children, they happily consented to wish their families a Merry Christmas over the air. But toddlers stared silently and then burst into tears. This happened so consistently that soon the little ones were omitted from this part of the program.[2]

As early as 1943, Harry Edelston, a psychiatrist at Leeds, charged that children were emotionally damaged by their hospital stays. His case studies were largely ignored. Ten years later, despite Bowlby's World Health report, despite the protest of L. A. Parry, whose 1947 *Lancet* article vigorously protested the restrictions on parental visits to hospitalized children, despite a 1948 editorial in *The Nursing Times* advocating hospital reform, Edelston wrote that many of his colleagues still refused to believe in "hospitalization trauma."[3]

The pediatricians and nurses who ran the children's wards regarded visitors as nuisances who disrupted hospital routines and as carriers of infection (although why parents should be more efficient germ carriers than hospital staff or student trainees was never explained). It was well known that children who had settled down after a few days on the ward typically began to cry and became unmanageable again after parental visits. The staff did not welcome such eruptions.

According to child psychiatrist Edward Mason, who began working at Children's Hospital in Boston in 1951, head nurses in some wards had immense power over which parents could visit, regardless of hospital policy. In many countries of the Southern Hemisphere, where medical facilities were typically less advanced and where family ties were extremely powerful, mothers had routinely slept at the foot of the bed when their children were hospitalized. But as hospitals improved technically, they began emulating northern practices.[4]

The suffering that parents and children endured because of such policies was great, especially when the child was very young and incapable of understanding his mother's disappearance for days on end, incapable of anticipating the next visit. To him, the abandonment seemed, on each parting, to be permanent. The feelings engendered in small children might (very loosely) be compared to an older child's learning that his entire family had been killed in a car crash or that everyone he loved on earth had intentionally abandoned him—and then having his rage, his sense of loss, and his feelings of being unwanted redoubled when the perpetrators returned for a surprise visit but refused to stay or take him with them.

One can imagine how such a state of affairs, going on for months or years, would finally exhaust one's ability to hope, lock one into a relatively permanent hardness, and cement one's anger against those who had formerly been so loved. Simultaneously, one's hunger for attachment would continue to incite jealousy and aggression and show itself in distorted forms, like theft. But even when such painful separations lasted for only a few days, they presented a problem, as these parents testified:

- I left John [twenty-one months old], on admittance, happily playing about the ward, quite fearless in his relationship with the Sister and the other children. He came home withdrawn and with no confidence at all. He would not go to his Daddy and I could not leave him at all, because he screamed and sobbed. He was frightened of being touched by me in any way (undressed etc.) and he cowered, literally, before neighbors and friends whom he knew hitherto.[5]
- When we arrived each day, as soon as she was beginning to recover that is, we used to see through the observation window that she was sitting in the cot listlessly staring at nothing in particular. When we went in she cried for a moment and then brightened up for the rest of our stay. As we prepared to leave she would stand at the end of the cot, desperately trying to climb out (something she never attempts at home) purple with rage and screaming with grief. We left her like that every day. . . .[6]

• When it was time for me to go, the child went nearly frantic, the Sister told me that she sobbed night and day, even in her sleep. . . . it was absolute torture for both of us when the time came for me to leave. I couldn't sleep knowing that my baby just layed and sobbed and only sleeping when her crying had exhausted her.

When she came home (after only 5 days) I thought all would be well, instead she wouldn't let me put her down to do anything, she wouldn't go to anyone (not even her father), she was terrified I was going to leave her, and when I took her upstairs to bed, and she saw her cot, she almost went hysterical. In the end I had to go to bed and have her with me, even then she didn't sleep for fear I would leave her.[7]

This last child's behavior on returning home would prove typical, although in many cases the clinging was preceded by rejecting the parent. The biologist Konrad Lorenz, whose theories about animal behavior would soon play a huge role in Bowlby's intellectual development, described a vivid example from his own life. Lorenz had left his daughter when she was three and did not see her again for almost a year. "She loved me very dearly and when we met again she seemed somewhat reserved, but she greeted me very politely and nicely and was very glad to see me. Then when I had left the room, very tactfully so that I could not hear her, she said to my wife, 'But our former Daddy was so much more beautiful.'"[8]

What could be at work in the mind of a little girl who experiences such abandonment, aside from anger and rejection? It would seem that the child, to protect herself against further heartbreak, dissociates from her emotional investment in the father. He becomes like a figure in a wax museum, a weak imitation that can arouse no emotion beyond disappointment that he is not the real thing and perhaps angry resistance if he tries to prove that he is. The rejecting behavior of children who had been hospitalized against their will by parents whose job it is to protect them from the intrusions of strangers was often more severe.

In most cases, however, rejection was quickly followed by clinging. The range of symptoms in this stage included timidity, lost confidence, pronounced fear of strangers, violent outbursts, often aimed at the parents, nightmares and nighttime fits, refusal to sleep alone, a furious jealousy over mother's attention ("She hated me even to speak to anyone else"). Parents often felt they were getting back a different child altogether, even though these children had all suffered only very brief separations compared to Bowlby's affectionless thieves. "It has completely changed her," one mother wrote. "I could hardly believe it was the same wee darling boy," wrote another. "He had lost so much weight, his face was pinched and haggard as if he'd been so miserable, and he could do nothing but hang on to me, and hug me tight. I'll never forget his first words to me—'Mummy, I thought you were never coming back for me.'"[9]

Even a child of four, old enough to understand that her parents would be back soon for another brief visit, able to look forward to that and know, despite her painful loneliness, that her misery would be temporary, showed how different a short period of time can seem to a person that age. Hospitalized for five days, one four-year-old, who had been visited by her parents daily, later told a neighbor that her parents had taken her to the hospital and left her there "for weeks and weeks." It was not uncommon for the small child to feel that being sent to the hospital was a form of punishment. "I'll be a good girl," one child pleaded with her parents, "please don't send me."[10]

Most of the parents who wrote these letters appeared to be patient and devoted. But dealing with a changed and rejecting child was trying. "At one time [the child's] attitude distressed me so much that I found myself wishing for another baby on whom to shower this surfeit of rejected mother love. Fortunately for him we did not have another, and now a year later I can say that we are quite normal again." Another mother wrote: "I think I got off lightly by loving him back to security instead of smacking him into a deeper sense of insecurity as I knew exasperated parents too often do."[11] Her insight speaks volumes about how a trauma like early separation, motivated by urgent need and surrounded by good intentions, can worm its way into the fabric of the mother-child bond, and through the tormented psychology of one working on the uncomprehending hurt and frustration of the other, destroy it.

In 1946, after reentering civilian life, Bowlby took a job at the Tavistock Clinic in London, which was going through a major reorganization[12] and quickly became deputy director, in charge of the children's department.[13] Here, he immediately instituted therapy with both children and parents and pioneered seeing whole families together—a mode of treatment he remained committed to for the rest of his life.[14] Child psychiatry was still a new field, and the government was eager to have services set up throughout the country. By the fall of 1946 Bowlby had the clinical services and training programs for new therapists operating. In 1948 he received his first research grants to launch a study of the effects of early separation.

That year he hired James Robertson, a young social worker, to observe children who were being sent off to the hospital. Robertson had unique credentials, having worked in Burlingham and Freud's wartime nursery. He proved to be an extraordinarily sensitive observer of children and their feeling states, and in short order his passion about their treatment in hospitals was at least as great as Bowlby's own.

> On 11 February 1948 I went in all innocence [Robertson wrote many years later] to the short-stay children's ward at the Central Middlesex Hospital, the parent hospital of the Tavistock clinic. This was solely for the convenience of observing a batch of children in one location, and not because of any awareness on my part that young children in hospital presented a special problem. The consultant pediatrician and his ward sister, for their part, welcomed me into their bright and tidy ward. The nurses who moved briskly about smiled at the young man in an ordinary suit who had come among them. The atmosphere was of orderliness and of everything being under control. I was told that this was a happy children's ward. But within a few hours I grasped the essentials of a problem of distress that was not being acknowledged in the hospital professions. It determined the direction of my professional life for many years to come.[15]*

In social background, outward manner, and life experience, Robertson was Bowlby's opposite. Angry about social injustice, deeply sensitive to and sometimes rankled by class distinctions, and touchy about attribution and credit, Robertson also had an open, rounded face, a ready smile, and a gift for gab that might have belonged to an affable TV host. In a

---

*Robertson may have forgotten when he wrote of his "innocence" here that his own daughter had been hospitalized for six days in 1945 when she was only thirteen months old, and that the enforced separation had been a bitter experience for the parents. "I offered to scrub the floors or do any task in the hospital so that I could be with her," Joyce Robertson later recalled, "but they wouldn't have me." (Milton Senn's Interview with James and Joyce Robertson, October 25, 1977.)

beautiful documentary film, *Where's Mommy: The Robertson Studies of Mother-Child Separation*, that Edward Mason made about Robertson, Bowlby is, by comparison, so dryly upper crust and in control of his feelings that the two men seem to come from different planets.[16]

One of seven children from a poor Scottish family, Robertson grew up in Clydesdale, near Glasgow, where housing conditions were among the worst in Europe. The family lived in a cold water flat and shared an outhouse with two other families. From age 14 to twenty-eight, Robertson worked in the steel mills to help support his family and read voraciously at night. At twenty-eight he attended a one-year school for the higher education of working men and women. When war broke out, Robertson, a conscientious objector, and his soon-to-be wife, Joyce, went to London to help out with the families of the dock workers, whose neighborhoods were being heavily bombed in the blitz. Shortly thereafter they were hired by Anna Freud to work in the Hampstead nursery around the corner from the Freud home where Sigmund Freud had died a year earlier.

Robertson had been disturbed by the evacuation of trainloads of children to remote parts of Britain (a process he had participated in), the distress of the children having been apparent to him. He was therefore attracted to the nursery's practice of keeping the children near enough for the mother to visit and to Burlingham and Freud's philosophy that the children were put at greater risk by being separated from their mothers than from being near falling bombs.

Robertson became the handyman on the property, tending to boilers and carpentry as well as organizing the fire-watching services, Joyce one of the caretakers, tending to the babies from 6 a.m. when they awoke until they were tucked in at night. In the meantime, with bombs falling in the background, the young couple attended staff meetings and seminars and learned psychoanalytic theory. By the end of the war, Robertson was doing social work with the families, helping to determine how the children would be resettled.

By the time Robertson, now a qualified social worker and training in psychoanalysis, went to work for Bowlby, he, his pregnant wife, and their first child were living in a hostel for homeless people, where they remained for two and a half years. "Surely very few psychoanalysts," Robertson later said, "had done the major part of their training in such strange domestic conditions."[17] Robertson now joined Bowlby's sanatorium study, an ambitious project designed to follow up children, aged one to three, who had been hospitalized. His job was to observe these children as they were being admitted and to record their reactions. He also observed children in a fever hospital and a residential nursery.

At the Central Middlesex Hospital Robertson saw desolate children silently sitting on their cots. He saw a kindhearted nurse rebuked for stopping to show concern for a silent toddler. He saw a child who was seriously ill in an isolated area attended to by a special nurse; the nurse sat quietly behind the child's cot so that the sight of her would not cause him to make exceptional demands. On Sunday when the parents came the silent ward rang with anguished cries. When Robertson expressed his concern to the hospital staff he was told that the children's distress was inevitable and that they all soon settled down. "Doubts I expressed were smilingly put aside as those of a sentimental psychologist. But if I followed some of the children back home I found invariably that the 'settled' state in the hospital ward had given way to difficult behavior— clinging to the mother, temper tantrums, disturbed sleep, bed-wetting, regression and aggression particularly against the mother as if blaming her."[18]

The hospital staff had an explanation for this, too: The mothers were simply less competent than the nurses in caring for children.[19]

In the course of the next two years, Robertson also observed children in a long-term ward, most of whom suffered from pulmonary tuberculosis, still a scourge at that time and regularly requiring long hospital stays, sometimes up to four years. Here he was able to observe the process that Bowlby and the other maternal deprivation pioneers only knew by its end product. These children typically went through three stages of emotional reaction to their separation. Robertson called the first stage "protest"—crying, clinging, screaming after parents had left. In this stage the child is frightened and confused and urgently looking for his lost mother, turning anxiously toward any sound that might herald her approach. This is gradually succeeded by "despair." The child becomes listless, loses interest in his surroundings, turns away from food, sheds only occasional tears. He desperately wants his mother, but, Robertson said, he is losing hope of getting her back. Robertson had already seen these two stages in the short-term wards. But in the children requiring long hospitalization, he observed a third stage that he first called "detachment." The child now seems to awaken somewhat to the possibilities of ward life. He interacts more. He smiles. He eats. But he has awakened a different child. He no longer seems to know his mother when she comes, to cry—or even to appear concerned—when she leaves. Gradually, he seems to become indifferent to maternal care altogether.

> On Sundays these "detached" young children seemed indifferent to the arrival of their parents. There was no crying, no clinging, no turning away. They were more interested in what their parents had brought than in the parents themselves. They searched bags and stuffed chocolate into their mouths. My impression was that feeling for their parents had died because of the passage of time and repeated disappointment of the wish to be taken home and had been replaced by hunger for sweet things which did not disappoint. "Don't be greedy," perplexed parents would say.[20]

Among the children Robertson observed during this period was Mary, a cuddly child of two and a half years. When she was discharged a year later, she seemed no longer to need her mother, squirmed out of her embrace, and then stood looking at her "as if not knowing what affection was about." Robertson, who had grown attached to Mary, was able to follow her for a number of years, seeing her turn into a self-centered girl, ruthless in her relations with her older brothers, and, as she grew older, increasingly solitary. Although Mary did well in school, Robertson was pained to find that, at twelve, she was unpopular with classmates and disliked by teachers and staff. He tried to enlist the compassion of the adults around her, earnestly explaining the ordeal Mary had suffered, but to no avail. "Disappointed though I was, I admitted to myself that I would not wish a son of mine to marry Mary."[21]

As he became more engrossed in his work, Robertson grew increasingly infuriated with the unwillingness of professionals, outside of Bowlby's team at the Tavistock, to believe what he was saying. The most painful blow came in 1951 when Robertson presented his findings to a group of pediatricians. Nervously aware of his low status, meager credentials, and poor, working-class roots, Robertson was crushed when the only doctor he thought he could count on as an ally, Sir James Spence, a pioneer in the humane treatment of hospitalized children who had already extended visiting rights and even overnight privileges to many parents, bitingly attacked him. "What is wrong with emotional upset?"

Spence said. "This year we are celebrating the centenary of the birth of Wordsworth, the great Lakeland poet. He suffered from emotional upset, yet look at the poems he produced."[22]

Bowlby would long recall the day in 1951 when Robertson told him that since nobody would accept his evidence he was going to make a film. It would be a primitive film, made with a Bell and Howell spring-wound 16mm camera—hand held and relying on window light. A child subject was selected by sticking a pin into the four-page waiting list for elective surgery at the Central Middlesex Hospital. Because there was some concern that Robertson might only show the child when distressed, he and Bowlby worked out a system whereby the toddler who'd been selected would be filmed during the same forty-minute periods twice each day, as shown by the clock, which was always in the frame.[23] The child's name was Laura. She was two years, five months old.

"When I saw Laura," Robertson later recalled, "I got a shock. For three years I had been talking to pediatricians about the states of acute distress little children invariably got into in pediatric wards, how when they lost their parents, when they were ill and in pain, these little children shouted, screamed, rattled their cots, their noses ran, their eyes streamed with tears, how they tried to climb out of their cots to get at the mother who had disappeared. [But Laura] was what we call in Britain 'a little madam,' a child of parents who were older than usual in having their first child and who had reared her with love but with strictness. At two years and five months, she was very well behaved, a very controlled little girl who, I saw immediately, was going to be the one child in a hundred who was not going to demonstrate what I had been shouting my head off for about three years."[24]

Robertson was tempted to go back and ask for another child, but he knew that that would destroy any hope of his being perceived as objective. He proceeded.

The Laura we see in the film, who is now known to child development experts throughout the world, is an exceptionally beautiful little girl with straight blond hair pulled back on top with a ribbon. She proved to be as self-contained as Robertson feared. She never wailed in a prolonged and uninhibited manner. But her feelings continually broke through her composure, which she then struggled to reassert. On the first day, after the routine bath, she ran naked to the door and tried to escape. Her expression, formerly bright, became dull, and she periodically sobbed quietly to herself, clutching her teddy or a favored blanket. Several times she quietly asked, "Where's my mummy?" She later looked more and more tense and miserable, despite heroic efforts to keep from crying.

Visiting was normally restricted to once a week, but because Robertson wanted to observe how her attitude toward her parents would change over the eight-day stay, at his request Laura's parents were allowed to visit every other day. On the second day of her hospitalization, her parents visited for the first time. On seeing them, she immediately burst into tears and pleaded with them to take her home. In one poignant moment, we see her looking into her father's face in a heartbreaking expression of supplication, as she clutches his tie—something she frequently did when distressed—and pleads pathetically, "Don't go, Daddy."[25]

In each successive visit the parents were greeted by a grayer, colder response, until she seemed frozen. On the fifth day she looked resentful and unsmiling when her mother appeared, and wiped away her mother's kiss. Her lip trembled when her mother said she was going home. When her mother waved good-bye on the seventh day Laura stood motionless with her head bent.

When her mother came to fetch her on the eighth day, Laura was apprehensive, as if not allowing herself to believe that she might really be going home. She greeted her mother shaking with sobs. When at last they prepared to leave, Laura scoured the ward for her belongings, including a tattered book her mother suggested she leave behind. She seemed determined to leave nothing of herself there. As Laura marched out of the hospital, clutching her belongings, she refused to take her mother's hand.

Two days after returning home, Laura was a bright-eyed child again, "as though a lamp had lit up inside her," thought Robertson at the time.[26] But like other children who experienced brief hospital, stays, she went through a period of anxiety and irritability after she returned, sleeping poorly, soiling herself, refusing to let her mother out of her sight, throwing violent temper tantrums, often just after seeking an embrace.

Five months after her surgery, Laura suffered something of a relapse. She was staying with her grandmother, someone she knew quite well, while her mother was in the hospital for five weeks because of complications following childbirth. For some reason, which was never made clear, her father thought it better not to visit her during that period, which must have contributed considerably to the stress of separation. When Laura's mother called the grandmother's house after returning from the hospital, Laura was excited to hear her voice and eager to go home. She went home in a state of excited expectation, but when her mother greeted her at the door, her excitement disappeared and she seemed to go blank. After a pause she said, "But I want my mummy." And for the next two days she continued in that vein, refusing to accept her mother, although she accepted her father instantaneously and without apparent problem.[27]

A month later, when she accidentally walked in on a portion of Robertson's film, which he was screening for her parents, she burst into tears and cried to her mother, "Where was you all that time?"[28]

In November 1952, James Robertson and John Bowlby went to a packed meeting of the Royal Society of Medicine in London to present the film. The film, which cost about eighty dollars to make, was low-key. Far from showing a distraught, hysterical little girl, it presented a child who remained fairly well in control throughout, her emotions revealing themselves mainly through little signs, like the twitching of her fingers or the narrowing of her eyes. Still, it was powerful, more powerful perhaps than the documentary of a more uninhibited child might have been. Although Laura was self-contained and Robertson's documentary caught only a few episodes of weeping, it nevertheless proved powerful evidence of Bowlby's theories on the dangers of early separations because of the poignant drama of the child's struggle with distress. Like Spitz's film of a few years earlier, it forced people to see that little children do indeed suffer a great deal. The audience, some three hundred pediatricians, nurses, and administrators, was outraged.

"I was immediately assailed for lack of integrity," Robertson said. "I had produced an untrue record. I had slandered the professions. I had tricked the hospital; I had chosen an atypical child of atypical parents; I had ... filmed selectively and I had edited it dishonestly. People stood up and said that their children's wards were not like that, two-year-olds were all happy, no parents ever complained, etc., etc."[29] Many demanded that the film be banned.[30]

Some wards to which Robertson had had access were now closed to him. "Pediatricians who had welcomed me into the wards from that day on did not welcome me. Some were personally hostile and walked across the street when they met me."[31] Attempts were made to discredit him. It was said that Laura was never filmed when she was happy. The Central Middlesex staff charged that Robertson had interfered with nurses trying to minister to Laura. A child health expert protested to Bowlby, saying that Robertson had failed to be objective, and citing as evidence his panning from Laura's emotionless face to her twitching fingers. As Robertson toured with the film, the reaction was similar throughout Britain. On two occasions, the chairman of the proceedings abandoned his neutral role to join the attacks on the guest. A Glasgow nurse told him, "Yon may be true of a wee English lassie, but it's not true of a Scottish bairn!"[32] Professor Spence, inexplicably, was as dismissive as before, but attempted to placate Robertson with the reassurance that he preferred Robertson's simple, misguided views to the "more dangerous attitudes" of Bowlby.[33] Resistance in the medical profession was so stiff that Bowlby and Robertson temporarily withheld *A Two-Year-Old Goes to Hospital* from general release to allow the turmoil to subside.

"The medicals, many of them, were in a dilemma because Dr. Bowlby was a respected medical and one of themselves," Robertson recalled, "whereas I was a nonmedical and an intruder. Dr. Bowlby and I, of course, were in complete agreement about the problem of the pediatric ward and about the truth of my film, but some of the medicals began to try and split us. It began to get around that Dr. Bowlby—decent chap and one of us—had modified his views, which of course he hadn't, and that it was this nuisance, Robertson, this interloper, who went on plugging the totally untrue, psychological, sentimental stuff about the dangers of early hospitalization."[34]

The reactions of the British analysts, who had seen an earlier screening of the film, was divided. Anna Freud was largely supportive, but the Kleinians rejected the hypothesis that the child's distress had anything to do with separation from the mother. Wilfred Bion, a prominent Kleinian who had served with Bowlby in the army, argued that Robertson and Bowlby had missed the point and that Laura was probably upset because her mother was pregnant.[35]

Surprisingly, the reviews that soon began appearing in the medical literature were uniformly positive. And younger nurses and pediatricians frequently buttonholed Robertson to tell him that they agreed with him and that they would do things differently if they were in charge. A few higher-ups were also sympathetic. The medical superintendent of Central Middlesex said, "Well, I am sorry it is my hospital. But I accept that it is an objective record which should be shown widely."[36] Such reactions gave Robertson the courage to persist.

In 1953 the World Health Organization made Robertson a short-term consultant and sent him on a six-week tour with the film to the United

States. There he was commended for having done an admirable job of documenting conditions in England but informed that his film had no relevance to the United States, where children were less cosseted and thus better able to withstand separations. Even where the problem of separation was understood, Robertson saw little interest in the obvious solution—allowing mothers onto the wards.

In 1955 pediatrician-psychiatrist Fred Stone returned to Britain after three years of training in the United States. "I arrived in this hospital," he told historian Alice Smuts, "one month after Jimmy Robertson had given his first presentation of his film *A Two-Year-Old Goes to Hospital* in Scotland. Can you imagine the atmosphere I arrived in? And I was greeted with howls of rage and despair and aggression—and, of course, 'You're one of us; you *know* that this is all rubbish.' And, 'We're going to get you a big research grant to disprove all this Bowlby nonsense.'"

At the time, visiting arrangements for parents at the Royal Hospital for Sick Children in Glasgow were two half-hour sessions per week. "I would drive up the hill here to come to an afternoon clinic, and there would be two hundred parents queueing up in the rain to get in for their half hour's visiting." Eventually, one of Stone's pediatric colleagues suggested a pilot study. The colleague had jurisdiction over two pediatric wards and was willing to allocate one of them for unrestricted parental visits for six months to prove that it wouldn't work. Stone readily agreed.

When the nursing staff got wind of the plan, however, they threatened to resign en masse. Stone suggested that meetings be set up between his staff and the nurses, twice a week for three weeks, before anything further was done. "And I think it's true to say that never has so much distress been aired in so short a time in our department. The aggression after the first meetings was unbelievable, truly unbelievable." But gradually, with the exception of one nurse, who did, in fact, resign, the aggressive posture gave way to tears.

"They said, 'You don't understand what you are asking of us. You're really meaning to say that any time of the day, no matter what we're doing, no matter what state of chaos we're in, a parent can just walk in and see how we're neglecting these poor kids, that they're lying there in their own excreta, that they're screaming because they have to have an injection, that somebody's forgotten to get their diet and we've got to do the whole procedure all over again—you want this?' And, of course, at that point we had to say, 'But what on earth makes you think that we're criticizing what you're doing? You're doing an impossible job remarkably well.' And, of course, then the tears came, as you can imagine."

The nurses had other causes of anxiety, too. "They talked about the mothers who were ungrateful and critical and dirty and lice-ridden—you can imagine. Well, they all agreed that there should be a pilot experiment to see whether it would work."

The experiment, however, was never actually concluded. In fact, Stone says, "I never heard any more about the issue at all. Nobody ever came back to me and said, 'The six months are up.' Nobody ever reported that it had been a success or a failure; all I knew was that somehow I heard that two wards were doing it, four wards were doing it, the whole hospital was doing it. And since then we've had almost unrestricted visiting in the whole hospital."[37]

Another early convert was Dermod MacCarthy, a pediatrician at the Amersham General Hospital outside London. MacCarthy had seen the initial screening of Robertson's film and had felt that it had slandered pediatrics. He complained about it afterward to his ward sister, Ivy Morris, who responded, "But what Mr. Robertson says is true." Later, he wrote, "I was angry, but after the film I really heard children crying for the first time."[38] MacCarthy's recognition that he had repressed all awareness of the young patients' suffering was a typical experience for many who view Robertson's film. An elderly nurse told Bowlby: "This film brings back to me the first child I ever nursed in hospital. This child was a little boy. He grieved for his mother and it simply broke my heart. After that I never saw grief again until I saw this film."[39]

MacCarthy soon opened his ward to unrestricted visiting and encouraged mothers of children under five to sleep in. Staff found that their anxiety about mothers' getting in the way, mothers stuffing their children with sweets, and the like were ill-founded. On the contrary, mothers were usually welcome as valued additions to the team.

The changed policy gave Robertson the opportunity for his next film, *Going to Hospital with Mother*. The film documents the five-day hospitalization of twenty-month-old Sally, whose mother is with her the whole time. Though she gets upset at times, Sally never shows the despair or rejection of her mother that was typical of children admitted on their own. We see the comfort she gains from her mother's presence in numerous situations—getting her face forcefully washed, being examined by a strange doctor, getting an injection, waking fitfully in an unfamiliar place. Sally never becomes fretful or withdrawn, and upon returning home, displayed none of the behavioral changes characteristic of other returning children. When released in 1958, *Going to Hospital with Mother* was well received by the profession, in marked contrast to its predecessor. This did not, however, herald the advent of major changes. Change came slowly, and restricted visiting lasted in various forms through the next three decades.

"Pediatricians had little dynamic understanding of child development," Robertson said later. "It would be said of my film, 'Yes, that is a pleasing film; the child was contented with the mother by her side, but these changes are too difficult and too costly to make. They are not, in fact, wholly necessary. Some more visiting will be enough.'"[40]

On the Continent, resistance was even stronger. It was not until the late 1970s that pediatricians there began considering the adjustments that were slowly taking hold in Britain and the United States.

In 1957 the British government established the Committee on the Welfare of Children in Hospital, chaired by the distinguished surgeon Sir Harry Platt. Two years later the committee accepted all of Robertson's recommendations, and the minister of health announced that they were henceforth ministry policy. He urged that all hospitals work toward implementing the recommendations. Robertson, meanwhile, had shaped recommendations into a book, *Young Children in Hospital,* which was quickly translated into nine languages. In the coming years he wrote influential articles for British newspapers, appeared on BBC-TV, and continued his travels. In the early 1960s, he spoke on BBC radio, and in a bold stroke told parents that "if they decided to stay quietly by the cot of their sick child they could not be evicted." Several parents wrote to say that they had tried it and that it had worked. In some cases hostility on the part of hospital personnel eventually gave way to sympathy and even the offer of a cup of tea.[41]

In the mid-1960s Robertson proceeded to make a series of films called *Young Children in Brief Separation,* which included an unusual and dramatic, not to mention labor-intensive, procedure: In four cases he and Joyce became the foster parents of small children whose mothers were hospitalized. They wanted to see what effects separations might have if they took place under near ideal circumstances—that is, without the potentially confounding variables of illness, a strange hospital setting, and inadequate substitute care.

In each case, the children were healthy and happily attached to their parents with no previous experience of separation. They were allowed to become familiar with the Robertson home before moving in, and Joyce found out all she could about their likes, dislikes, routines, and diets. Fathers were encouraged to visit, to dine with the children, to bathe them and put them to bed. In the case of the two-and-a-half-year-old Kate, Joyce visited the family a month before the separation and the child formed a strong attachment to her. Only gradually did Kate show signs of anxiety after moving in with the substitute family. In one poignant play episode, Kate re-creates her own family apartment, showing that she loves her parents and wants them back but the play parents do not seem to want her. "Throw them in the dustbin!" she cries. She demands that they be banished from the room but soon cries to have them back.[42]

For Jane the anxiety was somewhat worse. She displays it in the film with excessive unnatural laughter and with an exaggerated smile that seems designed to force smiles from the foster family. When her father visits, she becomes remote but then clings to him and cries when he tries to leave. She becomes distressed when she and Joyce walk past her home, which is nearby. The Robertsons believed that, at seventeen months, Jane had a difficult time both assimilating Joyce as a new person when Joyce made her advance visits and retaining a clear image of her mother once away. In the end, she became extraordinarily attached to Joyce, and remained so even after she went home—where she had to share her mother with a new baby. Although the Robertsons were concerned about subtle changes in her development, they believed that Jane's experience with the foster care was nevertheless largely positive. Despite her evident troubles, she functioned well enough in the Robertson home to learn new words. When her mother retrieved her after ten days, Jane went to her instantly, inviting her back into a maternal role.[43]

Of the four children, Thomas, the oldest, suffered the greatest conflict of loyalties and had the most difficulty accepting Joyce's care. In the film he displays his anxiety and ambivalence by mixing his affection toward her with aggression. He also avoids looking at his mother's picture. The Robertsons considered such emotional difficulties to be a state of "manageable anxiety,"[44] which the children were able to live with and, for the most part, work through. Narrating the aftermath of her caring for little Lucy, Joyce Robertson recounts that at Lucy's request she visited the family several times after the reunion. "My last visit was an outing to the park. Lucy invents a game which plays out the separation and reunion. She walks me away then runs back to her mother. Then she reverses the game. But she never returns to me."[45]

The Robertsons believed that "no matter how good the substitute mothering, separation from the mother remains a hazard for the young child because of the discontinuity in their relationship."[46] But each of these four toddlers was able to form a bond with Joyce, and after a separation of ten to twenty-seven days, reunite happily with his mother. The Robertsons were thus convinced that, if a substitute mother is available, the child will reach out to her and enter into a relationship that will both reduce the child's stress "and sustain his experience of responsive mothering-type care."[47] On the basis of such evidence they urged that foster care be the rule for children in brief separations and that hospitals have foster mothers on staff to be assigned to unaccompanied children.

In 1969 Robertson released *John*. The seventeen-month-old John was taken to a residential nursery for nine days while his mother was having a new baby. The nursery was well staffed and amply provided with toys. In the first day four different nurses attend to him, all of them kindly and cheerful, all of them apparently appealing to him. He is unable to keep any one of them by him, however, as this is not the way the system works. His tentative efforts at directing his love toward a new person are dashed as she abandons him and is eventually replaced by another. Most of the other toddlers, residents almost since birth, are accustomed to this life. They are noisy and aggressive, quick to defend themselves and to snatch things they want, unperturbed when a nurse leaves the room and unsmiling when she returns. John, initially interested in the new children, is soon perplexed by them and doesn't know what to do when they pinch or smack him.

On the second day, John is still coping well but unable to get a nurse to pay attention to him, often because the nurses are responding to more clamorous children. His distress building after the third day, he becomes gradually more isolated and moves about aimlessly. The nurses, accustomed to intermittent crying, miss his signals of despair. He seeks comfort from a large teddy bear. When his father visits, he is slow to respond but fights furiously to leave with him. On the fourth day a nurse who had comforted him two days earlier returns but he is no longer interested in her. His crying loses its edge of protest, becoming weak and pitiful. By the time the nurses recognize the seriousness of his condition, it is too late to help, especially since none of them is available for the continuous attachment he needs. By the fourth day he is refusing food and by the eighth he hasn't eaten for several days. When his mother at last appears to take him home, he begins to wail and throw himself about. He avoids looking at her and refuses to allow her to comfort him. When their eyes meet at last, he looks at her in a way she's never seen before.

"The making of the 'John' film" Robertson later said, "was a very, very distressing experience. We couldn't intervene any more than Joyce giving an occasional cuddle to the child. We couldn't take him over. Otherwise we'd have been thrown out of the institution." On returning home, John showed many of the signs of insecurity that had become familiar to Robertson, and they lasted for months. "This experience," Robertson said, "left John with a profound anger against his parents and a deep sense of insecurity." He feared the child would be permanently damaged by it.[48]

The reception of *John* was almost as tumultuous as the Laura film had been seventeen years earlier. Again professionals and government officials were dealing with a phenomenon that had been invisible to them before. Many reacted with outrage, but the period of resistance was shorter, and reviewers were almost uniform in their praise: "A horrifying film which forces us to look at what despair is for a young child"—*The British Journal of Psychiatric Social Work.* "No words can convey John's stress reactions as powerfully as the camera does. The impact of John's hour by hour increasing misery and deterioration becomes almost unbearable"—*The Journal of Child Psychotherapy. The Lancet* called the film a landmark and said it would do for residential care what Laura had done for pediatrics. Indeed, it soon helped put an end to the use of residential nurseries in Britain and promote foster care as the preferred alternative.[49]

Robertson had become by now something of a one-man institution, invited to give lectures and show his films around the world. For twenty years he needed a full-time secretary-assistant, much of whose time was devoted to the deluge of mail and telephone inquiries that poured into Robertson's little room at the Tavistock. In 1961 he oversaw the creation of the National Association for the Welfare of Children in Hospital. Robertson eventually quit the organization, angered by what he considered to be a slight, but it continues his work to this day.

Both he and Joyce had become markedly alienated from Bowlby as well. Part of the subtext of the making of the series on *Young Children in*

Brief Separation had, in fact, been a theoretical dispute with Bowlby. Bowlby had held that separations from the mother figure caused distress and despair in most children regardless of how they were treated during the separation, a point to which Anna Freud had strongly objected. When Robertson, who remained devoted to Freud, proposed the new series of films to investigate this issue, Bowlby apparently displayed a lack of interest, which struck Robertson as "very like resistance."[50] There was also speculation that he and Joyce resented Bowlby's appropriating or getting credit for James's ideas. At times their distaste for him seemed oddly impassioned. But, like it or not, their careers remained tied to his name.

Bowlby, true to form, continued to credit Robertson for his theoretical and practical accomplishments and to speak highly of him at every turn. In his 1973 book on separation, he acknowledges that the Robertsons' foster study caused him to modify his views on the traumatic consequences of separation, "in which insufficient weight was given to the influence of skilled care from a familiar substitute."[51] Although he was no doubt hurt and confused by their continued rejection, he gave no hint of it in his public utterances (and apparently not in private either). His blurb on the back of Robertson's last book, which appeared in 1989, the year after Robertson died, is a fitting epitaph: "James Robertson was a remarkable person who achieved great things. His sensitive observations and brilliant filming made history, and the courage with which he disseminated—often in the face of ignorant and prejudiced criticism—what were then very unpopular findings, was legendary. He will always be remembered as the man who revolutionized children's hospitals, though he accomplished much else besides. I am personally deeply grateful for all that he did."[52]

Bowlby's career had meanwhile taken some new and surprising turns. Always quick to grasp the theoretical implications of new data, Bowlby had right from the start begun including Robertson's formulations in his own writings. The stages of protest, despair, and detachment immediately became part of the standard language of maternal deprivation. But as early as 1951, Bowlby, wholly convinced of the truth of Robertson's observations—and believing that they called fundamental psychoanalytic assumptions into question[53]—was already off in another direction.

7

OF GOSLINGS AND BABIES:
THE BIRTH OF ATTACHMENT THEORY

When a duckling is hatched it attaches itself to the first moving object it sees. Almost invariably that will be its mother; although if a human scientist elbows his way into first view, the duckling will become hopelessly attached to him and follow him everywhere. Other instinctive behaviors can similarly be distorted, or fail to develop at all, depending upon what the young animal encounters or fails to encounter in its environment. We know this and many other facts about the bonding behavior of birds and mammals thanks to the work of ethologists like Konrad Lorenz and Niko Tinbergen.

Bowlby first heard of Lorenz, now considered the father of modern ethology, from Norman Hotoph, a young psychologist at the London School of Economics. Hotoph mentioned Lorenz's work on imprinting, the process by which early bonding takes place, and Bowlby, absorbed in questions regarding the infant-mother bond, managed to obtain Lorenz's 1935 article on the subject, "The Companion in the Bird's World."[1] The qualities of imprinting—a strong bond, which occurs quickly and firmly and is unrelated to feeding—had great appeal for Bowlby. Indeed, after reading Lorenz, it seemed that Bowlby had become imprinted himself.

In the summer of that year, John and Ursula Bowlby took their vacation in Scotland near Ursula's father, who was an ornithologist. Julian Huxley, the biologist, was visiting at the time. "I inquired tentatively," Bowlby said, "did he know anything about Lorenz and ethology? This led to an enthusiastic commendation from Huxley who knew him very well and who had done work of his own in this field."[2]

Since Darwin's time zoologists had been cataloguing the instinctual behavior of animals as a means of classifying them. Darwin, an ethologist before the name was invented, devotes a chapter of *The Origin of Species* to animal behaviors, noting that each species has its own peculiar repertoire of instinctual behavioral patterns, which are as fundamental to the species as its anatomy.[3] The problem with the term "instinct," however, as it came to be used by many biologists, is that it implied a rigid, inherited behavior, performed identically by every member of the species. Those who believed that animals were governed strictly by instincts reduced them essentially to machines that were programmed to behave in certain ways from birth.

But as naturalists began to study animal behavior in the wild, a new view, closer to Darwin's meaning, began to coalesce. Lorenz and Tinbergen moved away from the idea of rigid instincts, favoring instead "species-specific behavior." A species-specific behavior (a bird's peculiar song or nesting activity) is instinctive, but it is not preordained. In order to come into being it must encounter certain responses in the environment. Thus, the song a chaffinch will sing is limited to a certain range and quality by its genetic predisposition. But it must hear the song of an adult chaffinch if its song is to develop at all. What's more, it must hear the adult song within a certain sensitive period when it is receptive to this particular kind of learning. The same is true of imprinting. If a duck or gosling does not see a moving object within a relatively brief time after hatching, normal bonding will not take place.

The interplay between instinctual behavior patterns and events in the environment was found to exist throughout the animal world, with the young of each species prepared to react to significant symbols and events. Ethologists found that the mating behavior of the male stickleback fish is elicited by a shape resembling a pregnant female; the young herring gull opens its mouth wide in response to a red spot similar to the one found on the beak of adults of the species. Behavior involving mating and parenthood could in many species be modified by learning, turned off when no longer needed, or strung together in long sequences to produce complex social interactions that climax in copulation or that, when taken as a whole, comprise caring for the young.

To Bowlby it was immediately plain that the discoveries of the ethologists must apply in some form to human beings, that people, too, must have bonding behaviors and intergenerational cues, that they, too, must be prewired for some sort of relational experience, and that with them, too, nature's intentions could go awry if the environment failed them as it had with his young thieves. Intellectually, his encounter with ethology was the breakthrough of his career and the beginning of a lifelong love affair with Darwin, whose thinking formed the foundation upon which ethology was built.

"At that time," Bowlby recalled, "the conventional wisdom was that infants are only interested in mothers because mothers feed them." Anna Freud, without irony, called this "cupboard-love," a term that delighted Bowlby and that he used to great derisive effect for many years.[4] "I was profoundly unimpressed by that," he said. "I just didn't think it was true, I *knew* it wasn't true. There was a lot of fancy talk about breast-feeding and bottle-feeding and so on; I regarded it all as rubbish. It was completely contrary to my clinical experience. There were very loving mothers who had bottle-fed their babies and some very rejecting mothers whom I met in the clinic, women who were obviously very hostile, who had breast-fed their babies. And it seemed to me that the feeding variable was totally irrelevant, or almost totally irrelevant. So I was unimpressed with the conventional wisdom, but I had nothing particular to put in its place."[5]

He needed something. Critics were already insisting that the children in the maternal deprivation studies Bowlby had made famous were not suffering from the loss of their mother, were not even suffering from the loss of a mothering figure, but simply from a lack of adequate stimulation. Behaviorists in particular were making this point, and few of the studies were strong enough empirically to prove otherwise. Many of the babies who had suffered lengthy separations from their mothers had been placed in institutions where they were left in near total isolation for much of the day, with no one and nothing to play with. Behaviorists, therefore, were able to look at Bowlby's data and fit it comfortably into their own theories, where the love of a mothering figure was completely unnecessary to healthy emotional development. Most people who worked with children had a hard time buying that idea. It was hard to believe that all a child needed was enough stimulation and that it didn't matter where it came from or whether there was a single person with whom the infant could form a meaningful relationship. Such thinking seemed to be so utterly opposed to what intuition tells us about a child's needs. But science cannot run on intuition. It needs a theory grounded in data. The ethologists provided that. And Bowlby responded to it with enthusiasm: "I mean talk about *eureka*. They were brilliant, first-class scientists, brilliant observers, and studying family relationships in other species—relationships which were obviously analogous with that of human beings—and doing it so frightfully well. We were fumbling around in the dark; they were already in brilliant sunshine."[6]

In addition to improved strategies of investigation, ethology gave Bowlby an explanation: Separations from mother were disastrous developmentally because they thwarted an instinctual need. It's not just a nice thing to have someone billing and cooing over you, snuggling you, and adoringly attending to your every need. It is a built-in necessity, and the baby's efforts to obtain it, like the parents' eagerness to give it, are biologically programmed.

Bowlby would soon declare that sucking, clinging, following, crying, and smiling are all part of the child's instinctual repertoire, whose goal is to keep the mother close by. He saw the child's smile as a "social releaser" that elicited maternal care. And, like Ronald Fairbairn, he abandoned the Freudian notion of drives, based on hidden forces like libido and aggression, that accumulate within us and crave discharge. Instead he saw an array of innate behavior patterns—relationship-seeking patterns like babbling, looking, and listening—that are enriched and developed by the responses they receive from the environment.[7]

Bowlby introduced the formal term "attachment" to describe the infant-mother bond. Unlike bonding, which suggested an instantaneous event (and which years later was briefly and erroneously considered critical to a healthy mother-infant relationship[8]), attachment suggested a complex, developing process. Indeed, to Bowlby attachment was much closer to the idea of love, if not identical with it. He now proceeded to define a new series of developmental stages based on the maternal bond. During the first year the child is gradually able to display a complete range of "attachment behaviors," protesting mother's departure, greeting her returns, clinging when frightened, following when able. Such actions are instinctual and rooted in the biological fact that proximity to mother, because it is essential to survival, is satisfying. The formation, maintenance, and renewal of that proximity begets feelings of love, security, and joy. A lasting or untimely disruption brings on anxiety, grief, and depression.

In much of Freud's writing, the tie to the mother is curiously absent. He believed that after a brief love affair with the breast, the infant moves quickly into a stage of primary narcissism in which his main love object is his own body. Only much later, after the age of two, does the child become focused on the opposite-sex parent as an object of desire and love. The relationship of the child to its mother during the first two years of its life was a nonissue in classical Freudian thought.

Even when he did consider the power of early bonds, Freud was strangely fixated on father-love. It is not until 1938, just before his death, that Freud spoke with some feeling about the power of the early tie to the mother, describing it as "unique, without parallel, laid down unalterably for a whole lifetime, as the first and strongest love-object and as the prototype of all later love relations—for both sexes."[9]

But the idea that mother-love has such critical and lasting impact did not begin to take hold in orthodox psychoanalytic circles until Anna Freud began to move away from Freud's father-centered universe. Although she never married or had children of her own, she had had many maternal relationships, beginning with her nephew Ernst, whose mother, Anna's sister Sophie, had died, and continuing with the children of Dorothy Burlingham, her close friend and collaborator with whom she lived (platonically by all accounts) for decades. She was also, of course, a child analyst, her work with children much more focused on concerns with mastering reality than on Melanie Klein's arena, which was primitive fantasy life. She came to see the mother as playing numerous vital roles in the child's psychological development: the person whose relationship with the child forms the prototype for future relationships; an auxiliary ego, who helps the child cope with difficult situations; and the social legislator who inducts the child into the world of rules and standards (a modification of her father's view that paternal authority forms the basis of the superego). She believed that the loving attachment to the mother was ultimately more important to psychological development than the instinctual repression her father had emphasized.[10]

Anna Freud's nursery work in Vienna and then London during the war further convinced her of the mother's central role in the child's emotional development. These little children much preferred sleeping by their mothers' side in dismal air raid shelters—"a state of bliss to which they all desired to return"[11]—to the creature comforts of the Hampstead nursery. She discovered that children's responses to the war crises reflected their mother's responses—calm if the mother was calm, distraught if she was distraught. And it was plain to her that separation from the mother, not the father, was traumatic for the children in her care, a discovery that forced a new attitude among her analytic colleagues.

Anna Freud was a strong supporter of Bowlby's and Robertson's work on separation. She urged that mothers be admitted with their hospitalized children because otherwise, battered by illness, strange circumstances, and medical procedures, a child's ego resources—its ability to cope with the pressures of reality—are quickly overwhelmed.

By the 1950s most analysts were at least informally agreed that the relationship with mother is of critical psychological importance, that the child's first relationships are key foundations of his personality, and that his tie to his mother is, by the end of the first year, very strong. Among the classical Freudians, Erik Erikson was perhaps most eloquent on the subject. He believed that the infant's trust in the care he receives enables him first to achieve the bodily regulation he needs—in feeding, sleeping, eliminating. Later it enables him to let his mother out of sight "without undue anxiety or rage." In the end it "forms the basis in the child for a sense of identity" and of being "all right."[12]

But neither Erikson nor anyone else had a convincing theory to explain why any of this should be so. Four major theories were in vogue at the time, the most popular continuing to be that attachment develops because the mother satisfies the baby's physiological needs, mainly for nourishment and warmth. Others argued that the child has a built-in need to suckle at the mother's breast, and eventually it learns that there is a mother attached to the breast, and so relates to her as well. A third theory, advocated by the Hungarian analyst Imre Herman, presumed an inborn need to cling to another human being. The fourth was that infants crave a return to the womb and that this craving naturally draws them to seek mother and her embrace. (Bowlby could barely conceal his disdain for this concept: "It is difficult to imagine what survival value such a desire might have, and I am not aware that any has been suggested."[13])

Empirical researchers, like Charlotte Bühler, the great Berlin psychologist with whom Spitz had trained, had long noted that babies in their first weeks respond to the human voice and face in a totally unique way.[14] Klein had commented on the infant's tendency to gaze at her mother's face, and become engaged, through facial expressions, in what appeared to be "a loving conversation between mother and baby."[15] But none of this had worked its way into developmental thinking. Anna Freud had stuck by her father, arguing that love begins in the stomach and only gradually moves outward from there, and most analysts, even if the evidence of their eyes told them otherwise, followed suit. Thus, Budapest-trained analyst Therese Benedek, a brilliant and sensitive developmental thinker, believed the infant needed to be "smiled at, picked up, talked to, etc."; the American analyst Margaret Ribble, a major voice against maternal deprivation, believed that infants had an innate need for contact with the mother; Spitz believed in the importance of skin contact with the mother and decried its decline through much of the Western world. But all three held that such needs were built first upon feeding. This idea had become so entrenched, it was hard to think in any other way.[16]

Bowlby's theory had something in common with the sucking and clinging theories, but the views that were closest to his were expressed by a few object relations and interpersonal pioneers. Fairbairn, who saw our biological drives as aspects of our relational needs, once illustrated this point with an anecdote from a psychoanalytic session in which his patient cried, "You are always talking about my wanting this or that desire satisfied; but what I really want is a father."[17]

Michael Balint, a psychoanalyst of the Budapest school who later settled in England and with his wife, Alice, believed that the wish to be loved, totally and unconditionally, is a primary need of human beings from the time they are born. If they don't get it, they spend the rest of their lives searching for it. Balint saw this problem as rampant in civilized countries because the close mother-child tie is severed at too early an age.[18] Balint's analyst, Sandor Ferenczi, had been rejected by Freud toward the end of his career for trying to give patients the love they'd lacked in their early years (going so far in his abandonment of analytic neutrality as to hug patients and let them sit on his lap). Like Ferenczi, Balint believed that the deprivation of parental love underlies much neurotic phenomena, and he constantly saw patients trying to wrench from their analysts what their parents had failed to give them.

And then there was Winnicott. His thinking was also close to Bowlby's, but their relationship was perhaps the trickiest. Winnicott had come to psychoanalysis from pediatrics, and his intuitive gift for working with children was considered uncanny and inspirational by many. At the same time, his popular advice on child rearing made him the British equivalent of Dr. Spock, with a cult following of adoring women.[19] Winnicott, too, had taken strong positions, some of them predating Bowlby's, on both the centrality of the infant-mother bond and on the critical importance of the quality of mothering. Like Bowlby and Fairbairn, he believed that the baby had a built-in need to form an emotional relationship with the mother.[20] Unlike Klein, he was aware of the damage mothers could do, having treated thousands of mothers and children at the outpatient clinic at the Paddington Green Children's Hospital.[21] He saw the way the mother held the baby, both in the physical and psychological sense, as extremely important and had written that "the earliest anxiety is related to being insecurely held."[22] He and Bowlby had co-signed a letter in 1939 warning about the psychological dangers of evacuating young children from the cities during the war. Although strongly influenced by Klein, whom he considered a genius—he counted himself a Kleinian for many years and was apparently preoccupied with her approval[23]—Winnicott could not accept some of her main concepts (the idea of innate envy particularly infuriated him).

While his interest in Bowlby seemed minimal and his statements about him (mainly in private) were mixed, their views were so similar that years later Bowlby would repeatedly say that he felt that Winnicott stated in poetic terms many of the same things that he, Bowlby, was trying to express scientifically. But, while Bowlby concentrated on the environment and on the scientific underpinnings of intimate relationships, Winnicott focused on the child's subjective experience. He was in a sense the ground on which Bowlby and Klein met.

Winnicott's attention to parental impact was also evident in his concept of the "false self." A false self—grandiose, compulsively pleasing, precociously mature and competent, etc.—does not develop on its own. It is a response, Winnicott believed, to the mother's psychic intrusions.[24] Winnicott's delicate sensitivity to the child's needs, the intricacies of the mother-infant relationship, the ways in which a child forms a sense of self in the context of that relationship, and the numerous subtle avenues via which this process could go awry not only went a long way, in Charles Rycroft's words, toward resurrecting "the traumatic theory of neurosis,"[25] but would eventually contribute to a reputation that today places Winnicott higher than almost any other British analyst.

Although Winnicott was considered something of a maverick in the 1950s (both Freud and Klein considered him a lightweight and neither would allow her students to study with him on a regular basis[26]), he was not a threatening one, partly because he was not inclined to build theory at the expense of those to whom he felt some sense of loyalty. If Bowlby showed an implacable masculine spirit and a willingness to let the chips fall where they may in the single-minded pursuit of his idea, Winnicott's approach was essentially more feminine and maternal,[27] an inclination he readily noted in himself and which no doubt contributed to his clinical genius. As a result, his theoretical statements sometimes had a peculiar, obfuscatory quality about them, as he tried to maintain allegiances and build bridges, a tendency that Bowlby, for one, found maddening.[28] It was a cardinal tenet of Kleinian thinking, for instance, that the baby's first relationship is with the breast. Winnicott appeared to go along with this and yet differ with it at the same time. "When it is said that the first object is the breast," he wrote, "the word 'breast' is used, I believe, to stand for the technique of mothering as well as for the actual flesh. It is not impossible for a mother to be a good enough mother (in my way of putting it) with a bottle for the actual feeding."[29] This makes good sense, but it is not what Klein had in mind.

By the late 1950s Bowlby was ready to present the main themes of his new synthesis, and he did so in three papers addressed to his analytic colleagues, the first and most important of which was called "The Nature of the Child's Tie to His Mother." If we look at things the way the ethologists do, Bowlby said, there is no point any longer in thinking in terms of psychological drives, or energies that accumulate and require discharge. Freud, in keeping with the scientific thinking of his day, assumed that in order to explain the motivation behind a sexual or self-preservation behavior, one must postulate sexual and self-preservation drives. Bowlby said this way of thinking was now obsolete. You don't need an eating drive to explain eating. You don't need a seeing drive in order to explain the existence of the eye or phenomenon of sight. The eye works the way it does because natural selection favored physiological variations leading to improved vision. Mating and parenting behavior work the way they do because natural selection favored certain behavioral responses in these realms.

What's more, the trigger for many instinctual behaviors dwells as frequently outside the organism as within. Thus eating can be initiated or terminated only by certain chemical signals from within the body; but mating behavior may be elicited by the spread of another bird's tail, the color of its beak, or the song it sings. Between parent and child, between mating adults, certain actions naturally elicit certain responses.

The primary purpose of many of the infant's and young child's instinctual responses, in man as in other animals, is to ensure proximity to the adult, which is necessary to survival. Sucking, clinging, following, crying, and smiling—and perhaps cooing and babbling as well—are all instinctual responses that eventually coalesce to form the broad mosaic of attachment behavior. Initially unrelated to one another, in the course of the first year of life they gradually become integrated and directed toward a single purpose.

Crying and smiling do not actively attach the child to the parent; rather they attach the parent to the child. Bowlby noted the abundant evidence from animal studies that shows the mother responding immediately to the bleat, call, or cry of its young. (Bowlby observed that although the human baby's crying response is often terminated by food, babies frequently cry when they are not hungry and will stop when they are picked up, rocked, or spoken to.) The smile, Bowlby wrote, "has a comparable though more agreeable effect." Social smiling, which shows up at around six weeks, is activated by the human face—or, in the early days, by a simple gestalt composed of two dots—and it is a powerful social releaser of maternal behavior, beguiling and enslaving the mother. "Can we doubt that the more and better an infant smiles the better is he loved and cared for?"[30]

(By advancing this idea, that parents have instinctual responses to their young and that those responses are elicited by such things as smiles and cries, Bowlby was, indirectly, advancing an explanation for why nurses and other medical professionals could fail to hear or see the agony of hospitalized babies or deceive themselves into believing that the "settled" child who no longer cried for his mother was not depressed or suffering. To use Bowlby's language, the infants' cries activated the nurse's own attachment systems, making them feel compelled to offer maternal care. But because they could not possibly mother all the babies in their unit, they were placed in a biologically and psychologically untenable position, as if constantly having to listen to alarms and sirens and not being allowed to respond. Repression, rationalization, denial, and other defenses were the only recourse, the only refuge from a searing heart.)

From the baby's point of view, Bowlby said, none of its instinctual attachment responses is more primary than the other, and so it is mistaken to give preeminence to sucking or feeding, or to assume attachment follows strictly from their satisfaction. Clinging, to take one example, which is essential to the survival of most primates, sometimes shows extraordinary tenacity. In some species it is maintained both day and night in the first weeks of life and clearly has no relation to feeding. If an infant chimpanzee is kept from clinging to its mother, it will cry plaintively. The slightly older infant chimp will throw a temper tantrum. In human babies it is most pronounced when the child is afraid, when it is about to be put to bed, or after a separation from the mother.

The very young infant relies mainly on responses that will evoke maternal behavior—that is, crying and smiling. But as it grows older, it uses clinging and following to assure proximity. Following with the eyes shows up by the third month. Later, as it is able to crawl, then walk, following is activated if the child is tired, hungry, in pain, or afraid. Following reaches its peak, not, as many would assume, when the child is most helpless and dependent, but when he is becoming more independent, toward the end of the second year, because now he is able to crawl or walk into dangerous situations but not able yet to fend for himself in an emergency. With data like this, Bowlby was able to argue that attachment is quite separate from dependency based on feeding and not caused by it at all.

Bowlby saw sucking as another important element in the attachment repertoire, contributing to the child's sense of felt security. He disapproved of the modern tendency to wean children at six months. "In my experience most infants through much of the second year of life need a great deal of sucking and thrive on milk from a bottle at bedtime." He insisted, however, that breast-feeding is not the big deal it's been made out to be, nor are the early months of infancy so much more important than the later ones. "It is my impression that fully as many psychological disturbances, including the most severe, can date from the second year of life when clinging and following are at their peak as from the early months when they are rudimentary."[31]

Anxiety, fear, illness, and fatigue, Bowlby added, will all cause a child to increase these attachment behaviors.

Bowlby argued that neurotic disturbances arise out of distortions of the attachment system. The very sorts of maternal behaviors that cause a child to feel hostile toward the mother—minor rejections, for instance, or short separations—may also be expected to intensify following and clinging; hence the neurotically dependent behavior of some children and adults. When the mother figure is massively rejecting or totally absent, attachment behaviors may fail to mature or become totally repressed—the condition that Bowlby himself had seen in the affectionless thieves and assumed to be at work in adult psychopaths.

The attachment system does not exist for the purpose of creating love or for healthy emotional functioning in later life. Each of the instinctual responses Bowlby describes is present because of its survival value. Without them the child would die, especially the child that was born on the primitive savannahs where people first evolved. None of these survival behaviors is directed at the mother per se. In the early months individuals are vague presences. He argued, however, that the mother becomes the key player not because the baby is one day able to grasp that there is a person attached to the breast, but because she responds to and becomes the object of all the various attachment behaviors.

Before the baby is able to grasp the idea of a person, its suckling may relate only to the breast or the bottle, the smiling to any human face, and it is enough that the other attachment behaviors get responded to, regardless of where the response comes from. But gradually, as mother comes into view as an individual, their mutual history of dovetailed responses coalesces into the single phenomenon of love. The once separate, unrelated, instinctual patterns are now elements of a more complex system, attachment behavior, with a single direction and single purpose. And now there is a person to whom the baby feels attached and toward whom he consciously directs these behaviors. By a certain age, differing broadly among babies but probably six or seven months at the latest, "good mothering from any kind woman ceases to satisfy him—only his mother will do."[32] Subsequent studies of adoption in the first year tended to bear Bowlby out on this point, with children under six months of age tending to adjust to a new mother with much less distress.[33]*

Bowlby notes that throughout the animal world, species-specific behaviors, whether on the part of the child, the parent, or the mate, tend

---

*I find this idea, which remains a tenet of attachment thinking to this day—that "it is only during the second 6 months that these proximity and interaction promoting behaviors are integrated into a coherent system, organized around a particular figure or figures" (Bretherton, 1985, p. 7)—difficult to accept. My own son showed a clear preference for my wife and me from earliest infancy, and infant observations made by students at the Tavistock Clinic in recent years make the same finding (Juliet Hopkins, personal communication, February 5, 1993.) See also Mary Ainsworth's study of Ganda children in Chapter 10. However, as the adoption studies mentioned above indicate, the strength and quality of the infant's attachment does seem to go through some sort of important change in the latter part of the first year, at least in many infants.

to be focused on one individual (or in the case of the parent, one group of individuals, the children). Bowlby sees this neglected fact as so important, he gives it a name, "monotropy," which will live on in furious psychological debates for the next three decades.

By monotropy Bowlby did not mean, as many of his critics believe to this day, that the child becomes attached to only one figure. Rather that there is a hierarchy, with one figure, the chief caregiver, usually the mother, at the head. Even in adult life, most people live or seek to live by this hierarchical design, choosing one person who is their central attachment figure, one person who is loved above all others and whose presence most insures a feeling of security. When we are at our lowest, due to illness or emotional distress, this is the person we most want nearby.

In childhood the primary caregiver is crucial to healthy development. He believes that maternal deprivation and separation are damaging in the early years largely because the child's precious central figure has been removed, causing his attachment life and all its emotional and developmental derivatives to become disrupted.[34] Bowlby argued that, given this natural predisposition, threats to abandon a child who misbehaves, threats to send him away, or threats by a mother to kill herself—all of which he found to be distressingly common—are terrifying to the child, generating unbearable levels of anxiety. In the older child or adolescent they also arouse anger, which can so dominate the personality as to become dysfunctional. Years later, another researcher reported the case of an adolescent who, after killing his mother, cried, "I couldn't stand to have her leave me."[35] Bowlby thought this a fitting illustration of his theory.

Bowlby believed that babies were capable of true mourning, another controversial point with his analytic colleagues, despite the evidence of Anna Freud's wartime nurseries and a 1956 study by Christoph Heinicke, an American psychologist who worked on Bowlby's team. In 1958 Peter Marris published *Widows and Their Families*. Bowlby saw that the widow's reactions to loss that Marris described were similar to what had been observed in infants. The widow's pattern typically included rage, which might be directed almost anywhere—at a doctor, at herself, at the lost husband. The rage, Marris believed, while it lasted, gave the woman courage. Only afterward did she sink into depression.[36] Here, in grown adults, was the protest and despair that Robertson had observed in small children, proof to Bowlby that babies mourned like adults when they lost

a precious other and that this mourning of the loss of an attachment figure remained critical throughout life.

In healthy mourning, the individual gradually reorganizes. He allows
himself to separate from the lost person and begins to reach out to form
new attachments. Pathological mourning, in contrast, either never lets
up or is disavowed and continues to control the person unconsciously.
For the small child who loses his first attachment figure and is not given
a new one in time, like the institutionalized children Spitz filmed or the
affectionless thieves Bowlby treated, pathological mourning is the only
possible course, with results that distort the development of the child's
personality.

The detachment that Robertson had observed in young children
who'd suffered long hospitalizations and that Bowlby saw as the root of
affectionless psychopathy was one type of pathological mourning. It was
dangerous because it sealed off the personality not only from despair but
from love and other experiences that could disconfirm his feelings of
worthlessness, guilt, and bitter mistrust, thus precluding any working
through of the grief. In less severe cases, a prolonged and depriving separation in infancy will not lead to such profound character disorder. But
the pathological mourning process will show up when the child faces
separations or losses later in life and, as many classical analytic case studies had shown, predispose him not only to separation anxiety but to
depressive episodes as well.[37]

Bowlby now made an effort to interpret the sequence of reactions to
separation discovered by Robertson and to integrate them into his developing theory. If protest, despair, and detachment are the three primary
responses of the young child to separation from his mother, then we can
see in these reactions, he says, the basis for key emotional processes that
govern our psychology. Protest is an embodiment of separation anxiety,
despair is an indication of mourning, detachment is a form of defense.

In addition, Bowlby argued that separation anxiety, which had long
been a subject of debate in analysis—and which had been attributed to
all sorts of psychic processes, from Otto Rank's idea that it was a recapit-
ulation of the trauma of birth to Melanie Klein's proposition that the
child assumed that the absent mother had somehow been eaten up or
destroyed by the child itself[38]—was a natural, evolutionary-based childhood reaction. It was an intrinsic fear, like fear of the dark, loud noises,
isolation, and strange things and people. Separation anxiety, like

stranger anxiety, however, only becomes pronounced for many children in the second half of the first year. Bowlby explained this by noting that as the infant's attachment system becomes more organized around a particular mothering figure, so does his tendency to withdraw from or become upset by strange situations.[39] He believed that separation anxiety was particularly problematic for a child because in many cases attachment behavior was activated, but because the attachment figure was not present, it could not be shut off. He also saw such attachment frustration as the source of the hostility he had seen in so many young children who had either been separated from or neglected by their mothers.

Just as Freud, beginning with hysteria, outlined an entire theory of human psychology and psychopathology, Bowlby, building from his work on separation, was in the process of doing something similar. Unlike Freud, however, he had both Freud's and Darwin's shoulders to stand on.

Bowlby's theory was bold, full of common sense, speculative but grounded in science, and threatening to the older views. His papers were loaded with calls for research. Bowlby was unusual in this, as, of course, he knew, and he must have also known that such calls, aside from representing his true belief in what was needed, also tweaked the noses of his analytic colleagues. He was almost daring them: Here's what I believe; there's what you believe; let's see which position is borne out by the data. He could afford to state modestly that much of what he was saying was speculative and needed to be empirically confirmed; he was confident it would be. Meanwhile, in advocating research, he was also saying, in effect, "Let's play a game with which I am quite familiar and which you have never bothered to learn." Few psychoanalysts were also researchers; indeed it was quite rare for clinicians and researchers to speak the same language let alone be united in one person. Meanwhile, research on early separation undertaken by Robertson, Heinicke, and Rudolph Schaffer, former and current members of his team, were already lending support to his theories.

Throughout his papers, Bowlby made every effort to align himself with Freud and to offer citations from Freud to establish that he was plowing fields that Freud had sanctioned, even if Freud had never plowed them himself. He makes complimentary statements about the contributions of Anna Freud and Dorothy Burlingham and quotes from them approvingly where he feels in tune with their findings. On the other hand, he makes no bones about declaring certain views obsolete: Dependency is irrelevant to attachment and attachment behaviors. Mother and breast should no longer be equated nor should good mother and good feeding. It is wrong to speak of the earliest phase as oral or the relationship to the mother at that time as anaclitic, a popular term in psychoanalysis, coined by Spitz, and meaning simply that baby-love is built on the baby dependency. With these brief statements at the end of "The Child's Tie," he attacked sensitive elements of analytic orthodoxy, be it Freudian or Kleinian. There was something for everyone to be upset about.

8

"What's the Use to Psychoanalyze a Goose?" Turmoil, Hostility, and Debate

"All of us find security in being with people we know well and are apt to feel anxious and insecure in a crowd of strangers. Particularly in times of crisis or distress do we seek our closest friends and relatives. The need for companionship and the comfort it brings is a very deep need in human nature—and one we share with many of the higher animals."[1]

Thus began John Bowlby's first (and, as it would turn out, only) official advice to parents. A small pamphlet, called *Can I Leave My Baby?*, it was published in 1958 by the National Association of Mental Health. He continued:

> This need for companionship is even stronger in young crea-
> tures than in grown-ups. Whether it is a brood of ducklings on
> a pond, twin lambs in a meadow, or a human toddler around
> the house, the young are quickly distressed if they get lost and
> scamper to get close to their mothers as soon as anything hap-
> pens which frightens them.[2]

In his new pamphlet, Bowlby continued his assault on the stiff-upper-lip philosophy by which he had been reared and helped parents understand the implications of his and Robertson's work on early separation. He also wanted to offer some solace to mothers who were confused by the abundance of conflicting advice or who, because of their exposure to Bowlby's or Robertson's previous work, as filtered through the popular press, dreaded leaving their babies for an evening at the theater.

Bowlby, who by now had spent many years running a mother's group at a well-baby clinic from which he'd learned a great deal about mothers' experiences,[3] sympathized with parents regarding the relentless demands of young children, which seemed to grow worse rather than abate as the infant developed into a toddler. "If they are frightened and upset, they cling to their parents like leeches," he said. "All parents find this irksome and at times wish to be free of it. Some become alarmed lest it go on forever."[4] But he insisted that this process was natural and that if it was accepted, the demands would decrease and a secure child would emerge. "When you have a baby," he said, quoting an old adage, "you have five years of hard labor ahead of you. If you don't get it over at the beginning, you've got it coming to you later."[5]

Bowlby was not in the least opposed to a live-in nanny, as long as she was a good one, as long as it was recognized that she may become the true mother figure in the child's eyes, and—this he emphasized—as long as she stayed. For by the time the child reaches six months of age, his primary caretaker becomes a crucial and irreplaceable person who must be there fairly continuously for the next two and a half years. In a statement that seems particularly poignant in light of his own childhood experience, he warned, "For a child to be looked after entirely by a loving nanny and then for her to leave when he is two or three, or even four or five, can be almost as tragic as the loss of a mother."[6]

Bowlby favored separation in small doses. "It is an excellent plan," he said, "to accustom babies and small children to being cared for now and then by someone else."[7] It will prepare the child for future emergency separations and give the mother some breathing space. He told mothers that they should not worry about being away from their children for an evening or even, occasionally, for a long weekend. But until the age of three, longer separations are perilous and will usually have lasting ramifications in the form of insecure behavior. He thus opposed hospitalizing young children, advised seeking outpatient alternatives wherever possible, rooming with one's child if hospitalization is unavoidable, and making a fuss if this is resisted.

If the mother must be hospitalized, he urged that the child be taken care of by a familiar person, ideally the father or a favorite aunt or granny, but always someone who can serve as a full-time caretaker. But, upon return home, Bowlby cautioned, "Don't expect a cheerful welcome and a warm hug. Expect instead a rather bemused little person who keeps his distance and hardly knows what to make of things. He may even run away from you or claim that you are not his mother at all."[8] When the initial rejection is followed by night waking, clinginess, temper tantrums over the slightest separation, don't blame grandma for spoiling the baby while mother was away, Bowlby said. And don't try to correct such annoying behavior with firmness. The only corrective is "a lot of love and reassurance."[9]

Much of this was immensely controversial at the time, when the institutionalization, wartime evacuation, and sending of young children to boarding schools were consecrated practices. But, unique in the history of psychoanalysis, it had a rich body of research supporting it. In the vastness of psychoanalytic thinking, Bowlby's thesis might be considered small; but it was strong. It would remain controversial as increasing numbers of women entered the work force.

But it was in his discussion of parents and their roles that Bowlby may have seeded the ground for an even greater furor. In Bowlby's view, advanced for 1958 but relatively unchanged in later years, the father's role is mainly as a support for mother. The father becomes increasingly important to children as they get older, but because he is away so much during the infant's and toddler's waking day, he rates a poor second when they awaken in the middle of the night and seek reassurance. He urged fathers not to be too upset by that and to recognize that their role, keeping their wives happy, is a part of child care, too. To Bowlby, a nonstop worker himself, whose work *was* his life, and whose rare displays of temper were occasioned by the intrusions of his children,[10] it perhaps seemed inconceivable that a father could be more intimately involved, so that his presence, too, would be a source of security.

The mother, on the other hand, has a tougher and more exacting job, "perhaps the most skilled in the world."[11] She may be exhausted, overwhelmed, and short-tempered, but she gets great satisfaction from knowing how crucial and irreplaceable she is. Meanwhile, she must never forget that the job cannot be skimped without lasting damage to the child. "One cannot ever really give back to a child the love and attention he needed and did not receive when he was small. With understanding and affection, and perhaps skilled help, one can go a long way towards it, sometimes a very long way, but it will never be quite the same."[12]

Such pronouncements set teeth on edge. Among psychologists, Bowlby's insistence that what was missed early on could never be fully replaced was controversial and remains so to this day. There is evidence that sensitive periods do exist for human children, when, for instance, language skills must be acquired, and the same may be true for the ability to become meaningfully attached and thus able to give and receive love. But we are much more flexible in this respect than lower animals and much better able to make up our losses, a fact that Bowlby would come to recognize.

Some women, meanwhile, believed that Bowlby was determined to chain mothers to the home, and in this they were partially correct. He fully welcomed women into the professions—as the many women who worked for and with him have attested—but he expected them to face up to their maternal responsibilities when and if they had children and take a leave of absence. He did believe in a gradual return to work for those who wanted it, beginning on a part-time basis, after the child reached the age of three; and, as an employer, he went out of his way to make such arrangements possible. But such fine points were hardly acknowledged in the storm that soon swirled around him.

Bowlby's advice to parents and his recommendations regarding social policies affecting families and young children were less controversial among analysts, even seen as progressive. Indeed, he was having more positive impact on social policy and child care practices in England and around the world than any other analyst in history. For analysts it was the underlying theory that irritated them.

Both Melanie Klein and Anna Freud, now the rival doyennes of British psychoanalysis, found the analytic-ethological concoction Bowlby was brewing, with his constant references to birds and beasts, distasteful, and they let their followers know it. Analytic critics charged him, among many other things, with gross simplification of theory, with assuming that all pathology resulted from disturbances of the mother-infant bond (when it was well known that early medical and other environmental traumas could equally be at fault), and with overlooking the infant's ability to develop a negative concept of the mother on wholly irrational grounds—such as when she fails to relieve his suffering despite her best efforts, or when the arrival of a new sibling brings forth intolerable feelings of abandonment, rage, and guilt.

"An infant can't follow its mother; it isn't a duckling," said the Kleinian analyst Susanna Isaacs. "The human baby is very helpless for a prolonged period of time. And during this period it forms an internal image of the mother; this would be a mixture of memory, of fantasies, of the baby's response to the actual reality of the mother."[13]

To Bowlby reality was the cornerstone upon which fantasy was built. If a fantasy becomes terribly distorted—as he believed it did with his affectionless thieves, so that only a hateful picture of the mother is retained, regardless, in some cases, of how unfair it may be—that internal picture does not come about for nothing. It is based on an experience—in the case of the young thieves, early separation, hostile treatment, neglect, abuse, or some combination of the four. No matter how distorted infantile fantasies may be, negative internal images of mother will not grow out of an essentially positive, secure experience. But in the Kleinian view, fantasy did not depend on such links to reality. Using familiar Kleinian imagery, Isaacs argued that "babies are very capable of perpetuating a distorted view of the mother, of introjecting a 'bad mother' where none exists. It's their helplessness; helplessness and fantasy go together. And even the most perfect mother will frustrate the baby once in a while, keeping him waiting. This makes the baby angry, and the emotions of infants are terribly intense—it's so difficult for them to assess what's happening to them." Whereas the distortions of some babies tend toward the negative, other babies distort in a more positive direction, enabling them, according to Isaacs, to "introject a good internal picture when they haven't had a mother at all—just different people looking after them."[14] Such thinking, needless to say, was anathema to Bowlby.

The Kleinians, like the Freudians, protested that Bowlby ignored intrapsychic processes—and that it is just these processes that distinguish people from fish, birds, dogs, and rodents. As the leading Kleinian theorist of her day, Hanna Segal, recently said (quoting from Ogden Nash): "What's the use to psychoanalyze a goose?"[15]

The debate over such issues was very bitter, despite the fact that the participants were largely in the same camp, all of them psychoanalysts who accepted basic analytic principles, with Bowlby and Anna Freud in the forefront of the fight against maternal deprivation and Bowlby openly indebted to Klein for her views on early relatedness, fantasy, mourning, and depression.

But the debate was not taking place under normal conditions. The forties and fifties were an adventurous, incestuous, and, as some believe, a shameful time in British psychoanalysis.[16] The Anna Freudian and Kleinian camps were at such dagger points that it seemed they would split the Society apart, and, indeed, they would have if a "gentlemen's agreement" had not been worked out after the war that enabled the two groups to coexist. If Freud was a less combative personality than Klein, she was no less rigid in matters of theory and was, besides, a somewhat cool and aloof personality, ever conscious of the mantle of royal legitimacy she'd inherited. Intricate issues of loyalty and betrayal surrounded them both, and both were dogmatic, almost theocratic, in their views. ("Anna Freud worshipped at the shrine of St. Sigmund, Klein at the shrine of St. Melanie," Bowlby said.[17]) "These were not people you could disagree with," says Juliet Hopkins of the Tavistock staff. "If you disagreed, you were wrong."[18]

Anna Freud had been analyzed by her father, a practice that is not only considered grossly unethical today but violates commonsense strictures against boundary violation and incestuous intrusion. That she was never able to form a significant attachment to another man or a sexual connection with anyone, male or female, suggests the degree to which she remained stuck in her father's emotional orbit. As if not to be outdone by the founder, Klein had, in turn, analyzed her own children with horrendous results.[19] Winnicott, like Bowlby, had been analyzed by Joan Riviere and supervised by Klein. Klein asked him to analyze her son, which he did (from 1935 to 1939), while strenuously resisting her efforts to supervise the case. (She did, however, succeed in supervising the analysis of her grandson by Marion Milner.) Later, as Winnicott and Klein delicately dueled over theory and as Klein continued to reject him (even at one point refusing to allow his paper to be included in a special double issue of the *International Journal of Psycho-Analysis* in honor of her seventieth birthday because he refused to revise it in such a way as to more fully incorporate her ideas), his wife, Clare, also an analyst, went into treatment with Klein, which could only have been loaded with unconscious meanings and motives for all three of them.[20] Paula Heimann, initially a devoted follower of Klein's, found it necessary to publicly dissolve their connection after disagreeing with her mentor on a matter of theory.[21] Scientific meetings of the Society were often characterized by grotesque bickering and attacks, with the younger candidates, who were desperate for patient referrals from their superiors, often smirking to one another as someone from the opposing camp presented his views.[22] Meanwhile, Anna Freud and Melanie Klein sat in the front row "with barricades of people between them."[23] In 1962 Charles Rycroft, a brilliant and sensible analyst from the independent group, became so fed up that he stopped attending meetings of the Society and a decade later quit altogether.[24]

If it was a shameful time, it was also in many ways a fertile time, with British analysis experiencing a ferment that would not hit the States for another decade. Major questions were being asked not only about theory, but practice, and the fact that the Society had not split meant that all factions had to listen to and contend in some way with opposing views. Winnicott was extending the treatment hour for some patients beyond the standard fifty minutes, and, like some of his peers, was providing a more supportive, maternal stance for the patients who seemed to need it. The once monolithic analytic neutrality, which in practice often felt cold and distant, was now being questioned.

Meanwhile, analysts were seeing more and more of the type of patients mentioned earlier who did not fit the standard concept of neurosis. Instead of suffering from internal conflicts and being haunted by guilt—but otherwise having a pretty clear sense of who they were—they had trouble in relationships, often felt empty, detached, or worthless. Such patients, once considered inappropriate for analysis, were now being treated en masse, and the sources of their disturbances were invariably traced not to oedipal conflicts but to early, preoedipal, experiences, often related to faulty parenting.

It was into this agitated context that Bowlby—a Kleinian apostate—stepped with his new pronouncements.

It is understandable that Bowlby's views would not have been popular with his peers. It was not just his rejection of certain sacred psychoanalytic axioms. His ideas about ethology and prevention, because they tended to bypass intrapsychic processes, seemed vaguely unanalytic if not downright anti-analytic. To some it seemed, as Isaacs and Segal implied, that he was reducing a human child to a goose, with predictable, preset responses, and ignoring not only the richness and diversity of individual psychology but the ways in which an irrational inner world of guilt, fear, shame, identification, projection, and paranoia can serve as the distorting lens through which both the child and the adult perceive and experience reality.

Bowlby was a nuts-and-bolts man. He liked hard data and researchable concepts. He was proud that his forty-four juvenile thieves paper was the first psychoanalytic article to include statistics. He was unlike almost any other analyst in that respect. Although he was stirred by poetry and quoted it in his books, he saw himself as a scientist, one who would help (perhaps force) psychoanalysis to live up to its scientific pretensions. He preferred to work in the daylight where facts were facts and a man could feel in command of himself and his destiny; he was more wary of the darkness, with its shadowy ambiguities, where faulty and nonsensical notions, products of an overly active imagination, could gain credence and where disturbing feelings could not be easily warded off. Even some of those who saw value in his work (like the American analyst Otto Kernberg[25]) would fault him for failing to build a better bridge to thinkers like Klein, for whom the shadows were the main thing. But that was not where Bowlby wanted to be.

Evolutionary ideas spoke powerfully to Bowlby about the emotional needs of children. It was as if he had found a key he had been searching for all of his intellectual life, a key that would help him build a theory that would serve to avenge the wrongs done to him as a child by making it intellectually untenable for those wrongs to persist. But he went beyond that, demonstrating the necessity of intimate attachments throughout the life cycle and the critical importance to every human being of separation, loss, and mourning. In a vast work of reinterpretation (and stunning mental exertion), he plowed through the entire analytic canon demonstrating how early losses—especially the mother or father's dying when the patient was a young child—had been overlooked in one case study after another, resulting in fallacious assumptions and theory building. Although he was rarely acknowledged or cited at the time, his work on loss sparked in the 1960s the first flowering of analytic interest in this subject.[26]

In his 1980 book *Loss*, the third volume of the attachment trilogy that he would come to write, Bowlby summarized the conditions that he considered essential prerequisites for healthy mourning of a lost parent by a child or adolescent:

> [F]irst, that he should have enjoyed a reasonably secure relationship with his parents prior to the loss; secondly that . . . he

be given prompt and accurate information about what has happened, be allowed to ask all sorts of questions and have them answered as honestly as possible, and be a participant in family grieving including whatever funeral rites are decided on; and, thirdly, that he has the comforting presence of his surviving parent, or if that is not possible of a known and trusted substitute, and an assurance that that relationship will continue.[27]

Bowlby was able to demonstrate convincingly the successful coping of those rare children who had these conditions: They could be sad, they could talk about it, they could have their pain, perhaps for a long time, without having to dissociate from it and become prey to damaging unconscious processes. He was also able to demonstrate the disturbing consequences—the primitive defenses, the failure of subsequent development, the formation of phobias and other hysterical symptoms, the depression, the extreme mental disorders, the antisocial behavior, the irresolvable anger toward the living parent, the inability to form new relationships—for the many who did not have these protective conditions. Bowlby was a master at describing the environmental prerequisites to healthy emotional development and the psychological damage that followed their absence. But when it came to what went on in the psyche of the child, the path of the child's hatreds and aggressions and how they might get psychologically fixed in fantasy, or the torturous course of the child's identifications with his parents, living or dead, he was less creatively involved and ultimately less interesting. Even in the realm of early loss, it would be left to later analysts,[28] who built on his work, to describe in detail the complex fantasies and disturbing identifications that bereaved children are burdened with and how they can be helped with therapeutic attention.

At times Bowlby veered toward the utopian. One could almost assume by reading him that when the right conditions prevailed, mankind could finally master the bedeviling qualities that have always made the human animal such a problem to himself.

Bowlby did show interest in intrapsychic processes, more than his detractors give him credit for. His work on what he called "defensive exclusion" explored aspects of repression and dissociation. And he certainly put a great deal of effort into demonstrating how the child builds up an "internal working model" of self and other based on his experiences with the intimate people in his life (see Chapter 15). But if the inner world of Bowlby's child, buttressed as it was by research with lower animals, was more scientifically substantiated, it was less complex, less rich, less tormented and passionate than that conceived by some of his peers, especially the Kleinians, who would gain ground in England in the coming decades for the very reason that the seething they saw in the child—greed, aggression, envy, sexual possessiveness—was so helpful in understanding the seething that analysts saw in themselves and their patients.

But, again, that was not Bowlby's terrain. He was averse to any theory that could not be verified empirically, and beyond that I think he deeply disliked viewing the young child as Klein did, churning with wild fantasies and naturally inclined toward hatred and violence, as well as love and the wish for reparation. In the end, he narrowed his focus to the things that mattered most to him and did great work in that realm. Largely because of what he bravely rejected—drive theory, the death instinct—and partly because of what he quietly, perhaps avoidantly, omitted—a deeper look at fantasy life—few of his colleagues could see that what mattered to Bowlby mattered to them, indeed that he was onto something of huge consequence. Sadly, to this day senior people in the field can be found who believe that Bowlby was attacking psychoanalysis and that his goal was to destroy it.[29]

Bowlby always remained committed to psychoanalysis as a discipline that was concerned with certain questions—the role of the unconscious in emotional life, the meaning of dreams and fantasy, the psychosocial development of the child, the source of neurotic distortions. He felt that Freud had asked many of the most important questions. But he argued that every other academic discipline is defined by its realm of interest, not by a particular theory that must be adhered to.[30] Other analysts had struggled mightily with this problem, often twisting and contorting themselves in order to adapt new ideas to an overarching theory that often seemed at odds with the facts. Bowlby's ideas would not adapt, or perhaps more accurately, he was not the type to make a strenuous and circuitous adaptation when he saw a simpler, more direct route before him. This bluntness proved threatening to his colleagues.

Sometimes in science an overarching theory is recognized to be an "as if" proposition, a metaphor, or useful fiction. It lasts until fresh knowledge makes retaining the old metaphor more trouble than junking it and adjusting to something new. Those who devised the view of the universe with the earth at its center originally saw it as just this sort of useful fiction. It was a starting point for ordering one's ideas and building a cosmology.[31] But eventually it became a religious tenet, and those who opposed it were burned at the stake.

In psychoanalysis an allegiance to theory can represent an especially complex set of emotional commitments. As in other fields, it means an allegiance to things one has said in the past, to the way of thinking to which one has become accustomed, and to certain people with whom one has taken sides, including one's mentors. It may in addition entail a tie to one's own analyst whom one may love or venerate. It has often meant an allegiance to Freud, the worshipped founder, to whom one perhaps paid obeisance in all one's writings. And, most important, adherence to a particular theory also represents a loyalty to oneself and to the way one has worked with patients. To threaten an analyst's overarching theory—or "metapsychology"—therefore, is sometimes tantamount to threatening the very meaning of his work and his life.

Bowlby knew Anna Freud quite well and they were always on cordial terms. They were linked by a common concern for the treatment of small children, and Robertson, her loyal prote;aage;aa, worked for Bowlby. But she nevertheless considered herself the guardian of the flame, and she disliked heresy. Freud didn't go into outright attack when Bowlby elucidated his new theory; that was not her style. Besides, she believed "Dr. Bowlby is too valuable a person to get lost to psychoanalysis."[32] But "to say she cold-shouldered it," Bowlby recalled, "would be an understatement. She banned it."[33]

The key Freudian assault came after Bowlby's third paper, the one on mourning. The paper was published in *Psychoanalytic Study of the Child*, a highly respected annual, edited by the top people in the classical camp, including Freud herself. Without informing Bowlby or giving him a chance to reply, his paper was followed by three rejoinders—by Anna Freud, Max Schur, the analyst who had also been Freud's physician, and René Spitz, all of whom essentially dismissed Bowlby by arguing that what was valid in his thinking was not new and what was new was not valid.

On the whole, Freud's response was essentially defensive, using the royal "we" to enunciate where Bowlby was correct and where he had gone astray. She argued that very young children were not capable of true mourning, that Bowlby was too focused on environmental events in themselves ("as analysts . . . we do not deal with happenings in the exter-

nal world as such but with their repercussions in the mind"[34]), that he
misused and misunderstood analytic terms, and that he had naively discounted the pleasure principle. Strangely, she enunciated so many areas
of agreement that the uninitiated might miss the true purpose of her
exercise. Spitz, who saw himself as something of a rival of Bowlby precisely because of the similarity of their views,[35] was somewhat scolding
about Bowlby's lapses—including his failure to consider the developmental stages young children go through and his misunderstanding of
Spitz's own work. Schur was more openly disdainful, especially of
Bowlby's failure to appreciate the infant's "orality." Whatever validity
their objections may have had, in the annual's fifteen years of publication no replies like this had appeared before and none have appeared in
the thirty-odd years since. Clearly Bowlby represented a special sort of
threat.

The hostility that the Kleinians directed at Bowlby's ideas was more
severe and not made any easier for him by the fact that they had become
the dominant influence at the Tavistock Clinic where Bowlby was still
officially in charge. Trainees at the clinic, who were supervised by both
Bowlby and by a Kleinian analyst, sometimes felt, as one put it, as if they
were sitting "between two warring parents."[36]

Klein's followers exhibited neither Anna Freud's frozen cordiality nor
the gentlemanly restraint that Bowlby always maintained despite his
obvious and sometimes disagreeable self-certainty. They were particularly
hard on Bowlby when he read his papers at the scientific meetings of the
Society. In 1957, a few days before he presented it, Bowlby gave a copy of
"The Nature of the Child's Tie to His Mother," his key paper on ethology
and attachment formation, to a colleague whom he had previously considered a friend. The colleague turned out to be one of Klein's followers,
and apparently distributed the paper among them.[37] Their vociferous
opposition when Bowlby presented it struck him as having been organized in advance, with each speaker arriving at the platform with a different element of his theory to demolish. "Almost all the principal
people around Klein at that time had a bash," Bowlby later recalled. "I
don't think she spoke, but it was very much in character for her to get
her disciples to do her dirty work for her."[38] Bowlby's colleague and presumed friend was among those who joined in the attack.

Sadly, if not surprisingly, Joan Riviere, Bowlby's former analyst, was
also among those who protested, and Winnicott, who was then president
of the Society, wrote to thank her, expressing concern that to accept

Bowlby would mean to reject much of what Freud had fought for.[39] He also wrote to Anna Freud reporting that although he personally came out well in Bowlby's new papers, they left him with a feeling of "revulsion" nonetheless.[40] A year later, when Bowlby read his second paper, "Separation Anxiety,"[41] the response was even more heated, and two extra meetings had to be held to complete the discussion.

Bowlby, of course, had his defenders, including David Malan, then a young analyst, who was so upset by the hostile reactions expressed at the meetings that he rose to Bowlby's defense. Afterward, he recalled, "I went away somewhat terrified about the consequences of being so passionate a supporter of John's position—would I be excommunicated at once?" (Winnicott wrote to thank him, too!)[42]

Bowlby turned fifty in 1957. In certain respects, he was a force to be reckoned with. He was not only prominent because of his work on maternal deprivation, which had become an international cause célèbre in social work, child psychiatry, hospital pediatric units, adoption agencies, and ordinary homes, but his analytic papers were powerful, persuasive, clearly grounded in a thorough knowledge of psychoanalytic theory, and, unusual for analysis, based on scientific studies, most of them, of course, from outside the analytic realm.

Through all this, Bowlby had been active in the British Psycho-Analytic Society, and he was on good terms with many of his critics, having kept his hurt feelings to himself. He'd been training secretary from 1944 to 1947, and was deputy president under Winnicott from 1957 to 1961. He had helped keep the Society together after the war when the split between the followers of Anna Freud and Melanie Klein threatened to tear the organization apart.[43] It was at that time that a middle, or independent, group formed, composed of analysts aligned with neither Freud nor Klein, many of whom, as Bowlby liked to joke, still considered the center of the universe to be London, not Vienna. "Although in the natural course of things," he later said, "I might well have been elected the next president, it had become clear that there would be too much opposition and, with my agreement, those supporting me did not propose me."[44] Indeed, after the hellish response to his attachment papers, Bowlby stopped attending meetings of the society. Unread, uncited, and unseen, he became the nonperson of psychoanalysis and was lost to his peers for the better part of the next three decades.

By the late 1950s Bowlby was having trouble on other fronts as well.

Misunderstanding of his work was so widespread that mothers were warned never to leave their young children, and social workers and children's officers were keeping children in emotionally destructive homes rather than risk separation from the mother.[45] Bowlby himself was forced to admit in his careful way that "some of the workers who first drew attention to the dangers of maternal deprivation resulting from separation have tended on occasion to overstate their case."[46]

Problems persisted on the research front as well. Bowlby's work on maternal deprivation continued to stimulate an immense amount of study, research psychologists replicating and reexamining the studies upon which Bowlby had relied. Some reported successful replications.[47] But others were punching holes in much of the data. Doubts, for instance, were raised about the emotional, physical, and intellectual fitness of the children who suffered as a result of maternal deprivation ("In many cases the institutional population is a substandard one," one critic said[48]). Since many of the institutions in the early maternal deprivation studies gave the children precious little in the way of tactile or visual stimulation, not to mention a caretaker to love and belong to, opponents were able to maintain that good institutions would create happier, healthier children and might even, as one would later write, "facilitate proper social stimulation."[49] What's more, evidence was produced to show that some children did not seem to suffer any damage if deprived of maternal care. If some children survived such deprivation intact, perhaps the real problem of those who didn't lay within the children themselves.[50] (Of course, it could be argued with equal logic that since some people do not get tuberculosis after drinking infected milk, something is wrong with those who do.) In 1956, Bowlby published his report on the sanatorium study for which Robertson had been hired. Far from being able to solidly contradict the nay sayers, this study suffered from its own problems with research design, enabling Bowlby to only weakly support the premises he had hoped to prove.[51]

The fact that children reacted in a variety of ways to a separation from their mothers—some becoming clingy and others affectionless—fueled skepticism that both reactions could be caused by the same phenomenon. Even those who accepted the idea that an early deprivation could be damaging found it difficult to believe that problems would not disappear once conditions improved for the child. (One pair of researchers claimed that the mental retardation which seemed to befall severely deprived infants spontaneously reversed itself when the children got older, even without improved conditions.) The idea that severe or frequent separations from the mother may, in Bowlby's words, be a "foremost cause of delinquent character formation"[52] was taken as particularly hard to swallow.

Bowlby was, meanwhile, subject to frequent misreadings, with some critics assuming that he neglected to consider the contribution of distorted parent-child relationships or that he warned of the certainty of damage rather than the risk. The misunderstandings may have been so widespread because much was circulated by word of mouth or picked up from inaccurate secondary sources. Thus the British psychologist R. G. Andry could write with apparent innocence, "The concept of 'maternal deprivation,' as brought out clearly by Dr. John Bowlby, seems to imply that one of the most dangerous pathogenic factors in child development is the harm that may be done if a child has been deprived of the natural mother's love through separation."[53] Bowlby, of course, was talking not about the child in general but about the very young child, not about separation in general but about prolonged separation, and not about the natural mother but the mother figure. Errors such as these set Bowlby up as a convenient straw man.[54]

The big blow came in 1955, when psychologist Samuel Pinneau produced a memorable review of Spitz's work on hospitalism, including his now famous film on depressed institutionalized infants. Pinneau noted inconsistencies in the number of children Spitz reported studying; inconsistent and even contradictory descriptions of the children, the parents, and the institutions themselves; and failure to account for cultural, racial, and socioeconomic differences in the two populations of infants he studied. He pointed out that the children in the Mexican foundling home were available for adoption, which would have created a sampling bias, since presumably the healthier babies were constantly being removed. Finally, Pinneau questioned the validity of the developmental scale Spitz used to evaluate the children. From a scientific point of view the critique was devastating. The president of the New York State Psychological Association described the job Pinneau did on Spitz as "a kind of hydrogen bomb perfection of destructive criticism; not a paragraph is left standing for miles around."[55]

Although Spitz remained convinced of the truth of what he reported, he was unable to defend himself against this shattering critique, because in terms of scientific method his study was rickety at best. As his chief protégé, the American developmental psychiatrist Robert Emde, acknowledges, Spitz's 1946 paper would not be accepted, as is, in a professional journal today. As a sensitive clinician observing children who looked sad and lonely and ultimately hopeless, and who made him feel despairing when he was with them, Spitz could justifiably suggest that their emotional and physical decline was caused by the lack of maternal care.[56] But those who believed that the children were suffering from genetic deficiencies, malnutrition, birth complications, or simply a lack of stimulation, could counter with equal justification that Spitz's conclusions were completely unproved. Psychologist C. W. Eriksen, reviewing the debate in 1957, wrote, "Spitz, in this reviewer's opinion fails adequately to meet the questions that have been raised. While most of us will continue to believe in the importance of mothering during infancy, we must recognize that this belief has more the characteristics of a faith and less the basis of demonstrated fact."[57]

Flaws were found in other maternal deprivation studies as well. In some cases the institutions were not named or described; in others the ages of the children when the separations from mother occurred were omitted. While Bowlby might insist that the overall body of work sustained his thesis despite such flaws, many in the field, especially those whose theoretical inclinations lay elsewhere, were now able to dismiss the whole Bowlby-driven brouhaha about mother-love as so much sound and fury signifying nothing. A review of the literature by Lawrence Casler concluded that none of the studies Bowlby relied on offered "satisfactory evidence that maternal deprivation is harmful for the young infant." Asserting that "the human organism does not need maternal love in order to function normally,"[58] Casler argued that a child needs an adequate range of stimulation and experience and, although these are normally provided by people, they need not be.[59] He suggested that Bowlby's thesis on the central importance of mother-love had gained such wide currency less because of convincing evidence than because of the need of psychologists to believe in it.

Bowlby's ethological theory, meanwhile, was strictly speculative. True, it was built on empirical data, but it was data based on animals that were distant from man. He had made an imaginative leap, and many rejected it with little trouble. But in the midst of all this, two developments were taking place, in Africa and the United States, that would tip the balance in Bowlby's favor.

9

MONKEY LOVE:
WARM, SECURE, CONTINUOUS

In 1958 the psychologist Harry Harlow reported a series of experiments that every college student now learns about in introductory psych. Harlow, a researcher and theorist in animal learning at the University of Wisconsin in Madison and the president of the American Psychological Association at the time of his now classic report, had been losing many of his rhesus monkeys to disease. To overcome this he had decided to separate sixty of his infant monkeys from their mothers six to twelve hours after birth and raise them in total, germ-free isolation. They were fed with tiny bottles and they thrived.

But Harlow did notice some curious developments. The infant monkeys became ardently attached to the folded gauze diapers that were used to cover their cage floors. Much like children who become attached to blankets or soft toys, the monkeys clung to their cloth pads and protested violently if an effort was made to remove them.[1] Other baby monkeys, raised on a bare wire mesh cage floor, had a difficult time surviving their first five days. Strangely, they fared better if a wire mesh cone was placed in the cage and quite well if the cone was covered in terry cloth.[2]

Such phenomena aroused Harlow's curiosity and naturally brought to

mind Spitz's study of hospitalism. Harlow now decided to attempt a replication of Spitz, this time with monkeys. His purpose was not just to
understand the conditions under which withering away arises in infants
and how it can be abated but also, more broadly, the nature of affectional
ties and how they are reflected in biological conditions.

Until this time love had not received much attention from scientists.
Academic psychology was worlds apart from psychoanalysis and its concern for emotions. Its realm was ruled by behaviorists, heirs of Watson
and Pavlov, who considered behavior the only legitimate study for psychology. As a result, Harlow said, all we knew about love was based
on casual observation, intuition, and informed guesswork. Regarding
mother-love, sociologists and psychologists were in accordance with psychoanalysts: The baby loves the mother because she feeds it. Harlow
found this implausible.

"It is entirely reasonable," Harlow said, using the language of behaviorism, "to believe that the mother through association with food may
become a secondary-reinforcing agent, but this is an inadequate mechanism to account for the persistence of the infant-maternal ties."[3] This
was an important point. If, for instance, a monkey learns that a poker
chip can be used to obtain a banana, the chip will become a secondary
reinforcer, and he will respond to it with some of the same enthusiasm
with which he responds to food. But if the poker chip will no longer get
him a banana, after a while he will lose interest in it. But, as Harlow saw
it, human affection does not diminish when such associations cease. It
lasts a lifetime. Harlow similarly could not accept the psychoanalytic
emphasis on the breast and the infant's need to suckle as explanations for
baby-love.

Harlow believed he had in rhesus monkeys the perfect vehicle to test
some of these questions. Aside from being more mature at birth and
growing more quickly, the rhesus infant was almost identical to the
human infant in its responses related to feeding, physical contact, auditory and visual exploration, learning capability, and so on. (The similarity would cost many of these little monkeys dearly, for some of the
experiments that followed were cruel, intentionally duplicating the concentration camp-like miasma Spitz had observed in children.) Harlow
now devised an experiment that thirty-six years later remains one of the
benchmark studies in the field. He separated eight tiny rhesus macaques
from their mothers and raised them in cages where they were entirely

alone except for access to two contraptions he called "surrogate mothers." One of the contraptions was essentially a block of wood, softened
with a coating of sponge rubber, and covered with cotton terry. It had a
circular face with large eyes and a light bulb behind it to generate
warmth. The other surrogate was made only of wire mesh but also had a
face and a bulb. For four of the monkeys the cloth-covered mother was
fitted with a feeding nipple. For the other four the wire mesh mother had
the nipple. But regardless of which surrogate mother did the feeding, the
infant monkeys spent virtually all their time, some sixteen to eighteen
hours a day, clinging to the cloth mother. The monkeys' affectional ties
to their cloth mothers were sustained even after long separations. And
when the infant monkeys were placed in a strange situation, a room
filled with a variety of stimuli known to arouse monkey interest, they
always rushed initially to the cloth mother when she was available, clung
to her until their fear dissipated, and rubbed their bodies against her.
After several sessions like this, they began to use the cloth mother as a
base for explorations.

One of the experimental monkeys was born prematurely, before the
faces for the surrogate mothers had been constructed. This monkey was
thus forced to live with a faceless mother whose head consisted of only a
blank circle of wood. This did not seem to impede the little macaque's
attachment. But after six months it was given two new cloth surrogates,
one rocking and one stationary, both with completely detailed faces.
"To our surprise," Harlow said, "the animal would compulsively rotate
both faces 180 degrees so that it viewed only a round, smooth face and
never the painted, ornamented face. Furthermore, it would do this as
long as the patience of the experimenter in reorienting the faces persisted. The monkey showed no sign of fear or anxiety but showed unlimited persistence."[4]

The monkey's indomitable preference for the familiar face to gaze at is
indeed reminiscent of human love and some of its corollaries like home-
sickness. It also offered support for a view which Bowlby had expressed,
that part of the human baby's affectional tie to the mother was its search
for the mother's face.

Harlow's studies dealt the first scientific blow to the belief that affectional ties were based on nursing: For rhesus monkeys, at least, cuddly
contact proved far more important—a fact that brought great joy to the
Bowlby camp. But more than that they showed how important it is for

the infant to have someone to be attached to, and a particular someone, as the baby macaque with the blank-faced mother seemed to demonstrate. The surrogate mothers were woefully inadequate. They offered security but they were utterly passive, did no teaching, and did not relate to the babies, leaving them bereft of all the emotional skills that children naturally develop by being with their mothers. This relational vacuum would haunt Harlow's monkeys in later life, when future experiments found that they had difficulty relating to peers and more difficulty yet in raising children. And yet the surrogate mothers meant the world to these little monkeys. They seemed to love the cloth-covered mother dearly, despite the fact that she did so little for them, not even feed them.

Harlow was so impressed with the results of his study and the support it gave to the theories of the British analyst John Bowlby, of whom few in America had heard, that he wasted no time in generalizing to other members of the animal kingdom. Indeed, he became rhapsodic on the subject of mother-love, composing several bits of verse, like this one, accompanied by a picture of a baby hippopotamus with its mother:

The Hippopotamus

This is the skin some babies feel
Replete with hippo love appeal.
Each contact, cuddle, push, and shove
Elicits tons of baby love.[5]

In September 1957 Bowlby went to California for a year as a fellow at the Center for the Advanced Study in the Behavioral Sciences in Stanford. Having been alerted to Harlow's work by ethologist Robert Hinde, with whom, by now, Bowlby had been sharing ideas for several years, in April of 1958 he attended an American Psychological Association conference in Monterey, where Harlow gave his paper. "I heard him speak and I saw his films, which had a very powerful effect on me."[6] On his way back to England the following June, Bowlby visited Harlow for two days in Madison. The two were natural allies, and in the coming decades Bowlby and Harlow would remain intensely aware of each other's work. Each would inspire so much related research on both monkeys and children that the fields of ethology, comparative psychology, child development, child psychiatry, and psychoanalysis would become entwined in ways never imagined before.

* * *

Then in 1961, Ronald Hargreaves, the chief of the Mental Health
Section of the World Health Organization, who had commissioned
Bowlby's original 1951 report on maternal deprivation, decided to put
out a sequel. He asked authors in several disciplines, from pediatrician
Dane Prugh to anthropologist Margaret Mead, to consider all the new
research that had become available on the subject since Bowlby's bomb-
shell a decade earlier. Bowlby asked Mary Ainsworth, an American colleague who had worked on his staff, to stand in for him. Ainsworth
produced a brilliantly coherent statement of Bowlby's and her views. For
the first time in one place she clarified many of the misunderstandings,
successfully repudiated oft-repeated criticisms, and smoothed out some of
Bowlby's own apparent inconsistencies and dubious hunches.

Ainsworth broke the debate down into its constituent parts. She
noted that the catch-all phrase "maternal deprivation" was actually composed of three different dimensions—the lack of maternal care (insuffi-
ciency), distortion of maternal care (neglect or mistreatment), and
discontinuity in maternal care (separations, or the child's being given to
one mother figure and then another)—and that these three dimensions
were frequently confounded, making it difficult to study any one of them
alone. Carefully sifting through dozens of studies, she assessed what they
had to say about the effects of each of these conditions, and, in doing so,
she was able to disentangle many apparent contradictions.

To accomplish this Ainsworth had to chop through a forest of conflicting data and make sense of a hodgepodge of variables. The studies
focused on children of different ages, different IQs, different predepriva-
tion histories, different degrees and lengths of depriving experiences, and
they used a variety of measures to assess the emotional and social consequences of these experiences. The result was a massive confusion in
which it seemed that everyone could find something to support his point
of view. Ainsworth found that many of the studies that seemed to disprove one or another of Bowlby's hypotheses suffered from unreliable
measurements, sloppy research design, or a misunderstanding on the
authors' part of the phenomena they were studying, thus disqualifying
them from a voice in the debate. One research team, for example, took
the friendliness of maternally deprived children in the institution they
were studying to be a positive sign, apparently oblivious to the fact that
clinicians since Levy and Bender had cited indiscriminate affectionateness as one of the chief symptoms of psychopathic or affectionless chil-

dren. Flaws like this, based on carelessness or incomplete knowledge, abounded, and Ainsworth sniffed them out, one after another, like a bloodhound.[7]

Ainsworth did a better job of defending Spitz than Spitz had done himself, citing evidence from a French study, whose statistics and methods could not be faulted, that supported his contention about the severe deterioration of seriously deprived infants.

After more than sixty pages of sorting through all the data, making sense of what seemed a hopeless complexity, updating, clarifying, and indicating where more research was needed, Ainsworth was able to conclude—and to conclude convincingly—that Bowlby's 1951 assertions were essentially sound. It was a tour-de-force performance, which many considered to be the outstanding chapter in the new volume, and it won the respect of some who had withheld judgment until now. Bowlby could have had no doubts about what she had done for him.

Meanwhile, Harlow and Hinde were both reporting a stream of new experimental results with monkeys, which, if not exactly proving Bowlby's theories, at least gave them considerably more credence, especially since in the monkey studies variables that confounded the research on separation among human children could be much more carefully controlled. The monkeys Harlow had isolated for six months in early life showed persistent abnormalities into adulthood, particularly in social and sexual behavior, and proved to be abusive, even murderous, parents.[8] Hinde, meanwhile, found that infant monkeys suffered even from short separations from their mothers and that their distress caused by a thirteen-day separation was more pronounced than that caused by a six-day. The separated monkeys exhibited protest and depression and tended to be clingier after reunion, just like the children Robertson and others had observed.[9] Interestingly, the young monkeys' disturbance was greatest if there had been tension between mother and child before. Five months after a separation experience signs of stress remained, the young monkeys being more timid than controls when placed near strange objects or in strange situations.[10]

Within a few years Harlow and his wife, Margaret, were also reporting on the development of normal monkey attachment in a paper called "Learning to Love." "The outstanding quality of the good primate mother's behavior during this time," they wrote of the first months of life, "is total or near total acceptance of her infant—the infant can do no wrong—and she anxiously supervises its beginning sallies beyond her arm's reach." The monkey mother demonstrates "total, tender, loving care. She either does not punish her infant or at most punishes it with complete gentility." She handles her baby's physical needs, provides "physical support and intimate physical contact, which seems to be important to the development of childhood security." And she protects her child from all threats.[11] Coming on top of the Ainsworth review, such monkey studies, not to mention analogous studies of rats, dogs, and other mammals, quieted the opposition and placed attachment theory on a more secure footing. "Thereafter," Bowlby said, "nothing more was heard of the inherent implausibility of our hypotheses; and criticism became more constructive."[12]

But even if attachment theory had gained plausibility, nothing definitive could be said about the nature of human attachments based on monkey experiments. And given the restrictions on what a researcher could do with human babies, a more conclusive statement on the infant-mother bond seemed hopelessly out of reach. Unbeknownst to Bowlby, Hinde, and Harlow, however, Mary Ainsworth was about to change that.

PART II

BREAKTHROUGH: THE ASSESSMENT OF PARENTING STYLE

10

AINSWORTH IN UGANDA

Born Mary Dinsworth Salter in Glendale, Ohio, in 1913, Ainsworth grew up in Toronto, the oldest of three daughters in a model middle-class home. Her childhood was suffused with propriety, physical security, and educational opportunity. When she decided at three that she wanted to read, her mother enthusiastically purchased the requisite primers and flash cards. But there were troubling emotional currents in the home, and Ainsworth came to feel that in some fundamental way her upbringing had failed her, that it accounted for the nagging doubts and hesitancies she had about herself. Such troubling questions about her own home life would help set the course of her career.

When she entered the University of Toronto in 1929 at sixteen, Ainsworth encountered her first mentor, William Blatz, whose abnormal psychology class consisted almost entirely of his "security theory," and, troubled by insecurity, she was drawn to it. Blatz had made emotional security and the ways in which it is conferred or withheld the cornerstone of his personality theory. "I was impressed with his idea that the child derives security from being near his parents," Ainsworth told me. "And that that security enables him to move out to explore his world, to learn about it, and to acquire the skills to master what he encounters out there. I don't remember if he called that 'using the parent as a secure base from which to explore the world,' but that is how I finally came to phrase it."[1]

Toronto's psychology department was imbued with a messianic spirit, which Ainsworth quickly and joyfully shared and retains to this day: that the science of psychology could be used to fundamentally improve the quality of human life. She became a psychology major, did her doctoral dissertation on Blatz's security theory, and went on in 1939 to become a lecturer at the university, before doing a four-year stint as an army major in charge of personnel selection during the Second World War. In 1946 she returned to the university, where she and Blatz co-directed a team assessing security in various aspects of adult life. She also began training as a diagnostician during those years and quickly became such an expert on the Rorschach, the projective ink blot test, that she co-authored a volume with Bruno Klopfer, the leading Rorschach interpreter of the day.

Blessed with a quick mind and a keen eye, Ainsworth was a brilliant and eager researcher. But she had neither the hunger nor the disposition of a scientist on the make. Although she could be intellectually tough and, with her students, rigorous and demanding, she was nevertheless capable of discounting herself. In 1950, when she married the younger Len Ainsworth, who had recently completed his master's degree in psychology, she readily dropped her work in favor of his education. "It didn't seem like a good idea for Len to remain at the U of T"—where his new wife was on the faculty—"for his Ph.D., so we went to England. He got admitted to University College, London, and I went along."[2]

She assumed she would find work but was not able to get placed through the few letters she wrote before leaving. "Once in London, I looked up Edith Mercer, a woman that I had gotten to know in the army, my opposite number in the British forces. One day she phoned me up and said, 'You know, there is a job advertised in the *Times*.' It was for someone to assist in research on the effect on personality and development of separation from the mother in early childhood; and they wanted somebody familiar with development research and projective techniques."[3]

The ad had been placed by Bowlby. As Robertson's work had gotten under way, Bowlby needed a researcher who could analyze the raw data that Robertson was bringing in as well as a clinician with experience using psychological tests. When he interviewed her, Bowlby recognized at once that Ainsworth represented a perfect fit for his team, having not only the requisite skills but interests that coincided with his to a remarkable degree. Answering his classified ad would prove to be one of the most significant acts of her career.

Ainsworth was a scientist of Bowlby's caliber—brilliant, subtle, an independent thinker, sensitive to what empirical data demonstrated and what it did not. But their personalities, at least in terms of outward measures of confidence and extroversion, were markedly different. Bowlby was a leader with a commanding presence and a conviction in his correctness that only grew stronger in the face of opposition. Ainsworth, although tough-minded intellectually, was more retiring socially and prone to self-doubts when encountering rejection, which she would soon face on a grand scale.

If Ainsworth did not have destiny writ large in her features, she quickly recognized that Bowlby did. She was not only taken with his ideas, but struck, too, by his formidable and apparently secure personality. "He made no bones about the fact that he was single-handedly fighting the analytic establishment, that it pained him some, but that he was convinced he was on the right track. It was a long time before I felt any sense of getting close to him or being a friend. But I had no difficulty whatsoever making him into a surrogate father figure—even though he's not much older than I."[4] It was the beginning of a professional marriage that would prove as fruitful and enduring as any in the history of psychology.

During her three and a half years with Bowlby, Ainsworth got caught up in the issues that concerned him. Why does a baby need a mother figure to develop normally? Why is it so adversely affected by a prolonged separation from her after the relationship has been established? Why when they are reunited, especially after a depriving separation, is the child so deeply upset that the original relationship is not recovered for a long time, if ever? She had parallel questions about herself. She wanted to understand her own insecurity, which was clearly not based on any separations or losses but which she nevertheless suspected had something to do with her early years and her connection with a rather self-absorbed and distant mother.[5] And so the question formed, What goes on between the mother and child in the first year that lies behind all this? This question, brewing in a sense since Blatz, became so important to her now that she was determined that when she had her own project, it would be a study of the mother-child relationship in the first year of life.

Ainsworth's clinical background had been entirely the realm of psychological assessment. She was not a therapist and, unlike Bowlby's fellow analysts, was therefore not absorbed in the details of patient work. As a personality and developmental psychologist, she was more concerned with how a child progresses cognitively and emotionally, questions that analysts were also concerned with but had never studied scientifically. To her, therefore, the ethological model, and particularly the way ethologists had closely observed family relations in other species, proved a powerful attraction. Perhaps human infants and families could be observed the same way.

Robertson's method of observing children had an especially strong impact on her. "It was Jimmy's work that I most admired," she later said. "In studying separation he got acquainted with the families before the child was separated; he did observations of their behavior during separation, and followed them when they came home. And I made up my mind that whenever I went elsewhere and could start a project, it would be a study of this sort—direct observation in the natural environment."[6]

That is what she did in Uganda.

In 1954 Len Ainsworth got a job at Makerere College in Uganda (now the University of East Africa). Although Mary, again, had nothing lined up for herself there, she soon launched one of the pioneering studies in modern infant research. With no lab, with meager institutional support, with no help collecting or analyzing the data, with no one but her interpreter, she rounded up twenty-eight unweaned babies from several villages near Kampala and began observing them in the home, using the careful, naturalistic techniques that Lorenz and Tinbergen had applied to goslings and stickleback fish.

When Ainsworth arrived in Uganda in 1954, infant research was itself in its infancy. Babies had of course been studied, especially by such pioneer psychologists as Mary Shirley and Charlotte Bühler, and the neonate was just now coming under renewed attention. But in the previous two decades child development research had focused almost exclusively on older children, mainly four and up,[7] with the exception of Swiss psychologist Jean Piaget, who had given considerable attention to cognitive development in the first three years of life. Emotional and relational development during those crucial years had been neglected. In 1961 Rudolph Schaffer and Peggy Emerson, who did one of the important early studies of attachment, could summarize the hard knowledge about infant social development in one long sentence: "We now know that at the age of 4 weeks the infant will react to social overtures by a reduction of bodily activity; that at 6 weeks the first smile appears; that from 2 months on the mother will be visually recognized; that at 3 months the infant may vocalize in reply to others' speech; and that after 8 months he will no longer smile indiscriminately at all and sundry."[8] Longitudinal studies, in which infants were carefully observed going through the stages that brought them from newborns, with very meager relational abilities, to highly attached, eagerly related one-year-olds were unheard of. The processes and variables involved were largely a matter of conjecture.

The Ainsworths settled in Kampala, in the province of Buganda, which for centuries before colonization had been a powerful and independent kingdom with a highly developed and complex society. The families Ainsworth studied lived in six villages about fifteen miles outside the capital, in a thickly populated agricultural area. The houses, each of which were surrounded by about an acre of land, where the family grew its own vegetables and fruit, were rectangular dwellings with several rooms. The floors were earthen, the roofs thatched or corrugated metal. They had no electricity or running water. All the families were either Christian or Muslim, all the school-age children attended school. None of them spoke English.

The East African Institute of Social Research, located on the Makerere campus, gave Ainsworth a modest grant to support her work as well as the companionship of fellow researchers. According to the standard practice, new researchers spent a month in a Ganda village acquainting themselves with the customs and language, and Ainsworth followed suit. She picked up enough Luganda during this short period to engage in standard small talk, to understand much of what was said to her, and to speak to the local chiefs about her purposes. She told the chiefs she needed a sample of unweaned babies for her study. After overcoming their initial suspicions, they arranged meetings with local villagers, where Ainsworth gave her speech again.

In return for the mothers' cooperation, Ainsworth offered them transportation to the nearest clinic, not just for mother and baby but for all the children in the family, a valuable service in those days. Eventually, she also provided dried skim milk to the families at wholesale cost. Volunteers were few at first, but in the end, Ainsworth had to turn sub-jects away. Her final sample consisted of twenty-eight babies from twenty-three families (there were two sets of twins and two polygamous households). With her interpreter, Katie Kibuka, Ainsworth visited each home for two hours every two weeks for nine months. Mrs. Kibuka, a Ganda woman who'd been educated in the United States, conducted most of the interviewing of the mothers while Ainsworth observed. Their visits were more like social calls than scientific interviews. They made frequent shorter visits as well, sometimes to deliver medicine or to render some other service, sometimes just to preserve good working relations. In short order, Ainsworth was immersed in the lives of her subjects.

Ainsworth's original idea was to get to the bottom of the debate that raged around early separation. Was separation from the mother harmful, per se? Or was the real problem the deprivation of maternal care that usually accompanied separation? Ainsworth had heard that the Ganda separated infants from their mothers at the time of weaning, usually to be reared by grandmothers. This ancient custom, whose reported purpose was to encourage the baby to "forget the breast," appeared to offer Ainsworth what is known as an "experiment of opportunity." For here she would certainly find separation in its purest form, without the con-founding variable of deprivation. She assumed she would also find a group of modernized families who did not follow such practices with whom she could make a comparison. She further hoped to contrast the effects of abrupt weaning, which was reputedly the custom among the Ganda, with gradual weaning, which she expected to see among those who had abandoned ancient customs. But Ainsworth had not even fin-ished collecting her sample when she realized that the expected experi-ment of opportunity would not materialize. The European assumptions about Ganda child-rearing practices proved inaccurate; abrupt weaning was not a common practice after all, and very few children would be sep-arated from their mothers when taken off the breast.

Ainsworth had already begun collecting data, however. And she was observing everything: breast feeding, thumb sucking, bathing, general cleanliness, bowel and bladder training, bed wetting, soiling, sleeping arrangements, carrying and holding the baby, sharing of mothering, mas-turbation, distress, anger, crying, as well as how the babies responded to discipline, beatings, medical care. She was keeping tabs on the total amount of care given. She was tracking developmental milestones, like sitting, crawling, standing, and walking. And all this data, never before collected by a social scientist, was pointing her in a new direction: She was observing attachment in the making.

The baby is born and can be readily given to a foster parent without apparent harm. But sometime during the first year all that changes, such that even brief separations from the mother figure are a cause of distress. "How," Ainsworth asked, "does this attachment develop? What factors facilitate this development or delay or prevent it? What are the criteria which enable us to judge that an attachment has been formed?"[9]

When Ainsworth first arrived in Uganda she still adhered to the traditional view that attachment was born of feeding. But as she observed the families, her immediate impression was that Bowlby had been right. The baby is not a passive recipient creature who becomes attached to his mother because she satisfies his needs. "These were very active babies. They went after what they wanted. I began to see certain behaviors that indicated that the baby was becoming attached, and I was able to list them in chronological order of appearance. There was, for instance, the differential stopping of crying. The mother picked up the baby, the baby would stop crying, but if somebody else tried to pick him up at that point, he would continue to cry. Differential smiling. Differential vocalizations. I began to see different situations where attachment to the mother could be spotted; and you could differentiate an attachment figure from some other person, even a familiar person."[10]

For each child she now paid careful attention to a growing list of behavioral patterns that she saw as typical of attached babies. In addition to differential crying, smiling, and vocalizations, she included: crying when the mother leaves; following mother; showing concern for mother's whereabouts; scrambling over the mother; burying the face in mother's lap; using the mother as a safe haven when in a strange situation; flying to mother when frightened; and greeting her through smiling, crowing, clapping, lifting the arms, and general excitement. She noted the extent to which each baby demonstrated these behaviors and the age at which they first appeared. One baby, Samwendi, showed differential crying at nine weeks. "He was restless," Ainsworth wrote, "when I held him, despite my efforts to quiet him. When Mrs. Kibuka held him he was restless also, despite several shifts of position, and finally he cried violently. He stopped crying as soon as his mother took him."[11] Other examples from her notes:

- William (twenty-four weeks) began to crawl and to try to follow his mother whenever she left the room, letting out an immediate cry.[12]
- Muhamidi (thirty-three weeks) was brought into the room by a young girl and put down on the floor. He immediately crept to his mother, smiling and crowing with pleasure.[13]
- Nakiku (twenty-eight weeks) sat near her mother on the floor, bouncing about, smiling, and gurgling, and then crawled to her mother and buried her face in her mother's lap."[14]

Having been interested all her professional life in the subject of security, and having been indoctrinated early on in Blatz's security theory, which included the idea that the parents provide a secure grounding from which the child feels he can safely make excursions into the world, Ainsworth was sensitive to how the Ganda babies used their mothers in this respect. Again and again she observed that once they were able to crawl the children would make small excursions away from their mothers, always maintaining consciousness of her whereabouts and returning to her periodically, either physically or with a smile. Using the phrase that would become a cornerstone of attachment thinking, she wrote, "The mother seems to provide a secure base from which these excursions can be made without anxiety."[15]

If a child is attached, and secure in his attachment, she decided, he did not need to be glued to his mother. "He can even leave the room on his own initiative and his aplomb in so doing is sometimes in sharp contrast to his consternation when his secure base gets up and moves off."[16] It was just that consternation which demonstrated that exploratory behavior was an aspect of attachment dynamics, that the one could barely proceed without the other.

She witnessed one child after another using the mother this way. Some started exploring later than others, some took longer than others to wander off mother's lap when strangers were present. A brave baby might gain enough reassurance by making eye contact with his mother and exchanging smiles from across the room, but most would return for contact before going off on another jaunt. One little boy, Paulo, clamored away when his sisters left the house, but followed them only as far as the door, where he stood, holding on to the doorjamb, unwilling to go any farther. Paulo spent much of his time playing away from his mother but protested vehemently if she left the room. Information such as this, so familiar to sensitive parents, had never before been scientifically observed.

When a child felt threatened, as some did whenever Ainsworth and Kibuka entered the house, he would stay close to his mother, and exploratory behavior would cease. In strange situations, like the clinic where the children were taken periodically, they would often fly to their mothers when separated.

Ainsworth's observations led her to hypothesize five phases in the development of attachment. The first is an undiscriminating phase, in which the newborn baby has almost no social responses and then later responds readily to almost anyone. A phase of differential responsiveness follows in which the baby shows signs of knowing and preferring his mother. In the third phase the baby is able to respond differentially from a distance, crying when he sees mother leave the room, crowing when he sees her return. Ainsworth believed that the onset of separation anxiety in this phase heralds the beginnings of true attachment. During this period the children were also beginning to differentiate between strangers and familiar figures and would tend to stare at a stranger for prolonged periods. The fourth phase is one of active initiative—following, approaching, burying the face in mother's lap, scrambling over her. Children not only protest when mother leaves the room now but typically crawl after her. They greet her actively when she returns. And they begin leaving her, cautiously, to explore the world around them. Toward the end of this period, at around six to eight months, uneasiness with strangers becomes more conspicuous, thus initiating the phase of stranger anxiety. Some of the babies who had accepted Ainsworth and Kibuka when they were younger now stared at them, would not approach even when invited, and became tense when held. Babies who did not know them showed more conspicuous anxiety.

In the last three months of the first year, most of the Ganda babies became efficient initiators of attachment, bolder explorers of their environment, and markedly more alarmed by strangers. This was a time when clinging to mother became more pronounced in the presence of strangers or in strange situations. But there was enough variation among the babies for Ainsworth to note that the development of attachment differed from child to child and that methods of infant care and cultural factors both play a role in that variability.

Weaning was the most upsetting event for the babies, especially those who were accustomed to being fed on demand (a practice that Ainsworth nevertheless supports). The insecurity manifested around this time was worsened by mothers who withdrew somewhat from their children to drive home the point that breast feeding was now over. Clinging, crying, protests over the slightest distance from mother, and other aspects of insecurity now became more pronounced.

Parenting style seemed responsible for several broad differences among the children. Five of them, whose mothers were absent a great deal or who barely responded to them, did not develop any of the attachment behaviors that were so prominent in the others. Ainsworth called them "nonattached" or, perhaps more accurately, "not yet attached." Nora was left by herself in a crib much of the day and was not responded to when she cried, a fate typical of the nonattached group. She did not cry when her mother left the room, did not greet her mother when she returned, did not use her mother as a secure base, indeed seemed to be precociously independent. But Nora was not completely nonattached, for she delighted in seeing her father, who came home only on weekends. When he was there, she approached him again and again.

The causes of nonattachment seemed easy to identify. In the case of one pair of twins, Ainsworth recalled, the mother became extraordinarily upset and anxious over their demands. "She would be feeding one and the other one would be screaming, and she just didn't seem to be able to satisfy these babies for any length of time. She just gave up trying to respond the way a Ganda woman would respond normally to her baby, which is to be very sensitive to baby signals and to give the breast at any sign of wanting it—at least a great many of them would do that. She had a large baby carriage that she had gotten from somewhere. She put one child in one end and one in the other end and wheeled it out to the edge of their property so they could scream all they liked and she wouldn't hear them. Then when she thought it was time to feed them, she would bring them in and tend to them, and then off they went again. So she really was rejecting as well as neglecting."[17]

The other two nonattached babies were children of two wives in the same family, who had a total of five small children between them. "This was the most affluent family in the sample," Ainsworth would later note "and these mothers had learned from Europeans that each baby should have its own room, each baby should have its own crib." The room was shared by the mother, but during the day the two babies were often left there alone. "These two ladies rather liked polygamy—each could have completely free days. So one would go off shopping, and the other would take care of all these kids and not really give a lot of attention to the baby in the isolated room or heed its cries."[18] When Ainsworth and Kibuka came to visit, the babies would be brought out and set on the floor beside the mother, but they showed none of the attachment behavior so striking in the rest of the sample.

All of the other children were clearly attached, but, again, there were differences, and it was apparent to Ainsworth, especially when she assessed how the babies responded to separation—"Did the baby cry when his mother left the room? Did he follow her? Did he cling to her to try to prevent her going, or did he greet her return by clinging?"[19]—that some were more secure in their attachment than others. She noticed that certain babies seemed to cling and cry excessively, while others hardly responded at all when their mothers were about to leave them. "Were these babies less attached," she asked, "than the children who clung to their mothers and would not let them go? Or were they perhaps simply more secure in their relationships with their mothers?"[20] This would turn out to be a critical question, which she would not be able to answer until a decade later.

Ultimately, Ainsworth labeled seven children insecurely attached. They could not tolerate any distance from mother, needed almost continuous contact with her, and remained fussy and often continued to cry even when being held by her. Muhamidi was one such child.

Muhamidi came from a large, troubled, and disorganized home. The parents did not get along, the father did not help with the children, and he expected his wife to work in the fields with the coffee harvest despite her many other responsibilities. An older daughter was perpetually ill and occupied much of the mother's time. The mother was anxious.

Muhamidi slept with his mother and was breast-fed on demand, two factors that one might think would virtually guarantee secure attachment. He was healthy and well developed, and his mother took him everywhere she went, often carrying him on her back, even when she worked in the garden. Ainsworth gave her the highest possible rating in total amount of maternal care given to the child. But, despite having looked secure at thirty-two weeks, at eight months Muhamidi showed marked signs of insecurity. He cried a great deal. He demanded constant proximity to his mother, and he wept as soon as they were parted. He demonstrated little interest in anyone else. When he was tested at nine months with the Gesell Developmental Schedules (motor skills, language skills, social behavior, general adaptation), he was found to be a boy of high vitality with a Developmental Quotient 30 points above average. When he was tested again at twenty-two months, he showed less vitality and his Developmental Quotient had fallen from 130 to 109. At thirty-four months he seemed sad and dull and his DQ was 96. Muhamidi's brother, tested by the same doctor, experienced an even more dramatic decline from 142 to 76 over a similar period. One can only wonder, when reading such figures, whether insecure attachment had undermined the initially robust development of these children. Questions like this would be asked with increasing frequency as Ainsworth refined her work.

Ainsworth, meanwhile, struggled to understand why certain children, like Muhamidi, should be insecure. Anecdotal evidence was suggestive. She noted that some of the mothers of the insecure children "were themselves highly anxious, having been separated from or deserted by their husbands and finding it difficult to establish a satisfactory life apart from them."[21] One mother had to leave her child with a neighbor all day so she could work in the garden to raise food, a desperate necessity since her husband's desertion. Another mother was plainly rejecting of the child, a factor that Bowlby had called attention to years earlier. As for Muhamidi's mother, she was distressed that she could not give him the joyful attention she thought she should; she was invariably preoccupied by other things. Although she kept him with her all the time and gave him the breast when he wanted it, there was at times a perfunctory quality to her caregiving, as this observation by Ainsworth suggests:

> We found Muhamidi sitting outside the house crying bitterly. His sister was lying on a pile of cloths near him, appearing very ill and paying no attention to the baby. The mother appeared from behind the house where she had been working. She ushered us into the house, giving first attention to the polite greetings. She then went out to get him and put him to the breast immediately, without stopping to wipe his nose, which was streaming, or to wipe his face, which was muddy.[22]

Muhamidi's mother ultimately struck Ainsworth as disturbed herself —"a masochistic person who always did things the hard way and who compounded the difficulties that a malign fate had visited upon her."[23]

Despite such observations, Ainsworth could not confidently enumerate the specific maternal behaviors that made the secure infants secure and the insecure infants insecure. Sharp boundaries that might differentiate the two were hard to come by. Almost all the mothers were warm and affectionate, the only exceptions being two mothers of nonattached children. One factor that did prove a relatively dependable demarcation was the mother's enjoyment of breast feeding—twelve of the fourteen mothers who said they enjoyed breast feeding had securely attached children. But this factor is more in the nature of a predictor than a description of the quality of care that would lead to secure attachment. The total amount of care a child received—from mother, father, siblings, grandparents, nursemaids, father's second wife—proved not to be a significant factor. This finding was interesting from the point of view of the debate over whether a child needed a single main caregiver or would do just as well if not better with lots of caregivers. Margaret Mead had argued for the superiority of multiple caregivers.[24] But Ainsworth's data suggested that many providers were fine only as long as the care was not so diluted that no one person would become a significant attachment figure.

The amount of care provided by the mother herself, on the other hand, did clearly distinguish among the three groups of children. The mothers who gave the most care tended to have securely attached children, the mothers who gave the least nonattached, with the insecurely attached falling in between. Was this, then, the variable she'd been seeking? Ainsworth did not believe so. Who after all had received more care from his mother than Muhamidi? Although quantity often suggests quality, the two are not the same. Something about the care, the quality of the care, must have mattered. But how could that be factored out? She could not yet answer this question.

Infancy in Uganda, the book Ainsworth eventually wrote, was a unique document, rare in its meticulous attention to detail, original in its mixture of longitudinal and cross-sectional techniques, and the first to demonstrate the development of attachment, making sense of infant behaviors and developmental sequences that were poorly understood before. It also planted the concept of the secure base, which would gradually become more important in the way we think about the parent-child bond and about human ties in general.

The secure-base concept has proved particularly useful in recent years in understanding the maddening self-destructive behaviors of certain toddlers, behaviors formerly identified as "negative attention seeking." The tendency to get hurt repeatedly while exploring, to wander away from the mother in public places, or to simply walk out the front door and disappear down the street—behavior that recalls some of Bowlby's juvenile thieves—are now seen by psychologists Alicia Lieberman and Jeree Pawl as indications that the child does not feel his mother is providing a secure base for him. By behaving in these ways the toddler is asking, in effect, "How far do I need to go before my mother will bring me back? How much danger is too much so that my mother will protect me? How much fear do I need to experience before I'm helped to feel safe?"[25] Such issues, in different form, would prove to have meaning throughout childhood, adulthood, and old age as well.

Infancy in Uganda was not published until 1967, having been held up by personal upheavals and by Ainsworth's fastidious effort to make sense of the data she'd collected. But by that time she was deeply into something that would change the course of developmental psychology.[26]

1 1

THE STRANGE SITUATION

In 1956, for a third time, Ainsworth changed continents to follow her husband. This time to Baltimore, where, within a few weeks, a teaching and clinical job was patched together for her at Johns Hopkins University. It would be seven years before she managed to start her next longitudinal study, during which time she would divorce and enter psychoanalysis. The connection with Bowlby had grown thin, but when he visited her in 1960, just as her marriage was dissolving, he came face-to-face with the findings that she would eventually publish as *Infancy in Uganda* and understood for the first time how pertinent they were to his work. Indeed, this was the only major study outside his own unit offering empirical support for his theory. In terms of their relationship, says Ainsworth, "that made all the difference."[1] From being Bowlby's most capable adherent, she had become an equal colleague. In a few years she would be an acknowledged partner.

Ainsworth arrived at Hopkins when she was forty-three years old, without offers or prospects. She started out teaching an evening course in an area where she had great expertise and even some renown—personality assessment and intelligence testing. Supplemented with a couple of days a week at Sheppard Pratt, a private mental hospital near Baltimore, she gradually had enough work to keep her going, but none of it related to her true interest, which was now infant development. She looked back on Uganda with pleasure and longing. It had been a happy time for her. She loved doing research, and she loved contact with the babies, which her own marriage had failed to produce. As she later said, "I could hardly wait until I had the opportunity to replicate the thing."[2]

But it was not until another five years had passed, in 1961, that she was able to convince her department chairman at Hopkins that her true love was developmental psychology and that she wanted to return to it. In 1963 she received a modest grant to perform a pilot study for her next project, a longitudinal observation of mothers and infants in Baltimore. She managed with that meager funding to do the full study itself.

Although some eight years had passed since her last longitudinal research of infants and mothers in the natural environment, Ainsworth was still working in largely virgin territory. Psychologist Katherine Wolf had observed babies in the home in Boston and was widely believed to be the person who knew the most about infant development, but she had died before being able to get her data together and the notes she left behind were indecipherable to others. Psychoanalyst Louis Sander had also worked on a longitudinal study, much like Ainsworth's, which she herself considered superb. He had published several clinical papers referring to the work, in which he gave his impressions of certain developmental stages in infancy based on what he'd observed. But the study ran for a long time and funding was cut off before he was ever able to analyze his data. Other researchers, like Sylvia Brody, had observed infant-mother interaction in a lab or a play center. In Brody's case the lab was fitted out to look just like a home. But to Ainsworth a home in a lab was not the same as a real home.[3]

"Just take feeding. In the home environment, I could see how a mother responds to infant signals when she had a lot of other demands on her time, with the telephone and housekeeping and other kids if there were any. I saw one mother who was working very hard to put her six-week-old baby on three meals a day—and she was breast feeding at that! She would say, 'I don't know why the baby's crying. He was fed at seven o'clock this morning,' it now being after twelve. She would pick it up and play with it very nicely for a while and then put it down, and it would cry again. She would dangle a rattle, she would do this, do that, she even gave it a bath one day to fill up the time till one o'clock, with the baby off and on screaming. You would never observe that type of thing in the lab."[4]

The mothers' different responses to their infant's crying was also more obvious in the home environment. Some ignored 96 percent of their baby's cries, while others ignored only 4 percent; some mothers averaged two minutes in responding, while others averaged nine minutes. Sometimes Ainsworth sat and counted the minutes, waiting for what seemed an eternity while a baby howled in anguish. Some mothers steeled themselves to wait it out as long as they could, often because they believed that not responding would train their baby not to cry. Some were at times too engaged in other activities to be able to attend to the baby. Some, incredibly, simply did not register that the baby was crying, perhaps because they were too anxious or depressed themselves. (This proved particularly hard for an observer to sit through.) As Bowlby later remarked, "Had the observers not been present to see and hear what was going on but had relied instead on what the mothers had told them, the pictures they would have got would in many cases have been entirely false. . . ."[5]

Ainsworth put together a team of four observers and a total of twenty-six families with babies on the way. The researchers would make eighteen home visits of four hours each over the course of the infant's first year. As in Uganda, Ainsworth and her colleagues acted as friends, not furniture—talking, helping, holding the babies, becoming part of the family—in order to encourage the mothers to act more naturally. "To have somebody there for an extended period of time just watching and taking notes could be very tension producing. Besides, I wanted to see whether the baby would smile at us, whether he would cuddle when we picked him up, and how the baby would behave with us in comparison with the mother."[6]

In the Baltimore study, Ainsworth hoped to replicate the Uganda research and make it much more systematic. But she now had some specific questions she was eager to answer. First among them concerned the patterns of attachment behavior she'd observed among the Ganda. Were these patterns universal? Would American babies behave the same way?

Ethology stipulated that they should, that all human babies are born with a certain species-specific repertoire of instinctual behavior patterns. Ainsworth was clearly thinking along these lines: "The baby gives certain signals that he doesn't intend as signals; he behaves in certain ways under certain circumstances to bring the adult caregiver to attend to him and it all goes from there"—the meanings, the quality of relatedness, the feelings of love and security. "It's not that he is hungry and gives these signals for a purpose; he is upset about something. When he's alone, he is apt to give pretty much the same kind of signals as he does when he is hungry or has a pin sticking in him or is wet or whatever.* And the thing that was increasingly exciting to me after I had started the study of the American babies was to find that the behaviors that I had come to call attachment behaviors in the Ganda infants were essentially the same as for the American infants."[7]

Indeed, of the sixteen attachment behaviors she'd observed in the two studies, she found only two differences. The Ganda children clapped when greeting attachment figures, something the American children never did, and the American children hugged and kissed, something the Ganda children never did. These differences appeared to be culturally derived, as Ganda adults often clapped with pleasure when returning after an absence, while American adults frequently demanded that their babies give them a hug or a kiss, which Ainsworth never observed in Uganda.

If Ainsworth had stopped there, she would have produced another valuable and pioneering study, both replicating the Ganda research and demonstrating its cross-cultural validity. But she had a problem in making a certain critical comparison between the Ganda babies and middle-class American babies. "I all along had this idea about a secure base. It was so conspicuous with the Ganda babies. If the mother was there, the kid would roam all around the room and explore things, looking back at mother and maybe giving her a smile, but focusing most of his attention in the environment. And just as soon as the mother got up to leave the room, the chances were the baby would shriek and absolutely stop any kind of exploratory behavior.

"Now, the Ganda babies are much more used to having their mother with them all the time. Whereas the Baltimore babies were used to having their mothers come and go, come and go, and they were much less likely to cry when their mother left the room. So when they were happily exploring it wasn't clear if it was because the mother was there or not."[8]

These questions brought to mind a paper Ainsworth had read in 1943

---

*That the baby's cry is undifferentiated at first is a matter of debate. According to Barry Lester, a developmental psychologist at Brown University, the hunger cry of newborns is acoustically different from their pain cry and their distress cry. He adds that "by four to six weeks when they have more control over their vocal cords, babies develop a cry to communicate frustration and the 'fake cry' that is a bid for attention." (Goodman, 91–92, p. 27.)

called "Young Children in an Insecure Situation" by Jean Arsenian, who had put babies into a playroom, some with their mothers or mother figures and others by themselves. "She didn't talk about exploratory behavior, but she made it quite clear that the ones that were brought in with their mothers could take a constructive interest in the environment, while the ones that were brought in without a mother figure spent most of their time crying. I always remembered that, and when I started working on the infant stuff, I thought sooner or later I wanted to try this out.

"So I thought, all right, if you don't see the secure base phenomenon very clearly at home, that doesn't necessarily mean it doesn't exist. It could very well be different in a strange environment, such as Arsenian used—a playroom in a lab. If I could bring the children into the university with their mothers, maybe I could see how they used the mother to explore."[9]

Around this time Harry Harlow had reported yet another of his experiments with rhesus monkeys, which further confirmed Ainsworth's thinking. He had taken the monkeys raised with the cloth "mothers" and put them in an unfamiliar environment. If placed there with their cloth mother, they would rush to her and cling to her in terror, then gradually climb down, look around, and move off to explore. If alone, their crying and terror would not abate.

Now, it turned out that the Baltimore babies not only demonstrated less secure base activity than the Ganda, they showed less stranger anxiety, too, and they were much less likely to cry when their mother left the room. Ainsworth hoped that an unfamiliar setting might raise the threshold of threat on all three accounts and thereby ascertain whether these infant behaviors were indeed universal aspects of attachment.

"I thought, Well let's work it all out: We'll have the mother and baby together in a strange environment with a lot of toys to invite exploration. Then we'll introduce a stranger when the mother's still there, and see how the baby responds. Then we'll have a separation situation where the mother leaves the baby with the stranger. How does the baby respond to the departure? And when the mother returns, how does the baby respond to the reunion? But since the stranger was in the room during the first departure, maybe we'd better have an episode in which the mother leaves the baby entirely alone. Then we could see whether the return of the stranger would lessen whatever distress has occurred. Finally, we'll have another reunion with the mother. We devised this thing in half an hour."[10]

Thus the Strange Situation was born, a laboratory assessment that would come to be more widely used than any other in the history of developmental psychology. A room was set up at the psychology department of Johns Hopkins University with a one-way mirror for observation. It had three chairs, and a bunch of toys on the floor.

Ainsworth knew, of course, that the babies differed from one another: She'd seen variations in security among the Ganda and she'd seen it among these Baltimore infants, too. So she expected that they would behave differently in the inherently stressful strange situation into which she was now going to place them.

"The mothers who had been particularly good about responding to signals had babies who responded just exactly the way I had predicted babies would respond in this kind of situation." Indeed, she already had a script in mind: After the brief introduction, which she labeled episode one, came episode two—the baby alone in the playroom with its mother. Ainsworth expected that most of the babies would now fairly readily leave the mother to explore, that they would go to the toys, and that they would play with them. She expected that in the third episode, when the stranger entered the room, the babies would react to the stranger, some would go to the mother, and exploratory behavior would diminish. She anticipated that most of these babies would become distressed and probably cry when the mother left the room in the fourth episode, even though the stranger was still there. "I thought they might go to the door and try to follow the mother and search for her, or I thought they might go to the chair where mother left her pocketbook because that's what they had associated her with." In the fifth episode, when the mother returned, Ainsworth expected that the baby would approach the mother and want contact with her and then settle down. The mother was instructed to put the baby back on the floor if she'd picked it up during the reunion, and Ainsworth assumed the baby would become interested in the toys again at that point. During this episode the stranger slipped out of the room. In the sixth episode the mother left again, so that the baby was entirely alone for the first time, and Ainsworth expected that this would be even more stressful than the first separation. When the stranger came back and tried to comfort the baby in episode seven, Ainsworth did not expect the baby to be comforted. In the final episode, when the mother returned, she anticipated that the baby would demonstrate even greater eagerness for contact than it had shown before.

The very first child put through the Strange Situation behaved exactly the way Ainsworth had anticipated. "It was the only child I have ever seen who absolutely matched what I expected."[11]

Despite the surprising variability, Ainsworth's expectations were strongly validated. Although it was a strange environment, almost all the babies began to explore, usually keeping visual tabs on their mother at the same time. When the stranger arrived, exploration diminished markedly, and most babies spent more time looking at the stranger than the toys. Their wariness was evident mostly in gaze aversion but also in some cases in physical avoidance and crying. Still, the pleasant stranger also managed to get at least one smile from over half the babies.

When the mother walked out of the room the first time, half the babies cried at some point. A large minority of the babies were lured back into play by the stranger, but few of those who were truly distressed could be fully comforted by her. When mother returned, the vast majority of the babies greeted her by smiling, vocalizing, or crying, or more often with some combination of these reactions. About half of them wanted physical contact, the majority of them achieving it within fifteen seconds.

When the mother slipped out a second time, now leaving the baby alone in the room, the distress was usually very intense, with most of the babies crying, many of them so pitifully the episode had to be curtailed. When the stranger returned, she did not have much success in comforting the babies who are distressed, although many of them did accept her soothing attentions, allowing themselves to be picked up, and, although still upset, seeming to derive some solace from contact with her. The babies' responses to her efforts to get them to play were mixed.

When the mother returned the second time, the great majority of babies greeted her in some way, often with intensified crying. More than twice as many babies achieved contact with mother within fifteen seconds of her return this time than in the previous reunion, and almost all of them were picked up at some point, as indeed the instructions to the mother had recommended. Interestingly, almost half the babies also avoided the mother in some way during this episode, most prominently by turning away from her.

Since she and her colleagues had observed all these children in the home, Ainsworth knew that some of them were notably less secure than the others. How, she wondered, would their insecurity reveal itself? Two main variations emerged. Much as Ainsworth expected, one group of insecure babies tended to become extremely distressed in the separation episodes. Then, when they were reunited with their mother, they seemed to be going two ways at once. They eagerly sought contact with her, but also showed unmistakable signs of anger and resistance, often kicking her or arching away from her embrace, squirming and crying all the while, so that they were unable to derive any comfort from the contact.[12]

A little girl we'll call Suzie was such a child.[13] Suzie is inconsolable the second time her mother leaves the room, and even the stranger's return and soothing ministrations cannot prevent an almost panicked level of crying. Now Suzie hears mother's voice outside the room and stumbles toward the door.

Mother picks Suzie up at once, wipes her tears, and offers comforting words. Suzie does not mold to mom or fully embrace her. She remains fussy, keeps crying, squirms. Mom puts her down, picks her up again, wipes her hands with a paper towel; all the while Suzie is still crying. "What's the matter?" mother says. "What's the matter?" Still crying, the baby is struggling wildly and kicking at the same time. Again mom puts her down, then picks her up. "Suzie!" she says, her tone both imploring and scolding.

This impossible struggle between mother and baby continues for the full three minutes after mother's return. At certain moments Suzie seems on the verge of being comforted, and for an instant mother and baby actually seem attuned, as Suzie allows herself to be cared for while she cries. But suddenly her arms drop off her mother's shoulder and her body slumps. She has broken the connection, and mother is again exasperated. Four times the mother exclaims, "Suzie?" She tries to bounce her on her knee, to interest her in the world outside the window. But Suzie's cranky and irritable crying persists.

Ainsworth called such insecure babies "ambivalent" (or "resistant"). They were extremely distressed by the separations and eagerly wanted their mothers back, and yet resisted them at the same time. Their reactions were in keeping with Ainsworth's anticipations, based on the insecure behaviors she'd seen in the home. "I expected that some children were going to be more insecure than others, that they would cry harder, that they would cry more promptly, that they would cry longer, be harder to comfort, and that they would be angry. The thing that blew my mind was the avoidant response."[14]

* * *

Led by mom and squawking, a little fellow we'll call Donnie enters the room. He is an adorable, squiggly-haired toddler, who appears vital and engaging. His mother, as she was instructed to do, shows him the toys. "Look! Look!" she says, and then, "Go ahead. Go! Go!" The baby takes her cue and explores the toys, while mom, as instructed, retires to a nearby chair and pretends to read a magazine. He is very still as he examines the toys, looking back over his shoulder repeatedly to check on his mother. This is typical attachment behavior. He pauses, he looks around at the room, he vocalizes a little, and gradually settles in.

The stranger, a young female graduate student, enters and says, "Hi!" Donnie cranes his neck and watches her sit in the other chair, then goes back to the toys. He repeatedly looks up to keep tabs on mom. He continues to play as mother and stranger talk quietly, as called for in the protocol. Five minutes into the assessment, he remains in the same position, seated on the floor with legs outstretched before him.

The stranger sits down to play with him. He is easily engaged. He smiles, vocalizes, seems delighted with the mutual play. After a minute, mom rises and walks quietly toward the door. Donnie sees, turns, starts stretching into a crawl as if to follow, but it's too late. She's gone. He turns back to the stranger inquisitively, then bursts into tears. The young woman tries to comfort him. "I know, that's okay," she says in a soft, rock-a-bye voice. She reaches out and lifts him into her arms. He's still crying loudly. He does not protest the stranger's embrace, but he continues to cry, and she continues to try to sooth him, physically and with words. Gradually, she tries to reengage him in play.

The crying abates as little Donnie gets interested in the toys. He's on her knee now. She has one arm around him, the other free for play. He accepts a ball from her and cooperates by trying to drop it into a hole in a container. Eighty seconds after mom's exit, he is fully engaged in play, making only occasional little gasps, which seem to be remnants of his cry and a reflection of some ongoing distress. The stranger separates herself physically as he continues to play. He looks up at her and then starts playing on his own. She's behind him now and her supportive talk has tapered off. He's fully involved in the toys.

Donnie looks briefly at the door when he hears his mother's voice. A moment later she enters. Their reunion is not especially passionate, but he is soon in her arms, and shortly afterward she returns him to the toys.

Nothing seems to be amiss in any of this. But let's pause here and play the reunion back again. Because certain details, which might easily be overlooked, are telling.

When mother first enters, Donnie seems about to crawl toward her, and he lets out a little cry. He stretches out an arm in her direction. She stays by the door and says, "Come on, come on," urging him toward her. He crawls to her feet and, as he arrives, does something that doesn't seem to fit. In fact, an untrained eye will be tempted to overlook it and forget it happened. Arriving at his much missed mom, Donnie does not look up at her and demonstrate a desire to be lifted into her arms. Rather, he looks to his right, where one of the toy eggs he was playing with has rolled. Mom reaches down and puts her two hands in front of him palms up, and Donnie then willingly puts a hand on each of hers to accept a lift. But then again something odd, something like a word whispered out of place in an otherwise coherent sentence: As Donnie rises in her embrace, his eyes do not meet hers and he does not smile at her. Rather, he looks to the side, away from her, and then back in the direction of the stranger. Into these few seconds of reunion behavior Ainsworth will read a great deal.

Mother talks to baby softly and walks him back to the playthings, putting him down as the stranger quietly leaves. Still holding on to mother's hand, as she kneels alongside of him, Donnie gives a small yelp and seems interested in the toys again. A few minutes later, as Donnie is happily reengaged in play, mother quietly rises and leaves. Donnie shrieks and immediately follows her to the door crying. His way barred, he breaks into a loud, hopeless cry. Twenty seconds later the sympathetic stranger returns and immediately reaches down to pick him up. He seems slightly relieved but keeps crying loudly. She takes him to the play area and winds up a musical toy. He still looks distressed but stops crying. The musical toy engages him. He glances at the door. The stranger and Donnie stay in this position for a minute and a half. She has her arm around him as he sits on her knee and she shows him the toys. He remains interested and accepts the stranger, but his chest is heaving and he is obviously still upset. For a moment he gives her a smile. He takes a ball from her and tosses it down.

The stranger backs away from him while trying to keep him interested in the toys. He successfully drops a ball through a hole: "Good boy!" she says and claps. He's absorbed in play again, still gasping a little, and looking up frequently at the stranger.

A minute later he hears mom and turns to see her reentry. He vocalizes excitedly. He seems about to stand and go to her but doesn't. This is another telling moment. Donnie turns back to the toys. He looks again toward mom. The stranger leaves quietly while Donnie resumes exploration. He glances toward mom a third time. He's playing quietly now and seems absorbed, just as he was when the process started twenty minutes ago. Another whole minute passes before he looks again at his mother. He seems totally calm as the Strange Situation procedure comes to an end.

Donnie is a typical avoidant baby.

What was striking about babies like Donnie was how good they looked—in Donnie's case, adorable, accessible, resilient—if you ignored those peculiar moments when their behavior seemed strangely off, when they sought so little solace despite their distress. Such a baby seemed, as Ainsworth said, "a psychologist's dream baby"—competent, independent, unperturbed. Some of the one-year-olds whom Ainsworth rated as most secure were so distressed when left alone in the room that they could not even approach their mother when she returned but had to resort to sending her signals, like reaching pathetically with an outstretched hand, as if they were tiny infants again and unable to crawl or walk. But some of the babies in the avoidant group went through the entire twenty minutes with barely a ruffle. Even those who were evidently upset by the separation and searched for the mother when she was gone did not cling when picked up by her, and the few who did released her after a moment. Except for the fact that they occasionally hit their mothers at unexpected times—swatting her while smiling or giving a brief hostile kick in the midst of play, without any indication of mood change—these babies were amazingly blasé.[15]

The blasé response of the avoidant babies was such a shock to Ainsworth because of what she'd seen in the home. At home the secure babies generally cried infrequently, weathered small separations without great distress, and greeted their mothers positively upon reunion. They were inclined to seek close bodily contact, to enjoy it once they got it, and to happily give it up when released. By and large they did not display a lot of anger. Ambivalent babies like Suzie, on the other hand, tended to cry a great deal at home, to become markedly distressed during separations, to act disturbed in various ways when being held, and to be more angry. Astonishingly, the avoidant babies were just the same; indeed the Donnies were indistinguishable from the Suzies in the home environment. These children, who seemed indifferent to their mother's comings or goings in the lab, even to the point of ignoring her on reunion—who looked so extraordinarily independent—had appeared quite insecure in the home. They cried and showed as much separation distress and anger as the other insecure babies. Their cool indifference in the Strange Situation was reminiscent of adults who seem like pillars of strength until one realizes that they are cut off from their own feelings.

Ainsworth was familiar, of course, with all the attachment-related literature. She knew about the early history of the young thieves—those who had been sent to foster care after forming attachments to their mother and then icily avoided her when she visited, and those who came home after lengthy hospital stays and showed no interest in their mother or in being cared for at all, like Derek B. who called his mother nurse. She was aware of little Reggie in Burlingham and Freud's wartime nursery whose nurse had left him after having taken care of him for two and a half years, and of Reggie's snubbing her when she visited. ("My very own Mary-Ann! But I don't like her.") She was aware of the children in Robertson's studies, like Laura, who after a short hospitalization refused to take her mother's hand upon leaving, and who after a second short separation some months later refused to even recognize her mother for two days ("But I want my mummy!"). And, of course, she was aware of the children Robertson had observed in the long-term tuberculosis wards who, after going through a stage of protest and then despair, had proceeded to an eerie detachment in which they no longer seemed to know their mother when she visited or to show concern when she left.

Ainsworth now had a flash association: "The behavior of these avoidant one-year-olds, I realized, was similar to the older child who has had a long depriving separation and comes home and ignores mother. Here were these kids who had never had a serious separation behaving just that way."[16] The avoidant response suggested not only that both the infant and the older child had experienced a similar sense of rejection, but that they were using the same defense to cope with it when placed in a situation of heightened stress—an emotional cutoff that disguised their hurt and anger, even from themselves. Ambivalent children, in contrast, although also angry, had not crossed over into this protective state of indifference. They still hoped for solace and connection; but their anger spoiled the possibility of getting it. Ainsworth's ability to isolate and describe these reactions and their causes implied that she had hit upon the thing that Bowlby had only dreamed of—a procedure to assess the effects, not of drastic separations and loss, but of what he had called in his WHO report "the partial forms of maternal deprivation." She had opened a research window onto the quotidian details of parenting.

For the Baltimore study Ainsworth had developed four scales to rate a mother's way of being with her baby: How often was the mother sensitive to her infant's signals? How much acceptance of the baby did she demonstrate as opposed to rejection? Did she cooperate with the baby's desires and rhythms or did she tend to interfere, imposing her own schedule and her own pace when feeding, handling, or playing? And finally, how available to the baby was she, and how often did she ignore it? With this degree of specificity, she hoped to get beyond the vague concept of "maternal care," which she had come to regard as useless. As it turned out, a comparison of the mothers of the secure babies with the mothers of the insecure babies on these scales helped explain the puzzle of anxious attachment,* which had eluded her in Uganda.

Mothers of securely attached children were significantly more responsive to their infants' signals, quicker to pick them up when they cried, inclined to hold them longer and with more apparent pleasure. They were rated much higher in sensitivity, acceptance, cooperation, and emotional accessibility. In these four scales of maternal behavior seemed to reside the key to secure attachment, the key that she'd been seeking since her days with Bill Blatz in Toronto. The mothers of the two insecure groups rated equally low on all four measurements, the main difference being that, while the mothers of the ambivalent children were often maddeningly unpredictable, the mothers of avoidant children were substantially more rejecting. It was apparently the experience of rejection and the development of strategies to cope with it that gave the avoidant children their appearance of precocious independence when they had to deal with a stressful situation in the lab.

The behavior of the anxious mothers ranged from mean-spirited to merely cool, from chaotic to pleasantly incompetent. Many of these mothers were nice people and well-meaning parents who took pride in their babies and had various means of expressing their love. Some were good playmates or teachers; some were delighted by the positive qualities

---

*Ainsworth initially used the term "insecure attachment," but Bowlby, trying to keep attachment theory consonant with analytic concepts, preferred "anxious attachment," which also made sense given the anxiety that the child associates with the attachment. Ainsworth went along with that, but some of her students didn't. The two terms are now used interchangeably.

they saw in their children. But what they all had in common was difficulty responding to the baby's attachment needs in a loving, attuned, and consistent way. Inevitably this problem was compounded as the babies became more demanding and distressed, the mothers more irritated and overwhelmed. The power struggles that resulted inevitably brought out a more hostile and rejecting side of the mother's personality.

As Ainsworth and others spent more time analyzing the data over the coming years, a more refined picture of the three groups emerged. The mothers of the avoidant children, it was found, showed far less emotional expression, and, as Ainsworth's student Mary Main later suggested, they seemed to be rigidly containing their anger and irritation. They behaved less affectionately when they were holding their babies, and they were more inclined to reinforce their commands with gruff physical interventions. (Almost half of them handled their babies roughly on occasion, compared to only 8 percent of the mothers of secure children.) Some of the avoidant mothers, Main would write, "mocked their infants or spoke sarcastically to or about them; some stared them down. One expressed irritation when the infant spilled an imaginary cup of tea."[17] The mothers of secure and ambivalent babies did not behave this way.

Mothers of avoidant infants sometimes spoke of their dislike of physical contact and could be quite rejecting on this score ("Don't touch me!"[18]). Indeed, as Main reviewed the videotapes of avoidant mothers and babies, she sensed that many of the mothers had an aversion to physical warmth, so that that their infants eventually do not respond to most efforts to hold them. They don't cuddle or cling, and when held, they tend to go limp like a sack of potatoes. Late in the first year, their efforts to make physical contact with their mother are often limited to reaching for her arm or her foot. (None of this, it was found, was at all related to infant cuddliness at birth.)

Further analysis of Ainsworth's data revealed that the mothers who responded quickly and warmly to their babies' cries during the early months of life not only tended to have securely attached babies at the end of the first year but babies who cried less as well. Instead of crying, these one-year-olds tended to use gestures, facial expressions, and vocalizations to get their mother's attention. Similarly, the children of mothers who had been most affectionate in holding their babies and who had given them a lot of physical attention tended to seek less physical contact at twelve months than the other babies. As Ainsworth would later write, those infants, because they had been so consistently responded to, seemed to have developed confidence in their ability to control what happened to them.[19] Her findings seemed to disprove conclusively the advice that many psychologists and pediatricians had been giving to American mothers for decades—that they should not reinforce their babies' crying by responding to it. Such admonitions now seemed appropriate only for parents of babies who had already been spoiled or for limited purposes like sleep training when the baby was already several months old.

Feeding, too, revealed some sharp differences. Mothers of securely attached babies tended to feed them promptly on demand or to hold them off with gentle coaxing. They let the baby have some of the initiative when feeding on solids and were flexible in mixing solids and fluids. Less attuned mothers did not adjust well to the baby's pace, they overenlarged the bottle's nipple hole causing the baby to struggle and gag, and pushed solids on the baby in such a way that they ended up with a battle on their hands.

In face-to-face interactions mothers of securely attached children tended to be more skilled than the others in adjusting their own pace and behavior in accordance with the baby's cues. Not surprisingly, the mothers who smiled and spoke to their babies got more joyful responses, replete with bouncing and vocalizations, than those who merely looked at them.

Ainsworth had now clearly established that sheer quantity of maternal care was not the issue. On the whole, for instance, mothers of secure babies did not hold their babies appreciably more than other mothers. But there was a difference in the way they held them: They were much more affectionate, tender, and careful, rarely inept, rarely distressing their babies with an unpleasant experience of physical contact. And they held their babies when the babies wanted to be held.[20]

As Ainsworth analyzed the twenty-three babies who went through the first Strange Situation (three of the original twenty-six babies were not assessed due to illness or age), she was not satisfied with the three main categories of secure, ambivalent, and avoidant. The babies' behavior was too varied. She divided each insecure category into two subgroups and the secure babies into four subgroups.* Mary Main, who was there at the

---

*The anxious subgroups basically show different degrees or styles of avoidance or ambivalence. Some avoidant children completely snubbed their mothers on reunion, some showed some initial interest in contact. Some ambivalent babies were more angry, some more passive in their resistance. The secure subgroups allow for cases where a child is basically secure but shows some signs of avoidance or ambivalence.

time, later compared Ainsworth's rigorousness to that of Nobel Prize-winning geneticist Barbara McClintock, who was determined to explain the pattern of kernels on every ear of corn. "Mary was like that, too," Main said. "She had to explain every baby."[21] To Ainsworth's own amazement, the eight groupings she created would hold up for twenty years and thousands of children.

In the history of psychology's move toward an understanding of the impact of relationships, no one before had come up with a method of assessing relatedness. There were a myriad of procedures for assessing the individual and new ways of diagnosing, describing, and categorizing him were repeatedly being devised—but no one had found a way to assess how style of parenting contributed to individual differences. "I did not intend this as a way of assessing attachment," Ainsworth says, "but it certainly wound up as that. We began to realize that it fit in with our impressions after seventy-two hours of observation in an amazing way. But instead of seventy-two hours of observation we could do a Strange Situation in twenty minutes."[22] What's more, researchers could use her empirical base to launch new studies, investigating aspects of relatedness, how they are internally organized, how they are transmitted, how they affect future behavior. Through this ingenious project, capping years of research, Ainsworth had begun a revolution.

Ainsworth's discovery of attachment patterns would prove a bonanza to Bowlby. From the days of his supervision by Melanie Klein, when she had refused to consider the family relationships that contributed to the disturbance of the children he was seeing in treatment, Bowlby had wanted to show the world that early parenting was crucial in emotional development. He studied separations, not because he considered them more important than other damaging experiences of early childhood but because they were easy to research. No one could say they hadn't actually occurred. And once he got into the research, much like Freud's early grappling with hysteria, he found it opened many theoretical doors for him; so he pursued it as far as he could. His name became synonymous with early separation. But the big game in Bowlby's mind had always been the parent's attitude toward the child, the parent's everyday behavior, be it loving, rejecting, or some mixture of the two. Ainsworth's idea, of course, had been to do longitudinal research, like James Robertson. And indeed she was a pioneer—it may be fair to say the primary pioneer —in the observation of children in the natural environment. But Ainsworth had been interested first in emotional security and its sources.

And suddenly, almost as if by accident, the convergence of her interests had produced the very result that brought Bowlby's work full circle. She had gotten him, and attachment theory, into the home. For the first time, something could be said with scientific accuracy about the emotional impact that parents' everyday behavior has on their young.

The impact on Bowlby's status would be immeasurable. Until now his stature rested mainly on his work in maternal deprivation; and as a result of that work he was better known in Britain than most other psychoanalysts and fairly renowned abroad as well, though not in the United States. But his standing as a developmental theorist was modest. When his first volume of *Attachment and Loss* appeared in 1969, there were some who believed he was successfully building a sounder metapsychology—or overarching theory—which would one day replace other analytic models. Some of those who had worked on his Tavistock team—Robertson, Schaffer, Heinicke, Ainsworth herself—had done valuable research that lent support to his views. This empirical strength was more than almost any of the other analytic theorists could boast. But nothing resounding had happened to set him apart until Ainsworth's surprising Strange Situation, which applied the idea of separation and reunion in a wholly new way.

"The fact that the Strange Situation was not in the home environment, that it was in the lab, really helped," Ainsworth later said with a laugh. "I only did it as an adjunct to my naturalistic research, but it was the thing that everyone could accept somehow. It was so *demonstrable*."[23]

For the next twenty years, Ainsworth would be occupied with the fallout from this work. Because she and her co-workers had made such painstaking descriptions of each mother-infant pair, the statistical analyses would take years to work through. Meanwhile, she would be training others to use the technique, supervising and co-piloting new research, writing articles, teaching, giving workshops, and serving as the leader of a growing attachment community.

Of the Baltimore study, she later said, it "turned out to be everything that I hoped it would be, and it has drawn together all the threads of my professional career. Each piece of data analysis we did with very few exceptions had some sort of bang to it. It was always such a pleasure to find things working out, and we had an awful lot of things work out."[24] The constantly appearing evidence, meanwhile, was more raw material for Bowlby's grand synthesizing machine. It was fed into his three volumes of *Attachment and Loss*, which gradually made their way into publication between 1969 and 1982.

Ainsworth's work also held the potential of bringing attachment theory closer to its psychoanalytic roots. For what Ainsworth called "secure attachment" could also be understood as having something in common with healthy narcissistic development, a growing concern among analysts at that time, especially the followers of Heinz Kohut. They saw the infant as needing to be at the center of a loving caretaker's universe and that those who failed to get such consistent and dependable adoration would be at risk for developing a narcissistic personality disorder later (which typically includes a shaky sense of self-worth and clinging to an infantile need to be applauded and ministered to). One could even imagine the ambivalently and avoidantly attached children as representing in some way different variants of narcissistic disturbance.

Ainsworth's findings had the potential of promoting a rapprochement between Bowlby and Melanie Klein, too. The anxious children could, without great effort, be seen as struggling with some of the issues—paranoia, persecution, rage and its destructive effects—that Klein had explicated. And Ainsworth's secure base, which became internalized in the child as secure attachment, is not unlike Klein's view that the baby internalizes the good breast, or, ultimately, a warming sense of mother love, and that this activates the baby's pre-existing love-attuned circuitry that cause it to see itself as good and the world as a good place.*

Ainsworth, of course, framed the issues differently from either Klein or Kohut, speaking not about narcissism or internalization, but whether the developing child had faith in his mother's love, in his ability to get care when he needed it, and felt free to explore. But this evolving attachment view, although it added new dimensions, was hardly incompatible with those of her analytic contemporaries. In fact, much would be gained from free and regular interpollination, not to mention a full re-integration of attachment theory into the analytic fold. But that would not begin to occur for some twenty years, and then only slowly.

---

*It may be recalled that Bowlby's problem with Klein's point of view as it was originally formulated was that the baby's capacity to experience a good breast, and therefore a sense of himself and the world as being good, was not particularly dependent on the quality of mother love. The baby already had the love and the hate within him and he applied it to the suckling experience according to his own feelings of satisfaction or dissatisfaction, which might have little to do with the mother. But by the time Ainsworth was enunciating her ideas, Kleinians were more prone to take parental qualities into account.

Indeed, it would be a while before almost anyone would realize the importance of what Ainsworth had done. The findings of the Baltimore study, conducted from 1963 through 1967, did not begin to appear in published form until 1969, and her book *Patterns of Attachment*, written with several collaborators, was not published until 1978. The Strange Situation procedure, meanwhile, could not easily be learned from a manual, and developmentalists had to go through training to master it. It was sometimes difficult to recognize the avoidant response, partly because the avoidant children often look so good—independent, engageable, emotionally robust—that an observer might tend to rationalize or overlook the peculiarities of their reunion behavior; while some of the ambivalent children could also be quite hard at first to distinguish from the secure. It was hard for the untutored eye to pick up on the subtle cues that led a child to be placed in one subcategory or another and easy to overlook Ainsworth's strict precautions about not overstressing the child if a separation proved too much for him. The studies that Ainsworth's students conducted, which supported and extended her work, also took time; they did not start seeing print until the late 1970s. Beyond all that, scientists are cautious, new ideas are slow to catch on, and the attachment ideas turned out to be especially problematic for some, offending the reigning theorists and threatening others by calling specific parenting styles into question. Even Bowlby at first took Ainsworth's work in stride. As he himself would say, "I hadn't yet seen the payoff."[25]

12

SECOND FRONT:
AINSWORTH'S AMERICAN REVOLUTION

"I got interested in the field because I went to her lectures," says Inge Bretherton, who was a thirty-three-year-old undergraduate, returning to school after raising children, when she first heard Ainsworth speak in 1969. "I thought, Oh, here is somebody who's studying real children in real environments. Almost nobody else was doing that at the time. Back then, everybody was a behaviorist. You couldn't talk about the inner life, so to speak, or the internal world. Not in developmental psychology. I had gone to lectures in Cambridge where every time the person talked about consciousness, he made quotation marks in the air. That was the sort of climate in which this developed."[1]

Bretherton, now a leading attachment scholar and theorist, was just one of many bright students Ainsworth began attracting at that time, people who would carry attachment work with them to other universities throughout the seventies and eighties.

Everett Waters was an undergraduate in chemistry at Johns Hopkins when he met Ainsworth in 1971. Looking for a summer job, he told her that he would be willing to start out as a volunteer. "She said, 'Whoa-ho, a volunteer!' And she puts her arm around me and walks me down the hall to Mary Main, who's doing her dissertation."[2] Waters soon abandoned chemistry and entered the psychology doctoral program at the University of Minnesota in 1972. There he met a young assistant professor named Alan Sroufe, a soft-spoken and deliberate man with a commanding presence who over the next two decades would become one of the leading figures in developmental psychology.

Sroufe, who had only a passing awareness of attachment theory, had recently read a major paper by Ainsworth on attachment and dependency and was drawn to her ideas. He was thus particularly receptive to Waters' enthusiastic recounting of Ainsworth's work. The Strange Situation struck him as a potentially powerful tool, and he immediately got Waters all the lab space and money he needed to replicate the procedure in order to study whether an infant's attachment pattern would prove stable over time—an important question to anyone who, like Sroufe, had been trained in behavioral measures. Sroufe was equally impressed with the methodology Ainsworth had used in the longitudinal end of the study, in particular the various means she adopted to describe the maternal care she was observing in the home. He recognized that there was something new here, something that might alter the trajectory of his career.

Sroufe soon became the first significant "independent" to join the attachment group. He was neither a disciple nor student of either of the principals and was thus able to enrich attachment thinking with a wholly different orientation of his own. His placid face, somewhat reminiscent of the singer John Denver's, and his measured manner belie Sroufe's passion for ideas and for disseminating them. He had been a preacher for a small Protestant group as a youth, and some of his ideological opponents would find him overly dogmatic in promulgating the new attachment theology. But if this quality occasionally seemed a flaw, it was also an aspect of an extraordinary gift. For Sroufe has a talent that is rare in academia: He has the capacity to speak and write powerfully and accessibly, one idea building fluidly upon the other, illustrated by telling examples, and buttressed by a ready access to mounds of data. His 1977 article, "Attachment as an Organizational Construct," written with Everett Waters, would awaken many developmental psychologists to what attachment thinking was all about. Sroufe would also help seed psychology departments across the country with attachment scholars, becoming a mentor to a new generation of developmental psychologists. One of them, Dante Cicchetti, now a leading developmentalist in his own right, would later recall the "electric atmosphere" of his Minnesota years.

As Sroufe examined Ainsworth's material, he became convinced that she had achieved what no one had achieved before: the ability to study the complexity of relating in a way that could be quantified and used by other researchers. His enthusiasm for what she'd accomplished derived partly from his own history of difficulties with the research methods that preceded hers. His verbal mastery is evident in the way he discusses the originality of Ainsworth's work and the revolutionary potential he saw in it: "In the past, developmental psychology thought there were two ways of doing things—you either counted discrete behaviors, or you did global ratings. The problem with discrete behaviors is, while they're very reliable—you can code them very accurately and you can get every-one to agree, yes, he did seven of them, and he did four of those—it takes a tremendous amount of observation to get anything that's worth-while, and it's hard to know what they mean. They're very situationally influenced, very unstable over time, and of quite limited validity. To know that one mother picks up her kid more than another mother does, or that one child talks to other children more than a second child does, that may tell you something, but it probably doesn't. But if you know somehow that one child is able to emotionally engage another child and the second child isn't, that tells you a lot. Now how the heck do we measure that? It turns out counting frequency isn't an especially good way."

The problems that arose when trying to squeeze meaning from counted behaviors had caused some researchers to favor what was called "global ratings," which allowed an observer to make an overall judgment: how sensitive is this mother? how sociable is that kid? "But," Sroufe says, "global ratings always had the reputation of being subjective and unreli-able. People couldn't agree. Well, Ainsworth's methodology is actually neither of those.

"She has one scale called Cooperation and Interference. On one end, the cooperative end, these parents fit what they do to the child. They do things in a timely manner, they do things when the child is open to them, they don't do things at cross purposes to the child. On the other end, interfering, the parent is coming in doing things when the child isn't ready. Think of a feeding situation. You're feeding the child, he turns his head, and you cram the food in his ear. This would not be a cooperative behavior.

"So now you've got both things. You have ratings that are reliable and are based on behavior. But they're broader and more integrative and more attending to the *meaning* of behavior. Ainsworth showed that mothers of babies who are later avoidant hold their babies as much as mothers of babies who later are secure. So if you just measure frequency of holding you get no difference. But there's one circumstance in which mothers of babies who are later avoidant do not hold them, and that's when the baby signals that it wants to be held. So you could have counted a lot of holding and you would have gotten nothing."

Sroufe credits Ainsworth with enabling developmental psychology to recognize and measure the qualitative aspects of behavior, not just the mother's but the child's as well, so that in the Strange Situation one does not merely observe what the child does but how his behavior is organized—that is, what central themes and dynamics underlie it. "It isn't how much the baby cries," Sroufe says, "it isn't how much the baby looks at the mother, it isn't how much contact the baby seeks; it's when it does those things and with what other behaviors and to what end."

Sroufe now adopted Ainsworth's methodology to his own work: assessing such qualities as aggression and dependency in older children—in particular, children who had been through Strange Situations when they were a year old—in the hopes of seeing whether early quality of attachment would predict later psychological tendencies. "If you want to define aggression as one child comes up to another child and juxtaposes his hand, which is in a closed position, to the other child's body, that's all well and good, but if somebody goes, 'Hey, babe!'"—Sroufe throws a friendly punch at an imaginary shoulder—"that isn't aggression. And it can also be aggression if you just go up and stand next to the kid and never hit him. You can keep redefining your behaviors to rule one thing or another out, but it's so much easier to let a coder attend to the meaning of the thing and take into account the various cues that are available."

In Ainsworth's methodology, however, Sroufe saw a shift not just from counting behaviors to assessing a deeper quality of the child's psychological organization but also from studying the child in isolation to studying the bond between mother and child. "This movement of psychology from studies of individuals as units to thinking of relationships as units, that's a profound change in the field. And here's Ainsworth who comes along and has a way of conceptualizing and assessing a relationship. The thing that's profound about her assessments, both the home observations and the lab assessments, is that she is assessing the quality of the relationship between the infant and the caregiver. Not the baby, not the mother, the relationship."[3]

Waters' study was the first of many to come out of Minnesota. He assessed a group of babies at twelve months and then again at eighteen and found that 48 of 50 fell into the same Ainsworth attachment category on each occasion.[4] This was a significant finding that flew in the face of the predictions of leading developmental theorists, who assumed that the attachment classifications were transient and situational rather than incorporated into the child's psychology. Most interesting from Sroufe's point of view was that the classifications remained the same despite the fact that eighteen-month-olds behave very differently from twelve-month-olds and thus manifest their security or anxiety in entirely different ways.

Before long Minnesota was buzzing with attachment research. That the Institute of Child Development, prestigious and centrist, had gotten into attachment, was enormously helpful to Ainsworth, who needed the support. For her findings were not universally accorded this friendly reception. Behaviorist thinkers found her conclusions flawed and unacceptable and lost no time pointing that out.

In 1969 the world of psychoanalysis in which Bowlby operated and the world of developmental psychology that had become Ainsworth's home were almost completely foreign to each other. Although psychoanalysis had a theory of human development, it was mainly a clinical discipline dealing with patients. Its concepts of psychological progress from infancy through childhood and adolescence—whether Sigmund Freud's, Anna Freud's, Melanie Klein's, or Erik Erikson's—were based largely on inferences about what the developing child must have experienced at various stages. These inferences were first built on clinical experience with adult patients—their fantasies, their memories, their feelings when in regressed states. They were later reinforced by clinical experience with children. But they were almost never based on the direct observation of infants or of children outside the consulting room.

Developmental psychology, on the other hand, was strictly an academic discipline, centered in the psychology departments of universities, and interested in the actual experiences of normal children. Developmentalists had wanted to break away from the testing and measuring of groups of children, which had been the purview of child psychology, in favor of observing children in the natural environment and discerning the laws of maturation, stages of their growth, and how early experience might affect later behavior. Their special tool was the longitudinal study, which was providing numerous insights into the processes of normal development. Ainsworth herself had come out of a developmentally oriented program in Toronto.

By the late sixties, however, when she was beginning to make her views known through American publications, the dominant ideology of the psychology departments where developmentalists did their teaching and research was behaviorism, and, in particular, learning theory. Unlike psychoanalysts, behaviorists were not concerned with what the infant felt or any other aspect of its internal experience. They focused mainly on behavior and learning—aspects of the child's being that were more readily accessible to direct observation; and counting behaviors was the standard means of research.

Behaviorism had grown out of the turn-of-the-century work of Edward Thorndike and Ivan Pavlov, and later James B. Watson, who first coined the term and who believed that psychology should be a hard-nosed, empirical science. Watson rejected the value of introspection—a technique for exploring mental functioning that had been acceptable in psychology up to his time—denounced the concept of inherited personality traits, and insisted that all behavior, animal and human, was the result of environmental stimuli. Watson also belittled the concept of consciousness as unscientific and saw mental processes as bodily movements. Thoughts in his view were merely subvocal speech.

Watson had been impressed with Pavlov's experiments in Russia, in which a dog was made to salivate at the sound of a bell because the ringing of the bell occurred repeatedly just before the dog was fed. This conditioned response became the core of classical behaviorism. Watson promoted much important experimentation on conditioned responses, perhaps most notoriously, conditioning an eleven-month-old child, Little Albert, to become terrified of cuddly animals. This was achieved by sounding a loud clang over his head each time he reached out to touch a small white rat. Classical behavior therapy assumed that if people could be maladaptively conditioned, they could be deconditioned and thus made well. This approach sometimes proved effective, especially with phobias like the one Watson induced in Little Albert (although, unhappily, Albert's mother took him away before he could benefit from the reverse treatment).

One of behaviorism's most brilliant modern adherents, B. F. Skinner, believed that almost all behavior, from language acquisition to attachment, is shaped by rewards. It has little to do with inborn tendencies, capacities, or needs or the way such things might mix with experience to produce unconscious fantasies and desires. If a hen happens to peck a disk or if a rat happens to depress a lever and each then gets a pellet of food, and if this happens consistently, the animal will eventually come to associate the behavior with getting fed. Much the same happens with people, Skinner said, but in a more complex and subtle way. Experiments with animal conditioning, many of them done in the famous Skinner box, have enabled researchers to shape animals' behavior in astonishing ways, such as teaching chickens to play Ping-Pong. Such feats demonstrated not only how potent a force rewards are but also how far afield they can take an organism from its instinctual behaviors, accounting, in human beings, not only for complex athletic and scientific endeavors but for neurotic distortions as well. What Skinner called "operant conditioning" became an important tool of behavior therapists. In child treatment, for instance, the rewards could be systematically applied by the therapist and taught to parents or teachers in order to reshape the child's behavior. Beyond that, Skinner's behaviorism was also a philosophy for the rational management of society, and throughout his career he offered suggestions, sadly unheeded for the most part, for ways in which public policy could make use of rewards to improve social functioning without needless coercion.

For Skinner and other learning theorists the forces of conditioning explained it all. Speculation about what went on inside the individual—his emotions, his insights, his imaginings—was needless, useless, and detrimental to science. They were similarly unimpressed by the theories about biological maturation, which suggested that certain biologically timed abilities clicked in at certain ages. Development, they said, was not a succession of stages, as Arnold Gesell had argued, but a smooth progression based on the gradual impact of the environment. To behaviorists, the child was almost completely malleable, was inclined to seek pleasure and avoid pain from the first moments of infancy, and was exquisitely attuned to the subtle conditioning forces that most of us overlook.

Bowlby and Ainsworth did not deny the importance of behavioral theory—Bowlby had made it a key element of his system. But they saw learning as just one part in the complex web of human nature and relatedness. Like Noam Chomsky, who was battling Skinner over the issue of speech acquisition, arguing that speech was not randomly learned but something that the child was biologically prepared for and actively participated in through innate abilities, Bowlby and Ainsworth made similar claims for attachment. Attachment developed because of instinctual needs and had little to do with the rewards and punishments that mediated many forms of learning. Indeed, they argued that attachment will develop in the face of very little reward and a great deal of punishment, as is the case with abused children who show very strong attachments to their parents.

Learning theory, however, saw nothing inherent in being human that caused people to seek intimate attachments. Attachment was simply a remnant of dependency. In the classical behavioral view, the child associated his mother with taking care of him and eventually came to feel that he needed her as much as food or water. In the more recent Skinner model, dependency came about because certain dependent behaviors—crying, clinging, seeking attention, seeking praise—were constantly rewarded by the mother. At normal levels such reinforcement accounted for all normal human ties; excessive reinforcement, for all the negative aspects of dependency, from clinginess to spoiledness to lack of self-reliance. But in both views one theme remained constant: Relationships were a secondary phenomenon and not particularly important in themselves.[5]

In the battle that developed between Ainsworth and her behavioral colleagues, the infant's cry became a central point of contention. In learning theory, crying is a random activity that means nothing until it is reinforced by a mother's responsiveness. Like the rat that learns to depress a lever to get a food pellet and is soon pressing the lever like crazy, an infant has no initial reason to cry and would not continue doing so unless the crying were reinforced. Because he learns that crying gets him what he wants, he cries all the more. A random, accidental behavior thus becomes a furious habit. Hence the injunctions since Watson's day against spoiling children with too much responsiveness: If you picked up your baby every time it cried, you'd soon have a ferocious crybaby on your hands. This warning, Dr. Spock notwithstanding, remained a feature of American baby-rearing ideology (and, indeed, lingers on today). Bowlby's idea, as it arrived on the developmental psychology scene in the United States through the articles of Ainsworth and her students, that the infant is prewired for attachment and has certain inborn attachment behaviors that must be responded to by the caregiver if the child is to develop emotional security—in other words, that the baby cries for a purpose and requires a response—struck behavioral theorists as pitifully misguided.

Ainsworth's Baltimore research was similarly incomprehensible to them. Her statistics suggesting, for instance, that babies cried less at twelve months if their cries had been responded to conscientiously when they were younger flew in the face of learning theory logic. If you reinforced a baby's crying, proximity seeking, and the like by responding to it positively, you should get more of such behavior, not less. But Ainsworth insisted that warm, sensitive care does not create dependency; it enables autonomy. "It's a good thing to give a baby and a young child physical contact," she would later say, "especially when they want it and seek it. It doesn't spoil them. It doesn't make them clingy. It doesn't make them addicted to being held."[6] This was stark disagreement—and the fact that it had such immediate consequences for real-world issues of child rearing heated the debate up all the more.

Ainsworth did not deny that excessive dependency existed. But she held, as Bowlby had, that dependency and attachment represented different realms of relatedness, attachment being closely synonymous with love; dependency more often representative of neurotic anxiety. "Does a phobic wife who clings to her husband and consistently seeks his proximity," she asked, "love him more than a woman who is less neurotic and more competent loves her husband?" The answer, she said, was not necessarily. Indeed the phobic wife might actually love less than the healthier wife. Similarly, she asked: "Is the child who especially clings to his mother more attached to her than a child who clings less—or is he merely more insecure?"[7] Again, as her own studies had shown, clinginess did not indicate greater attachment or love but greater anxiety.

Ainsworth repeated what Bowlby had been at pains to insist: that attachment itself should not be confused with attachment behavior. The anxiously attached child shows heightened attachment behaviors—crying, seeking, clinging—but he is not more strongly attached. He doesn't love his mother more than the securely attached child. Rather, his love (which is not weaker either) is riddled with uncertainty and anger. Indeed, the anxiously attached group that Ainsworth labeled ambivalent seemed on their way to becoming dependent characters, in the negative, clinical sense, like the clingy, phobic spouse.

With the results of her Baltimore study in hand, Ainsworth could state with assurance what her early mentor, Bill Blatz, could only propose as theory: that the responsive mother provides her baby with a secure base. The infant needs to know that his primary caregiver is steady, dependable, there for him. Fortified with the knowledge of his mother's availability, the child is able to go forth and explore the world. Lacking it, he is insecure, and his exploratory behavior is stunted.

Although numerous methods had been devised to measure conceptual and cognitive development—many of them introduced by Swiss psychologist Jean Piaget—until now there had been almost no measurement or assessment procedures for an infant's social and emotional development, certainly not at this level of complexity. Although it was widely assumed that real-life events shaped personality, no one had been able to come forth with evidence about exactly which events or experiences mattered. To a few visionaries like Sroufe it seemed that Ainsworth, in a stroke, had changed all that. But in the behaviorist-dominated atmosphere of developmental psychology in the late 1960s, her assertions about the baby's knowledge of the mother's availability or about the security to explore the world that such knowledge confers bordered on the mystical and fell on deaf ears.

To many mothers Ainsworth's prescriptions might seem as natural as maternity itself. (Of course you pick up your baby when it cries!) But as pleasing as it may be for some to discover that psychology is catching up to what has always seemed intuitively correct to them—that little children do indeed need nurturance and consistency, that the way you are with your baby will profoundly affect its personality development, that what happens to it when it's little will influence what it becomes later— it is equally displeasing to come face-to-face with a body of evidence that suggests that you yourself didn't or aren't or won't be doing it right. Her statements were thus not only threatening theoretically but personally as well, for there was no shortage of developmental psychologists who were also parents.

In any case, prominent developmentalists, most of them trained in learning theory, attacked her on every front. They insisted that the patterns of attachment that Ainsworth thought she had demonstrated would not prove stable and, even if they did (as Everett Waters' study seemed to demonstrate), that they should not be thought of as representing the child's quality of attachment but merely the way the child behaved when given certain cues from the mother. Take the mother away, and the child would look entirely different. Any other conclusion could only mean that Ainsworth had misread her data. They further contended that any assessment based on twenty minutes of behavior was inherently flawed because the data base was too small.[8]

During those years Ainsworth sought funds to replicate her work, but the funding agencies, while respectful of her research capabilities, replied that there was no point replicating something of so little value. It was a depressing development, and it fueled her own self-doubts.

But the Strange Situation's value did not escape a handful of infant researchers, who saw that they had been given an extraordinary tool, a Rosetta Stone of sorts, with which they could decipher the residue of the infant's experience with its parents. For the first time they had three categories of children who demonstrated distinct behavior patterns in a laboratory procedure:

- The *securely attached*, who sought their mother when distressed, who seemed confident of her availability, who were upset when she left them, who eagerly greeted her upon her return, and who warmly accepted and were readily comforted by her soothing embrace.
- The *avoidantly attached*, who seemed to depend less on their mother as a secure base; who sometimes attacked her with a random act of aggression; who were far more clingy and demanding than the secure children in the home environment; and who, despite in some cases being just as openly upset by the mother's departure in the Strange Situation, showed no interest in her when she returned.
- And the *ambivalently attached*, who tended to be the most overtly anxious; who, like the avoidant children, were also clingy and demanding at home; who, like the secure, were upset when abandoned by the mother in the Strange Situation; but who, despite wanting her desperately when she returned, arched away angrily or went limp in her embrace, so that they could not be soothed.

Once researchers had these three categories and knew what sort of caretaking the three types of children had experienced—sensitively attuned and reliable in the case of the secure children; rejecting and somewhat harsh in the case of avoidant children; inconsistent or chaotic in the case of the ambivalent children—all sorts of questions previously confined to theoretical speculation were suddenly accessible to empirical study. Because now children whose quality of attachment had been assessed at twelve months could be followed and tested for other qualities as well in order to compare how anxiously attached and securely attached children developed. In the coming years psychologists would—sporadically at first, then with greater frequency, and finally in a flood of empirical excitement that would make Ainsworth one of the most cited authors in the history of developmental psychology—use the Strange Situation to correlate attachment style (and hence the mother's parenting style) with the child's character development, schoolwork, problem-solving ability, self-reliance, self-esteem, peer relations, general sociability, and just about every other important issue in his young life, with some stunning results. None would be more prolific at this than Sroufe.

PART III

THE FATE OF EARLY ATTACHMENTS

13

THE MINNESOTA STUDIES:
PARENTING STYLE
AND PERSONALITY DEVELOPMENT

Armed with Ainsworth's published data, Bowlby was able to advance his attack on the unfeeling style of child care he deplored and in particular the assumption that a stoic, somewhat depriving upbringing built autonomy, self-reliance, and strong character. Bowlby could now argue with greater force that just the opposite was true — that self-reliance both in childhood and later life rested not on benign neglect or stern disciplinary regimes but "on secure attachment to a trusted figure,"[1] which was, in turn, built on sensitive responsiveness to a baby's needs. He predicted that the babies from Ainsworth's most securely attached subgroup, the ones who had received the most consistently positive care, "would be most likely in due course to develop a stable self-reliance combined with trust in others."[2] Bowlby was obliged to acknowledge that his argument could only be considered speculative, that the empirical data were "still woefully insufficient." But it was just this empirical data that Alan Sroufe was equipped to provide.

As a result of Waters' study, Sroufe now had a group of toddlers whose attachment histories were known. His goal was to construct a follow-up that would determine what benefits or disadvantages their quality of attachment had conferred. The problem was, What to look for? Certain behaviors that were prominent indicators of well-being or disturbance at one age (like failure to coo as a baby) could hardly be expected to persist as strong indicators later (failure to coo as an adult). Indeed, the immense changes that children go through as they develop had led many in the field to dismiss the very idea that some form of stable personality existed from one developmental stage to the next.[3] They held that there was little if any connection between what happened in the early years and what happened later. Sroufe believed that there were connections and that an underlying pattern did persist. It could not be found in particular behaviors but rather in the quality of the child's adaptation at each stage of life. Indeed, he felt that he and Waters had already established that when they determined that quality of attachment was stable between twelve and eighteen months.

"If you think about it," Sroufe related some years later, "the differences between twelve-month-old babies and eighteen-month-old babies are dramatic. In fact, eighteen-month-old babies are more like you and I than they are like twelve-month-old babies. At age twelve months infants that have a secure attachment history are, generally speaking, very distressed by separation, especially if they're left alone. If a mother leaves a twelve-month-old baby, even for two minutes, when the mother comes back, that baby wants to be held and wants to be held for some time. He crawls over, he's crying, he climbs up her legs, and when he gets picked up, he hugs in and holds on. At eighteen months, infants who have secure attachments with their caregiver, generally speaking, are not so distressed by separation, they don't so much need physical contact upon reunion, and the most dramatic change is that contact need not be long. An eighteen-month-old can be upset, the mother comes back in, the baby comes over and gets picked up, couple of seconds, that's good enough, back down to play. And in fact, many times what an eighteen-month-old needs is interaction with the mother upon reunion, not physical contact — he'll actively greet her, maybe show her a toy, maybe smile, maybe take her a toy. But those relationships have the same quality in that in both cases you see activity initiated by the infant to reachieve contact — on the one hand more physical, on the other hand more psychological. Secondly, you see that reachieved contact is effective in settling the infant and returning the infant to exploration and play."[4]

Sroufe believed that if he could show stability in the quality of the baby's relationship with the mother, he could also show stability in the general quality of the child's adaptation. This would include the child's orientation toward others, his ways of dealing with stress, his expectations, and his overall approach to the world.[5]

Working with Sroufe, graduate students Leah Albersheim and Richard Arend rounded up forty-eight two-year-olds whose security of attachment had been assessed by Waters six months earlier. Leaning on the work of Erik Erikson and psychologist Jeanne Block, they expected that children of this age should display greater autonomy, flexibility, resourcefulness, and be able to use the assistance of their mothers without being unduly dependent on it. To test this, a series of activities was created. The team predicted that the well-adapted two-year-olds would become readily involved in the play tasks, be able to persist when frustrated, resist succumbing to self-defeating behaviors, and use their mothers' help when they got stuck. They would not automatically comply with mother: Some opposition was normal at this age, especially when asked to do something onerous, like stop playing and clean up the toys. But they would gradually cooperate with her, or at least try to, especially in a difficult play problem where her assistance was crucial to success. Sroufe expected that they would share their enthusiasm with their mother and frequently with the experimenter, too.

"The main task was well suited to children at that age," recalls Albersheim, now a child psychologist. "And for the most part they responded with a lot of enthusiasm. There were two sticks, each one too short to poke a toy out of a tube. So they had to figure out how to put them together to make one stick. Usually kids that age will play around with the tube and put the little sticks in, and after a while they figure out that it's not working the way it's supposed to, and through trial and error they get to where the two sticks will fit together to make one long stick." She still remembers how they struggled with the problem. "It's a wonderful age and a wonderful time to see kids trying to do a task that's going to challenge them and watch their pleasure as they see themselves succeed at what they're trying to accomplish. That's a really exciting thing for a two-year-old."[6]

In almost every respect, however, the securely attached children* did

---

*This is an inaccurate but convenient shorthand. All we know about the attachment status of these children is their assessment at age twelve or eighteen months in the Strange Situation with their mothers. I will often use "securely attached" as a shorthand description for children with secure attachment histories with their mothers. But it should be kept in mind that a child who was assessed as securely attached at twelve or eighteen months is not necessarily securely attached at two years or later and may have a different quality of attachment with another significant figure, like the father. I will also sometimes use the shorthand "secure" or "anxious" when referring to attachment status. But this, too, is not quite accurate, since one can be secure materially or intellectually or in physical ability without being securely attached.

better. They were all able to flexibly manage their impulses and desires, while few of the anxiously attached children had this capacity, many of them falling apart under stress. The secure group also showed substantially more enthusiasm, more persistence, more responsiveness to instructions, and less frustration. And they were much more likely to be rated high in the display of positive feelings. None of the ambivalent children smiled, laughed, or expressed delight at the same level, and almost half the avoidant children engaged in prominent displays of pouting, whining, and hitting. "I remember one avoidant boy," Albersheim says, "who just got so upset with the task he started to hit everything, including his mother, with the stick."[7]

Securely attached children also engaged in more symbolic play — pouring an imaginary cup of tea and offering it to mother to drink, putting a toy man in a toy car and having him drive around, placing animals in a barn. Such symbolic play is an important aspect of the child's mental and emotional development. As Albersheim says, it's a measure in part of the child's ability to tune in to his own inner life, a precursor of self-expression. Also, by creating an imaginary world, and temporarily living within it, the child practices his understanding of how the world operates and has a chance to work out problems, both emotional and practical.

Securely attached children also showed more opposition initially at cleanup time. This might not seem desirable, especially to a parent struggling to get compliance, but it nevertheless indicated that the children were doing pretty much what they needed to do at this age — expressing their growing desire for autonomy, as well as a certain confidence in themselves. Indeed, despite their open resistance, securely attached children displayed less anger during cleanup than either of the anxious groups. They were able to assert what they wanted — even if it differed from mother's wishes — rather than mix compliance with aggression. What's more, during the tougher problem-solving tasks, when compliance with mother could make the difference between success or failure, the secure children were the most cooperative.[8]

But what about the mothers? How were they affecting their children's performance?

Many of the key relationship issues for two-year-olds and their mothers were being worked out at this time by Margaret Mahler, the distinguished psychoanalyst who was observing infant-mother pairs in a playroom. Mahler emphasized the importance of the mother's "emotional willingness to let go of the toddler — to give him a gentle push, an encouragement toward independence."[9] In this her thinking was close to Ainsworth's, who believed that a sensitive parent picks up on the child's cues that "he enjoys the adventures of exploring ... and he is gratified when he masters a new skill or problem on his own."[10]

Such sensitivity becomes particularly critical in what Mahler called the "rapprochement" phase, which overlaps much of the second year. At this stage, Mahler believed, the child is developing a clearer sense that the mother is a separate individual whose wishes do not always coincide with his. As eager as he is to expand his newfound autonomy, he is also flooded at times with both anxiety and a feeling of loss: He and mommy are no longer one. He senses, Mahler wrote, that "the world is *not* his oyster, that he must cope with it more or less 'on his own,' very often as a relatively helpless, small, and separate individual."[11]

During this period he wants his mother to participate in everything he does and to share his things with him. He insists that she come with him on his explorations. He brings her one toy after another for her appreciation, often piling them in her lap. He shadows her incessantly. He darts away from her, sometimes under perilous circumstances, demanding, in effect, that she follow and catch him. But at the same time, Mahler said, he is constantly on guard against being reengulfed by her. By the latter part of the rapprochement phase, conflicts and crises frequently develop, in which the toddler demonstrates, in Mahler's words, an "alternating desire to push mother away and to cling to her."[12]

Mahler observed that, while some mothers cannot tolerate the child's growing separateness, others cannot stand his mounting demands and begin to withdraw. But the less emotionally available the mother is, "the more insistently and even desperately does the toddler attempt to woo her,"[13] with disruptions, displays of babyishness, and full-blown tantrums. As a result the mother's life becomes more miserable and the child's energy is drained away from explorations and the tasks of independence.*

Assessment of the Minnesota mothers suggested that they were nego-

---

*Mahler's assumptions about this age period are still debated. While not disputing the behavior Mahler observed or its importance, analyst and developmental theorist Michael Basch questions her interpretations. "A child at this age looks back at the mother to see if her face displays an approving, mirroring appreciation for his achievement. The recognition that 'the world is not his oyster' is something that comes, if it comes at all, at the end of the oedipal phase, when the child should face and accept his relative smallness vis-à-vis his parents' and other adults' power." (Personal communication, June 1993.)

tiating the toddler period with the same degree of sensitivity they'd shown in the first year. The mothers of secure children were, for instance, rated almost twice as high in both "supportive presence" and "quality of assistance." They did not simply tell their child what to do — they gave him the information he needed to complete the task himself and helped him to see the connection between his actions and the results. Highly rated mothers gave minimal assistance along the way, just enough to keep the child engaged. They seemed to know how to love at a greater distance now, without withdrawing or impinging.

The mothers of the anxiously attached children, by contrast, seemed unwilling or unable to maintain an appropriate distance. Some became intrusive and made it impossible for the child to have his own experience. "They couldn't tolerate the child having any frustration," Albersheim says. "They would just get in there and almost solve the problem for him because it was too painful for them to watch the child struggle. But if children don't get to struggle a little bit — and be able to see either that they can accomplish it or that they need a little help, and to be able to figure that out on their own — if that's interfered with, it's a real loss for the child."[14]

The mothers of other insecure children hung back, giving no assistance even when it was needed, or got involved in ways that the child couldn't use, with the result that some passive children never got the push they needed and others became so frustrated that the experience was ruined for them. In either case their confidence could only have been undermined by such experiences, and the Minnesota team felt they were observing incompetence in formation. The consistency they saw in quality of parenting suggested that the benefits of secure attachment in the first year and the handicaps of anxious attachment would in many cases become solidified with age.

The correlations that came out of this early study convinced Sroufe that he was on to something. Correlations, of course, do not prove causality: That height correlates well with reading ability in people under twelve does not signify a causal relationship between height and reading ability; both just happen to increase with age. Similarly, small correlations often demonstrate no more than gross tendencies of populations — slightly more Jewish men, for instance, may lose their hair than Italians, but that statistic means very little to any particular individual. But the correlations from this early Minnesota study were very powerful — the differences between the secure and insecure children so pronounced on some scales as to show almost no overlap (comparable to: all Jewish men lose their hair and no Italian men do), as if two different breeds of children were being observed.

The children had a different style of relating to their mothers as well. In another study, this time of eighteen-month-olds, Minnesota researchers found that the secure children were much more likely to share positive feelings with their mothers. Almost all the securely attached children (eighteen of nineteen) smiled spontaneously at their mothers during a play episode, while less than half of the anxiously attached children did so. Almost half of the secure kids showed their mother a toy; while only three of the seventeen anxious kids did so. And only secure children both showed a toy and smiled — or showed a toy, smiled, and cooed all at the same time.[15]

In a third study, assessing children at three and a half, the secure group appeared considerably more advanced in other relationships, too, being almost twice as likely to suggest activities, to be sympathetic to peers' distress, and to be sought out by other children.[16]

Sroufe and his students were now convinced that Ainsworth's twenty-minute assessment had not been just twenty minutes of random behavior but that she had tapped into a profound issue in early development. They looked forward to seeing if the correlations would hold up at later ages and approached each new study with growing enthusiasm.

They were not disappointed.

Until now, all the Minnesota studies used samples of children from middle-class homes. But in 1974 psychologist Byron Egeland, a colleague of Sroufe's at Minnesota who was studying risk factors in child abuse, began putting together a new sample. He recruited 267 expectant mothers, all of them with low income and few resources, who were receiving prenatal care at a nearby public health clinic, to participate in a longitudinal study. For the next two decades these mothers and their children (whittled down by attrition over the years to some 179 families) would be the subjects of innumerable studies by Egeland, Sroufe, and their graduate students.

The women were young (average age just over twenty) and mostly single, with few social supports. Many had dropped out of high school. Very few had planned their pregnancies or were well prepared for parenthood. Eighty percent were white, 14 percent were black, the rest Hispanic or Native American.[17]

Egeland and Sroufe lavished enormous attention on this "poverty sample," Egeland with a view to abuse and its precursors, Sroufe looking for the correlates of secure and insecure attachment. They did prenatal measures, obtained nurses' ratings of each mother's degree of interest in her newborn, and assessed the children at birth with numerous measures to rule out constitutional liabilities. Psychological tests, interviews, questionnaires, and third-party observations soon followed at regular intervals.

One of the first fruits of the new study was the ability to predict security of attachment at birth. The child's constitutional and genetic make-up, based on neurological, motor, and cognitive tests, proved largely irrelevant, although one neurological assessment was able to predict later ambivalence, a fact that would explode into a huge debate in coming years.[18] But mother variables were more powerful. Depressed mothers and those who had been rated by nurses as having a low interest in their baby before it was born were more likely to have anxious children at one year.[19]

When the children in the poverty sample reached aged four and a half to five, Sroufe launched his most ambitious study to date,[20] enrolling forty of them in a specially created nursery school on the Minnesota campus. Two groups of children were observed over a period of fifteen to twenty weeks in a variety of contexts — playing outdoors, during free playtime, all together during circle time (when children and counselors got together for songs, games, and announcements), and during small group activity. There was one teacher for every six children, allowing for a lot of teacher-child contact and the opportunity for teachers to get a good feel for how each child expressed himself and managed his impulses and feelings. In addition to the teachers and videotapes, some twenty specially trained observers were used as well, keeping tabs on the children from a discreet distance. "We even set up booths to observe the kids," Sroufe says. "We observed every speck of their behavior."[21] Numerous qualities were singled out for assessment, and in the end the teachers were asked to select a single phrase to describe each child. As usual, none of the teachers or raters knew anything about the children's prior attachment classifications.

The world of the preschooler is quite different from that of the toddler. Children at this age tend to be actively engaged with one another and to get by with significantly less adult assistance. Most are able to contain their impulses and to follow rules. Sroufe predicted that children with secure attachment histories, because they had been sensitively responded to, would be more likely to enjoy themselves and less inclined to be whiny, aggressive, or have tantrums. He predicted that, because they had developed positive expectations of others based on their experiences at home, they would also have positive ways of displaying their needs for attention and would thus present fewer management problems. On numerous measures these predictions proved accurate — not for every one of the secure children, but certainly for the group as a whole.

Indeed, children with secure attachment histories scored higher in every area, from ego resiliency, to self-esteem, to independence, to the ability to enjoy themselves and respond positively to other children. They were seen as having superior social skills — initiating more interactions with other children, sustaining them for longer periods, and, when approached, reacting with positive feelings. They had more friends. Indeed, they held the majority of the top positions in popularity — an important finding in light of the fact that degree of popularity among one's peers in third grade had been shown to be a strong predictor of emotional well-being or disturbance in adulthood.[22]

The secure preschoolers also seemed to have more empathy for peers in distress. Ambivalent children, by contrast, seemed too preoccupied with their own needs to have any feelings left over for others, and avoidant children sometimes seemed to take pleasure in another child's misery. "When a child was injured or disappointed in the nursery school," Sroufe recalls, "since we were filming, we were able to go back and study the reactions of different children. We found that a number of ambivalent kids had difficulty maintaining a boundary between themselves and the distressed child. That's customary for really young children — two-year-olds would do this — but these kids were four or five. So, for example, a little girl fell and hurt her lip, and one of the ambivalent kids immediately put his hand to his own mouth and went and got up on a teacher's lap. It was as though it had happened to him. In the same situation an avoidant child would do something like call her a crybaby. Whereas a secure kid would get a teacher and bring the teacher to the child or stand by and look concerned."[23]

Some of the ambivalent children, because they were thrown into a tizzy by aggressive encounters, became easy targets for bullies. And their unpredictable, sometimes disruptive behavior often made the other children antagonistic toward them. The aggressive avoidants tended to be widely disliked, especially by the secure children, who saw them as mean.[24] Only a few of the children were considered severe disciplinary problems; they all had anxious histories.

None of the behavioral patterns that the Minnesota team witnessed in these children was new to them. They were observing the normal spectrum of childhood qualities. But what neither they nor anyone else had had before was empirical evidence regarding the way the children had been raised and thus, presumably, the source of their differing social responses.

Sroufe identified three types of avoidant children at this age — the lying bully who blames others; the shy, spacey loner who seems emotionally flat; and the obviously disturbed child, with repetitive twitches and tics who daydreams and shows little interest in his environment.[25] Sroufe was also able to identify two ambivalent patterns — the fidgety, impulsive child with poor concentration who is tense and easily upset by failures; and the fearful, hypersensitive, clingy child who lacks initiative and gives up easily. None of these children were as damaged as Bowlby's affectionless thieves. But each of the five troubling behavioral styles Sroufe witnessed suggests a degree of pain and haunting separateness in these preschoolers that is sad to contemplate.

Contrary to the predictions of behaviorists, who attributed dependency to pampering, both groups of anxiously attached children — who, in Ainsworth's study, had experienced anything but pampering — turned out to be highly dependent. When the children were ranked in terms of dependency, anxious kids held almost all the top positions. From the beginning, Ainsworth's critics had claimed that avoidant children were not anxiously attached but precociously independent. That was why they hadn't greeted their mothers or seemed much interested in them on reunion. This argument (which persists to this day) exasperated Sroufe. For it was apparent in the preschool nursery that avoidantly attached babies grew up to be four- and five-year-olds who were just as dependent as ambivalent children, seeking attention in negative ways and making frequent contact with their teachers, climbing into their laps or sitting next to them at circle time at nearly three times the rate of the secure group. "We looked at it every which way," Sroufe says, "teacher ratings, observer ratings, frequency of child-initiated contact with teachers — and by every measure those avoidant kids were highly dependent."[26]

Avoidant children were least inclined to behave dependently, however, when they were injured or disappointed. One avoidant child, after having banged her head, crawled off into a corner by herself. Another folded his arms and withdrew when disappointed. Still others expressed their needs for adult attention in bizarre ways. One approached his teacher "through a series of oblique angles (much like one tacks a sailboat into the wind)," until finally, backed up right alongside her, he would wait for her to initiate contact.[27] Such behavior, much like their reunion functioning in the Strange Situation three or four years earlier, spoke poignantly of an expectation that they would be rejected when in distress.

Sadly, their expectations often acted as self-fulfilling prophecies. Because avoidant children frequently tended to be sullen or oppositional, because they sometimes preyed on other insecure children, and because they tended to come across as arrogantly self-sufficient, they were least likely to elicit their teachers' concern and most likely to incur their wrath. One little boy stole a toy, hid it in his pocket, did everything he could to elude the teacher, and then absolutely denied knowledge of the toy when questioned.[28] Such behavior infuriated the teachers. The phrases that teachers used to describe avoidant children expressed the frustration they felt. Of one little girl the first teacher wrote: "Mean to other children, kept things which didn't belong to her." The second wrote: "The most dishonest preschooler I have ever met." The third: "Mean, lying — everything is hers."[29]

According to Sroufe, the teachers generally did not expect the avoidant children to comply or follow rules. "The teacher would say, 'John, I want you to put those toys away over there; John, come on, I want you to put those toys away' — she wouldn't even leave any time between the first request and the second because she had no expectation whatsoever that the child would put the toys away because she asked."[30] The consistency of the teachers' response was such that Sroufe would later say, "Whenever I see a teacher who looks as if she wants to pick a kid up by the shoulders and stuff him in the trash barrel, I know that kid had an avoidant attachment history."[31]

Although the teachers' summary statements for the ambivalent children were equally disturbing, their behavior toward them was usually more indulgent. They saw them as ineffective, emotionally immature, and incapable of following rules, and so they held them to a lower standard. Little Paulie, for example, was a "wild-eyed man," perpetually anxious, with almost no frustration tolerance, and little ability to cope. Paulie's immaturity, his inability to engage in the ordinary give and take, and his impulsiveness alienated the other children. But Paulie, as Sroufe put it, "wore his heart on his sleeve. . . . He was so clear about his desire for closeness and care that his behavioral and emotional problems did not alienate the teachers. In fact, they were continually supportive."[32]

On the whole, the teachers reacted with a poignant consistency when dealing with each of the three types of children (although they knew nothing of their classifications). They tended to treat securely attached children in warm, matter-of-fact, age-appropriate ways; to indulge, excuse, and infantilize the clingier, more scattered ambivalent children; and to be controlling and angry with the avoidant children, despite the fact that they were equally needy.

The findings were such that Sroufe and his students at times felt depressed and guilty as they examined the tapes, especially when they considered what the future was likely to hold for some of these children.

Subsequent studies of preschool children, coming out of Minnesota and elsewhere, confirmed and elaborated their findings. It was discovered that children's fantasy and play themes,[33] their family drawings,[34] their concentration, their exploratory behavior,[35] and their ability to negotiate short separations with their mother[36] all looked significantly healthier or more fully developed if they were securely attached. Former Sroufe student Dante Cicchetti found a similarly divergent development among securely and anxiously attached retarded children.[37]

In the Minnesota studies early secure attachment did not in most cases prove a ticket to a problem-free life. Many of the children with secure attachment histories seemed to have problems, some of which may have been attributable to unstable or troubling home circumstances, including a distressed mother, lack of adequate attention and stimulation, and frequently an absent father, all of which were characteristic of Sroufe's sample. But, on the whole, they showed more competence, flexibility, resilience, empathy, and enough relational abilities to keep them from appearing emphatically disturbed. For instance one of the secure girls was considered a "sparkplug" by one teacher and a "queen bee" by another. She had difficulty waiting her turn and she overstimulated the other children at times with her antics. But she was seen as a competent child and none of the descriptions suggested the anger or aggression that might imply a seriously impaired ability to relate to others. Other children with histories of secure attachment presented a more troubling picture — "a spacey, undersocialized kid," "dependent, sad, frail" — not as troubling as some of the anxious children perhaps, but disturbing enough to make clear that security of attachment in the first year is not a guarantee of future emotional well-being.[38] Indeed, the security itself might not last, especially if the environment is as volatile as in the Minnesota poverty sample.

The preschool study was a landmark in attachment research and in the validation of Ainsworth's work. From very small differences in behavior — over the course of just twenty minutes or so in the Strange Situation — very large differences were now apparent in the children's adaptation as four- and five-year-olds.

Certain caveats must be kept in mind, however. First, in the excitement over the Minnesota results, it was easy to forget that questions were going unanswered, partly because no one was doing for subsequent years the sort of careful observational studies that Ainsworth had done for year one. How is anxious attachment that develops in the second, third, or fourth year different from anxious attachment that takes hold in the first? What is retained, if anything, of the initial security? What unique problems arise depending on the month or year of anxious onset? And how does the child deal with the loss of his secure love? My own clinical experience, like that of others, suggests that although much is retained and much more can, ideally, be rekindled later, the loss of early security is a major cause for emotional distress in adult life. It may be occasioned by the arrival of a new sibling, or the disappearance of a loving grandmother from the home, or the harsh reemergence of the mother's narcissistic needs with the end of infancy, any or all of which can leave the small child feeling bereft and abandoned. Loss is a big word in the attachment lexicon, but it has not been applied in this context.

Also, is there a time for most children — at the end of the second year? the third? — when the attachment question is largely settled, regardless of what new problems may arise in the family? Could it be said, for example, that the acquisition of attachment patterns is largely a factor of infancy and toddlerhood, when the child is most dependent and susceptible; that unlike the lower animals studied by ethologists, there is no rigidly set sensitive period but that the receptivity to change rapidly decreases after a certain age? This makes a lot of sense, but there is as yet little in the way of research data to substantiate it.

Regarding the Minnesota studies, it should be noted, too, that some of the children only showed subtle signs of their attachment histories, while a few others did not behave at all the way the theory predicted. What's more, neither the preschool study nor the others that preceded it proved a causal link between secure attachment and healthy emotional development; others could argue — and indeed would — that the child's inborn temperament was the cause of both. And, finally, Sroufe's research did not prove a link between sensitive, responsive parenting and secure attachment: Anxious attachment might after all arise for other reasons, various unfortunate circumstances, like the family's moving or suffering financial trauma, or, as mentioned above, the unhappily timed arrival of a new sibling or the loss of a loved grandparent, any of which could cause emotional problems that might drive a wedge between parent and child.

But none of these limitations slowed the enthusiasm that was developing for attachment research. Nor could they prevent attachment theory, at least as interpreted by those with a political agenda, from acquiring an even more strident moral imperative than Bowlby had endowed it with, with the result that mothers were given new cause to feel guilty or inadequate. Coming at a time when women were asserting their rights to a career and to equality in the workplace and when many families found they needed two incomes to get by, the new attachment research, inspired by Ainsworth's revolutionary work, engendered anxiety and hostility once again.

It should be remembered that the driving force behind attachment thinking was a quest to discover what children need, and Sroufe's research was designed to show what happened if they got it and what happened if they did not. In our society mothers tend to be the vehicle through which the community nurtures its young, often in a more exclusive way than earlier or elsewhere on the planet. If a child is not being properly nurtured, blame could just as logically be placed on our social organization, which fixes too many burdens on the mother, on family disruptions, on paternal absence, on poverty, or on the human condition itself, which leaves us eternally vulnerable to losses and other tragic hurts. But attachment theory, as it was evolving, could be quite logically taken to imply that mothers were the problem. It was studying the infant-mother relationship and showing, in study after study, the miseries that befell the child when that relationship was disturbed. Despite cautionary words from its spokesman that mothers needed more support, or that the real issue was the primary caregiver, regardless of sex, or that fathers and other attachment figures mattered, too, attachment theory was being seen as a vehicle for blame. Opposition to attachment theory in developmental psychology would eventually coalesce around this issue.

But at the time when the Minnesota papers were first seeing print, attachment research in the United States was still young, its momentum was high, and it was not looking over its shoulder. The Minnesota team had amassed some of the most powerful evidence yet about the importance of early environments. More would follow.

14

THE MOTHER, THE FATHER, AND THE OUTSIDE WORLD: ATTACHMENT QUALITY AND CHILDHOOD RELATIONSHIPS

One day in 1988 an eleven-year-old girl named Amy was talking excitedly with three friends. They were making plans to open a "craft store" at their summer day camp, where they could barter some of the jewelry they'd been making.

> Amy surprised her friends when she revealed a small bag of necklaces she had made at home the night before. She explained she had been thinking about it at home and decided that the store would 'look better if there were lots of things to display.' The other girls agreed that more merchandise would make the shop look more attractive. As they quickly scooped up their belongings in a joyous response to a camp counselor's call to prepare for swimming, they all agreed to take some yarn and beads home with them that night, so that they could make even more items to display on the next day of camp. Walking toward the lockers to get their swimming gear, Amy noticed that Clarissa did not have any yarn and offered to share some of hers. Clarissa gratefully accepted

the yarn, put it in her locker, and the two girls rushed to catch up with the rest of the group, now on its way to the pool.[1]

By the late 1980s the children from the poverty sample had reached their eleventh year. This is an age when Erikson stressed the importance of industriousness in a child's life and when the American psychoanalyst Harry Stack Sullivan spoke of the emergence of loyal friendships, or "chumships." It is a time when group membership becomes critical to a child and when he learns self-confidence and constructiveness in social settings. Now forty-seven children from the sample spent several weeks attending a summer day camp, and were closely watched by the Minnesota team. Among those selected for this study—by graduate students James Elicker and Michelle Englund—was the girl they called Amy.

Amy and her friends, like the rest of the Minnesota poverty sample, had been studied and evaluated in one way or another since they were born. When Amy was one she had been observed with her mother in the Strange Situation and was found to be securely attached. The mother's behavior in those few minutes was taken to be representative. She was encouraging when Amy exclaimed over a new toy, reassuring when Amy became momentarily disturbed, pleased to watch Amy's explorations. Mother and daughter were smooth and relaxed with each other and, as Amy picked up a toy to mouth or shake, she sometimes looked back and smiled at her mom.[2]

The researchers assumed that, as a result of their mothers' sensitivity and responsiveness, children like Amy develop positive social expectations, come to understand the idea of reciprocity, and develop a sense of self-worth and efficacy. Assuming no jarring changes in this relationship, this positive experience should make it possible for them to enjoy the spontaneity, ease, and giddy pleasures that Amy shared with her friends at eleven and a half years.

Relationships with peers had been a component of attachment studies for some time now. As early as twenty to twenty-three months of age securely attached children were rated as more sociable.[3] By the age of three it became apparent not only that anxiously attached children were less sociable but that other toddlers didn't respond as positively to them.[4] When they were four years old, a time when social skills and sensitivities are rapidly developing and true connections with other children begin to form, Sroufe and his students divided up a group of preschoolers into same-sex playmate pairs, carefully arranging for every combination of secure, avoidant, and ambivalent children, and videotaped their interactions. The children with secure attachment histories consistently participated in the best functioning pairs. They were more sensitive and attuned to their partners, developed true friendships with them, and engaged in creative and elaborate play. Indeed, the secure children had the most healthy partnerships across the board, even when they played with children who had anxious histories.

The avoidant children on the whole made the worst partners. Not only did they have difficulty forming a mutual, positive connection, but they sometimes took advantage of their less competent, more vulnerable playmates—by tricking them during a swap, for example, or attempting to steal their toys.

Many of the secure children refused to be put off by the rebuffs of their anxious partners. Former Sroufe student Van Pancake recalls a case like this: "The boy with the secure history would initiate play, with blocks or with cars, and the other boy would ignore him or say something rejecting. But the secure boy continued to initiate. And he was very creative. He kept coming back in a way that had variety in it and that took into account the kinds of activities and interests of his playmate; and, eventually, these two boys became very good playmates."[5]

Anxiously attached children on the whole lacked this ability. The avoidant children tended to show little interest in closeness. On one occasion the teachers had made a "space capsule" out of cardboard and aluminum foil. An avoidant boy saw it across the room, asked the teacher about it, and became interested. But as he started toward it, he saw the movements of other kids inside and turned and went back to his Legos.[6] The ambivalent children, on the other hand, were drawn to relationships but often were not competent in them. They usually did well with secure partners, but they ran into problems with avoidants. "I remember one of these children with the ambivalent history was very interested in engaging her partner," Pancake says, "but the initiations were repetitive and when they were irritating to the partner, the child did not modify them and find some other way of connecting."[7]

The most disturbing material to come out of these four-year-old playmate pairs were repeated acts of cruelty. Lucy, a little avoidant girl, frequently antagonized Nancy, her ambivalent playmate, by saying no to every comment Nancy made. At other times she froze Nancy out when she sought interaction. Once, when Nancy complained of stomach pain, Lucy poked her in the aching spot. When Nancy cried out, Lucy poked her there again.

Sroufe and student Michael Troy reviewed the videotapes of fourteen of the preschool playmate pairs for evidence of victimization. In all five cases where an avoidant child was paired with another anxiously attached child victimization was noted, usually by all three judges. None of the judges saw victimization in the remaining nine pairs.

Elliot and Oscar both had avoidant histories. Elliot continually tormented Oscar, who was gullible and passive in the face of Elliot's aggression. In one play session, Elliot whispered expressions like "bugger nose," "bugger face," and "Hey, poop!" into Oscar's ear. He then became more hostile, throwing Oscar's toys or claiming they were his. When Oscar somewhat meekly called Elliot a liar, Elliot acted shocked and said, "Oh, you said a naughty word, I'm telling my momma, you said bad words, I'm telling the teacher, I'm gonna tell everyone!"[8] Oscar became more flustered and upset.

The securely attached children did not allow themselves to be bullied or even pulled into a relationship that had hurtful dynamics. They either found a way to make the relationship positive, withdrew, or met the aggression with just enough force to discourage it. It was as if such behavior was foreign to them and they would have nothing to do with it. The anxious children who became victims, on the other hand, seemed at times to facilitate their own exploitation. In the case of another pair of little boys with avoidant histories, Ronnie repeatedly victimized Ralph. At the beginning of one session, after the two had been playing separately for a minute, Ralph approached Ronnie and said with an imploring voice, "Why don't you tease me, Ronnie? I won't get mad."[9] In another pair, the victimized child made 119 overtures, of which only nineteen received positive responses.

To Sroufe it was self-evident that such piteous behavior patterns had their origin in the rebuffs the children had suffered when they'd taken their needs to their mothers. These children must have experienced emotional unavailability, rejection, or physical abuse at home such that it only seemed natural to experience or inflict it in other relationships. "It's unlikely," Sroufe said of Lucy, "that the child's mother actually hit her in the stomach when she had a stomachache, but she has had countless experiences with what happens when a person is vulnerable and needy. Does a partner exploit that vulnerability? Is a partner rejecting because you're feeling vulnerable? If that's been my experience of what a partner does, that's what I know to do as a partner when I'm in that situation."

The behavior of securely attached children who reacted sensitively to their playmates and supported their more vulnerable friends also must have derived from their home experience. "If you're in a relationship, the relationship is part of you, there's no way around it," Sroufe said. "How do you get an empathic child? You get an empathic child not by trying to teach the child and admonish the child to be empathic, you get an empathic child by being empathic with the child. The child's understanding of relationships can only be from the relationships he's experienced."[10]

As the children reached preadolescence, the superior relational abilities of the children who had been securely attached in infancy continued. Elicker and Englund found that secure children spent more time with each other and less time with adults, and the interpersonal sensitivity they displayed at four continued to develop. Seventy-six percent of the securely attached eleven-year-olds made friends, compared to only 45 percent of those who had been anxiously attached.[11] When groups formed, like Amy and her friends, they were composed almost exclusively of children with secure histories, sometimes with one anxiously attached child included.[12] The emotional demands of group functioning —status, role apportionment, conflict resolution—were apparently too difficult for most insecurely attached kids to negotiate without arousing more anxiety than they could effectively handle or behaving in ways that alienated their peers.

The secure children were also more able to hold on to their friendships while participating in a larger group. They could play near others or invite others to join them without fearing that they would lose their friend. Ambivalent pairs could not do this. In the course of three summers, only one pair of avoidant children formed a friendship: "Their play often took place in private areas at a distance from the others or behind some sort of barrier. They were jealous of the advances of any other child and did not invite others to play with them. When one or another partner was absent from camp, the other appeared 'lost,' unable to join in with the others."[13]

Ten-year-olds with behavior problems—who were hostile, noncompliant, hyperactive, who tended to give up and cry, who displayed nervous habits, who were passive and withdrawn, or who were worried and unhappy—were usually children who had been anxiously attached to their mothers.[14] But quality of attachment seemed to affect boys and girls differently. In the poverty sample, for example, aggression was particularly marked among avoidant boys. They were more likely to bully, lie, cheat, destroy things, brag, act cruelly, disrupt the class, swear, tease, threaten, argue, throw temper tantrums, become defiant. (Ambivalent boys, on the other hand, were more prone to be shy, apathetic, and withdrawn.) The picture was quite different with avoidant girls, perhaps because they are biologically less aggressive and because girls, for a variety of reasons, are more inclined to cope with their anxiety by behaving in socially approved ways. They tend to internalize their feelings more—blaming themselves, becoming depressed, or feeling ashamed as opposed to fighting off such feelings by striking out at someone or through some other behavioral strategy.[15]

Patricia Turner, a doctoral student at Cambridge University working with Joan Stevenson-Hinde, wife of ethologist Robert Hinde and a leading attachment researcher herself, has performed one of the few studies that have attempted to build on this question. Turner found that some of the stereotyped qualities we associate with boys and girls—such as smiling compliance in girls and angry aggression in boys—may actually represent the ways in which insecure attachment works itself out in each group.

The anxiously attached boys, for instance, were off the charts on every measure of aggression, assertion, and control seeking. They appeared to be very hungry for attention and approval (their dependency scores were also the highest), but they were unable to seek attention openly, perhaps because their hunger for it and their expectation of rejection were both too terrible to allow into consciousness. They thus sought attention in indirect ways, which were often disruptive and aggressive. Their peers would either resist them or forcefully ignore them, which only heightened their frustration and need, reconfirmed their expectation that they would be rejected, and increased their offensive behaviors. Secure boys did not behave this way and, in fact, they were no more assertive, controlling, or angrily aggressive than secure girls (although they did show twice as much playful aggression).*

---

*The number of dependent behaviors among anxiously attached boys was almost twice that of the anxiously attached girls and approximately three times that of the securely attached children. Unfortunately, Turner did not distinguish between children with avoidant and ambivalent histories. It is hard to know, therefore, whether her findings conflict with the Minnesota finding that boys with ambivalent attachment backgrounds are very different from the aggressive avoidants. See Note 16 for figures.

Secure boys and secure girls were also about equal in the degree to which they expressed positive feelings. Insecure girls, however, by a huge margin—about two to one—expressed vastly more pleasure and conferred many more smiles on their peers than any other group. Again the management of relationship anxiety—the sense that one wants to be loved and connected but that one will not be treated well—seems to explain this behavior. It has been found in other studies, for instance, that low-status, low-pecking-order children in a nursery school tended to be big smilers when initiating contact with higher-ranking children. The smiles of such children, far from being expressions of pleasure, are most likely a demonstration of submission and plea not to be maltreated.[16]

Although the data linking secure attachment with better peer relations in childhood has been impressive, Ainsworth has cautioned against jumping to conclusions. "There is evidence that the securely attached child will do better with other kids, but it's not true across the board. There are kids that are doing much better with their same-aged peers than you'd expect from the nature of their attachment to their parents." She believes that something besides the attachment system is at work here—what she laughingly calls "the sociable system"—and that no one has yet fully grasped the complexity of what's going on.[17]

It should be remembered, too, that the Minnesota sample consists of hard-pressed families, over 60 percent of them headed by a single parent. Many of the children have presumably suffered more than the insensitivity, inconsistency, or rejection of attachment needs that Ainsworth observed in her middle-class Baltimore homes. Such circumstances would naturally exaggerate their problems in relating to others, suggesting more drastic consequences to anxious attachment than is necessarily the case.

By the early nineties the children in the Minnesota study had reached their teenage years, and Sroufe found that whatever relationship advantages secure attachment does tend to confer persist through age fifteen.[18] He sees in his longitudinal study the opportunity to trace the fate of early attachments into later years as well. If the funding for the research can be maintained, he will be able to keep additional generations of graduate students studying the poverty sample at successive ages right on through adulthood. From the point of view of the National Institute for Mental Health, which has been providing much of the funding, the study would seem irresistible. "You couldn't name an NIMH priority," Sroufe says, "that we can't access with the data coming up: drug abuse, delinquency,

AIDS, teenage pregnancy."[19] He will also, before long, be able to assess what kind of parents they become and whether their children's attachment status mirrors their own. If, as he suspects, attachment history plays a role in predicting such a wide variety of outcomes, the payoff of this research will have proven to be considerable.*

In the mid-1970s attachment workers began showing an increased interest in the child's attachment to his father—a person who tends to get overlooked in most developmental research, either because he is considered less important or because he is less available for observation. (In Sroufe's poverty sample only 12 percent of the biological fathers were present at eighteen months and many were reluctant to participate; assessments of their impact could only be indirect.)[20] One of the first efforts to overcome this was made by Michael Lamb, a former student of Ainsworth's. Observing children in the home at seven, eight, twelve, and thirteen months of age, he found that on most attachment measures —proximity seeking, touching, crying to, signaling a desire to be held, protest on separation, greeting on return—infants showed no preference for mothers over fathers. When infants are distressed, their attachment behaviors become more pronounced, but they display them in the same way to both mother and father, depending on who is present. When both are present, distressed infants consistently prefer their mothers,† even little boys who otherwise prefer their fathers. Thus, Lamb's work seemed to support Bowlby's contention that children arrange their attachment sympathies in a hierarchy.[21] (This certainly seems to be the case in my home.) Most children, however, are flexible enough to switch the father to the top of the hierarchy if the mother is unavailable for a period of time.[22]

The first study to assess *quality* of attachment to the father was reported by Mary Main and Donna Weston in 1981. They found the percentage of children securely attached to their fathers was about the same as that for mothers. But there was no correlation between the two.[23] A child could be securely attached to one, both, or neither of his parents. While one secure attachment, especially if it was to mother, was better than none, children who had been found to be securely attached to both

---

*A chart briefly summarizing the findings to date regarding secure and anxious attachment appears in the appendix.

†Or, probably more accurately, their primary caregiver, assuming secure attachment to both parents.

parents tended to be the most confident and competent. When empathy was measured, the children with two secure attachments were notably superior. This has since been supported by other studies.[24] On the whole, it seems that everything that has been learned about mother-child attachment relates in some way to father-child attachment as well, as many readers have no doubt already assumed. And yet there are differences.

The primary caregiver—and therefore the mother in most cases—is, of course, especially important. Something fundamental seems to get established in the infant's relationship with her during the first year or two that often considerably outweighs the contribution of any secondary attachment figure. But the formative power of the second parent— whether he is harsh or accepting, tyrannical or easygoing, highly involved or abdicating, living at home or long gone—is critical, too. This fact has been established over and over again in clinical work, where unsatisfactory relationships with or abandonment by fathers often require years of working through. Today 27 percent of American children are born to single mothers, many of them poor teenagers.[25] We know from Sroufe's studies that many such children do not do well.

Although fathers are usually secondary caregivers, they are not merely secondary mothers. They usually provide a higher level of stimulation, are often seen by children as more exciting playmates, and their (on-average) somewhat lesser degree of intimacy with the child and greater resistance to coddling makes them more of a stepping-stone to the outside world where the child will have to relate to people who are not in perfect sympathy and attunement with him.[26] Fathers' growing involvement with their children (especially sons) during the toddler period, which has been documented in many cultures and even in primate studies, may facilitate the child's ability to move outside his mother's orbit.[27] Finally, of course, fathers are men and therefore able to offer something to both sons and daughters that mothers cannot.

Fathers are role models for their sons; they are sought after, imitated, competed with, worshipped. Boys hunger for this relationship and are extremely attentive to everything that goes on within it—acceptance, rejection, cooperation, degree of openness, limit setting, respect and self-respect. Both the quality of the father's life and the quality of his relationship with his son will deeply affect the developing boy's sense of self and possibilities. Which is to say that boys identify with their fathers. Identification is not an area much explored by attachment theorists, but its psychological effects are huge. It will certainly have much to do with a boy's character structure, influencing it in ways that attachment theory cannot now predict. (Of this, more later.)

A father's impact on his daughter tends to be somewhat different but is also profound. Whether and how he is able to express his love and show that he values her will affect the extent to which she feels valuable and lovable herself, especially to other male figures. The sexual attraction between father and daughter can be a source of self-confidence or shame and guilt. If the father is emotionally estranged from his wife and becomes overly seductive with his daughter, that may adversely affect her development, skewing it toward seductiveness or enmeshment.

There is every reason to believe that husbands also have an impact on the quality of mother-child attachments. Marital satisfaction, for instance, as well as the father's general support of the way the mother handles their child, have both been associated with the quality of the child's relationship to the mother.[28] And even troubled girls, if they later marry relatively supportive husbands, are found to be adequately nurturant mothers.[29] Thus, how the father relates to the mother; whether he supports her caregiving efforts; whether he acquiesces in or collaborates with her unfairness, imperiousness, or other failures; whether he demonstrates love and respect for her, distances himself emotionally from her, gets involved in manipulations and power struggles with her may all have a lasting impact on the child's psychology. Studying that impact, which may be different for boys and girls, is an important direction for future attachment studies. It will be promoted if attachment workers begin performing for later years the sort of home studies Ainsworth did in the first year—because many fathers only become significantly involved with the child when it is older.

Other attachment workers, notably former Ainsworth student Robert Marvin, at the University of Virginia, and John Byng-Hall, a colleague of Bowlby's at the Tavistock, have attempted to include more complex family dynamics. Their work suggests that family secrets, covert family alliances, the way conflicts are managed, the solidarity of the parents in maintaining their roles as authorities in the family—all the issues to which family theorists have drawn attention—affects the formation, maintenance, and quality of attachment bonds. This, of course, puts parental sensitivity and attunement—the principal factors measured by Ainsworth—in a different perspective. Needless to say, all of this begs for further study.[30]

* * *

By the late 1970s, Minnesota papers had begun appearing with regularity in the child development journals. That the quality of early attachment correlated so powerfully with so many important aspects of the child's emerging personality brought attachment theory a level of interest and recognition it had not known before. For many in the field, Sroufe's data, as well as his dramatic way of organizing and presenting it, permanently altered the contours of the nature-nurture debate. Evidence of this sort, about the impact of early experience, emerging from solid empirical research, had never before been available.

Students getting their Ph.D.'s in psychology while working with Ainsworth, Sroufe, and Main in the seventies, as well as others who only read their work, became enchanted by the potential of this new area of investigation to answer age-old questions about what children need. Attachment research offered them something that was rare in academic psychology—combining the pleasure of testable hypotheses with the prospect of changing the world. And at the center of it was this amazing device—the Strange Situation—which could be performed in twenty minutes and which could presumably reveal something fundamental about a baby's unfolding psychology and the way it had been raised. By the early eighties, universities all over the United States were populated with attachment scholars.

15

STRUCTURES OF THE MIND:
BUILDING A MODEL
OF HUMAN CONNECTION

Why do we persist as we are? Why is change so difficult? Why should we assume that many of Sroufe's anxiously attached children will not find in other relationships what their parents failed to give them? If the avoidant child has dreams of one day finding his fairy princess or her knight in shining armor, why shouldn't those dreams come true? Why should a child who's been neglected, rejected, or abused form relationships that seem to reenact those conditions? Why should the rich get richer and the poor poorer, even in emotional life? Why does the past so often predict the future?

Psychoanalysts had long assumed that the answer to such questions lay in the unconscious processes that begin early in life. It's not simply a matter of learning—in the sense of being conditioned to repeat certain behaviors—or imitating elsewhere what one has seen at home. One forms images of the self and others and of how they fit together, which have a powerful hold on the personality and serve as a blueprint for future relationships. The analytic literature was crowded with terms and metaphors that tried to grasp this inner process, much of it centering around the concept of "transference," which we will return to later when we discuss adult attachment. With his usual audacity, Bowlby hoped to clear away the tangle of analytic terminology with a new concept, "the internal working model," which, unlike the others, would be grounded in hard science.

Eclectic as usual, Bowlby cited evidence that lower animals like the digger wasp make such internal models in the form of a mental map of their environment, which enables them to navigate in their world without having to work everything through from the beginning each time they encounter a familiar situation.[1] If this were true for lower life forms, Bowbly argued, then certainly much more sophisticated models must exist in humans, including our understanding of how intimate relationships work, how others can be expected to treat us, and how we perceive ourselves. This line of thinking led him inevitably to the Swiss cognitive psychologist Jean Piaget.

Piaget argued that we are born with a system of extremely flexible mental and behavioral programs, which he called schemata, that enable us to explore and make sense of our environment. It is upon this inborn framework that all future learning is built. In Piaget's view, as in Bowlby's and later Ainsworth's, the infant is not a passive creature who is shaped by his environment, but is constantly exploring, striving to learn, and struggling to bring the environment under his control.

The baby's earliest programs, according to Piaget, include sucking, grasping, listening, vocalizing, and moving the limbs. To learning theorists these were random behaviors. To Piaget they were tools specifically designed to enable the baby to interact with, investigate, and master his environment. They were, in effect, sensorimotor blueprints with a behavior at one end, a mental representation at the other, and an immense capacity to absorb and adapt. The infant uses each program to explore and process information from the world around him. He sucks on a variety of things, he grasps them, he makes noises, and through these efforts he constantly picks up new information not only about his environment but about the impact of his behavior. As he observes the consequences of his behavior, his inborn programs become modified and more sophisticated—the tools themselves change. Because sucking won't work on a glass of water, for example, the sucking program gradually expands through trial and error to include drinking—and the child not only becomes more proficient at getting what he wants but has developed an expanded vehicle for exploration.

It is upon this highly flexible and modifiable framework, which gains in complexity with increasing physiological maturity (enabling the child to develop new programs like walking and talking) that all intelligence is built and continues to be built throughout life. And it is through these mental abilities that the child is able to engage in a distinct class of behaviors that Piaget called "exploratory" and that he believed are as essential a component of our inborn behavioral repertoire as mating and feeding.[2]

The parallels with attachment theory were apparent to Bowlby from the beginning. Both theories started with the idea that the child is not a blank slate, that he has inborn mental capacities, structures, needs, and that he is striving toward various things—toward relatedness in Bowlby's sphere of interest, toward mastery in Piaget's.

Bowlby's encounter with Piaget enabled him to speak in what he believed were more scientific terms about internal representations. Through sucking, clinging, following, smiling, crying, and, when older, by going to mother when in physical or emotional distress or simply when he wants attention, the child explores his relationships and builds a model of the way they work. The internal working model, like the wasp's internal map, reflects the child's relationship history, codifying the behaviors that belong to an intimate relationship, and defining how he will feel about himself when he is closely involved with another person.

Bowlby saw attachment as essentially complementary to exploration. When attachment behavior is activated, often because of fear, exploratory behavior is shut down. When attachment—in the form of proximity or felt security—is achieved, attachment behaviors are shut down and exploration may begin again. This complementarity between attachment and exploration was observed repeatedly by Ainsworth in Uganda and Baltimore, by Harlow with rhesus monkeys, and by Margaret Mahler, who saw children early in the second year constantly returning from their explorations to spend a moment with mom and "refuel."[3] Thus, Bowlby wrote, parents who are "encouraging, supportive and cooperative" not only enable a child to feel securely attached, but also enable him to confidently explore his environment and develop a sense of competence.

When the child became old enough to have insight into his mother's feelings and motives, he was able to form a much more complex relationship with his mother, what Bowlby called a goal-corrected partnership, which meant essentially that now mother and child could negotiate and make plans together, based on their respective needs, a fact that Robert Marvin would later verify with a number of ingenious experiments.[4]

This, too, would be fed into the child's model, updating it with a more sophisticated sense of the complex give and take and the subtle mutuality of relationships.

There were some important differences, however, between the purely cognitive schemes Piaget proposed and attachment's internal working model. Most important, a person's model of relationships is often a much poorer guide to reality. Ideas and memories get distorted when love, hate, anguish, and shame come into play; when we repress memories, cut ourselves off from feelings, and develop defenses. The attachment models of anxious children in particular, Bowlby argued, become rigidified and difficult to update. Secure children may recognize that some people are cold and unwilling to befriend them, but children whose attachments are predominantly anxious, who have no experience and therefore no model of secure relating, may have a hard time recognizing, may not want to recognize, that another person is able to be steadily loving and available.

The rigid internal models of anxious children may also act as a self-fulfilling prophecy.[5] The person who expects to get rejected gives little of himself, acts mistrustful, ignores or misreads friendly overtures, appears superior and standoffish, and others back away from him. Such experiences confirm his early expectations: This is how other people treat me; this is all I am worth.[6] The anxiously attached girl may become quietly hypnotized by fairy tales in which an unloved child, like Cinderella, achieves the true love she deserves, but her habitual modes of feeling, perception, and communication may turn such dreams sour in the end.

The internal models of very young children are particularly subject to distortion, because they readily misinterpret the meaning of their parents' communications. They feel hated and rejected as a result of untimely separations; they interpret outwardly rejecting behavior as proof that they are not loved. They draw conclusions—"I am responsible for mommy's drinking; if I were a better child she'd be a happier person"— that bear no relation to the facts. Under three, they lack the cognitive sophistication to think through the implications of what they feel. As Mary Main notes, anyone will feel unlovable if the person he is most attached to is rejecting. But an older child, who can recognize the distinction between appearance and reality, can use his logic to hold out some hope for himself: "I may be unlovable, but who knows? Mom's been wrong about other things."[7]

The false unconscious beliefs about himself to which the small child is vulnerable can be reopened for consideration and working through at later ages. This sometimes happens when adolescent girls confide in each other; when adults fall in love, experience a rebirth of trust, and feel liberated to explore previously forbidden internal terrain; or when they become parents and gain a new perspective on their early life. But built into the very nature of shameful self-feelings is a desire to ignore them. Indeed, we often construct our lives in such a fashion as to keep them out of consciousness and away from the view of others. So it is not uncommon, even in adulthood, to be burdened with unexamined and hateful self-concepts first incorporated at a young age.

As the child builds up defenses to ward off unmanageable thoughts and feelings, his working model of relationships is subject to further distortions. He may, for instance, consciously believe his mother is the most wonderful and loving mother he knows and unconsciously see her as insensitive and inconsiderate. He may consciously fear that his brutal father will abandon him and unconsciously wish it.[8] Other distortions may be imposed on him by adults. Extreme instances of this were documented in a study of forty-five children who had lost a parent by suicide and subsequently became psychiatrically disturbed. It was found that about one fourth of them had witnessed the suicide or seen evidence of it but had been pressured to believe that the parent had died in some other way.

> A boy who watched his father kill himself with a shot-gun . . . was told later that night by his mother that his father died of a heart attack; a girl who discovered her father's body hanging in a closet was told he had died in a car accident; and two brothers who had found their mother with her wrists slit were told she had drowned while swimming.[9]

When the child related what he had seen, the surviving parent typically tried to ridicule the memory or discredit it by attributing it to a TV show or a bad dream. They themselves, it seems, were unable to deal with the reality of what had happened, and thus forced their own disavowal on the child. Other children see sexual scenes they were not supposed to see; they are drawn into nocturnal incestuous liaisons they are not supposed to remember during the day; they have hurts they're not supposed to have. A little girl is rejected by a father who once actively adored her because he is overwhelmed by his sexual feelings for her. His horrible about-face is continually discounted by the mother, who not only insists that daddy loves her but denigrates the child for thinking otherwise.

> Evidence shows [Bowlby wrote] that many of these children, aware of how their parents feel, proceed then to conform to their parents' wishes by excluding from further processing such information as they already have; and that, having done so, they cease consciously to be aware that they have ever observed such scenes, formed such impressions, or had such experiences.[10]

The resulting confusion, mistrust, self-doubt, and guilt can play havoc with their psychology.

The study of anxiously attached children suggests that many of them fail to develop cognitive capacities that might enable them to reevaluate and work through such distorted models. Main has found, for instance, that insecure six-year-olds have a reduced capacity for self-reflection, for thinking about feelings, and thinking about thoughts. Secure children are more likely to be able to acknowledge having more than one feeling at a time, they can imagine how feelings might change, they recognize that different people might feel differently in the same situation, and that people can say one thing while meaning just the opposite. Anxious children often lack such awareness. By age ten their options for working through are further impaired because they have difficulty even recalling the past.[11]

The power and persistence of negative models, and the impact they have on the child's capacities for self-reflection and complex thought, help explain why change can be so difficult and life so unfair. But such models are not completely dominant. Their power is presumably affected by how extreme is the the child's anxious pattern with the parent and whether he has other attachment relationships that are secure. (I say "presumably" because these factors have for the most part not been considered in the literature.) Even a child who has built negative internal models based on experiences with both parents may retain an island of secure functioning as the result of repeated experiences with a third person, of far less importance, like a grandparent or baby-sitter. Psychoanalyst Janet McKenzie Rioch reported such a case five decades ago, in which a patient was helped in later life by having had a secure attachment to her childhood nurse:

During the many hours when she was with this nurse, she was able to experience a great deal of unreserved warmth, and of freedom for self-realization. Her own capacities for love and spontaneous activity were able to flourish. . . . This, which one might call her *real self*, although "snowed under" and handicapped by all the distortions incurred by her relationship to the parents, was finally able to emerge and become again active in analysis.[12]

With his work on internal models and mental processes, Bowlby helped bring psychoanalytic concepts about inner processes closer to the mainstream of developmental thinking. A brilliant synthesizer, Bowlby was proud to have built bridges from Freud to Piaget and to numerous other areas of scientific inquiry. Ainsworth, like Bowlby, was also committed in her way to a psychoanalytic view. She had been analyzed in the early 1960s after her divorce, and she had read Freud's vast collected works during this time. To her, the bridge from Freud to Piaget made great sense (even if Piaget himself regarded psychoanalysis as an unscientific mythology that would soon be dead[13]). As developmental psychology finally began taking interest in Piaget in the 1970s, her Baltimore research, with its powerful empirical base, helped make the bridge from Piaget to Freud a sturdy crossing for other developmentalists.

But the way he constructed it, Bowlby's bridge was a narrow one. His internal model seemed to lack contact with the complexity, irrationality, and passion of intrapsychic processes. If it had something to teach his analytic colleagues, it also had much to learn from them about, for instance, the processes of identification by which a child could adopt for himself the most hated aspects of a parent, especially a parent who was unavailable through emotional distance or loss; the ways in which we cleave to bitterness, like a hellish security blanket we cannot bear to give up; the endurance of early paranoia. His internal working model was an important contribution, both as a step toward giving analytic concepts firmer grounding in science and as further proof of the formative power of early experience. But, as I suggested in Chapter 8, it glowed a bit too much with the logic of the day, where goodness if given a chance can only prevail and where the night's disturbances are but a dream.

In 1969 Bowlby published his book *Attachment*, a vast reworking and updating of "The Nature of the Child's Tie to His Mother." This would be volume one of his attachment trilogy, followed by *Separation* in 1973,

Loss in 1980, and a revision of *Attachment* in 1982. In a review of the second volume, analyst Charles Rycroft would write:

> Dr. Bowlby is almost unique among psychoanalysts in believing in the principle of economy of hypothesis and in preferring simple, commonsensical explanations to ones which are complex and obscure. As a result, his findings are refreshingly straightforward and tend, perhaps rather boringly, to be precisely what warm-hearted but naive nonintellectuals have always thought.[14]

This was, of course, Bowlby's limitation and his great strength, and Rycroft meant it as praise. It was Bowlby, after all, who had recognized how often the early loss of a parent or other loved person was the precursor of depression and other clinical states when others had missed it; it was he who had determined that love is a biological necessity and not, as so many others had assumed, an accident built on dependency. Time and again Bowlby took the direct route where others were circuitous and mistaken. He was unusual among analysts in choosing to study other disciplines and make use of their findings. He was unusual, too, in that he relied on research and inspired so much of it. Because of these strengths, his concept of the internal working model caught on in developmental psychology where analytic ideas had traditionally been shunned. One attachment paper, published in 1985 by Mary Main and her colleagues at the University of California at Berkeley, would be particularly influential in this regard, bringing the concept of the child's inner life to the forefront of academic psychology as perhaps never before.

16

THE BLACK BOX REOPENED:
MARY MAIN'S BERKELEY STUDIES

By the early 1980s, the Minnesota research had been widely reported and extremely influential. Indeed, the model that Alan Sroufe had pioneered was now so extensively employed that new data were continuously appearing in the journals about apparent consequences of secure or anxious attachment. Sroufe had spawned an industry.

"People kept trying to do what Alan was doing," Jude Cassidy recalls. "Alan has talked about attachment and peer relations, but Alan looked at it in two-year-olds, I'm going to look at it in three-year-olds. Or Alan looked at it with best friends, I'm going to look at it with strangers. Or nobody's looked at it in five-year-olds, or nobody's looked at it in the kindergarten. By the time I came along, it was getting pretty thin. I was referring to it as the 'do it to the right, do it to the left' school of social research. I had the sense that we needed a shot in the arm—people are going to be measuring shoe size next! And then Mary Main came along."[1]

Mary Main was one of Ainsworth's most creative and prolific students. A graduate of the Great Books program of St. John's College in Annapolis, her first love had been linguistics, but due to poor grades she had not been able to get into the linguistic graduate program at Hopkins. "But I was married to a lofty professor who said that if I was interested in language I should go back to babies, that everything interesting probably started with babies," and that caused her to accept a friend's suggestion that she try to study with Ainsworth. "It was an arranged marriage," she now says of her graduate work with Ainsworth—observing and classifying babies in Strange Situations not at all what she originally had in mind for herself.[2] But she would eventually return to language (as we will see in greater detail in Chapter 24), and when she did, she did so in tour-de-force fashion.

Main's cheerful, occasionally breezy style and her girlish voice belie a consuming dedication we tend to associate with driven scientists. When Main moved to the University of California at Berkeley in the mid-1970s, she and graduate student Donna Weston began an ambitious longitudinal study of middle-class families. Children were assessed at twelve or eighteen months for security of attachment to both mother and father. In the spring of 1982, with the children in her longitudinal study now six years old, Main and her colleagues—graduate students Carole George, Nancy Kaplan, and a young English assistant named Ruth Goldwyn—brought them in for a two-hour assessment. Forty families participated. Everything was videotaped.

One segment of the study was conducted by Nancy Kaplan. A Sarah Lawrence graduate who had recently spent two years working with psychoanalyst Sibylle Escalona observing prematurely born infants in the South Bronx, Kaplan, today a practicing clinician, had hoped by studying with Main to combine her interests in clinical work and research. "My wish," she says, "was to try to get at the unconscious, to explore the sorts of things that all clinicians work with but that are very hard to nail down empirically."[3] Kaplan showed each of the six-year-olds a series of photographs. The photos depicted children who were undergoing separations from their parents. The parents are saying good night at bedtime, going away for a weekend, bringing the child to the first day of school, or, in the most extreme case, going away for two weeks. They were asked what the child in each of the photographs might feel and do in response to the imagined separation.

Once again the three major patterns emerged—secure, avoidant, ambivalent—and Kaplan found that for 79 percent of the children she was able to accurately surmise their original attachment classification with their mother by how they reacted to the photographs. (Early quality of attachment to father, taken alone, proved not to be significant.) Some of the children who had been rated securely attached to their mothers at twelve months spoke touchingly of the sadness, loneliness, or fear associated with separation, and some had constructive ideas about how the pictured child might respond. When asked how the child in the picture feels, one boy said, "Sad, because they are going away. If he had permission to, he could follow them." When asked what the child might do, he responded, "Make sure that his Dad or Mom give him a phone number that he knows just in case if something goes wrong."[4] In recognizing that the separation was unhappy but not beyond his management, this boy — the only child in the study who responded with such exemplary security —exhibited to an extraordinary degree the balance between attachment seeking and self-reliance that Bowlby took as the hallmark of healthy functioning.

The securely attached children were sometimes able to relate the experience of the child in the picture with their own experiences: "I'll tell you about this picture," said one six-year-old. "I know 'cause when I started school at my first kindergarten class, boy, I was just like this girl!... I mean, I just didn't want to go to school. At first, I was happy, but then I got sad. . . . I was gonna miss my mom and I just didn't know about school and couldn't go to kindergarten yet. This little girl feels sad . . . 'cause she doesn't really know everybody yet."[5]

The securely attached children generally took their feelings seriously, but did not find them too upsetting to talk about. Thus, one six-year-old said the pictured child would stamp her feet "'cause she's mad." Another simply said that she was "a little angry at her mom and dad 'cause they are leaving her."[6]

Avoidant and ambivalent children also noted the unhappiness and loneliness of the pictured child but their responses were very different. Avoidant children often seemed overstressed by the discussion and were at a loss for what to do. One boy who had been classified avoidant five years earlier, when asked how the boy in the photo felt, said, "Sad," in a high-pitched voice. When asked why, he responded more emphatically:

> He FEELS SAD!!! [Why?] Because his parents are leaving [whimpering voice]. Oh, God, he doesn't want to sleep all by himself! He's a crybaby. He doesn't want to sleep all by himself. [What's he gonna do?] Quack, quack, stay home, that's all.

Another avoidant child said of a pictured boy, "He feels sad because he doesn't know if his mom will come back or his dad will come back." What can he do? "I don't know." This response, "I don't know," or "Nothing" was typical of the avoidant children.[7]

It may be recalled that mothers of avoidant children tend to downplay or be put off by attachment demands. When the children snub them on reunion in the Strange Situation, such behavior suggests that in moments of stress, when attachment needs are highly activated, they've learned to shut their attachment behavior down. Their response, like that of the young child who's been sent away to the hospital for a week or more, seemed to be a defense against further disappointment, as well as against the destructive power of their own rage. At twelve months their defensive strategy seemed to work; they did manage to cope with the Strange Situation separations fairly well, even if they did need to put a clamp on their need to be comforted. But now, at age six, their surface detachment no longer seemed so successful in the face of attachment stresses. They seemed flooded with anxiety. What's more, their inaction had become solidified, as if infusing their being. They could not even imagine a useful response to a painful separation. They believed that an attachment stress could only leave them miserable and paralyzed.

The ambivalent children seemed very similar at six to what ambivalent children look like at twelve months, especially in the intensity of their involvement with their parents and their contradictory impulses toward them, often combining proximity seeking with rage. When one ambivalent child was asked what to do about the pictured separation, he responded:

> "Chase them." [Who?] "Mom and dad in his new toy car." [Then what?] "And then he's gonna toss a bow and arrow and shoot them."

Another ambivalent boy suggested that the pictured child could "shoot his gun at him."

> [Then what will happen?] "Then he's gonna die." [Who?] "His dad."[8]

The depth of the tragedy of such responses is reminiscent of the boy who killed his mother because he couldn't bear for her to leave him. In pain over a temporary separation, some of these children imagine killing off one or both of their parents and thus losing them for good. This anger, which arises presumably because someone they love has repeatedly disappointed them, is so overwhelming that it would seem they already feel, when confronted with separation, as if that person is lost forever.

A fourth category of more disturbed children (see Chapter 17) spoke not so much of sadness or loneliness but of inexplicable fear. They imagined that they or one of their parents would be severely hurt or killed. And their responses were often contradictory, strangely repetitive, accompanied by aggressive behavior, or expressed in nonsense language. Asked what the child in the picture could do, one of these six-year-olds said,

> "Probably gonna lock himself up." [Lock himself up?] "Yeah, probably in the closet." [Then what will he do?] "Probably kill himself."[9]

For some of these children it seemed that any attachment stress quickly reached annihilating proportions.

What happened next in the Berkeley study was inspired by the work of James Robertson, and in particular his 1971 film *Thomas: Ten Days in Foster Care*, about a two-year-old whom James and Joyce Robertson had taken in for ten days when his mother was in the hospital. Thomas had what appeared to be a secure and loving relationship with his mother, and Joyce tried to keep it alive by regularly showing him his mother's photograph. At first he kissed the photograph and handled it tenderly. A few days later, he seemed to become nervous in its presence, fiddling with something, his eyes downcast. By the end of his stay with the Robertsons, he avoided the photograph entirely, moving away from it, obviously anxious. Main found all this arresting. She reasoned that the behavior of the mother in the photograph hadn't changed, so it must have been something in Thomas himself, something about his feelings toward her, his sense of his relationship with her, and perhaps his sense of himself in the context of that relationship. In other words, his internal model had gone through a transformation, what might be called a malignant transformation (although Thomas was gradually able to recover a more favorable model after his mother returned).

Now, after being shown the separation drawings, the six-year-olds in the Berkeley study were presented with a Polaroid photograph of them with their parents taken earlier, when they'd first arrived in the lab. It was introduced with the words, "But here's a photograph of yourself and your family, and you see, you are all together."[10] Securely attached children tended to take the photograph readily and smile or show some interest in it, while the anxiously attached were more inclined to passively avoid it or actively move away. Some clearly became depressed while viewing it. "One child who had been playing cheerfully with the examiner, took on an immediate depressed aspect and bent silently over the photograph for 12 seconds."[11]

Kaplan and Main believed that with these assessments they were taking an X ray of the children's internal representations of their attachment experience with their parents, particularly the mother—a representation of how attachment experiences lived within them as a set of beliefs about themselves and others and about what is possible for them to do within the context of an intimate relationship. Will mom or dad be accessible if I need them? Will they respond to my feelings? Do I have the power to affect them or to do other things that will be helpful to myself in their absence? It was assumed that the attitudes the children exhibited about the availability of their parents, the usefulness of their anger, their ability to manage their loneliness, would be carried into other relationships—indeed, already had been, thus accounting for the Minnesota findings on how they behaved with peers and teachers.

Until this time, despite Bowlby's and Inge Bretherton's writings on the child's internal working model, the differences between anxious and secure children were largely understood in terms of the different behaviors they exhibited in the Strange Situation or in the various longitudinal follow-ups. Main said, in effect, No, the behaviors are not the key; they are just a manifestation of the way the child has mentally encoded information relevant to attachment; it is the psyche we want to look at. The child's early attachment experiences, she said, cause him to establish an internal model that organizes and directs not only his feelings and behavior "but also attention, memory, and cognition," to the extent that such mental functions are related to attachment. As a result, people with different attachment histories not only have different patterns of behavior but different "patterns of language and structures of the mind."[12] Main believed that the internal model reveals itself in different ways at different ages, but that it is always there and that it is a pervasive force in each person's psychological make-up.

The idea that what people say about themselves and their feelings could be scientifically meaningful had fallen into almost irretrievable disrepute since the early days of the field in the last century when introspection was believed to be a legitimate research tool. Behaviorism had so thoroughly disparaged the idea, likening the mind to a black box the contents of which could never be scientifically investigated, that it seemed almost inconceivable to base a study on such data. But Main believed that we reveal our inner life in what we say, and she has devoted much of her career to proving it.

How does the way a child talks about an imagined separation reflect his expectations about life and close relationships? What can we learn about how an adult approaches love and connection based on how he talks about his childhood? How does the way a parent remembers his own childhood become reflected in his behavior toward his own child, and how is it reflected in the child's quality of attachment? Nothing like this had ever been attempted before; and, especially with the emergence of the material from the adult interviews, which came out gradually over the course of the next decade, it represented a second revolution in attachment studies.

When Kaplan had finished with the children and the interviews with the parents had been completed, the parents returned to the playroom—first one, then three minutes later the other—the total reunion period lasting about six minutes. Jude Cassidy, a former ballet dancer and now a student of Ainsworth's, came to Berkeley to work on the project that summer. A determined, Florida-born young woman with exceptional qualities as an observer and a voice that becomes soft and lilting when she talks about children, Cassidy's job was to make sense of the reunions.

For babies and mothers in the Strange Situation, the reunion had, of course, provided stunning information. But these were six-year-olds. They were going to school. They were accustomed to separation. And, in any case, they were not likely to wear their feelings on their sleeves. They were not going to crawl, or cry, or beg to be picked up, or seek comfort in any obvious ways. Main acknowledged that she had doubts about whether anything could be found, especially since the behavior of these families when reunited all appeared to be within a normal range of acceptable parent-child interaction. But she gave Cassidy some of the tapes, put her in a room with a video machine, and told her to look.

"And so I looked at them. I looked at them a thousand times. That was all I did that summer, working full-time. And at first it really didn't seem like there was much there. But I kept looking and kept looking. Finally, differences just started to emerge."

The lack of overt variability in behavior meant that Cassidy had to keep studying the five hours of videotaped reunions, hoping to find some underlying patterns that would differentiate the relationships. "First I looked at all the tapes, there were about sixty or seventy, until I knew them really well. Then I found a tape that I just thought, This dyad" (or mother-infant pair) "was really secure. It looked like a really great dyad. It made me feel great just to look at them. The child seemed glad to see the parent, very comfortable, casual, interested in interaction and contact, but in a real calm, subtle kind of way. If the parent asked a question, the child would do things that we came to call 'expansions.' These kids were not just answering, they would say, 'Yeah, plus, you know what? I did this with them and then I did that.' Or inviting the parent to join in play. And so, on this first one, I said to Mary, If there's a secure kid in the whole bunch, it's got to be this kid. So she went and looked it up and said, you're right, it is a secure kid. Then she said, Try to find some other kid, somewhere, that you can label.

"So I found a kid who, the mother was asking questions and she wouldn't answer. And it was really painful and embarrassing. The mother was trying to get something going, and the child just would not answer. So I thought, Okay, this is avoidance at six. And Mary looked it up and, in fact, it wasn't avoidance. It had been a disorganized child. So I said, Hmm. But later I found a child who was being very neutral. She was answering her mother's questions, but just maintaining neutrality—'fine, thank you'—no expansion, no invited play, but not rocking the boat by being really obnoxious about it. So I said, maybe this is avoidance at six, this sort of cool neutrality. So Mary looked it up, and, yes, the child had been classified avoidant as a baby.

"So I continued through the tapes like that. I said, let me go find another kid who looked like that kid who was secure, who made me feel the same way. And I did. Then Mary would tell me, Yes, that had been a secure child, or, No, it wasn't, it was something else, and we built a system based on my mistakes and my correct hits."

Working in this way, Cassidy eventually labeled every one of the children. In 85 percent of the cases the classification she gave the child with mother or father was the same classification the child had received at twelve months. When I interviewed her eleven years later, it was apparent that that summer, working with Main, had been one of the peak experiences of her career.

"The thing that was so wonderful was that there were these meaningful parallels. A secure baby wants contact with his mother and wants to show her that he's interested in her, that he missed her, that he's glad she's back, and that he wants some comfort. And for a six-year-old, it's the same thing, but it's displayed differently. I think about half of the six-year-olds who had been secure babies at some time or another touched their mother or their father during the reunion. So they were interested in physical contact, but it wasn't, I've got to sit in your lap. It was so subtle, and it was so *cute*. This one little girl, her daddy was sitting on the floor; he had his legs stretched out in front of him, and his foot was kind of near her, and she just reached out and took the toe of his great big size-fourteen shoe and wiggled it back and forth for a second and then went back to playing. A boy needed to get a cookie, which was on the other side of this father, and he had to lean across his father, and as he did, he just put his hand on his father's knee, like for balance, and then he reached across and came back. And then it was gone. It was no big deal. But in that instant he displayed a comfort with his father's body. Or one little girl shows a picture to her mother, and she leans in and puts her hand on her mother's shoulder, and their faces are side by side, just a few inches apart. No child classified as avoidant did that."[13]

On the whole, Cassidy found that the anxiously attached children showed little flexibility in their communication with their parents. While secure children and their parents treated each other in a relaxed and friendly way, readily engaged in conversation on a variety of topics, and fell into an easy intimacy that was not at all clingy, the anxiously attached children communicated far less, with little spontaneity, and a very restricted range of feeling and subject matter. The ambivalent children, not surprisingly, tended to mix intimacy seeking with hostility, and they often seemed affectedly cute or ingratiating. Avoidant children also showed a pattern reminiscent of how they'd behaved at twelve months in the Strange Situation. They tended to keep their parents at a distance, to keep greetings brief, and to choose strictly impersonal topics of conversation. By keeping busy with toys, they were able to ward off whatever advances their parents tried to make. The disorganized children were most likely to try to control or dominate the parent, by acting in an either rejecting or humiliating way, or to strangely reverse the roles and becoming solicitous and parental. One can imagine how such anxious patterns of relating to parents might become amplified a few years later in the cauldron of adolescent emotions.[14]

Sroufe's studies had shown that in their relationships with playmates, children tend to perpetuate aspects of the relationships they had learned at home. It was certainly suggestive of an internal working model, but this study added a new dimension. For what Cassidy was able to show was that the children, in their relational behavior, were no longer merely responding to their parents' leads. With their mothers and fathers, they were now full partners in the relationship, equally responsible for its tone in the current moment. The child's model of relating, as Bowlby asserted, was no longer owned by the parent or hovering somewhere between them. It now fully belonged to the child.

While Kaplan studied the children's responses to imaginary separations, as well as the family drawings they'd created, and as Cassidy pored over videotapes of the reunions, Ruth Goldwyn spent her summer attempting to make sense of the interviews that had been done with the parents. The results of her work with Main on those transcripts would not only demonstrate the intergenerational transmission of attachment styles but also provide a way of understanding how attachment experiences reach their final stage of mental and psychological incorporation in adulthood. Of this, we will speak more later. All told, this single piece of research opened attachment studies to a new level of discourse, closer perhaps than it had ever been to its psychoanalytic roots—although it would still be some time before analysts recognized it.

17

They Are Leaning Out for Love: The Strategies and Defenses of Anxiously Attached Children, and the Possibilities for Change

The behavior of six-year-olds in the Berkeley reunion, like the behavior of one-year-olds in the Strange Situation, suggested that insecurely attached children have developed unconscious strategies for dealing with mother's neglect, rejection, or inconsistency and with the intolerable furies and hatreds that boil up within them in response. It is hazardous to make assumptions about what is going on in the minds of small children and even more hazardous to generalize too broadly, especially when influences are coming from so many different directions, both inside and out. But certain patterns do suggest themselves when a particular style of anxious attachment becomes entrenched and thus a key factor in the person's developing psychology.

The ambivalent children (who represent about 10 percent of middle-class samples, 20 percent of Sroufe's poverty sample)[1] seem to be desperately trying to influence their mother. Many of them seem hooked by her haphazard, unpredictable style and the fact that she does come through on occasion. They pick up that she will respond sometimes— perhaps out of guilt—if they plead and make a big enough fuss. And so they are constantly trying to hold on to her or to punish her for being unavailable. They are wildly addicted to her and to their efforts to make her change, they become enmeshed with her in various unhealthy ways, and later in life they become similarly addicted to other potential attachment figures, such as teachers in the school years and, in all probability, romantic figures after that. But through it all they do not believe they have what it takes to get what they need from another person.

Ambivalent children fret for themselves, and, often, they fret for their mother: Where is she? What is she doing? Is she okay? Not surprisingly, some of them become what family therapists have called "parentified"—that is, caretakers for their own parent. Bowlby argued that such extreme ambivalence is the true source of school phobia, not because, as is commonly thought, the child is afraid of school, but because he fears that he will lose his mother or that she will be unbearably lonely if he dares let her out of his sight.[2]

According to Main, the predominantly ambivalent child emphasizes his feelings of helplessness in order to elicit care. He learns to scan the environment in search of threatening elements that will enable him to become fearful and thereby get attention. Gradually, the ordinary takes on a frightening cast, leading in some cases to chronic fretfulness or anxiety.[3] Meanwhile, he is highly attentive to attachment-related signals, to any hope that some succor and connectedness may be in the offing or to any danger that it may be removed. This extreme attentiveness saps energy that might have been available for play or work, compromising intellectual development and giving the personality a dependent and highly emotionalized cast. Ambivalent children are not turned off. Their longing for connection is always on "high." But they often alienate others with their impulsiveness; and, in those relationships where hope is kindled, they may alienate them with their hypervigilance and clinging.

Attachment theory does not tend to address itself to the cauldron of rage and aggression, including in some cases sadistic and masochistic aggression, hatred and envy, self-hatred and persecutory anxiety that must churn within these children. This is partly a legacy of its coming of age within developmental psychology, where the emotional life has not traditionally been examined in depth, and partly a legacy of John Bowlby's limitations in this realm, as exemplified by his split with Melanie Klein. Klein's main concern was studying just such churning passions and the relationship fantasies that accompanied them, which she saw as prominent in every small child. One of her key early insights was that extreme passions are inherent in our make-up and a natural response to feelings of deprivation or persecution, real or imagined. Much to Bowlby's horror, of course, Klein ignored whether they *were* real or imagined and seemed to care little about the environmental conditions that might promote such violent inner storms or stand in the way of the child's mastering them to the extent that love could prevail. But Bowlby's political differences with Klein notwithstanding, he was, as I have said, not drawn to this subject matter. He seems to have successfully lidded his own cauldron and was not eager to get reacquainted with its contents. Not that Bowlby entirely ignored aggression: He knew it was important. The reader may recall that years earlier Bowlby had discussed how much the child needs to be able to express hatred and aggression toward the parent (see Chapter 4). Being allowed to have these feelings without being overwhelmed by guilt or anxiety helps the child to accept the ambivalence that is part of every close relationship and gives him the confidence that he can control his negative impulses, that they do not have to destroy him or those he loves. Although this early insight of Bowlby's has not been adequately applied to anxious attachment (for an exception, see Kobak's thinking mentioned in the following chapter), it seems obvious that an avoidant or ambivalent child would lack just such confidence. How can he satisfyingly voice his belligerence to a parent who is too dependent on the child's glowing love, who cannot tolerate rejection, who feels turned off by need, who caves in to depression when the child is tantrummy or oppositional, who desperately needs the child to be a perfect narcissistic reflection of herself?

There is another implication here, too, perhaps especially for the ambivalent child, whose hurt and rage and hatred are so volatile and so quickly unmanageable: He never develops the sense that mom is there to contain his overwhelming emotions; that he can have a tantrum; that he can hate her and feel as if he and mom are through, but that she will be soothing and convey the sense that the tantrum will soon pass without causing permanent damage and that even his wish to annihilate her will not have devastating consequences. In other words, even if his extreme negative feelings are too much for him, they are not too much for her; she can (in Winnicott's word) "hold" them, and through his relationship with her he will learn to manage them one day himself.

What then becomes of the ambivalent child's rage, a rage that already at age one in the Strange Situation was so disorganizing that the child could not take in the comfort that the mother offered and that the child himself so desperately sought? Studies do not exist to answer this question, and even if they did, we would probably find so many variables within the ambivalent syndrome as to make a single answer impossible. But work with patients in psychotherapy does offer some clues regarding the internal processes of at least some of these children. In these paradigmatic cases, where the mother behaves in just the way expected by Ainsworth and Main, the relationship with the mother herself probably remains stormy, because the child is still desperately trying to get her to be what he needs her to be, which means in many cases, I think, not just getting her to be available, accepting, attuned, but also to contain his distress, to perform the holding function that the child has still not learned to perform for himself even though he may be technically capable of it.

In many cases grisly power struggles will follow, leaving this ambivalent child burdened with unconscious fantasies of mutilation, dismemberment, retaliation, and desertion—the sorts of fantasies that disturbed young children revealed to Klein in play therapy. These unconscious fantasies about what happens in close relationships will haunt the growing child's sense of self, making him feel shamefully unworthy of being close to others without quite knowing why. And they stand ready to corrupt future intimate relationships, for the fantasy does not just relate to me and mommy, but to me and anybody with whom I am close or by whom I long to be loved. Because most ambivalent children are so anxious about abandonment, their aggression toward others is, I suspect, most apt to come out in disguised or passive-aggressive ways, with extreme outbursts still being reserved for mom or for those moments with highly valued others when there is too strong a whiff of betrayal. Meanwhile, I suspect that many ambivalent children remain prey to persistent feelings of envy and resentment which further foments their rage and their sense of themselves as poisonous. (We'll talk more about the ambivalent style in adulthood in Chapters 24–26.)

Ambivalent attachment is a very broad category and can take up residence in the personality in an endless variety of ways, but consider the psychological dynamics in some adolescent girls who suffer from anorexia. Often, the anorectic stance grows directly out of the impossible power relations the child has had with the mother, including feelings of persecution, neglect, and cruelty. In many cases the anorexia develops into an angry refusal not only to take in food but to take in any caring, any emotional nutrition, from another person, even though, deep down, that is what is most wanted. This refusal, so reminiscent of the ambivalent baby's reaction in the Strange Situation when she seems unable to absorb her mother's efforts to comfort her, is, among other things, a way of hating, a subtle but powerful form of aggression, that can last even after the eating disorder itself has passed. Any therapist who has tried to jump through hoops to nurture a patient like this only to be thwarted by confused grimaces or shrugs, or who has experienced a sisyphean sense of losing the very connection with the patient that he confidently thought had been built up over previous months or years, knows eventually that the anorectic is not just starving herself, she is starving those who love her, too. By refusing to connect—or to stay connected to her own connectedness—she is acting out, albeit unconsciously, a form of sadism.

When I have seen women in treatment who I assume have had ambivalent relationships with their mothers, they usually have a strong identification with their mother as well. The identification is another aspect of the child's, and later the adult's, fantasy-emotional-relational life, with the result that many of these women feel doomed to the worst aspects of the mother's destiny, including in some cases a bitterness toward men or toward fate in general.

With his bids for loving contact repeatedly frustrated and sometimes angrily rejected, the child with a history of avoidant attachment to his mother (about 20 percent of middle-class samples) finds himself in a special box. He doesn't feel he can be openly angry with her, despite the fact that anger, according to Bowlby, is the natural response when a child's attachment needs are thwarted. Experience has taught him that his anger will only cause her to become more rejecting. And so he has learned to turn himself off. At the slightest hint of pain or disappointment, he shuts down his attachment system and experiences himself as having no need for love. Unlike the ambivalent child, whose attachment antennae are always up and receiving and who seems to have no defenses to ward off painful emotions, the avoidant child, Main believes, has made himself deaf to attachment related signals, whether they are coming from within himself or from someone else. He avoids any situation and perhaps any topic that has the potential for activating his attachment needs.[4]

Even later on, as a child who seems to have accepted life on the edge of human connectedness, who seems to many observers to prefer detachment, the prospect of further rejection is too terrible to risk. The predominantly* avoidant child cannot be warmly affectionate with his mother or go to her when in need. But by keeping his attachment system dampened, he is at least able to stay near her without risking more pain or ruining the connection with his disappointment and anger. Thus, despite appearances, the strategy of the avoidant child still seems to serve the purpose of preserving proximity. Psychologically, he is firmly in his mother's orbit, his thought, feeling, and behavior shaped by the claims of that relationship, but, like Jupiter or Uranus, he abides at a distance that affords him little warmth.

This constricted way of life, in which positive displays of feeling are curtailed, can often be managed, especially if the avoidant child develops solitary interests. But when he's most distressed and needing care, his efforts to minimize or turn off the strong, biologically based attachment needs emanating from within can be a terrible struggle, which leaves him stressed to his limit. Now the rage that he feels toward his rejecting unavailable mother is no longer so easily repressed. He becomes taut; his trigger is held by a thin hair; and it is possibly at such moments that he is most likely to unleash his anger at other children.[5]

To the outside world, the avoidant child seems to say, Who needs you —I can do it on my own! Often, in conjunction with this attitude, grandiose ideas about the self develop—I am great, I don't need anybody —which have little in common with secure independence. For some parents it is useful to promote such grandiosity in the child. If the mother can convince herself that the child is superior to other children because of his amazing autonomy, she can feel reassured about her own lack of nurturing attention: This kid is special, he barely needs me, he's been doing his own thing practically since he was born.

It is not hard to imagine the fury that engulfs a child whose attachment needs are so profoundly frustrated. We know that the avoidant child seems to abandon his overtly rageful stance in favor of a defiant "I don't need you!" But when anger toward a parent is stifled, as it often is, for instance, when a parent dies, the child tends to turn the anger against himself, creating a stubborn pocket of guilty or shame-ridden

---

*I use this word *predominantly* to emphasize that there are degrees of anxious attachment. In generalizing about ambivalently and avoidantly attached children, I am talking about children who are very solidly in an anxious category. Even then it should be remembered that all children are different, each with special vulnerabilities that may pull them into more disturbed realms and special strengths that may pull them out of an expected disturbance. And they may have other attachments with other adults that gives them alternate modes of relating.

depression. The depression may be masked by compulsiveness, aggression, or other symptoms. Meanwhile, the "I don't need you!," begun as a rageful, wounded pout, now becomes an unconscious stance toward people in general, even loved people. This too is a form of self-starvation and is probably intensified by an identification with the depriving parent, such that the avoidant child now becomes the agent of his own deprivation.

As with the ambivalently attached, it is hard to imagine the avoidant child or adult being able to express anger while simultaneously retaining a feeling of love and connection. We still have a lot to learn about why various children become avoidantly attached to their mothers, but to the extent that the relationship fits the picture that emerged from the Baltimore study, we can assume that in the avoidant person's fantasy, to express anger over one's hurts or unmet needs is to be rejected, swatted down, disparaged. His anger is, therefore, likely to remain unexpressed (except in outbursts of temper), because the consequences of expressing it are too terrible. Instead there may be an unspoken withdrawal—"I don't need this person any more; he's history"—which may in turn be covered by an outward amiability that suggests nothing has happened. This is not to say that avoidant anger can't also be cold and dooming (perhaps like the parent's) or even murderous, but it will rarely be accompanied by a sense that anger and love can go together: that I can hate you and still know I love you, that I can be confident even as I'm fuming that things will be right with us. The avoidant personality thus feels that his anger is always putting his relationships in jeopardy. In a sense, it could be said that he is in hiding from his own attachment storms and the inner representations that go along with them.

The avoidant child may be afraid to get too close. He may unthinkingly wander away from his connections, unaware that he is starving himself in the process. Or he may become openly rejecting, especially if he has been rejected by the parent with whom he is most identified; and his rejecting style may be sadistic or exploitive in the manner of that parent. As with ambivalence, the ways in which avoidant rage can get played out, both in fantasy and behavior, are endless, depending on the unique set of circumstances with which the child is presented both in infancy and later on.

Given the distortions of thought, feeling, and relationship style inherent in anxious attachment, there is understandably a great deal of concern

about the tenacity of attachment patterns. That they often seem to persist through childhood and into adulthood is hardly surprising,[6] if for no
other reason than the fact that the environment most children start out
with doesn't change. Early anxious attachment can be assumed to arise
from several sources: trying circumstances, such as an overtaxed, under-
supported mother not having the time or the peace of mind to be sensitively and consistently available to each of her children; ignorance,
which might cause otherwise caring parents to let a baby cry for prolonged periods, to leave him repeatedly or for too long a time before he is
able to handle it, or to become prematurely concerned with training for
independence; unhappy events in the child's life (deaths, separations,
sibling rivalries), which might create emotional problems the parent
cannot handle; some innate need in the child that the parent is unable
to satisfy; and, finally, parental psychology, which easily works its way
into and complicates the other conditions. Indeed, what begins with
ignorance, unfortunate circumstances, or infant need is often prolonged
by psychology, as the parent reacts or overreacts to the child's anxious
pattern.

Circumstances and ignorance, of course, can change much more readily than parental psychology. But, even if the miraculous happened, and
parents with all their deeply ingrained psychological baggage were suddenly liberated and able to let their love flow without the anxieties, conflicts, sore points, and poor habits that have been built up and reinforced
over the course of a lifetime, the child might have a hard time seeing the
change. The avoidant child doesn't want to be tempted to open himself
to hope or trust when he's worked so hard to close himself down and
when so much is at stake in terms of the agony of renewed rejection.
Indeed, he may feel the temptation itself is so pernicious, arousing
agonies of renewed ambivalence, that the person who seeks his trust
may become the object of his sorry rage. The ambivalent child, meanwhile, whose care has been inconsistent or chaotic, cannot believe that
a caring gesture is any more than a passing fancy. So he is likely to keep
testing and testing, keep mixing clinging with hostility and unreasonable
demands, perhaps driving away the parent who wants to initiate something new.

Throughout their early years insecurely attached children are believed
to be relatively amenable to change. Avoidant children, for example,
will seek attachments with teachers and other adults, and, if they are
lucky, they will find a special person who will provide them with an

alternative model of relatedness. Research has shown that if they are securely attached to their father (or to another secondary caregiver), that will be the best insurance in helping to overcome insecure attachment to the mother. But even if it's only an uncle they see occasionally, the knowledge that he cares will keep a different model of relatedness alive in them. Indeed, studies of resiliency indicate that a child's having had such a person in his life can make a significant difference in his ability to believe in himself and to overcome adversity.[7]

But it may be hard for the insecurely attached youngster to find such an alternate attachment figure because the strategies that he has adopted for getting along in the world tend to alienate him from the very people who might otherwise be able to help. The behavior of the insecurely attached child—whether aggressive or cloying, all puffed up or easily deflated—often tries the patience of peers and adults alike. It elicits reactions that repeatedly reconfirm the child's distorted view of the world. People will never love me; they treat me like an irritation; they don't trust me; or, I always feel that I need them more than they need me.

But if adults are sensitive to the anxious child's concerns, they can break through. Sroufe believes that teachers in particular can be trained to bypass the child's resistance. He cites the example of an avoidant child named Eddie. Eddie's "acts of hostile aggression toward weaker children, his devious behavior, and his blunt, matter-of-fact noncompliance ('No way, José!') infuriated" the teachers. According to Sroufe, his

> malicious, antisocial behavior, his apparent pleasure at others' distress, and his fearless contesting of wills with the teachers had all the marks of incipient sociopathy. His elaborate deviousness and his swaggering style seemed to confirm that he was beyond reach. But in fact, of course, no four year old can genuinely be a sociopath. And beneath the swagger was a desperately needy child. . . .

Sroufe instructed the teachers not to punish Eddie but to be patiently available to him despite his provocations.

> The teachers quickly learned to see opportunities for closeness with [Eddie] and explicitly disconfirmed his feelings of low self-worth by not rejecting him. As often as possible, the teachers prevented [Eddie] from engaging in hostile behavior.

And when it was necessary to separate [Eddie] from other children, which was often the case early in the term, a teacher would stay with him.

Eddie soon stopped being a behavior problem, formed a strong attachment to one of the teachers, "and made remarkable progress toward learning to meet his basic needs for closeness."[8]

How much of this Eddie will be able to carry over to other relationships is hard to say. But the difficulties involved are suggested by another avoidant Minnesota child with whom the same strategy was applied. About fifteen weeks into nursery school this little girl, who had become very close to one of her teachers, had a dream. "In the dream," Sroufe related, "her teacher hurled her against the wall. She told the teacher the dream and the teacher said to her, 'I would never do that.' And it absolutely shocked me—I was in an observation booth hearing this—the little girl asked the teacher, 'Why wouldn't you do that?' For her to understand a nurturant, responsive relationship was beyond her mind at that point."[9]

One way or another, it would seem important to reach insecurely attached children by adolescence, because that's when it is believed their patterns become more firmly set. Even then they can still be changed; there is still the possibility of psychotherapy, not to mention other vital relationships, and the emotional flux of the adolescent years sometimes opens children up in new ways. But clinical experience strongly suggests change is most easily accomplished during the earlier years, when a steadfast parent or an available teacher can turn a child around.

In childhood, a strong component of provocative behavior, like Eddie's, is a plea for the adult world to be different. "Love me, show me your love, change," the child is saying. The child wants to have his pain soothed, he wants the relationships with those he loves to be whole again, and he is ready to forgive. This is still true for the adolescent, and even for the adult, but with age we become much more committed to keeping things as they are. As we will see later, when exploring adult attachment, bitterness and resentment become hardened into a new kind of security, and the hope for change is dimmed. A small child like Eddie may seem difficult but is wonderfully open and flexible by comparison.

Parents, of course, have great difficulties with the negative patterns their anxiously attached children develop. The off-putting communicative styles described by Jude Cassidy among the middle-class six-year-olds in Berkeley, not to mention the more disturbing patterns seen among the underprivileged Minnesota children, can be tormenting to parents. Some may convince themselves that nothing serious is amiss or rationalize what they see as an inevitable part of growing up: Kids are difficult, they don't get along with parents, and that's just the way it is. Others only see the child's contribution, are unhappy with his glumness, artificial or cloying sweetness, hostile defiance, withdrawal, or manipulation, are hurt by his lack of open affection, and make things worse by pulling away or coming down on him for it. Indeed, as I've suggested, one of the tragedies of the development of anxious attachment in the first year is that it generates behavioral styles in the child that not only disappoint, annoy, or infuriate his parents but that pushes the parents' buttons, bringing into play (or further into play) disturbed aspects of their own psychology.

Virtually every attachment researcher has noted the melancholy consistency with which parents of insecurely attached children misinterpret their behavior. According to Sroufe they often feel depressed and discouraged because they believe their kids don't love them. Nothing, of course, could be further from the truth. Virtually all children, even abused children, love their parents. It's built into the nature of being a child. They may be hurt, disappointed, caught in destructive modes of being that ward off any possibility of getting the love they yearn for, but to be attached, even anxiously attached, is to be in love. Each year the love may become a little more difficult to access; each year the child may disavow his wish for connection more firmly; he may even swear off his parents and deny that he has any love for them at all; but the love is there, as is the longing to actively express it and to have it returned, hidden like a burning sun.

Even a mother who has sought therapy, who's found a stable mate, who's overcome distracting financial distress—who has in one way or another become ready or able to take a more responsible, consistent, nurturant role toward the child—may find it hard getting through to the child who has adopted such survival strategies. She may find it difficult, for example, to convince him to give up his angry, cut-off stance and be open to receiving love from her again; or to let go of the clinginess, the guilt, and the power struggles and trust that mother has changed, that she will not neglect him this time, that they can be separate people and she will be there to meet his needs. Getting this message through takes much patience and consistency, until the child builds up a new set of expectations, a revised model of the way love works.

When the child actively rejects the parent's advances, the parent's job is complicated. For he must not only keep faith in the possibility for an open and loving connection and persist in his newfound responsiveness in the face of painful rejection, but he must also deal evenly and fairly with destructive aspects of the child's behavior. The mother or father whose own emotional problems were responsible for the anxious pattern to begin with finds both ends of this task difficult. To keep loving in the face of rejection is contrary to the parent's own internal model. To want to hug a distressed toddler, only to have him squirm away, to speak lovingly to the six-year-old, only to see him look at the ground and fidget impatiently, seems beyond endurance. By the same token, to be respectful and to steadfastly demand respect; to discipline a child in a moderate way; to neither indulge, seduce, manipulate, nor explode—all this is contrary to emotional habits built up over a lifetime.

I recall an incident from my own childhood. I believe I had an anxious attachment to my mother, which was perhaps mainly ambivalent but had certain avoidant features and looked more and more avoidant as I got older. My mother, in turn, was, I think, avoidantly attached to her mother, a hardworking but somewhat distant woman who attended to everyone's physical needs but was not especially warm. In those days my friends and I played a game called Skelzy, which required shooting weighted bottle caps around on a pattern we chalked on the ground. We weighted the caps by melting bits of crayon into them, usually by placing them on a hot radiator. One afternoon my mother, who was busy elsewhere in the apartment, had left water boiling for rice in the kitchen, and I saw an opportunity. I placed the bottle cap filled with crayon bits on the lid of the pot. To my chagrin, the lid tipped and everything fell in. I called my mother in a fearful and guilty state. I fully expected a blast of temper. Although I could hardly have expressed it this way at the time, I felt reemerging from within me, as I awaited her response, a familiar aspect of my self. It had been out of mind for a while but now seemed a deeper truth about me than whatever I'd been feeling a minute before: I was an ugly problem child.

My mother has since told me that she felt guilty about her temper and the hurt it might have caused. It seemed on this occasion that she worked mightily to restrain it and be patient. In any case, I was surprised to encounter a warm, slightly indulgent reaction, as if my effort to make

a Skelzy cap in this way was amusing if impractical and certainly a forgiv-
able error coming from a child she loved. I was lovingly sent on my way.

What I did next seemed like nothing so much as a confirmation of my
badness. I decided to try again. Again the cap and crayon bits fell into
the rice water, and this time my mother obliged me with the reaction I
had originally anticipated.

This, I believe, is typical of the way in which a relational style is per-
petuated even when the parent makes a stab at something new. My
mother's first reaction must have struck me as needing further testing. I
had to know whether I could trust the change in her, whether it was
safe to see the relationship in a new way. Besides, it would be nice to
get that indulgent smile again. My mother thought I was a wonderful kid
—smart, independent, competent—and would have been incredulous at
the thought that beneath my confident smile I sometimes felt needy and
unhappy and completely uncertain about how or whether to approach
her. Meanwhile, she had her own demons to struggle with, including this
irrational temper she could not control and didn't know where it came
from. Now, feeling under assault by a taxing child who seemed bent on
ruining her afternoon, her temper was reemerging. If she had indeed been
trying something new, she had underestimated how much work she would
have to do to get me to see her and our relationship differently.

The avoidant child does not tend to come to his mother when in distress. This is another way in which the changing mother has a difficult
job. She may want to respond sensitively now, but she has fewer opportunities to do so and is likely to be rebuffed for her efforts. The child does
not have a good feeling about opening himself up to his mother when he
is in pain. He does not have a good feeling about letting her into his
domain of vulnerability. He associates such experiences with rejection
and shame.

Nevertheless, I do believe that the avoidant child offers his parents
opportunities for new beginnings. He is hurt by a playmate and makes an
oblique mention of it. The mother who has not tended to the child's
hurts in the past has an opportunity to question him now in a sensitive
way and to sympathetically speak his unspoken feelings—suggesting for
the first time that they are not shameful but a natural human response
that can be shared with another person. The child may not seem to like
the experience or to accept whatever words are offered, but a second
opportunity may arrive after a shorter interval. At some point the
avoidant child, trusting in the mother's availability, may spill his hurt

and insecurity in a shocking way: The adolescent, having fallen in love and been rejected, for instance, may reveal that he feels thoroughly dependent and weak. This is a challenge for the mother to hear, for these are the qualities that rankle her. But it is an opportunity—not only to lovingly explain that there is nothing wrong with wanting to be loved or to be hurt when his love is spurned, but also to give him a rewarding experience of depending on her, an experience that could affect his model of what relationships can be about.

That these opportunities can be assisted and promoted by psychotherapy is strikingly revealed by a case reported by child psychotherapist Juliet Hopkins. Hopkins, a quietly attractive woman with soft, penetrating eyes, is Bowlby's niece, and, like him, she too found a professional home at the Tavistock Clinic. Trained to work and think psychoanalytically, she finds that attachment concepts add a valuable layer of meaning to her work, as is apparent from her report on a young patient named Clare, who was referred to the clinic when she was six years old.

Clare's mother had not wanted her. She had found her physically repellent as a baby, prop fed her, and confined her to a playpen until she began nursery school. The mother was not totally rejecting, however, and did gradually come to enjoy talking with Clare and playing with her. She believed that Clare resisted cuddling.

> As soon as Clare could walk [Hopkins wrote] she walked away from her mother and was liable to get lost. She had always been stoically independent, never asking for help except when she had hurt herself. Her mother described her as "accident prone" and felt that she had accidents to gain the attention which she had no other means of seeking. Even when she had hurt herself she did not cry.

Clare had the uncanny ability to reproduce her mother's way of talking and gesturing, as if, Hopkins surmised, by becoming her mother she could do without her. When she started treatment, she did the same with Hopkins, interpreting her own behavior so that she would not need the therapist. "Once, when I spoke to her of her hidden wish to cry, Clare explained, 'I never cry because if I started I would never stop.' I understood this to mean that she feared there would never be anyone to comfort her."

Clare was preoccupied by lepers, and her nightmares were inhabited by them. She believed that they were contagious and that "if they touch someone they die." She nevertheless thought "they could be cured by the laying on of hands." These fantasies spoke volumes to Hopkins about Clare's extreme, avoidant history.

> As therapy proceeded Clare became aware that she felt herself to be a leper whom no one wanted to touch because she would kill them, and she also became aware of her longing to cry and to be comforted. In her session she was tortured by the longing to touch and be touched by me which conflicted with her terror of it, and by her longing to cry which she fiercely resisted because it was "so silly and only babies do it."

After nearly a year of therapy an accident occurred that Hopkins believed was intentional (if unconscious) on Clare's part, allowing her "to translate some of her longings into action." Clare fell heavily from Hopkins's desk onto the floor. "As she lay there she raised her arms beseechingly towards me and burst into tears. I picked her up and she sobbed for some minutes on my lap, though keeping her head averted from me."

The next day Clare's mother told Hopkins that Clare had come to her in distress, seeking comfort for the first time. "Mother, who had been greatly helped by her own therapist, was ready to respond to Clare and thereafter Clare continued to turn to her mother when upset and began . . . to confide her worries to her. She became cuddly and, before long, very clinging and demanding, and no longer accident prone."[10]

If reaching and redirecting anxiously attached children is difficult as they get older, the problem of repair is especially thorny for abused children, because the messages they get and the working models of relatedness they develop are more confused and more sealed off against intrusion. "An abusing mother," says Pat Crittenden, "tends to be fairly coercive and demanding, even hostile, but to come across almost sickly sweet. She is unlikely to scream and yell at her child. She is far more likely to paste a smile on her face and with gritted teeth demand that her child do something. The child then learns to associate a positive expression of feeling with a really negative experience. And so when he goes off to school, or meets other members of his family, or maybe later meets a peer or a potential lover, he will misinterpret positive expressions of feeling. He will assume that people who appear to be nice are being coercive."[11]

If unanswerable attachment alarms go off for the avoidant child whose mother is averse to holding and comforting him when he wants it and makes him feel rejected when he reaches out to her, one can barely imagine the painful dilemma faced by the child whose object of love thrashes him, often at just the moments when he is most in need of connection. It is hardly surprising that these children seem to fall into a fourth attachment category, not part of the original Ainsworth classification system. Labeled "disorganized/disoriented" by Mary Main, they display behaviors typical of both the avoidant and the ambivalent baby.* In the Strange Situation they seek proximity with the mother in a disoriented, herky-jerky, semiparalytic way—they approach her backwards, or they freeze suddenly in the middle of a movement, or they sit for a while and stare into space. As they grow older, their mode of relating to others becomes contradictory and infuriating, such that if they are eventually removed from an abusing home, they fail in one foster care family after another. Because love for them is fused with aggression, and because they are so hardened against themselves—and therefore against other wounded beings in pain—the rate at which they repeat the misdeeds done to them with their own children is high.[12]

Selma Fraiberg, the child psychoanalyst whose book *The Magic Years* helped generations of parents to understand the process of early development, attempted to address this problem by inventing a form of treatment for mothers and their babies where neglect and abuse had already become serious enough to have come to the attention of community clinics, agencies, or courts. Into Fraiberg's Ann Arbor clinic came bleak and cynical young mothers, who showed no reaction to their baby's cries or no interest in handling them. They often revealed such indifference toward their infants that it was painful for the therapists to observe. Eventually they were asked to recount their own experiences as children.

After repeated invitation, they told their stories, heartrending recitations of beatings, abandonment, psychologically cruel punishments, and painful disregard; but they told them flatly, as if reading from the phone book. At one point a sixteen-year-old mother who often forgot to buy

---

*While some studies suggest that a significant portion of these babies have been abused (Cassidy and Berlin, 1992), Main also found that many of the mothers experienced tragic early losses that they had never been able to properly mourn. The result, she believed, was a pervasive sense of anxiety and fearfulness that was subtly communicated to the baby (Main and Weston, 1981; Main, 1991).

milk for her baby and fed him Kool-Aid or Tang cried, "But what's the use of talking? I always kept things to myself. I want to forget. I don't want to think."[13]

As the mothers told their stories, the therapists intervened to speak the missing feelings: How hard it must have been for you to be all alone; how terrified you must have felt; how horrible not to be heard by anyone. Gradually, "grief, tears, and unspeakable anguish" for themselves as cast-off children began to emerge, and as this happened, the wounded mothers reached out to their babies. One mother, while pouring out her long disavowed grief, picked up her baby, "held her very close, and crooned to her in a heart-broken voice."[14] Another mother, angry and tearful as she reexperienced emotions she'd sealed up years earlier, spontaneously went to pick up her little boy, "enclose him in her arms, and murmur comforting things to him."[15] It was as if the mothers' attachment feelings, dammed up for many years, were flowing again.

Psychologist Alicia Lieberman studied with Ainsworth at Johns Hopkins in the mid-seventies before going on to work with Fraiberg, first in Ann Arbor and later at the Infant-Parent Program at San Francisco General Hospital where she still works today. Lieberman, who was raised in Paraguay and whose enthusiastic, refreshingly open style of speech carries an Hispanic accent, saw in Fraiberg's work an opportunity to combine her interests in attachment research and psychotherapy. In recent years, she has taken Fraiberg's model and applied it to a non-abusing group of families whose babies had been assessed as anxiously attached.

In 1991 Lieberman reported the case of a mother who often provoked her eighteen-month-old by teasing him and taking away his favorite toys. Typically, the baby threw a tantrum on such occasions, but the mother did nothing to alleviate his distress, explaining her apparent indifference by saying he should be able to take care of himself. Lieberman was eventually able to ask the mother if that was the way it was for her as a child. The mother gradually recalled that throughout her childhood she had been "mercilessly teased and physically abused by her psychotic older sister." If she asked for help, her mother would say: "You girls work it out yourselves."

Lieberman spoke to her tenderly "about a young child's needs to be believed and protected when she asks for help." At this the mother began to cry profusely: "Nobody listened to me. I was so scared and I had to take care of myself." Lieberman asked, "Do you think that is why you feel that Andy should get out of his tantrum all by himself?" The mother seemed surprised and thoughtful. She said, "Maybe; I need to think about it." She then became considerably more tender toward her son. During the next session another tantrum occurred. The mother, for the first time, embraced him while he cried.[16]

Bowlby could only have been pleased by such developments. For they brought full circle his own clinical work in the London Child Guidance Center of five decades earlier. But now, not only were parents being treated along with the children, but attachment principles were informing the work and also being used to evaluate the results. In a study of one hundred mother-infant pairs who had been assessed in the Strange Situation at twelve months, Lieberman found that after one year of this type of treatment the anxious pairs were virtually indistinguishable from those who had been rated secure.[17]

Reading all this, some parents may understandably wonder, Should I get a Strange Situation done on me and my kid? As a general rule, most attachment workers would, I think, recommend against it, preferring instead that parents simply make an effort to be more sensitive to attachment issues or speak to a knowledgable therapist if they are worried. Knowing a child's quality of attachment may relieve some parents and spur others to take action, but the relief may yield an ill-founded complacency (even securely attached parents and children have problems), while the action may be compromised by onerous levels of parental guilt. Besides, the Strange Situation was devised as a research tool, and its power is based on percentages. Some infants who receive sensitive care look anxiously attached (they may have had a bad day), and some who have neglectful parents look secure (they may have some irrepressible positiveness that is not yet understood). Sroufe has been asked by the courts to help settle custody cases by putting the child through a Strange Situation with each parent, but he has steadfastly refused.[18]

18

UGLY NEEDS, UGLY ME:
ANXIOUS ATTACHMENT AND SHAME

In the studies coming out of Minnesota and elsewhere, efforts were repeatedly made to measure the self-worth of securely and anxiously attached children at various ages, and the differences were unmistakable, with secure children scoring higher in every measure of self-esteem.[1] Attachment theory held that getting love, reliably and consistently, makes the child feel worthy of love; and his perception that he can attain what he needs from those around him yields the sense that he is an effective person who can have an impact on his world. Sroufe's findings seemed to confirm this.

The child whose needs are not met, who feels ineffective in his efforts, or who, worse, is rejected or put down in various ways, according to Bowlby, builds up a negative set of assumptions about himself. He is not worthy of love or respect. He is, in effect, ashamed of what he is. In attachment writings, the word "shame" is rarely if ever used; indeed, attachment studies and shame studies have been largely unrelated fields of inquiry. But there can be little doubt that shameful feelings about the self are an important component of relational insecurity.

Shame rises up from several sources. The anxious child must inevitably feel that there is something wrong with him and something wrong with the immense love that flows out of him toward his parents and is somehow not accepted.[2] The very fact of not being attuned to, so central feature of anxious attachment, is in itself a shame-inducing experience, and some studies have found what looks like an early expression of shame in infants whose mother does not appreciate, echo, or elaborate the feelings they express. (For more on the subtleties of attunement, see Chapter 23.) The anxiously attached child may also feel, at some level, misshapen by his unwanted feelings. He is mistrustful, he is bitter, he is retaliatory, he is violent, and, perhaps, worst of all, he is very, very bad for harboring a secret hatred of his mother, a hatred for which in all likelihood he has been made to feel guilty and monstrous whenever he has dared to show it. Greed, natural in infancy and, in most children, modified through gratification, may become a perpetual disgrace or a dirty secret for him. Rage that he has not been able to satisfyingly express turns inward, such that he, rather than the parent, becomes the villain. For any or all of these reasons, he may come to hate himself and to want to keep the secret of his defectiveness from the world.

Laura, a sixteen-year-old treated for depression and overeating by Juliet Hopkins at the Tavistock Clinic, had, like Hopkins' other young patient, Clare, a mother who had shunned bodily contact with her during her infancy. If Clare saw herself as a leper, Laura came to see herself as a tortoise and her little sister (who had been caressed as a child) as a cuddly bunny. Laura had dreams in which she was alone on a desert covered with a revolting skin disease. She had a concern for India's Untouchables and had set up a collection box for them. "I have found it common," Hopkins observes, "for physically rejected children to dramatize or draw themselves as physically repellent or unstrokeable creatures, like tortoises, toads, crocodiles and hedgehogs."[3] This sense of deformity, degradation, or worthlessness is a central feature of shame.

Shame theorists believe that neglect and rejection, especially if early and extensive, generate a self-feeling in the child of ugliness and undesirability. Parental rejection can be global, it can be limited to specific aspects of the child that the parent dislikes, or it can be a subtle combination of the two. Is the child accepted and valued for what he is—slow, placid, squirmy, delicate, dark-skinned, plain? Is he allowed to be dirty, funny, needy, silly, proud, aggressive, weak, defiant, creative, uncertain? To the extent that such qualities arouse anxiety in the parent and are responded to with coldness, punishment, or ridicule, they will become sources of shame.[4]

A defensive parent's own limitations can also translate into shame for the child. A mother who is self-centered and ungiving may ward off her own feelings of guilt by finding fault in her daughter. She perceives her little girl as overly demanding and repeatedly scolds her for being selfish. The child comes to believe that she is selfish and despises herself for it. Her natural self-assertion is compromised as she comes to feel that she should not take, should not ask, should not calculate in her own behalf; for any of these things may exhibit the hated quality. What's more, she finds that if she is restrained and solicitous, her mother likes and approves of her. Nevertheless, her unmet needs keep rising to the surface and she acts them out in ways that cause renewed displeasure in her mother and renewed self-hate in herself.

As she gets older, the girl compensates for her supposed defect with rigid displays of generosity. She remembers everyone's birthday, she's always ready with a compliment, she seems content to settle for second best. No one must ever know what she truly is; no one must ever see that clawlike third hand reaching out of her pocket with "Selfish!" written all over it.

Because this inner dynamic proceeds largely outside of awareness, the shame image often persists into adulthood in a strangely unevolved form. If not understood or worked through, it retains the terrible charge of parental rejection. The girl becomes a young woman who unconsciously believes not just that she suffers from a troubling flaw, but that she is revolting and untouchable and that her selfishness is a deformity that makes her unfit to live among other human beings.

People differ in the degree to which they defend against shame. Some obsessively avoid it by restricting their lives and narrowing their consciousness. Through an addictive or compulsively busy life-style, unwanted self-images can be kept from impinging upon awareness. Others are more aware of their shame and tormented by it, sometimes to the point of depression. Perhaps the best evidence that these two styles of living with shame are associated with avoidant and ambivalent attachment comes from a study of six-year-olds by Jude Cassidy. Cassidy found that securely attached children have a strong feeling of self-worth and competence, but when pushed were able to acknowledge imperfections. In other words, they seemed to be neither tormented by shame nor rigidly defending against it. Avoidant children, in contrast, persistently portrayed themselves as perfect and refused to admit to any shortcoming; while the low self-worth of ambivalent children was prominent and undisguised.[5] This study suggests that from an early age quality of attachment may be connected not only with the degree of shame formation but with the development of fundamental dysfunctional personality styles.

Shame formation does not end with infancy but persists throughout childhood. In any family the ways in which differences get worked out are particularly fertile breeding grounds for shame, for they tell the child a lot about his rights, his dignity, his worth. Is he allowed to feel he's still okay when saying no, when complaining, or when expressing the normal hostility or aggression that children inevitably feel at times toward their parents? Can the parent set limits or punish without spilling disgust or rage all over the child? Chicago analyst Michael Basch, who has integrated shame and infant studies into psychoanalytic thinking, has argued that these highly charged moments are critical, for, as he puts it, "Shame is the response to emotion that is not being dealt with effectively."[6]

In a telling parallel, one that recalls Bowlby's early thinking on the subject, Roger Kobak has held that secure attachment is linked to the child's ability to successfully express negative emotions.[7] A secure child can cry, shout, or fall silent and know that he will be responded to in a meaningful way. His negative emotions are thus an effective part of his repertoire and do not become ugly to him and have to be disavowed. He can say, "I hate you," or "You don't love me," or "You're mean," or "You like the baby better than me," with confidence that he will not be met with an icy stare, the silent treatment, a slap, an order to go to his room, or various forms of guilt: "How can you say that?" "Don't you know that hurts mommy's feelings?" "You ingrate!" "You nasty, selfish, rotten little boy!" "You apologize!" None of this means that the parent must tolerate destructive acts of aggression on the part of the child, like biting or hitting. But rather that such behaviors can be curtailed without stigmatizing the feelings behind them and ultimately the child himself.*

Evidence suggests that mothers of secure children seem much less threatened by the child's negativity. Their early sensitivity to the infant's signals reveals itself in later years in their ability to spot negative emotions even when they are unspoken and to help the child to give them voice. Robert Marvin found that in Strange Situation observations done with three- and four-year-olds, mothers of secure children were much

---

*A parallel aspect of secure attachment is no doubt related to the giving and receiving of authentic positive emotions such as love, joy, appreciation, and enthusiasm. Many parents, of course, have trouble participating with the child in these dimensions, too. See Chapter 23.

more likely, as part of their display of concern upon returning, to ask about the child's anger at her for leaving.[8] The mother of the insecure child does not behave this way, and he, in turn, may lack the confidence that if he speaks of his hurt or anger she will be receptive. Karin Grossmann similarly found that mothers of avoidantly attached infants tend to ignore the negative feelings their children express during play, only giving them friendly attention when they are in a positive mood.[9]

Parents of anxiously attached children seem to have difficulty with their own negative emotions as well. In a small study at the Barnard College Toddler Center in New York, Lawrence Aber and Arietta Slade found that

> mothers of secure children were far more likely to express anger directly to their children; furthermore, they reported that when they became angry they would say so: "Mommy gets angry when you do that," "I'm angry at you," and so on. Mothers of anxious (predominantly avoidant) children rarely reported that they got directly angry at their children nor did they report that they were likely to describe these feelings to the children when negotiating conflicts. . . . Interestingly, these were also the mothers who experienced their children as most aggressive and who reported that their children would bite and hit them.[10]

Unleashed anger, expressed with venom, is abusive to a child and will leave him feeling like a worthless thing. But unexpressed anger is damaging, too, for it leaks out in insidious ways—a look, a tone, an abruptness of manner—which the child experiences as rejection. Sometimes the subtler it is the worse it is, for both the sense of rejection and the shame get planted at a deeper, less accessible level. The child does not burst into tears or seek condolence from the other parent. There is no memory of parental meanness, which might be available for the child to work through—in play, in ruminating about fairy tales with witches and demons, or even consciously at a later date. There is no concept like, Mommy doesn't want me to be this way, no opportunity to keep the unwanted aspect of the self alive through some form of rebellion. There is only the subterranean certainty that he is no good and the relentless supression of some dynamic aspect of the personality that might otherwise reveal one's deformity to the world.

Findings about parental attitudes toward negative emotion give us not only a better understanding of shame formation but are suggestive of some of the critical factors that may be at work in the continuation—and creation—of secure attachment in later childhood. To be understood instead of punished, to express anger and not be rejected, to complain and be taken seriously, to be frightened and not have one's fear trivialized, to be depressed or unhappy and feel taken care of, to express a self-doubt and feel listened to and not judged—such experiences may be for later childhood what sensitive responsiveness to the baby's cries and other distress signals are for infancy.

The first emotions that the parent deals with are the attachment emotions themselves—the baby's desire for connection, his need to be taken care of, his need to be responded to when hungry, when in pain, when wanting love or attention. Many parents, because their own dependency needs were rebuffed as children, still live in unresolved pain over them. But the pain is not felt, it is dissociated, and they structure their lives to keep it that way. An avoidant boy who is ashamed of being needy may grow up to be a man who is a caricature of independence, unable to ask for help or closeness or even to feel those longings within himself without risking the disintegration of his self-respect. Will he be warmly receptive to moments of clinginess or dependency in his own little boy? Clinical evidence suggests that parents cannot tolerate seeing their unmet needs expressed by their children, and they cannot tolerate the anger and distress the child expresses when those needs go unmet again. They either overreact or become dismissive, with the result that the child's attachment feelings—as well as his anger and distress—are either walled off from his consciousness or revved up to the point where they overwhelm him. His ability to communicate his attachment-related feelings is gradually shrunken and distorted until it demands misinterpretation. This fairly well describes the avoidant condition, further complicated by shame.

Two incidents from my own childhood may help illustrate this point. I grew up in a large city housing project with hundreds of kids. One winter afternoon, when I was seven or eight, the ground was covered with snow and all the boys were out in force playing and fighting. Gradually, as it got darker, one kid after another went home. When none of my own friends were around anymore, I wanted to go home myself, but my mother was still out and the apartment locked, so I kept hanging out with the others. Finally, it was completely dark, and I was the last kid. I felt lonely and bleak. I thought of going to visit my best friend's family. I went to their building and up to their door. I could hear the happy sounds of family life coming from inside. But I could not bring myself to knock. I could not present myself to them this way, a needy little boy, so pathetic and alone.

The terrible thing for me in all this was not that my mother stayed out late and that I was stranded. That was painful, but it only happened once; it was not a pattern. But the experience caused my attachment needs to surge dramatically, and, because of the way attachment issues were dealt with in my home (and in my parents' homes when they were children), where autonomy and "strength" were emphasized and signs of dependency either ignored or found revolting, I felt pathetic and undesirable when my need for comfort, security, and care surfaced.

The second incident occurred a few years later—I was perhaps eleven now—when my parents were going to dinner at my uncle and aunt's and I was being left home alone. I had no interest in going but for some reason, which I could not understand at the time, I whined and complained continuously and demanded to be taken. Finally, a call was placed and I was brought along. In retrospect, I think this was another moment when my attachment needs were surging, perhaps because of something that had happened in school earlier that day, and as a result I did not want to be left alone. But I had no experience negotiating such feelings, either with myself or with my parents. Another child might have conveyed that he was down and needed comforting. If he could talk about what was bothering him, be told that he was loved, be kissed or held, he might not have felt so alone when his parents left. But I could not ask for these things and may have had difficulty tolerating them if they had been offered. Instead, I ended up with a victory I didn't want and a lousy feeling about myself—a whiner and complainer, a big baby, needy and greedy, who upsets the plans of others by making a fuss over what he doesn't even want and is in no better mood after he gets it.

I think repeated incidents of this sort give one a strong, if disavowed, impression of who and what one is. Most of us repress a shameful self-image because it is so painful, often building up a contrary, conscious self-image, which we broadcast to the world through various false displays and which we devote considerable psychic energy to maintaining. But the negative self-feeling remains, and the fact that it is unconscious gives it tremendous lasting power, if for no other reason than it can never be examined anew, can never be felt, shared, or worked through.

The defenses that the avoidant child erects—as well as the manipulative and devious ways he develops for getting his needs met—and the anxious displays of dependency to which the ambivalent child is prone are both causes for additional layers of shame, as first family members, then neighbors, and then teachers and schoolmates all begin to react to him as if he were annoying, hateful, inadequate, or odd. Aggressive, defiant children do not like themselves for being that way. At some level of consciousness they view themselves as angry, spiteful, unlovable beings. They don't know that they are also sad and desperately hungry for love. Necessity has forced them to disavow such feelings and often to repress the memories that go with them. They thus have little basis for sympathizing with themselves. Meanwhile, the seeds of self-disdain are nourished by the punishments, harsh words, and overt exasperation of others.

Clingy, panicky children, who are pitied or ridiculed, can only devalue themselves as well. Their fundamental experience is rejection. The inevitable accompaniment is an ever-present sense of inferiority. If they are also victimized, as some ambivalent children are, their self-worth, already compromised, suffers further depreciation. For the ambivalent child who is enmeshed with his mother, a different sort of shame may strike later, in young adulthood, when he finds himself lacking in self-reliance, overly dependent on his mother, and plagued by insecurity in his relationships.

But what about the child whose degree of early neglect or rejection is more extreme? Or the child who has been subjected to ridicule or severe punishment whenever he complains, protests, or acts angry? Or the child who is violently rebuffed when he exhibits the annoying and manipulative styles of expressing need that follow in the wake of early rejection? For him the feelings of shame that attach to the identity are proportionally worse: I get treated like shit because I am shit; I come from hateful people and I am like them.

This tightening grip of shame is apparent to anyone who has worked with such children in therapy. I recall an adolescent boy I'll call Juan whom I treated some years ago. His father had left the home when Juan was very young and showed little interest in him thereafter, a blow of inexpressible enormity. His mother was controlling and fault-finding and seemed to favor his younger brother. In his behavior—isolated, sheepish, occasionally bullying (he enjoyed being called the Gorilla and liked to knock down other skaters at the rink); his complete inability to approach anyone, especially when in need (he sat alone in the lunchroom for weeks after being transferred to a new school and failed to make a single friend in the four months he was there)—Juan was in every respect an example of a boy with an extreme avoidant attachment history. Although Juan hid his shameful sense of defectiveness under a layer of grandiosity, his low self-worth was apparent in the way he hung his head as he lumbered about, in his conviction that he would always be rejected, in the fact that he pinned all his hopes for love on an unlikely scenario of stardom but otherwise expected very little of life. On one occasion I asked Juan to draw a picture of an animal. Although his first thought was a tiger, he settled on a pigeon, which he described as a garbage-eating bird, a flying rat. He then told a story, snickering as he did so, of the horrible things that boys did to this pigeon, ending with its being killed and tossed off the roof. It is not difficult to imagine the various ways in which such a model of the self will get played out in later years.

The late psychologist Helen Block Lewis, one of the pioneer explicators of shame, saw in the Bowlby-Ainsworth theory a means of grounding the shame concept in evolutionary design. The ability to vicariously experience the feelings of another, she said, "is the foundation of attachment (on both sides), and the price we pay for it." Shame is the vicarious experience of the rejection. To the infant, separations (and losses) are experienced as rejections and therefore as blows to the self. We would not be human if this weren't so.

Lewis believed that shame was always accompanied by what she called "humiliated fury" and that this helped account for the angry resistance of the ambivalent child in the Strange Situation. The avoidant child, on the other hand, "may be showing the forerunner of a pattern of reaction that involves bypassing the shame of being rejected. They do not directly express humiliated fury. Rather, they behave as if they were turning the tables on the rejecting mother by rejecting her."[11]

All told, the accumulating evidence from attachment research in the 1970s and 1980s and the theoretical work it stimulated was yielding a powerful sense in the field that quality of attachment is a lasting, core issue for the personality. It seemed to encapsulate something vital about the nature of one's earliest relationships, which, in turn, related directly to one's feelings about oneself and one's expectations of others. When

combined with the knowledge gained from decades of clinical experience, and with the work being done by Main and her students on internal representations, it seemed plain that attachment quality must affect
how one approaches human connections at later stages of life and in
periods of crisis.

Clearly, quality of attachment was not everything. It did not govern
the development of one's intellect or ability to play, which are affected
more by other aspects of the parent-child relationship. And it was certainly only a fraction of one's psychological life, which rested on numerous other factors in one's makeup and development. In the emotional
complexity of any single person, quality of attachment, assessed at age
one and only to the mother, left out much of the complexity of any individual life, and it left out much of what arises later in childhood that
makes a lasting impact on one's psychology—negotiating a growing separateness from mother in late toddlerhood, coping with the sometimes
tormenting or traumatic conflicts of the oedipal period, making and losing friends, finding oneself rudely replaced as the baby of the family by a
younger sibling who co-opts everything that we thought rightfully ours,
and so on through all the challenges of adolescence. Attachment category said nothing about the child's inherent resiliency, his luck in finding
other, alternative attachment figures—or his determination to do so—
or his ability to hold on to and nurture a kernel of positive experience
with a teacher or relative. It said nothing about the choices he might
make in adolescence or adulthood—in marriage, in career, in habits or
pastimes—or the misfortunes and bad influences that may befall him.
Nevertheless, to a growing number of developmentalists, the quality of
early attachment to the primary caregiver stood out, like the key in
which an otherwise complicated piece of music is played, imbuing the
personality of many children with a characteristic inflection that is present from movement to movement.

19

A New Generation of Critics:
The Findings Contested

To many young developmental psychologists, reading the work of Ainsworth, Sroufe, Main, and their students and to others who heard about attachment principles through popular authors and popular books by experts like Selma Fraiberg, Penelope Leach, or T. Berry Brazelton, one of the beauties of the material has been its great common sense. It seems only natural that infants would seek attachments as part of their biological makeup; that our earliest relationships become a part of us; that something like an internal working model would account for the types of relationships we develop later in life.

"It's intuitively pleasing, that's what's getting in the way," says the internationally renowned developmentalist Jerome Kagan. "Because it makes intuitive sense people are assuming it's right. But most of the time intuition is wrong. I mean, intuitively the sun goes around the earth, right? Intuitively, the earth is flat, right? Why is psychology the least advanced science? Because our intuitions aren't very good."[1]

Kagan, a hugely influential Harvard psychologist who eschews ideological labels ("I'm part of the *reasonable* school"), is the author of *The Nature of the Child*, which casts a critical eye on such popular assumptions as "a mother's love for her infant is necessary for the child's future mental health" or "that the events of infancy seriously influence the future mood and behavior of the adolescent."[2] At sixty-four Kagan is ebullient, enthusiastic, and likable. He is combative in his views, enjoys making others defend theirs, and seems keenly aware of the impact he has as a speaker. He occasionally sports an ironic half-smile as he raises his eyebrows, cocks his head, and scrutinizes an opponent's arguments for a weakness. Kagan is also prolific, and his work has been widely hailed. His accessible writing style, his breadth of knowledge, his ability to integrate insights from anthropology, sociology, and philosophy, not to mention developmental psychology, into a grand and persuasive theme have made him a formidable and at times maddening antagonist to the attachment community.

By the early 1980s Kagan had emerged as the spokesman for the growing body of attachment critics, rejecting almost every assumption upon which attachment theory was based. He does not believe that early experience is particularly important. ("I was rejected by my parents" has become, he charges, "a rationalization for distress and incompetence."[3]) He spurns the idea that early experience forms any lasting psychological structures, such as Bowlby's internal working model. And even if early experience did matter, Kagan doesn't believe that the Strange Situation measures it. ("Is it reasonable that a history of interaction between mother and infant comprising over a half-million minutes in the home would be revealed in six minutes in an unfamiliar room?"[4]) He sees secure and insecure attachment, at least as those terms are currently used, as misnomers and believes that what's actually being measured are aspects of the child's behavior that reflect either its inborn temperament or its assimilation of parental values. Finally, he believes that attachment theorists are too concerned with what they call security and have allowed their own values to skew their work. ("In the forties and fifties, the children now called attached were called overprotected and that was a bad thing."[5]) His position on attachment is complicated because he attacks it from several different directions, which are not always consistent with one another, but all of which he argues with great verve and authority.

Kagan believes, for instance, that the modern concern for attachment and for the general impact that parents have on their children is an ephemeral aspect of this time and this place and should hardly be the basis for a general psychology of development. Because of the uncertainties inherent in modern society, Kagan argued in 1978, we have latched on to the idea of the importance of early experience in order to regain some sense of control.[6] In the process, mother-love has been elevated to something of an icon:

> Every society needs some transcendental theme to which citizens can be loyal. In the past, God, the beauty and utility of knowledge, and the sanctity of faithful romantic love were among the most sacred themes in our society. Unfortunately the facts of modern life have made it difficult for many Americans to remain loyal to these ideas. The sacredness of the parent-infant bond may be one of the last unsullied beliefs.[7]

By taking the debate to a higher plane, where the cherished beliefs of our culture may be seen as fleeting, Kagan was able to strike at the foundation of attachment thinking. He objected to Bowlby's claim that the "loss of a loved person is one of the most intensely painful experiences any human being can suffer." He dismissed Bowlby's belief that "intimate attachments to other human beings are the hub around which a person's life revolves, not only when he is an infant or a toddler, but throughout his adolescence and his years of maturity as well, and on into old age."[8] According to Kagan, such is not the human condition but merely the way it is for certain people, raised certain ways, in certain cultures. A high-caste Hindu, he argued, who has trained himself to avoid attachments of all kinds, would hardly feel this way.* His dismissal of Bowlby, like many of his arguments, had an Olympian tone that must have caused teeth to gnash from London to Berkeley:

> Although many nineteenth-century observers would have understood and probably agreed with Bowlby, few would have written three books on the theme of attachment because, like the blue of the sky, the idea was obviously true. Bowlby's conclusions are newsworthy in the last half of the twentieth cen-

---

*This strikes me as somewhat facile. That the Hindu monk must struggle mightily to extricate himself from feelings of attachment suggests that attachment is indeed a basic and powerful element of human nature. In Christopher Isherwood's *Ramakrishna and His Disciples*, a Hindu holy man speaks of the unexpected personal torment even he feels over the loss of a loved one and voices renewed compassion for the emotional pain experienced by ordinary folk when they suffer a loss.

tury because historical events have led many citizens to question the inevitability of maternal devotion to the child and of the child's love for the family. Parental abuse and adolescent homicide of parents have undermined the nineteenth-century faith in the naturalness of familial love. Modern citizens have begun to question the universality of deep affection and continued loyalty, whether between adults or between parents and children, are saddened by the conclusions implied in that inquiry, and are eager to hear a wise commentator on human nature assert that the love between child and parent is an absolute requisite for psychological health.[9]

Kagan acknowledges that "the concept of attachment remains useful and should not be abandoned,"[10] and yet it is plain from much else he says that he thinks little of the concept and less yet of the work that's been done in its name.

As for quality of attachment, Kagan sees it simply as a matter of contemporary mores: "My view is, if you're attached, you are motivated to adopt the values of your parents. If your parent values autonomy, you'll be autonomous; if your parent values dependency, you'll be dependent."[11] He argues that the children whom Ainsworth has labeled securely attached become upset when left alone in the Strange Situation not because they're securely attached but because they're less able to deal with uncertainty. They've been trained for dependency, and are showing its ill effects.

Like Bowlby, Kagan is a great synthesizer, but despite his acumen, it sometimes seems that Kagan has assimilated just enough attachment theory to discredit it, rather than to wrestle fully with its meaning. His writing on attachment shows a number of errors and misunderstandings, more typical of the fault finder and antagonist than the reasoned commentator, and that may have hindered his ability to be heard. His distaste for attachment thinking is such that when I called him for a first interview in 1989, for a piece on attachment for *The Atlantic Monthly*, he was incredulous that I would wish to write a popular article on such a theme. In 1982, according to Sroufe, he convinced the W. T. Grant Foundation to stop funding attachment and similar research on early development.[12] But regardless of cracks in some of his arguments and the ire he arouses, his views cannot be ignored.

A researcher who studies inborn temperament and who strongly believes that genes contribute to much of what we become, Kagan argues that too much attention has been wasted studying the effects of early environments. He cites studies demonstrating that even maternally deprived children, raised in institutions, could make surprising recoveries when given a superior environment and adequate treatment. Research by Stephen Suomi, Harlow's successor at the University of Wisconsin, seemed to support these findings, showing that severely deprived rhesus monkeys who were frightened and unsocialized could become virtually normal if placed in the company of a group of younger, "therapist" monkeys, where they could gradually learn social skills.[13] Such stories of rehabilitation caused many in the field to claim that Bowlbyism had been cut off at the legs, for they assumed that attachment theory was based on the assumption that early inadequate care always caused irreversible damage.

This misconception, which dogged Bowlby since he first wrote about maternal deprivation, was largely, I think, the responsibility of attachment workers themselves, and especially the ardor with which they reported the predictive power of Ainsworth's classifications. To predict, of course, does not mean to determine. It does not even denote a causal relationship. (The rising sun fairly consistently predicts an increase in automobile traffic on certain parts of the planet.) But this was more and more the implication.

As Bowlby saw it, anxious attachment in the first year did not necessarily breed future difficulties, but it was a liability for the child, especially since the future is in some way built upon the foundation laid in the past. The fact that the parental psychology that may have contributed to anxious attachment in infancy and the parental behaviors that went with it usually remained in some form throughout childhood increased the liability. That parents often had negative reactions to the behaviors of their anxiously attached children, and that parent and child became involved in an escalating pattern of negative interaction as a result, made the risks of disturbed emotional and social development that much more severe. Finally, the fact that the child built a model of relating based on such experience and tended to become committed to that model, perpetuating it at home and replicating it with others, made change that much more difficult. Yet things do change, and the complexities multiply to such a degree that no hard predictions can be made about the future.

The Minnesota studies had shown that after the first year, mothers of anxiously attached children continue to respond to them inadequately, so that at subsequent stages of their development—when they need to establish a healthy autonomy, manage their frustration in dealing with challenging situations, know what to do when their feelings were hurt by a playmate—they were still not getting the sort of parental care they needed. What's more, qualities in the children themselves were now adding to the impediments, frustrating parents when they wanted to be helpful. This was evident as early as one year, when avoidant children would not make themselves available to maternal soothing (by acting as if they didn't need it) and when ambivalent children drove their mothers nuts by alternating a momentary cuddle with arching away and kicking, such that nothing the mother did seemed to alleviate their misery. Given all this, it was logical to see anxious attachment in the first year as having the potential to set the tone for much of the child's emotional and interpersonal life.

But the question of causality was a murky one, and in the enthusiasm of attachment presentations—where one naturally wanted to give the importance of one's findings as bright a shine as possible—the implication was often left hanging that maternal rejection in the first year in and of itself caused dependency or bullying in the sixth, and did so regardless of what might happen in years two through five or in the child's other relationships.[14] If Kagan and other critics made the first year sound inconsequential, attachment theorists and their followers in the press sometimes made it sound insurmountable.

Sroufe's own early reports could have dispelled such notions, for unlike children in middle-class samples who showed remarkably consistent attachment styles not all of the children in his high-risk sample maintained the same attachment classification between ages twelve and eighteen months.[15] Change occurred rarely, but when it did, it usually reflected the upheavals, both negative and positive, to which these families were prone, like the disappearance of a father or the single mother's forming a stable partnership with a new man. In another Minnesota study, in which the mother's behavior was assessed alongside the child's, the quality of the relationship clearly continued to play a critical part in the quality of the child's adaptation. A number of children who had been securely attached as infants exhibited behavior problems at two and a half. It turned out that their mothers no longer behave like the mothers of secure children. They were neither warm nor encouraging, were ineffective teachers, failed to provide suitable playthings, and by the time their children were four sometimes confessed to feeling confused and bewildered.

Similarly, some children with anxious attachment histories did not display the behavior problems that were typical of anxious children in the poverty sample. The mothers of these children respected their strivings toward independence, allowed them to explore without being intrusive, were warm and supportive teachers, and provided the children with a healthy, stimulating environment. In most respects, they looked just like the mothers of securely attached children. And perhaps that is what they now were.[16]

Sroufe not only believed that fundamental changes can take place after the first year, he had to repeat this point again and again in an effort to shake off the charge that he was a first-year determinist.

But as far as critics like Kagan were concerned, such protestations only enhanced their own arguments. For if attachment status can change as care changes, then why make such a fuss over the first year? Why pursue all this data showing correlations of year-one attachment classifications with later emotional health? Kagan and others found the idea of an internal working model, which acts like a flywheel, tending to keep a child on his established course, at best unproven, at worst ludicrous. They maintained that the disturbances caused by an inadequate or rejecting environment lasted only as long as the child remained in that environment.

It was not that Kagan believed a child was infinitely malleable. Quite the contrary. But he argued that those characteristics of the child that are most enduring are the ones he brought with him from birth. Environmental influences come and go, but heredity lasts. In stark contrast to Bowlby, who believed that present adaptation is always a weave of developmental history and current circumstances and that early experience is especially formative, Kagan saw early experience with parents as having much more transient effects. "A particular quality in a young child," he wrote in 1978, "is not likely to persist unless the environment continues to support it."[17] Or, as he put it on another occasion, experience was like material on a tape; if it could be recorded, it could be erased.[18]

If it were true that the effects of early experience only endured as long as the environment remained unchanged, then except for the fact that no one wanted to see little children suffer or feel insecure, there was less urgency to one aspect of what Bowlby and Ainsworth had been fighting for: loving, responsive parenting in the early years. It would be nice if it were there, and everyone would like to have it so, but infancy is just one of many phases the child will go through and his parents just two of the many relationships he will have. This point of view had policy implications, too—for orphans, hospitalized children, children being fought over in custody battles, and babies in poor-quality day care, to cite some obvious examples. Certain conditions might cause insecure attachment or even psychopathic behavior, but that is less cause for concern if the disturbance will pass as the child grows older and has new experiences.

For example: Should a two-year-old, or even a four-year-old, who has been living happily with foster parents that want to adopt him be returned to his biological mother who hasn't seen him since early infancy but has now gotten her life together and wants her child back? Heart-rending cases like this come up in the courts repeatedly. Some, including most attachment thinkers, argue that the interests of the child demand that he stay with the foster parents, that it would be criminal to rip him away from the people to whom he has formed his primary attachments. In 1989 Ainsworth supported foster parents in just such a struggle, arguing that it would be heartbreaking for the child and perhaps emotionally damaging for him in the long run to be extracted from his family and returned to parents he didn't know. Others insist that children will adjust to such painful changes without lasting damage.

Sroufe tried to counter the argument that the effects of early experience could be virtually erased by examining children whose level of functioning had shown marked declines or improvements. Some children in the poverty sample, for instance, had had secure attachment histories but deteriorated in the preschool years to the point where they could not be distinguished from children with anxious attachment histories. Sroufe found that these children were more likely to rebound later than children who had been anxiously attached from the beginning.[19] He also found that children who had been anxiously attached as infants but who were functioning well in later years, such that they could barely be distinguished from secure children, tended to suffer from underlying problems with their self- esteem.[20] "Even when children change rather markedly," he wrote, "the shadows of the earlier adaptation remain."[21] He believed that in times of stress those shadows were most likely to appear—and he, too, was able to cite monkey data, indicating that

Suomi's rehabilitated macaques do indeed relapse under some conditions.[22]

The experience of adults in psychotherapy, who have to struggle mightily to overcome the relational styles, attitudes, expectations, and a sense of self learned in the home; the proneness to depression in times of loss or separation of those who have suffered the early loss of a parent; such things would seem to attest to the enduring power of early models. But that does not mean the shadows of the past always linger. What is more, we still know remarkably little about the effect of other attachment figures, most prominently the still largely overlooked father, where the relationship may be good enough to overcome insecurity with the mother, at least to the extent that other aspects of development to go forward relatively unhindered. Nor do we know much about changes in attachment status. We don't know if there is a tendency for the number of secure children to decline as parents are faced with more and more complex challenges—toilet training, the terrible twos, the child's growing assertion of autonomy, oedipal conflicts, relating to peers, struggles with schoolwork, the complexity of adolescent emotions; or if many children who had been insecure as infants become securely attached later as parents' life situations change or as hidden strengths—of parents or child—come into play at later ages. We do not know, partly because, as Ainsworth has noted with some chagrin, no one has done for later periods of childhood the sort of naturalistic longitudinal study in the home that she did for the first year.[23]

But certainly evidence exists for change in both directions. Indeed, in Sroufe's sample, although impressive correlations between infant attachment status and current functioning hold good for later ages—especially regarding dependency (where the correlations to early attachment status were as strong at fifteen as they were at four and a half[24]) and peer competence—some of the correlations do decrease steadily as the children get older, suggesting the persistent impact of developmental and environmental changes. Critics may seem cavalier in dismissing the power of early experience or suggesting the ease with which its effects can be reversed. But whether something—in the form of an underlying vulnerability or strength—must always remain of the earlier attachment experience is still a matter of legitimate debate.

With the development of a method of assessing adult psychology vis-à-vis attachment (see Chapter 24) and the growing up of the first children put through the Strange Situation, it has become possible to address this question of continuity in a new way: by comparing attachment status in infancy with attachment status in adulthood. Results from longitudinal studies in Germany have been inconclusive, revealing major reversals of attachment status and no correlations. But when Judith Crowell and Everett Waters, who re-examined the grown children, age 20 to 22, from the first (middle-class) Minnesota sample, they found something very different. Sixty-nine percent retained in adulthood the Strange Situation classifications, secure or insecure, they had as infants (ambivalent vs. avoidant was not assessed). When major life events that might be expected to disrupt attachment status in childhood were accounted for (such as the death of the mother when one child was four), the correlation rose to 77 percent.[25] All this is, of course, still preliminary.

But if we put aside for the moment the various empirical uncertainties, what stands out as important here? To me it is this: First, that there do seem to be patterns of attachment, secure and insecure, and that they matter a great deal, such that we would naturally want our babies to have a secure attachment to us if we possibly could and that we would want that security to persist. Second, that these patterns show up as early as age one and that they grow out of the quality of the parent-child relationship. And, third, that they continue to be an issue for people later in life (see Chapters 24–26), such that they can be seen as representing an aspect of our psychological structure. Thus, no matter what damage we might do as parents, and we are bound to do some, perhaps much, knowing that our children feel confident of our love and availability at least insures that they have a good foundation for self-esteem and non-avoidant self-reliance and for building secure and loving relationships with others. This in itself seems worth knowing, regardless of whether the early pattern is destined to endure or how easy or difficult it is to change. My own clinical experience and training, like that of many others, also tell me that anxious attachment to the primary caregiver that begins in the first year and persists thereafter is the worst case for any child, especially if there are no mitigating attachments to others. For it is our earliest wounds that are most deeply unconscious, that are almost unknowable, unattached as they often are to memory or language, and therefore the hardest to question, to symbolize, to verbalize, or to change. Change, of course, is possible, especially if there is a healing source of love elsewhere or if the parent makes an early and radical shift. There is no reason to believe the primary issues of early development are closed at the end of the first year. Whether they are understood in terms of narcissism or infantile paranoia or secure attachment, all of early childhood will be important in determining how they get worked out, and trends begun in the first year can take a turn for the better or worse in the next. (One of the grown children interviewed by Crowell and Everett, who had been anxiously attached to his mother at age one, seemed to have emerged into a secure adult because at age eight, when he developed diabetes, his mother become for him the loving caretaker she had not been before.[26])

But I think we can also say that the more entrenched a position is in the first year or two, the harder it will be to change. And many apparent changes will represent the ability of some children to successfully move on to other things—sports, school work, friendship—that veil their wounds. It will only be later, perhaps in adolescence, when these children again long for closeness, that the early damage will be apparent. While attachment critics have been justified in pointing out the fallacy of interpreting follow-up studies in such a way as to assume that every pattern seen in older children flows *ipso facto* from quality of attachment to the mother in the first year, I think they have been too sanguine in dismissing its importance. The reports of child therapists, describing the enormous struggles they go through to help young children deal with disturbed relationships with their parents, are sobering in this regard: Yes, change is possible, but it is often difficult, and we should value every effort to get the parent-child relationship off to a good start.

Because of Ainsworth and her followers, we now have considerable information about what yields secure attachment in the first year, and as we shall see in subsequent chapters, that information keeps growing. This, too, is important. It is valuable in helping parents, and in helping society to help parents, to relate to their babies in a healthy way. That parents and society should want to make that effort seems self-evident. It does not depend on proving that the effects of the first year necessarily last forever, and it seems unfortunate that the debate should get stuck there for even a moment.

Like many other attachment critics, Kagan was particularly dubious regarding the interpretations that were being made about the avoidant child. He could not accept the idea that these children, some of whom had little trouble separating from their mother in the Strange Situation, many of whom settled down eventually once she was gone, and all of whom showed little interest in her upon reunion, were revealing some kind of insecurity. Such kids were either bold, or precociously independent, or had been trained by their parents to control their fear.

> A child whose mother has been otherwise attentive and loving [Kagan wrote] but has successfully encouraged self-reliance and control of fear, is less likely to cry when the mother leaves and, therefore, is less likely to approach her when she returns.... Although some psychologists might regard these latter mothers as less nurturant, the mothers may have behaved as they did because they valued control of fear and sturdy self-reliance in their children.[27]

Kagan saw Bowlby, Ainsworth, and Sroufe as narrowly preoccupied with security and not attentive enough of the advantages American society confers on being able to handle adversity. Thus, a parent rated as insensitive on Ainsworth's scales might actually be giving a child superior training for the modern world, and all those children that attachment researchers had been labeling securely attached may be poorly adapted to real life.[28]

The debate over the avoidant child made the findings of the German attachment studies a source of much concern. These studies were the work of a husband-and-wife team, Klaus and Karin Grossmann. A disgruntled Ph.D. student in psychology at the University of Arkansas in the late 1960s (he disliked behaviorist rigidities), Klaus's interest in ethology led him to a second doctorate at the University of Fraiburg, combining psychology with behavioral biology, and ultimately to Ainsworth's longitudinal studies. "I thought this is exactly what ethologists would do if they worked with human babies," he says. He decided to launch what would be the most comprehensive replication of her research ever undertaken. Karin gave up her studies in mathematics to become a psychologist and join him. "We decided that if we did a study like Ainsworth's," she says, "we would have to see the children right at birth. Because otherwise how would we know that these children were not different from the beginning? But at that time in Germany it was practically impossible for a strange male to enter the maternity ward. So we started to work with a hospital, and I was present at all the births of the infants."[29]

The first sample of children studied by Klaus and Karin Grossmann in

Bielefeld in northern Germany seemed to confirm Kagan's view. Fully two thirds of these children were classified insecure and half of the entire sample were classified avoidant—two and a half times the typical figure for avoidant children in middle-class American samples. In conversation with the Grossmanns, Kagan discovered that they attributed the large number of avoidant classifications to the fact that in this part of Germany early independence was highly prized. "Should we conclude from these data," Kagan asked rhetorically, "that many more German than American children are 'insecurely attached' . . . ?"[30]

The Grossmanns ultimately did a second study in Regensburg, in southern Germany. Here the percentages of the children in each attachment classification group were, much to their relief, similar to the American breakdown. But the data from the southern study came later and so were not available when the researchers attempted to understand the high rate of avoidants in the north and what this might suggest about German child-rearing practices and German culture in general.

At first the Grossmanns were inclined to take the view they reported to Kagan and that he, in turn, wrote up in *The Nature of the Child*: that an avoidant classification in this part of northern Germany, where people tended to "distance themselves a bit from each other," should not be a matter of great consequence. The British ethologist Robert Hinde, Bowlby's "tutor in ethology" and an important attachment theorist himself, was inclined to agree. To be avoidantly attached here should not be seen as a psychological liability but rather representative of an appropriate adaptation to this culture. So when the Grossmanns published their data in 1985, aware of the prejudices against the German character as being cold and authoritarian, and hesitant to be in the position of providing ammunition for those who might see the huge number of avoidant children as evidence for this view, they were cautious and protective in their conclusions: "We simply said that it may be caused by the fact that these mothers wanted to have their children self-reliant as early as possible."[31]

The wish to train their babies for early independence would explain why the Bielefeld mothers looked so different from many of their American counterparts. They were quite sensitive to their children when they were newborns, only becoming less responsive in the latter part of the first year. Indeed, according to Klaus Grossmann, "Most of these families that had avoidant children are actually very nice families, and they are very nice to their children in other ways."[32] On Ainsworth's maternal acceptance scale, for example, the mothers of these avoidant children were average to low average, considerably higher than their American counterparts, where low sensitivity was always accompanied by very low acceptance.

"You can still think your child is a nice child," Karin Grossmann explains, "and that you're going to cherish him and support him, but you just don't want him clinging to you. We have studies that show that these mothers are quite sensitive when the child feels good; what they can't stand is a crying child coming to you, clinging to you, and wanting contact. So they push that out."[33] She notes that it's quite possible to "imagine a whole culture functioning on the avoidant principle: You mind your own business, you don't show your emotions, you don't go to anyone for help. In old Prussia I think it would have been a high ideal to keep a stiff upper lip and never bother anybody else with your problems."[34]

Nevertheless, the Grossmanns came to believe that the avoidant attachment could not be so easily discounted as culturally normative. To have to achieve the required level of physical independence at ten months—to abruptly cease displays of love, need, emotional hunger, and distress—is something that the human baby adjusts to at a cost.

The latter part of the first year is a time when many observers, including Ainsworth, have noted the onset of separation anxiety. It is a period when the baby's perception of his parents as unique individuals is fully coming into being and his love affair with them is reaching a peak. He follows like a puppy, wants to be held a great deal, climbs onto his mother with glee. In a book addressed to mothers, Penelope Leach writes of the extreme emotions that frequently prevail at this stage:

> The baby has learned to know and love you better than anyone else and now he wants you all the time. . . . His ideal would be your continual presence and constant attention. He feels passionately for you physically. He will sit on you, play with you, stroke and pull you, pop food (and worse) in your mouth, behaving as if your body belonged to him. . . . [He demands] to be cuddled and kissed, patted and stroked. He holds out his arms for more, laughing with glee when he is tickled, sucking his mother's nose if it comes within range and purring like a sensuous kitten when it is time for a bath or a new diaper. . . .[35]

Leach warns that even a mother who enjoys and reciprocates this intense love affair may find the baby's extravagant demands and incessant shadowing difficult to take at times. According to Bowlby, of course the baby behaves this way because all of his instinctual attachment behaviors have by now been unified into one coherent system, and they are directed toward specific favorite persons, with the primary caregiver being the apple of his eye. And because of his helplessness, and his inability to soothe himself with images of the absent mother or to delay gratification, there is an urgency to his love that is beyond anything we can fathom in later life. It is just at this moment that many parents in northern Germany feel it necessary to pull back and shut the door on this all-consuming baby-love.*

It is interesting in this respect to note what the mothers of the *securely* attached children in the Bielefeld sample looked like. To the Grossmanns, they seemed unlike the average German mother. "They were not so eager to present themselves as a perfect household," Karin says, "clean child, clean house, clean mother. The mothers were less dressed up, the children were less dressed up, they weren't overeager to serve coffee or tea right at the beginning. I actually had the feeling that they were more secure with themselves."[36] There was no indication that these mothers or their children were poorly adapted to this society. Indeed, quite the opposite.

To the "shock and disbelief"[37] of their German colleagues, follow-up studies demonstrated the same sorts of continuities in Bielefeld and Regensburg that Sroufe was finding in Minneapolis, the secure German children demonstrating numerous psychological advantages. At five the Regensburg children, for example, played with greater concentration and quality, they were better able to manage conflicts with their playmates, they had a better understanding of social situations. What's more, they felt free to go to their parents when they were lonely, sad, or distressed. The avoidant children, in contrast, were left alone with their negative emotions.

---

*Most American parents can, I think, understand the impulse behind the stop sign erected by the Bielefeld mothers. Our culture has mixed feelings about closeness and dependency, and besides, we are busy people. On the cultural spectrum we are much closer to the citizens of Bielefeld than to many traditional or primitive societies where babies and mothers are inseparable for years and where physical and emotional intimacy is the norm. Every culture requires that its children adapt in different ways in order to live successfully in that society, and the human being is malleable enough to adapt well to an extraordinary variety of conditions. But that does not mean that every adaptation is healthy or useful or that culture cannot be organized in harmful ways.

Unlike Sroufe's sample, however, there were few behavior problems among the anxious German children. They were essentially normal kids from normal families, with none of the stresses of poverty, single parenthood, or extreme neglect. Also some of the avoidant children in the Bielefeld sample may have been different even from avoidant children in American middle-class samples, a reflection of different parental motives. Many of the parents of the avoidant Bielefeld children supported them in school and in sports and were generally accepting of them. Certain feelings could not be displayed or discussed, but unlike many of the avoidant American families, there may not have been the same buildup of rejecting experiences. The avoidant children in the U.S. had mothers who rebuffed them despite a general cultural attitude that is accepting of warm responsive care to children under one. It implied a more deep-seated psychological aversion to having a warm connection with their child. Because the mothers of avoidant children in north Germany were behaving according to a cultural norm, their psychological qualities may in some cases have been less of an issue and the rejection less pervasive as a result.

This, of course, raises a question about the Minnesota studies. Do their follow-ups demonstrate the expectable effects of anxious attachment? Or are they more properly the effects of severe anxious attachment? Clearly, after Bielefeld, it could now be said that if a child qualifies as anxiously attached in the Strange Situation at year one, this can imply a large variety of outcomes, some far less grave that what Sroufe's follow-ups might suggest. (More on this in Chapter 25.) That many of the German parents raised avoidant children because of the dictates of culture rather than psychology might also help account for the fact that the Grossmanns found so many more reversals of attachment quality when assessing these children as adults.

As the Grossmanns continued to follow the Bielefeld sample, they nevertheless became convinced that these children paid a lasting price for their avoidance. At age ten, unlike their secure counterparts, the avoidant Bielefeld children did not form close friendships. They reported many more problems with peers, like being excluded, taken advantage of, or ridiculed. They had less confidence, less self-reliance, less resiliency.[38] Although the avoidant pattern was less pronounced than among the Minnesota children, "When put under stress, the patterns of withdrawal and reduced peer interactions so vividly described by Alan Sroufe," Klaus Grossmann recently said, "can also be readily observed in our children."[39] The Grossmanns, therefore, have come to agree with a point Bowlby made when accepting an honorary doctorate at the University of Regensburg in 1989—that the mere fact that parents are behaving in accordance with a cultural norm does not necessarily spare the children any harm. (Bowlby, however, was strikingly out of touch, I think, when he stated, "No matter where the rejection comes from, it is bound to have the same outcome.")[40]

As a result of such findings, the Grossmanns are urging changes in certain strongly held German opinions about child rearing. "We fight the notion," Klaus says, "that crying doesn't matter, that it strengthens the lungs. We fight the notion that independence has to be trained, or that you must punish a child by withdrawal of availability or love. We've explained over and over again that those children who get the most sensitive responsiveness on the part of the mothers are the ones who will be least clinging."[41]

In 1975 Ainsworth, then sixty-one, left Johns Hopkins for the University of Virginia at Charlottesville. She had been dissatisfied at Hopkins (and made nervous by their official retirement age of sixty and the need to get yearly waivers). As someone who readily turned students into members of an extended family, Ainsworth found Virginia's appeal enhanced by the fact that Robert Marvin was already teaching there and that another former student, Mark Greenberg, was studying with him.

Leaving Hopkins when she did meant that Ainsworth would no longer be able to work with a bright South African student named Michael Lamb (who would soon go on to do the early research on attachment to father). Lamb had been eager to study with Ainsworth, but was only able to complete one year at Hopkins before she left. Lamb immediately moved to Yale, and his relative lack of experience with Ainsworth, including never getting Strange Situation training from her, would become a matter of heated concern ten years later when his name appeared as the lead author of the most global critique of Ainsworth's Baltimore research that had ever been made—and the first to stir bad blood. Lamb, who subsequently became chief of the Section on Social and Emotional Development at the National Institute of Child Health and Human Development, accurately noted that the consequences of anxious attachment were much better documented than the causes. He questioned not only Ainsworth's sample but her methods and numbers, and questioned whether the Strange Situation is complex enough to "capture all significant variance in infant behavior." Lamb was hardly alone in having doubts about the Strange Situation. Psychologists of many different stripes and persuasions had voiced strong doubts about it, even ridiculed it. The English developmentalist Michael Rutter referred to it as a curious procedure "involving mother, caretakers and strangers not only going in and out of rooms every minute for reasons quite obscure to the child but also not initiating interactions in the way they might usually do."[42] But the Lamb critique of Ainsworth's work was the most comprehensive and, some felt, the most insolent. ("He just slandered her," Sroufe said.[43]) That it was made by her former student and written in a tone that could be read as suggesting there was little value to her contribution was a personal blow to her. "There was a time," Inge Bretherton says, "when it was difficult for her to talk about anything else, because she was so hurt."[44]

Lamb recommended that a new procedure be devised to replace the Strange Situation, warned that we really don't know what much of the attachment findings really mean, and suggested that, considering its small sample size and other failings, Ainsworth's original research be downgraded to a "pilot study."[45] This was perceived as an intolerable insult. It must have been especially stinging to Ainsworth, since, unbeknown to people in the field, her Baltimore research had, in fact, been funded only as a pilot study—she was unable to get any more money for it—and she had taken secret pride in the fact that she had, with such limited resources, achieved such a huge scientific triumph.

The leading attachment theorists found Lamb's tone so debunking and dismissive toward Ainsworth and claimed that the article was so full of misstatements of fact that they refused to submit the usual comments or rebuttals to the journal (*Behavioral and Brain Sciences*) that published it. Ainsworth herself maintained a stony public silence. Lamb, despite his own valuable contributions, instantly became, in Bretherton's words, "the black sheep of attachment theory."[46]

But Lamb had raised legitimate points. Ainsworth's study was not unimpeachable. It was difficult, for example, to get perfect reliability checks on each observer in the home situations (were they definitely measuring the same thing?), and there were no videotapes to review for greater certainty. Also, at the time Lamb was writing, it could justifiably be argued that Ainsworth's study had seen virtually nothing in the way of replication, which was quite surprising when you think of the skyscraper of research and theoretical conclusions balancing on its small base. It must be kept in mind that in every study that began by assessing infants in a Strange Situation at twelve or eighteen months and that continued to evaluate those children for years afterward, assumptions were being made about the style of parenting each child had received, and conclusions were being drawn about the effect that style had had on the child. But the style of parenting was never assessed the way Ainsworth assessed it. A number of studies, including Sroufe's, assessed maternal sensitivity in the first year, sometimes over the course of a number of hours when the baby was six months old, and those assessments predicted attachment classifications in the expected way. But there was nothing like Ainsworth's seventy-two hours of in-home observation over the course of the whole year. In many other cases there was no assessment of the quality of care at all; it was only inferred from the infant's Strange Situation classification. And that inference was possible mainly because of Ainsworth's twenty-three Baltimore families. If her study was flawed and the correlations it demonstrated opened to question, the whole attachment edifice would begin to wobble.

Ainsworth was not insensitive to this and wanted to see more replications. She regretted not having had the opportunity herself. But longitudinal studies of that magnitude take time, money, and patience. As Bretherton says, "If you have thirty children and you're observing them once a month for four hours, there's just an incredible amount of material that you have to go through and analyze"[47]—which may require more funding, and more grant proposal writing, for several years hence. Young workers prefer to expend such efforts breaking new ground rather than tilling the old. Since Lamb's critique, however, the Grossmanns have reported their replication in Germany with home visits throughout the first year,[48] and Ainsworth rightly asserts that much has been established in partial replication by researchers who performed detailed clinical ratings of maternal sensitivity if only for a few hours.[49] Nevertheless, legitimate questions have lingered.

PART IV

GIVE PARENTS A BREAK! NATURE-NURTURE ERUPTS ANEW

20

BORN THAT WAY?
STELLA CHESS
AND THE DIFFICULT CHILD

By the 1950s it was becoming increasingly rare for young parents in urban America to be living with or near their families of origin. And even if they were nearby, the cultural bonds that had held them together had loosened to such an extent that, far from being models and accepted figures of authority, the parents, grandparents, uncles, and aunts of young adults were often seen as imperious and intrusive. As a result, many new parents, especially among the nontraditional urban middle class, no longer had the guidance (or interference) from older generations in caring for their children.

At the same time, the largely new fields of psychology, sociology, anthropology, and education had all developed huge funds of knowledge about child rearing and were eager to impart them to the masses. Parents received instruction on proper baby care from the child guidance clinics, which had by now spread all over the country and had had a huge effect on child psychiatry; from nursery school teachers; from social workers; from books written by various experts; from magazine and newspaper articles written by authorities, nonauthorities, and ignoramuses alike.

For many years, John B. Watson's behavioral formula had held sway, favoring a strict regime and warning parents against coddling. These ideas had waned after the thirties but still carried weight. By the early 1950s a countertrend developed advocating a much more permissive child rearing. It had been influenced by new ideas in progressive education; by the continuing popularization of psychoanalytic theory (which was quoted frequently by people who had only the faintest understanding of it and often cited aspects of it that had long ago been abandoned as obsolete); and by cultural anthropologists, some of whom had discovered that certain primitive tribes whose members were happily adjusted— indeed quite free of the anxieties typical in industrialized countries— raised their children without imposing any of the discipline common in the West. The permissive crusade advocated leniency in all things to avoid unnecessary frustration, prolonged breast feeding (just recently considered a barbaric throwback), feeding on demand, and relaxed bowel and bladder training. The new regime was considered not just a happier, less pressured way to raise a baby, but essential to good mental health.[1]

As a result of all the advice, much of it conflicting, that now bombarded parents, as well as a parallel onslaught from advertisers who swooped in to exploit parental anxieties in order to sell all manner of products, many new mothers, especially those who were educated and sought to be well informed, felt overwhelmed and more uncertain of themselves than ever. The result, as Benjamin Spock noted (in 1953), was that they had even more problems raising their children. To some observers at the time, the atmosphere seemed positively totalitarian. It was as if parents were cringing in their own homes, while some ethereal outside authority judged their every move.[2] Bowlby's report on maternal deprivation, once in the hands of more zealous crusaders than he, became fuel for this fire, contributing to the anxieties parents felt about making a wrong move. Indeed, at the very moment that he was trying to prove that mothers are terribly important to their babies and that what they do or fail to do has lasting impact on their children's personality and adaptation, a ferocious caricature of his philosophy was already taking shape.

Millicent McIntosh, president of Barnard College, concerned that young women were becoming frightened at the prospect of becoming mothers by what they were learning in child development courses, was among those who protested: "Even the most innocent-appearing act or a carelessly spoken word may 'harm' a child or 'damage' his future happiness. You hurt them by comparing them to other children; you hurt them by not comparing them and praising them for being special; you hurt them by being too affectionate to them and by not being affectionate enough."[3]

While some of this avalanche of advice was useful, much of it was meaningless because it attempted to tell parents what they should feel. Hilde Bruch, offended by the widespread misuse of psychoanalytic theory, wrote, "It is fallacious to assume that psychological advice can be carried out in this way.... Children respond to the genuine, though often unconscious emotional attitudes of their parents and are not fooled by intellectualized and pretended feelings."[4]

It was in this uniquely American atmosphere that Stella Chess, the child psychiatrist who had worked with Loretta Bender on the children's ward at Bellevue in the thirties, began the study that would define her career. Chess was disturbed by the assumption common among mental health workers that if the child had a problem one need only look at the mother for its source. "Many of the mothers of problem children," she reported in 1958, "develop enormous guilt feelings due to the assumption that they must necessarily be solely responsible for their children's emotional difficulties. With this guilt comes anxiety, defensiveness, increased pressures on the children, and even hostility toward them for 'exposing' the mother's inadequacy by their disturbed behavior."[5]

In an editorial in the *American Journal of Orthopsychiatry*, deliciously titled "Mal de Mère," Chess cited several cases of childhood disturbance in which speculations were made "concerning the mother's relationship with her own parents, her degree of immaturity, her presumed rejection of this child and her overcompensations for this rejection." In each case, however, further examination revealed that the problem lay elsewhere. In one case, of school failure, the child turned out to be retarded, a condition that had gone undiagnosed through age eight. In another, that of a fourteen-year-old delinquent girl, the pressures of poverty and racial discrimination had been overlooked. The third case follows:

> An 11-year-old boy is argumentative in class, fights the teacher's statements of fact, and is greatly upset by marks less than superlative. When criticized by his parents he becomes angry, storms into his room only to emerge cheerfully ten minutes later. He is a "sore loser," yet is very popular with friends. In the course of psychological testing he describes his figure drawing as a boy, age seven. Mother is then asked whether anything important happened at age seven, and she

recalls that this is the year in which she returned to her suspended magazine editorial work.[6]

This creates an immediate "Ah-hah!" among those assessing the case
who now quickly attribute the boy's problems to maternal desertion. It is
assumed that the boy needs psychotherapy and that the mother needs to
resolve "her ambivalence toward the maternal role," by giving up her
job.[7] What is not known, because no one bothered to look into it, is that
the boy has been inclined toward stormy episodes from earliest infancy.
Far from being a reaction to his mother's return to work, his bursts of
temper at school and with friends appeared to be a manifestation of an
inborn personality trait.

As far as Chess was concerned, the child always brought with him a
great deal of who he was. This obvious fact had long been plain to parents, especially if they had more than one child, as well as to nurses and
pediatricians who worked with newborns and saw the striking variety of
temperamental types that emerged at birth. Chess did not believe that
genes were destiny, but that the child's inborn qualities interacted with
the type of care he received and other aspects of the environment,
including the cultural milieu, to produce his ultimate constellation of
personality characteristics.

Like Bowlby, Chess had been influenced by the work of David Levy,
but in the opposite direction. A former supervisor of hers, Levy had written one of the pioneering works on maternal deprivation. He was also
one of the first psychiatric researchers to take note of inborn temperament. In his studies of "maternal overprotection," Levy found that children whose mothers tended to fret over them needlessly often had
significant personality problems. But they were not all of the same type.
Some of the children became tyrants, dictating their bedtimes, their
menus, when they would come in from play. The mothers catered to
their wishes, meekly offering a new food if the first one was rejected. The
other children, equally coddled, seemed like little robots. They passively
accepted their mothers' excessive ministrations and seemed to have little
initiative of their own. Levy held that the parents were not that different
from one another but that they were dealing with different types of children. So that it was not maternal overprotection per se that determined
the child's personality, but rather the child's reaction to it, based on his
innate proclivities. Children who are inherently active react to such

mothers by becoming domineering; children who are inherently passive react by becoming automatons.[8]

Many others had held that personality traits were inherited. Plato argued (metaphorically) that men were composed of gold, silver, or baser metals and that the men of gold should rule. Hippocrates, addressing himself more to temperament than to intelligence or general worthiness, divided mankind into four inborn personality types: phlegmatic, melancholic, sanguine, and choleric. Francis Galton, the great nineteenth-century English scientist and the father of modern behavioral genetics, did a pioneering study of hereditary genius, which helped launch the eugenics movement, whose name he coined.[9] Carl Jung proposed that people were inherently introverts or extroverts. More recently, William H. Sheldon, an American psychologist and physician, had argued that human beings fall into one of three constitutional types—endomorph (round and soft), mesomorph (strong, athletic), or ectomorph (thin, delicate)—and that each had certain emotional styles—easygoing and tolerant; dominant and aggressive; sensitive, cerebral, and high-strung.[10] But Levy's empirical data—and his recognition of the interplay between heredity and environment—were unique.

"I saw it in my own children," Chess recalls, speaking of inherited styles. "If one of them came yelling and shrieking, I just knew automatically that you couldn't tell by the amount of yelling and shrieking how important it was, because that's the way things had always been with that particular child. If another one came running into the house with a puckered and pouting mouth and went directly upstairs, I knew something dreadful had happened. And I knew that the difference between the reactions of these two children had nothing to do with the environment, because they had always been that way."[11]

Another of her children showed marked stranger anxiety. "If he was eating in his high chair and somebody came to visit, I'd turn around and there he was, frozen. It was like the game of statues. He was frozen in the exact attitude and nothing was going to happen until this stranger went. I might say, Could you just go out until we finish with the meal? And as soon as the stranger was gone the movement came back. That's the way he was. And then I began to see the same kind of individuality in the children I was treating and in my friends' kids whom I'd seen while they were growing up, and began to talk with my husband about his adult patients."[12] The power of heredity seemed unmistakable.

*   *   *

Chess, a thin, attractive woman, and a grandmother many times over, turned eighty in 1994, the year after we met. She has a delightful, straightforward, refreshing style. Her speech is loaded with parenthetical statements, and you can get a whole education in child psychiatry or the history of the New York psychiatric community before she finishes a sentence. Her husband, Alexander Thomas, also a psychiatrist and former chief of Bellevue Psychiatric, speaks adoringly of her and reveres her achievements. Because he is the superior writer, he received first authorship on many of their joint works, but he readily credits her as the creative force.

During the late thirties and early forties when Chess and Thomas were beginning their careers, the atmosphere in New York psychiatric circles was so decidedly environmentalist that the interest they were taking in inborn traits seemed retrograde. "Our friends accused us of going back to the nineteenth century—constitutional psychopaths, the constitutional inferior, the bad seed. Why are you bothering with that?"[13]

In the mid-fifties Chess and Thomas, later joined by Herbert Birch, a pediatric researcher, began the now famous New York Longitudinal Study to determine how infant temperament might contribute to later clinical problems. The first 136 infants came from eighty educated, middle-class families; an additional ninety-five came from working-class Puerto Rican families. Mothers were interviewed extensively about every aspect of their children's behavior and responses. The families were followed at regular intervals until the children reached adulthood, making the NYLS one of the seminal studies in child development.

The team found nine variables upon which they could assess the children's temperamental characteristics:

Activity level. "I can't leave him on the bed or couch because he always wriggles off"; "He kicks and splashes so in the bath that I always have to mop up the floor afterward" versus "In the bath he lies quietly and doesn't kick"; "In the morning he's still in the same place he was when he fell asleep."

Rhythmicity. How regular is the baby's sleep-wake cycle, his eating times, elimination, and other biological functions.

Approach or withdrawal. Positive reactions to the new: "He always smiles at a stranger"; "He loves new toys" versus negative: "When I gave him his orange juice the first time, he made a face"; "Whenever he sees a stranger he cries."

Adaptability. Not the child's initial response to the new, but how he adapts to it over time: "At first he used to hold himself perfectly stiff in the bath, but now he kicks a little and pats the water with his hand" versus "Every time he sees the scissors he starts to scream and pull his hand away, so now I cut his nails when he's sleeping."

Intensity of reaction. "He cries loud and long whenever the sun shines in his eyes"; "Whenever she hears music she begins to laugh loudly and to jump up and down in time to it"; "When he is hungry he starts to cry, and this builds up to a scream, and we can't distract him by holding or playing with him" versus "He squints at the bright light but doesn't cry"; "If he does not like a new food he just holds it in his mouth without swallowing and then lets it drool out"; "When other children take a toy away from him, he plays with something else; he doesn't try to get it back or cry."

Threshold of responsiveness. How intense does an external stimulus have to be before the child reacts? "You can shine a bright light in his eyes and he doesn't even blink, but if a door closes he startles and looks up"—high visual threshold, low auditory threshold. "He doesn't pay any attention to new people; he doesn't cry, but he doesn't respond to them either"—high threshold for social relations. "He laughs and smiles at a stranger, and starts to cry if they don't play with him"—low threshold.

Quality of mood. Positive: "Whenever he sees me begin to warm his bottle he begins to smile and coo"; "He loves to look out of the window. He jumps up and down and laughs"; "If he's not laughing and smiling, I know he's getting sick." Negative: "He cries at almost every stranger, and those that he doesn't cry at he hits"; "I've tried to teach him not to knock down little girls and sit on them in the playground, so now he knocks them down and doesn't sit on them"; "Every time he sees food he doesn't like he starts to fuss and whine until I take it off the table."

Distractibility. If he's about to chew up the electrical cord can he be thrown off course with a toy? If he's hungry and crying, will he stop when picked up?

Attention span and persistence. How long does he tend to stay involved in an activity once begun? And how determined is he to stay involved regardless of obstacles? For example, will he continue to struggle with a new toy even though he can't get it to work? This category, at a later age, includes frustration tolerance.[14]

Any parent reading this list will immediately recognize aspects of his own child and will probably have little trouble determining whether the child is high, low, or middle on many of the scales. But Chess and her co-authors went a step further, creating four broad categories into which they were able to fit each of the babies in the study. "Difficult babies" (about 10 percent) were those who displayed negative mood, were irregular in biological functioning, were slow to adapt, tended to withdraw in new situations, and reacted with high intensity. Another group of babies, who were also negative in mood, slow to adapt, and inclined to withdraw from novel situations she labeled "slow to warm up" (about 15 percent). Unlike the difficult babies, these children were not necessarily high in activity and reacted with low to moderate rather than high intensity.

Chess defined "easy babies" (about 40 percent of the sample) as those who were positive in mood, regular in body functions, and quick to adapt. They also tended to approach the novel rather than withdraw, and to react with low to moderate intensity. The remaining babies (about 35 percent), displayed various mixes of the temperamental qualities.

Parents, teachers, and researchers associated with the study all used pejorative terms, including "mother killers," to characterize the children who fell into the difficult temperament group.[15] They slept irregularly. They were hard to train regardless of the techniques used. They typically reacted to frustration with violent tantrums and were just as likely to cry loudly over a scratch as a serious wound. They became obsessed with certain foods to the exclusion of all others, then abruptly changed, would not touch the favored food, and would have to eat something else all the time instead. Toilet training was often an ordeal because they lacked biological regularity. They were slow to adapt, needing repeated exposures to anything before accepting it. (And if parents were timid and introduced a new thing only sporadically, the initial negative reaction would only be prolonged.) Adverse responses to the new meant an endless stream of shrieks and wails because so much in a baby's life is new. If, with long and patient effort, he comes to like the bath he hated at first, the difficult baby may now howl when taken out. Parents could never know what the baby might like in the end, because he disliked everything in the beginning. Going to school of any kind was certain to elicit howls and protests. Each new demand invited a new tantrum. Some of these children ended up having learning problems as a result of not adapting to the school environment. Of these, some were wrongly seen as mentally slow.

Chess found that parents of difficult children were no different on the whole from other parents, neither in their attitudes about having a child nor philosophy about raising them; although some of them did develop unfavorable attitudes after having lived with their difficult child for a time. But no parent is free of emotional hang-ups, and the difficult children were much more likely to push the buttons of their parents and cause those hang-ups to get worked into the relationship with the child. One mother, guilty that she's not giving or maternal enough, is determined to respond to the child's every cry, stay up with him at night, and virtually become his slave—a course of behavior that might placate the child in the short run, but is ruinous to both his personality development and ultimate adaptation. Another mother, competitive and needing control, sees the child's negative mood, failure to fall asleep when put down at night, and food refusal as an attempt to control her or as a conscious defiance. But her insistence on compliance only heightens his negative responses. Yet a third is thrown into a rage by the child's strident altercations with his younger siblings, and soon brands him a troublemaker. Whatever the parents' emotional makeup, they are likely to find a hook in the difficult child to hang their hang-ups on.

The difficult children in Chess's study needed patience and consistency and only a few parents seemed able to give it across the board. The successful parents were either remarkably free of the sorts of intense emotional reactions these children tended to elicit or, more likely, they were able to control those reactions and remind themselves that many of their reactions were inappropriate. Resourceful parents would spell each other, the father staying home with the screaming child while the mother had time away to recuperate, and they would alternate in taking him on excursions with their inevitable tantrums. Clearly, it seemed to take an unusual parent—patient, good-humored, consistent, firm—to handle these children well. (And since the problems seemed to be inherited, the parent might have the same temperamental difficulties as the child.) In an exceptional book, written for parents, the first of its kind to integrate the nature and nurture perspectives, Chess, Thomas, and Birch offered reassuring examples of how difficult some children can be and how best they can be handled:

> Jane's mother seemed inexhaustibly patient and consistent with her. When Jane was one, two, and even three years old, a denial in the supermarket would turn her into a screaming, kicking little fury. But her mother almost never blew up. She would patiently pick Jane off the floor, take the purchases to

the check-out counter, and go home without screaming or
fussing back at Jane. These tactics were markedly successful,
and neighbors were frequently amazed to see the youngster
playing contentedly a few minutes later. . . . When, time after
time, her violent demands brought firm, consistent, and quiet
removal, her tantrums diminished. In time they began to look
more and more like token attempts at self-assertion. Fortunately, neighbors and relatives took their cues from Jane's
parents. They let her scream, but refused to let her inconve-
nience others. They were pleasant and ungrudging when the
child made her lightning switch to positive behavior.[16]

Jane's mother alerted her nursery school and kindergarten teachers to
her temperament, and they too learned to react to her with firmness and
calm. Jane continued to display intense reactions at times, but on the
whole she became a cheerful and cooperative girl.

Tommy, another child who fit into the difficult group, had very different parents:

They felt harassed from the beginning. When the child's
pattern persisted as he passed his first, then his second, and
finally his third birthday, they grew increasingly upset. Nothing seemed to satisfy Tommy, even though they were constantly trying to make him happy. They gave in to his
demands, reasonable or unreasonable. If he wanted a toy in
the supermarket, his mother bought it quickly to avoid trouble. But no matter how much his parents tried to satisfy him,
every excursion, every visit, indeed every play period was
marked by some commotion. . . .

[Tommy's mother] could take just so much and then would
explode, screaming: "You always make trouble. Nobody can
satisfy you." She would also make endless threats but would
not carry them out. Tommy's father kept aloof from this frantic interplay between mother and child. One fuss from his son
and Daddy left him to his own devices. As time went on there
was less and less contact between the two. Both parents were
convinced that Tommy was impossible to please or satisfy.
Indeed, this had become true, not only at home, but at play
and in school.[17]

Chess was particularly critical of the impact psychoanalysis and related theories were having on the beleaguered parents of such children:

> In these theories, a loving and accepting mother should have a happy and contented child, from which it follows that an unconscious maternal attitude of rejection could be the only explanation for a difficult screaming child. As a result of reliance on these theories it was not unusual for the mother of a difficult infant who screamed frequently and who made all routines a crisis, to develop self-doubts and feelings of guilt, anxiety, and helplessness unless she was unusually confident in her adequacy as a woman and a mother.[18]

Just as Bowlby had said, in effect, that behavioral theory was fine and useful as long as it didn't overreach its boundaries and apply itself to areas where its explanatory power was nil (as in attachment or speech acquisition), so Chess was saying that psychodynamic theories were fine as long as they didn't overstep their boundaries and attempt to explain temperament in terms of maternal influence. It is only later, when we see how the child with a given temperament has fared, that we can begin to see what impact the parents have had.

The slow-to-warm-up child also presented a challenge to many parents. The initial negative response of these children is typically quiet. They cling, they withdraw, they turn away, they fuss mildly. "Their first few weeks in nursery school," Chess wrote, "are typically spent on the sidelines, quietly watching the activity of the group. In elementary school, a new academic subject may evoke the announcement, 'I don't like it,' or, more typically, initial silent nonparticipation."[19]

She recalls that it was common when she first started work for nursery school teachers to tell parents that a child who was shy and slow to warm up was anxious and needed treatment. Such parents often brought their children to see Chess for an evaluation. Invariably she would ask the parents of these shy children to bring a toy from home so the child would not have to use a toy that was not familiar. "I'd say, 'Oh, I see you brought a toy from home, is this the way you use it?' and I'd do it all wrong. The kid would forget he was supposed to be shy and say"—Chess uses a reprimanding falsetto—"'That's not the way you're supposed to do it! This is the way you're supposed to do it!' 'You mean like this?' And we'd be interacting." Further inquiry of the parents might reveal that something had happened which had compromised the child's adaptation. He may, for instance, have been out sick a lot and never had a chance to feel familiar at school. "So the school only saw this child who was standing at the periphery. Well, I also saw a child who was standing at the periphery, but he wasn't scared of me. Otherwise how could he come out and tell me I was doing it all wrong?"[20]

One slow-to-warm-up child was four-year-old Stanley who, with his two older sisters, was taken on a weekend trip to a seaside motel.

> The three children [Chess wrote] were put to bed in the same room, and when the parents opened the adjoining door a half hour later to check on them, the two older children were asleep in their respective beds while Stanley was sitting in the middle of the floor, solemn but not crying. Their attempts to induce him to get back into bed were fruitless. He simply repeated "I don't like that bed." The parents, prepared for this response by similar incidents in other new places, picked him up, tucked him into bed, made soothing noises, sat with him for a bit, and then left. As his mother was on her way out of the room, she heard the child climbing out of the bed again. When she asked him his intentions, he said, "Sit on the floor," and was apparently prepared to sit out the night. When he was brought into the parents' bedroom and provided with a bed more closely resembling his crib, he promptly fell asleep.[21]

The patient acceptance of such parents paid off handsomely as children like Stanley grew older. By the time he was five, Ralph, another slow-to-warm-up boy,

> was a well-adjusted member of his kindergarten group. He looked forward to going to school, greeted his playmates pleasantly, and visited back and forth with his friends after school. He continued to be placid rather than exuberant, even with good friends, but he was clearly contented and happy. When he visited in a new home, went to a new place, or met new children, he still took a long time to function easily. But both he and his family had learned that his shyness would wear off in time, and everyone was willing to wait.

Ralph's parents had come to understand very early that his hesitancy about accepting the unfamiliar needed to be honored.[22]

Different parents, of course, react differently to the slow-to-warm-up child, based on their own temperament, philosophy, and psychology. Some mothers are impatient and fast-moving, can't understand why their child is not the same, and unwilling to make what seems an excessive accommodation to his needs. Other parents are disturbed that their child is hesitant and unsure of himself in new situations and take it as an intolerable reflection on themselves. Still others give up too easily so that the child never has a chance to get used to new things, thereby surrendering him to a narrow range of foods, friends, and activities—and hence a narrow life and diminished self-concept. Teachers are likely to see the slow-to-warm-up child as insecure or maladjusted, which could create additional problems for him.

Jerry's parents, like Ralph's and Stanley's, were also nicely attuned to his temperament, but his mother's attitude changed when she began taking him to the playground and was embarrassed by his clinging, anxious reaction to new situations.

> The mother was dismayed, since to her, as to many other American mothers today, this moment was a big test of social maturity and healthy personality development. She felt that Jerry had failed this test and was sure that the other mothers in the playground were blaming her for having such an "anxiously" timid baby. They probably were.
>
> ... Instead of holding the child in her lap or giving him a familiar toy to play with near her until he warmed up to the new setting, she began to push him insistently to play "like the other little boys." The more she pressured, the more he clung. The more he clung, the more pressure she applied. Finally she gave up taking him to the playground at all.

In kindergarten Jerry did not participate with the other children. He dreaded going, cried, and clung to his mother. "He had in fact, become the anxious, fearful child his mother dreaded."[23]

* * *

If difficult children could make otherwise reasonably normal parents into tyrants or saps, easy children seemed to be able to make almost anyone into a paragon. They fussed little, smiled a lot, fell into regular patterns of eating and sleeping, including daytime naps, enjoyed new experiences, smiled and babbled at strangers, and rarely cried unless hungry or sleepy. As they got older, they were more able than other children to see the good in an otherwise disappointing situation and were most likely to comfort other children in distress.

Nevertheless, some easy children did develop problems. They were not immune to traumatic events, such as death of a family member or lengthy separations. But also their very adaptability made them susceptible to the neurotic demands of parents and to replicating the dysfunctional qualities they see in them, "sometimes," as Chess notes, "to the point of caricature."[24] It would seem that this type of child would be particularly vulnerable to the demands of an insecure mother who wants to be taken care of herself, leading to a false caretaking self (and perhaps in later life into a caretaking profession). Some of these children developed a mode of functioning at home that met with disapproval or even derision from peers or teachers. (Chess cites the case of a mother who had turned her easy, adaptable three-year-old into a perfectly mannered little aristocrat.) Easy children were not immune to disappointing their parents either—if, for example, they turned out to be not as bright as the parents hoped or if they learned a behavioral style from the parents that the parents hated in themselves.

Easy children can also run into problems with well-meaning parents who fail to give them what they need. Chess cited the case of Pammy, a winning baby who was raised by parents who felt their own childhoods had been spoiled by perfectionistic parents for whom nothing was ever good enough. Wanting to spare Pammy the pain they'd suffered, they failed to set limits for her. "Whenever they tried tentatively to do so, Pammy's charm would always divert them from their purpose."[25]

Pammy not only failed to learn limits and responsibility, she began relying on an ever more grating cuteness to avoid every sort of request. She did not learn the rules of games, and so, when she went to school, did not play with the other children. Although her IQ was normal, she began to experience herself as stupid. By age seven, she was a virtual misfit.

In studying these cases, where parents' reactions to their children turned out to be contrary to their temperamental needs, Chess came across a number of cases where the temperament of the parents and the temperament of the child seemed to represent a poor fit. She cites the case of the child who is very high in activity. Some parents are delighted by such a child. He may be always getting into things he shouldn't be, always disappearing to run off in some new direction, always on the verge of some physical disaster, but they are charmed by his energy and patient in teaching him rules. Other parents find the highly active child intolerable. They may have less stamina, need more control, or be unwilling to put their fine breakable objects in storage. They find themselves constantly correcting the child, criticizing him, admonishing him to "Sit still," "Don't touch," "Put that down," "Stop running."[26] As a result their child not only becomes resentful of all instruction, he fails to learn the difference between important and unimportant commands. He develops a chip on his shoulder, which carries over into his relations with teachers and peers.

Another example of a poor fit occurs between lively, exuberant parents and a child who is low in positive affect and high in persistence. Susie, for instance, would work for long periods on a task that interested her, but never seemed, as her parents said, "really enthusiastic." They wanted her to lighten up, to be less fussy, to show some feeling. By the time Susie was four, her mother had become so fed up with her lack of demonstrativeness she would exclaim, "Aren't you ever satisfied? I'm not going to take you out any more because you don't really like anything I do for you." To make matters worse for Susie, she had two younger brothers who were much more like her parents in temperament and to whom they gave more and more of their positive attention. Susie began to believe that she was stupid and couldn't do anything right. "Quiet persistence," Chess wrote, "was her strength, but it earned her little positive recognition from her father and mother."[27]

As the study progressed, Chess found that a number of the children displayed emotional or behavioral problems that required attention. Children born with difficult temperament predominated. Indeed, 70 percent of them ended up with behavior problems—phobias, learning difficulties, stealing, lying, defiance, excessive concern with pleasing others. Not, Chess insisted, because this is the inevitable fate of children with this temperament, but rather because they were more likely than other children to encounter an unsatisfactory environmental response.[28]

Although Chess and her colleagues found that temperament made a powerful contribution to personality, and that difficult or aggressive temperament may predict adjustment problems later, the environment always played a role. Their close scrutiny of the children and their parents over the years revealed what enormously different psychological outcomes were possible for children with very similar temperamental profiles.

Chess also found that family influences could either be attenuated or compounded by outside forces, like peers and teachers. "A parent may be fostering negativistic tendencies in a slowly adaptive child by insisting on quick adaptations to various new situations that are either very difficult or impossible for that youngster to make. If the nursery school teacher makes similar demands, the influences encouraging negativistic trends will be intensified. If she allows [him] to adapt at his own pace," however, the negative parental influence will be alleviated.[29]

Culture had to be considered a factor as well: "It must be emphasized," she wrote, "that the temperamental constellation we label as difficult is difficult in those cultures such as ours in which demands are made on the young child for the early establishment of regular sleep and feeding schedules, for quick adaptation to new situations and new people, and for cheerful acceptance of the rules and routines of the family."[30] To illustrate this point, she referred to a study of families in rural Kenya where researchers had identified a group of children who were biologically comparable to the children considered difficult in her sample:

> However, for the Kenyan mothers, these babies were not difficult to manage. Irregularity in sleep or feeding rhythms was no problem, since the infant was always with the mother or an older sib, slept beside the mother and was nursed whenever he or she awoke during the night. Fussing and slow adaptability were not issues of concern, because these parents, unlike so many American parents, did not view such behavior as alarming signals of a beginning behavior problem. Rather, their common statement was that "one cannot know about personality until the child is old enough, about 6 or 7 years, to take responsibility in household economic chores."[31]

To Chess, interaction was all. Although she had impressive statistics on the power of inborn temperament, she did not want to fall into the trap that she'd seen psychiatry fall into so often before, of launching a general theory based on a fragment. Rather, she saw temperament and environment as continually interacting and modifying each other. Children have an impact on their parents, causing them to be certain things they might not be otherwise, at least not so strongly. They have traits that may push their parents' buttons, eliciting reactions another child might not get. How easy it is to care for a child, how well his temperament dovetails with the parents', how well his behavior fits with their prior expectations will all influence their behavior and their attitude toward the child. By the same token, children can change. Parents and others can help a child to learn how to deal with himself. They can help him to adapt to situations that are hard for him. A tendency toward negative mood may become more positive if caretaking has been benign. Similarly, a highly adaptable child, repeatedly confronted with impossible demands, may become less and less adaptable over time.[32]

Chess's work on temperament and its interaction with the environment has continued for over three decades. Reports on the New York Longitudinal Study and the new conclusions drawn from it have appeared in the 1960s, 1970s, and 1980s, as the children from the sample have reached adulthood and formed their own families. The work she's done with Thomas and Birch has moved child care away from the one-style-fits-all recommendations formerly given to parents by pediatricians and other advisors to a recognition that different children have different needs. Some children do well being fed on demand, others do not. Some can easily be toilet-trained at an early age, some do better later. Some easily adapt to new learning situations in school, some need encouragement, persistent pressure, or repetition of the new activity before they will get fully and effectively involved. Sensitivity to such differences in children is apparent now in books such as those addressed to parents by pediatrician Berry Brazelton, in which he illustrates childhood development by following several children with different temperamental styles.[33]

In an age where deviations from the cultural ideal (uptightness with the new, anxiety about change, the lack of assertive self-confidence, a high level of aggressiveness) are quickly seen as character flaws, Chess and her colleagues have also been a force for tolerance. She has helped make parents and child care workers more aware of the fact that a child can have a disposition that the culture does not value without that disposition having been created in some way by pernicious parenting. Her work has helped ease the pressure on parents. With knowledge of temperamental differences, they could perhaps see a tantrumy baby without feeling ashamed or guilty or enraged, but just know that this is biologically natural and they face a difficult task.

Chess's work could also be seen as a reconfirmation of certain aspects of the Bowlby-Ainsworth thesis, for it reinforced the importance of sensitive care. Indeed, it took the issue to a higher level of sophistication, because she not only recognized that sensitive care means different things to different babies (as Ainsworth did), but documented in detail what those differences were for specific temperamental types.

But it was not seen this way by either camp. For one, Bowlby and Ainsworth were viewed by Chess and her allies as radical environmentalists and parent blamers. It seemed to Chess and to those who followed her in the examination of hereditary traits that behavior in the Strange Situation was as much a factor of temperament as anything else. In the data that Sroufe reported, children in the behavior problems group could easily be seen as children who were difficult from birth, while the secure group looked an awful lot like the easy child, right down to the capacity for empathy and the good peer relations. Even the percentages were similar. Chess also believed that attachment theory was overly focused on the first year and ignorant of how radically things could be altered, for better or worse, thereafter; and that it was overly concerned with the mother to the exclusion of other family, community, and social influences. In such views, she was hardly alone.

For their part, attachment theorists saw problems with Chess's methodology: not collecting data on temperament until the child was three months old, by which time mothers would have left a considerable imprint; not appreciating the immense impact of the mother in the earliest days, especially in enabling the baby to achieve stable biological rhythms; relying too much on parental reports, which are notoriously biased (Ainsworth felt particularly strongly about this from her own experience); and mistaking the effects of environmental influence (schoolyard aggression, for example) for inherited traits. Others, including fellow genetic researchers, doubted whether the nine temperamental criteria reflected actual biological traits or simply convenient groupings of characteristics. The strongest objections from environmentalists were reserved for the "poorness of fit" concept. Attachment theorists and like-minded clinicians were hoping to educate parents about their babies' needs and how best to respond to them. They grudgingly acknowledged that responding sensitively might be harder for certain parents with certain babies, but what good could come of a concept that seemed to acquiesce to those hardships, as if there was nothing a poor-fitting parent could do? Part of good parental attunement meant adjusting to achieve a good fit with the baby. What's more, it appeared at times that Chess only saw parent-child conflict in poorness-of-fit terms and was insensitive to the fact that many parents are anxious, self-centered, depressed, angry, imperious, manipulative, detached—and that, without outside help, they cause their children to become disturbed.* In Levy's work, after all, when babies were faced with an anxious, intrusive, overprotective mother, they became disturbed. The baby's temperament only affected how, not whether.[34]

More radical environmentalists saw the poorness-of-fit idea as a pernicious effort to place baby and parent on the same plane, with equal responsibility for adjusting to each other and making the relationship work. Presumably, now, parents could throw up their hands and say of their child, "We just weren't meant for each other," rather than face the fact that they are the ones, regardless of their own temperaments, attitudes, or countervailing emotions, who must struggle to give of themselves in the way the baby needs them. Chess, had not, of course, meant the fit doctrine to be taken this way, but it was as if the concept was born on a slant and could barely be probed without rolling in that direction.

The debate over goodness or poorness of fit, which soon engulfed developmental psychology, spilled over into the more relationship-oriented wing of American psychoanalysis, which was slowly influenced by the wave of infant research taking place in the 1970s. Fashions in analysis had swung widely on the nature-nurture question, from Freud's early environmentalist view (the seduction theory) to Klein's extreme genetic view (which assumed that the baby arrived with images of people and fantasies of relationships already in place). In an influential 1983 work on object relations theory, New York analysts Jay Greenberg and Stephen Mitchell warned against another overarching swing of the pendulum:

> Sullivan and Fairbairn both write as if the only crucial variable is the caretaker, anxious or not, emotionally available or not. They do not emphasize the extent to which the care-

---

*When Stella Chess read this in manuscript form, she wrote in the margin, "I do blame parents at times—really!" (July 12, 1993).

taker's responsiveness or lack of responsiveness is keyed to the *particular* baby's style and rhythm.[35]

The authors argued that, according to the latest infant research, the mother's success or failure in meeting the infant's needs must be understood in terms of goodness of fit:

> Each baby brings to encounters with caretakers his own particular rhythm of engagement, level of activity, distinct affective and behavioral displays. Each caretaker brings to his encounter with the baby his own style and intensity of responsiveness, attention span, level of interest, anxieties, and so on.[36]

Such an even-handed view of of the parent-child relationship made another New York analyst, Gerald Schoenewolf, seethe: "To attribute failure to a bad fit is to absolve mothers of responsibility and blame. In doing this Greenberg and Mitchell are bowing to a feminist trend of the 1970s and 1980s, a trend that in my opinion has been quite destructive to child rearing."[37]

The table was set for war.

21

RENAISSANCE OF
BIOLOGICAL DETERMINISM:
THE TEMPERAMENT DEBATE

Attachment thinkers had made various efforts over the years, mostly *pro forma*, to account for inborn temperament. Bowlby spoke of it in his earliest papers. In 1940 he wrote, "It should not be assumed that I ignore inherited difficulties, which are almost certainly significant in a large number of cases." (Although in most cases, he added, neurosis was still unlikely unless the environment had exacerbated whatever problems the baby started out with.[1]) Later he described one of his juvenile thieves as having been "difficult from birth," while another "was said to have been quite an easy baby."[2]

Similarly when Bowlby first presented his theories of attachment, he displayed an awareness of the fact that certain babies smiled more than others, which, he said, caused them to get more love and attention. This, too, reflected an acceptance of inborn temperamental difference—in this case regarding the display of positive feeling—and of the fact that children influenced the kind of care they received. In 1973, in *Separation*, he acknowledged that genetic factors may play a role in susceptibility to fear, which, he said, had been "well-documented in the case of other mammals, e.g. dogs."[3]

Ainsworth, too, was aware that babies were different from birth. In evaluating maternal behavior in her Baltimore home study, she wrote that "babies differ in the kinds of signals they give" and that "it may take some time before a mother can learn to read the signals of her baby." She believed that if mother and baby were to be optimally attuned, a "mutual adaption" must take place.[4]

But neither Bowlby nor Ainsworth believed that inborn traits accounted for all that much in the average child. They were thus unprepared for the surge in genetic research among psychologists in the 1970s and 1980s and the degree to which inherited qualities would be taken as fundamental in adult personalities. The evidence accumulated in these studies seemed to offer a stunning refutation of many of their most fundamental assumptions.

Male twins, thirty years old, were separated at birth, put up for adoption, and ultimately raised in different countries. They had no contact with each other. Yet when psychoanalyst and personality researcher Peter Neubauer caught up with them at age thirty, they were so similar as to make the whole concept of environmental influence seem superfluous. Both demonstrated conspicuous obsessive-compulsive traits. They were highly preened, religiously punctual, and so anxious about cleanliness they both regularly scrubbed their hands just short of bleeding.

Neubauer asked each twin independently to account for his unusual fastidiousness. The first blamed his mother, noting that throughout the years of his childhood she had been fanatically well ordered, insisting that everything be returned to its place and that all the clocks ("We had dozens of clocks") be "set to the same noonday chime." The second twin was equally certain of the origins of his personality style. "The reason is quite simple," he said. "I'm reacting to my mother, who was an absolute slob."[5]

Since the first reports from the New York Longitudinal Study, the idea of temperament as a quality that the child brought with it from birth had begun to catch on in developmental circles. Psychologist Richard Bell had taken up Chess's idea that the influence between parent and child is not just one-way, that the infant and its qualities have a strong impact on the parent and affect the quality of care it receives, and his work on this subject was widely influential.[6] All this had contributed to a rising concern that mothers were not being treated fairly, neither by psychologists nor by the general public, as evidenced by the assumptions of the hand-washing twins.

Developmental psychology, meanwhile, had spawned a new discipline. Called behavior genetics, it occasioned a revival of interest in the idea of inborn personality not seen since the last century. The new researchers did longitudinal studies of twins reared together, compared adopted and nonadopted siblings, and, perhaps most dramatically, examined adult twins who had been raised apart.[7]

Finding identical twins who were separated at birth is a difficult task, but it offers a rare and dramatic opportunity to sort out the environmental from the hereditary. Because identical twins have identical genetic material, it's almost like raising the same person in two different environments and seeing how powerfully the genes shine through. Finnish twins Daphne Goodship and Barbara Herbert, for example, were separated at birth and did not meet again for thirty-nine years. They arrived at their first meeting wearing the same outfit (beige dress and brown velvet jacket). They discovered that they both suffered miscarriages with their first pregnancy, then had two boys and a girl (in that order). Both had weak ankles from falling down stairs at fifteen, and both met their husbands at sixteen. Their mannerisms seemed identical, as did their shapes and weight. Identical twins, of course, are as prone to coincidence as anyone else, and much of such informal data may be little more than that. But there was more: Their personalities also had prominent echoes, like their habit of giggling, the fact that they are both penny-pinchers (despite being raised in diametrically different socioeconomic circumstances), and their marked guardedness about revealing their opinions.[8]

University of Minnesota psychologist Thomas Bouchard and his co-workers, who, since 1979, have examined over 120 pairs of adult identical twins who were separated within a few months of birth,[9] believe that individual qualities like imagination, leadership, curiosity, tolerance, sociability, alienation, and vulnerability to stress are all strongly heritable. "When we set up the study," Bouchard says, "we just assumed that social attitudes wouldn't show a genetic influence." But he noted with excitement that he found otherwise: Religiosity and traditionalism also seemed to have genetic links.[10]

Bouchard began studying identical twins reared apart after reading a newspaper story about Jim Springer and Jim Lewis. When these "Jim twins" first met, also at age thirty-nine, they found that each had constructed a similar circular white bench around a tree in his yard. They were each affectionate and sentimental and had the same habit of leaving love notes around the house for their wives to find. They had similar wood-working shops in their basements. They both drove Chevrolets, drank Miller Lite, and chain-smoked Salem cigarettes. Both had worked as sheriff's deputies. Both had had vasectomies. The first wives of both men were named Linda, and their second wives were both Bettys. One had a son named James Allan, the other James Alan. They both had had dogs named Toy.[11] "I thought for sure the story in the newspaper was exaggerated," Bouchard told me. But he discovered it was not. The finding of such uncanny similarities in twins reared apart (who until then had been mainly compared in terms of IQ) altered the direction of Bouchard's career. He would soon find more uncanny material to match it.[12]

Bouchard put all the twins through a huge battery of standard assessments, such as the Vocational Interest Test, the major personality inventories, a life stress interview, and measurements of interest, values, and expressive style, all of which yielded impressive correlations.[13] But it was the anecdotal material—much of it reported in the press—that was often most captivating: Twin men, living in New Jersey, meet for the first time in adulthood. They find that they are both volunteer firemen, both like hunting, both married women with the same first name, both drink only Budweiser and grasp their beer with the pinky lodged underneath. "We had the same moustache," said one, "the same sideburns, even the same glasses."[14] Another pair of male twins, reported by Neubauer (who, unlike Bouchard, followed his subjects from infancy), are introduced to each other for the first time at nineteen. Both had won boxing championships, both had artistic interests; even the cavities in their teeth were in the same location. A third pair of twins, introduced later in life, share an extreme chameleon-like capacity for adaptability. Although quite different from each other, they are eerily similar to the people in their surroundings.[15] A fourth pair find they like to play the same oddball practical joke. A fifth that they share a phobia about water and that they have an identical means of coping with it when they want to go for a swim—wading in backward.

It is difficult to overestimate the impact the twin studies have had on the field. They seem to have established that a great deal of what we think of as personality traits have, at the very least, a genetic component. Other evidence, including the wealth of material coming out of the Colorado Adoption Project, has been equally compelling. Judy Dunn and Robert Plomin have reported that biological siblings are quite different despite having been treated the same way at the same ages by their mothers. "What little resemblance there is among siblings," they concluded, "is due to hereditary similarity, not to the experience of growing up in the same family."[16] Recently, more physiologically based studies — of variability in brain chemistry, heartbeat, and hormonal levels in infants — have added a new level of confirming data. University of Wisconsin psychologist Richard Davidson, for instance, has found evidence that people with greater activity in the right frontal cortex of the brain are prone to be gloomy, while those with more left frontal activity are prone to be cheerful.[17] Although newborns cannot be tested to determine if this pattern is present at birth, some researchers feel strongly that it is an inherited quality that may make some people more at risk for depression. As a result of work like this, it is now frequently assumed that not only certain types of severe depression but other mental disorders — hysterical character, hyperactivity in children, manic-depressive illness, vulnerability to addiction, schizophrenia, the obsessive-compulsiveness disorder of the two hand-washing twins — are genetically based.

Temperament research is still in its infancy and there is much confusion and disagreement among researchers. What is a trait? What is personality? What is temperament? How can it be measured? Perhaps most important: Are behavioral or biochemical variations observed or measured at birth stable traits; are they susceptible to environmental influence; do they change over time?[18] No one knows for certain what the building blocks of temperament are. Chess still prefers the nine temperamental variables she and her husband worked out with Herbert Birch. Others favor the more parsimonious categories — emotionality, activity, and sociability — worked out by Plomin and Arnold Buss.[19] Still other researchers favor different categorizations.

Most genetic behaviorists give at least a passing salute to the environment, acknowledging, to cite an obvious example, that not everyone whose heredity makes them more vulnerable to addiction becomes a drug abuser, that something else, something experiential, is needed as well. They describe temperamental traits as "heritable," which means having a genetic component (as opposed to "inherited" — applicable to traits like eye color — which means fully determined by genes). But the clear trend has been toward more and more emphatic demonstrations of the power of heredity — and a dismissal of work, such as that being done on attachment, which places such a large emphasis on the child's experience.

In this debate, too, Jerome Kagan has figured prominently. Early in his career Kagan had been an environmentalist and a strong proponent of maternal influence but had come to believe that the primary constituents of personality are genetic and constitutional (present at birth but not necessarily genetic) and that many important personality variables are determined by the chemical broth of hormones, neurotransmitters, and brain peptides in which the brain sits.[20]

In 1978 Kagan began studying a sample of children, representing some 15 to 20 percent of the population, who were similar to Chess's slow-to-warm-up group. According to Kagan, such children all display a cluster of behaviors and emotional states that can be summarized as a tendency toward fretfulness, anxiety, and inhibition. As early as two months of age these infants are easily hyperaroused, cry, or become fretful in the presence of novel stimulation, and are often difficult to soothe. Like fearful strains of laboratory rats, long known to researchers (and quite easy to breed), they have a distinct, excitable brain chemistry.

In his longitudinal study, begun in the toddler period, Kagan found that young children with this shy, timid, fearful profile are reluctant to interact with others and tend to play apart from other children in play groups. When an unfamiliar event occurs, they're more anxiously reactive than other children, clinging to their mothers, stopping play, and cutting short their own chatter, humming, or other vocalizations. When observed again at age seven and a half, 75 percent retain the pattern, revealing prominent anxieties, like fear of going to camp, of watching violent TV shows, of sleeping over at a friend's house. At ten they still prefer to play alone rather than in groups. At thirteen, the anxious profile remained. "And, as you might expect," Kagan says, extrapolating from other evidence, "extremely shy, phobic children, are likely as adults to select bureaucratic jobs with minimal risks."[21]

Where Ainsworth sees ambivalent attachment, Kagan sees the inherited susceptibility to stress typical of his fretful children. Where Sroufe sees children displaying the emotional consequences of secure or anxious attachment, Kagan sees the unfolding of inborn traits. His work has led him to the conclusion that people, like dogs, come in a variety of breeds—some cocker spaniels, some Dobermans, some terriers, some Labradors—and no matter what happens to us, we don't change breeds. ("Every dog owner knows," he has said, "that it's hard to make a terrier behave like a police dog."[22]) The implication of such tenacious patterns has at times been upsetting to him. "I've struggled with this a lot," he told me. "My training, my beliefs, my upbringing all came together when I was a younger person to lead me to minimize the role of biology. I believed that even if you started with a little bit of biology that your will and experience could overcome it. I've now seen many children for whom that's difficult."[23]

Although he often sounds as if he believes that temperament is destiny, Kagan denies that he is, as some attachment people charge, a radical genetic determinist. In particular, he has begun in recent years to acknowledge the power of family influence, noting, for example, that inhibited children, if they are lucky enough to grow up in families that value education, often go far. "Some," he says, will "select rewarding careers that require solitary intellectual activity—science, computer programming, history, music, and art. T. S. Eliot and John Maynard Keynes, who were very inhibited children, both won Nobel prizes."[24] In his thirteen-year assessment, Kagan found one inhibited child from an intelligent, well-educated family who said he wanted to be an astrophysicist. Why? Because he likes to work alone. Another boy, from a disadvantaged family, was clearly less well adjusted, and seemed to be on his way to a conduct disorder. While acknowledging such important environmental influences, Kagan nevertheless maintains that the underlying, inherited style remains. Thus, all of the children in the anxious, inhibited group, "whether they are headed for a conduct disorder or president of the class," are low in the expression of positive feeling and display very few spontaneous smiles.[25]

Behavior geneticists like Kagan see their work as providing a source of optimism. If the fundamental message of attachment research is that children need to be cared for in a consistent and sensitive way, that they love their parents powerfully and need to have that love returned and sustained, then the fundamental message of temperament research is that people are inherently different, that those differences need to be tolerated and respected, and that much of what we once saw as parentally induced is actually part of the natural range of human differences. "I think if we recognize that individuals differ from each other in these fundamental ways," Bouchard says, "we're going to have a lot more respect for one another. We know that we're physically different. We respect and understand that a kid who's only four and a half feet tall is not going to compete with a kid who's six feet tall. Well, the same may be true for many psychological traits and characteristics."[26]

Kagan agrees. "There are some people with a very short fuse. They blow up easily; it's hard to get along with them. Many people assume that it's a function of their past and they should be able to control it. So then you get angry at these people. But if you believe that this is partly temperamental, and that their biology prepares them for this, then you become a little more forgiving."[27] Kagan also expects temperament research to take the pressure off mothers who, he believes, have gotten a raw deal as a result of decades of behaviorist and psychoanalytic influence. He quotes with pleasure the words of a famous scientist who suffers from terrible stage fright whenever he makes a speech. After hearing Kagan present his data, he said, "I've been blaming my mother for fifty years, but after hearing this, I'm going to stop."[28]

The sudden rise of behavior genetics and its direct attacks on attachment theory caused distress in the attachment ranks. No one was more roiled by the new trend than Sroufe, who, with Ainsworth's gradual retirement, was becoming attachment's chief spokesman in the United States. His distress over the issue was apparent the first time we spoke in 1988: "There's a tremendous wave of biological determinism," he said. "Everything's genes these days. There have been dozens of papers saying that all this stuff is just temperament. Hell, we'll find a gene for security of attachment any day here!"[29]

The behavior-genetic challenge to attachment theory was essentially two-pronged. One prong indicted the attachment idea for blaming mothers and ignoring the fact that infants could be difficult or that there could be a poor fit. This charge still causes feathers to fly: No one will admit to blaming mothers, and Bowlby himself was at pains to point out the sympathy with which he, as a clinician, viewed both the mothers and the children in anxious pairs and the awareness he always retained of the mother's own hardships and psychological burdens. What's more, most attachment workers readily concede that the father or another person can be the primary caregiver, so that mothers are not really the issue except for the fact that in most families they do in fact play that role. Be that as it may, attachment theorists have not been so eager to let mothers—or caregivers in general—off the hook: They want it understood that sensitive, consistent parenting is vital, and they see proclaiming that as part of their mission.

The blame issue is similar to the poorness-of-fit concept in that it has been highly charged politically, and the antagonists are often more concerned about the impact certain types of statements will have than whether or not they are true. Many developmentalists recognize that, of course, parents are sometimes to blame for their children's suffering, but they believe that making an issue of it will only tend to generate guilt—and a guilty parent is more likely to do a poor job than one who had been reassured and encouraged. Because they believe— and I think for the most part rightly so—that an atmosphere of guilt is so destructive, they lean toward never saying anything, even in professional contexts, that might suggest that mothers ever behave badly. Poorness-of-fit and other temperament-based explanations are more reassuring.

This prong of the opposition's thinking has made some inroads into the attachment canon. Alicia Lieberman, firmly in the attachment camp, has narrated a training video, *Flexible, Fearful, or Feisty?*,[30] to help acquaint child care workers with temperament. She readily acknowledges that some babies make it easier for parents than others. "There are children," she says, "who are more resilient and who forgive more easily and for whom the momentum toward mental health is stronger. They make a mother into the kind of mother who provides security of attachment because of who they are, because of how easy they are to read, because of how predictable they are, how rewarding they are, how easily they respond to even awkward soothing. So that the mother has her own wounds healed by the baby. And I think there are children who temperamentally are much more fragile, for whom smaller deviations in sensitivity or predictability have a bigger cost."[31] Bowlby summarized the attachment position this way:

> An easy newborn may assist an uncertain mother to develop a favorable pattern of care. Conversely, a difficult unpredictable newborn may tip the balance the other way. Yet all the evidence shows that a potentially easy baby is still likely to develop unfavorably if given unfavorable care and also, more fortunately, that with only few exceptions a potentially difficult baby can develop favorably if given sensitive care. The capacity of a sensitive mother to adapt to even a difficult unpredictable baby and thereby enable him to develop favorably is perhaps the most heartening of all recent findings in this field.[32]

Although Sroufe has staunchly resisted the notion that a child can be born inherently difficult and cites compelling evidence that parental input or lack of it—even in the very first days—plays a significant role in at least some of the difficult infant profiles, he, too, has made an accommodation:

> If Karen is ambivalent about being a mother [he wrote with colleagues in a recent developmental text] and Meryl is cranky as a newborn, interaction between the two will tend to intensify these traits. As long as Karen's situation does not improve, Meryl is apt to become a truly difficult child, even though her initial irritability could have been only temporary in different circumstances.[33]

This interactionist view, now given at least lip service by everyone in the field, albeit with different emphases, has been supported by various studies among humans and lower primates. In one study, neither the infant's susceptibility to stress nor the mother's desire for control alone predicted quality of attachment, but taken together they did.[34] Steven Suomi, now at the Institute for Child Health and Human Development in Washington, found that heredity seems to determine whether a rhesus monkey will be socially forward or retiring and that monkeys with excessive timidity—similar to the fearful profile observed in some human children—will often tend to have problems later in relationships. But these are only tendencies, he says. A nurturant mother can often erase temperamental deficits. The exceptionally nurturant mother, Suomi has found, takes the time to teach her fretful child coping styles, such as how to get help from others when he becomes afraid. As a result, Suomi says, the fretful baby "later in life becomes a very effective and high-ranking member of its social group."[35]

The second prong of the behavior-genetic attack struck more forcefully to the core of the attachment idea, not necessarily by denying that something which might reasonably be called "attachment" existed or that it developed in better or worse ways, but by dismissing virtually all of the research done in its name, beginning with Ainsworth's Baltimore study. It asserted that what Ainsworth measured in the Strange Situation was really temperament—or that whatever she measured was so confounded by temperament as to make her assessments meaningless.

"Ainsworth's Strange Situation could be appropriately rated," Chess and Thomas wrote, "under the temperamental categories of approach/ withdrawal, adaptability, quality of mood, and intensity." Subsequent descriptions of older children done by Sroufe and his students, they said, "could also be rated under the same four temperamental categories, plus persistence."[36]

The idea that inherited temperament might be determining attachment outcomes was preposterous to Sroufe. If this were so, why is it that some infants come out with different patterns of attachment with each parent—that, indeed, only a small correlation has ever been found between attachment to mother and attachment to father? If this were so, how could we explain the fact that quality of attachment can change? And, finally, if this were so, why would depressed and unresponsive mothers almost always have anxious babies? In one study, Sroufe evaluated the newborns of such mothers. "We could show—really clearly— deterioration in those kids," he said. "They looked pretty good at three months, but at six months they didn't look so good. About half of them were anxiously attached at twelve months and all of them at eighteen months. We're talking a serious downhill slide. What are you going to say? The baby was *born* a downhill slider?"[37]

Sroufe does not hold much stock in the whole idea of inherited temperament, at least not in terms of the qualities in children that interest him, and he does not believe that temperament and quality of attachment are worth discussing in the same breath: "I believe that temperament is a useful concept, that is, that infants and children differ in terms of preferred tempo and so forth. . . . [but] more meaningful individual differences are best captured by other concepts."[38] And he is just as good at dismissing temperament research as the behavior geneticists have been at dismissing his. He (among others) argues that Kagan's data on the continuity of temperamental behavior at different ages are vastly inflated by studying a small group at the temperamental extreme and that for the majority of the population such continuities are insignificant.[39] He is particularly scornful of the huge amount of temperament work based on parental reports, noting that a parent's concept of what a baby is like has been shown to have little in common with the appraisals of neutral observers. In one study, expectant parents were asked—before the fetus had begun moving in the womb—what they thought their baby would be like. The parents' imaginary descriptions of their unborn infants tended to be similar to how they described their actual baby many months later, suggesting, at the very least, that their expectations played a role in their perceptions.[40]

The temperament-attachment debates soon focused on the avoidant babies. Kagan, among others, insisted that many children classified as avoidant appeared to be indifferent to their mother's comings and goings in the Strange Situation not because they've given up getting anything from her but because they are truly indifferent. Unlike their counterparts who have been labeled secure or ambivalent (with equal injustice), the so-called avoidant children are simply constitutionally less fearful.

Sroufe countered such arguments by pointing out that the children who were classified avoidant only looked calm and independent in the Strange Situation; at home they were as clingy and tantrumy as those who were classified ambivalent. And, of course, he had his poignant observations in preschool and later that indicated ongoing dependent behaviors, of an often pathetic character, among these supposedly fearless and independent kids. Even in the Strange Situation, there was evidence that avoidant calm was only superficial and that avoidant children were masking more powerful underlying feelings. One Minnesota study, confirmed later by the Grossmann team, showed that the heart rates of avoidant one-year-olds go way up when the mother leaves the room and way up again when she returns, even as their behavior remains calm, data that seem to suggest that the avoidant child is indeed in a state of angry emotional cutoff from the parent.[41] Kagan would have none of this, arguing that heart rate acceleration in such situations may also be a function of temperament and that his own data suggest just that.[42] Sroufe countered that if the elevated heart rates of the avoidant child illustrate a temperamental style, it is just the opposite of the bold, fearless child Kagan perceives him to be. And indeed, it would seem that Kagan is trying to have it both ways in this case, for the type of child to whom Kagan is referring here, whose heart rate tends to be elevated in such circumstances, is the shy, inhibited child, not one that could be called bold or precociously independent.

The ambivalent child has been, if possible, an even greater source of contention because it seems to display the fussy and irritable style of the one temperamental group that Kagan has spent most of his time studying and that has, on the whole, been more firmly documented than any other. Behavior geneticists took note when attachment workers in Japan found that the majority of Japanese babies were classified ambivalent—

an extraordinary finding when one considers that ambivalence turns up in only one tenth of the middle-class American babies. Kagan immediately charged—as he had with the north German sample—that it would be absurd to assume that the child-rearing practices of an entire nation were at fault. Rather he took this as another sign of temperament at work, in this case picking up a racially based constitutional inclination to be more easily distressed. In an unusually pointed response, which suggests the degree to which Kagan's arguments and the way he expresses them can get under the skins of his opponents, Jay Belsky, a rising young attachment star at the Pennsylvania State University, wrote: "What Kagan has not acknowledged, although making this inference that sounds sensible, is that research on constitutional differences between Japanese-Oriental and North American-Caucasian infants would" lead to just the opposite conclusion, since "Japanese newborns are actually *less* susceptible to distress."[43]*

It did not take long before attachment workers were setting up their own studies to try to settle this question directly. In one, Belsky found that certain aspects of the mother's personality, assessed before her baby was born, were a more reliable predictor of the child's later attachment status than the baby's temperament. Mothers who showed greater empathy and concern for others, mothers who were more mature and stable, were more likely to have securely attached children. Indeed Belsky found that none of the direct assessments of infant temperament, including fussiness and alertness, measured at various times during the first year, had any predictive value in terms of Strange Situation classification at twelve months. But mother's *appraisals* of their infants' temperaments were predictive. Although it is impossible to know for sure what the mothers' appraisals were really all about—the mother, the infant, the relationship between the two—what was particularly interesting in Belsky's study is that the mothers' appraisals often changed over the course of the year. The mothers of children who would later be classified as secure did not see their babies as any less challenging or more attractive than the mothers of children who would later be classified as anxious—indeed, they rated them as somewhat more challenging and less

---

*Many attachment researchers now assume that the early Japanese studies of attachment were flawed because Japanese children, who were not accustomed to being left alone for even a minute, were—contrary to Ainsworth's instructions—allowed to get overstressed and cry too long in the separation episodes of the Strange Situation. Thus, they were inaccurately classified ambivalent. In fact, Japanese babies tend to be raised with an extraordinarily high level of attunement and attentiveness on the part of their mothers.

attractive. But over the course of the year their assessments changed, and they saw their babies becoming more adaptable and less difficult. Just the opposite was true of mothers whose children were destined to be classified as anxiously attached. While many of them rated their babies higher in the beginning, they tended to see their babies becoming more difficult as the year wore on.[44]

Belsky further found that although laboratory assessments of the infant's temperament could not predict whether the child would be securely or anxiously attached, they did seem to predict the style of secure or anxious attachment. Fussy and irritable infants who later became anxiously attached were more likely to be ambivalent than avoidant. If securely attached, the fussy child was more likely to fall into the more clingy and excitable subgroup. Belsky felt he had squared this circle with this study, creating a rapprochement between behavior geneticism and environmentalism, without giving up any of attachment's tenets. His finding—essentially, that temperament affects the way secure or anxious attachment is expressed—has become widely accepted in attachment circles. (Strange when you consider how directly it seems to contradict a fundamental attachment tenet—that babies become avoidant or ambivalent based on the style of parental care.)

In Germany Klaus and Karin Grossmann have also attempted to unravel this problem, assessing the children at birth by using state-of-the-art temperament measures. "We did establish that some children make it easier for mothers than others," Karin says, with the result that positive correlations did exist between certain temperament styles and secure or anxious attachment. They found, however, that the mother's sensitivity as a caregiver was the more powerful predictor. The Grossmanns also assessed the levels of cortisol, a stress-related hormone, in children going through the Strange Situation. Their findings further supported the idea that avoidant children were distressed but not showing it.[45]

Other studies, including one by former Sroufe student Brian Vaughn, discounted any association between inborn temperament and attachment classification. Vaughn found that early assessments of temperament —whether determined by a widely used temperament questionnaire or by measurements of hormonal secretions—could not predict whether the baby would be securely or insecurely attached.[46]

The overlay of inherited temperament and parental psychology, not to mention family circumstances and cultural differences, all came into play with the report of a huge study by Dymphna van den Boom at the University of Leiden in the Netherlands. For five years, van den Boom had been a teacher of children with learning and behavior problems and had been impressed with the fact that children who ended up in special schools had usually exhibited problems when they were quite small and that their mothers frequently complained of their having been difficult. She became interested in parent-child interaction, began reading widely in attachment theory, and became concerned that attachment theory seemed indifferent to the effects of the child's inborn characteristics, a problem she was determined to remedy in her own doctoral thesis.

Van den Boom waded through 588 neonatal assessments in order to find and study one hundred babies who were all highly irritable at birth, displaying a low threshold for the expression of negative feeling, as assessed on Berry Brazelton's Neonatal Behavioral Assessment Scale. Since critics of attachment theory had repeatedly alluded to studies showing that children assessed as irritable at birth were more likely to be classified anxious at one year, this was an important target population. Van den Boom's children were particularly at risk. Not only were they inherently more trying than more placid and smiley babies, they were born into low-income families, where uneducated and pressured parents might not have the time, the knowledge, or the emotional reserves needed to guide their babies through to a solid adaptation.

Van den Boom now asked all the key questions: Is this select group of irritable children destined to be classified anxiously attached at one year regardless of how they are raised? If so, will they, in keeping with Kagan's thinking, belong to the ambivalent group, a manifestation of their fussy, fretful style? Will the quality of attachment be at all affected by how sensitively they are responded to? If so, by how much?

In order to answer these questions she divided the hundred pairs of children and mothers into two groups of fifty each. One group of mothers received three counseling sessions of about two hours each between the child's sixth and ninth months, the purpose being to enhance the mother's sensitivity and effectiveness. The other mothers were left to their own devices.

Because the irritable babies were less responsive to their mothers, smiled and made pleasing sounds less frequently, van den Boom found that the mothers tended to become discouraged and give up on them in various ways. One mother, van den Boom recalls, "turned on the radio to help her shut out the crying and fussing" as soon as the baby became upset. Van den Boom educated the mother in the importance of soothing a crying baby, and then worked with her to determine what soothing strategy would work best. Like most mothers in the study, this mother found her success at soothing her baby rewarding and that encouraged her to keep at it. Another mother, apparently rattled by previous failures, responded to her baby's cries by trying to soothe it every which way she could, using one strategy after another in quick succession. In short order, both baby and mother were at wits' end. Van den Boom helped the mother determine which soothing strategy was most effective and encouraged her to keep doing it until the baby calmed down. Other mothers, exhausted from failed soothing efforts and fearful of disrupting a quiet infant, had stopped interacting with their babies when they were not crying. Van den Boom encouraged such mothers to play with the child. But because the mothers of irritable babies turned out to be very interfering, often by pushing one toy or another on a resistant baby, she asked them to begin play without toys, a process that helped promote attunement.[47]

The outcome was stunning. In the families that received these simple interventions, 68 percent of these fussy children were classified securely attached at one year. In the control group, only 28 percent were classified secure. There could be no doubt that quality of care was a key variable in quality of attachment, but it was not the only one, and it was influenced by other factors. Also, that forty-eight of the one hundred turned out to be securely attached refuted any idea that it was their temperaments that were being measured in the Strange Situation. They all displayed the fussy, easily stressed, quick-to-cry style, but almost half of them were classified secure. If this study stands and is replicated by others, it would seem to have settled some major questions.

But while settling some questions, van den Boom immediately raises others. Attachment theorists assume that in many cases the mother's deep-seated psychology determines her behavior toward her baby and thence the baby's quality of attachment. If that is the case, how can six hours of intervention be enough to insure security? It leaves one incredulous. Will a secure relationship built on such a foundation be quickly eroded as unaltered aspects of the mother's psychology come into play in later months and years? Or will a solid start help mother and child to remain securely related thereafter? The fact that many mothers do better with their second child than their first suggests that, at least for some parents, just knowing the ropes makes a difference. (Other parents do better with a second child because they enact all their psychological needs and hang-ups with their first.)

But Van den Boom's evidence indicated that extreme temperament also plays a role in anxious attachment. Her study confirmed what Stella Chess would have expected: that irritable children did indeed seem to place additional stresses on their parents (who, in turn, no doubt, became more rejecting) thereby making it harder to establish a secure relationship, a fact suggested by the phenomenally low secure rate of the nonintervention group.*

Van den Boom also found a surprising breakdown among the anxiously attached children: In both the experimental and the control groups, the great majority (77 percent) of the anxious children were avoidant, not ambivalent as Kagan, Chess, and others would have predicted and as Belsky had found in his study. In the Strange Situation, van den Boom's irritable children looked nonchalant. Why this should be so remains a mystery, as does so much in the interplay of biology and experience. It may be that the mother's style of impaired caregiving is in most cases ultimately a more powerful influence than the baby's temperament in determining whether the baby will be ambivalent or avoidant and, further, that mothers of irritable babies tend to respond to them differently based on the cultural setting. This is what van den Boom believes.[†]

Genetic research has been an important corrective, not necessarily because it has all the answers its proponents claim to have, but because it forces us to reconsider simplistic environmentalist assumptions. Unfortunately, as of this writing, the corrective seems to be turning into another huge swing of the pendulum. At this moment behavior geneticists are excited by their own successes and, with some important exceptions, not

---

*Ainsworth also noted the tendency of some mothers to become more rejecting when dealing with a fussy infant, although it seemed to her that in the cases she observed the fussiness began with the mother's frustrating the baby. "In all of these cases there seemed to be a vicious spiral in which the baby's fussy demands exasperated the mother, who then overtly or covertly rejected the baby, who in turn responded to the rejection by anxiety and by increasing his demands. The mother's and the baby's anxiety seemed to be in a spiraling interaction." Ainsworth, 1967. See also Chapter 11.

[†]Van den Boom, 1988, 1993. Van den Boom notes that in Japan, where irritable babies usually end up classified as anxious-ambivalent, mothers tend to encourage a high degree of emotional dependence in their small children. If a factor like irritability should become involved, the mother is more likely to become inconsistent than totally cut off. In Germany, on the other hand, especially northern Germany, where irritable babies often turn out to be anxious-avoidant, early independence is highly valued. Thus the baby is more likely to face a total ignoring of his attachment-related signals.

yet ready to integrate an environmental view. Meanwhile, their work has struck a responsive chord in the culture.

Biological explanations of who we are have a compelling quality. They offer hard science rather than ambiguity; they circumvent questions of inner conflict or anxiety about self-worth; and they hold out the promise of an efficient way to deal with problem people like alcoholics, depressives, or children diagnosed with attention deficit disorder. According to Dr. David Comings, a medical geneticist at a Los Angeles hospital, interviewed for the PBS documentary *Medicine at the Crossroads* in 1993, "One could argue that up to twenty percent of the population has some type of genetic behavior problem." He envisions a time when one could send a behavior-problem kid "to the laboratory and find out if he has any of these abnormal genes."[48] (Then what?)

Biological explanations have become dominant in psychiatry where it is commonly assumed that moderate depression, relationship difficulties, neurotic anxiety, and other common emotional problems are based on malfunctions of the brain and nervous system, even though little evidence exists to support this view. Biologically based research into emotional problems now gets the majority of government funds, while research on psychological or sociological factors often suffers.[49]

The press is particularly susceptible to news of genetic breakthroughs (which make an easily grasped newspaper or TV story), and it often gives little attention to later withdrawals. As a result, the public is probably much more aware of claims that a specific gene was found to cause manic-depressive illness than the later retraction or that excessive drinking is inherited despite studies that indicate otherwise.[50] If the press reports that some human quality, like homosexuality, optimism, criminality, or anxiousness has a "genetic component," the public often assumes that this quality is inborn, when in fact, for most people who display it, the hereditary component may be very small.

In developmental psychology, biological determinism reached an apotheosis of sorts in April 1991, when Sandra Scarr, an old bridge-playing friend and intellectual antagonist of Ainsworth's from the University of Virginia, took the podium to deliver her presidential address to the Society for Research in Child Development. A behavior geneticist who had become interested in inherited differences as an undergraduate (when "I was told there were none"[51]), Scarr's central theme was that "being reared in one family, rather than another, makes few if any differences in children's personality and intellectual development."

Smiling, cheerful infants who evoke positive social interactions from parents and other adults seem likely to form positive impressions of the social world and its attractions. Infants who are fussy, irritable, and who receive negative or neutral interactions with their caregivers and others would seem less likely to form the impression that social interactions are a wonderful source of reinforcement.[52]

Citing recent studies, Scarr went on to emphasize that at every stage of development our genetic makeup more or less determines how people respond to us. Two toddlers from the same family get different responses from their parents because of their different inborn personalities. Children raised in poverty will receive more attention and encouragement from their teachers if they are spunky and intelligent. "Adults who are considered physically attractive by others are more likely to be chosen as dates and mates than others considered less attractive. Attractive adults are also more likely to be hired for jobs and more likely to be promoted on those jobs than their less physically attractive peers." Thus, the environment does not form us, we form it.[53]

This view does acknowledge that there are powerful influences at work within the family, but only in one direction: from child to parent. In the family Scarr portrayed, a parent's psychological makeup or his conscious efforts to adjust his caregiving to a particular baby's needs have little impact on the child's emotional development.

Such a major playing down of environmental influence has caused uneasiness in the field, because of the message it sometimes gives to the general public. Ever since Arthur Jensen used a genetic argument to oppose compensatory educational programs for blacks as a waste of public funds,[54] people have worried that the contributions of genetic behaviorists might be used to suggest that whole groups are poor, downtrodden, burdened with high crime rates, drug abuse, or family violence, because they've found their rightful genetic niche; that people are what they are and cannot be changed. Scarr does not endorse this view as applied to ethnic or racial groups, and her research with black adopted children has helped refute it. But for individuals within a group, she sees heredity as the primary cause for individual differences, including social class status.

In one of their papers, Bouchard's team quotes, with evident triumph, a pre-twin-study comment (1981) by psychologist Walter Mischel, a prominent behaviorist: "Genes and glands are obviously important, but social learning also has a dramatic role. Imagine the enormous difference that would be found in the personalities of twins with identical genetic endowments if they were raised apart by different families."[55] The implication of quoting Mischel this way was that their work had so obviously proved him wrong. But, in fact, Mischel was right: there are substantial differences. On the average, according to Bouchard's data, 50 percent of the personality traits displayed by identical twins reared apart are divergent.[56] But because the similarities have been so arresting—and so supportive of the inborn temperament theory—not much has been said about the differences or how they come about. Even less is said about the fact that the similarities may have been promoted by similar or parallel environmental experiences. Less still about evidence that temperament itself may not be immutable and may be altered by experience.[57] "They make generalizations about the environment," Cornell's Urie Bronfenbrenner protested at one point, "but don't analyze the data to determine what influence the environment had."[58]

For instance, many of the similarities in twins, to the extent that they do have an hereditary component, may represent the way a person with a certain genetic makeup develops when he has encountered a certain type of environment while growing up. What's more, it's not always the surface trait but the way it is manifested that is most critical in a person's life. What may be more important to the twin Jims and their families than the fact that they are both highly sociable men who leave romantic notes around for their wives to find is that they have both managed to develop a warm and secure connection with their wives. Where does this capacity come from? Attachment research suggests it evolves from secure attachment early in life—feeling loved, feeling that one's love is valued, expecting good things to come of close relationships, feeling good about oneself, feeling that one has the power to have a positive effect on another person. Is it not possible that both twins had such an early environment? A child who is endowed with great linguistic potential will barely learn to speak if not regularly spoken to by a certain age. That both Jims have a tendency to be demonstrably affectionate and that both men have the same unusual way of displaying it may owe a great deal to their temperamental makeups. But the fact that they are able to get to the point with another person where those traits can manifest themselves probably reflects similar secure attachment histories.

Also, although the two men may achieve similar scores on certain personality inventories, we don't really know very much about how they experience themselves or what they are like to be with in a relationship, since such in-depth analysis is beyond the capacity of most studies like this. We do know that both Jims leave affectionate notes for their wives to read; and yet these notes may have a different effect on the two women. One may feel that her husband is playful and secure in his love. The other may feel that he is too much like a puppy, maybe even a whipped dog at times, constantly wagging for affection. The notes, which she sees as emblematic of a nagging insecurity, could thus become a secret source of embarrassment or disgust for her, which she wouldn't mention in a superficial interview about her husband's qualities and habits.

Psychopathology raises similar questions. Some of the earliest of the twin studies found that when identical twins are raised separately and one is later found to have become schizophrenic, there is a 50-50 chance that the other will also be found to have become schizophrenic.[59] That is an extraordinarily powerful argument for genetic involvement, because only one person in a hundred normally contracts this disease. Such findings have largely discredited the once popular notion of the "schizophrenogenic mother" who drives her child crazy with interpersonal torments, such as the famous double-bind form of communication.* Indeed, it has so discredited that theory that many experts in the field are now scornful of the idea that parental influence can make any contribution to this condition.[60] But the fact that another 50 percent of those siblings—with an identical genetic makeup—do not become schizophrenic is an equally powerful argument for the impact of the environment. Finnish psychologist Pekka Tienari attempted to assess the genetic and environmental components by comparing adopted children whose biological mothers were schizophrenic with those who came from healthy families. The first group became disturbed at a much higher rate, suggesting a genetic component, but severe disturbance developed only among those children who were living in homes that were evaluated as emotionally dysfunctional.[61]

Consider again the case of the hand-washing twins. Many will take as the moral of their story that the twins' blaming of their mothers is wholly mistaken, that, in reality, they were destined to be compulsive neurotics from birth. This is clearly what Neubauer believes: "Neither the mother

---

*For example, the parent invites the child to openly express a courageous opinion and then disparages it. Or the parent says, "I love you, darling," with hate in his eyes. The child feels entrapped by this form of communication, unable to react in any direction. How can you hate a mother who loves you? How can you love a mother with those eyes?

who was compulsive nor the one who was slovenly made any difference in the eventual behavior of their sons."[62] But even behavior geneticists will generally agree that the environment can play a critical role in bringing inborn predispositions to flower; so what else can we say about the origins of the twins' condition?

The most economical explanation for their similarity is certainly genetic. Their genes may have dictated both how much stress it would take to push them over the edge, as well as what symptoms they would display once they got there. But what was the stress? The stress that the first twin met up with may well have included an adoptive mother who coincidentally had the same symptoms to which he was prone in full flower. How might an obsessive-compulsive parent, who insists that every knickknack be kept in its inviolable place, affect a child? In all likelihood, she cannot tolerate the child's natural messiness, she reacts with disgust when his hands or face are dirty, she makes changing a diaper an ugly necessity rather than a playful and sensual exchange, with loving pats, nuzzles, and kisses. The child's cheerful smiles and other efforts to engage her get cut off because she is easily distracted by a dirty sleeve, a sock half off, or sticky hands. Although she may love her baby very much, her behavior has a rejecting quality to it. And it continues that way, into toilet training, room cleaning, playtime, and dinner manners. Eventually, the young child feels that he himself is dirty and shameful and must constantly be hiding, disguising, and cleaning away the evidence of who he is.

Avoidant attachment would seem a plausible result. We've seen that avoidant children often seek something to focus on in order to keep their attention away from attachment concerns. They are able to stay in proximity to their mother if they are concentrating on a toy or a coloring book. Extreme avoidance would thus seem to provide a natural pathway toward obsessive preoccupations. If the child has an obsessive-compulsive predisposition, the stress of a relationship with an obsessive mother might push thus him in that direction, causing him to take on his mother's concerns with a vengeance.

Now let's consider his brother, raised in an antithetical environment. A mother who is an "absolute slob" is not necessarily rejecting. A messy mother can be loving and consistently responsive, and her messiness need not get in the way of secure attachment. But something in the second twin's experience caused his genetic weakness to give way. It could have been that he falls into the small minority of the population who will become psychologically disturbed in almost any environment. It could have been a cruel and authoritarian father or an excessively rigid or rejecting nanny. Or the young man could have been right in assuming that in some way his slovenly mother played a part.

A slob may not only be slobby about material things. She may be as neglectful and forgetful of the baby as she is of the dishes, the clothes, and everything else. She may not be able to provide the baby with the feeling that he is contained in a secure and well-managed environment —Winnicott's "holding" environment—which gives him a sense of safety and regularity and which enables him to build his own steady rhythms. Again, she may love her child very much, but her behavior is the essence of neglect. Not feeling securely held and contained, the child's own impulses, feelings, and bodily functions may feel overwhelming and out of control, and at a certain point he may find a "solution" to this problem in various forms of rigidity, especially if he is prewired to respond to unbearable stress in this fashion.

Messiness may also grow out of an uncontrolled emotionality. In such a person, every feeling may run to excess in the way it is expressed and yet little is felt profoundly and even less is understood. She is scattered. She does not tune in well to those around her, being perpetually preoccupied with and perhaps fascinated by herself. Not being tuned in to or given a stage for his feelings, the baby's feeling side may never have a chance to develop. Indeed, he may rigidly contain his feelings in an effort not to be overrun by hers; he erects, in effect, an inner wall against her intrusions. He forms an avoidant attachment to her in part to hold on to his core integrity, to protect his vulnerable self from her impingements. The wall he builds takes the form of the rigid obsessiveness toward which he is genetically inclined.

None of this is to say that the hand-washing twins were not headed for some form of compulsive behavior regardless of the environment they came from or that it might not have taken extraordinary parental efforts to prevent it. But parental input should not be ignored. If one is genetically vulnerable to phobias, obsessions, or other disorders, parental input and the attachment style that follows may in many cases either dampen those proclivities or be the fuel that keeps a pathological disturbance burning. On the whole, one's first relationships would seem to remain a primary force in all those issues—whether you trust others or not, whether you anticipate love or rejection, whether you feel good about yourself as a person—to which attachment theory has drawn attention. Nothing in genetic research suggests otherwise.

New investigations, meanwhile, indicating that brain biology and even developing brain structure are sensitive to the earliest environmental inputs, may radically alter the terms of this debate. For there is growing evidence that very early attachment experiences influence some of those temperamental traits that were previously seen as genetic. We now know that the brain is rapidly organizing itself in the first months of life, and the latest research suggests that it does so in intimate concert with the responses it receives from the caretaking milieu. The baby's ability to regulate itself, especially in all those areas related to emotion, depends on parental attunement and empathy; and if the mother fails to attune to the baby emotionally, the baby's brain may exhibit lasting physiological deficits. These may show up early in the chronic dysregulation of a "difficult child" and later in various personality deficits.[63] All of this, obviously, raises major questions about what we have assumed to be inborn.

This is not to say that genetics are irrelevant. Far from it. And, attachment workers have been as guilty of ignoring (or giving lip service to) genetic influence as behavior geneticists have of disregarding the environment. And they certainly have done little to understand the minority of children who don't fall into the expected attachment category given the quality of care they received, or who don't show the expected behavior in later years to match the attachment group they belong to. Rather, there's been a too convient tendency to dismiss such anomalies as resulting from measurement error. (Ainsworth would eventually come to believe that she had been too rigid in rejecting the temperament view.) For these reasons, despite the frequent rancor and misunderstanding, the struggle between the two developmental camps seems to have been beneficial to both. In recent years, some behavior geneticists, like Robert Plomin, have become more interested in the *differences* between people with similar genetic makeups and the role the environment may play in their creation. Stella Chess is undertaking a major re-analysis of her data to determine the ways in which temperament itself, not just adaptation, can change. Meanwhile, the hard-core environmentalism that has often characterized attachment thinking has softened, as it has become more apparent that we bring certain qualities with us from birth and that those qualities influence how we respond to the world and how the world responds to us. Exactly what those qualities are, though, and how malleable they are, still demands considerable investigation.

22

A RAGE IN THE NURSERY:
THE INFANT DAY-CARE WARS

By the time Sandra Scarr addressed the Society for Research in Child Development in 1991, the blaming and defending of mothers had become a central subtext of the nature-nurture debate. In the 1970s and 1980s mothers were beginning to feel extraordinary pressures to provide optimal environments for their children. Like the mothers Stella Chess was concerned about several decades earlier, these mothers faced persistent and contradictory admonitions about how to raise healthy children. Only now, the desiderata had multiplied, and a new obsession had arisen over intellectually stimulating books, gadgets, and exercises for infants and preschoolers, the absence of which might condemn the child to a lower IQ and diminished opportunities throughout life.

The mothers of the seventies and eighties were also likely to have jobs. Vast numbers of them were returning to work within the first months or weeks of their baby's birth, in a social transformation of revolutionary proportions.[1] (By 1992, almost 54 percent of mothers with children under one were working outside the home, as compared to about 25 percent in 1970. As of 1990, according to one survey, over 40 percent of American babies receive their primary care from someone other than a parent—65 percent of them by a relative or neighborhood mother who takes in kids, 22 percent in commercial day-care centers, and 13 percent by nannies.) The new working mothers were particularly sensitive to how their absence might affect their babies, they were susceptible to guilt, and there was no lack of voices telling them what to do. Indeed, perhaps no debate in the history of the twentieth century's drawn-out conflicts on the proper ways to raise children generated more heat than that over working mothers and day care.* Once again, attachment theory was in the thick of it.

In her 1984 book on the subject, *Mother Care/Other Care*, Scarr, who had herself raised four children while working, attempted to debunk the idea that a mother was uniquely important to a child and that any disruption of the bond between them might be ruinous to its future well-being. She objected to the notion that a baby had a special need for its biological mother; that the best thing for a baby was an exclusive relationship with its mother, undiluted by other attachments; that mothers are somehow better equipped than fathers or other caregivers to tune in to the infant and its needs; that the ideal mother finds "passionate personal fulfillment in fulfilling the needs of her child."[2]

Much of this Scarr intended as an attack on Bowlby and Ainsworth, neither of whom believed any of these things (with the exception that Bowlby did see women as naturally better than men at child care[3]). But such ideas were in the air, and they arose with ever more ferocity as the debate over day care heated up.

> Why should working mothers feel guilty or deprived? [Scarr wrote.] Working mothers spend four to six hours a day with their babies, rather than all eight to twelve of the baby's waking hours. Are they missing significant developmental phases? Should they "suffer" from being away part-time from maternal responsibilities, if they also have paying jobs that are important to them and to the rest of the family? Why the guilt trip? Working mothers spend as much time as nonemployed mothers in direct interaction with their babies. What are they missing, except redundancy?[4]

---

*The new preferred term among many experts is "child care." The two terms are often used interchangeably now.

Developmental research, including attachment research, contributed to the defensiveness that many mothers felt. It was not just that the studies, in keeping with population norms, spoke continuously of the impact of the mother and failed to adequately emphasize that the father could also be the primary caregiver, but, perhaps more important, they neglected to speak of the huge impact of the father even if he was not the primary caregiver. It sometimes seemed as if there was only one parent in the two-parent home, only one whose influence counted, and that the other one, the father, did not really have to concern himself much with the parenting role or the lasting effect he was having on his children.

This problem was aggravated by a conservative political movement that wanted women to stay at home with their babies but rarely considered what it might mean for them to do that. What do you do if you are a single mother (as over 22 percent of mothers now are)? What do you do if, like a woman I saw in therapy, you bought a house just prior to an unexpected pregnancy, and two salaries are essential to meeting the mortgage? What do you do if you are a lawyer or a Wall-Street analyst or a professor on a tenure track? Will you be able to get your old job back? Can you opt out of all the competitions and let your peers walk past you? What does a psychotherapist or internist do with all his or her patients? Ask them to come back in a year?

Feeling burdened by this insensitivity and attacked by those who believed that their absence from the home undermined the family and scarred their children, working mothers felt obliged to justify themselves. Some legitimately cited studies that demonstrated the benefits of day care or the fact that, for many women, work is an important ingredient of their self-esteem and a protective factor against depression.[5] As Scarr wrote, "some women at home full-time are lonely, depressed, and not functioning well" and "high-quality day care settings have in fact been shown to compensate for poor family environment."[6] Other day-care advocates went further, denouncing housewifery and full-time motherhood as indentured servitude. Mothers who stayed home felt humiliated by such attacks. And they felt left out by a swiftly changing culture, one in which virtually every article in women's magazines on family matters was now addressed exclusively to working women. Some argued that child care was not a sacrifice but a pleasure, and, for all its hassles, a peak experience they wouldn't miss. Others joined the attacks on working mothers with appeals to biology and tradition, sometimes showing insensitivity to those mothers, often single and without extended-family support, who had no choice but to work. Soon, it seemed, both sides were debating more and more with the extreme wing of the opposition and seeing themselves as oppressed and abused.

Throughout the 1970s psychologists attempted to compare children in day care with children reared entirely at home, but there were so many confounding variables that it was hard to draw conclusions. The findings were at times contradictory, with some studies showing that day-care children were more positive and less tense in social interactions and had better relationships with peers, while others showed that they were less cooperative and more aggressive. Jerome Kagan reported no difference in separation anxiety between children raised at home and those who had day care. What's more, the day-care children in his study played more easily and with less apprehension in a strange environment than those raised at home (which, opponents argued, may have been simply because they were more used to doing so). The mothers of day-care children found them more patient and less shy with strange adults.[7] Research by Mary Blehar, a student of Ainsworth's, indicated that day-care children cried more and showed more anxious attachment, but her study had some methodological shortcomings and was not confirmed by later research. Other attachment researchers, like Jay Belsky and Mary Main, had found no problem with day care, and, indeed, Main had found that whatever problems children first display diminish the longer they are in day care. There was one important caveat: For children under three there was some concern about anxious attachment; but this had not been definitively shown.[8]

In almost every case it was difficult to make generalizations or be sure of what a finding really meant. Were the day-care children in some studies more secure or did they simply look that way because they'd had the opportunity to develop their social skills? Were personality differences in the children a reflection of their differences in daytime experience or a reflection of the fact that mothers who tended to put their babies in day care were different from those who did not? If children with extensive day-care histories displayed a higher rate of anxious attachment in some studies was it because, as Sroufe suggested,[9] repeated early separations made them more vulnerable to inadequate or inconsistent parental care at home? Or was it a reflection of the fact the children in day care were more likely to come from financially stressed and unstable homes?

Then too there were such vast differences in the nature and quality of the child care that using a single term to describe all the variations seemed pointless. There was part-time and full-time care. There was day care in a family setting, with just a few other toddlers, and day care in a large facility. There were situations in which the child had a specific caregiver assigned to him, which provided him with many of the benefits of an attachment figure (assuming the person stayed), such as comfort and security when he was stressed, and those—far more numerous as it turned out—where he had no special person, where he felt lost and uncared for, and where he was at the mercy of bigger, more aggressive children whom he would eventually succumb to or emulate.[10] There were facilities with high staff turnover and facilities where the staff was stable. The ratio of caretakers to children ranged from a handful, some-times a large handful, of toddlers to a single adult—who had to spend so much time managing, controlling, and disciplining them that she had little time for loving or stimulating interaction—to the caretaker who handled as few as two or three babies at a time. (There was also the nanny, sitter, or housekeeper who came into the home where the child lived, who, in effect, served as a substitute mother, and who was often found to be more stimulating and responsive and less controlling than the mother herself. But this option, which Scarr herself had used,[11] was not normally considered under the heading of day care, which had essen-tially come to mean "group care.") And then, of course, there were chil-dren entering care at different ages. None of the studies attempted to assess the mother's emotional state, her feelings about leaving the child each day, or the quality of her home life, all of which would naturally have an impact on the child and on her relationship with him.[12]

To complicate matters further, numerous studies were flawed. For one thing, many of them used the Strange Situation, often in modified form, to look for evidence of insecurity in children two or older. But, as Brian Vaughn noted, the Strange Situation had been designed for one-year-olds, the idea being to put them through a series of stressful separations to see how their attachment system manifested itself. There was no evidence that the procedure had any validity for assessing quality of attachment in children over twenty months old, who were presumably much better able to withstand such short separations.[13] Other researchers, meanwhile, had modified the Strange Situation in ways that may have destroyed its use-fulness; some had (incredibly) used it in the child's home where short sep-arations from mother are common and thus unlikely to stress the child; and still others had resorted to the meaningless task of counting behaviors rather than using Ainsworth's carefully constructed scales.

The only two studies that used the Strange Situation as it was intended did find more anxious attachment in those children who had begun day care before their first birthdays.[14] Indeed, in Vaughn's 1980 study, 47 percent of these children were anxiously attached, and all of them were avoidant, the form of insecure attachment associated with an inaccessible or unavailable mother.

Nevertheless, when the two major surveys of the day-care literature were written—in 1978 by Jay Belsky and Larry Steinberg, and in 1981 by Michael Rutter—the authors seemed justified in concluding that high-quality day care did not compromise the child's bonds with the parents or appear to pose any serious risks. Thenceforth, Belsky in the United States and Rutter in Great Britain were widely cited as having given day care the green light. Both authors had raised important caveats, however, which were frequently ignored. Rutter, for instance, wrote that while the risks of day care had been "greatly exaggerated in the past," it did raise some questions. There was some concern, at least for a minority of children, that day care for the very young child could lead to emotional disturbance. There was also some indication that day care caused behavioral change, sometimes for the better, but not always. Both he and Belsky were careful to point out that whatever we knew about day care was the result of relatively crude research—day care versus home care—that paid no attention to the many variables in quality and quantity of care. Finally, and perhaps most important, virtually all of the studies had been done in high-quality, university-based centers that had little relationship to the day care that was available to the average person, which was almost universally of a much lower, even dismal, quality, with lower staff ratios, high staff turnover, poor training, and more cramped conditions. The research had, in effect, been conducted in an ivory tower. It was unrelated to the choices facing most parents.

While the evidence was by no means certain, opinions were. Many were opposed to day care in principle and assumed it had lasting deleterious effects. Bowlby was especially wary of separating mother and baby for long or repeated stretches before the age of three, and wished to see a campaign, equivalent to the surgeon general's crusade against smoking, to convince parents that day care was bad for their babies. His concerns were exaggerated as they were picked up and spread by others of a more dogmatic frame of mind.

Meanwhile partisans on each side were carefully selecting quotes and partial conclusions from the research to bolster their own arguments, such that academic work was being picked over by cultural advocates and journalists with an angle for bits and pieces to use as ammunition. When I published a lengthy article in *The Atlantic* on attachment theory in 1990, which assessed some of the debates on day care without forming any firm conclusions, the founding editor of the magazine *Working Mother* wrote a letter to the editor of *The Atlantic* denouncing Bowlby, Ainsworth, and the magazine for claiming that mothers shouldn't work and used an out-of-context quote from Rutter as proof that day care had been given a clean bill of health.[15] A similar distortion was made by the other side, who, in Belsky's words, take any evidence that certain kinds of child care may be deleterious for certain children, and proclaim, "Aha, this demonstrates that only mothers can care for babies, that day care is bad and we shouldn't have working parents."[16]

In Britain, the great sinner from the pro-infant-day-care, feminist perspective was, of course, John Bowlby, who remained obdurate on the issue and seemed unconcerned about whom he offended. "This whole business of mothers going to work," he said, "it's so bitterly controversial, but I do not think it's a good idea. I mean women go out to work and make some fiddly little bit of gadgetry which has no particular social value, and children are looked after in indifferent day nurseries. It's very difficult to get people to look after other people's children. Looking after your own children is hard work. But you get some rewards in that. Looking after other people's children is very hard work, and you don't get many rewards for it. I think that the role of parents has been grossly undervalued, crassly undervalued. All the emphasis has been put on so-called economic prosperity."

Bowlby believed that "an affectionate, stable person who will act as a substitute mother over a period of years"—the nanny—is an appropriate solution for women who preferred to work or who could not afford to interrupt their careers. But finding someone to fill that role is no longer so easy. Especially if she is expected to stay until the child is old enough to leave home, which Bowlby saw as important—because otherwise the child would be struck with a traumatic loss. "You get a nice girl who stays a year or two and then moves on; this is very, very bad."

Even many of his own followers would part company with Bowlby over the contention that the full-time nanny becomes the primary attachment figure, supplanting the parents in the child's affections; while the idea that she must stay till the child is grown and leaves home strikes others as preposterous. As Alicia Lieberman says, "Normal parents cherish their babies more than anybody else can cherish them, and this passionate commitment is recognized and responded to by the baby. [It] is not lost just because they may spend the day apart."* Virtually every working parent knows the truth of this. But that the nanny is still an important figure to the child, in many cases an attachment figure, and that her early loss or abrupt replacement can sometimes be traumatic would find little argument.

"You see, I'm all in favor of mothers' having assistance," Bowlby told me, "the more assistance the mother gets, the better. My wife was the chief carer for our four children, and we always had a girl, a university student, and we didn't expect that girl to stay. That worked out well, because they were just assistants, they were never playing a major part in a child's life."

If a child was not going to have a long-term nanny and if the mother was going to remain the main caregiver, Bowlby believed she should not work at all during the first few years. For mothers of older children, Bowlby was more flexible than many people realized. "A child of three can make use of a nursery class, nine-thirty to three-thirty even—that's maximum."[17] But then he felt it was essential for the mother to be home at 3:30 when the toddler returned. This, of course, meant part-time work, at best, during the preschool years and perhaps for several years thereafter.

Such views made Bowlby a household name in Britain all over again, but more of a demon now than a saint ("the notorious Dr. Bowlby," as one female journalist wrote[18]). In the United States day-care advocates saw the culprit as psychoanalysis in general (for placing so much emphasis on the mother-child bond) and attachment theory in particular (virtually unheard of before). Then, in 1986, the demon's horns were passed to Belsky.

Jay Belsky is a dynamic, witty, bearded man with a warm smile and substantial presence, some of which comes from his command of the data, some from his power with language, which barrels out of him in whole paragraphs of tanklike intensity. Belsky had studied developmental psychology in the mid-seventies at Cornell, where he first read Ainsworth,

---

*"There is a great deal of research regarding children in the kibbutz," Lieberman says, "showing that these children are preferentially attached to the parents rather than to the metapelet (or caregiver). My own clinical experience and observations of normal children in child care arrangements indicate that whenever the parents are adequately emotionally invested in the child, *they* become the preferred attachment figure even if the child spends eight to ten hours a day with someone else." (Personal communication, September 28, 1993.)

whose writing he found refreshingly clear and direct. Despite the mild resistance of his mentor, Henry Ricciuti, who saw attachment as a spent force by that time, he was drawn to her ideas. He considered himself a hard-core empiricist, however, and, believed, with Michael Lamb and others, that there were "serious limitations" in Ainsworth's Baltimore study. He determined that when he had the chance he would do larger-scale replications of her work in order to test her fundamental assumptions about the origins of attachment differences.

As a young professor at Pennsylvania State University, Belsky proved that he was not only energetic, fast-working, and prolific, but that he was an excellent proposal writer who could pull in large grants. He quickly had several huge longitudinal studies under way. Having studied with Urie Bronfenbrenner at Cornell, he brought to this research some of Bronfenbrenner's interests in the broader family and social context in which the mother and child live. Thus, Belsky was the first to evaluate the impact of the marital relationship on the baby's attachments.

Although Belsky had not been mentored by any of the major attachment figures or by their students, in a remarkably short time he became an attachment figure to be reckoned with himself. This was a notable accomplishment, especially when one considers that in attachment circles, as in other academic coteries, genealogy—who studied with whom and for how long—can sometimes play an excessive role in the accordance of both respect and cooperation. But Belsky was not to be put off. "He runs a big shop, with a lot of graduate students, and he cranks out a lot of data," says Jude Cassidy, also at Penn State, although across campus in another department. "You can't write an attachment paper today without quoting him, because he has a lot of the basic data for whatever case you're trying to build."[19]

In his 1978 day-care review, written at twenty-six when he was barely out of graduate school, Belsky had been critical of the Strange Situation, but reversed himself after Sroufe alerted him to the Minnesota studies, just then coming out, which suggested strong predictive validity for the Strange Situation classifications. Belsky immediately capitulated, and Sroufe was disarmed. In his next letter to Belsky he wrote: "It was a rare experience for me to get an open response to a critical message. You are in a very small group of academics who have the ability to honestly change their position (that is, without pretending that they haven't). I think this bodes well for your career."[20] This comment would prove to be perversely prophetic.

A leading commentator on day care, Belsky wrote and spoke frequently on the issue, his outer-borough New York accent and spirited, rapid-fire speech becoming known to a variety of audiences, including the United States Congress in 1984. As a result of his expert status, he was constantly having to evaluate new evidence, some of it suggesting that group child care might be more of a problem, especially in certain situations, than he had believed before. The new data, all of it related to children who had begun extensive care—more than twenty hours a week—in the first year, described preschoolers with higher rates of avoidant attachment; first-graders who were more difficult, argumentative, and aggressive—hitting, kicking, swearing, shoving; and nine- and ten-year-olds who were seen as troubled by their peers—in other words many of the sequelae of anxious attachment found earlier by Sroufe.[21] Although at least one of the new studies was clearly done with children who had inferior day-care experiences, another had studied children with high-quality care, while others were mixed.

"There was a slow, steady trickle of evidence," Belsky told me. "I would acknowledge the disconcerting evidence and, like everyone else, I would explain it away. In fact, I had this lovely correspondence with a psychologist named Judith Rubenstein. In 1981 she and Carolee Howes found that kids with infant day-care experience threw more temper tantrums, had more fears and that kind of thing. And they argued in their work that these kids were having difficulty negotiating the developmental task of autonomy. I wrote about it, but I wasn't willing to embrace it, because I felt at that point there wasn't enough data to substantiate it. I was saying, Judith, I think the data are interesting, but, in the face of other data, these aren't enough to turn me around."[22]

In 1985 Belsky was preparing to give a talk at the University of Minnesota, outlining his thinking on day care and about the new data that were continuing to trickle in and cause him to scratch his head. "All of a sudden I realized, what am I spending all this time explaining away every piece of disconcerting evidence? A lot of energy was going into explaining away data, and every year there's more explaining away to be done."[23] At that talk and at the next one, before the American Academy of Pediatrics the same year, he voiced a concern. The data were suggesting to him that more than twenty hours per week of day care in the first year placed a child at a somewhat increased risk for anxious attachment and future behavior problems, with the child tending to display aggressive and noncompliant behaviors between the ages of three and eight.* There were caveats, however. Some of the findings were based on community day care, which was mainly low quality. The data could be reflecting the fact that families who tend to put their children in extensive day care in the first year are under more stress than families who don't, and those stresses rather than the day-care experience itself could have been causing the anxious attachment. There could be other confounding variables as well. Nevertheless, there was cause for concern. The distinguished Yale developmentalist Edward Zigler, who was in the audience, told Belsky he had come to a similar view, and asked him to contribute a chapter to a new book he was editing on the parental leave crisis.

Also in the audience was the associate editor of *Zero to Three*, the bulletin of an organization by the same name that reports on childhood issues to policymakers. The editor asked Belsky if he would write up his new thoughts for them. He was reluctant, partly because he considered *Zero to Three* to be a marginal publication and was unaware of the prominence the organization and its newsletter had achieved both in the professions and in government. "At the time, I had a piece under review at *The American Psychologist*"—the flagship journal of the American Psychological Association—"and I begged off. But she was very persuasive, she said, Oh, come on, and I finally agreed to do it."[24]

The article that Belsky wrote for *Zero to Three* was an excruciating exercise in walking on eggs. He began by talking about the huge variety of day-care options and how difficult it was to draw conclusions about the institution as a whole. He discussed how emotionally charged the issue is and the warnings he'd received against saying anything negative. He carefully stated that no irrefutable conclusions were possible, that someone looking at the same evidence might justifiably see it differently, but that "a relatively persuasive *circumstantial* case can be made that early infant care *may* be associated with increased avoidance of mother, *possibly* to the point of greater insecurity in the attachment relationship, and that such care *may* also be associated with diminished compliance and

---

*Belsky chose the figure of twenty hours because that was the way the available studies were structured (i.e., "under twenty hours" vs. "over twenty hours" per week). But clearly there is a vast difference between a baby's being in group care, even poor group care, four hours per weekday and a baby's being in group care, even good group care, eight, nine, or ten hours per weekday. And yet, strangely, this overly encompassing hourly range has not figured prominently in the debate; few have complained that day-care experiences of twenty or twenty-five hours a week should not be lumped in with whole days away from the mother without a stable and available substitute figure to depend on. I suspect this is so because supporters of early infant day care are usually concerned about the needs of full-time working mothers who usually require the longer hours.

cooperation with adults, increased aggressiveness, and possibly even greater social maladjustment in the preschool and early school-age years." (Italics are all Belsky's.) He even went so far as to allow "that my *gender* and the more or less *traditional* nature of my *family structure* could bias my reading of the evidence."[25]

At this time it was not at all difficult to find pediatricians and developmental psychologists who were openly critical of infant day care, and who did not couch their message as carefully as Belsky had. Urie Bronfenbrenner, who was opposed to most day-care options as they currently existed, had said, "You can't pay for an irrational commitment, and yet a child needs that. He needs somebody who will not just be there certain hours and then say, 'I'm off now, I work nine to five.'"[26] But neither Bronfenbrenner nor any other day-care critics had endured the onslaught that Belsky was about to suffer.

"As far as I was concerned," Belsky recalls, "*Zero to Three* was nothing, who was going to see it? But it ended up on every congressman's desk because ZERO TO THREE knows how to play the Washington game. And then it ended up in the *Wall Street Journal* as a big story." According to Eleanor Szanton, the executive director of ZERO TO THREE, "This was definitely more controversial than anything we'd ever published."[27] Emily Fenichel, the editor who had invited Belsky's contribution and found it quite moderate before publication, remembers thinking afterward, "Oh, my God, what have I done?"[28]

Belsky's article was political dynamite, for it represented an important reversal by an iconic figure. The person who had reassured the public that day care was okay now warned of risks. The risks were only for extensive day care begun in the first year, but the warning was perceived as a crack in the wall of the day-care defenses. Later that year Belsky reported his own day-care study that showed higher avoidant attach-ment among early day-care babies, thereby confirming his belief in that warning.[29]

In the political climate that existed at the time, and still exists, such a warning is not merely the statement of a scientist evaluating new evidence. It was taken as a political move. In a subsequent issue of *Zero to Three* four prominent developmentalists teamed up to rebut Belsky, accusing him of the selective use and misinterpretation of data.[30] In an additional rejoinder Stella Chess reflected the underlying political anxieties when she wrote: "An unsupported dictum that such day care is a 'risk factor' can only cause unnecessary guilt among working mothers and provide ammunition for the many elements in our society who are hostile to the idea of spending public funds sufficient to provide good day care facilities for all young children."[31] Belsky, a supporter of better day-care options for all ages and a believer in the value of day care for many children over age one, was stunned by such attacks, as if a scientist should not report an uncomfortable truth. What good are we doing mothers, he asked, if we tell them full-time infant day care is okay if it turns out that it isn't?

The *Wall Street Journal* article appeared in March 1987. In it the noted developmentalist Tiffany Field characterized Belsky's views as "bunkum." Sandra Scarr dismissed them as part of a "backlash against the women's movement." She said: "The advice for women has always been to get out of the work force. This is just another way of saying the same thing."[32] The intensity of feeling surrounding the issue was such that ZERO TO THREE organized a "summit meeting," chaired by Edward Zigler, to try to get the opposing sides to speak to each other and at least hammer out some minimal basis for agreement. The research guidelines that emerged from that meeting were adopted by the National Institute of Child Health and Human Development for use in a major collaborative research project on infant day care that continues to this day. But the quarrels and polemics would not die down.

At a conference at the University of Virginia later that year, Scarr, who was quoted as saying that infant social and intellectual development is rendered nearly invulnerable by biological design,[33] ridiculed the idea that early day care was worse than later day care: "If parents had to choose a time to take off a few months to be with their babies, for the baby's benefit, it would not be the first few but the end of the first year and any time in the second year." Before that, she told the *New York Times*, children's "brains are Jell-O and their memories akin to those of decorticate rodents."[34]

Belsky's opponents pointed out that many parents, due to financial necessity or lack of a spouse, have no choice but to put their babies in child care. So why denigrate it? Better to work to improve it. Belsky responded that he was all in favor of improving it but meanwhile what-ever risks there may be should be known, especially to parents who do have choices. Such parents, he said, may be "trying to decide whether two incomes are absolutely necessary and whether it might be wiser to defer the return of the second parent (typically the mother) to the labor force until after the infant's first year," especially given the quality of day care currently available.[35]

As the controversy grew, the gray fell out of the picture. Belsky was no longer issuing a limited warning, he was blackballing all of day care. That spring Kagan was quoted as saying, "Ten years ago, I wrote a big book on day care that said essentially that 'Day care is safe.' When I read ten years later that suddenly day care is bad, it makes me symbolically cry. . . . No one can say day care is blatantly bad." Yale psychologist Deborah Phillips asked rhetorically, "Have we raised a bunch of thugs so far in day care?"[36]

In the furor that followed, one began to hear new things about Jay Belsky in psychology departments, in private conversations, and at conferences where developmentalists gathered. It was said that Belsky purposely sought out *Zero to Three* so that his anti-day-care message would have the maximum possible impact. In a caricature of his own earnest search for possible bias, it was said that Belsky, who was married at the time and whose wife stayed home to care for their two sons, then four and six, thought everyone should raise kids the way he did. Also, that he was opposed to women working and that he was antiwoman in general. Brian Vaughn's contention that the child experiences being left off at day care each day as a rejection was now wrongly attributed to Belsky as well.

"I constantly heard these comments," Jude Cassidy told me. "Jay Belsky says that if a kid is in day care he'll be scarred for life. Jay Belsky says that day care really screws up kids. Or Jay Belsky hates day care and says that day care is like death. As I say to my students, what Jay Belsky actually says is that the evidence at this point seems to suggest that if children in the first year of life are in day care more than twenty hours a week, it's an increased risk for insecurity. While at the same time noting that most babies in day care are securely attached, over 50 percent. It's just that the percentage for home-reared babies is better. Jay says: 'I believe that most day-care babies are secure.' But it gets translated as, Day care just stinks and if you put your kid in day care it's horrible."[37]

Belsky: "The interesting thing is, in the 1978 piece, when we essentially gave day care a green light, we made it very clear that we were talking about research on day care which was done on high-quality programs in universities and that therefore we didn't know anything about community day care. The fact that that work got publicized in the media as 'No risks for day care,' without the appropriate qualifications and caveats, nobody had any problems with that. That was a politically correct thing to say, so it didn't need caveats. When it came to politically incorrect things, even if you gave the caveats, it was as if you hadn't given them."[38]

It was not long before Belsky felt a shift in the atmosphere around him. "I was at SRCD [Society for Research in Child Development], the year after, 1987, in Kansas City. This was the first big meeting after this thing had broken. I have a fear that I'm going to be attacked, that I am the enemy. I could feel and hear the hissing. And I don't cow. I make my arguments and basically say, I'm not against day care, this is a scientific issue to me. I see Urie Bronfenbrenner, and I go over to say something. It turns out he's sitting with my biggest nemesis at that point, Sandra Scarr.

"I really want to avoid her, but Urie tries to make peace. So we start talking and Sandy starts to bait me on day care. I finally say to her, 'You know what I don't understand, Sandra? You're so certain that what I'm saying is absolutely wrong.' I said, 'To tell you the truth, I'm plagued with doubts. I called my argument circumstantial, I called it inferential. I'm not convinced of this. But you have no doubts.' She says: 'Don't play Hamlet with me, Jay!' So I figure, Hey, this is not the type of encounter I wanted, it's time to disengage. I say—and I'm just trying to be collegial in the worst sense of the word—I say, 'Well, Sandy, you know this has been an interesting discussion, we should have more of these, it's important to talk, you know.' I hate that kind of bullshit, but at that point I just wanted to get away. And Sandy says, in an angry voice, 'We don't have to talk anymore, you just have to figure out why you're so angry. Why are you so angry, Jay? Why are you so angry about all of this?'"[39]

Scarr, who does not recall this encounter and has been surprised to learn that Belsky found her such an antagonist (she notes that others dislike him more), did—and still does—believe that he had an axe to grind. If not, he would have reported the data differently, emphasizing the urgency of improving infant day care rather than "how can we make mothers feel guilty and stay at home."[40] But whatever happened at the SRCD and at similar meetings during this period, and however much Belsky may have invited it by dint of his own style—perceived by many as brash, cocksure, abrasive, even obtuse at times—there can be little doubt that he stepped on a raw feminist nerve and took a lot of heat for it.

"People say to me, How do you take it? They say, why'd you get involved in this? And the naive truth is, I had no idea. I had no idea that what I had to say was going to be that controversial."[41]

Even in the professional journals, where the debates were much more polite and well reasoned, Belsky sometimes felt he had become a target.

One of the most important articles replying to him, by Alison Clarke-Stewart in *The American Psychologist*, bore the title "Infant Day Care: Maligned or Malignant?," implying, Belsky felt, that he hadn't merely raised a concern about early day care but had smeared it. But Clarke-Stewart, who had dedicated her book on the subject to her son who "spent his first year in day care so that this book could be written," went on to offer a series of reasoned objections. She argued that critics of infant day care tended to overstate the degree of risk—her reading of the various studies placed the actual increased risk of anxious attachment at 8 percent (Belsky placed it at 10 to 15 percent, while some evidence suggests it could be as high as 22 percent); that the aggression and noncompliance seen in some children who had spent their infancies in day care might actually be a reflection of the increased independence that day care promoted; that insecurity with the mother did not necessarily mean a child who had many other relationships was altogether insecure; that, for children who were getting inadequate care at home or who had difficult relationships with their mothers, a daytime spent with a pleasant, competent caregiver could improve their chances for healthy development; and, perhaps most important, that the Strange Situation might not be the appropriate tool for assessing security of attachment where day-care children were concerned.[42]

The debate placed the Strange Situation back at the center of controversy. How could this brief, artificial procedure, some asked, measure the quality of an entire relationship? Belsky, who had himself initially doubted the validity of the Strange Situation, now found himself its most embattled defender. "This business about its being artificial is the dumbest scientific critique I have ever heard. Does anybody protest the cardiovascular stress test because it's artificial and short? Does anybody say that a thermometer can't work because it's a silly piece of glass with some mercury in it and you only keep it in your mouth for a couple of minutes? The issue here is not what it looks like, not its face validity, the issue is its empirical utility."[43]

In a recent paper written with Jude Cassidy, Belsky was able to show how consistent the Strange Situation has been in assessing the effects of various risk factors. "If you take the data on the Strange Situation, in terms of rate of insecurity first for kids who were abused, then for kids who have depressed mothers, then for kids who have early and extensive day care and then for just regular kids, you get this nice linear function." (Eighty-five percent insecure among maltreated children; 50 percent insecure among children with clinically depressed mothers; 40 percent insecure, on average, among children with over twenty hours per week of infant day care; 25 to 30 percent insecure among children in "low-risk" samples—that is, children from stable, middle-class homes with less than twenty hours of outside care.[44]) "And I make the argument, I say, You people who are so ready to call this an invalid assessment, you show me another developmental assessment of twelve-to-eighteen-month-olds that is this sensitive not only to variation in care, but to conditions that one would think would be greater or less risky. It's gotten to the point where the Strange Situation is like an IQ test; it's a procedure everybody loves to hate. And I think they hate it because it works and it tells them things they don't want to believe. What if we found that kids who went to day care were more likely to be securely attached? Would all these people be going nuts over the Strange Situation? Of course not."

Alison Clarke-Stewart, Jerome Kagan, and others, however, argued that because children in day care were accustomed to daily separations, they were less stressed by their mother's departure during the Strange Situation and so they cried less, played more, and were relatively unconcerned about their mother's return. To label such children avoidant was therefore a terrible misnomer. Belsky dismisses this argument much as Sroufe had dismissed earlier arguments that children labeled avoidant were actually more independent. "If you go to the 1983 *Handbook of Child Development*," Belsky says, "Alison Clarke-Stewart actually tables the data on this question by looking at how much kids in day care and not in day care cry in Strange Situation-like procedures. Her analysis clearly shows that there is no difference in the amount of overt distress shown by kids with and without day-care experience in these separation paradigms. That's her data that she's amassed. And yet, she has the intellectual audacity again and again to make the argument that these avoidant kids in day care are falsely appraised."

It wasn't long before Belsky had his own study up and running to test this proposition in an even more thorough way. "And we found no support for it. The avoidant kids with day-care history were not spending more time playing and were not less stressed than avoidant kids without day-care history. In fact, it was just the reverse. So that argument collapses. It doesn't stop people from using it, because, see, it's a political debate. The idea is to keep throwing darts, undermining Jay Belsky's arguments with these darts. It's a political dialogue, it's not a scientific dialogue."[45]

Some believe that Belsky thrives on controversy and wades in where others loathe to tread. ("I think he did ride this horse for quite a ways," an erstwhile supporter says.) It is impossible to miss the enjoyment he takes in presenting his data, being in the spotlight, smiting the opposition. When I asked University of Alabama psychologist Brian Vaughn why other people like himself did not get into trouble for their reports on the problems of babies in day care, he said, "How many of those people went on *Good Morning, America?*"[46]

Belsky's verve in speaking out has caused him to rush headlong into an area of acute female sensitivity. Many mothers find it agonizing to leave their children, especially if they are very young; they constantly second-guess themselves about their choices; and they feel jealous of the people who replace them during the day. Mothers like this do not want or need to be told that they may be harming their babies, especially by a man, especially one more inclined to hammer out conclusions than to tread gingerly or to soothe.

The contrast Belsky creates with the rest of his profession is stark. Other psychologists approach the day-care issue with a delicacy that borders on dread. "I'm a little leery these days of being put into the pigeon hole of being anti-the-advancement-of-women," a famous developmentalist says when I point out the care with which he chooses his words and the disclaimers that adorn his speech. "You're going to trap me," laughs another when I question her about her feelings regarding the quality of the debate that has taken place on this issue. I asked one researcher what he would do, given what he now knows, if he were a young man just starting a family. How would he feel about his and his wife's both working full-time through the child's first year? There was an extended silence. Then: "I can't answer that. I can't imagine myself as a young man."

"Well, what if a young couple should ask you your opinion: Should we try to work it out so that one of us can stay home during much of the first year? Would you say it really isn't that important?"

Another protracted silence. "No, I wouldn't have any opinion."

"You wouldn't have any opinion or you wouldn't have one for publication?"

"I wouldn't have one for publication."

I asked psychiatrist Peter Barglow if he thought that people censored themselves when talking about day care, especially if they have anything cautionary to say. "I think they do" he said. "The reason is one gets quickly bashed by people who are politically correct." When Barglow published findings about the risks of anxious attachment with nanny care, he himself was criticized "by feminist researchers" as well as by "some personal friends and colleagues." His wife, who was assisting him at the time, was warned by friends, "You can't say things like that."[47]

For his part, Belsky recognizes that he does not behave like the typical academic. He points out that his parents were not college educated. They owned a luncheonette in Manhattan's garment district where he worked for many years when he was growing up, and his family life was riddled with open conflicts more typical of a milliner's shop than a university department. "The last thing I ever envisioned myself being was a scientist or an academician. In many ways," he laughs, "the personality doesn't fit the job." But rather than brash or abrasive he prefers to see himself as a rugged individualist, someone "who's not willing to say all the right things," who doesn't play the "smile in your face stab you in the back" academic game, who doesn't see "achieving high levels of cohesion" as "the ultimate goal of intellectual discourse." Meanwhile, he believes that while growing up in a "high-conflict family" did not help him develop the correct personality for academia, it has enabled him to weather its storms. "I know how to fight back," he says, "and while it has been stressful, it's not obliterating, as it apparently would be to a lot of people."[48]

And yet "the day-care wars," as he calls them, have been costly. His reputation for the most part remains intact. He is still a professor with many graduate students, getting grants for big studies, prolifically published, and a member of the Multi-Site Day Care Consortium, the huge study sponsored by the National Institute of Child Health and Human Development that will hopefully get to the bottom of the day-care question in future research. But there has been a subtle change in his status as viewed by many of his peers. He is a known quantity now, a man with a flag, the wrong flag.

"What this whole thing has been is an effort to marginalize me, and it's been remarkably effective. By 1985, if I went to a child development meeting, I had lots of people coming up to me, wanting to talk to me, wanting to talk to me about my work, wanting to talk about their work. I can remember standing in a hallway and not being able to finish a conversation because of all the interruptions. I mean, don't get me wrong, I enjoyed it. Now I walk through a meeting like Hamlet's ghost. Nobody sees me, nobody comes up to me. I'm exaggerating—nobody I don't know, nobody who isn't a good friend of mine. I'm a pariah. I violated the Eleventh Commandment of Developmental Psychology—Thou Shalt Not Speak Any Ill of Day Care, whatsoever, ever.

"And I think the second good example of this is that my friend Larry Steinberg and I—he was the guy who co-authored the first day-care paper with me in 1978—we published a textbook two years ago. And you know at the beginning before the textbook came out, I said to the publishers, we should think about leaving my name off this book. They said, No, don't be ridiculous. Well, lo and behold, sales people walk in wanting to sell this book. And whose offices do they go into? Assistant professors, associate professors. And who are they? They're working females. 'I don't want a book by Belsky.' They show them what it has to say about infant day care, its reasons. 'I don't care, I don't want it.' In fact, it's gotten to the point where the sales manager has told them, 'Don't even bother pushing that book, you're just going to lose credibility.'" Belsky's next text, also a collaboration, did not have his name on it.

"Urie Bronfenbrenner said to me: 'You know, Jay, what you have to do is always make it clear, up front, that day care is here to stay and that you're not against day care.' I said, 'Urie, c'mon.' I was in the Soviet Union with him in 1983. I was amazed that everybody who got up and gave a talk on the Russian side had to start off with something about Marx and Lenin. I said, 'I'm not against day care, and if raising concerns is going to be taken as being against day care, let it be. We can't have a climate in which everybody kowtows.'

"The whole thing has opened my eyes to the nature of academia, and how low-brow it really is. How people can pontificate and just be so full of shit. I expected better out of academics, and I was probably naive in that regard. They're no different, I guess, from anybody else. But it really burst my bubble about what the academy was all about. When honest disagreements are not treated as things worth having, but as a battle between good versus evil—with the evil claiming to be good, as far as I'm concerned—that's been disappointing. You know, Wait a minute, we're supposed to be having an intellectual discourse here, we're supposed to be considering."[49]

*   *   *

Although few have come forward to say, Count me with Jay, Belsky's views are not considered controversial by most attachment workers, and even outside the attachment camp they are recognized by many as quite moderate. Meanwhile, he has won some admirers for voicing them. "I think Jay did the field and women an enormous service," says Arietta Slade, a clinical psychologist and attachment researcher at the City University of New York. "Because in subtle ways the women's movement has encouraged women to minimize attachment experiences during the child's early years. And that's very destructive. Mothers who leave their children for long hours each day often convince themselves that what-ever arrangements they came up with for their kids are just fine." Slade believes the 1980s were a damaging time for child rearing, because many working mothers overrode their best instincts in an effort to simplify an inherently difficult situation.

"It's hard for women to have a career and be a parent. Very hard. It's horrible that it costs money to have good day care, it's horrible that women don't have the same freedom that men have, it's horrible that you can't have it all and raise kids who still feel confident that there's going to be somebody there for them. But it's better to say it's hard and struggle with it than to say, Well, it feels hard but it's really simple and I'll just do what I need to do."[50]

Eleanor Szanton of ZERO TO THREE also believes that Belsky did the right thing, and despite the fact that he has not made many friends in psychology, others have been affected by his views. "It's interesting to see how people's minds have changed," Szanton says. "When I came into the organization in 1979, Selma Fraiberg, who was one of our founders, had just published *Every Child's Birthright*"—which urged mothers to stay home with their babies, opposing even part-time group care until the fourth year—"and she was persona non grata after that with the women's movement. The book was seen as a putdown of women and an effort to push them back in the kitchen. I think many people now— because of a combination of Belsky, and the tremendous upset with the quality of child care, and more women realizing that they can't do it all —are much more willing to listen."

Speaking of professional child care advocates like herself, many of whom were distressed and enraged by Belsky's original article, Szanton says, "I think everybody feels now that Belsky did a service. It has made policymakers at least begin to consider whether parental leave"—the bill finally passed into law in the opening months of the Clinton administration—"is more appropriate than they had previously thought. It's forced them to consider whether there should be more funds for better child care."

Also, partly because of the controversy Belsky stirred and, perhaps even more because of the tireless educative efforts of Berry Brazelton and others, there is a greater appreciation of the importance and delicacy of the infant period. "I remember meeting Senator David Durenberger [Republican-Minnesota] in the early eighties," Szanton says. "He was always a friend of child care. And I made a remark to him that infants and toddlers, of course, needed more expensive care, because the ratios" —of children to staff—"needed to be lower. And he looked at me and said, 'Why would that be?' He thought they just needed baby-sitting at that age. I think that mentality has begun to change."[51]

Lieberman elaborates: "The caregiver must have the time, the talent, the experience, and the training to learn to know a baby." That includes "treasuring this baby's most charming, endearing attributes," and helping the baby cope with potentially problematic aspects of its temperament. The fussy baby, she says, needs to learn to cope better with its fussiness, the shy baby needs to be encouraged to explore, the reckless baby needs someone attentive enough to build in safeguards.[52]

The real world of infant day care rarely provides this, at least not in the United States. As of 1992, day-care workers averaged $5.35 an hour, less than parking attendants and kennel workers, which would help account for the huge turnover rate (41 percent per year in 1988). Only three states set staff ratios that met ZERO TO THREE's hardly utopian standards (one to three for infants, one to four for children under three). Nine states still allow one caretaker per six infants; nineteen one per eight toddlers.[53] Meanwhile, few knowledgeable parents who could afford better would consider even the approved ratio of one to three for their own babies when they are first learning about loving relationships and whether people can be trusted. (Any mother who's cared for triplets can tell you why.) In recent years, study after study has found the quality of care in this country—in centers, with relatives, with the kindly neighborhood woman—to be wretched, humdrum, or barely adequate. In a major 1994 study of family day care by Ellen Galinsky of the Families and Work Institute, only 9 percent of the homes she rated were good, with 56 percent rated adequate/custodial, and 35 percent developmentally harmful.[54]

What Scarr said in 1986 still appears to be true: "Most families find it far easier to purchase quality cars and refrigerators than to buy good day care."[55]

Meanwhile, in academia, the day-care hostilities drag on. Belsky continues to be the man the media contact when they want a negative view, and he continues tracking the data. The trickle of evidence that disturbed him in the mid-eighties, he says, has now become a steady stream, adding ever more confirmation to his warnings. In a huge study of suburban Dallas families, psychologist Deborah Vandell, now at the University of Wisconsin, found that third-grade children who had had 30 or more hours of day care begun some time in infancy scored the lowest in emotional well-being, work habits, peer relations, and compliance (as assessed by parents, by teachers, by a child's self-report quiz, by peer evaluations of popularity, and other measures). Texas, it turns out, has some of the worst standards in the country for day care, so many of these children were probably in poor care. But Vandell found that the day-care effects held regardless of the income level, marital status, and race of the families involved. (Vandell had an arduous time getting this study published, more so than any of her other work, which surprised her, "because I'd never had such strong findings.")[56]

In a 1994 study, Jack Bates at the University of Indiana reported that the more day care a child has received (regardless of when it occurred) the more likely he is to display problematic levels of aggression at age five. Bates, too, studied children from all social classes and told me that there is nothing in his data "to suggest middle class families can be sanguine on this subject."[57]

Critics continue to point out that quality is the real issue. And they too can cite studies to bolster this point, many of them from Western Europe where the quality of care is typically beyond almost anything known in the United States, and where early day care was found in one study to enhance development. Belsky himself concedes now that if nonparental care for babies is good enough, there is no need for parents or society to be concerned, and he too favors a federal program that offers quality day care to all Americans, as well as subsidized parental leave. Where he differs from his critics is in his insistence in pointing out how far we are from having such care and how damaging it is for children when they don't get it. "Everyone says that kids need good quality care," Belsky argues. "But no one is willing to take the next step and point out that poor quality care is bad for kids—and that most care in this country is poor quality, so a lot of kids are possibly being harmed."[58]

Belsky's overall assessment of the data on day care remains complex and carefully qualified. Regarding timing of entry: "As I look at the most recent studies, the problem seems to be with extensive care begun in the first year and continued thereafter. So, it's really an entire infancy and early childhood of full-time or near full-time nonparental care. Twenty, thirty or more hours. If it's just the first year, the effect can go away." Regarding quality of care: "What kids need are stable, enduring, sensitive relationships. That's really what's critical here. And in American day care, especially in infancy, especially in the opening years, that's more the exception than the rule."[59] If children receive early and extensive high-quality care from a nonparental figure, Belsky sees no great cause for alarm—but the parents need to recognize that the alternate attachment figure may now count more prominently in the child's development. Belsky, meanwhile, speaks of day care versus "parental care" rather than "maternal care," in order to emphasize his belief—and the evidence of the research—that fathers can also be primary caregivers and that in terms of security of attachment children do just as well when fathers play that role.

"The real risk of early and extensive [day] care as we know it in this country," Belsky says, "is when risks accumulate. We get unstable care, turnover in care givers, poorly paid care givers who are unresponsive and impatient. We get parents who are exhausted at the end of the day who have no wherewithal to care sensibly for their kids. We have employers who have no tolerance for the fact that their employees are parents, too."[60] As these risk factors accumulate, the chance of anxious attachment rises.

To Belsky the idea that people should soft-pedal the facts about full-time infant day care because they may disturb mothers smacks of "yuppy narcissism." He was particularly upset by journalist Anna Quindlen's column in the *New York Times* after that paper reported the Galinsky study on the poor quality of family day care. Quindlen argued that mothers do not necessarily provide better care themselves, so perhaps we need not get all worked up about the quality of nonmaternal care. "My response," Belsky says, "is wait a minute! She's so busy taking care of the emotional needs of the mothers, she's forgetting about the kids. It's a good case of what I consider disseminating intellectual Prozac. We're going to regulate your anxieties here, not give you anything to worry about!"[61]

Belsky recalls the scathing 1982 federal report on the state of the nation's schools. "Nobody worried about making teachers and principals feel guilty. Nobody pulled punches when they found the schools weren't very good and that kids did badly in bad schools. And here we have a perfect parallel, and people won't acknowledge that care is bad. And even when they do, they don't tie it together, so that you come to a conclusion, like with schools, *a nation at risk*. If we were looking at any other issue, teenage pregnancy or cocaine use, the same statistics would be a cause for tremendous alarm. But when it comes to day care everything is explained away."[62]

Belsky recognizes that all of the data are based on correlations, and so it has to be remembered that while the findings may apply to some children, they do not apply to all. Indeed, the difference in rate of anxious attachment between day-care and home-care infants is small to moderate. Why some day-care children seem to be more at risk for anxious attachment no one can currently say, although it seems reasonable to assume that they face some other stress as well, such as a relationship with their parents that is otherwise only borderline-secure or a temperament that requires a higher level of nurturant attention. Whether there are subtler risks as well, affecting children who come out looking securely attached despite full-time day care begun in the first year (Do they move into a less secure subcategory? Do they develop a negative trait, style, or preoccupation that is not picked up in the Strange Situation?) is still unknown. The question has not yet been asked.

Bowlby approached the problem of working mothers and day care at the social level. He recognized that "career girls are placed in a difficult situation" if they miss too much time and wished to see the workplace restructured so that the choices facing them would not be so stark. "At the Tavistock, when I was the chairman, we had a very able woman psychiatrist who, when she had two boys, gave up work almost entirely for two or three years, and then we were able to arrange for her to do two half-days a week. She kept her hand in, she remained part of the department, and then, gradually, as the children got older, she came back. Unfortunately, this is not the way most employers operate. And I think it's a thousand pities."[63]

Bowlby did not defend himself against personal attacks, but Freda

Martin, a psychiatrist who worked with him, insists that, despite his reputation, "he was very supportive in the most practical ways" when faced with the problems of working mothers. "I can think of no other institution in the 1970s," she wrote in tribute to him, "where because the incoming Chairperson of a Department (myself) had young children, the time of the Clinic Professional Committee Meeting, by long tradition held at 4:00 in the afternoon, was altered without a murmur to 11:00 in the morning."[64]

That such options and adjustments are not available to most women may be reflected in a disturbing figure: 97 percent of male executives have children, compared to only 35 percent of female executives. These statistics seem to suggest that for some women succeeding in the corporate world means giving up having children. And, of course, those who do have children will have to give up their rearing to surrogates.[65] The business world, and our culture as a whole, does not yet take the process of parenting seriously enough to give mothers—or fathers—the flexibility they need to care for their babies without insufferable losses in their careers.

Bowlby was not insensitive to the argument that a mother who comes home happy and fulfilled is better for the child than one who stays home bored and resentful. But, despite the rage that swirled around him, it did not sway him much, because as far as he was concerned the children still suffered. Better to alter social thinking and expectations, so that women would naturally want and expect to stay home in the early years and have less cause for envy or resentment. When I told him that in the United States it had become virtually unthinkable for many women not to have a career—which under current circumstances does indeed pull them away from the home—he said, "Well, times change. I mean people don't smoke; they used to. I think women will realize that if they have children, then they have responsibilities, and if they want to have happy relationships with their children in later life, then it's important to do a lot of work with them when they're small. But I give it another twenty years."[66]

From his strong words and firm position, one could easily assume that he felt anything less than what he recommended would be harmful to every child—and perhaps at some gut level he did. But he acknowledged that studies showed that only a few children were likely to be harmed by extensive infant day care. According to Scarr, "Eight percent, if you believe that Alison Clarke-Stewart figure, is a very small difference. Is that the stuff of which public policy is made?"[67] To Bowlby it was. Indeed, what separated him from many of his opponents was how seriously he took the idea of five, eight, or ten additional children in a hundred becoming anxiously attached. "The proportion of people left with a crippling illness after polio is minute," he said. "But because we know that that is a risk factor we take tremendous precautions. Well, now we have ample evidence that certain types of experience in childhood are risk factors. Plainly, there is every reason to abolish those risk factors if you can."[68]

Ainsworth, a "career girl" herself, is more flexible about early day care, more open to the possibility that supplemental mothering can be arranged without harming the baby. "From the point of view of the child's general welfare, the mother should be pretty consistently available. That doesn't mean she has to be there every moment, can never go out, never have anybody else look after the child, or anything like that. But fairly consistently available. It's very hard to become a sensitively responsive mother if you're away from your child ten hours a day. It really is. Women's-lib people have been finding it comfortable to assume that it doesn't matter what you do and that a woman owes it to herself to work and do what fulfills her. People who focus primarily on the welfare of children tend to ignore what suits the mother. But it's really a matter of how do we adjust these two things. Had I myself had the children I longed for, I like to believe I could have arrived at some satisfactory combination of mothering and a career, but I do not believe that there is any universal, easy, ready-made solution."[69]

In recent years many attachment workers, Sroufe included, have noted the positive things day care has to offer, and, although wary of day care in the first year, they have come to believe that for toddlers and older children, even full-time day care is not only not harmful, but may, at least in the case of good-quality care—with high staff ratios, well-qualified workers, low turnover, and each child assigned to a particular caregiver—provide children with a range of stimulation and experience that promotes their cognitive and social development.[70] In other words, if done in the right way at the right time, day care can be a boon to the whole family. In this they are largely in agreement with Scarr, Kagan, Clarke-Stewart, and other day-care advocates.

The need for a balance between the unconditional love and support parents can give and the exposure to the outside world that group care can provide is captured in an observation by Urie Bronfenbrenner:

"It's good for a child to be in the company of people who are crazy about him for a substantial number of hours every day. I'm sure of that. But it is also good to be with people who are not crazy about him. He needs both kinds of experience. He needs some mothering, some father-ing, some day care, even some coolness toward him.... All of these needs must be met."[71]

There is much to consider for both sides in this debate. For those who are wary of infant day care it should be kept in mind that although the statistics may be on their side—the risks are higher—statistics do not determine the fate of any individual baby. More babies may thrive in home care, but some do fine in alternate care, while still others do better in day care than they would have done at home. Not every baby has the option of a willing, nurturant mom. To be home with a depressed mother who would rather be elsewhere is not a great thing, and studies have shown that a mother's satisfaction with what she is doing is a key vari-able in determining how well children do.[72] If her baby is taken off her hands for 30 or 40 hours a week, it may free her to be a better mother when they are together.

Parents need to know that it is possible for both of them to work, that they can put their baby in some form of high-quality nonparental care and still have an emotionally sound child. There does not seem to be a hard and fast rule, written into our genetic code, requiring that a baby be cared for full-time by its mother or father until it is a year old. Many par-ents, especially if they are at ease with themselves and their decisions, and many babies, especially if they have an easy temperament and an alternate caregiver who loves them and makes them feel secure, can maintain a solid relationship despite beginning extensive nonparental care at some point during the first year. Even in the studies of run-of-the-mill out-of-home care, 50 percent of the children seem to be doing all right.

But those who prefer not to worry about infant day care need to face some facts as well. Most infants, in order to feel that their love is recipro-cated, that they are valued and accepted, and that they are secure enough to happily explore the world, seem to need a lot of unhurried time with at least one person who is steadily there for them—preferably, as Bronfenbrenner says, with someone who is crazy about them. And for many babies that need may not diminish as quickly as we might hope. Because so much gets established in that early period, most developmen-talists, regardless of their public stance on day care, recommend that one parent spend some months at home after birth, and the number of months they recommend is often far less than what they would want for their own child.

Even under what might be considered normal conditions, it can take a lot of relaxed, deep-time familiarity to understand a baby's quirks and preferences; to know, for instance, that he's only rejecting his bottle because he wants his blanket first, or that he's willing to nap only if held in a tight, rocking embrace until he stops his struggling and cranky crying and drops off. If the child has a difficult temperament, or the mother, for whatever reason, has a hard time adjusting to the baby and reading its signals, or if she is simply slow to develop her confidence, the two will need long periods of time to get in synch with each other and become a secure pair.

It has been argued that anxious attachment to a mother or father might not be the worst thing for a young child, especially if he forms secure attachments elsewhere. But it is certainly not a happy development for the parent-child relationship itself. And because anxiously attached kids have a way of pushing their parents' buttons and resisting overtures toward change, a vicious cycle may set in that keeps the relationship from getting righted. What's more, in our primitive state of knowledge, we cannot be at all sure that anxious attachment is the only outcome to be feared.

Given all this, no parent can afford to listen to generalizations or make a decision based on ideological preference.

Since 1980 the major increase in working mothers with small infants has come among college-educated women. For many couples who can afford it—including most psychologists I know—hiring a nanny is a common solution. This option is rarely discussed because it is open to so few, but it is believed to be the least risky.

Nevertheless, a study of 110 families by Peter Barglow found a shocking correlation. When full-time nanny care began in the first eight months, it was associated with a much higher incidence of insecure attachment to the mother at the end of the first year—46 percent insecure, compared to 29 percent insecure among home-reared children.[73] This figure emerged, according to Barglow, under optimal conditions, with all the parents being "well-educated" and "deeply involved in parenting."[74] And yet the results are about same as what is typically found among babies in routine day care.

A six-year follow-up, reported in 1994, gave Barglow more cause for optimism. He still found "traces of adversity"[75] in the way nanny-reared kids related to their peers at age seven (unfortunately, the only variable he studied), but the percentage differences were small. This improvement could be understood in several ways. One, that nanny care in the first year has some built-in protective factor—such as secure attachment to the nanny—that was not assessed in the original study. Another, that sensitive and involved parents are often able to undo many of the ill-effects of early insecurity in the child-parent relationship. More than likely, it is a combination of the two.

My son, Raphael, was born during the writing of this book. My wife, Thaleia, a partner in a small architectural firm, stayed at home full time during the first year, with part-time care from a succession of baby sitters —who took him off her hands for several hours each day—and frequent help from me. By six months, we had a nanny coming in 30 hours a week. By the end of one year, Thaleia was more than eager to resume work, although she was prepared to adjust her hours, depending on the baby's reaction. When she started working about twenty-five hours a week at the beginning of the second year, we increased the hours of the nanny, who had become a valued person to the baby, not to mention us. Rafie thrived with this arrangement. At this age we still did not feel comfortable putting him in group care for the better part of each day— although, happily, he had plenty of children to play with in the building where we live and in the playground nearby. At age three he started preschool in the mornings and still had his nanny in the afternoons and all day in the summers. All in all, hardly an ideal Bowlbian solution— which Thaleia would have found unendurable—but closer to his model than some of the alternatives.

The political climate in academia has not always been helpful to parents struggling with such concerns. Not much is being addressed, for instance, to the parent who wants to hire help (what to look for in a sitter or a nanny, what to avoid) or be sure that a baby cared for at home has adequate peer interaction, because so much attention is focused on maternal care versus day care, with complex issues repeatedly reduced to slogans. What's more, it is difficult at this time for anyone who has negative things to say about early infant day care—and therefore working mothers, and therefore women's rights—to present the data in a straightforward fashion. They either soft-pedal the facts or leap on them with obvious ideological gusto.

In this atmosphere it is acceptable to favor a parent's taking several months off work after childbirth, as Berry Brazelton does, but to suggest a parent take a full year or more (as many in the field privately do) seems pointless, not only because one will be seen as crossing the line from supporting women to oppressing them, but because economic realities do not allow for that in the case of many families, and one must not seem elitist.

National politics also plays a role. It has been hard enough getting a family leave bill passed that allows mothers and fathers in large companies to take off twelve weeks (without pay) without losing their jobs; to favor the year or more of family leave that other countries have instituted has, until now, been seen as jeopardizing one's chances of getting anything.

Meanwhile, the position of the poor has become more precarious. Without going into what causes people to seek welfare, how many of them are cheating or unhealthily dependent, or what proportion are capable of being good parents if able to stay at home, the fact is that poor children, like all others, need the love of a dependable caregiver, and when their mothers work, they need high-quality alternative care. When poor single mothers are required to work without adequate provision for their children, as they are under recent welfare legislation, many children will suffer. There are no easy solutions to the problems of poverty and welfare, but whatever benefits are achieved by forcing single mothers off the welfare rolls are probably offset by the costs that society will incur as their children get older. Unless and until universal high-quality day care is available to American families, it will be in the best interest of society and probably more cost efficient, as well, to keep welfare mothers on the rolls and give those that need it yet additional support—educational, psychotherapeutic, medical, even financial—to help assure the secure attachment and healthy emotional development of their kids. (Of this, more in Chapter 27.) But there is not a politician in the nation who would say this or a government official who would entertain it.

Nor is this view adequately reported in the press. Journalists, too, are sensitive to the prevailing winds, and certain truths do not get spoken if they seem to violate correct thinking. When Public Television aired its documentary *Childhood* in 1991, a brief excerpt from René Spitz's landmark film on the ravages of maternal deprivation, which helped change the way a generation of child care workers looked at the needs of infants, was used as a passing illustration of the point that early researchers had gone overboard in their concern for the continuity of maternal care.[76] That maternal deprivation and early separation had proved a legitimate cause for alarm was not mentioned, presumably because the producers did not want to complicate their message that mothers should not be anxious about working. Because the topic has become so politicized, no parent can allow this decision to be made by experts. Mothers' needs are different, every baby is different, and there is a lot at stake.

23

ASTONISHING ATTUNEMENTS: THE UNSEEN EMOTIONAL LIFE OF BABIES

The loving mother teaches her child to walk alone. She is far enough from him so that she cannot actually support him, but she holds out her arms to him. She imitates his movements, and if he totters, she swiftly bends as if to seize him, so that the child might believe that he is not walking alone.... And yet, she does more. Her face beckons like a reward, an encouragement. Thus, the child walks alone with his eyes fixed on his mother's face, not on the difficulties in his way. He supports himself by the arms that do not hold him and constantly strives towards the refuge in his mother's embrace, little supposing *that in the very same moment that he is emphasizing his need for her, he is proving that he can do without her*, because he is walking alone.

—Søren Kierkegaard, 1846[1]

When Bowlby first began arguing in the mid-fifties that the infant had innate social capacities, that it was a primary actor in the creation of the relationship with the parent, his ideas met with little resonance among his peers. But in the early seventies, a new interest began to emerge for observing the infant and for analyzing the infant-mother bond. Over the course of the next decade, developmental researchers discovered that what had been widely considered a suckling blob was in fact a surprisingly social creature. They found that newborns by the eighth day are able to distinguish the smell of their mother's milk, and, if offered two breast pads taken from nursing mothers, would consistently turn to the one that came from their own.[2] In an ingenious experiment, newborn infants were given the opportunity to choose what to listen to by their rate of sucking on an electronically rigged pacifier. They invariably sucked at the rate that caused them to hear a recording of the human voice—and, if given a choice, selected their mother's voice above others.[3] It was similarly found that they prefer to look at the human face over other visual patterns. That they are able to distinguish among certain emotions on the face. That they are also able to distinguish between faces, and that by five to seven months they can recall a week later the picture of a face they were shown for less than a minute. This was far from the long-accepted "blooming, buzzing confusion" proposed by William James.

The presence of complex social capacities in the infant brought new interest in what Ainsworth had called maternal attunement. For it made sense that a sensitive and responsive presence was needed for the socially prepared newborn to develop into a truly social being. Winnicott had perhaps been most eloquent on this score, holding that the mother's ability to tune in to her baby was central to every aspect of its psychological development.

In timing with her baby, Winnicott believed, the mother (or primary caregiver) struggles to bring the world to him in understandable form. She gives him a sense of achieving what he is incapable of achieving on his own. By knowing what he wants and responding to it, she gives meaning to his cries and other signals, so that eventually he knows what he wants and learns to signal with intent. She puts words to his feelings. As the American analyst Heinz Kohut argued, the baby experiences her as an extension of his own self,[4] her assistance contributing to his sense of competence and keeping his still fragile self from being overwhelmed by the stresses and tensions that constantly impinge upon him. Her devotion, her ability to be intricately in tune with his wants, enables the infant to experience himself as the master of his world,[5] to feel quite confident and wonderful despite his helplessness, and to evolve a healthy sense of self. The sensitive mother figure also helps the infant to stretch his capacities by communicating with him at a level that is a little bit—but never too far—beyond his current abilities. She reaches down to his level while at the same time presenting him with opportunities to grow—responding to his nonsense syllables as if they had real meaning or encouraging him to walk for just a few steps without holding on.[6] A long period of intense and harmonious involvement with a sensitively attuned mother is, thus, essential to the baby's emotional health. She could be considered the lattice on which much of his psychology and mental organization develops. But aside from Ainsworth's Baltimore study and the attachment classifications that grew out of it, there was little empirical evidence to support this view.

Then in 1971, the year Winnicott died, Daniel Stern, a psychoanalyst and infant researcher who had been studying infant-mother interactions at the Cornell University Medical Center in New York, decided to slow down his film of infant-mother pairs and examine it frame by frame. He soon discovered finely synchronized behavioral patterns that no one in the field had quite attended to before. He saw, for example, one mother-baby pair after another play their own variation of an intricate dance of threat and delight he dubbed the suspense game. "I'm gonna get ya!" says the mother, over and over again, with rising intensity, her fingers perhaps marching up the baby's chest matching the rhythm of her words. "I'm gonna get ya!" she says with more threat, her eyes gleaming as she looks into his, her head shaking slightly from side to side. "Here I come, I'm gonna get you, yes I am!" as her hands form a threatening semicircle over his chest. And throughout all this, the baby coos and giggles with ever more glee.[7]

The microanalysis of film and video of infants and mothers engaged in such ordinary, everyday interactions was soon picked up by others — most notably Psychologist Edward Tronick, now chief of the Child Development Unit at Children's Hospital in Boston; Hanus and Mechthild Papoušek at the Max Planck Institute for Psychiatry in Munich; Berry Brazelton at the Children's Hospital in Boston; and Beatrice Beebe, at Yeshiva University in New York. The world of intricate communication they discovered in what had once been dismissed as rather charming but meaningless babble turned out to be as rich and unexpected as the universe of "cavorting beasties" that Anton van Leeuwenhoek observed when he put an ordinary drop of water under his newly invented microscope.

According to these researchers, infants and mothers continually engage in lengthy reciprocal exchanges, with the mother matching the infant's intensity and tempo, adding variations to elaborate the communication, and attending to the infant's cues, such as the desire to initiate an exchange with a coo or a gaze or the wish to terminate it when he feels he's had enough, often by turning away.

"I have videotape of me interacting with a six-week-old infant," Tronick says. "When I purposefully get too close, the baby narrows his eyes, looks off to the side and sort of purses his mouth. He won't look at me. I get even closer and the baby turns his head away. When I move

back, he starts to peek at me. I keep talking to him and move back a little farther. He makes eye-to-eye contact and, since he can't yet fully
smile, he gives me a sort of half smile. Then, when I come closer again,
he looks off to the side. The infant is not only responding, he is actively
behaving in a way to modify what I do. When I am too intrusive and fail
to respond to his signals, he turns away. When I am sensitive to his
needs, I am rewarded by his looking at me, smiling, and vocalizing—
behavior that would encourage me."[8]

According to psychoanalyst Louis Sander, like Ainsworth a pioneer in
the naturalistic observation of mothers and infants, one of the crucial
results of such nicely synchronized exchanges is that the baby learns to
regulate himself—biologically at first, in the form of regular patterns of
sleeping, eating, and eliminating, but gradually on a psychological and
social level as well. He comes to know when he needs to reduce or
increase his arousal and how to achieve it.[9] It has since been discovered
that mothers who are responsive when their babies signal "Enough!,"
have children who are able to sustain longer periods of attention, an
important capacity for cognitive development.[10]

Stern found that, as the infant gets older, the mother introduces into
their dialogue new complications. She continues to match the baby's
feeling level, but now adds color and depth by doing it through a different mode of expression:

> • A nine-month-old girl becomes very excited about a toy
> and reaches for it. As she grabs it, she lets out an exuberant
> "aaah!" and looks at her mother. Her mother looks back,
> scrunches up her shoulders and performs a terrific shimmy
> with her upper body, like a go-go dancer. The shimmy lasts
> only about as long as her daughter's "aaah!" but is equally
> excited, joyful, and intense.
> • A nine-month-old boy bangs his hand on a soft toy, at first
> in some anger but gradually with pleasure, exuberance, and hu-
> mor. He sets up a steady rhythm. Mother falls into his rhythm
> and says, "kaaaaa-*bam*, kaaaaa-*bam*," the "*bam*" falling on the
> stroke and the "kaaaaa" riding with the preparatory upswing
> and the suspenseful holding of his arm aloft before it falls.[11]

Through such creative echoes the mother not only reinforces the
baby's behavior, but she communes with him, which helps define for him

what he is all about, builds their relationship, and shows him that his experience can be understood and shared with another. Perhaps, most important, such communion gives the infant a sense of being appreciated, validated, and approved, which seems to be such a vital need at this time of life. Stern found attunements like these embedded so subtly in maternal behavior that they often go unnoticed. But he believed that they account for the impression we form of how well a mother and her baby are relating.[12]

The burst of scientific knowledge about the mother-baby relationship coming out of the universities in the 1970s established Winnicott's prescience in point after point and further validated Ainsworth's emphasis on maternal attunement and "mutual delight." It was now found that the baby not only looks to the mother to participate in his play, to echo his feelings, and thus to have his experience affirmed and understood, he also depends on her to take him to levels of emotional experience that he could not achieve on his own. The shared experience helps usher the baby into social exchanges and the richness of relating to another person.[13] Even knowing what to feel in many ambiguous situations is developed through this primary relationship. If a baby is confronted with a strange object, like a walking, flashing, beeping robot—is it dangerous? is it fun?—he looks to the mother for guidance. If she smiles, the infant will smile; if she looks frightened, he will become more apprehensive.[14]

Ainsworth had studied attunement across a number of variables—feeding, face-to-face encounters, bodily contact, response to infant crying. With the microanalysis of video it now became possible to perceive that such attunements take place in different *dimensions* as well, including intensity, rhythm, and duration. Most of the time mothers seem mainly interested in participating in a shared experience with the baby. They explained their behavior to Stern with phrases such as "I just wanted to join in."[15] At other times they are trying to slip into the infant's experience in order to adjust his emotional state. But how they do it—the specific techniques revealed in the video analyses—is as invisible to them as the numerous muscular contractions and coordinations that enable them to drive a car or brush their teeth.

The power and importance of this shared experience is illustrated by the famous "still-face" experiment. Tronick asked mothers to make their faces expressionless in the middle of an interaction with their babies. By three months of age, the infants typically reacted to their mothers' blank expressions with distress.[16]

Babies notice milder forms of misattunements as well. Stern asked mothers to purposely misattune to their babies by responding to them with an intensity that over- or undershot the intensity the baby was displaying in its behavior. In one example a mother is watching her nine-month-old play excitedly with a new toy. She jiggles his bottom, matching with her jiggle the level of his excitement. She does this again and again, and each time the baby responds to her jiggles with no response at all. He just goes on with what he was doing. But when asked by the researchers to jiggle somewhat more slowly than would match his emotional state, the baby stops playing and turns to give her a perturbed look. Every time the procedure is repeated, with the mother over-shooting or undershooting his intensity, the baby responds this way. When she then gives him a nicely matched jiggle, he goes on as before, doing what he was doing. Babies also notice verbal misattunements, and they seem to be equally perturbing to them. "What is at stake here," Stern wrote, "is nothing less than the shape of and extent of the share-able inner universe."[17]

The revolution in empirical knowledge about the infant came down heavily in support of Bowlby and Ainsworth. Researchers, like Jay Belsky, applying the new techniques, soon found that well-synchronized mother-infant interactions predict secure attachment.[18] This work enriched the attachment idea and gave further credence both to the relevance of the Strange Situation and to Bowlby's and Ainsworth's emphasis on the quality of care in the first year.

The findings added a powerful new dimension to the day-care debate. For given the complex world of mutual influence in which the infant's psychology evolves, it would seem critical, to use Bronfenbrenner's words, for the baby to have plenty of time each day with "somebody who's crazy about him." And, of course, the new findings fortified the whole environmentalist position, providing data that were as dramatic in their way about parental influence as the data the behavior geneticists had presented regarding the influence of genes. The evidence clearly suggested that a mother who fails to attune across a broad emotional spectrum will not only adversely affect the baby's emotional and social development, but its initial biological regulation as well, creating in some children qualities similar to what Chess saw in the difficult child, qualities that might be mistaken for inherited temperament.

Winnicott had long held that it was important for the mother to give the baby the space to be with himself when he is not making demands on her. Out of this quiet state, which Winnicott called "going on being," emerges not only the child's capacity to be alone but authentic and spontaneous expressions of his self. "It is only when alone . . ." Winnicott wrote, meaning, usually, alone in mother's presence, "that the infant can discover his own personal life."[19] Mothers who intrude on the baby because they are more attuned to their own needs than his cause him to be more attuned to her needs, too, and thus more inclined to develop a false, compliant self. Stern's research appeared to validate this view.

Stern cites the case of Stevie, whose mother continually forced face-to-face interaction with him no matter how desperately he turned away. Sometimes she chased him from side to side with her face so insistently that he ended up crying.[20] Whatever the cause of her behavior—she may have been hostile, she may have had a neurotic need for control, she may have been deficient in her sensitivity to the feelings of others, or she may have been hypersensitive to rejection, such that each time the baby turned away she took it personally—Stevie's developing sense of relatedness was impaired. "From observation of many infants such as Stevie," Stern wrote, "it is clear that they generalize their experience, so that they are relatively overavoidant with new persons."[21] He believed that children like Stevie gradually discover that they are able to be most fully themselves when they are alone, leading to a well-functioning but relatively isolated life, what might be called an avoidant life.*

Molly's mother was controlling in a different way. She constantly told Molly how to play with toys ("Shake it up and down—don't roll it on the floor"), and, in effect, rode roughshod over Molly's natural rhythms of interest and excitement. Her exertion of power over the baby was such that Stern and his colleagues often experienced a tightening knot of rage in their stomachs as they watched the tapes. Molly's solution was compliance: "Instead of actively avoiding or opposing these intrusions," Stern wrote, "she became one of those enigmatic gazers into space. She could stare through you, her eyes focused somewhere at infinity and her facial expressions opaque enough to be just uninterpretable, and at the same time . . . by and large do what she was invited or told to do.

---

*This suggests an alternate avenue to avoidant attachment, one based on impingement and intrusion rather than insensitivity to attachment needs; although it seems plausible that the latter would accompany the former. (See Chapter 25.)

Watching her over the months was like watching her self-regulation of excitement slip away."[22]

When the researchers saw Molly again at age three, she struck them as emotionally flat; and Stern offered a troubling but hopeful observation: "At some point in her development," he predicted, "anger, oppositionalism, hostility, and the like will be sorely needed to rescue her."[23]

The special predicament of a child with a depressed mother is illustrated by a baby named Susie whose solution to dealing with her mother's lack of responsiveness was to lean all the more heavily on her own natural spunk and persistence. Susie would exert herself strenuously to make her mother come alive, and because she occasionally succeeded, she continued in this effort year after year. To her, being with an intimate partner is not a matter of dread, as it is for Stevie, or a cause for tuning out, as it is for Molly, but rather an impetus to hard work, in order to bring the other person to life. By three years of age, Stern wrote, "She is already a 'Miss Sparkle Plenty' and precociously charming."[24]

As the child acquires language, his early sense of self becomes solidified by words. In cases like those of Stevie, Molly, and Susie, language helps solidify a false self. Phrases like

> "Aren't you being gentle with the teddy bear! Sally's always so gentle." Or "Isn't this exciting! We're having such a wonderful time." Or "that thing is not so interesting, is it? But look at this one"[25]

tell the child what to feel, what to be interested in, what inner modes are acceptable, reinforcing previous manipulative attunements. They build a verbal foundation for the false self, a way of thinking about oneself that becomes locked in and taken for granted. Other ideas such as "I love to explore visual patterns," or "I love speed and action," which may better express who the baby, and later the adult, truly is, remain inchoate and therefore more difficult to access.

By the time the child is six months old, the mother's attunement with the baby has begun to educate him about the emotional states that are acceptable to share with other people. The mother's fears, desires, ideas about propriety, feelings of shame, and personal fantasies all come into play in determining which aspects of her baby's being will be reinforced and which will, in a sense, be banished. The mother who only tunes in to a certain range of the child's inner life—who only values his arousal and engagement but not his passivity or who relates to him fully only when he's down, not when he's up—tells the child what part of himself to bring forward in interpersonal experience.

Consider the subtlety of such influence: When ten-month-old Sam became excited and flapped his arms at his mother, she responded with, "Yes, honey." The intensity of her response consistently fell just short of Sam's own intensity, which surprised Stern's team because the mother was otherwise a dynamic and vivacious person. Asked about her level of response, she confessed that she saw Sam as being too passive and was afraid he'd turn out like his father. She hoped that by behaving as she did, Sam would rely on his own fire, not hers. Ironically, she was probably having just the opposite effect. Sam would likely come to feel that his dynamic side, never adequately responded to, was not something he could share with others, and it would probably atrophy as a result.[26]

Such findings echoed elements of attachment research. As Bowlby wrote of avoidant children, who snubbed their mothers upon reunion in the Strange Situation no matter how pitifully they'd searched for her when she was gone: "Already by the age of 12 months, . . . [they] no longer express to their mothers one of their deepest emotions or the equally deep-seated desire for comfort and reassurance that accompanies it."[27]

The dynamics that Stern was able to capture in his video analyses brought to empirical life issues that psychoanalysts had speculated about for years. Can we trace certain obdurate, difficult, and strangely self-defeating behavioral styles to a time beyond memory when we first learned how to relate? In the past such questions could only be answered with shrewd guesses about the early experiences of adult patients. Now there was more tangible evidence:

> The baby takes a doll [Stern wrote] and starts to chew on its shoes with gusto. The mother makes a number of attunements to his expressions of pleasure, enough so that she is seen as a mutually ratified member of the ongoing experience. This membership gives her entrée to take the doll from the baby. Once she has the doll she hugs it, in a way that breaks the previously established chewing experience. The baby is left hanging.

The mother is essentially saying, "No, don't chew on the doll's shoes!" and, also, "Dolls should be hugged." But instead of openly prohibiting or teaching, Stern wrote, "she slips inside the infant's experience by way of attunement and then steals the affective experience away from the child."[28] Such manipulative misattunements take many forms and are, Stern argued, the likely origin of later lying, evasions, and secrets. The child, and later the adult, comes to feel that if people are allowed access to his true inner experience, they will be able to manipulate it, distort it, undo it. Only by freezing them out can he keep his inner experience unspoiled.

Stern points out, however, that the mere fact that mothers will frequently be out of tune with their babies, even for selfish, foolish, or neurotic reasons, does not necessarily bode ill for the child. No parent is perfect, and as long as the poor attunement is not dominant, it will be useful in teaching the child the facts of intimate life: that attunement unlocks the doors that separate people, that it can enrich one's life, but that it has certain built-in hazards against which one will, at times, have to guard.[29]

What, meanwhile, are we to conclude about the relationship between imperfect maternal attunements and anxious attachment? If Sam, for example, becomes passive like his father, and if his mother is disappointed in him for this, does that necessarily mean that they will be insecurely attached? Obviously not. Such limitations and such wounds seem too common, perhaps even bordering on the universal, to serve as a marker for disturbed attachment. My guess is that the hurts have to reach a certain critical mass or be concentrated in attachment-sensitive areas (such as the parental response to the child's caretaking needs) before the child experiences a fundamental doubt having crept into his relationship with his mother, such that he is no longer certain of her love and availability.

Stern's clinical examples reveal the hidden tragedies of misattunement, and by doing so, they suggest the subtle processes by which anxious attachment *may* come about. They also suggest avenues for future research in this realm. In a pilot study that was influenced in part by his work, Wendy Haft and Arietta Slade found "a pattern of selective misattunements" among mothers with anxious babies. Those whose babies tended to be ambivalently attached to them misattuned to a broad spectrum of the baby's emotional expression, but were extremely attentive and well attuned when the baby was afraid. They were, in effect, training him to see fear as a primary means of achieving a sense of relatedness to another person. Mothers whose babies tended to be avoidantly attached to them, on the other hand, were most likely to misattune to the infant when he was expressing a negative feeling, especially toward them, or when he was seeking comfort or reassurance. Such mothers excelled, however, in attuning to their baby's exuberance, especially when he was mastering some new toy or game.[30] This is consistent with Karin Grossmann's findings, first referred to in Chapter 18, on the behavior of many of the mothers she observed with avoidant children:

> If the [avoidantly attached] infant played well [she reports], the parent attended joyfully and tried to join in. Many times, though, the parent's play interfered with, dominated, or frustrated the infant. If, subsequently, the infant showed signs of distress, frustration, or boredom, the parent retreated, observed from a distance, and waited until the child had pulled himself together again and had overcome his negative emotions by himself.
>
> Thus, the avoidantly attached infants experienced friendly attention mostly when they were busy playing by themselves, and when they showed positive emotions; but they were left alone when they displayed negative emotions. The securely attached infants, in contrast, experienced acceptance and consolation when they displayed negative emotions, but when they did not signal helplessness during play, the parent did not interfere and accepted his interest in the world around him.[31]

Findings like these support the idea that what we have been calling "parental rejection" may often be a subtle process, one that the parent himself may easily bar from awareness. Such findings also suggest that attachment themes play an important role in the development of what Stern called the child's "shareable inner universe."

Winnicott saw the early infant period as a time when the mother is largely selfless in her relationship with the baby, that, from her last trimester of pregnancy, she becomes increasingly absorbed with the baby and its needs, so that by the time the baby is born she is utterly preoccupied with him ("primary maternal preoccupation,"[32] he called it; "enslaved" was Bowlby's word). But gradually, he said, the mother awakens from her insane and exhausting devotion, and seeks to reclaim her life. In tandem with the baby's growing capacities, she stops shaping the world in perfect accordance with his wishes. The child loses his sense of omnipotence, learns that he is not the center of the world, and begins to see others as having an independent existence. This painful lesson is softened somewhat by the child's own striving toward separation and the excitement he finds in his new autonomy.

To ease the transition, the child typically becomes attached to what Winnicott called a "transitional object." This is often a blanket or a bear, which he now carries with him everywhere, talks to, and loves. Winnicott saw great psychological importance in the transitional object and believed that parents must not only treat it with care but collude with the baby's emotional investment in it and his fantasies about it.[33]

With his term "good-enough mother,"[34] Winnicott expressed the idea that no mother can or need be perfect and, indeed, mustn't be perfect if the child is to abandon his grandiosity, not be a lifelong nuisance, and become his own person. (How much imperfection can be tolerated and at what point will, of course, vary from one mother-child pair to the next.) The phrase is now famous and has been adopted by people who play down the importance of maternal attunement—Sandra Scarr uses it to support the idea of early day care. Yet the functions Winnicott's good-enough mother serves are plainly immense. Winnicott makes it clear that built into mothering is a strong tendency to suppress her own needs in favor of the baby's. The new infant research of Stern and others suggested that mothers do seem to be naturally drawn to provide just the sort of care he described. When mothers fail severely enough, the result is often anxious attachment.

Quality of attachment, as important as it is to the child's self-esteem, access to his feelings, and future relationships, is of course not the only aspect of the parent-child bond. Parents are also playmates and teachers, and these aspects of their caregiving can go well at times even if the attachment is insecure. But it is the attachment side of the relationship that is most emotionally charged for parents and the most difficult to control. Many mothers cannot master their anger, for instance, although they try. They cannot keep from acting out their anxiety. They cannot stop themselves from being controlling or hostile, even though they love their children dearly. One of the unspoken trials of parenthood is that it brings out elements of our psychology that seem to take over despite our best intentions, often compelling us to behave in ways with our children that replicate what we experienced with our parents. It remained for another branch of attachment studies to explore this phenomenon.

PART V

THE LEGACY OF ATTACHMENT IN ADULT LIFE

24

THE RESIDUE OF OUR PARENTS:
PASSING ON INSECURE ATTACHMENT

Bowlby believed that when a baby is born, it evokes feelings in the parents that are as profound as those of a young child for its mother or as the passions of new lovers. But, like other analysts, he recognized that, inevitably, those feelings are not all positive. Along with overpowering feelings of love, come resentments, hatreds, and anxieties as well, which are usually associated in some way with feelings first felt in the distant past. Thus, wrote Bowlby, a mother who is obsessed with the fear that her baby will die may unconsciously harbor an impulse to kill it, and,

> adopting the same solution she adopted in childhood perhaps in regard to her death wishes against her own mother, struggles endlessly and fruitlessly to stave off dangers from elsewhere—accidents, illnesses, the carelessness of neighbors. The father who resents the baby's monopoly of his wife and insists that her attentions are bad for it is unaware that he is motivated by the same kind of jealousy that he experienced in childhood when a younger sibling was born. The same is true of the mother impelled to possess her child's love who, by her

endless self-sacrifice, tries to ensure that her child is given no excuse for any feelings other than those of love and gratitude. This mother, who at first sight appears so loving, inevitably creates great resentment in her child by her demands for his love, and equally great guilt in him through her claims to be so good a mother that no sentiment but gratitude is justified.[1]

Like other analysts, Bowlby did not believe that the negative feelings parents have toward their children are necessarily harmful. They exist in some measure in virtually every parent. When my son was three months old, I noticed one afternoon that he seemed to be more in love with his mother than with me. I found myself becoming jealous when, while holding him in my lap, he constantly looked off to the side to gaze and smile at her. It rankled me that he did this, and it rankled me that it rankled me—for at some level I felt that my jealous response was infantile and that it might spoil the love between us. But the important question from Bowlby's point of view was, Could I tolerate such feelings in myself or were they so threatening that I would have to banish them? For it's in the banishment that the feelings become treacherous.

A father might find himself so powerfully jealous of his son that he needs to disavow it, for any number of reasons. Most likely, he felt deprived of love himself as a child and has created a life for himself where deprivation remains a constant, if unseen, issue. In some respect he has continued to feel like a baby, hungry for attention, and in this way comes into direct, if unconscious, competition with his son. But these feelings seem shameful and threaten his sense of competent adulthood. If he has never attended to this part of his psychology and it remains a threatening stranger, the situation with his wife and son puts him in an intolerable emotional turmoil, requiring the mobilization of his defenses. But when feelings like jealousy or resentment are disavowed and defended against (perhaps, in this case, by the father's being scrupulously supportive— even a cheerleader—whenever the rotten kid turns to beam at his mom), they do, in the end, emerge in some way. The father might become subtly unavailable, unconsciously rejecting the little boy and wanting to be pursued. Or he might become impatient with some real or imagined aspect of his son's personality or innate capacities; so that now, instead of feeling jealous, he finds himself angered by signs of slowness, dependency, or lack of assertiveness in his son. However his resentment emerges it will very likely have the flavor of his own childhood home.

The father may have dreamt of a fresh start when he became a parent and determined never to fall into the traps that snared his dad. But as Selma Fraiberg wrote, "In every nursery there are ghosts," such that "a parent and his child may find themselves re-enacting a moment or a scene from another time with another set of characters."[2] As criticism and judgmentalness leak or pour out of him, the resentful father may feel as if he has become trapped inside his own father's skin.

Various efforts have been made over the years to evaluate the extent to which a parent's attachment style is transmitted to the child. That is, if the father was insecurely attached to his parents, will his son have an insecure attachment to him? In one study, mothers from Sroufe's sample were interviewed about their attachment histories. "Scales were constructed," Sroufe says, "to assess the amounts of chaos and uncertainty in the child care, the amount of nurturance that was available, and whether this adult portrayed an image of her own mother as confident and competent in the maternal role. If she had that view of her, she turned out to be sensitive with her infant and her infant was securely attached."[3] Indeed, a clinically trained judge was able, in thirty-one of thirty-six cases, to correctly predict whether the mother's child was securely or anxiously attached based on the information from these interviews. In another study mothers were assessed to determine how accepted or rejected they felt by their own parents.[4] The acceptance-rejection factor just about perfectly divided the mothers of secure and anxious babies. But the most influential, in-depth, and complex study of intergenerational factors in attachment was done in Berkeley under the direction of Mary Main.

The Berkeley Adult Attachment Interview was the final element of the effort to assess the internal working models of parents and their six-year-olds discussed in Chapter 16. Devised by Carol George, Nancy Kaplan, and Mary Main and analyzed by Main and Ruth Goldwyn, it posed a series of ever more probing questions about each parent's early relationships. It asked for a detailed account of his family situation, descriptions of mother and father, what he did as a child when he was upset or ill, experiences of separation or loss, feelings of rejection, and feelings about the parent's relationship with his own six-year-old. The interview, which lasted between thirty and ninety minutes, sought not only to discover what the adult's early attachment experiences were like, but, perhaps more important, how he thought and felt about intimate attachments now—that is, how he *represented* them in his mind, what his internal model was like, and whether he could give himself the freedom to access painful memories in this realm and open them up for inspection or whether the whole business was too distressing and needed to be warded off. To that end, transcripts of each adult responding to questions about early and current attachments and what they mean to him were carefully analyzed for such issues as coherency, quality of memory, and anger; and these variables—not what happened or didn't happen in the past—were what Main ultimately used to determine adult attachment status. More than an interview, it was a psychological assessment, almost like a Strange Situation for adults.

Main was able to identify three major patterns—or, as she puts it, states of mind with respect to attachment—patterns of adult attachment that directly paralleled Ainsworth's childhood attachment categories. Adults categorized by Main as "secure-autonomous" presented a believable picture of their parents, often using what she called "fresh and lively language." Usually, but not always, they presented at least one of their parents as having provided them with a secure base in childhood, but the childhoods they portrayed were not trouble-free. These adults were able to be objective about their parents' positive and negative qualities and could offer convincing examples to illustrate their points. Their communication style was clear and direct, showing that they understood what the interviewer was asking, and they gave an appropriate amount of information to provide an adequate answer. They seemed to be comfortable discussing attachment themes and able to reflect on themselves and their relationships.

If the secure adults had unhappy attachment histories, they seemed to have understood and worked them through, at least to the extent that they could speak about them without getting into a stew, often demonstrating insight into the effects their negative experiences had had on them as well as some forgiveness or understanding of the parent's behavior. One mother who had been rejected by her parents as a child laughed when asked to elaborate and said, "How many hours do you have?" She then continued, "Okay, well, to start with, my mother was not cheerful, and I can tell you right now, the reason was that she was over-worked."[5] The secure parents showed little evidence of self-deception, seemed willing to depend on others, had a balanced view about their own role in their relationships, recognized that they were similar to their parents in various ways, not all of them positive, and generally seemed to accept the importance of relationships in their lives.[6] The great majority of the children of these parents turned out to have been rated securely attached in the Strange Situation five years earlier.

Adults categorized as "dismissing of attachment" seemed unable or unwilling to take attachment issues seriously. They answered questions in a guarded way, without much elaboration, and often had trouble remembering their childhoods. They seemed to dislike and distrust looking inward. Some exhibited an underlying animosity that seemed to imply: "Why are you asking me to dredge up this stuff?" or "The whole point of this interview is stupid!" The dismissing adults spoke vaguely about their parents, frequently describing them in idealized terms. But when pressed for incidents that might illustrate such descriptions, their memories contradicted their assessments, as negative facts leaked into their narratives. Thus, one parent called his mother "nice" but eventually revealed that she was often drunk and swore at him. When asked if that bothered him, he replied, "Not at all. That's what made me the strong person I am today. I'm not like those people at work who have to hold [each other's] hands before making a decision."[7]

This stalwart, anti-sniveling response was typical of the way dismissing subjects played down the affect of early hurts or embraced them as having built their character. Another dismissing father described his mother as "loving," "caring," "the world's most affectionate person," "invariably available to her children," "an institution." But pressed for details, he could not recall a single instance of his mother's warmth or nurturance.[8] A third father described his mother as "excellent" and his relationship with her as "fine." Yet when probed on the point, he eventually recalled having broken his hand as a child and being too afraid to tell her about it.[9] A dismissing mother said she had never been upset as a child. Never? "No, because nobody died." As the interview progressed, however, she revealed a number of painful facts. Her father had been upset that she had not been a boy and she'd once overheard him say that the family would not have lost their farm if they had had a son. She also reported that she had often been left alone as a child and typically came home to an empty house. Finally, it emerged that her father was an alcoholic, that he beat her mother, and that one of those beatings, delivered when her mother was pregnant with her, caused her to be born with a crippled foot that required surgery.[10]

The dismissing adults could equally have been called avoidant. They were reminiscent of the children Bowlby had studied decades earlier who had suffered terrible separations from their families at an early age and then became indifferent to affection or hurt. And they were reminiscent of the avoidant children in the Strange Situation who turned away from their mothers on reunion, as if their mother's return was no big deal, despite in many cases their having cried and searched for her desperately when she was gone. Like the avoidant children, the dismissing adults seemed to have warded off crucial parts of their feeling world through various defensive processes, so that they no longer felt the pain of rejection or the longing for love. Approximately three quarters of the children of these dismissing adults turn out to be avoidantly attached to them.

A third group of parents, whom Main classified as "pre-occupied with early attachments," seemed like the ambivalent child grown up. Often they spoke as if the feelings of hurt and anger they had had as children were as alive in them today as they had been twenty or thirty years before. The childhoods they described were often characterized by intense efforts to please their parents, considerable anger and disappointment, and by role reversals in which the child had tried to parent the adult. But these memories were expressed in a confused and incoherent manner, as if they had never been able to get a grip on what happened to them and integrate it into a comprehensible picture. They seemed still so enmeshed with their parents that infantile feelings flooded and bewildered them as they recalled the past. At times they would launch into an angry diatribe, seeming to lose themselves in feelings of resentment and to forget that they were participating in a formal interview with a stranger. ("I thought here I am getting married and she's not bloody prepared to give. I thought every mother would sort of want to give the best—but not her!")[11] Unable to see the forest for the trees, these preoccupied parents seemed to have no sense of their own role in any of their relationship difficulties.[12] The vast majority of their children were ambivalently attached to them.*

In subsequent studies, similar correlations were found. Meanwhile, several researchers, in the United States, England, and Canada, have turned the research around and studied not parents of six-year-olds but expectant parents. Peter Fonagy, working in London with Howard and

---

*Main also identified a fourth group of adults all of whom had suffered a profound early loss, like the death of a parent, that they seemed unable to understand; in some cases they seemed unable to integrate the knowledge that the long-lost parent was truly dead. Their relationships with their children were the most distressed, usually falling into the disorganized category.

Miriam Steele, was able to correctly predict infant Strange Situation classifications in 75 percent of the cases—a figure in keeping with research done elsewhere—based on interviews with the mothers prior to giving birth.[13]

Arietta Slade, who's begun analyzing data from a similar study, has found many differences in the way women face the emotional upheavals of pregnancy. Women classified as secure in the adult interview are for the most part more open psychologically to becoming a mother. They can accept that the child will be dependent on them and that they themselves will experience pain and distress. "They expressed anxiety about the changes they were facing, they complained about the physical discomfort, they worried about their marriages, and they fretted over their competence as parents." But, Slade says, these concerns "were balanced with a sense of hopefulness and joyful anticipation."[14] Indeed, the secure women had already begun a relationship with their unborn babies, had nicknames for them, and felt pleasure and fulfillment in imagining what their babies were like.

On the other hand, women from the two anxious categories found it difficult to derive pleasure from the knowledge of becoming a mother. They either pushed aside any anxiety and insisted that all would be well, or became overwrought with fears. Their descriptions of joy or excitement were often constrained. And their fantasies of what their babies would be like suggested that the unborn baby had already become a figure in old struggles. One pregnant woman, who had had terrible power struggles with both her parents, already imagined her baby as willful and uncontrollable. Another, who had always felt distant from her own mother, could not imagine anything about her unborn child.[15] Discussing this, Slade told me, "It's so interesting that a mother who's felt controlled by her mother her entire life is already preoccupied with whether she can control her fetus. Or that a mother whose own mother pushed her aside is already convinced that her child won't have any needs, won't change her life, and will be autonomous early on. Chills go up and down your spine when you hear these things." (Anyone who has found himself behaving as a parent in the very way he detested one of his own parents for behaving—fretful, intrusive, moralistic, overprotective, imperious— can certainly appreciate the dilemma of these expectant mothers.)

Slade has found a need for control typical among the anxious mothers she has studied thus far. It has sometimes showed up in rigid ideas about whether they wanted to have a boy or a girl. "It's another example of how these kids don't have much autonomy, even before they're born. You should be a boy, you should do this, you should do that—the baby doesn't really have a chance to come out and be heard and be listened to and be seen. The secure mothers have much more curiosity about who the baby's going to be. They bring the past into their expectations, too, but they do it in more flexible ways."[16]

We don't know from Main's work exactly why the adults become secure or insecure. We certainly don't know how likely it is that a secure adult, as measured by Main's interview, was secure with his mother as baby, although giving the AAI to people who went through the Strange Situation in infancy promises some answers in that regard. We don't even know for sure how well Main is tapping into with the adult what Ainsworth tapped into with the child. It should be remembered in this regard that while the Strange Situation assessed a relationship, the AAI focuses on an individual, apparently assessing some aspect of his psychological structure. Some believe the AAI is strictly cognitive. Judith Crowell, the child psychiatrist at the State University of New York at Stony Brook, who has given the AAI to adults who were assessed with the Strange Situation as children (see Chapter 19), argues that the interview measures how well and how much attachment issues were discussed in the family as the person was growing up. "That's not quite the same thing" she says, "as measuring an attachment relationship. I think it's a closely parallel thing, in that people who can do that well are the people who can help their child be secure, but I think it's more cognitive and not so rooted in the behavioral system."[17]

Like others, I tend to believe that the AAI taps more deeply into the subject's psychological dynamics, probably reflecting the cumulative history of the adult's attachment-related experiences, or perhaps, for some, the aspects of that history that are most activated, most dominant when the interview is taking place. If it were possible to plot a graph charting the quality of a child's attachments by evaluating them every few years from infancy onward, I assume we would see a varied tapestry, composed of winding and changing paths, eventually coalescing into certain dominant and subordinate themes. One of the problems with Main's classification system, however, is that it does not allow for such multiplicity. Even some of her staunchest supporters would eventually take issue with this.

The adult classification system and the conclusions Main and others have drawn from it have not gone uncontested. The interview is complex and difficult to rate. Unlike the Strange Situation, which shows over 90 percent reliability between raters, the reliability of the adult interview is in the 70 to 80 percent range, still high but with many more disagreements between raters over how to classify any one individual. Thus, although the correlations between the parent and child classifications are impressive, the number of adult transcripts that seem fuzzy and difficult to categorize call into question the rigorousness of the correlations. Finally, no effort has been made to understand the significant minority of parent-child pairs whose attachment classifications do not match up. Meanwhile, not surprisingly, skeptics in the field find it hard to believe that how a parent talks about the past can indicate anything about the quality of his relationship with his child. Despite such objections the Berkeley interview has rapidly become the most influential piece of attachment research since Ainsworth's Baltimore study.

Main has devoted much of the past ten years to poring over the transcripts of adult interviews. She has become particularly obsessed with modes of speech, seeing them as a gateway into that invisible realm that both psychoanalysis and attachment theory have uniquely sought to understand—the internal representations, or models, we have of ourselves, of significant others, and of our relationships. Does the person speak in run-on sentences without taking a breath? Do his sentences run out of steam at the end as if he's lost faith in what he has to say or hopes that his listener will finish the sentence for him? Does he speak in the first person (immediate), the second person (more removed), or the third person (detached)? Does he use certain vague phrases that are supposed to convey a lot of meaning? Is he prone to slips of the tongue ("I died when my father was ten")?

"The more I look at the interviews," Main told me, "the more I'm astonished by the degree to which aspects of adults' speech will correlate precisely with their child's score on some variable in the Strange Situation, like resistance to the mother on reunion."[18] Ainsworth, meanwhile, has found that in certain cases she can predict not only the child's general attachment classification but its subcategory as well by studying the parent's use of language.[19]

Main has attempted to understand how linguistic mannerisms and quirks fit into a person's entire psychological profile—not only the quality of his relationships, but his access to feeling and to memory, his ability to direct his attention toward or away from certain subjects, his capacity to engage in the normal, cooperative give-and-take of conversation. A sensitivity to metaphor has enabled her to make subtle associations—for instance, that the avoidant infant's shifting its attention away from the mother on reunion is equivalent to the dismissing adult's changing the subject away from attachment themes. No one has toiled with equal fervor to make such links.

"She absolutely believes that there are these connections," Jude Cassidy says. "Annie Dillard talks about carving up the Panama Canal with a teaspoon, and I think that's what Mary Main would do. She believes that there's this kernel of truth underneath there, that the way parents talk about their own childhood attachment relationships has got to be related to the way their babies are attached to them. And if it's covered up by the Panama Canal and she has to dig away with a teaspoon until she finds that kernel of truth, she's going to keep digging. And if it takes her five or six or seven years, that's all right."[20] (This portrait recalls Main's own description of Ainsworth in Chapter 11.)

Main's work supports an assumption on which much of psychoanalytic treatment is based: that being able to put feelings, especially unwanted feelings, into words makes them available for review and transformation. (Indeed, some of the more reflective, introspective secure adults sound like people often do when they have experienced some years of introspective therapy.) To have this ability means, in effect, that your internal model is still a "working" model—open, flexible, able to assimilate new information. It means not only an ability to rethink the past but to recognize that people can be different and that their behavior doesn't always mean what we think it does. The criticism of a husband or wife, for example, may feel like an intentional assault on one's identity. If you are able to attend to the feeling and put it into words—"I feel worthless and debased, convinced he wants to get rid of me, and insanely anxious and needy"—then you are in a much better position than the person who reflexively acts out such feelings by becoming depressed and overeating or becoming uncontrollably rageful. It gives you the space to recognize that your feelings may be somewhat irrational in the current context. That Main found this capacity present in secure adults but absent in those who still seemed controlled by their early anxious attachments helped convince her that without reflection there is little opportunity for change.

To the younger generation of attachment workers, like Roger Kobak, such findings have been a source of inspiration. Kobak, who studied philosophy and history as an undergraduate, went to divinity school after that, took a year to study psychoanalytic theory at Yale, then began a Ph.D. in community psychology, seemed in danger (as Ainsworth, a strong admirer of his, once remarked) of becoming a perpetual student. He finally turned to attachment research and completed his doctorate with Ainsworth "because it was the only place in academic psychology where psychoanalytic ideas were being utilized."[21] In Main's work those ideas are being utilized and integrated to an unprecedented extent.

"She created a window," Kobak says, "on these mental processes that have been talked about for years but never studied empirically."[22] He believes that it will take some time before her work is understood and assimilated by others, that it is as alien as Ainsworth's findings initially were, but that it is equally revolutionary. The excitement it has generated, meanwhile, has given attachment studies a third wind, one that is pulling in analysts and other clinicians. Arietta Slade is one example.

"Hearing Mary Main present some of her preliminary findings in 1985," Slade says, "was a pivotal experience for me. As a clinician, I got very excited. It was the first time I'd heard these kinds of phenomena addressed in an empirical fashion." Slade, inspired to begin her own attachment research, eventually took Main's training workshop. "My training in the Adult Attachment Interview," she says, "has completely changed the way I listen to how people talk. I hear language differently, because the scoring system of the interview is focused on language—on the kinds of words people use and the ways they back up what they say. These subtle things can tell you a great deal about a patient's defenses and the way he constructs his reality." And, of course, it also suggests something about the patient's past. "If I hear someone being really dismissing, I tell myself I better find out about rejection. I know this is someone who's probably been really shut out in some profound way, someone who must have felt terribly alone."[23]

In 1956, as part of the British Psychoanalytic Society's celebration of the centenary of Freud's birth, Bowlby gave a lecture on "Psychoanalysis and Child Care" in which he stated:

> Time and again we hear it said by teachers and others that a child is suffering because of the attitude of one of his parents, usually the mother. We are told that she is overanxious or down on the child, overpossessive or rejecting, and time and again such comments are justified. But what the critics have

usually failed to take into account is the unconscious origin of these unfavorable attitudes. As a result, all too often the err-ing parents are subjected to a mixture of exhortation and crit-icism, each as unhelpful as the other.[24]

Now, almost four decades later, attachment research has begun ad-dressing itself to some of the psychological forces driving the parents of anxious children. Although new to developmentalists, understanding parental psychology and how it affects the child was hardly new to psy-choanalysis. But the understanding had never been systematic before, providing an overview of certain broad tendencies in parental psychol-ogy and their counterparts in the child's developing psychology.

Both Fonagy and Main believe that the most important quality distin-guishing the secure from the anxious adults* is their capacity to under-stand what makes themselves and others tick. They are better able to recognize their own inner conflicts and to have a sense of why their par-ents behaved as they did. One secure adult, for instance, when asked how she thought her experiences as a child affected her behavior as a parent, responded with a clear sense of her own inner workings. She explained that she feared her tendency to fluctuate from one extreme to the other—from being too withdrawn with her child, as her own mother had been, to "smothering him with constant attention."[25]

Anxious adults either failed to have insights into themselves and their parents or offered explanations that were platitudinous, self-deceptive, or self-serving. Thus, one anxious mother, when asked about the relation-ships between her parents, responded: "I am the apple of my father's eye and . . . he does absolutely idolize me . . . and I think it's amazing that my mother has never been remotely jealous of me in any way at all!. . . She's just genuinely never held that against me at all and is fantastic!"[26] Compare this to the deeper, more aware, less denying response of a secure parent to a related question: "It was difficult for her to like me. He adored me so much and treated me as someone so special. It would have been super-human of her not to feel jealous."[27]

Fonagy found that neither education, intelligence, social or economic status, nor ethnic background have any relationship to this capacity to

---

*As with the labeling of children, the terms "secure" and "anxious" represent a convenient but inac-curate shorthand. An adult may be secure in his attitude toward attachment issues but be insecure— and exhibit all sorts of prominent anxieties—in other respects, and vice versa.

reflect openly and clearly on the inner state of oneself or others. With studies like this, which do the indispensable work of re-integrating attachment theory with its analytic roots, Fonagy, who is himself an analyst, is rapidly becoming one of the most prominent and important attachment thinkers.

Winnicott had emphasized the importance of the caregiver in helping the infant to understand his own feelings and impulses. In the beginning the mother does the reflecting for the baby; gradually he takes it over himself. The work of infant researchers like Stern seemed to corroborate Winnicott on this point. Fonagy now related this to secure attachment. For clearly only the parents who had the capacity to reflect on inner states could provide this function for their children. He concluded that the child's confidence that its emotional and mental states would be accurately assessed, clearly reflected, and appropriately responded to were a central feature of secure attachment.

What happens when a parent lacks this capacity? First, of course, the child may fail to become familiar and comfortable with his inner world. He may not develop the self-reflective ability that will enable him to understand and work through at a later date faulty models of relating he learned at home. (See Chapter 15.) Meanwhile, the parent, unable to be self-reflective himself, is more likely to instill such faulty models. For he will continue to be a slave to his own early patterns, persisting in strategies and maneuvers with his own child that he first learned when dealing with a rejecting or erratic parent.

Both Ainsworth and Main found the mother of the avoidant child to be distant—rejecting of the infant's attachment needs, hostile to signs of dependency, and disliking affectionate, face-to-face physical contact, especially when the baby desired it. Her aversion to nurturance would seem to be a logical outgrowth of the neglect she probably experienced when she herself was young. Needs and longings that were painfully unmet have become a source of hurt and shame for her. Having cut herself off from them, they make her angry, depressed, or disgusted when she sees them in her child.

Unfortunately, unreflective parents don't realize what is happening to them. They may love their baby, they may talk about it in glowing terms, they may be good playmates, they may readily compliment the child when it is doing well, they may be diligently concerned with the baby's feeding, sleeping, and physical comfort. But when attachment needs arise, they find themselves being impinged upon by an intolerable sense of threat. Perhaps because to be fully open to the baby's emotional needs is to become reacquainted with oneself as a baby, to reexperience the pain of being totally dependent and desperately in love and yet being shut out and feeling unwanted. People construct their defenses in order to prevent being reengulfed by such feelings. But when one becomes a parent, the buried, unresolved pain is shaken loose, the defensive wall is breached, and new defensive efforts are required, which, in the case of the dismissing parent, means keeping the baby and its needs at some distance.

A dismissing mother may find a solution to the clash between the baby's emotional needs and her own—and to whatever guilt she may unconsciously feel about this conflict—by seeking the haven of a belief system that disdains introspection as naval gazing, favors early training in autonomy, and stands guard against spoiling. Meanwhile, if, like so many avoidant children, she is somewhat grandiose, the idea of a superior kid, who has no needs, will feed her own superiority.

Jay Belsky found mothers of avoidant children to be intrusive with their babies. Given the understanding of the avoidant mother that has been developing since Ainsworth's Baltimore study, his data have been received with some skepticism.[28] Belsky acknowledges that intrusiveness may be an artifact of the research process—behavior that comes about when a certain type of mother finds herself being observed by a psychologist and wants to look the perfect parent. But Jude Cassidy has attempted to make sense of it by stressing Main's theme of unconscious strategies.

"An avoidant mother," Cassidy says, "wants to keep her baby from getting too close. She feels really uncomfortable when the baby comes over crying. She doesn't like the baby crawling on her lap. So why would she become intrusive? I think two things are going on. One is an unconscious recognition that if you badger somebody repeatedly, they'll go away. It's like this idea of dysfunctional marriages where the wife nags and the husband pulls back. In some unconscious way the wife really wants the husband to do just that. Another reason is that by coming at her baby repeatedly the mother can control the interaction and keep her baby from initiating care seeking. It's like you're out on a date and you don't want the guy to kiss you, so you just talk constantly and don't give him a chance to get a kiss in. I think it's the same with these mothers. Here, play with this, no play with this—it's directing the focus, and she wants the focus away from attachment issues."[29]

A certain type of ambivalent, or preoccupied, mother is haunted by different demons. The inconsistency and incompetence that may characterize her caregiving suggest a lack of involvement with her baby, but something more complex is probably occurring. For example: A mother who has never worked through her own ambivalent attachment has probably been struggling all her life to find stable love. When she was a child, she may have been pained by the competent, steady caring that she saw friends' parents give to them. As an adult she may be prone to a nagging, uncontrollable jealousy in any close relationships where she feels cause for doubt. She may want to love deeply and steadily, but it is hard for her because she's never been filled up enough with patient, reliable love to be in a position to give it. When she becomes a mother, such unresolved, tormenting issues may play havoc with her emotional life.

This mother may care for her baby as much as any other mother, but she finds her caregiving impaired by her own rankling needs, which make it hard for her to be consistently available. If, unconsciously, she envies the baby's position as the one who is meant to be coddled and cared for, that may further impede her ability to give of herself freely. If she harbors an underlying wish that the child remain tightly enmeshed with her, that he beome for her an attachment figure who will never separate or betray, she may find herself interfering with her infant's efforts toward autonomy. The existence of such inner conflicts seems to be corroborated by the observation that some preoccupied mothers frequently intrude when the baby is happily exploring on his own and push for interaction even when the baby resists it.[30] A mother doesn't do such things out of a lack of love. But to see her child separate—become his own person—in these small ways is painful to someone who feels deprived of love. It is to feel the knife in the chest all over again, of being a small person, desperately hungry for care, tormented by a mother who is careless about her needs and who thus makes every separation a daily torment.

Cassidy believes that such conflicts best explain the apparent incompetence of many mothers of ambivalent children. For if a mother unconsciously wishes to keep a baby addicted to her, there is no better strategy than being inconsistently available. Nothing makes a laboratory rat push a pedal more furiously than an inconsistent reward. Without being fully aware of it, some preoccupied mothers may know this.

The immature, dependent, babyish behavior that Sroufe observed in some ambivalent children may, thus, represent the sort of child his parent unconsciously wishes for, one who will not grow up and separate from mom, who will always be clingily demonstrating his need for her, and who will anxiously seek to appease her. The child, meanwhile, suspended perpetually in his attachment anxieties may, if he gets stuck in his mother's orbit, grow into a similar sort of person, who constantly seeks succor and devotion from another—much more than the average person is likely to put up with. Without enough countervailing influence, he may eventually become a parent who repeats the pattern with his own children in order to finally get the devotion he missed. This is certainly as a good a theory as any as to why some parents become so invested in keeping their children preoccupied with them. Throughout all this, a lack of experience with self-reflection—and, in all likelihood, an aversion to it—keeps these dynamics unconscious and therefore unresolvable.

As I write this, however, I am aware of how much is missing and how much effort I am making to qualify my statements. For one thing, we are talking here about a certain tendency which may exist among mothers of ambivalent children; how prominent it is, we do not know. It is a compelling explanation, it resonates with our understanding of human nature, it seems to capture a broad trend in personality as we know it, but it is too speculative, it is too simple, and it cannot account for everyone in this category. Other children may sense an underlying depression in the parent and feel that only their love and attention and good performance can keep that parent from emotional collapse. This, too, could generate an unhealthy pre-occupation, even in a child who has received all the appropriate adoration, and may be carried through to adulthood in the form of a haunting, perhaps unnameable, separation anxiety. Main has found that many children classified with the most severe form of anxious attachment, disorganized/disoriented, had mothers who had failed to mourn a significant loss, like the death of a parent. But I suspect that unmourned losses, perhaps of a lesser degree, are rampant among adults with anxiously attached children and that they have a thousand ways of passing on their own, often hidden, separation anxieties to their kids, such that they grow up terrified of abandonment, fearful that they will disintegrate if left alone, convinced that the people they love will die if they are not always present to save them, or some other variation on this theme.

It should be remembered, too, that anxious children do not always replicate the anxious category of their parents. They are often anxious but in different ways. The mismatch rate, some 30 to 40 percent in most samples, may be related in part to the child's temperament, but it may also be accounted for by other factors, like gender. Some research suggests that the emotional systems of boys and girls are innately dissimilar in certain respects. Boys and girls may also react differently to the mother for psychological reasons. "Mightn't it be the case, as I have observed in our sample," Slade asks, "that a preoccupied mother might drive her son to withdraw and avoid? Mightn't it also be the case that a dismissing mother's withdrawal could inspire clinging, neediness, and ambivalence in her daughter?"[31]

Also, in trying to show how a certain attachment experience with the mother can reverberate throughout a child's interpersonal existence, we inevitably leave out many other complexities, including the complexities of family life as a whole, and particularly the effect of the father. Whom, for instance, does the child most identify with? (To raise again one of the eminent missing questions of attachment theory.) What is the nature of that identification? And what course does it take over time? If the child is a boy who feels strongly identified with an emotionally withdrawn and avoidant father, he may start out in an ambivalent relationship with his mother but then move to a place where his relationship with her is much like his father's. The underlying ambivalent current may persist, but his predominant style will now look avoidant-dismissive. All this will be further complicated by the boy's struggles and disappointments with his father, the way his oedipal conflicts get worked out, the degree to which his love, despite such disappointments, is able to thrive in these relationships or with other family members or intimates, not to mention betrayals, separations, unresolved losses, and so on. It will be complicated to the point where trying to tell a paradigmatic story of attachment-related development looks more and more pointless, even more so when illustrating it with the child's relationship with just one parent.

The efforts to understand what makes unresolved parents raise insecure kids, or, put another way, why love falters, hurts, gets wasted or forgotten, or becomes a chalice that can never be retrieved, underscores a subtext that runs throughout this literature: Being a parent is difficult. It is easy to judge parents, and some are certainly awful, making little or no effort to protect their children from themselves. But, as self-aware parents know, the effort to shield our children from the damaged parts of ourselves (the fears, the unmourned injuries, the unbearable longings) is arduous. And it is constantly undermined by our entrenched dissociations and indispensable armor, which have kept us as we are for so long. We love our children, we dread harming them, and we dread losing them. This is true for the educated and the uneducated, the rich and the poor, those who have some understanding of their own psychology and those who do not. "The poor single mothers in our study," Sroufe told me, "all want the best for their kids. They maybe can't do it. They may be so beaten down by their histories and their circumstances that they're doing a terrible job, but I've never seen one that didn't want to do it right."[32]

Doing it right is, of course, a major concern for Americans of all social levels. Millions of books on child care are consumed every year, not to mention magazine articles, television shows, and video cassettes. Parents learn about how the baby is likely to behave during each new week or month, what it needs to eat, what the variations are in physical and cognitive development, how to sleep train it, how to toilet train it, and so on down to the last detail. But, as useful as this is, none of it will help parents do the one thing they most need to do—gain a deeper understanding of their own motivations, conflicts, and inner needs. In the self-help literature directed at parents virtually no attention is paid to the emotional upheavals that the parent is likely to face—the disturbing return of long festering feelings, the sense of being driven to behave in ways that one would rather not think about, the haunting sensation of being inhabited by the ghost of one's own mother or father as one tries to relate to one's child.

"It's very American," says Slade of the child care advice now available. "You just have to do X, Y, and Z, and your child will be fine. Parents have a fantasy that they're going to do it differently, that they're not going to repeat the past and they are going to overcome the obstacles. And I think most people don't exactly repeat the past and they do certainly do things differently. But to really deal with these emotions requires a willingness to let the past into your consciousness."[33] That not only means giving up the fantasy that we as parents are completely unlike our parents, but struggling with those very things in ourselves we have always hated and have not wanted to admit to consciousness.

The problem we have as parents, then, is not usually a lack of love or good intentions, but more often an unwillingness to face who we are. Obviously, this failure has other implications for adult psychology, as well.

25

ATTACHMENT IN ADULTHOOD:
THE SECURE BASE VS.
THE DESPERATE CHILD WITHIN

In 1992, a prominent New York jurist, considered a likely nominee for the United States Supreme Court and a potential gubernatorial candidate, was arrested on charges of extortion and harassment. Married for thirty-five years, he seemed a model family man, but he had been having an affair for many years with a younger woman. When she broke it off, he began a bizarre campaign to terrorize her with anonymous phone calls, letters threatening embarrassing disclosures and harm to her daughter, and extortion demands. This went on long enough and became egregious enough for the FBI to become involved and to apprehend him. He was compelled to resign immediately from the state's highest court, seemed to suffer an emotional collapse afterward, and was later sentenced to fifteen months in prison.

To many people such behavior by a powerful, respected, and well-liked figure seems utterly inexplicable. How could a man who had so much go berserk over the loss of a mistress? Why would a man known for his good character and fair dealings become so brutal and infantile? From a distance, it is impossible to say anything about this particular judge. But the tragedy of a successful, late middle-aged man ruining his life for a younger woman is very familiar in our politics, folklore, and literature. It is, I think, evocative of attachment issues gone awry.

An imaginary example: An avoidant child grows up undervaluing attachment relationships and experiences. He is intellectually gifted and applies himself to school. He has rough edges at first but he learns to be charming. Although everyone admires and likes him, no one feels particularly close to him. And because he is isolated emotionally, the deprivation that began in infancy persists into young adulthood. Starved for affection, though unaware of it, he fantasizes about a great, all-encompassing love. Once perhaps, in his early twenties, he thought he found it and was so bitterly wounded afterward that, without being conscious of his decision, he only allowed himself to date women who were immediately enthralled by him. Unfortunately, he didn't respect such women. Gradually, he concluded that the love he once dreamed of did not exist; in the end, most people are too flawed or bound to disappoint. Be that as it may, it was good to have someone around. He made a "sensible" marriage, much like his parents, to a woman whose presence gave him the emotional support he needed to pursue his career, a need he would have been embarrassed to admit to himself. He became a father, continued to be charming and admired, rose rapidly in his profession, and gained considerable power. Although sometimes taken aback by a streak of insensitivity or dictatorialness, people valued him and took him seriously, but, emotionally speaking, he did not take himself seriously. He fed himself on a stimulating but lopsided diet of power, achievement, and praise, meanwhile allowing his deeper self to starve. He was attached to his wife and children and would have been deeply hurt to lose them. But at home he was a star, a figure to be more venerated than intimate with, and they were frightened of his capacity to turn cold when disappointed with them.

Sometimes, in the morning, he awoke from dreams in which he was disturbingly alone. When he went on business trips and was stuck in the airport without any work and no admirer or person of influence to chat with, he felt strangely isolated and detached, as if he didn't have a wife and family back home, as if he was the only man on earth without a friend. This loneliness of the soul distressed him, and he pushed it out of his mind.

Then, at the height of his powers, he met an impressive younger woman who worshipped him and by whom he was sexually captivated.

Unlike the first time he fell in love, he was now starting from a much more secure position. He was confident. His hated feelings of neediness, which subverted him when he fell in love as a young man, were kept at bay because of the secure base provided by his marriage. And because power is a great aphrodisiac, his new lover perceived him in the most positive glow, almost like the adoring, unquestioning love a child has for her father. What's more, because he was loyal to his wife and had no intention of disrupting his comfortable home life, the new relationship was never tested in the cauldron of mundane daily existence or the rigors of true commitment. He remained the impressive charming man of power. She remained the wide-eyed acolyte. Neither ever knew the other in three dimensions. In effect, there was no main course in this relationship, only dessert.

But, like so much else in his life, the dessert became addictive, the affair another way to escape from his haunting loneliness, even, in this case, while seeming to feed it. It was as if he had finally found true love, the total, accepting, maternal love he'd never had enough of. But it was not true love. It was an exciting, tantalizing, delicious mirage in which he invested very little of his genuine self. His partner, who wanted something more lasting, eventually outgrew her infatuation and left.

The affair lost, he was thrown back on his emptiness, confronted with the terrible aloneness he felt as an infant before he had perfected his avoidant rituals. Indeed, he now seemed in some ways more ambivalent than avoidant, consumed by jealousy, hunger, and desperation, like the crazily dependent people who murder a lover over an infidelity and get immortalized in country and western songs. And, accustomed as he was to getting his way, he behaved like an infant, wretched, vengeful, and full of narcissistic rage.

In 1970 Bowlby gave a lecture on "Self-reliance and Some Conditions That Promote It," which made it plain that he saw secure attachment in adulthood affecting not only the quality of one's parenting but the quality of one's entire emotional life. "Evidence is accumulating," he said, "that human beings of all ages are happiest and able to deploy their talents to best advantage when they are confident that, standing behind them there are one or more trusted persons who will come to their aid should difficulties arise."[1] He called the trusted person an attachment figure and, borrowing from Ainsworth, said that such a figure offered the

companion a secure base. He believed that the ties to the parent gradually weaken as the child gets older and that the secure base function is
slowly shifted to other figures, eventually resting fully on one's mate.

Sifting through evidence from several disciplines, Bowlby argued that
self-reliance and healthy or mutual dependence were inexorably linked.
Studies of the American astronauts had found that these most self-
reliant and capable young men were "comfortable when dependence on
others is required" and that they were able to maintain their trust in
those they depended on even in trying circumstances. They had grown
up "in relatively small well-organized communities, with considerable
family solidarity and strong identification with the father."[2] Other studies done in the 1960s also suggested that emotionally healthy young people, who were both self-reliant and able to rely on others, had had home
lives in which both parents were loving and emotionally generous and
the mother had given them a feeling of complete security.

The importance of being able to rely on someone—and of having
someone to rely on—is illustrated by the behavior of women who cope
successfully with the immense demands of pregnancy and early motherhood. One study found that the women who fared best were able to ask
for help from appropriate people and to do so directly, without hints or
manipulations. They had relationships with their husbands whose support they happily sought, and they themselves had the capacity to give
spontaneously to others, including their babies.

Those women whose pregnancies were marred by emotional difficulties had a much harder time with dependency. They either did not ask
for support or did it in demanding and aggressive ways, suggestive,
Bowlby argued, of their lack of confidence that true support would ever
be forthcoming. Typically, they were dissatisfied with what they received
and, in the end, not adept at giving themselves.[3]

Although Bowlby rarely spoke of solitude, of the importance of being
able to be happily alone, of the creativity and self-knowledge that can
come in times of stillness, he did believe that, like self-reliance, the
capacity for healthy solitude in adult life arises from being secure in the
realm of attachment and having a secure base to return to.[4]

But implicit in all this is that the one builds on the other, that having
an internalized secure base, a strong sense of having been loved and of
having confidence in one's essential ability to love and be loved, enables
one to both enjoy solitude and to confidently seek nourishment when
one needs it.

The ways in which an internalized secure base operates in the passage to adulthood has been studied by Roger Kobak, who has used the Adult Attachment Interview to assess attachment in teenagers. Kobak found that secure teens—those who were able to speak coherently and thoughtfully about their experiences with their parents—were better able to handle conflicts with both mother and father. They were more assertive and more capable of listening to their parents' point of view. And they showed less dysfunctional, critical anger. They also made an easier transition to college. "We found," Kobak says, "that the secure kids were rated by their friends, who had known them for the first seven months of the college year, as much more ego resilient—that is, much better able to cope with stress, study when they needed to study, have a good time when they needed to have a good time." The dismissing freshmen—who had trouble remembering early experiences with their parents and played down the importance of attachment issues in their interviews—"were seen by their peers," Kobak says, "as more hostile, more condescending, more distant." The preoccupied students—embroiled, angry, and incoherent when speaking about their parents—"were seen by their peers as more anxious, introspective, ruminative."[5]

This study suggests that young adults, like the astronauts and the pregnant women, continue to be aided by the secure base they have had at home. It gives them the strength to do the adult equivalent of exploration—take risks, face challenges, be open to the new. In all likelihood, it also puts them in a better position to find a new attachment figure—and thus a new secure base—and to serve that role themselves.

The lack of a secure base would seem to leave one struggling with a profound and painful loneliness. The person with a largely ambivalent style knows it's there and is driven nuts by it, as if on fire and convinced he can never put it out. The predominantly avoidant person disavows it. But both, I think, are haunted by a fear of loneliness, some form of separation anxiety, occasioned by panic attacks or depressions, and a hungry search for a sense of internal goodness. I would speculate that for that reason the two attachment styles seem prone to certain types of addiction, the ambivalent becoming addicted to people, the avoidant to work, power, acquisition, achievement, or obsessive rituals. Ultimately, the control their loneliness has over them shows up in surprising ways, such as in news stories about famous people, like the ruined New York judge, who seem to have it all and then bring disaster upon themselves through their behavior in passionate attachments.

* * *

To Bowlby, mourning in adulthood remained as important as mourning in infancy, for even in adulthood the loss of an attachment figure, such as a parent or a spouse, is a powerful blow that rips away our secure base and, in a sense, undoes our world. His work with Colin Parkes, a psychiatrist known for his work on bereavement who joined Bowlby's staff at the Tavistock in 1962, further extended attachment research and thinking on the subject and eventually influenced Elisabeth Kübler-Ross, who incorporated attachment concepts into her famous 1970 book *On Death and Dying*.[6] Parkes has since used attachment principles in both bereavement counseling and in developing programs to help people through the process of dying.[7] Both Parkes and Robert Weiss, a Boston sociologist who studied loss due to divorce, found that protest, despair, and detachment, which James Robertson saw in hospitalized children, are the standard responses to loss of an attachment figure at every age. Healthy reactions to loss in adulthood entail a gradual emotional reorganization and a refocusing of one's attachment feelings to new figures.[8]

When mourning fails, and such a reorganization does not take place, it may well be related to early anxious attachment. If someone grew up in a home where attachment needs were played down and considered babyish, feelings of grief are likely to be stifled and not worked through. The approach to loss, whether it's of a pet, a best friend, or parent, is an immediate and premature "We can't dwell on these things; let's move on"; and so the loss is never truly experienced. A man like this stifles all his pain when his wife dies because the only means he has of coping with emotional pain is avoidance. His loss does not seem to make him suffer; he just becomes a more distant, compulsive, and strangely flattened personality. If the avoidant personality says "Let's move on" prematurely, someone who grew up in an enmeshed home may never feel ready to say it. Instead, he is more likely to suffer from chronic, unresolvable grief. Tears and laments spill out on every occasion, but they never get resolved so that life can begin anew. The ambivalent clutching that characterized the relationship with the living person now characterizes the relationship with the dead. Years later, tears of despair come just as readily as before. Nothing is changed.

If a spouse is away for a period of time, it is natural to miss him. If a move is made to a new place, it is natural to feel a loss over friends and family who have been left behind and to work assiduously to create new ties to replace the old. But with separations, too, anxious attachment can deform the process. Clinical work suggests that people with what appears to be an avoidant or dismissing psychology often fail to recognize that separations have an emotional impact on them. We see this when a therapist goes on vacation and the patient becomes depressed without having any idea that this may be related to the therapist's absence. Instead, he feels a worsening of his emotional condition and an inexplicable indifference to or anger with the therapist upon his return. When a spouse is away, a person with this psychology may become obsessively focused on work, may even celebrate the separation as an opportunity to get more work done, but then be strangely, perhaps even cruelly, distant from the spouse when he or she returns. Young people like this go to college far from home, emigrate to a new country, readily leave friends behind to take a job in a new place, never anticipating that they will suffer any feelings of loss as a result. And, because they don't take attachment needs seriously, they don't take care of them. They fail to make the concerted effort needed to maintain old connections or build new ones. In the end they may be brought low by their unmet attachment needs and by an attack of separation anxiety, experienced as a sense of depression and inner collapse. Feeling too weak, too desperate, and too ashamed to approach anyone for love, they may allow this condition to worsen and persist.

Others, who display what appears to be an ambivalent or preoccupied attachment style, are hypervigilant about separations, likely to become anxious or even panicky when left, and to become overwhelmed by feelings of clinginess and impotent rage. They do not readily venture forth or take chances, for they do not believe their attachment needs will ever be met. They cling tenaciously to what they have, often using guilt and blame to keep their attachment figures on a short leash.

On July 26, 1985, social psychologists Cindy Hazan and Phillip Shaver of the University of Denver published a "love quiz" in the *Rocky Mountain News*, a local paper. Designed to test the impact of attachment quality on romantic love, the quiz asked readers to identify themselves with one of three statements that Hazan and Shaver believed would represent the emotional styles of secure, avoidant, and ambivalent attachment in adulthood:

- I find it relatively easy to get close to others and am comfortable depending on them and having them depend on me. I don't often worry about being abandoned or about someone getting too close to me. [Secure.]

• I am somewhat uncomfortable being close to others; I find it difficult to trust them completely, difficult to allow myself to depend on them. I am nervous when anyone gets too close, and often, love partners want me to be more intimate than I feel comfortable being. [Avoidant.]

• I find that others are reluctant to get as close as I would like. I often worry that my partner doesn't really love me or won't want to stay with me. I want to merge completely with another person, and this desire sometimes scares people away. [Ambivalent.][9]

Respondents were then asked about their childhood relationships, the emotional styles of their parents, and fifty-six questions regarding their most important romantic relationship. Hazan and Shaver found that the subjects whose responses suggested a secure attachment style were happier in their love relationship, saw their partner as a good and trusted friend, were able to accept him despite his flaws. Their relationships lasted longer and they had far fewer divorces. Subjects whose responses suggested an avoidant style revealed a fear of intimacy. They did not believe in head-over-heels romantic love, were often doubtful of whether romantic love existed at all, and found their relationships to be full of emotional highs and lows and jealousy. Ambivalent-looking subjects reported more intense roller-coaster romances, tended to fall in love easily, and became obsessively involved with their lover, so that it became difficult to take their minds off him.

Unfortunately, there was a tautological quality to these findings—if people think of themselves as secure or anxious, they are going to say a lot of things about themselves that are consistent with that view. The results were nevertheless intriguing, partly because when the three categories were studied in detail, patterns emerged that fit well with one's expectations and that seemed to add a fuller picture of attachment quality in the adult years. If the avoidant style seemed very much like the distant, self-sufficient man "who refuses to commit," the ambivalent style seemed to embody such popular phenomena as "women who love too much."

The Hazan-Shaver report caused a huge stir in social psychology that continues to this day. Numerous studies have been conducted using their self-report measure or modifications of it. In one study, reminiscent of the Strange Situation, dating couples were brought into the lab. The woman was separated and told she was about to go through an anxiety-provoking procedure. She was then sent back to the waiting room to be with her partner. Sharp differences emerged between the self-described secures and the avoidants, with the women in the secure group more likely to seek emotional support and physical contact and the secure men much more likely to give it.[10]

Hazan and Shaver, meanwhile, wanted to see if they could find a link between security and exploration in adults, as Ainsworth had found in infants. To that end they launched their "love and work" study. Once again, those in the secure group seemed to be doing fairly well, while the anxious subjects had problems. Those in the ambivalent group, for instance, tended to procrastinate, they had difficulty concentrating, and were most distracted by interpersonal concerns. They also had the lowest average income. "It's very parallel to infants in the Strange Situation," Hazan says, "where the ambivalent kids are not able to engage in exploratory behavior because they're so preoccupied with where their mother is and what she's doing."

The avoidants, meanwhile, were most likely to be workaholics and most inclined to allow work to interfere with their social life. Some said they worked too hard to have time for socializing, others that they preferred to work alone. Not surprisingly, their incomes were as high as the secures, but their satisfaction was as low as the ambivalents. "Again," Hazan says, "it's like the avoidant infants—they're not exploring happily, but they're putting all their energy into it."[11]

There has naturally been a great deal of skepticism in the field about whether one's attachment pattern could be meaningfully assessed by the simple self-report procedure that Hazan and Shaver used. Nevertheless, it came as something of a shock when researchers subsequently found that when adults are assessed using both the Hazan-Shaver methodology and Mary Main's Adult Attachment Interview, there was virtually no correlation between the results.[12] No one has as yet been able to figure out exactly why. One problem, of course, with the self-report, which both Hazan and Shaver readily acknowledge, is that people are defensive, they say all sorts of positive things about themselves, but unless they are probed in depth the truth is likely to remain hidden. This seems to be a major difficulty with avoidant adults, many of whom rate themselves as secure on the questionnaire but turn out to be dismissing on the AAI. When this trend is accounted for, Shaver believes, the two assessments show much more congruence.[13] Meanwhile, studies by social psychologists all over the world have found consistent results with the Hazan-Shaver measure, even, surprisingly, in the avoidant category: If someone calls himself avoidant in the self-report, he tends to feel and behave in ways one would expect—to be low in self-disclosure, low in relationship enjoyment, more likely to get divorced, and more likely to be promiscuous (and thereby evade intimate attachments) than people with either of the other two relational styles. So, there is a real muddle here.

Kobak believes that what Hazan and Shaver tapped in to for many subjects was the specific attachment feelings aroused by their current relationship. The idea is that when we're with a noncommittal person who's always threatening to leave, we are prone to feel like a clingy, ambivalent child—regardless of our previous attachment experience. When we're with an insecure, punishing nag, we're prone to become somewhat distant and avoidant. Indeed, Kobak has found that in marriages people don't always act the way their Berkeley adult attachment category would predict. As a result he believes that "adult romantic style may be more the product of adult romantic experience than of childhood relationships."[14]

To the extent that this is true, it also suggests a possible limitation in the classification system devised by Main. For unlike the childhood attachment categories Ainsworth developed, which label not the individual but the relationship (secure relationship with mother, avoidant relationship with father), Main's system identifies each adult with a single attachment style. This may be legitimate as far as it goes. It could, as Klaus Grossmann suggests, represent an integration of past experience with all attachment figures, as well as the tendency to revert to the style learned with the primary caregiver when under stress.[15] But it neglects the possibility that we can draw on different models when relating to different people, and it may not, therefore, be enough to capture the varieties of the adult experience.

It thus seems reasonable to assume that there is more to adult attachment status than the AAI tells us. A predominantly dismissing adult, for instance, may have hidden realms of security or pre-occupation that the interview, at least in its current form, is not yet able detect. Also, in most research like this, people do not fall neatly into the available categories; there is usually some squeezing involved on the part of the scorer. The assumption is that individual psychology exists on a continuum, that various people might fall somewhere between dismissing and secure, or between secure and pre-occupied, and that lines must be drawn in order place them into some category. But maybe it is not just a continuum. Different self-states may be involved. The AAI may even pick up on these different self-states, but it does not yet know what to do with such data.

An example here may help. I have a patient who much of the time seems remote and unattainable. He does not make connections easily, and most of his friends do not know him deeply. He does not trust that people's interest in him is sincere, and with new lovers he demands extraordinary displays of devotion before he will consider making a felt commitment. It is not as if he does not care for these people. He does. But, as a mode of self-protection, he does not allow himself to experience how connected he is with those he cares about, including me. Thus, throughout most of his relationships, he superficially displays the avoidant-dismissive style, and I think an AAI scorer might be tempted to categorize him as such if he was interviewed at the right time. But once he acknowledges to himself that someone really matters to him, especially a woman, it is almost as if another personality or self-state emerges: he becomes desperately dependent and fearful of separation or loss. In our work together, it has become clear that he is fundamentally like a puppy who wants a lot of attention all the time, but in most relationships he does not seek it actively, preferring to starve himself than risk the sorts of wounds and humiliations he suffered as a child.

"According to the current system of classifying adults," Arietta Slade says, "you're either an apple, an orange, or a banana, and there's no such thing as mixed fruit. But that doesn't jibe with clinical experience. It doesn't jibe with the way people are. You see somebody in one relationship who's been clinging and demanding and needy, and then you put them in another relationship with a clingy, demanding, and needy person, and you watch them turn around and become unavailable and closed off and rigid. There's an interrelationship between the styles that is not accounted for in the categorical system."[16]

No one equates anxious attachment in infancy with emotional disturbance. True, severe disruptions of early attachment—prolonged maternal deprivation, harsh separations, the untimely death of a primary attachment figure—can, under certain circumstances, lead to serious disorders, including psychopathic personality, agoraphobia, or depression, as Bowlby attempted to establish in great detail.[17] But in childhood, anxious attachment alone does not predict behavior problems in school unless it is also accompanied by high stress, such as experienced by many of Sroufe's poverty children.[18] And even where behavior problems do arise, the child will still have many new influences and many opportunities to take a different path.

How then are we to understand anxious attachment's relationship to emotional disturbance? To begin with, anxious attachment is connected to those issues which psychoanalysts have defined as "pre-oedipal." That is, they arise in infancy and toddlerhood, before the pre-school era when triangular problems with mom and dad gain in importance and when a whole new array of potential psychological disturbances come to the fore. Indeed, at some point when psychoanalysis and attachment are rewoven together, pre-oedipal and attachment disturbances may come to be synonymous. Either way, we are dealing with a vast realm, from people who are essentially whole but have certain types of struggles in the realm of intimacy to those who are so badly damaged by crazy, violent, depressed, rejecting, or absent parents that they were never able to internalize enough sense of goodness about themselves and others to keep rage, paranoia, and panic from spoiling their lives.

When the anxious quality is severe enough to warrant thinking in terms of a pathology, it may still be impossible to draw meaningful correlations between attachment category and diagnosis. Nevertheless, the anxious categories are suggestive of the personality distortions to which adults are prone, and it is interesting to see how well the attachment idea overlaps with our understandings of character disorder. Bowlby, for instance, believed that an entrenched avoidant attachment lay at the core of the narcissistic personality disorder, one of the primary diagnoses of our era. And, indeed, the overlap is evident in the way clinicians think about the origins of this condition. Like Winnicott, Heinz Kohut, one of the foremost explicators of narcissistic disturbances, believed that infants need deep and consistent appreciation. Babies crave having their performance validated, they need to be seen and loved for who they truly are, and they need to be given an ongoing sense of belonging, of being a valued fellow being in the family.[19] If a mother fails consistently to attune to her baby in this way and to respond to his complex emotional needs, the young child, feeling unknown and unappreciated, is unable to know or appreciate himself. He shrinks back into a sense of helplessness, smallness, defectiveness, and shame, which he may then defend against by clinging to his infantile grandiosity, a grandiosity one or both of his parents may promote.[20] Without corrective experience, he grows into an adult who constantly seeks the adulation and perfect union he never had as an infant. Outwardly self-important, prone to pomposity, self-adoration, and an annoying attitude of entitlement, he is haunted by a fragile self-esteem. His friends complain that he's only interested in talking about himself, his boss that he takes frustrations too personally, his neighbors that he's pushy and conceited. None of this is inconsistent with Sroufe's descriptions of obnoxious, entitled, and wounded preschoolers with avoidant attachment histories.

Avoidant attachment would also seem to be a component of compulsive personality traits. At its extreme, the compulsive personality is the nightmare version of the uptight, authoritarian father who is determined to banish all emotions. He lives in a constricted world, his attentions narrowed to schedules, rules, and tidiness; and he is obsessed with trivia. He is continually peeved by what he considers to be the unethical or substandard behavior of others, and he gets more pleasure out of making lists, cataloguing his belongings, or going to the toilet than in comradeship or play. If he lives in an apartment building, he always puts his garbage out in the proper bags at the correct time and remembers with pinched disapproval the garbage lapses of each of his neighbors. We can see a kernel of the compulsive character in the avoidant child's narrowing of his focus to a toy or some other object in order to escape his painful attachment conflicts.*

The isolated preschooler Sroufe describes, who also has an avoidant attachment history and perhaps certain genetic leanings, may, if things continue to go poorly, develop into a schizoid personality. A loner who has no friends, the schizoid adult prays there will be no one on the elevator when it lands at his floor. Annoyed by casual social encounters and the demands of small talk, he cannot understand what pleasure people can possibly extract from their tedious and demanding entanglements with one another. For him, avoidance seems to have become a religion and his unconscious wish for connection a disturbing and tightly hemmed-in desire.

At the other end of the emotional spectrum, married perhaps to the compulsive list maker who balances her account and monitors her behav-

---

*The obsessive or compulsive personality should not be confused with someone who suffers from obsessive-compulsive disorder, or OCD. The latter is a more severe condition, usually involving phobias (e.g., of germs), rituals (e.g., hand washing), is often treated with medication, and is not considered a personality issue. Similarly, the hysterical character should not be confused with hysterical paralysis and other such anxiety-induced physical symptoms that were prominent in Freud's day.

ior, is the live wire. Seductive and engaging, she can often make people feel there's no one on earth they'd rather be with. Often diagnosed as an hysterical character, she is scattered, charmingly incompetent, and easily thrown into a tizzy by schedules, details, and responsibilities. Her dramatic flair makes her popular. Male neighbors delight in meeting her in the hall, and they wonder: "Why is she married to *him?*" But she flees from intimacy, and, like the ambivalent child, she tends to be demanding or clingy, immature, and easily overwhelmed by her own emotions.*

Perhaps the most extreme condition to which early ambivalent attachment may be a contributing factor is the borderline personality. Unlike the schizoid, she's had an intense relationship with almost everyone in the building but they've ended badly and she now considers them all "shits." Impulsive, self-destructive, and rageful, patients with this diagnosis are often dreaded by psychotherapists, as Peter Fonagy suggests:

> It takes but one patient with severe borderline pathology to shatter the equilibrium of the therapist's life with unending demands for "special" treatment, round-the-clock availability, physical and sometimes sexual contact, perfect attunement, heroic efforts to prevent self-injury or suicide—only to be repaid by contempt, reproach, hostility and at times outright physical attack.[21]

They seem to be at the extreme edge of ambivalent attachment, where preoccupation with attachment signals—Do you really care for me? I'm going to make you prove it! What's the meaning of what you just did? You've turned against me! I'm utterly alone and unwanted!—readily reaches the point of panic.[22]

Few people, of course, perfectly fit these stereotypes (although some come very close). Narcissistic problems wend their way through all the personality disorders, and many people exhibit a mixture of compulsive and hysterical traits. As we've seen, there are myriad contributors to personality, and much depends upon each person's inborn temperamental leanings, the unique circumstances in which he was raised, and what

---

*Just as the compulsive personality seems to be more common among men, the hysterical seems to be more common among women. This may be reflective of a biological gender difference or of the fact that such traits are more acceptable in women and therefore get played out in a less guarded way. The same gender issues may be at work in avoidant and ambivalent attachment patterns in adulthood, with fretful ambivalence being more plainly apparent in women and stoic avoidance more apparent in men.

transpired at each developmental stage from infancy through adolescence and perhaps beyond.

The intensity of personality problems also varies greatly. There are, for instance, well-functioning people who have some narcissistic traits and those who are crippled by their grandiosity and shame. Roger Kobak has proposed a similar continuum for quality of attachment, ranging from the highly dismissive to the highly preoccupied on one scale and from the very secure to the very insecure on another. This is a matter of great controversy in attachment circles, but I find it appealing partly because it suggests what many readers of this book will have already concluded—the extent to which the problems of anxious attachment are in some way relevant to all.

26

REPETITION AND CHANGE: WORKING THROUGH INSECURE ATTACHMENT

Early in Freud's development of psychoanalytic technique, he discovered that his patients relived aspects of their childhoods through their relationship with him, often responding to him as if he had been one of their parents. It soon became a standard assumption of analytic treatment that the patient frequently relates to the analyst the way he would to an important early figure, no matter how unlike that figure the analyst may be in most respects. Working through this distorted perspective—otherwise known as the transference, but obviously related to what Bowlby would later call the internal model—is considered a key feature of analytic work.

How transference manifests itself is still a matter of debate, but a number of features are widely recognized: Transference does not only apply to the analytic relationship but to virtually all relationships that are close or involve a figure of authority; it can be triggered by certain types of interactions that are especially charged for the individual; it can be positive (irrational love or veneration) or negative (irrational hate or contempt); and its valence can change, accounting not only for the intensity of falling or being in love but also for the intensity of mistrust or loathing that can be directed at the same person. Finally, it is not only our early self that we replay in adult relationships, but the parental role as well, a fact that is particularly evident when, inexplicably and seemingly against our will, we act like one of our parents with our own children.

Transference feelings emerge in different ways with different people. Harry Stack Sullivan, a founder of the interpersonal school of American psychoanalysis, believed that, as children, we develop different senses of self in each of our primary relationships and that in later life we relate to others through these selves. (This corresponds nicely with subsequent attachment findings that a child can have different qualities of attachment with each of its attachment figures.) There may be a self-in-relation-to-mother pattern, a self-in-relation-to-father pattern, a self-in-relation-to-older-brother pattern, a self-in-relation-to-nanny pattern, depending on who was important to the child when he was young.[1]

A girl who is brought up by a cold, domineering mother and a kind but ineffectual father will tend to see similar qualities in others, with the result that she behaves toward them at times as if they were emotional and behavioral copies of her parents. An act of coolness by a close female friend causes her whole painful relationship with her mother to be activated within her: Suddenly she is drenched in feelings of being small, oppressed, and helpless, while her friend appears all-powerful and coldly dismissing. The friend may indeed have been cool, even somewhat rejecting, but there is an irrational intensity to the woman's reaction. Meanwhile, she persistently sees the men in her life as weak despite their evident strengths and accomplishments. And the power of her expectations is such that she actually brings out the weakness in many of the men who are close to her, so that their weak side is all she ever knows or relates to. At the same time, she may be unaware of the rage she feels over dad's ineffectualness and the subtle abandonment this constitutes.

Freud observed that, despite our conscious protests and longings, we often seem to prefer relationships that repeat our early experience, no matter how unsatisfying. People can, of course, change, and their early models can be modified. But, as Mary Main's work has shown, by the time some people reach adulthood their models have become relatively closed and their capacity for self-reflection and change compromised. We see Freud's "repetition compulsion" in people who seek the same sort of partners again and again, exhibiting behavior that remains disturbingly consistent across relationships. Bowlby explained this as a natural bias in favor of what we already know: No matter how painful or unfulfilling it may be, it offers the second-rate security of being familiar. Fairbairn explained it as an unconscious commitment to those we worshipfully loved as children. No matter how much they hurt us, we don't want to give them up. Many, including Freud, have seen in repetition an effort to master an early trauma. In the process of repetition, however, the very meaning of love becomes subtly perverted. It may come to mean pining after the unavailable; being seduced and rejected; being treated with contempt; being engaged in sado-masochistic warfare; being worshipped and adored as a paragon of strength even as one's true self lies hidden, glutted with ugly needs and emotions; and so on.

The fact that many people find romantic excitement in a lover who displays the qualities of a rejecting parent, an excitement that they do not find in others, suggests the degree to which they remain not just committed to but enthralled by early attachment figures. They can't let go of the mother or father who didn't love them the way they needed to be loved. And they continue to be bewitched by the hurtfulness that compromised their care. They are caught in the parental orbit, a hurt child still leaning out for a love that can never be, and blinded to what they are doing by the belief that they have no feelings toward their parents at all or have washed their hands of them.

The issue of loss is important here. Bowlby talked a great deal about the child's need to be able to mourn a lost parent and how hard that can be if conditions are not right (see Chapter 8.) But losses come in many shapes: We once had an adoring, available mom, but when we became two and over-taxed mom's patience, the good mom was replaced by an irritable, rejecting disciplinarian. She only became more so when the second baby was born, which increased the demands on her and made us furiously jealous. That kind of loss also needs to be mourned, but the child is rarely able to do so. Instead, a twisted attachment forms, in which the child may become magnetized by the rejecting quality, and to give that up feels like giving up love itself. And so one seeks love in repetition.

But that is not all. An obvious corollary is that the prospect of being given to in a truly loving way is undermined at every turn; indeed it feels perversely unacceptable. There are many layers to this: We don't deserve it. We'll be rejected. It's not the way mom did it. And getting it now would not only deprive one of one's beloved bitterness but would also activate the long dissociated pain of that early loss.

For many people, therefore, adult sexual attachments do not give birth to a renewal of trust; or, if they do, the trust recedes as it is overpowered by earlier patterns.

What implications does this have for the a sense of having an internalized secure base in adulthood? That is, for having a feeling of okayness, of healthy independence, of trust, self-reliance, and confidence in one's ability to love and be loved—all those qualities that are the hallmark of secure attachment? A secure base is not a yes-or-no proposition; that is, for most people, the issue is not that you either have it or you don't. An exception might be psychopathic personalities, like orphans raised in institutions, who never had a loving caregiver and therefore never internalized a loving and self-loving aspect, or some of Bowlby's juvenile thieves who, because of terrible losses or separations, are so trapped in their rage that they cannot access part of themselves that feels loved and capable of love. But for others who are not so fundamentally disturbed, including those who would be characterized as avoidant-dismissing or ambivalent-preoccupied, the capacity to love and be loved in a nourishing way is more like a channel that one has trouble tuning in to. In intimate relationships, perhaps especially with the opposite sex, one is fixated on another, more compelling, channel. Here, always playing, is the drama of the rejecting parent and the longing child who is some combination of angry, bad, inadequate, manipulative, and spurned. Living for this drama, one moves into each relationship playing one or both sides of the pattern. This obsession, this repetition compulsion, inevitably intensifies one's sense of being bereft of internal goodness, of seeing such goodness as only existing in desperately sought after others, whom one hates and envies as well as loves and desires. The result is that the internalized secure base, which is indeed there in some form or shape, does not have a chance to develop. It lies dormant or underutilized and thus fails to become a foundation that can be built upon and strengthened by adult experiences of secure relating. This pattern, I think, is what accounts for the sense of total collapse and emptiness, of depression and doom, that often occasions separation or loss—or the fear of it—in adulthood. One feels as if there is no internalized security or goodness at all.

Needless to say, shame also plays a part in all this. For someone whose predominant attachment orientation is ambivalent, core feelings of shame are probably closer to consciousness, and the desperateness he feels about relationships is probably heightened by the sense that he is not worthy of love. The person whose dominant attachment mode is avoidant has more likely cut himself off from such anxieties. But he is no less motivated by them—because staying cut off from shame, which is crucial to him, absorbs a lot of his interpersonal energy.

A number of years ago I wrote a book, *Top Dog/Bottom Dog*, about the ways in which these processes of desperation and cutoff operate in daily life, and, in particular, how people exploit each other's feelings of inadequacy in order to alleviate their own self-doubts. The book told the story of several fictional characters, including a couple named Martin and Georgette Grodin. Although I wrote their story before I became acquainted with attachment theory, it is plain to me now that they each represent, to different degrees, a version of an anxious child grown up. Their ways of being with each other illustrates, I think, some of the problems of anxious attachment in adult relationships.

Georgette is a popular, attractive, thirty-five-year-old working mother, whom friends like to confide in, but who doesn't get the respect she should, especially from her boss and husband and even on occasion from her best friend, all of whom are very attached to her. Martin is a dynamic, successful man, supremely confident, addicted to work, intolerant of his wife's depressions, and intolerant of his own feelings and needs if they disrupt his otherwise steady course.

It is the evening of Georgette's thirty-fifth birthday. She has been feeling depressed for several weeks. She and Martin have not been getting along, distance has been growing between them, and, to make matters worse, Martin comes home late from work. Hoping that sex might bring them closer together, Georgette prods Martin into bed. They make love, but it's not satisfying because they remain unconnected; and afterward there's an uncomfortable silence.

> MARTIN: "How was it?" [I can't bear the thought that I'm not a good lover.]
> GEORGETTE: "Fine." [I'm ashamed to admit I'm dissatisfied.]
> MARTIN: "You don't sound fine." [You're ruining it again, Georgette.]
> GEORGETTE: "I'm sorry." [I hate myself.][2]

Both people in this relationship suffer from self-doubts—Martin, that he's not a good lover, that he's a disloyal husband, that he's selfish;

Georgette that she's a bringdown, that she's never satisfied, that she's pathetically needy. But whereas Georgette ruminates and torments herself about her inadequacies, Martin thinks he's superior to her and most other people in innumerable ways. He is particularly proud of his independence and the fact that he is not ridden with the pitiful insecurities he sees in his wife, his child, and his subordinates at work. But to maintain his superior posture, he has had to perfect strategies to keep his insecurities and self-doubts at bay, in this case by making Georgette the problem. Such maneuvering around feelings of shame is, I think, a frequent legacy of avoidant attachment.

Anxious children learn to manipulate to get their needs met, and inevitably their manipulations get carried over into adulthood. The ambivalent child may become seductive or cute, act fretful, or make others feel guilty for not giving him the attention he wants, all depending on what strategic styles are modeled or succeed in the family. Georgette makes Martin feel guilty about working late and neglecting their daughter; she stops doing things that he likes and that had always been a part of their life together, under the ruse that she no longer has the time; she becomes depressed and overeats. Such passive aggressive behavior is partly a retaliation for the way he treats her, partly the only way she knows how to make demands of a withholding person.

An avoidantly attached boy, like the Minnesota child who backed gradually into a teacher's lap when we needed attention, will probably learn to disguise his care seeking. He may become adept at using various forms of control to get another person to be there for him; he may seek out people whose needs are more apparent and who give without having to be asked. When Martin is feeling low and wants attention from his wife, he cannot be direct about it. He expects her to magically anticipate his needs, and, because of her keen sensitivity, she often does. If Georgette is planning to be busy with a friend on a Saturday, Martin does not say, "I don't want you to leave me today because I'm feeling dejected and blue." First, because he does not want to know that that is his condition and, second, because, if he did know, he would be too ashamed to disclose it. So he cajoles and wheedles, expresses irritation over the way she spends her time, maligns her friend, finds some pretext to get angry, all with the idea of maneuvering her to stay with him.

Having grown up with parents who could not tolerate any signs of weakness or dependency, Martin has trained himself to be invulnerable. Somewhere within him may be the potential to feel and behave like an overwrought ambivalent child, but, like a child in the hospital who has shifted from protest to detachment, Martin has steeled himself and moved on. He learned through repeated rebuff as a young child that there is nothing more shameful than being an anxious apron-string-puller with needs hanging out all over the place. It may be okay for other people, he may even be drawn to it in the people he chooses for sexual partners, but, although he can be attracted to such people at times, although he may become attached to them and care for them, he has a hard time respecting them—because, unconsciously, he hates those qualities in himself. Meanwhile, to maintain his rigid invulnerability, he is willing to jettison almost anyone who threatens to disturb his equilibrium by challenging his domination or his view of himself. This need for control is one aspect of his addictive life-style.

Georgette, whose father died when she was young and who had an enmeshed and caretaking relationship with her alcoholic mother, is nevertheless a warm and attractive woman with a spontaneous streak that draws people to her. She has a greater capacity for self-reflection than Martin, and she has managed not to repeat her mother's mistakes with her own daughter. But when it comes to her marriage, her insecurity and befuddlement is pronounced. In her relationship with Martin she is preoccupied with attachment issues, easily convinced of her own shortcomings, and quick to take the blame.

Georgette sees Martin's hidden, hurt side; she sees the unrealized potential, the creativity that's been suppressed along with his cut-off self; she believes she could heal him. But, while she wishes the best for Martin and wants to see him develop into what she knows he can be, she is confused about her motives. Does she want him to open up for her benefit or for his? Martin is confused, too. He loves having someone attuned to him, who knows him well, who is so appreciative of what makes him happy and why. But when she pushes too far, starts messing around with his supposed insecurities, he distrusts her, convinced that her Delilah-like ministrations are designed to tame, declaw, and enmesh him. And there's something legitimate to his distrust, for there's a compulsive, self-serving quality to what Georgette does, a repetition in some ways of what she did with her mother.

As a child, Georgette felt that if she could be her mother's therapist, she could tame the beast in her. She could induce her mother to be steadier and more nurturing, cure her of her alcoholism, and put an end to her unpredictable rages. Her efforts did gain her a measure of safety and control, but they became her addiction, and that has carried over to her marriage, as she hopes to succeed with her husband where she failed with her mother. But, of course, she never does quite succeed. Because she fails to heal Martin and make him into a more caring, devoted partner, Georgette believes she is an inadequate wife, just as she once believed she was an inadequate daughter. Nevertheless, she drives on.

Georgette assumes that by struggling with Martin this way, she will eventually work something out for herself; that if she can just convince him to be sensitive, caring, and consistent she will have achieved her mission and be at peace. But she has little sense of the magnetic allure his inconsistency has for her, of how her reactions to him are amplified and distorted by her unresolved feelings toward both her mother and the loss of her father, or how her own maneuvers and retaliations keep their pattern alive. Meanwhile, the power struggles that she and Martin engage in re-create the flavor of their childhood homes, Martin taking the role of his disapproving mother, Georgette that of her own childhood self. Their failure to achieve a satisfying intimacy with each other appears to be typical of many couples with anxious attachment histories.[3]

If we look again at the findings of Main and others who have assessed adult attachment, it is important to remember that the key quality of the secure-autonomous adults is not that they had secure attachments with their parents. Rather they were all distinguished by an open and coherent way of reflecting on their attachments. To the extent that they felt wounded by a parent, they had managed to work it through, so that they were no longer either rigidly cut off from their true feelings about that relationship or still embroiled with hurt, rage, and blame. Somehow they had arrived at the point where they could let the past rest and move on with their lives.

Some of them appear to have been able to go beyond what they experienced with their parents because they had other relationships in childhood that kept an alternate perspective alive in them. According to Main, some of these adults spoke of

> the kindness of relatives who they saw only occasionally, the parents of friends who provided alternative models of parenting when they were very young, or teachers who took a personal interest. One father cited a cold night in early childhood when his visiting grandfather had gotten up to bring

him an extra blanket: "*Nobody* had ever done anything like that for me before, and, at that moment, I realized that not everybody was alike."[4]

But for many children, such alternative models do not exist, which makes their task much more difficult. It is, therefore, not surprising that some of Main's subjects attributed their change to psychotherapy.

Therapy can do many things. It can provide a new model of what a close relationship can be; it can teach one to reflect on feelings, events, and the patterns of one's own behavior in a way that one was unable to do before; it can compensate to some degree for nurturing experiences one never had as a child; it can provide the guidance, persuasion, and pressure one needs to break an addictive pattern and attempt something new (such as recognizing, tuning in to, and beginning to use the strong, nourishing parts of oneself that have been disavowed and seen as existing only in yearned-for others); it can be an opportunity to face some unpleasant facts about how one really operates in relationships; it can provide a context where that portion of the self that has always been ready to relate in a new, more trusting, more direct and healthy way can emerge and take what may be its first tentative steps; and it can offer a safe haven where feelings of shame no longer present such a terrible barrier to self-exploration. It is the last of these functions that I would like to comment on here, because I think shame is a critical barrier to the entire working-through process.

I had a patient in treatment who was prone to rageful fits with her husband and children. She wanted to know who "the real me" was but was afraid to find out. She didn't think she'd like whatever true self she'd find. And yet the experience of therapy suggests that being able to come out of hiding and speak of hated aspects of oneself can be a healing process. A patient who is able to face the shameful fact that she is a shrew to her husband and children is free to stop the endless litany of blame and to feel again. The constant complaints, the incessant demands that the therapist see things from her point of view, the guilt-inducing accusations that he always takes "their side"—such defenses are part of her flight from feeling, fueled by the desperate fear that she will be found in the wrong. An early goal of treatment will thus be to get her to relinquish these defenses and to know what she feels, including her self-hatred.

To stop running and experience the shame is painful, but it is also an opportunity. It gives her the chance to recognize that being in the wrong for acting like a shrew does not mean that her husband or daughter aren't also wrong in their way, nor does it make her into a poisonously deformed and unlovable thing. That's a legacy of how she experienced being wrong when she was a child. But it's a legacy she cannot overcome so long as the shame remains unconscious and unspoken. Once she speaks about it, to someone who is able to listen and absorb without becoming anxious, judgmental, or compulsively helpful, something changes. She is able to view herself from a freer, less tyrannical perspective, able, perhaps for the first time, to feel some sympathy for herself and her predicament. She is able to see that her cruel lack of sympathy for herself is in part what fuels her rages and her desperate need to blame. Gradually she may find that she is able to look at deeper issues of shame, closer to her core—of feeling, as a little girl, unwanted, a piece of excess baggage who constantly had to prove her worth. For the first time, she is able to see herself as she was as a child and to grasp the importance of her attachment needs, which somehow got thwarted at that time. The clarifying, sympathetic, clean relationship with the therapist helps guide and contain this process, and may help liberate her self-love. If it goes well, her therapy will gradually enable her to be self-reflective in a way that was impossible before and to be more appreciative of the mental states of others—both of which have been found to be key ingredients of the secure adult.

How might such a therapeutic experience affect Martin or Georgette? In Martin's case, it would encourage him to relinquish his addictions and power games and risk standing still with his unfelt pain, first in the therapy office, gradually on the outside. It would mean recognizing how wrapped up he still is in his mother's orbit, despite the fact that he rarely thinks about her and doesn't even like her very much. It would mean embracing the rejected child he once was, the insecure little boy who couldn't take his needs to his parents. It would mean giving up his pose of unruffled poise and revealing some of his self-doubts and anxieties about shame to his wife—a process that would not only help balance the power between them but would also enable her to serve as a much better attachment figure for him.

For Georgette such a process would mean learning to stand next to her fear of abandonment without becoming panicked. It would mean reexamining her hated inadequacies—weakness, neediness, perpetual dissatisfaction—from an adult perspective. It would mean recognizing that not only is she not hopelessly deformed but that she's really quite normal in these respects and that her relentless self-hatred is an act of unremitting cruelty against herself. It would mean seeing that her constant fear of abandonment—and the appeasements that grow out of it—allows people to take her for granted, to act disrespectful, and to constantly reinflame her self-hatred and shame. It would mean trading in her obsession with Martin's acceptance and approval for a firmer, cleaner, less manipulative, less caretaking, less clutching stance with him, by which she gains the best chance of winning the respect and steady caring she wants and deserves.

Becoming conscious of shame and other early unresolved anxieties in this way, allowing oneself access to needs and parts of the self that were put off limits ages ago, can also go on outside the therapy room. Close friends and marriage partners can sometimes serve this function, when the trust is such that they can disclose things to one another and explore them in ways they haven't before. This is perhaps taking the secure base function to the highest possible level in adulthood.

In Main's study, some of the secure adults who believed they had been anxious children attributed the change to their relationship with their spouse. Something new and special happened there that overcame pulls they may have experienced toward transference and repetition. As Alicia Lieberman puts it, "With a love partner one can go over and over the kinds of things that one's mother and father didn't respond to well, and if the partner responds well, it's like a release, and one can finally lay old conflicts to rest."[5] The preoccupied wife who had ambivalent attachments to her parents cannot believe her husband when he says, despite their fights and mutual dissatisfactions, that he genuinely loves her and wants to stay with her. She cannot assimilate it to her worldview, her internal model. She is sure that he will abandon her, either because he already wants to or because her impossible and anxious neediness will eventually drive him out. But his steadfastness over the years builds her trust. It causes her to remember her relationship with a great uncle, whose love was precious and unwavering, and to think more and more about him and how good she felt about herself around him. Gradually, she assimilates her marriage to this model, and it becomes more central. Feeling more secure, she finds herself freer to reflect on the past—about how her parents made her feel, how it affected her behavior with others.

She is able to consider what she's feeling when her husband criticizes her, because she is not unconsciously convinced that she is worthless and he wants to get rid of her. And she is able to use her husband as a secure base for this process.

A growing body of evidence indicates that these three variables—having had a loving, supportive figure available in early childhood, having undergone in-depth psychotherapy, and/or being in a stable relationship with a supportive spouse—are perhaps the most important elements in breaking the intergenerational cycle of emotional damage. Several studies have shown this to be the case with women who were abused as children but have not become abusing mothers.[6]

Selma Fraiberg believed that having a baby is a key developmental stage for adults and that it too represents an opportunity for change. Having a baby can offer a new perspective on one's own childhood—what one felt, what one's parents must have felt, how psychologically delicate the process is, how inevitably imperfect. Finding oneself dealing well with the emotional challenges of parenthood can also be a transforming experience. "The wounds can really be healed in the context of raising a baby," Lieberman says. She believes that one's sense of self can be lifted by being with a baby who seems to be saying, "You're doing okay, Mom, you're really doing okay."[7]

Given the considerable struggle that seems to be involved in resolving the past and becoming our own person, where do we, as adults, stand in relation to our parents, especially if our childhood attachments were not secure?

That our parents have such immense impact on our lives, that they affect the types of people we become and the way we behave with our mates, that their anxieties often live within us in some fashion and emerge in the way we experience, or fail to experience, our children—all this is naturally the cause for much emotion. In our society impassioned attitudes toward parental flaws tend to flow in one of two directions, which, not surprisingly, echo the two major styles of anxious attachment. Some people hold that we should never speak ill of our parents. They may not be perfect, but they did give us life, they did struggle to feed us and take care of us, and to carp or complain reflects ingratitude and betrayal. In my experience, people who hold this view rarely have a warm and open relationship with their parents. The form may be there, the dutiful visits, the gifts, the cards, the helping hand, but the feeling is not. They seem to be defending so rigidly against feeling any anger that they often have difficulty experiencing other feelings as well.

A second response to parental flaws is unrelenting anger and blame. In recent years Alice Miller, whose excellent book, *The Drama of the Gifted Child,* introduced many people to the ways in which self-absorbed parents wound their sensitive children, has become a proponent of this response. In a series of works, culminating a few years ago in *Banished Knowledge,* Miller has become committed to exposing parental abuse and denouncing mental health workers who whitewash or make excuses for it. Her message is that parents do a great deal of harm and that we, the children, must be willing to remember and embrace our rage if we are ever to be whole.

A friend, a woman in her forties, attended a workshop in which she had an important insight on this subject. She had been speaking bitterly of the ways in which her mother had disappointed her since she was a child, when another woman, in her seventies, asked her, "What would you think of me if I attacked my mother at such length?" My friend said, "I guess I would hope that by your age you would have come to terms with all that." The older woman said, "That's exactly what the women here in their twenties are thinking about you."

I relate this incident because nowhere in Miller's recent work is there the suggestion that persistent anger at parents can work against us, even when its roots are valid. In *The Drama of the Gifted Child,* Miller equated a person's ability to mourn with the ability "to give up the illusion of his 'happy' childhood." This makes good sense; it is a useful prescription for the avoidant adult. But holding on to anger and blame is another impediment to mourning. It prevents the grown-up child from feeling the loss of what he never had. His anger, in effect, shields him from his sadness, and it also, paradoxically, keeps him enthralled with the very parent he blames and hates and denounces. This is the ambivalent, enmeshed position, and, in adopting it, Miller, who in her old age is seething over what her mother did to her, has fallen into a writing style typical of the incoherent, muddled interview transcripts of preoccupied adults.

Miller is right, I think, that early wounds must be fully experienced at some point in one's life, but carrying them like a banner is not a symbol of health or maturity. Eventually, one must separate, in the positive sense of becoming one's own person, which means not just letting go of the unconscious, neurotic tie to the parent, but letting go of the wound that perversely sanctifies that tie and letting go of the ways in which one's own behavior with others (including with one's children) replicates it.

The cards that people get dealt—in terms of the blessings and curses of heredity, the supportiveness of their families, the quality of their early social encounters—are terribly unequal. And yet no one comes away with the perfect childhood. Even those that attachment theory labels secure are not without troubles, anxieties, annoying habits, self-doubts, phobias, depressions, or obsessions. Securely attached children can have an overly sexualized relationship with a parent, be too encouraged in their aggression, fail to experience adequate limit setting, have their intellects overemphasized or dismissed, feel tormented by parental conflict, and by the inner conflicts that result from allegiances, betrayals, and identifications with a damaged or hurtful parent. They may experience unfortunate sibling rivalries, suffer inadequately mourned losses, be troubled by conflicts outside the home, and so on. Various estimates put the securely attached as high as two thirds of the middle-class population. As Arietta Slade and Larry Aber have written:

> Given our knowledge of human nature and of our fellow men and women, it would be foolish to assume that such a large proportion of individuals would be free of neuroticism or character pathology. In fact, in reading the adult attachment transcripts of secure individuals, neurotic conflicts, problematic identifications with parents, evidence of character problems, etc., are quite evident. And, yet, at a fundamental level these do not interfere with the capacity to recognize and integrate the importance of early relational experience, to remember the effects of that experience, even if it was negative, and to respond to their children in a way that is relatively free of the burdens of the past.[8]

The willingness to remember and reflect is at least as important in keeping the past from weighing too heavily on our relationships with our children as it is with our mates. This was brought home to me recently in my own experience as a new father. In the early months of my son's life I found myself haunted by the fear of losing him. It often came upon me just at those moments when I felt most in love, when he was most unbearably cute. I would be hit by a fantasy that something terrible would happen to one of us. Initially, I tried to shut this fear out and convince myself it wasn't important, just a "rogue" thought, as a friend's psychologist once put it. When I finally decided to face it, I remembered what actually happened to me and my father. We had a warm connection until I turned nine or ten. Then we became antagonistic, and for several years our relationship was rent by battles.

Recently, my father commented that he liked little children mainly until they reached what he called the end of the age of innocence. I thought, yes, after that their independence can become trying and thence begins the struggle for control. For the first time I recognized that I had already begun to fear repeating this process with my son, who is willful, assertive, and full of beans. Unconsciously, I expected that aspects of his personality would represent a poor fit with mine (which is quite similar) and, rationally or not, I was anticipating struggles that would put an angry wedge between us. As this issue became more conscious for me, the concern did not go away. I still recognize it as something I may have to deal with in one form or another. But being able to reflect on it and talk about it has helped dissipate some of the haunting anxiety about permanent loss, and it gives me more confidence that when we do come into conflict my reactions are less likely to emanate from old destructive patterns.

An important lesson emerging from adult attachment research, then, would seem to be this: We cannot change our childhood. But we can let go of the defensive and obsessive postures formed at that time. We can make sense of what has been repressed and forgotten. We can reexperience dissociated feelings with a new appreciation for ourselves as we were as children, for the situation that existed at the time, for the parents who may have caused us to suffer. And we can successfully mourn our losses. If we've managed to hold on to an alternative model, and if we are wise or lucky in love, we may be able to work through our childhood experience in the context of a marriage or something like it. If the grip of the past is too strong, we may work it through in therapy. In either case, if we remain conscious of ourselves and of the pull of early models, even if hang-ups of various kinds remain, as inevitably they must, we have a better chance of creating satisfying relationships with our mates and secure relationships with our children. To that extent it seems that in emotional life, much as in history, we are only doomed to repeat what has not been remembered, reflected upon, and worked through.

PART VI

THE ODYSSEY OF AN IDEA

27

AVOIDANT SOCIETY:
CULTURAL ROOTS OF
ANXIOUS ATTACHMENT

Before the modern era, most life tended to be family life. In preindustrial Europe, production was carried on in family farms or small shops. Hired laborers lived with the farmer, the baker, or the cobbler and his next of kin and were considered family members themselves. Servants fit into the family affectional system. Their relationships with their master's children were often like that of an uncle or aunt, and their own children like that of siblings or cousins. Apprentices were treated like sons, obliged to obey the master, and were completely dependent on him until they turned twenty-one. Few people went out to work. The old did not become segregated in retirement villages or institutions, but lived out their days within the family they'd been a part of all their lives. The setting may have been claustrophobic, with the intense hatred, resentment, and murderous jealousies that inevitably arise under such conditions; but there was also love, familiarity, and unquestioned belonging.

> Time was [Peter Laslett has written], and it was all time up to 200 years ago, when the whole of life moved forward in the family, in a circle of loved, familiar faces, known and fondled

objects, all to human size. That time has gone forever. It makes us very different from our ancestors.[1]

Preindustrial society was hierarchical, authoritarian, and unjust and characterized by a degree of bullying and submission that we would find intolerable. Personal freedom was severely limited. And the opportunity to rise above the conditions into which one was born, to even hope for a materially better future, was almost entirely absent. But although existence was precarious in many ways, with poor nutrition and primitive medical practice placing life and health at risk at every turn, and although personal misery and psychological disturbance could no more be averted than today, people experienced a kind of security that until our era could be taken for granted in most stable societies. They were guided by traditions and values that they accepted for the most part without question. And they belonged; they had people they could count on and a milieu they felt a part of.

It wasn't just that parents stayed together and were always in or near the home, or that extended families were often tightly knit, an ever-present factor in one's life. There were larger communities as well. People identified strongly not only with their family or clan but with their church, their village, their guild if they belonged to one, and their social class. They worked, worshipped, celebrated, and amused themselves in the context of these groups. They did not consider themselves to be special or apart, but cut from the same cloth as their peers. Indeed, personal identity was inconceivable outside these affiliations,[2] which were emotionally and spiritually sustaining and saturated with mutual help. They were in every respect *attachments*, social attachments, as imbued with love, rage, hurt, and happiness as a child's attachment to his parents.

In many traditional societies, there was a familiarity and intimacy even among nonequals. People lived in such close daily proximity and were so mutually dependent that little of what one was could be hidden. In late-nineteenth-century Russian novels, it is apparent that even the roles of master and servant or landlord and peasant did not preclude feelings of affection, devotion, dependency, and deep familiarity. Goncharov's Oblomov is particularly poignant on this score, lamenting the passing of the traditional order with its warmth, its certainties, and its timeless routines in favor of the energy, opportunity, and calculations of a newly mobile and enterprising society.

The industrial revolution and the shift in customs and ethics that went along with it caused the world to gradually change from one in which people were born into a God-given place, with clearly ordered roles and duties, to one in which they had to make their place. Competition became a new organizing principle, and in one sphere of life after another it was becoming impossible to feel quite the same unity with one's fellows. No longer cradled by unchanging, familiar connections, by homey surroundings, and by the known rhythms of nature, men went out to work in impersonal, often crushing environments. Frequently, they had to steel themselves and swallow their emotional needs. "Dependency," an unnecessary concept before, became an undesirable quality in men and, much later, in women. Meanwhile, as old bonds dissolved or became less central to one's life, the sphere of intimacy that surrounded each person shrank.[3]

In the world that commerce and industry were creating, there was less time for nonproductive pleasures. Daydreaming, chatting away the afternoon, taking long midday naps, and other idle pastimes no longer fit the quickened schedules of life and were frequently stigmatized as lazy or lower-class.[4] As the opportunity for success and the fear of failure became a bigger factor in people's lives, parents became anxious about formerly acceptable qualities in their children that were now deemed slothful, clingy, or immature. The passivity that allows one's feelings to come to the surface and get worked through in fantasy and contemplation was now more likely to be seen as a waste of time. One had goals to achieve. If one became cut off from one's feelings, passivity became not just a waste of time but a threat, and one's busyness something of an addiction.

The history of the family is so complex with so many contradictions and so many variations from era to era, from place to place, and from one social group to the next, that it is difficult to make generalizations.[5] But if we think of the family as the child of society, we could say that modern conditions have often tended to make the increasingly isolated nuclear family anxiously attached to the culture that gave birth to it. Meanwhile, as each home became a more private and unique place, without the protocols and rituals that had governed life before, parental psychology became far more critical in determining whether a child would be securely or anxiously attached.[6]

In the last century our society has become more child-conscious perhaps than ever before, concerned with what children need, and aware of the importance of early environments. We have struggled to eliminate the routine mistreatment of children, the diseases that once ravaged them (and that in prior times caused some parents to hold off becoming too attached to them when they were little lest they die), and the wretched poverty and ignorance that often deformed family life. Our accomplishments in these areas have been huge. As historian John Sommerville has observed, "Some children are probably better cared for now than ever before in history."[7] But the social organization of the modern era has thrown up new sorts of challenges, many of them stemming from isolation and alienation, which present new barriers to secure attachment.

The middle-class patients who sought help from Freud, Janet, Jung, and the other pioneering psychotherapists at the turn of the century and for several decades afterwards tended to know who they were, or at least who they thought they should be, and to feel a natural sense of belonging and of responsibility to both their families and their social milieux. They suffered from annoying symptoms—compulsions, hysterical paralyses, phobias, fetishes—that they hoped to discard, but otherwise experienced themselves as emotionally intact.[8] The new analytic patients, as the reader may recall, did not display these obvious symptoms. They were haunted by feelings of self-doubt and emptiness, were prone to dislike or hate themselves, and were unclear about who they were or should be. During this era many of the character neuroses we discussed in the previous chapter—schizoid, narcissistic, borderline, as well as Winnicott's false self—came to the fore.

Heinz Kohut believed that during the early part of this century, when psychoanalysis was first coming into being, problems in child care were more apt to arise when the child's first sexual stirrings began. Hence Freud's emphasis on oedipal conflicts and the neurotic problems that sometimes developed in their wake. In recent times, Kohut argued, parental failures start earlier when the parents lack the time, the energy, the inclination, and the cultural support to provide the attuned, baby-oriented environment infants need in the earlier years.* Such failures are more likely to impair the child's developing sense of self.[9]

As early as his World Health report Bowlby struggled with the societal

---

*Kohut was probably speaking mainly of middle- and upper-class families. Very poor or financially destitute families, especially those with a lot of young children or where the mother had to take in work, would have had a hard time providing a baby-oriented environment either in Freud's day or earlier. The poor, however, were rarely seen in treatment.

changes that militated against secure attachment. In previous generations, Bowlby noted, mothers were surrounded by teenage sisters, cousins, and their own mothers, all of whom pitched in with the child care.
Such helpers not only gave mothers much needed breaks from the ordeal
of taking care of one or more children, but also companionship, guidance, and confidence. The child, meanwhile, had alternate attachment
figures; and less pressure was, therefore, placed on the bond with the
mother to provide him with all his needs. "It has taken the world's rich-
est societies," Bowlby said, "to ignore these basic facts."[10]

The loss of community ties also disturbed Bowlby. "Mobility is the
great enemy," he told me. "In days gone by, people stuck around, they
saw a lot of each other. But this business of moving every five years from
one place to another is exceedingly destructive. I'll give you an example.
The Israeli kibbutzim look after small children in an awfully silly way."
(Infants have traditionally slept in a dorm overseen by a caretaker and
only spent limited time with their parents. An unusually high number of
them have turned out to be ambivalently attached.[11]) "But once the
children are older, it's a wonderfully stable community where everyone
knows each other and where there's a great deal of mutual support, like
a small town. Any small town in days gone by was a community where
people knew each other, and you constantly met all your friends—
when you went shopping or to church or to school or whatever. And
there was a lot of mutual help. If people know each other and have long-
term relationships, mutual help makes sense, because I can help you
today and five years hence you can help me. But if you aren't going to be
here in five years, and the community is constantly changing, it is by
definition not mutually helpful."[12]

The pace of life can also be a hardship. Speaking of a time no more
distant than the 1970s, Ainsworth says, "People used to have more
leisure, more time for fun, sociability. Now everybody's too busy to be
sociable. It's sad."[13] We seem to be, more and more, a busy, time-con-
scious people, occupied with goals of all kinds and habituated enough to
work and advancement or other forms of stimulation that, for much of
the population, sociability has lost some of its former pleasure.

The effect on children of our increasing emphasis on ambition is perhaps most apparent in athletic prodigies, who often lose their childhoods
in training and competition,[14] but it reaches most children in some way.
Even infants, naturally joyful learning machines, are sometimes pressured
to learn faster and better.[15] New devices are being marketed to improve

mental capacity, including a strapped-on-the-belly tape player for preg-nant mothers to stimulate the nervous systems of the unborn. In Phila-delphia the Better Baby Institute trains infants who can't yet crawl to become intellectual powerhouses and instructs their parents on how to carry on the process at home.[16]

"I don't think it's a very healthy thing to be *at* the child too much," Ainsworth says, "to have him taste this and smell that and feel this, try-ing to enrich all aspects of his life. It's intrusive. The normal kind of interactions that take place in the course of routines, where there is some conversation and smiling back and forth and perhaps a little play—or in periods that are consciously devoted to play—I think that's what the child needs in terms of stimulation. That doesn't mean that the child's interest in other things shouldn't be encouraged, but he'll have that interest if he just has a chance to explore. Stimulation is something you *do* to somebody else. It's experience the child needs."[17]

There's a simplicity and naturalness to Ainsworth's message. All your child needs in order to thrive both emotionally and intellectually is your availability and responsiveness. You don't need to be rich or smart or tal-ented or funny; you just have to be there, in both senses of the phrase. To your child, none of the rest matters, except inasmuch as it enables you to give of yourself. And yet this does not seem to be an easy message for our culture to absorb. For many parents it seems simpler to apply themselves to beefing up the baby's IQ or working overtime to ensure that they can pay for the best schools.

In 1975 an American writer, Jean Liedloff, wrote a book called *The Con-tinuum Concept*. Liedloff spent two and a half years in a South American jungle living with the Yequana, a stone-age tribe, and was transformed by the experience. She saw people who were at ease with themselves, who took great pleasure in whatever they did—even ordeals, like rowing a canoe against an impossible current, which we might consider intolera-bly frustrating. She saw a graceful people, living in the moment, who were not preoccupied with everything they had to do.

The Yequana infants were carried everywhere by their mother and in constant physical contact with her until they started to crawl. Whether doing daily chores, dancing excitedly at a party, or sleeping at night, the mother kept the baby attached to her. Children were not fretted over or given training in obedience. But they were never far from loving atten-tion. And they grew up to be extraordinarily self-reliant and at ease with both themselves and their environment. They were also well behaved, "never fought, were never punished, always obeyed happily and instantly; the deprecation 'Boys will be boys' did not apply to them."[18]

The society Liedloff described was a world of Bowlby's theories come to life, where attachments were deep and natural, where children followed their mother like ducks, where "the younger generation" took "pride in becoming like its elders,"[19] and where attachment behaviors persisted fully and openly over the course of a lifetime. The capacity of Yequana adults for mutual caring and dependence is captured by an incident Liedloff describes with a young man of twenty:

> I was doing my best to excise the beginnings of gangrene from his toe by flashlight. The pain must have been excruciating. While offering no resistance to my scraping the wound with a hunting knife, he wept without any sign of restraint on his wife's lap. She ... was completely relaxed, not putting herself in her husband's place at all, but serenely accessible, as he buried his face in her body when the pain was greatest or rolled his head from side to side on her lap as he sobbed. The eventual appearance of about half the village at the scene did not appear to affect his reaction either toward self-control or dramatization.[20]

Her encounter with the Yequana caused Liedloff to question our entire way of life but especially our child-rearing practices. With a Bowlby-like emphasis on the ancient conditions under which our species evolved, Liedloff urged her readers to return to what she called the "continuum," the natural biological flow in which we came into being. She urged mothers not to work, if possible, during the baby's first year; to carry him next to their body while doing their chores; to instantly respond to his cries, just as their heart naturally dictates; and to sleep with him at night, as mammals and primitive peoples who haven't lost touch with their nature have always done.

> At this moment in history, with our customs as they are, sleeping with one's baby seems a wildly radical thing to advocate. And so, of course, does carrying him around, or having him held by someone, at every moment, asleep or awake. But in light of the continuum and its millions of years, it is

only our tiny history which appears radical in its departures from the long-established norms of human and pre-human existence.[21]

Liedloff and similar thinkers have inspired many people. More mothers now use Snugli-like devices to carry their babies rather than strollers or baby carriages, and one recent study suggests that this practice alone may help promote secure attachment.[22] Some parents have even begun taking their babies to bed, and the influential developmentalist Melvin Konner has endorsed it.[23] And yet, how much can we import the methods of a primitive tribe to our own culture where the demands of social life and the meanings we attach to what we do are so different? While there may be limits to human adaptability, it seems to me that letting a baby be on his own at times, letting him nap and sleep alone, do not stretch those limits too far, as long as his care is, as Ainsworth has said, consistently warm and responsive.

Karin Grossmann agrees with Liedloff that a very close mother-infant connection in the first year is ideal. "It's what the Japanese do, it's what many other cultures do. These children are very secure. When they are distressed, they will go and seek comfort right away; they will not be very afraid of strange people. But, of course, this is not enough to make you a capable member of our society. You have to learn to be on your own. That's the way life is structured here. So it would be silly to raise a child in America for the first three years in this style. He would not be able to go to preschool. He would not be able to negotiate with his mother and to give a little when she does return to work. He would not be fit to live in this culture."[24]

To emphasize this point, Karin refers to the five weeks she and Klaus spent working among a tribe on Trobriand Island in Papua New Guinea. The children of the Trobrianders were secure and confident in their home environment, but when they tried to move to the more bustling and competitive society next door, they generally failed.

It is important to remember, too, that we come to parenthood not as blank slates but as people with specific experiences and feelings. A thousand years of therapy would not turn any of us into a stone-age parent even if we were certain that was a worthy goal. We can be inspired by other peoples, but change has to be organic and begin with who we are, both culturally and psychologically. Without that we are bound to stumble. That is why when a mother decides to behave in a totally different manner from her own mother, she often finds her mother's shadow hang-ing over her in unforeseen ways. As Karin Grossmann observes, a mother may give up her own life and career on the child's behalf, in attempted imitation of primitive child care, because of her own need for a cuddly object of security. She then becomes "so invested in the child that she expects him to bring her instant and eternal happiness in return. And she has a hard time letting the child go when it needs to explore."[25] Such parents may also find it impossible to accept or react constructively to the child's natural aggression. None of this is to disparage the efforts of American parents who are attempting to adopt Liedloff's ideas to their own homes. We do not yet know how well this is working, and each fam-ily no doubt goes about it in different ways. But replicating the Yequana in contemporary society is virtually impossible, and numerous compro-mises will have to be made.

To read about the Yequana is nevertheless to feel a sense of loss. We miss having a deeper, more satisfying contact with ourselves; and, despite our belief in individualism, our tendency to look down on those who need social support, and our disdain for government programs, we miss having a community that surrounds us with love and security. Some of that loss can be dealt with on the personal level—by coming to terms with the past in ways described in the previous chapter. Some of it can be dealt with through social adjustments, by mobilizing ourselves to make our society more supportive and caring, especially in light of what we now know about attachment needs.

Since Bowlby's World Health report in 1951, he and his followers have had a huge and steady influence on child care practices around the world. Adoption policy, hospital policy, social-work policy, not to mention the everyday behaviors of parents, have all been affected. That infants become profoundly attached to parents or parental figures, that they love them with every ounce of their being, that they need to be loved and affirmed by them and are wounded by losses and lengthy separations is perhaps better understood now than ever before. But this enlightenment has been patchy, inconsistent, and often in conflict with other social needs or wants, like the importance of careers to mothers, industry's wish not to be disrupted by lengthy parental leaves, and the general reluctance to spend lavishly to assure high-quality child care programs. That a U.S. court in 1993 could order a two-and-a-half-year-old child (the famous "Baby Jessica") returned to biological parents she did not know, thereby severing her ties to the adoptive parents who raised her, without a consideration of the child's feelings, suggests that our courts and our laws remain ignorant of important issues in child development.

In the World Health report Bowlby stated, with what now sounds like utopian optimism, that, having conquered most of the diseases caused by malnutrition and infection, society was free to turn its attention to mental health. He advocated supporting families with a helping hand or financial assistance in times of need, with psychotherapy, and with other services, so that children would not have to suffer the deprivations and other torments that are both harmful and preventable, and so that they would not grow up to be the sorts of parents and fellow citizens one would not wish to have in one's midst. In the post-war period many industrialized countries have developed such supportive family services. Nevertheless, some developmentalists warn that child welfare is in crisis, perhaps especially in the United States, which has lagged significantly behind on all fronts.

That social policy and social interventions can make a society more humane and give parents a better chance to raise secure children has been demonstrated in numerous studies. People respond in remarkable ways when they feel that someone is there to help them. A series of studies have now found that when mothers have solid social supports—whether from the extended family or an outside helper—the likelihood of secure attachment is enhanced, particularly, one study found, when the infant has a trying temperament.[26] Even Dymphna van den Boom's simple six hours of helpful instruction over the course of several months to poor Dutch mothers of temperamentally difficult children (see Chapter 21) seem to have been a godsend to them, enabling them to form secure attachments where avoidance would otherwise have been predicted. Alicia Lieberman's therapeutic work with troubled mother-infant pairs, where the mother learns not so much better techniques of child care but how her own emotions, based on her own childhood experience, may be getting in the way of providing responsive care, has also been shown to make a huge difference in the development of secure attachment. Studies of women giving birth in a Guatemala hospital—where they had previously been left alone for much of the time—demonstrated that the constant friendly support of an untrained female helper enabled them to have a much shorter labor (8.7 hours on the average as opposed to 19.3), to have half the perinatal complications, and to be better able to enjoy the early hours of their baby's life.[27] Such support—educative, therapeutic, and warmly attentive—if provided to children, parents, the sick, and the dying, could help relieve the sense of isolation, alienation, and insecurity that troubles our society.

In Syracuse, New York, an extensive program of child care and family support was offered to a group of low-income families until their children reached the age of five. A follow-up study when the children were fifteen found them doing much better than a control group of kids from similar backgrounds. They performed better in school and were more apt to report liking their teachers. Adolescent boys from similar families who did not have access to the program during their early years committed four times as many offenses, and the offenses were more severe. A similar program in Connecticut provided health and social services to poor families with infants and toddlers. Ten years later the children and their mothers were doing far better than those who had not received such early support. The other families were costing the state an average of almost three thousand dollars more each year in welfare and special education.[28]

Most parents have some social support. It takes the form of friends; close relatives, including brothers and sisters who may also be parents and can give them hand-me-downs and advice; and their own parents, who may be in the position to help out with child care and to help them financially. They may not have a lot of support, but enough to get by and to give their children the kind of care they need. Other parents lack these supports entirely. Many would benefit from community assistance of the sort offered in the Syracuse and Connecticut programs. But when it comes to providing such services, the United States is particularly impoverished, the only industrialized country that has not instituted a system of child care for working parents, a guaranteed minimum family income, and national health care for families with small children. While we now have a parental leave law, it is small in comparison to Sweden where mothers can take a year off with full pay and the guarantee that their job will be there for them when they return.[29] A report in the *New York Times* on the Australian health care system offers one small example of the routine support other nations provide:

> When a baby is born . . . the hospital notifies an infant health center in the family's neighborhood. Within days, the parents are visited by a highly trained nurse. Typically these "sisters" try to get to know the mother, offer a phone number where they can be reached for advice on everything from bathing to

breast-feeding, and make an appointment for the baby at the
health center. These nurses take care of all the baby's routine
health needs.[30]

In such an environment, parents are probably more secure and less likely
to let anxieties impinge upon their relationships with their children.

Poverty per se does not breed disturbed family relationships. Attachment research has tended to show that people can have very little materially and yet be excellent caregivers as long as they are not overwhelmed
by deprivation. But if they have to deal with the stresses of poverty, have
suffered early maltreatment or neglect themselves, and are isolated as
well from sources of support, then the chance of their children becoming
securely attached and well functioning declines sharply. Even the ability
to learn is impaired by such conditions. According to a ZERO TO THREE
report, which echoes two decades of attachment research and other studies in early development, students do well in school if they arrive having
already developed in their early years confidence, curiosity, self-control,
a sense of effectiveness, the ability to relate well to others, the capacity
to communicate, and the ability to cooperate. Children from overstressed homes, with few resources and little social support, often fail to
develop these qualities, leaving them with bad feelings about themselves
and little hope of success later.

And this is not a marginal issue. According to Urie Bronfenbrenner,
in the United States, unique among developed nations, a quarter of all
young children, from newborns to five-year-olds, have the added burden
of poverty. Studies, like Glen Elder's *Children of the Great Depression*, as
well as a host of more recent investigations, have documented the toll
that poverty and family instability can take on the lives of such children.
(Paternal unemployment alone has been associated with unstable, unhappy, unproductive lives among sons.)[31] Economic privation has been
associated with serious medical, psychological, and social problems that
could have been prevented. These problems include disturbed family
relationships; child abuse; lonely children coming home to empty
houses, being kept company for hours on end by television, and coalescing into destructive groups with similarly deprived youngsters; and eventually, of course, more alienated, dysfunctional adults who have little
stake in society, who, it could be said, lack a secure attachment to the
society, and act out their anger by being uncaring, uninvolved citizens or
worse.

Developmentalists have made numerous proposals to ameliorate these conditions. ZERO TO THREE whose board of directors includes many of the nation's leading child development experts—Berry Brazelton, Robert Emde, Stanley Greenspan, Joy Osofsky, Arnold Sameroff, Edward Zigler, among others—recently put forward a series of recommendations that are modest by Western European standards: that every parent have the opportunity to take at least six months off from work after the birth of a child to help promote responsive caregiving; that the government establish strong, meaningful standards for day care, mandating appropriate staff ratios and training and including family subsidies to "bridge the gap between what families can afford to pay and what child care really costs if staff are paid appropriately";[32] that comprehensive health care be available to all families, as well as decent affordable housing, and income support for families below the poverty line. Equally important, it recommends an integrated network of services that would enable parents—including foster parents, some of whom are caring for babies handicapped by traumatic early experiences, like being born addicted to cocaine—to benefit from all that we have learned about what children need in their early years. Such services would provide easy access to parenting education; to a developmental specialist who works with their pediatrician and could help them understand what their baby is experiencing or why it behaves as it does; to treatment of the kind Alicia Lieberman provides to disturbed mother-infant pairs; and to a friendly person who is familiar with their circumstances and can point them in the direction of the various social services that are available to them.

Bronfenbrenner has lamented the fact that in the United States age segregation of children makes it impossible for many adolescents to relate to small children. He believes that not only should they have constant opportunities to be with younger kids, but that a "curriculum in caring" should be instituted from grade school on up and that this should include special tasks, like taking care of old people and sick people, which children are naturally good at if given the chance.

Teachers could also be given better training in the meaning of the disturbing, sometimes maddening, behavior they see in their classrooms. They could work more closely with school psychologists so that anxious children don't get driven more deeply into their early attachment models, as is now typically the case, but are encouraged to open up and see the world of people anew. Having additional lay adults in the schools, hired on the basis of their ability to relate to children, to serve as potential attachment figures to the children who need them could, as Sroufe has suggested, facilitate this process and take a huge burden off teachers. The school years are a unique opportunity for troubled children to be redirected emotionally, but that opportunity has not been seized.

There are other ways, of course, in which our society can become more responsive, especially in relation to how we care for the sick, the dying, and the bereaved. In each of these conditions, attachment needs soar and we hunger for someone to hold our hand or show us the way. Such support was once more available, provided to varying degrees by the extended family, by the church, or by neighbors whom one knew and trusted. The recent success of hospices in helping people to die in a positive frame of mind, the success of bereavement counseling in preventing suicide,[33] the rage people experience over the unfeelingness of doctors all suggest the importance we place on being cared for in a kindly way when we need it.

Governmental efforts, of course, can never adequately fill a gap where warmth and connection are wanted. The emotional challenges of the current era will still need to be faced in other, more personal, ways. But social programs can perhaps create conditions where human connections have a better chance to flourish.

Implementing programs that take attachment needs seriously would be very expensive—a lot more than the supercollider, though perhaps less than the Savings and Loan bailout or going to war. There would be savings, too, just as there always are when preventive programs are instituted, especially where children are concerned. The bills for later welfare services would probably be reduced, as would the destruction caused by alienated youths and the cost of expensive incarcerations. We would also have a better-earning, tax-paying work force among the groups at risk. But, most important, it would offer us a different quality of life, where we would be taking care of human needs that most societies attended to before the industrial era; strengthening the family, which is the best institution we have for meeting the needs of children; enjoying a greater social cohesion, with less cause for segregation and fear.

But we are nowhere near making any of these commitments because our social policies are shortsighted. Americans, for instance, are livid about crime, infuriated by beggars, indignant at the antisocial behavior of minority or poverty youths. But our response to these social ills is like that of Aladdin's uncle who, you may recall, sent the boy into the underground chamber in search of the magic lamp. With Aladdin struggling up the stairs, the uncle made louder and louder demands that he hand up the lamp while refusing to give Aladdin the hand he needed to emerge from the cramped stone stairwell. When Aladdin could not produce the lamp because he was too weighed down, his uncle, impervious to the obvious solution and incensed at being thwarted, ragefully slammed shut the overhead door, thereby abandoning his nephew and the lamp in one swat. This is America today, stubbornly committed to threats and punishments (and moralistic exhortations regarding family values) as the preferred method to bring about changes to problems whose causes are in large part social, economic, and psychological. Although police action and criminal justice is always important, no amount of threat or punishment can reverse the alienation and hostility of those who have paranoid or infantile character structures, who are overwhelmed by feelings of being cheated and deprived, who have no faith in their ability to nourish or be nourished, and who face every encounter with a lover, a child, or society itself with the expectation that they will exploit or be exploited. People like this will cost their communities a bundle whether or not they are handled in an enlightened way. But at least by providing psychiatric and social supports, we can hope to improve their behavior, lessen future damage, and perhaps give them some release from their inner demons. Meanwhile, nothing would serve us better than to pay *whatever it costs* to help families give their children adequate, loving care so that such personalities will be less prevalent in the next generation—and to keep doing so even if some unworthies take advantage. Investing in secure attachment is not a cure-all by any means, but it is a win-win proposition for everyone involved. Unfortunately, like Aladdin's uncle, we would rather pay through the nose in punishing.

28

LOOKING BACK:
BOWLBY AND AINSWORTH

John Bowlby died of a stroke on September 2, 1990, at the age of eighty-three. He was staying at his beloved vacation home on the Isle of Skye in Scotland where he had spent many summers with his family, gardening and taking long walks over the rugged, majestic landscape. He was buried there, as he wished, before a group of family and local friends, in the graveyard of a ruined pre-Reformation church. At the service, which took place at another church nearby, which he and Ursula had attended for many years, the minister read a passage from *Pilgrim's Progress* about the passing over the river of the character, Valiant for Truth, as "the trumpets sounded for him on the other side."

Earlier that year Bowlby had seen his last work, a biography of Darwin —a surprising departure into a new realm—published to near universal acclaim. Frank Sulloway, himself a Darwin scholar, called it "a remarkably sensitive and revealing portrait of Darwin by a self-trained admirer who came to know more about the man than many Darwin scholars do."[1] He considered it a model psychobiography, a significant improvement over Freud's efforts in that genre.

Bowlby's *Charles Darwin* is both a biography and an attempt to clear up a medical mystery, for Darwin had all his life suffered from a debilitating anxious condition, which included bouts of nausea and vomiting and which had never been, in Bowlby's mind, satisfactorily explained. Bowlby attributed Darwin's troubles to a sequence of unhappy childhood experiences, of which the most telling was the loss of his mother at age eight. After her death his father and sisters were so aggrieved they refused to speak of her or allow her name to be uttered, and the "wall of silence" made it impossible for Darwin to mourn her loss. Years later he seemed to have even forgotten that she'd existed or that the trauma had ever occurred. Add to this, difficult relationships with his father, of whose love and respect he never felt certain, and his reproving older sister, who undertook to fill the maternal role, and Darwin becomes a poignant study in spoiled attachment.[2]

Bowlby had many reasons to feel connected to Darwin. He believed that much of his struggle with organized psychoanalysis had represented his effort to "recast" analysis "in terms of modern evolution theory."[3] He saw himself as an evolutionist and believed that the formation of affectional ties—the development of love—was one of the greatest achievements of human evolution.[4] Bowlby also admired Darwin's personal qualities, many of which foreshadowed his own—the courage, the tenacity in the face of staunch and hostile opposition, and the warm and generous style with which Darwin conducted himself in his writings.[5] But knowledge of Bowlby's own childhood experience—the coldness and emotional unavailability of his parents, his being sent away to boarding school at age eight—might lead one to believe that the connection he felt to Darwin was also based on a shared sense of loss, a shared sense of not having had his deepest self responded to. One can imagine that he made much the same connection with the maladjusted children at the progressive schools where he briefly worked as a young man and with the child patients he treated for many years thereafter. Their pain had something in common with his.

Bowlby acknowledged that he was not an intuitive therapist and that he had to rely on theory to discern what his patients were struggling with.[6] But despite this and despite his cocksure intellect, he was not full of himself, he was not puffed up, he was, as his wife says without irony, "a very plain, simple man."[7] A colleague, Hyla Holden, similarly referred to "the straight-forward and loving simplicity which lay behind his formidable intellect."[8] Surely, his patients must have appreciated this in him. He rated himself a good listener, and one can imagine his asking earnest and sympathetic questions as he homed in on a point.

Friends and colleagues remember him as having been reliable. "You could count on him in every way," wrote his former subordinate, psychiatrist Freda Martin.[9] "I have images of him, even last winter," Tavistock familty therapist John Byng-Hall wrote the year Bowlby died, "shaking the rain off his green mackintosh and hat as he arrived on time for some evening meeting, while others sent their apologies."[10] Despite his severe and sober countenance, he could readily loosen up and be fun. "I can vividly see him," yet another colleague recalled, "leading the Scottish reel with Mattie Harris at the magnificent Christmas parties held at the Institute of Psychoanalysis."[11] But he was not emotionally accessible, was unable to express affection verbally, and outside the therapy room with its carefully prescribed roles, he was not drawn to the emotional affairs of others. He valued his many friends, thought only well of them, and preferred not to go any deeper. Regarding his personal relationships, Ursula Bowlby has said, "John wasn't curious about people, about 'how they ticked,' and he was very *in*curious about himself. This seems an absurd statement, considering his career, but anyway it is true.... Perhaps he was fascinated by patterns—how the pieces fitted into the jigsaw."[12] All this, of course, is a hallmark of the avoidant personality. But, no doubt like many avoidant personalities, Bowlby did manage successful and fulfilling relationships. His well of feeling, shapeless and unarticulated as it may have been, could be touched by others. And perhaps especially with children—including those who had become detached, mistrustful, and mean—he could resonate with their suffering, even if he was not able to suffer himself.

Bowlby lived long enough to see many of his once heretical views widely accepted. Hotly disputed for many years, his early work on separation and deprivation is barely questioned now, except by those who argue not that such experiences aren't damaging but that the damage may be reversible under optimal conditions. In psychoanalysis, the idea that parental neglect or mistreatment is a source of later emotional disturbance is no longer questioned by anyone. And in developmental circles, behaviorist objections to other aspects of attachment theory no longer command attention. It is perhaps a measure of how thoroughly some of his concepts have been absorbed that a review in *The Psychoanalytic*

Quarterly of a collection of his short pieces faults him for stating the obvious, the reviewer apparently unaware that what is obvious now was anathema when Bowlby first spoke it.[13] He took pride in the fact that even some former detractors quietly admitted to him that he had been correct all along.

In his last decade, his status as a significant innovator, reformer, and theory builder was recognized throughout the West, while his recommendations were built into the practice of social work and became part of the standard advice that baby doctors give to parents and lawmakers. Many honors were bestowed on him, the one he valued most being the honorary degree he received from his own university, Cambridge, in 1977. "Fortunately," he said of the belated acceptance, "I come from a long-lived family."[14]

After completing the third volume of his trilogy, Bowlby offered a reporter the following, typically understated assessment of his accomplishment: "Look back thirty years, and there were four theoretical paradigms that were totally distinct from each other"—psychoanalysis, learning theory, cognitive psychology, and ethology. "There was no conversation between any of these four fields, and they each had a different set of assumptions. . . . One of the things I've been concerned about is to try to develop some sort of theoretical framework that does justice to the contributions each has made, so that there could be interchange and communication, and data drawn from different fields. I think that's a useful thing to have attempted."[15]

In a more formal, if less restrained, review of the final volume Rycroft wrote: "Few people, it seems to me, are today as persistent and consistent, as single-minded, as Dr. Bowlby has shown himself to be; his attitude towards his life's work and achievement has a Victorian monumentality about it which is enviable and all too rare."[16]

Bowlby's influence has extended to many disciplines, from ethology, where animal studies based on his theories have been conducted, to clinical work with patients, to personality psychology, to social psychology, where ever more basic attitudes and conditions, such as the way one conceives of one's relationship to God, are found to relate to attachment style. (One can easily imagine that the quality of one's patriotism is related as well.)

Bowlby was perhaps most proud of his gradual acceptance by his psychoanalytic family, which had once driven him from home. He always wanted to be considered an analyst and must have been hurt by those who said he wasn't (one analytic journal referred to him disingenuously as an ethologist).[17] It pleased him that, especially in later years, he was asked to speak repeatedly to analytic audiences around the world, including the Anna Freud Center in 1988. When he turned eighty the British Psychoanalytic Society, somewhat belatedly, held a celebration in his honor, which at least one former Bowlby antagonist recalls as "a convincing and moving reunion."[18] Bowlby's name is still distasteful to some stalwarts in the Kleinian camp, so that one can still hear dismissing comments about him at the Tavistock Clinic, where they remain in the majority. But even there the mental framework has changed, and the influence of the eminent Kleinian analyst Wilfred Bion has allowed a focus on the early real-life experiences that were Bowlby's passion. Some analysts, however, continue to believe that he abandoned psychoanalysis or turned hatefully against it. And only a tiny few are aware that he and his followers have succeeded in making a science of something that analysts deal with every day in their clinical work but have tended to ignore in their theory: the influence of the early environment. Most, as of this writing, have not even heard of Mary Ainsworth.

And yet this state of ignorance has begun to change, especially among the younger generation. Articles have begun appearing in some analytic and psychiatric journals attempting to integrate attachment concepts into the main body of analytic thinking or offering introductory overviews of attachment research.[19] Eminent Freudians, like Americans Fred Pine, Otto Kernberg, and Albert Solnit refer to attachment contributions with respect.[20] And others have begun to realize that far from being a threat to psychoanalysis, attachment research offers a degree of scientific support that it has never before enjoyed. Toronto analyst Morris Eagle, for instance, notes that research on avoidant attachment provides the best empirical evidence on repression and its consequences.[21] The work that Main initiated on how we internalize early experience offers similarly powerful confirmation of traditional analytic concepts like transference and repetition, while simultaneously providing a means to explore them further scientifically. As more children from the Sroufe, Grossmann, and Main samples are given the Adult Attachment Interview, new sources of data, of special interest to analysts, will be available about how early experience is incorporated psychologically. If some of these subjects, whose early attachment histories are known, can eventually be seen in some form of research-oriented psychotherapy, as Nancy

Kaplan hopes to do one day with the Berkeley sample, the results might certainly captivate the psychoanalytic world. Meanwhile, Peter Fonagy and his colleagues in London, with their work on self-reflection, internal representations, borderline states, and other forms of psychopathology, has pioneered the long-overdue integration of attachment theory with more traditional analytic thinking, yielding important developmental and clinical insights.[22]

Politically, things have changed, too. Anna Freud and Melanie Klein are dead, as is the sanctity of drive theory (see Chapter 7). As many analysts, unencumbered by the old debates, come across Bowlby's ideas today, they find in them a natural extension of their own thinking. The third issue of the New York journal *Psychoanalytic Dialogues* noted Bowlby's passing with a strong appreciation. The statement, written by Lewis Aaron, ends, "The editors dedicate this issue to John Bowlby, who taught so much about the importance of mourning our losses."[23]

Indeed, those who champion his views in the analytic community believe not only that he deserves to be considered a genuine psychoanalyst but an invaluable one. "To my mind he is one of the three or four really great psychiatrists of the twentieth century," the British analyst Anthony Storr wrote in *The Lancet*.[24] Storr later told me: "I think he really saved psychoanalysis from being totally discredited. By writing as he did, and giving scientific status to everything he said, he took his findings out of the morass that psychoanalysis got into and gave it some scientific respectability. He had a much more commonsense approach to many of the things that Freud postulated, and where he disagreed with Freud, I think he was nearly always right."[25] This is, needless to say, a minority view, especially in England, where Bowlby is still less appreciated among analysts than elsewhere, but one that is no longer unthinkable.

In 1984 Jeffrey Masson published a book called *The Assault on Truth* in which he accused Freud of having been dishonest and cowardly in abandoning his original theory of neurosis—and in particular that hysterical symptoms in adulthood were caused by childhood sexual molestation. In reviewing the book, which he called "distasteful, misguided and at times silly," Rycroft wrote, "If Masson had really wanted to reintroduce a traumatic theory of neurosis, he would have done better to base it on Bowlby's work on separation and loss, instead of attempting to resuscitate Freud's seduction theory."[26]

On October 16, 1991, the British Psycho-Analytic Society held a memorial in Bowlby's honor. Three people spoke, but, according to Ursula Bowlby, "It was the middle paper, by Eric Rayner, that hit the jackpot." Rayner reviewed the development of Bowlby's ideas, his struggle with Melanie Klein, his report on juvenile thieves, his explosive monograph for the World Health Organization on maternal deprivation, his development of attachment theory, the supporting research on secure and insecure attachment coming out of the United States, the writing of his trilogy, *Attachment and Loss*. Rayner also spoke of the shameful organized attack that drove Bowlby from any further presentation of his views at the Society's scientific meetings; the extraordinary value that child therapists had found in attachment ideas; and the usefulness of the attachment metaphor in understanding social issues—such as the disaffection that a whole portion of society can experience when it feels left out, demeaned, uncared for. He noted that in terms of social policy Bowlby was the most influential psychoanalyst that had ever lived, but that most psychoanalysts had ignored him because his scientific interests didn't seem to have much relevance to their clinical work. Rayner challenged his fellow analysts to decide whether an evolutionary, biological orientation and an openness to scientific research should have a place in analytic thinking. "Perhaps we should . . . debate his theories again," Rayner concluded. "If nothing else, our therapeutic frame of mind is altered by theory. John Bowlby was a great alterer of frames of mind."[27]

Rayner's was a modest eulogy. But "when he sat down," Ursula Bowlby recalls, "there was spontaneous applause. Even the ranks of Tuscany," she adds, delightedly quoting Macaulay, "could scarce forbear to cheer."[28] Although most of those present were analysts from the "middle group"— that is, independents like Bowlby himself who had not aligned themselves with either Melanie Klein or Anna Freud[29]—Rayner was amazed by the strength of the response.

Bowlby did not investigate the subtleties of clinical experience, which is the everyday bread and butter of analytic work. Indeed, in later decades, he largely gave up doing treatment altogether, in favor of writing, training an army of psychotherapists, assessments of incoming patients, and clinic management. (He once told Ursula that sitting for five hours a day and listening to patients was "no life for a man."[30]) Given his interests, it is hardly surprising that Bowlby has not achieved the status among working analysts of the other great innovators of his era, like Fairbairn and Winnicott. He offers something different, something that analysts are beginning to cautiously consider from a distance. It's not what they're used to, but with interest in infant research rising throughout the analytic world, their appreciation is growing.

Inge Bretherton has written, "One notable talent that stood Bowlby in great stead throughout his professional life was his ability to draw to himself outstanding individuals who were willing and able to help him acquire expertise in new fields of inquiry that he needed to master in the service of theory building."[31] Ethologist Robert Hinde is the outstanding example there. But Bowlby generally drew outstanding people to himself, not just experts from other fields. These included Jimmy Robertson, who had the passion and energy to tackle hospital policy; Peter Marris, whose book *Widows and Their Families* had so influenced Bowlby; Colin Parkes, who has used attachment principles with the dying and bereaved; among others. None, however, compared to Ainsworth.

When I met her in 1988, Ainsworth was a bright-eyed woman of seventy-six whose mode of engagement changed readily from intellectual delight to professorial instruction, from easy laughter and fluency to a flustered search for the right word. She lived in semiretirement near the University of Virginia in Charlottesville, where she had taught for many years. She still attended child development meetings, where her voice and analysis carried great weight. (That activity was halted by a series of small strokes in 1992.) In discussing her work, Ainsworth revealed a strong, sometimes bristly pride and an uncommon willingness to credit others. The penetrating gaze she trained on me at times was suggestive of her years as a teacher and clinician. Although more self-aware, more interested in herself as a psychological being, Ainsworth seems to share some of Bowlby's avoidant features and, like him, has never found it easy to express feelings. Her former student Robert Marvin, also of Charlottesville, who, along with his wife, Cheri, has been like family to Ainsworth, feels that he was aided in becoming close to her because he himself came from a family in which feelings had to be read between the lines.[32]

With her two pioneering longitudinal studies, Ainsworth made the most dramatic effort to take attachment theory into the field. But she did much more than that. She gave Bowlby early theoretical support—one thinks of her seminal papers on maternal deprivation (1962) and dependency (1969)—and was instrumental in introducing his ideas to developmental psychologists. With her clinical and diagnostic skills (it should be remembered that she was an established Rorschach expert before she ever met Bowlby) she led the way to a practical study of attachment themes, enabling other scientists to consider and explore them further. That was the great meaning of her ingenious creation, the Strange Situation. With that in hand, she was able to mobilize the better part of an entire discipline to follow in her footsteps.

Bowlby described his extraordinary connection with Ainsworth as one of the happiest he's had ("a mutual admiration society," in the words of his wife[33]). Her visits to London were a treat for him, as the two of them barricaded themselves in his office in the Bowlby home and read each other's work. He saw their four decades of nearly unbroken collaboration, with manuscripts regularly flying back and forth across the Atlantic for critiquing, as having been invaluable. He did seem to harbor a touch of guilt about her long comparative obscurity. When we spoke in 1989, he still recalled with regret a ground-breaking report she wrote for him that, because of prior commitments he had made, was published in an obscure journal. His final book on attachment, *A Secure Base*, was dedicated to her.

Although she never had children of her own, Ainsworth did become the matriarch of the far-flung but close-knit family of attachment researchers, many of whom were intellectually nurtured by her since their graduate school days and continued to see her as a guiding force in their work. They, in turn, have helped make her one of the biggest names in developmental psychology since Piaget. Although still unknown to the general public and to most clinicians, her fame in the world of infant development exceeds that of Bowlby himself.

"Bowlby does the theory,"[34] Ainsworth used to say, as if he were the commander in chief and she the field marshal. It was an arrangement that reflected the side of her that emerged in this relationship. Despite her own prominence, with many followers who barely know Bowlby's work, to Ainsworth he remained the senior partner. That they were not riven by the jealousies and competitiveness that have destroyed so many other scientific enterprises may have something to do with a supportive femininity that came out with Bowlby and that men like Bowlby thrive on. "I think that women on the whole are much readier to take the lead from a male mentor than the other way around," Ainsworth says. "It's not just Bowlby. I saw this with Bill Blatz in Toronto, way back when. He had a great following of women who worked in the nursery school or with parent education and who seemed to be disciples. But he could never find a man to work with him for any length of time."[35]

Like Bowlby, Ainsworth is an impressive thinker and writer. The success of attachment theory no doubt owes a great deal to this concentration of communicative talent. She writes as if the material has personal meaning to her, a quality that must have contributed to the influx of students who came to study with her and carry on her work. That she was also a creative teacher with a unique approach to child development caused some of her undergraduates to want to continue in the field. And, like Bowlby, too, she was able to attract outstanding people—Mary Main, Inge Bretherton, Alicia Lieberman, Jude Cassidy, Roger Kobak, to name but a few, and, indirectly, Alan Sroufe, who has also attracted outstanding people. If attachment research in American universities is "zooming," to use her word, it is partly the result of the personal power of this shy, strong-minded woman.

To her students, Ainsworth has always been a formidable and dominating figure, no-nonsense in her approach to the research, and hardly self-effacing in the presentation of her views. But there has always been the self-doubting side. "I was pretty insecure as a child, and I suppose I never really let it go. If a paper was turned back with a severe criticism or a grant proposal turned down as having no value, I would immediately think, well, maybe I'm just no good; maybe there isn't anything at all to this thing I value so much."[36] It seems fitting, when placed alongside Bowlby, who seemed blissfully unfamiliar with the experience of self-doubt, that, while he did the grand synthesis, she was the one to clarify the origins of some of the commonplace insecurities that haunt our daily lives.

Through many of the early years, Ainsworth's work was subject to blistering attacks. The revolutionary style of her research—the shrewd move from counting behaviors to attending to the meaning of behavior and the context in which it occurs—not to mention the conclusions she drew about the importance of sensitive, responsive, consistent parenting, so broke with the conventional frame of mind in developmental psychology, and so challenged the popular wish that both parents could work full-time with little impact on their children, that many were angered by it. Like Bowlby, who weathered vitriolic attacks for suggesting that children are harmed by prolonged separations from their families, many of the attacks on Ainsworth were bitter and impassioned. Sroufe, who observed the vindictiveness at professional meetings, was impressed with her "grace and dignity" under fire.[37]

"One of the things that gave me more and more confidence," she told me, "was that things always worked out the way we hypothesized they would. We gave negative evidence every chance to emerge if it was there, but the whole thing has been so reliable in that sense." But hers was never the implacable Bowlby-style confidence. When Ainsworth says, "Imagine the surprise I had, beginning in the eighties, when I began to get awards!"[38] it does not sound coy. She did not expect them. But by the end of the decade, few psychologists had as many.

Entering the spotlight both pleased and embarrassed her. Unlike Bowlby, who held the light as if he were born to it, Ainsworth never seemed at home. "It sounds corny and modest," she told me with a touch of urgency, "but it's the ideas I've been so enthusiastic about and so eager to put forward, not myself. You ask whether it took a lot of patience to do those longitudinal studies. Well, yeah, it takes patience, because I don't think there are any useful shortcuts. But it never felt that way to me, because I find the firsthand details so awfully interesting. The data collections for those longitudinal studies were among the most interesting things I've ever been into in my life."[39]

The change that Ainsworthism has wrought in developmental psychology in the last fifteen years can hardly be measured. "Our whole developmental approach was cognitive until she came along," Berry Brazelton says, referring to psychology's pre-Ainsworth emphasis on such functions as perception, memory, and abstraction. "She enabled psychology to look at the emotional development of children in a reliable, quantifiable way."[40] Sroufe goes further: "I've always said that if there were a Nobel Prize for this kind of thing, she would get it. It'll never happen. Some of the implications are too subtle. It's not characterized by a specific, in-time breakthrough, like the isolation of a gene. But when I went to school I was taught that only behaviors were real, not relationships—they didn't exist. Ainsworth demonstrated that there can be a psychology of relationships and that relationships can be measured. That's why you get Nobel Prizes, isn't it?"[41]

Even those who strongly support the attachment idea have reservations about various aspects of the theory or research. Roger Kobak has stressed to me repeatedly his concern that attachment theory does not take enough account of later developments in childhood and adolescence, and the ways in which each new stage brings new energies and new opportunities to work through earlier problems. Morris Eagle, one of a handful of psychoanalysts who have made a serious study of attachment themes, believes, as I myself do, that in focusing so much on experience Bowlby eventually lost touch with the child's fantasy life and its inevitably irrational components.[42] Also, partly as a legacy of Bowlby's battles with Kleinians and orthodox Freudians, who were very interested in such matters, and partly because of Bowlby's own limitations, attachment theory, as it now stands, does not take much account of the child's sexuality or aggression.

Bowlby complained that he could hardly be faulted for not studying everything. He studied what interested him and he took it as far as he could. But, as Rycroft notes, one does get the impression at times that he sees attachment not as being one factor in emotional life, but the key to it all.[43] And when this happens one becomes more troubled by the elements it leaves out—from the complexities of fantasy life to the turmoils of the oedipal era—and thus more troubled by the possibility of oversimplification. Chicago analyst Michael Basch sees development as progressing in sectors—attachment, autonomy, creativity, psychosexuality, and the feeling-thinking system—sectors that influence one another but develop along separate lines. "I think it is important to emphasize that attachment is only one very important aspect of development," he says, "albeit one that significantly affects the other sectors."[44]

Clearly, then, attachment theory is by no means without flaws, holes, and huge unanswered questions. Various studies suggest that we cannot be as confident as we once were about the parenting styles that lead to ambivalent vs. avoidant attachment or the degree to which inborn temperament or cultural mores may also play a part. (Is the ambivalent child constitutionally irritable? Is the mother erratic in her attentions? Is she overly attuned to the baby's signals of fear?) We still do not know enough about the critical role of the father—a legacy of Bowlby's mother-centric views and of the fact that mothers have been much more accessible to study. We do not know how quality of attachment to same-sex or opposite-sex parent plays out in later development or how the child's identifications affect his attachment patterns. We know even less about attachment issues with siblings and other nonparental figures, like grandparents and nannies. We do not know what goes on in the parent-child relationship in the years after age one that may contribute to the security or insecurity of the older child's attachment.

How is attachment played out during the second year, which must still be loaded with attachment issues, including the period that Mahler has labeled "rapprochement," when the child is full of internal conflict over his growing independence? Is it still a fundamental factor, and therefore still readily accessible to change, during the oedipal years, or is it now more entrenched and acting to help or hinder the child's and parent's capacity to deal with new struggles that arise? What about the school years of middle childhood? What about puberty? And how does an insecurely attached child of one develop qualities that suggest security later on?

How central is quality of attachment to character? How does it relate to sexuality and aggression, two aspects of emotional life long regarded by analysts as playing a central role in development but about which attachment theory has so little to say? Does insecure attachment necessarily lead to neurotic character? Does a consistently secure attachment necessarily preclude it?

Quality of attachment seems to be an important factor in those problems of identity and relatedness that are believed to develop in the first years of life (the "pre-oedipal period"). Does that mean it is not a factor in problems that develop later on? Does it mean that early security precludes early disturbance? I think the answer to both these questions is no; but if that is true, then pinpointing early attachment's role in adult psychology becomes even more complicated.

What are the implications for character development of a child who has an ambivalent relationship to its mother, an avoidant relationship to its father, and a secure relationship to its nanny or grandmother or sister? Why do we recognize that such multiple internal representations can exist in children and yet give adults only one attachment classification? Are the four major attachment categories or the eight or nine subcategories distinct and separate, as Ainsworth believes? Or do they become fuzzy at the edges and tend to blend like colors in a spectrum? Does it make sense to talk of the securely attached as having avoidant or ambivalent leanings? And there is more.

But I think even the unanswered questions suggest the impressive scope of attachment's reach, how important future attachment research will be, and how useful are its metaphors. Also, there is no reason to believe that at least some of what is missing in attachment theory as it now stands cannot be incorporated once the appropriate attention has been paid. That longitudinal studies in the home have not been extended yet beyond the first year means that attachment theory still has a lot to learn not only about what sorts of parental behaviors sustain secure attachment in later childhood or how attachment issues manifest themselves in the evolving parent-child relationship, but about how later developmental issues—all the changes that are going on in the child's mind and body—get incorporated into its internal model. Alicia Lieberman, author of *The Emotional Life of the Toddler*, has been struggling with this question as it pertains to the second year. "I've been very interested in the question of assertiveness in the second year of life," she says. "And in sexual curiosity—exploring one's genitals and checking out the differences between boys and girls, worries about how one was made versus how others are made—and the effects all that has on mood and self-concept. All these cognitive and emotional developments must have an effect on the parent-child bond and on the internal organization of attachment. I think attachment has become a little too isolated from other motivational systems within the child, and this becomes particularly apparent in the second year of life."[45]

Much has been debated about Ainsworth's categories of attachment, which in the beginning seemed too simple to represent complex humanity. The idea that they were simplistic has, I think, been refuted, both by their enormous metaphorical power and the way in which the same three or four styles show up in so many areas of thought, feeling, and functioning. But, like the parallel classification of parents—sensitive and responsive, inconsistent or chaotic, hostile and rejecting—they do inevitably miss much of the poetry and texture of any individual life.[46] Anyone who treats patients in psychotherapy will find a knowledge of anxious attachment useful and at times enlightening. But it is only one piece of the puzzle that any personality presents. In discussing the avoidant-dismissive attachment style throughout this book, I have tried to give some breadth to the category and acknowledge that it can encompass many different personalities from the well-functioning person for whom certain portions of the inner world are off limits to the person suffering with a schizoid disorder for whom any act of relating arouses anxiety and threat. But who would guess it might also include a John Bowlby, who could write so movingly about mother-love and the feelings of small children and of whom a colleague could say after his death that it was "hard to imagine a more fulfilled or completed life"?[47] The mysteries and special adaptations of any individual are unavoidably compromised by classification.

The fact that much of the impressive data coming out of attachment research is based on correlations must also give one pause. Even high correlations, like Sroufe's data on the number of anxiously attached babies who act overly dependent in later years or Main's on the number of parents whose children fall into an attachment category analogous to their own, still include a lot of individuals who do not behave in the expected manner. Some of this is no doubt due to the fact that measurement tools in the social sciences are always imperfect. But it also seems reasonable to assume that more is operating here than meets the eye.

Bowlby himself was well aware of the fragility of all theories, that, no matter how good for their time, their usefulness must one day come to an end. But, for now, the usefulness of attachment theory seems to be rising. The work on family relations, the impact of fathers, the differential effect of insecure attachment on boys and girls, the differential impact of mothers and fathers on the same- and the opposite-sex child has all only just begun. The investigation of adult attachment, how it affects personality style and relationships—and the fact that the way a parent represents his own attachment experiences in his mind predicts the quality of the relationship he will have with his child—interest and research in this area is nothing short of explosive. The use of attachment principles in child, adult, and family treatment is also growing. That clinical work can be assessed to some extent by the use of the Strange Situation—as Lieberman has done in her work with distressed Bay Area families (see Chapter 17)—suggests the uniqueness of this tool.

Although Bowlby was a great theory builder and fascinated by all the questions psychoanalysis and attachment theory touched upon, his first concern seems to have remained what it was for him as a young man, the well-being of children. "I'm the kind of person," Bowlby told me, "who identifies a typhoid bacillus and says, Look, if you let typhoid bacilli get into the water supply, there'll be trouble. That's been my job in life."[48] His monumental efforts at theory building were thus mainly in the service of social change. He hoped that the lasting value of attachment theory would "be the light it throws on the conditions most likely to promote healthy personality development. Only when those conditions are clear beyond doubt will parents know what is best for their children and will communities be willing to help them provide it."[49]

As wedded as she is to scientific method, Ainsworth, too, has the heart of a reformer. It has been her mission to prove that how we respond to our children when they are very young is of singular importance. Of her work and the work that has grown out of it she has said, "It's more a matter of faith than anything else, but I do think it has great relevance to the well-being and happiness of mankind. It sounds corny, and I don't go around shouting it from the rooftops, but that's what's behind the whole thing as far as I'm concerned."[50]

In his review of James Agee's 1957 novel, *A Death in the Family*, Dwight Macdonald wrote that it was "an odd book to be written by a serious writer in this country and century," partly because of the way it dealt with love. "It is not sexual, not even romantic; it is domestic—between husband, wife, children, aunts, uncles, grandparents."[51] This was the love that stirred Bowlby and Ainsworth.

Starting with a simple concept, which seems self-evident now that it's been stated—that a child needs to be lovingly attached to a reliable parental figure and that this need is a primary motivating force in human life—the work of Bowlby and Ainsworth and the many others they inspired has helped fill an unseen void that wended its way through much of social and medical science. It's a void that still exists in many respects, and it's a concept that still meets with resistance: It doesn't always fit comfortably with the lives we have built for ourselves. Modern society has taken many of us a long way from a life centered on the pleasures and pains of being connected to others. Our focus is often on other things—achievement, power, acquisition, romance, excitement. But the need for proximity, for felt security, for love; the need to be held, to be understood, to work through our losses; these basic themes of attachment are to some degree built into us biologically. We have mixed feelings about them. But they are there.

APPENDIX

Typical Patterns of Secure and Anxious Attachment

NOTE: The following chart is meant only as a convenient guide and does not take into account many of the complexities and exceptions found in the research. It should be remembered that anxious attachment (avoidant and ambivalent) is not always associated with the styles of parenting described here, but can sometimes come about for other reasons; that a child often has a different pattern of attachment to mother and father; and that attachment patterns can change, so that, while many avoidant babies, for example, continue in their early pattern, others do not end up behaving like an avoidant six-year-old or develop later into a dismissive adult.

Securely Attached	**Avoidantly Attached**	**Ambivalently Attached**
Mother (or primary caregiver) is warm, sensitively attuned, consistent. Quickly responds to baby's cries.	Mother is often emotionally unavailable or rejecting. Dislikes "neediness," may applaud independence.	Mother is unpredictable or chaotic. Often attentive but out of synch with baby. Most tuned in to baby's fear.
Baby readily explores, using mother as secure base. Cries least of three groups, most compliant with mother, and most easily put down after being held.	By end of first year, baby seeks little physical contact with mother, randomly angry with her, unresponsive to being held, but often upset when put down.	Baby cries a lot, is clingy and demanding, often angry, upset by small separations, chronically anxious in relation to mother, limited in exploration.
Strange Situation: Actively seeks mother when distressed, maintains contact on reunion, readily comforted.	*Strange Situation:* Avoids mother when distressed, seems blasé.	*Strange Situation:* Difficult to soothe after separation—angry and seeking comfort simultaneously.
Preschool: Easily makes friends. Popular. Flexible and resilient under stress. Spends more time with peers. Good self-esteem.	*Preschool:* Often angry, aggressive, defiant. May be isolated, disliked. Hangs around teachers. Withdraws when in pain.	*Preschool:* Fretful and easily overwhelmed by anxiety. Immature, overly dependent on teacher. May be victimized by bullies.

Securely Attached	Avoidantly Attached	Ambivalently Attached
Teachers treat in warm, matter-of-fact, age-appropriate ways.	Teachers become controlling and angry.	Teachers indulge, excuse, and infantilize.
Age 6 with parents: Warm and enthusiastic. Able to be open and to engage in meaningful exchanges. Comfortable with physical contact.	*Age 6 with parents:* Abrupt, neutral, unenthusiastic exchanges. Absence of warm physical contact.	*Age 6 with parents:* Mixes intimacy seeking with hostility. Affectedly cute or ingratiating. May be worried about mother when apart.
Middle childhood: Forms close friendships, and is able to sustain them in larger peer groups.	*Middle childhood:* No close friends or friendships marked by exclusivity, jealousy. Often isolated from the group.	*Middle childhood:* Trouble functioning in peer groups. Difficulty sustaining friendships when in larger group.
Secure Adult	**Dismissive Adult**	**Preoccupied Adult**
Easy access to wide range of feelings and memories, positive and negative. Balanced view of parents. If insecure in childhood, has worked through hurt and anger.	Dismissing of importance of love and connection. Often idealizes parents, but actual memories don't corroborate. Shallow, if any, self-reflection.	Still embroiled with anger and hurt at parents. Unable to see own responsibility in relationships. Dreads abandonment.
Usually has securely attached child.	Usually has avoidantly attached child.	Usually has ambivalently attached child.

ACKNOWLEDGMENTS

I was fortunate in writing this book to have had the assistance of numerous researchers, clinicians, and theorists, including many of the leading attachment scholars. I am indebted to all of them and thankful for their cooperation. Without it a book like this would have been impossible. Mary Ainsworth has spent countless hours discussing her work and her life with me over the course of several years. Her open and generous assistance has been an immeasurable help. The late John Bowlby welcomed me into his office and home for two memorable afternoons, as he discussed the development of his thought and the intellectual struggles of his career. Alan Sroufe has been available for many hours of interviews. His ability to vividly conceptualize key issues in the attachment debates and his feedback on the manuscript have been a great help to me. Ursula Bowlby, a wonderful and enthusiastic correspondent, has trusted me with her memories of her husband, providing me with insights into his character and motivation I could not have gotten elsewhere. Arietta Slade first introduced me to attachment concepts in her exceptional class on infancy in the Doctoral Program in Clinical Psychology at the City University of New York. She has been an invaluable supporter and adviser, helping to clarify many of the key issues, and generously critiquing the manuscript.

Roger Kobak, Jay Belsky, and Klaus Grossmann made themselves available for repeated questioning. Each of them has helped me understand subtle aspects of the theory and of their own work and has generously read and responded to the manuscript. Inge Bretherton, Mary Main, Juliet Hopkins, Michael Basch, Alice Smuts, and Edward and Jean Mason have similarly undertaken to educate me about various important realms that this book has touched upon. I am grateful both for their guidance and their careful reading of the manuscript.

I also wish to thank Stella Chess for the time she spent with me discussing both her own work and the early days of Child Psychiatry at Bellevue Hospital in New York, and for reading and commenting on the chapters relating to temperament, day care, and the critiques of attachment theory. I am similarly indebted to Karin Grossmann, Jerome Kagan, Jude Cassidy, Nancy Kaplan, Everett Waters, Alicia Lieberman, Patricia Crittenden, Eleanor Szanton, Robert Marvin, Charles Rycroft, Cindy Hazan, Sandra Scarr, Leah Albersheim, Van Roy Pancake, Philip Shaver, Morris Eagle, and Thomas Bouchard for the time they spent speaking with me. Charles Rycroft, Katherine Coker, and Mary McKinney read the book in manuscript form. They provided me with valuable feedback, as did Eleanor Szanton who read the chapters on day care and society.

Others who have shared their thoughts with me at various times in ways that have enriched the book are Dymph van den Boom, Anthony Storr, Colin Murray Parkes, Lawrence Aber, Robert Emde, Dante Cicchetti, John Byng-Hall, Steven Ellman, Michael Lewis, Elizabeth Bott Spillius, Eva Spitz-Blum, Otto Kernberg, Fred Pine, Albert Solnit, Hanna Segal, Susana Isaacs Elmhirst, T. Berry Brazelton, Annelies Reiss, Emily Fenichel, and Richard Billow.

I am grateful, too, to my editors at *The Atlantic*, Michael Curtis and William Whitworth, who responded encouragingly to my proposal for an article on attachment theory and gave me the space to present it in the length and manner I felt it needed. Without them and their very special magazine this book would not have happened. My editor at Warner Books, Jamie Raab, has been supportive throughout and a pleasure to work with. I would also like to thank my agent, Kris Dahl; Deborah Huntington, Vickie Wingfield, and Wendy McCormick, who transcribed some of my interviews; and Jennifer Patton, who assisted me in getting my notes and bibliography together in the harried final days.

My closing thanks go to my wife Thaleia who has read the manuscript through all its stages and has helped me to understand how someone outside the field might respond to what I've written. She has also made my life a lot easier and happier throughout.

NOTES

INTRODUCTION

1. Gesell, 1928, p. 328, cited in Labarba, 1981, p. 179.
2. Watson, 1928, pp. 81–82.
3. Bowlby, 1966, p. v. Forward in Ainsworth, 1967. Note that new studies have shown that the infant, even the neonate, does have the capacity to distinguish the smell of his mother and to recognize her voice.

CHAPTER 1: Mother-Love

1. Levy, 1937, p. 644.
2. Cited in Spitz, 1945, p. 53.
3. Levy, 1937, p. 645.
4. Levy, 1937, p. 644.
5. Bender and Yarnell, 1941, p. 1169.
6. Interview with Chess, October 21, 1991.
7. Bender and Yarnell, 1941, p. 1169.
8. Bender and Yarnell, 1941, p. 1169.
9. Bakwin, 1941, p. 31.
10. Spitz, 1945; Bakwin 1942; Interview with Robert Emde, March 14, 1991.
11. Interview with Chess, October 21, 1991.
12. Bakwin, 1942, p. 31.
13. Smuts's interview with Senn, September 1980.
14. McNemar, 1940, cited in Ainsworth, 1962.
15. Skeels and Dye, 1939, cited in Ainsworth, 1962. Note that the fluctuations in IQ score do not necessarily reflect fluctuations in intelligence but rather on how well one is able to function intellectually, which might be affected by one's emotional state.
16. Mary Ainsworth, personal communication, August 7, 1993.

17. Spitz claimed to have been analyzed by Freud, but there was no independent record or corroboration of this, and according to his daughter, he enjoyed telling tales. Interview with Eva Spitz-Blum, October 8, 1991.
18. Interview with Robert Emde, March 14, 1991.
19. LaBarba, 1981.

CHAPTER 2: Enter Bowlby

1. Bowlby, 1940, p. 155.
2. Interview with Chess, October 21, 1991.
3. Bowlby, 1988a.
4. Bowlby, 1940, p. 155.
5. East and Hubert, cited in Bowlby, 1940, p. 156.
6. Bowlby, 1940, p. 164.
7. Bowlby, 1940, p. 169.
8. Hamilton, 1990.
9. Interview with Colin Murray Parkes, May 8, 1992.
10. Sutherland, 1990.
11. Ursula Bowlby, personal communication, February 7, 1992.
12. Hamilton, 1990.
13. Ursula Bowlby, personal communication, July 6, 1992.
14. Ursula Bowlby, personal communication, February 19, 1992.
15. Kraemer, S., 1990.
16. Ursula Bowlby, personal communication, February 19, 1992.
17. Interview with Juliet Hopkins, May 7, 1992.
18. Scarf, 1976, p. 151.
19. Ursula Bowlby, personal communication, August 23, 1993.
20. Interview with Hopkins, May 7, 1992.
21. Hopkins, personal communication, August, 1992.
22. Alice Smuts's Interview with Bowlby, June 6, 1977.
23. Bowlby, 1979, p. 13.
24. Smuts's Interview with Bowlby, June 6, 1977.
25. Bretherton, 1992.
26. Smuts's Interview with Bowlby, July 23, 1977.
27. Riviere, cited in Bowlby, 1985, p. 26.
28. Grosskurth, 1987, p. 396.
29. Although Bowlby gave no indication that he respected Riviere, valued his experience with her, or was influenced by her intellectually, he did send one of his sisters (Juliet Hopkins' mother) to Riviere for analysis. (Personal communication, Juliet Hopkins, 1993.) Was this in the first blush of treatment when he still had hopes that it would be a valuable experience for him? Was this indicative of a belief that psychotherapy or psychoanalysis was good for other people but not necessarily for him (an attitude that would seem consistent with other aspects of his personality)? Or did this suggest that Bowlby got more out of his experience with Riviere than he knew or cared to let on?
30. Bowlby, 1985.
31. Ursula Bowlby, personal communication, July 4, 1992. According to Charles Rycroft: "Joan Riviere impressed many people by her insistence that she was 'county' and 'top drawer,' but I don't think she really was. Distinguished academics on her father's side, but no baronets, barons, medieval Welsh princes, etc., as Bowlby had." Personal communication, March 16, 1993.
32. Smuts, personal communication, August 14, 1992.
33. Bretherton, 1991.
34. Bowlby, 1988b, p. 44.
35. See Bowlby, 1979.
36. Rycroft, 1992, p. 74.
37. Freud, 1900, cited in Bowlby, 1979, p. 8.
38. Bowlby, 1988b, pp. 43–44.

CHAPTER 3: Bowlby and Klein

1. Bowlby, 1979, p. 5.
2. Riviere, 1927, p. 374. Bowlby did not much care for this and wrote forcefully in the margin of his copy, "Role of Environment = Zero."
3. Klein, 1959, cited in Caper, 1988, p. 151.
4. Klein, 1927, cited in Caper, 1988, p. 154.
5. Klein, 1933, cited in Bloch, 1978, p. 2.
6. Segal, 1981, p. 13.
7. Bowlby, Figlio, and Young, 1990.
8. Grosskurth, 1991.
9. Interview with Bowlby, January 14–15, 1989.
10. Klein, 1933, cited in Caper, 1988, p. 166.
11. Riviere, 1927, pp. 376–377.
12. Interview with Bowlby, January 14–15, 1989.
13. Klein, 1975, p. 78.
14. Interview with Bowlby, January 14–15, 1989.

CHAPTER 4: Psychopaths in the Making

1. Bowlby, 1979, pp. 5–6.
2. See Vaillant, 1977, for a discussion of these themes.
3. Bowlby, 1979, p. 12. Bowlby is working here strictly with the conflict side of the equation. He is leaving out the equally critical issue of shame formation. See Chapter 18.
4. Bowlby, 1979, p. 12.
5. Smuts's Interview with Bowlby, July 23, 1977.
6. Bowlby, 1944, pp. 113–115.
7. Bowlby, 1944, p. 40.
8. Bowlby, 1944, p. 38.
9. Bowlby, 1944, p. 41.
10. Bowlby, 1944, p. 38.
11. Bowlby, 1944, p. 38.
12. Bowlby, 1944, p. 39.
13. Bowlby, 1944, p. 49.
14. Bowlby, 1944, p. 123.
15. Bowlby, 1944, p. 35.
16. Bowlby, 1944, p. 19.
17. Ainsworth, 1962.
18. Ainsworth, 1962; Rutter, 1981.

CHAPTER 5: Call to Arms

1. Bowlby, 1951, p. 31.
2. Burlingham and Freud, 1944, cited in Bowlby, 1979, p. 10.
3. Burlingham and Freud, 1942, cited in Bowlby, 1979, pp. 89–90.
4. Bowlby, 1951.
5. Burlingham and Freud, 1944, cited in Bowlby, 1951, p. 20.
6. Ainsworth, 1962.
7. A. Freud, cited in Bowlby, 1951, p. 132.
8. Bowlby, 1951.
9. Bowlby, 1951, p. 47.
10. Bowlby, 1951, p. 76.
11. Bowlby, 1951, pp. 67–68.
12. Bowlby, 1951, cited in Rutter, 1981, p. 15.
13. Bowlby, 1951, p. 100.
14. Bowlby, 1951, p. 157.
15. Bowlby, 1951, p. 71.
16. The book did not do well in the United States, where it had an unlucky publishing history.
17. See Rutter, 1981.

CHAPTER 6: First Battlefield

1. Robertson, 1962, pp. 58–59.
2. Robertson and Robertson, 1989.
3. Edelston, 1953, cited in Robertson and Robertson, 1989.
4. Interview with Edward and Jean Mason, April 12, 1990.
5. Robertson, 1962, pp. 57–58.
6. Robertson, 1962, p. 110.
7. Robertson, 1962, pp. 61–62.
8. Lorenz, in Tanner and Inhelder, 1971, p. 232.
9. Robertson, 1962, pp. 67–68.
10. Robertson, 1962, p. 69.
11. Robertson, 1962, pp. 63–64.
12. Senn's Interview with Bowlby, October 19, 1977.
13. Bowlby, Figlio, and Young, 1990.
14. Bowlby was proud of having written the first paper on family therapy, although he never had the time to pursue the matter further and is thus not included in anyone's pantheon of family treatment founders.
15. Robertson and Robertson, 1989, pp. 10–11.
16. Mason, 1991. This film has unfortunately been withdrawn from distribution at the insistence of Joyce Robertson.
17. Senn's Interview with James Robertson, October 25, 1977.
18. Robertson and Robertson, 1989, p. 13.
19. Robertson and Robertson, 1989, p. 13.
20. Robertson and Robertson, 1989, p. 15.
21. Robertson and Robertson, 1989, pp. 16–17.
22. Robertson and Robertson, 1989, p. 20. This is Robertson's recollection. Why was Spence so cold to him? Perhaps he disliked someone else adopting his issue and taking it further than he had. Or did Robertson, who could be quite touchy at times, misinterpret Spence?
23. Bretherton, 1987.
24. Senn's Interview with James Robertson, October 25, 1977.
25. Robertson and Robertson, 1989, p. 32. Fourteen years later, when Robertson showed the film to a gathering of Laura's family, the sixteen-year-old Laura stood up at the end and said of the experience she'd just watched, "That meant nothing to me." But as she spoke, she leaned over and clutched her father's tie.
26. Robertson and Robertson, 1989, p. 41.
27. Tanner and Inhelder, 1971, pp. 230–231.
28. Robertson and Robertson, 1989, p. 42.
29. Senn's Interview with James Robertson, October 25, 1977.
30. Mason, 1991.
31. Senn's Interview with James Robertson, October 25, 1977.
32. Robertson and Robertson, 1989, p. 46.
33. Robertson and Robertson, 1989, p. 45.
34. Senn's Interview with James Robertson, October 25, 1977.
35. Grosskurth, 1987. Bowlby said of this episode: "We do not think this was due to pregnancy, because we have got so many other anecdotal stories of exactly this kind."
36. Robertson and Robertson, 1989, p. 45.
37. Smuts's Interview with Stone, August 1, 1977.
38. Robertson and Robertson, 1989, p. 54.
39. Tanner and Inhelder, 1971, p. 223. This is obviously not a direct quote but Bowlby's memory of what she said.
40. Senn's Interview with James Robertson, October 25, 1977.
41. Robertson and Robertson, 1989, p. 67.
42. Robertson and Robertson, 1989, p. 111.
43. Robertson and Robertson, 1989.
44. Robertson and Robertson, 1973b.
45. from Mason, 1991.
46. Robertson and Robertson, 1973b, p. 3.
47. Robertson and Robertson, 1973b, p. 10.
48. from Mason, 1991.
49. Robertson and Robertson, 1989, pp. 90–91.

50. Senn's Interview with James Robertson, October 25, 1977.
51. Bowlby, 1973, p. xiii.
52. James from Robertson and Robertson, 1989.
53. Ainsworth, 1962.

CHAPTER 7: Of Goslings and Babies

1. Smuts's Interview with Bowlby, July 23, 1977.
2. Smuts's Interview with Bowlby, July 23, 1977. Huxley had written the foreword to the English translation of *King Solomon's Ring*, Lorenz's new book, which was due out the following winter, and promised to get an advance copy for Bowlby.
3. See Bowlby, 1958b.
4. See, for example, Bowlby, Figlio, and Young, 1990.
5. Smuts's Interview with Bowlby, July 23, 1977.
6. Interview with Bowlby, January 14–15, 1989.
7. Bowlby, 1958b.
8. Inspired by animal studies, in which—to cite one example—mother goats rejected newborns who had been separated from them immediately after birth, Marshall Klaus and John Kennell held that there is a critical period during which mother and baby have the opportunity to bond, and if they are separated by hospital policy, the necessary intensity of connection may never develop between them. The idea has been widely recognized in the field to have been hugely overstated and downright false in many respects. Mothers have plenty of time to bond to their babies, even if they adopt them months after birth. Nevertheless, the work of Klaus and Kennell enabled a greater appreciation for how wonderful early post-partum contact between mother and newborn can be and how emotionally valuable it can be to some mothers. Their work has convinced hospitals to allow mothers and babies to remain together rather than persisting in the senseless policy of isolating them after birth. See Ainsworth, 1985.
9. Freud, 1938, cited in Bowlby, 1958, p. 352.
10. Sayers, 1991.
11. A. Freud, 1944, cited in Sayers, 1991, p. 169.
12. Erikson, 1950, pp. 247, 249.
13. Bowlby, 1958b, p. 369.
14. Bowlby noted that Ian Suttie, a British psychotherapist who had worked at the Tavistock Clinic before the war, had argued that the child's need for his mother was a primary motivation, related to the desire for company and the dislike of isolation, and was independent of the bodily needs that mothers satisfy. That Suttie was not an analyst and that he had coupled his theory with an attack on Freud probably insured that his theory would be ignored. He also died young. Suttie, 1935, *Origins of Love and Hate*, cited in Bowlby, 1958b.
15. Klein, 1952, cited in Bowlby, 1958, p. 354.
16. Klein, 1952, cited in Bowlby, 1958.
17. Fairbairn, 1952, p. 137.
18. Greenberg and Mitchell, 1983.
19. Rycroft, 1985.
20. Winnicott, 1975, p. 314.
21. Hughes, 1989.
22. Winnicott, cited in Hopkins, 1991, p. 187.
23. Grosskurth, 1987.
24. Phillips, 1988.
25. Rycroft, 1992, p. 80.
26. Hughes, 1989.
27. Rycroft, 1985.
28. Juliet Hopkins observes: "I don't easily associate JB with the use of such an ill-tempered word as 'maddening' but that may well be correct. He once told me that he found DWW difficult because he was completely content with paradox, whereas he himself, as a scientist, could not be." Personal communication, August, 1992.
29. Winnicott, 1975, p. 239.
30. Bowlby, 1958b, pp. 366–367.
31. Bowlby, 1958b, pp. 369, 370. Regardless of the pleasures and health benefits breast feeding may provide, Bowlby did not see it as essential to healthy attachment either of baby to mother or vice versa. The fact that the hormone prolactin, secreted in substantial quantities when a

mother breast-feeds her baby, has been shown to promote nurturing behavior in laboratory animals is considered by some to be proof that breast feeding is the sine qua non of mother-infant bonding. But the work of comparative psychologist Jay S. Rosenblatt suggests that prolactin is not a crucial element in the bonding of mother to infant in mammals. While the hormone may give some initial impetus to mothers who need it, the presence, appearance, and behavior of the young seem to be more significant in sustaining the maternal bond. Personal communication, 1990.

32. Bowlby, 1958b, p. 370.
33. Yarrow, 1967.
34. Bowlby, 1958.
35. Burnham, 1965, cited in Bowlby, 1973, p. 251.
36. Bowlby, 1960.
37. Ainsworth, 1962.
38. Klein, 1935, cited in Bowlby, 1973.
39. Bowlby, 1973.

CHAPTER 8: "What's the Use to Psychoanalyze a Goose?"

1. Bowlby, 1958a, p. 3.
2. Bowlby, 1958a, p. 3.
3. Bretherton, 1987.
4. Bowlby, 1958a, p. 3.
5. Bowlby, 1958a, pp. 5–6.
6. Bowlby, 1958a, p. 7. Ursula Bowlby had lost her nanny at five and a half and felt that it had scarred her for life. Ursula Bowlby, personal communication, August 23, 1993.
7. Bowlby, 1958a, p. 6.
8. Bowlby, 1958a, p. 9.
9. Bowlby, 1958a, p. 10.
10. Ursula Bowlby, personal communication, July 27, 1993.
11. Bowlby, 1958a, p. 6.
12. Bowlby, 1958a, p. 6.
13. Isaacs, quoted in Scarf, 1976, p. 151.
14. Isaacs, quoted in Scarf, 1976, p. 152.
15. Interview with Segal, January 13, 1989.
16. Interview with Rycroft, May 8, 1992.
17. Grosskurth, 1987, p. 325.
18. Interview with Hopkins, May 7, 1992.
19. Grosskurth, 1987.
20. Grosskurth, 1987.
21. Interview with Rycroft, May 8, 1992.
22. Grosskurth, 1987.
23. Charlotte Balkanyi, cited in Grosskurth, 1987, p. 406.
24. Interview with Rycroft, May 8, 1992.
25. Interview with Otto Kernberg, February, 1988.
26. Rita Frankiel, personal communication, October 1996.
27. Bowlby, 1980, p. 276.
28. See, for example, Furman (1981) and Lopez and Kliman (1979).
29. This opinion was expressed to me by both Hanna Segal (interview, January 13, 1989) and Susana Isaacs (personal communication, June 19, 1992).
30. Bowlby, Figlio, and Young, 1990.
31. Ellenberger, 1970.
32. A. Freud, cited in Grosskurth, 1987, p. 404.
33. Interview with Bowlby, January 14–15, 1989.
34. A. Freud, 1960, p. 54.
35. Interview with Robert Emde, March 14, 1991.
36. Hamilton, 1990, p. 21.
37. Grosskurth, 1987. Bowlby characteristically refused to name the person he suspected of the treachery.
38. Interview with Bowlby, January 14–15, 1989.
39. Bretherton, 1991.

40. Bretherton, 1991.
41. Bowlby, 1959.
42. Malan, 1990, p. 7.
43. Trowell in 1990.
44. Smuts's Interview with Bowlby, July 23, 1977.
45. Rutter, 1981.
46. Bowlby, cited in LaBarba, 1981, p. 493.
47. LaBarba, 1981.
48. Casler, 1961, p. 30.
49. Casler, 1961, p. 30.
50. Casler, 1961.
51. Interview with Ainsworth. (Regarding interview dates with Ainsworth, see notes for Chapter 10.)
52. Bowlby, cited in Ainsworth, 1962, p. 115.
53. Andry, 1960, cited in Ainsworth, 1962, pp. 103–104.
54. Ainsworth, 1962.
55. Stone, 1954, cited in LaBarba, 1981, p. 492.
56. Emde, 1983.
57. Eriksen, cited in Casler, 1961, p. 9.
58. Casler, cited in Rutter, 1981, p. 15. While Casler's review quoted here appeared in 1968, it was typical of what the opposition had been already saying ten years earlier.
59. Rutter, 1981.

CHAPTER 9: Monkey Love

1. Such contact needs had been reported earlier by others.
2. Harlow, 1958.
3. Harlow, 1958, p. 673.
4. Harlow, 1958, p. 685.
5. Harlow, 1958, p. 677.
6. Smuts's Interview with Bowlby, July 23, 1977.
7. Ainsworth, 1962.
8. Suomi and Harlow, 1978.
9. Bowlby, 1979.
10. Hinde and Spencer-Booth, 1970 and 1971, cited in Rutter, 1981.
11. Harlow and Harlow, 1966, pp. 244–245.
12. Bowlby, 1988b, p. 23.

CHAPTER 10: Ainsworth in Uganda

Note: Interviews with Mary Ainsworth took place on the following dates: June 6, 1988; June 16, 1988; September 1, 1988; December 28, 1988; January 27, 1989; January 26, 1992; January 30, 1992; February 2, 1992; August 11, 1993; August 20, 1993. Much of the material relevant to chapters 10 and 11 was covered in the interview of December 28, 1988.

1. Interview with Ainsworth.
2. Interview with Ainsworth.
3. Interview with Ainsworth.
4. Interview with Ainsworth.
5. Interview with Ainsworth.
6. Interview with Ainsworth.
7. Ainsworth, 1962.
8. Schaffer and Emerson, 1964, p. 5.
9. Ainsworth, 1967, p. 331.
10. Interview with Ainsworth.
11. Ainsworth, 1967, p. 270.
12. Ainsworth, 1967, p. 337.
13. Ainsworth, 1967, p. 341.
14. Ainsworth, 1967, p. 343.

15. Ainsworth, 1967, p. 345.
16. Ainsworth, 1967, p. 345.
17. Interview with Ainsworth.
18. Interview with Ainsworth.
19. Ainsworth, 1987, p. 331.
20. Ainsworth, 1987, p. 331–332.
21. Ainsworth, 1987, p. 392.
22. Ainsworth, 1967, p. 144.
23. Ainsworth, 1967, p. 141.
24. Mead, 1962.
25. Lieberman and Pawl, 1990, p. 382.
26. Ainsworth, 1967.

CHAPTER 11: The Strange Situation

1. Interview with Ainsworth.
2. Interview with Ainsworth.
3. Interview with Ainsworth.
4. Interview with Ainsworth. This baby later turned out to fit into one of the less secure subgroups in the securely attached category. Given the mother's overall responsiveness, Ainsworth could not have understood this outcome if she hadn't visited the home.
5. Bowlby, 1988b, p. 49.
6. Interview with Ainsworth.
7. Interview with Ainsworth.
8. Interview with Ainsworth.
9. Interview with Ainsworth.
10. Interview with Ainsworth.
11. Interview with Ainsworth.
12. Ainsworth et al., 1978.
13. Both Suzie and Donnie, who follows, were not part of Ainsworth's original study, but were observed—and videotaped—some years later. Ainsworth did not videotape her original sample, but the phenomena she observed were essentially the same.
14. Interview with Ainsworth.
15. Ainsworth et al., 1978.
16. Interview with Ainsworth.
17. Main and Weston, 1982, p. 46.
18. Main and Weston, 1982, p. 45.
19. Bell and Ainsworth, 1972.
20. Ainsworth et al., 1978.
21. Interview with Main, December 18, 1988.
22. Interview with Ainsworth.
23. Interview with Ainsworth.
24. Ainsworth, 1983; interview with Ainsworth.
25. Interview with Bowlby, January 14–15, 1989.

CHAPTER 12: Second Front

1. Interview with Bretherton, January 22, 1989.
2. Interview with Waters, January 5–6, 1989.
3. Interview with Sroufe, December 20, 1988.
4. Waters, 1978.
5. For an overview of behaviorist thinking at this time see Ainsworth, 1969; Hartup, 1963; Maccoby and Masters, 1970; also Dollard and Miller, 1950; Gewertz, 1961.
6. Interview with Ainsworth.
7. Ainsworth, 1969, p. 1015.
8. Interview with Sroufe, December 20, 1988.

CHAPTER 13: The Minnesota Studies

1. Bowlby, 1979, p. 109.
2. Bowlby, 1979, p. 102.
3. Clarke and Clarke (Eds.), 1976; Kagan and Klein, 1973.
4. Sroufe, 1989.
5. Sroufe, 1983.
6. Interview with Albersheim, April 23, 1993.
7. Interview with Albersheim, April 23, 1993.
8. Matas, Arend, and Sroufe, 1978. (Albersheim's married name at the time was Matas.)
9. Mahler, Pine, and Bergman, 1975, p. 79.
10. Ainsworth, 1984, p. 568.
11. Mahler et al., 1975, p. 78.
12. Mahler et al., 1975, p. 95.
13. Mahler et al., 1975, 80.
14. Interview with Albersheim, April 23, 1993.
15. Waters, Wippman, and Sroufe, 1979.
16. Waters et al., 1979.
17. Sroufe, Carlson, and Shulman, 1993.
18. Sroufe found "virtually no differences" between avoidants and secures "on Apgars, Brazelton neonatal exams at 7 and 10 days, nurses' ratings in the hospital, behavioral observations at 3 months, or Carey temperament questionnaire responses (derived from Thomas, Chess, & Birch, 1968) at 6 months." Sroufe, et al., 1993, p. 71.
19. Interview with Sroufe, December 20, 1988.
20. Sroufe, 1983.
21. Interview with Sroufe, December 20, 1988.
22. Cowen, 1973, cited in Eagle, 1992.
23. Interview with Sroufe, December 20, 1992.
24. Elicker, Englund, and Sroufe, 1992.
25. Sroufe's third category of avoidant children who looked almost psychotic at times would probably have been considered part of a fourth category by other researchers, more disturbed than the avoidant or ambivalent children.
26. Interview with Sroufe, December 20, 1988.
27. Sroufe, 1983, pp. 74–75.
28. Sroufe, 1983.
29. Sroufe, 1983, p. 66.
30. Interview with Sroufe, December 20, 1992.
31. Sroufe, at City University of New York, February 10, 1989.
32. Sroufe, 1983, p. 76.
33. Rosenberg, 1984, cited in Sroufe et al., 1993.
34. Fury, 1992, cited in Sroufe et al., 1993.
35. Interview with Main, March 5, 1993.
36. Interview with Marvin, March 19, 1993.
37. Cicchetti and Beeghly, 1990.
38. Sroufe, 1983, p. 66.

CHAPTER 14: The Mother, the Father, and the Outside World

1. Elicker et al., 1992, pp. 77–78.
2. Elicker et al., 1992.
3. Pastor, 1981.
4. Jacobson and Wille, 1986, cited in Turner, 1991. Note that this study, unlike the previous one, didn't find such differences until age three.
5. Interview with Pancake, March 23, 1992.
6. Sroufe, personal communication, July 11, 1993.
7. Interview with Pancake, March 23, 1992.
8. Troy and Sroufe, 1987, p. 169.
9. Troy and Sroufe, 1987, p. 169.
10. Sroufe, 1989.
11. Elicker et al., 1992.

12. Sroufe et al., 1993.
13. Sroufe et al., 1993, p. 25.
14. Erickson et al., 1985.
15. Renken et al., 1989.
16. Turner, 1991. Here are some of the data from Turner's study, expressed in the number of occurrences of each type of behavior in the ninety-minute observation time. There were thirteen securely attached girls, 11 securely attached boys, 9 anxiously attached girls, and 7 anxiously attached boys in the study, all second-borns. Unique among such studies, attachment status was based on current relationships, using a modified Strange Situation adapted especially for four-and-a-half-year-olds.

	Secure Girls	Secure Boys	Anxious Girls	Anxious Boys
Dependent Acts	7.2	6.0	13.9	22.4
Assertive Acts	10.7	9.6	4.0	27.6
Controlling Acts	18.8	20.8	13.1	51.6
Acts of Aggression:				
Mild	8.1	4.4	7.7	29.0
Strong	2.8	1.5	2.3	15.0
Playful	5.1	10.4	7.0	18.9

17. Interview with Ainsworth.
18. Sroufe et al., 1993.
19. Interview with Sroufe, December 20, 1988.
20. Sroufe, personal communication, July 11, 1993. When the children in this study turned thirteen, Sroufe's team got "every available man into the lab (N = 44)" and assessed his interaction with the child and with the child and mother together.
21. See Bornstein and Lamb, 1992, for complete list of Lamb references, p. 419.
22. Klaus Grossmann, personal communication, August 10, 1993.
23. A subsequent effort to pool the data from all the mother-father attachment studies has found a modest correlation between the child's quality of attachment to mother and father. Sroufe, personal communication, July 11, 1993.
24. Main and Weston, 1982; Easterbrooks and Goldberg, 1991; Suess, Grossmann, Sroufe, 1992.
25. ZERO TO THREE, 1993.
26. See, for example, Smolak, 1986, on the differences between mothers' and fathers' speech patterns with young children. Cited in Sroufe, Cooper, and Detlart, 1992.
27. Sroufe et al., 1992.
28. Belsky, 1984.
29. Sroufe et al., 1992.
30. Marvin and Stewart, 1991; interview with Marvin, March 19, 1993. Salvatore Minuchin, one of the pioneers in family treatment and theory, has identified families as falling into one of three types: adaptive, in which family members are sensitive to, open with, and supportive of one another; disengaged, where they tend to be uninvolved, insensitive, and somewhat angry; or enmeshed, in which they tend to ignore one another's boundaries, behave in intrusive and disrespectful ways, and feel ambivalently toward one another. As Marvin points out, this bears a remarkable similarity to secure, avoidant, and ambivalent attachment patterns.

CHAPTER 15: Structures of the Mind

1. Bowlby, 1982.
2. Bowlby, 1982.
3. Mahler et al., 1975.
4. Marvin, 1977; interview with Marvin, March 19, 1993.
5. See Bretherton, 1991.
6. Bowlby, 1988; Wachtel, 1977.
7. Main, 1991.
8. Main, 1991.
9. Cain and Fast, 1972, cited in Bowlby, 1988, p. 102.
10. Bowlby, 1988b, pp. 101–102.
11. Main, 1991.
12. Rioch, 1988, p. 40.

13. "Piaget Sees Science Dooming Psychoanalysis," by John L. Hess, *New York Times*, October 19, 1972, p. 49.
14. Rycroft, 1985, p. 149.

CHAPTER 16: The Black Box Reopened

1. Interview with Cassidy, February 9, 1993.
2. Interview with Main, March 5, 1993.
3. Interview with Nancy Kaplan, September 9, 1993.
4. Kaplan, 1987, p. 7.
5. Kaplan, 1987, p. 8.
6. Kaplan, 1987, p. 9. Children who had been classified secure five years earlier, however, were not uniformly healthy or creative in their responses. Some disavowed their feelings and lacked creative solutions, suggesting, perhaps, that their security had been compromised.
7. Kaplan, 1987, p. 11.
8. Kaplan, 1987, p. 13.
9. Kaplan, 1987, p. 17.
10. Main et al., 1985, p. 89.
11. Main et al., 1985, p. 90. Main cautions that these procedures are meaningless if attempted in the home.
12. Main, Kaplan, and Cassidy, 1985, p. 67.
13. Interview with Cassidy, February 9, 1993.
14. Main and Cassidy, 1988.

CHAPTER 17: They Are Leaning Out for Love

1. Campos et al., 1983, came up with an average of 62 percent secure, 23 percent avoidant, and 15 percent ambivalent based on a summary of all the American studies assessing quality of attachment, not just middle-class samples.
2. Bowlby, 1973.
3. Cassidy and Berlin, 1992.
4. Main and Weston, 1981; Main, 1991.
5. See Sroufe, 1983. Avoidant aggression is different from the anger of the ambivalent children, who, as Sroufe points out, lack self-control, who are frustrated and flail about, haphazardly seeking connection. The avoidant child is very controlled, and his anger more likely to be cruel and bullying, a reflection of an underlying hostility that has been redirected toward a safer target.
6. Longitudinal studies have yet to show that for any specific person the pattern formed in childhood still exists in adulthood. But adults do show the same patterns (see Chapters 24 and 25).
7. See, for example, Egeland et al., 1988.
8. Sroufe, 1983, p. 77.
9. Sroufe, 1989.
10. Hopkins, 1991, p. 190.
11. Interview with Crittenden, January 9, 1989.
12. Thirty percent, according to recent research. Cited in Fonagy, unpublished.
13. Fraiberg, Adelson, and Shapiro, 1975, p. 125.
14. Fraiberg et al., 1975, p. 110.
15. Fraiberg et al., 1975, p. 127. By being freed to express the negative emotions that had been walled off for so long, each mother seemed to go through what Fraiberg called a "momentous shift in her identification with the baby. Whereas before she was identified with the aggressors of her childhood"—and convinced that she was destined to behave as they did—"she was now the protector of her baby" (p. 127). It could also be said that the mother's ability to experience her long-walled-off attachment feelings, in the form of anger and grief, had enabled her natural attachment feelings for her baby to flow. What linked her childhood attachment feelings with her maternal attachment feelings seemed to be the mother's ability to sympathize with herself as a child. For the caring she finally felt for herself as a wounded child was analogous to the caring she now spontaneously gave to her baby. The therapy could thus be seen as representing the conquest of extreme avoidance by enabling attachment feelings to flow once more.
16. Lieberman, 1991, pp. 268–269.
17. Lieberman et al., 1991.
18. Interview with Sroufe, December 20, 1988.

CHAPTER 18: Ugly Needs, Ugly Me

1. See, for example, Sroufe, 1983.
2. Lewis, 1987.
3. Hopkins, 1991, p. 191.
4. For an overview of this subject, see Karen, 1992.
5. Cassidy, 1990. See also Ainsworth, 1985.
6. Interview with Basch, September 22, 1990.
7. Kobak, 1987.
8. Interview with Marvin, March 19, 1993.
9. Grossmann, 1989.
10. Slade and Aber, 1987, p. 21.
11. Lewis, 1987, p. 32.

CHAPTER 19: A New Generation of Critics

1. Interview with Kagan, January 9, 1989.
2. Kagan, 1984, p. xii.
3. Kagan, 1979, p. 9.
4. Kagan, 1984, pp. 62–63.
5. Interview with Kagan, January 1, 1989.
6. Kagan, Kearsley, and Zelazo, 1980.
7. Kagan, 1984, pp. 56–57.
8. Bowlby, 1980, pp. 7, 442.
9. Kagan, 1984, pp. 55–56.
10. Kagan, 1984, p. 63.
11. Interview with Kagan, January 1, 1989.
12. Interview with Sroufe, December 20, 1988.
13. Suomi and Harlow, 1972.
14. "It is, of course, not being argued that anxious attachment causes later overdependency," Sroufe wrote in 1984; "that is, were the caregiving environment substantially changed we would expect greatly reduced continuity in adaptation.... Quality of attachment in infancy does, however, *predict* later dependency behavior (as nothing else has yet been shown to do), and it seems reasonable to assume that behavioral organization builds upon earlier foundations in a coherent manner." Sroufe et al., 1983, p. 1625.
15. Interview with Sroufe, December 20, 1988.
16. Erickson et al., 1985.
17. Kagan, et al., 1980, p. 147.
18. Kagan, 1980, cited in Sroufe, Egeland, and Kreutzer, 1990.
19. Sroufe et al., 1990.
20. Interview with Sroufe, December 20, 1992.
21. Sroufe, 1983, p. 74.
22. Sroufe et al., 1990.
23. One result is the lack of a truly valid method for assessing the attachment status of older children, although several ingenious methods have been devised, most notably by Jude Cassidy and Robert Marvin and by Pat Crittenden.
24. Sroufe et al., 1993.
25. Interview with Judith Crowell, MD, February 27, 1997. See also Crowell (1995).
26. Judith Crowell Interview, February 27, 1997.
27. Kagan, 1984, pp. 60–61. His comment overlooks the fact that many of the avoidant infants did not just fail to approach their mother, but didn't greet her at all, didn't interact with her, actively snubbed her.
28. Kagan, 1982.
29. Interview with Karin Grossmann, July 12, 1991.
30. Kagan, 1984, p. 62.
31. Interview with Klaus Grossmann, July 12, 1991.
32. Interview with Klaus Grossmann, July 12, 1991. This was in stark contrast to the mothers of ambivalent children in Bielefeld, many of whom behaved in odd and disturbing ways—stuffing the child at mealtimes, teasing him excessively, and engaging in other strangely insensitive behaviors.

33. Interview with Karin Grossmann, July 12, 1991.
34. Interview with Karin Grossmann, July 12, 1991. One might suppose that the repressed emotions would then fester and become bigger, maybe emerging later in destructive ways. "That's what we would expect," Klaus said. "But if you have a very highly regulated culture then all these eventualities will be taken care of—by very rigid behavior."
35. Leach, 1990, p. 190.
36. Interview with Karin Grossmann, July 12, 1991. Grossmann credits Ainsworth's strict rules on how to conduct a home observation for enabling them to notice this variable.
37. Grossmann and Grossmann, 1991.
38. Grossmann and Grossmann, 1991.
39. Klaus Grossmann, personal communication, May 24, 1993.
40. Reported to me by Klaus Grossmann, personal communication, May 24, 1993.
41. Interview with Klaus Grossmann, July 12, 1991.
42. Rutter, 1981, p. 160.
43. Interview with Sroufe, January 5, 1989.
44. Interview with Bretherton, January 22, 1989.
45. Lamb et al., 1984.
46. Interview with Bretherton, January 22, 1989.
47. Interview with Bretherton, January 22, 1989.
48. Grossmann et al., 1985.
49. Bates et al., 1985; Belsky and Isabella, 1988; Egeland and Farber, 1984; Kiser et al., 1986; Barglow and Hoffman, 1985.

CHAPTER 20: Born That Way?

1. Bruch, 1954.
2. Bruch, 1954.
3. McIntosh, cited in Bruch, 1954, p. 727.
4. Bruch, 1954, p. 726.
5. Chess et al., 1959, p. 801.
6. Chess, 1964, p. 613.
7. Chess, 1964, p. 614.
8. Levy, 1943.
9. Galton, 1869, 1979.
10. Sargent and Stafford, 1965.
11. Interview with Chess, October 21, 1991.
12. Interview with Chess, October 21, 1991.
13. Interview with Chess, October 21, 1991.
14. Thomas, Chess, and Birch, 1969, pp. 20–24.
15. Chess now regrets that she reported that term. Personal communication, July 12, 1993.
16. Chess, Thomas, and Birch, 1965, pp. 37–38.
17. Chess et al., 1965, pp. 38–39.
18. Thomas et al., 1969, p. 79.
19. Thomas et al., 1969, p. 92.
20. Interview with Chess, October 21, 1991.
21. Thomas et al., 1969, p. 93.
22. Chess et al., 1965, pp. 35–36.
23. Chess et al., 1965, pp. 36–37.
24. Thomas et al., 1969, p. 87.
25. Chess et al., 1965, p. 40.
26. Chess et al., 1965, p. 43.
27. Chess et al., 1965, pp. 44–45.
28. Further analysis revealed that other combinations of inherited traits also put a child at risk for later disorders. Other risky temperamental configurations include: 1) a combination of irregularity, nonadaptability, withdrawal responses, and predominantly negative mood of high intensity; 2) a combination of withdrawal and negative responses of low intensity to new situations, followed by slow adaptability; 3) excessive persistence; 4) excessive distractibility; and 5) markedly high or low activity level. Thomas et al., 1969.
29. Thomas et al., 1969, p. 73.
30. Chess and Thomas, 1987, p. 188.

31. Chess and Thomas, 1987, p. 189.
32. Thomas et al., 1969.
33. Brazelton, 1983.
34. Levy, 1943.
35. Greenberg and Mitchell, 1983, p. 229.
36. Greenberg and Mitchell, 1983, p. 228.
37. Schoenewolf, 1990, p. 19.

CHAPTER 21: Renaissance of Biological Determinism

1. Bowlby, 1940, p. 157.
2. Bowlby, 1944, pp. 39, 41.
3. Bowlby, 1973, p. 187.
4. Ainsworth et al., 1978, p. 142.
5. Neubauer and Neubauer, 1990, p. 21.
6. Bell, 1968.
7. In the United States, among the key studies to follow Chess, Thomas, and Birch, were the Louisville Twin Study, a longitudinal study of some five hundred twins from birth through fifteen years (begun in 1963, it started assessing temperament in 1976); the Colorado Adoption Project, another large-scale longitudinal, which compared the temperamental characteristics of adopted children to their biologically unrelated siblings raised in the same family; and the Minnesota Study of Twins Reared Apart.
8. Todd, 1985; Rosen, 1987.
9. Segal, 1984.
10. Interview with Bouchard, November 11, 1990.
11. Jackson, 1980; Rosen, 1987.
12. Interview with Bouchard, May 5, 1993.
13. Bouchard and McGue, 1990; Bouchard et al., 1990; Tellegen et al., 1988; Waller et al., 1990; Arvey et al., 1989.
14. Rosen, 1987, p. 38.
15. Neubauer and Neubauer, 1990.
16. Dunn and Plomin, 1990, p. 78.
17. Goleman, 1991.
18. Most psychologists agree that temperament is an inborn predisposition that is stable across time and that shows up in almost any situation. This includes genetic as well as constitutional components, which may be influenced by such variables as the mother's hormonal levels during pregnancy or her having a disease like rubella.
19. Plomin, 1987.
20. Kagan estimates, based on the many different recipes that can comprise this broth, that we may ultimately discover sixty or seventy temperamental types.
21. Kagan, 1989. (No page numbers are available for this source as I was using a tape transcript and not Kagan's paper.)
22. Quoted in Galvin, 1992, p. 41.
23. Interview with Kagan, December 21, 1990.
24. Kagan, 1989.
25. Kagan, 1989.
26. Interview with Bouchard, November 11, 1991.
27. Interview with Kagan, December 21, 1990.
28. Interview with Kagan, December 21, 1990.
29. Interview with Sroufe, December 20, 1988.
30. Lally and Mangione, 1979.
31. Interview with Lieberman, March 1, 1993.
32. Bowlby, 1982, p. 368.
33. Sroufe et al., 1992, p. 217.
34. Mangelsdorf et al., 1990.
35. Interview with Suomi, November 11, 1991.
36. Chess and Thomas, 1982, p. 220.
37. Interview with Sroufe, January 5, 1989.
38. Sroufe, 1983, p. 42.
39. Sroufe, personal communication, July 1993.

40. Vaughn et al., 1987; Zeanah et al., 1987.
41. Sroufe and Waters, 1977b.
42. Interview with Kagan, January 9, 1989.
43. Belsky and Isabella, 1988, p. 52, emphasis in original. The Japanese study was reported by Miyake, Shing-jen, and Campos, 1985.
44. Belsky and Isabella, 1988. At nine months the mothers of babies who would later be classified as insecure rate them as significantly more fussy.
45. Interview with Karin Grossmann, July 12, 1991.
46. Vaughn et al., 1989.
47. Van den Boom, personal communication, March 1, 1993.
48. Moore and Freeth, 1993.
49. Letter to The APA Monitor, April 1993, p. 3, by Joseph Richman. See also Kohn, 1993. The trend is such that former U.S. Surgeon General C. Everett Koop warned against the power of the "pharmaceutical-medical complex" in the mental health fields.
50. In a study of adults whose fathers had been heavy drinkers, it was found that 85 percent consumed very little alcohol or none at all. Cited in Kohn, 1993.
51. Scarr and Weinberg, 1993, p. 94.
52. Scarr, 1991, p. 16.
53. Scarr, 1991, p. 16.
54. Jensen, 1973.
55. Mischel, 1981, cited in Tellegen et al., 1988, p. 1037.
56. Waller et al., 1990.
57. Interview with Stella Chess, October 21, 1991.
58. Bronfenbrenner, quoted in Adler, 1991, p. 8.
59. Gottesman and Shields, 1972, found the concordance rates to be anywhere from 20 percent to 60 percent depending on the study.
60. See, for example, E. Fuller Torrey's otherwise excellent *Surviving Schizophrenia: A Family Manual*, 1988.
61. Tienari et al., 1990, cited in Sroufe et al., 1992. Considering this and other studies, psychiatrist Lyman Wynne, a schizophrenia researcher at the University of Rochester, now believes that although heredity plays some role, "the evidence for genetic effects" in schizophrenia "is not overpoweringly strong." Kohn, 1993, p. 30.
62. Neubauer and Neubauer, p. 22.
63. See Schore, 1994.

CHAPTER 22: A Rage in the Nursery

1. Clarke-Stewart, 1989. Today almost a third of mothers with children under three are working full-time.
2. Scarr, 1984, p. 98.
3. Interview with Bowlby, January 14–15, 1989.
4. Scarr, 1984, p. 100.
5. Rutter, 1981.
6. Scarr, Phillips and McCartney, 1993, pp. 373–374.
7. Kagan et al., 1980.
8. Rutter, 1981.
9. Sroufe, 1988.
10. ZERO TO THREE, 1993.
11. Interview with Scarr, August 19, 1993.
12. An example of the complexities involved is illustrated by a study which found that working mothers of securely attached toddlers showed better emotional integration than working mothers of anxious toddlers. Benn, 1985.
13. Vaughn, Gove, and Egeland, 1980.
14. Schwartz, 1983, and Vaughn et al., 1980, cited by Vaughn, Deane, and Waters, 1985.
15. Vivian Cadden, Letters to the Editor, *The Atlantic*, May 1990.
16. Belsky, quoted in Wattenberg, 1992, p. 8.
17. Interview with Bowlby, January 14–15, 1989.
18. Interview with Bowlby, January 14–15, 1989.
19. Interview with Cassidy, February 10, 1993.
20. Letter from Sroufe to Belsky, March 2, 1979.

21. Schwartz, Strickland, and Krolick, 1983; Willie and Jackson, 1984; Barglow, 1985. All cited in Belsky, 1986.
22. Interview with Belsky, December 4, 1992.
23. Interview with Belsky, December 4, 1992.
24. Interview with Belsky, December 4, 1992.
25. Belsky, 1986, p. 6.
26. Bronfenbrenner, quoted in Byrne, 1977, p. 43.
27. Interview with Szanton, May 5, 1993.
28. Interview with Fenichel, May 6, 1993.
29. Interview with Belsky, December 4, 1992.
30. Phillips et al., 1987.
31. Chess, 1987, p. 25.
32. Scarr, quoted in Ricks, 1987, p. 35.
33. Collins, 1987.
34. Scarr, quoted in Evans, 1987.
35. Belsky, 1987, p. 23.
36. Kagan, Phillips, both quoted in Jackson, 1987, p. 3.
37. Interview with Cassidy, February 10, 1993.
38. Interview with Belsky, December 4, 1992.
39. Interview with Belsky, December 4, 1992.
40. Interview with Scarr, August 19, 1993.
41. Interview with Belsky, December 4, 1992.
42. Clarke-Stewart, 1989.
43. Interview with Belsky, December 4, 1992.
44. Belsky and Cassidy, in press. Note that the 40 percent figure for children in day care includes children from all sorts of homes, not just low-risk, middle-class homes.
45. Interview with Belsky, December 4, 1992.
46. Interview with Brian Vaughn, 1994.
47. Interview with Peter Barglow, 1994.
48. Belsky, personal communication, August 31, 1993.
49. Interview with Belsky, December 4, 1992.
50. Interview with Slade, March 3, 1993.
51. Interview with Szanton, May 5, 1993.
52. Interview with Alicia Lieberman, 1994.
53. ZERO TO THREE, 1993.
54. *Zero to Three*, April/May 1994, p. 33; Chira (1994).
55. Scarr et al., 1993, p. 369.
56. Interview with Deborah Vandellm May, 1994. See also Vandell, (1990).
57. Interview with Bates, May 1994. See also Bates (1994).
58. Interview with Belsky, April 25, 1994.
59. Interview with Belsky, December 4, 1992.
60. Belsky, quoted in Wattenberg, 1992, p. 8.
61. Interview with Belsky, April 29, 1994.
62. Interview with Belsky, April 29, 1994.
63. Interview with Bowlby, January 14–15, 1989.
64. Martin, 1991, p. 65.
65. Figures from Felice Schwartz, of Catalyst, interviewed on National Public Radio, Weekend Edition, February 13, 1993.
66. Interview with Bowlby, January 14–15, 1989.
67. Interview with Scarr, August 19, 1988.
68. Interview with Bowlby, January 14–15, 1989.
69. Interview with Ainsworth.
70. Sroufe, 1992.
71. Bronfenbrenner, quoted in Byrne, 1977, p. 43. Bronfenbrenner might have added peer experience as well.
72. Interview with Lieberman, April 25, 1994.
73. Barglow (1995).
74. Interview with Barglow, 1994.
75. Interview with Barglow, 1994.
76. Haines-Stiles, 1991.

CHAPTER 23: Astonishing Attunements

1. Cited in Sroufe, 1979, p. 462.
2. MacFarlane, 1975, cited in Stern, 1985.
3. Siqueland and DeLucia, 1969, cited in Stern, 1985; Goodman, 1991/1992.
4. Kohut's actual term was "self-object."
5. Stressing the importance and healthiness of this early grandiosity, Kohut argued that the narcissistic personality disorder develops in those who have never had their grandiosity adequately supported as infants and thus are unable to outgrow the need for it.
6. The eminent Yale developmentalist Jerome Bruner refers to mother's ability to help the child unfold by being just a tiny step ahead of him as "scaffolding"; the great Russian psychologist Lev Vygotsky referred to the phenomenon as the "zone of proximal development." Sroufe et al., 1992.
7. Stern, 1985.
8. Tronick, quoted in Goodman, 1991/1992, p. 27.
9. Sander, 1964.
10. Brazelton et al., 1974.
11. Stern, 1985, p. 140.
12. Stern, 1985.
13. Abramis, 1990.
14. Stern, 1985.
15. Stern, 1985, p. 148.
16. Tronick et al., 1978.
17. Stern, 1985, pp. 151–152.
18. Isabella and Belsky, 1991.
19. Winnicott, 1958, p. 34.
20. Stern, 1985.
21. Stern, 1985, p. 195.
22. Stern, 1985, pp. 196–197.
23. Stern, 1985, p. 197.
24. Stern, 1985, p. 198.
25. Stern, 1985, p. 227.
26. Stern, 1985.
27. Bowlby, 1988b, p. 132.
28. Stern, 1985, p. 214.
29. Stern, 1985.
30. Haft and Slade, 1989.
31. Grossman, 1989, p. 2.
32. Winnicott, 1958, p. 300.
33. Winnicott, 1958.
34. Winnicott, 1965.

CHAPTER 24: The Residue of Our Parents

1. Bowlby, 1979, pp. 19–20.
2. Fraiberg et al., 1975, p. 387.
3. Sroufe, 1989.
4. Morris, 1983; Ricks, 1985.
5. Main et al., 1985, p. 96.
6. Fonagy et al., unpublished.
7. Shaver and Hazan, 1992, p. 43.
8. Fonagy et al., unpublished, p. 7.
9. Main et al., 1985, p. 97.
10. Fonagy et al., unpublished.
11. Fonagy et al., unpublished, p. 8–9.
12. Main and Goldwyn, in press.
13. Fonagy, Steele, and Steele, 1991.
14. Slade, September 1992, p. 4.
15. Slade, September 1992.
16. Interview with Slade, February 18, 1993.

17. Interview with Judith Crowell, February, 1997.
18. Interview with Main, March 5, 1993.
19. Ainsworth and Eichberg, 1991.
20. Interview with Cassidy, February 9, 1993.
21. Kobak, personal communication, August 24, 1993.
22. Interview with Kobak, July 8, 1993.
23. Interviews with Slade, January 6, 1989; February 18, 1993.
24. Bowlby, 1979, p. 17.
25. Fonagy et al., 1991b, p. 209.
26. Fonagy et al., 1991b, p. 210.
27. Fonagy et al., 1991b, p. 111.
28. Because Ainsworth and Main were analyzing mothers' behavior in the home and Belsky in the lab, one way of making sense of this conflicting evidence is to assume that mothers who are normally rejecting in the home may behave in an intrusive, out-of-synch way during a short structured play period in a university setting, in order to be the interactive mother they think a psychologist expects. Karin Grossmann (1989) also found mothers of avoidant children to be intrusive.
29. Interview with Cassidy, February 9, 1993.
30. Ainsworth et al., 1978.
31. Slade, 1993, p. 8.
32. Interview with Sroufe, December 20, 1988.
33. Interview with Slade, March 11, 1993.

CHAPTER 25: Attachment in Adulthood

1. Bowlby, 1979, p. 103.
2. Korchin and Ruff, 1964; Ruff and Korchin, 1967; cited in Bowlby, 1979, p. 108.
3. Bowlby, 1979.
4. Interview with Anthony Storr, author of *Solitude*, July 14, 1993. (He spoke with Bowlby on the subject.)
5. Interview with Kobak, June 9, 1993.
6. Bretherton, 1992.
7. Interview with Parkes, May 8, 1992.
8. Weiss, 1975, 1982.
9. Hazan and Shaver, 1987, p. 515.
10. Simpson, Rholes, Nelligan, in press, cited in Shaver and Hazan, 1992. No clear pattern emerged for ambivalents in this study.
11. Interview with Hazan, July 20, 1993.
12. Interview with Kobak, June 9, 1993.
13. Shaver, personal communication, September 1, 1993.
14. Kobak, personal communication, August 24, 1993.
15. Grossmann, personal communication, September 3, 1993.
16. Interview with Slade, February 18, 1993.
17. See Bowlby, 1973; 1980.
18. Lewis et al., 1984.
19. See Basch, 1988.
20. This is a revisionist reading of Heinz Kohut's work on narcissism. He did not see grandiosity as a defense against shame, but rather the other way around. See Morrison, 1989. Note that it is commonly accepted that healthy infant development includes a grandiose sense of self. It wanes as the young child becomes better able to handle daily challenges on his own, develops a secure sense of himself, and is simultaneously confronted with the fact the world does not exist to serve and applaud him.
21. Fonagy et al., 1992, p. 18.
22. It could equally be argued that borderline pathology begins with disorganized attachment. See Slade, 1993, for a valuable discussion of these issues and in particular the way early modes of coping with negative emotion typical of the avoidant and ambivalent child may contribute to neurotic character. See also Liotti, 1992, for a discussion of how disorganized/disoriented attachment may lead to an increased vulnerability to dissociative disorders, like multiple personality.

CHAPTER 26: Repetition and Change

1. Rioch, 1988.
2. Adapted from Karen, 1987, p. 27.
3. Slade, 1993, writes: "It is my strong impression—having read many [Adult Attachment Interview transcripts]—that insecure adults generally have more difficulties with intimate relationships. . . ." (pp. 5–6).
4. Main and Goldwyn, in press, p. 23.
5. Interview with Lieberman, March 1, 1993.
6. See Belsky et al., 1989; also Egeland, Jacobvitz, and Sroufe (1988), and Hunter and Kilstrom (1979), both cited in Belsky et al., 1989. Belsky studied an average population. The other two studies were of women who had a history of abuse as children.
7. Interview with Lieberman, March 1, 1993.
8. Slade and Aber, 1987.

CHAPTER 27: Avoidant Society

1. Laslett, 1962, p. 93.
2. Sennett, 1977.
3. See Fromm, 1955, for a discussion of some of these issues.
4. Lasch, 1979.
5. Sommerville, 1990.
6. Maccoby and Martin, 1983.
7. Sommerville, 1990.
8. Erikson, 1950.
9. Kohut, 1980.
10. Bowlby, 1988b, p. 2.
11. Sagi et al., 1985. A more recent report by Sagi and co-workers suggests that elevated levels of ambivalent attachment only occur in those kibbutzim where children sleep separately from their parents. With only a single caretaker listening for disturbance over a monitor at another location, the babies' cries often go unheeded or are only responded to after a long delay. Sagi, 1991, cited in Belsky and Cassidy (in print).
12. Interview with Bowlby, January 14–15, 1989.
13. Interview with Ainsworth.
14. Greenspan, 1983.
15. Interview with Sroufe, December 20, 1988.
16. Mitchell, 1991.
17. Interview with Ainsworth.
18. Liedloff, 1977, p. 9.
19. Liedloff, 1977, p. 139.
20. Liedloff, 1977, p. 78.
21. Liedloff, 1977, p. 157.
22. Anisfeld et al., 1990.
23. Konner, 1989.
24. Interview with Karin Grossmann, July 12, 1991.
25. Interview with Karin and Klaus Grossmann, July 12, 1991. The reader may also recall the case of Muhamidi, one of the insecurely attached Ganda children whose mother carried him everywhere, fed him on demand, but was herself emotionally disturbed.
26. Crockenberg, 1981; Jacobson and Frye, 1991.
27. Sosa et al., 1980; Klaus et al., 1986, both cited in Bowlby, 1988b.
28. ZERO TO THREE, 1993.
29. Interview with Sandra Scarr, August 19, 1993.
30. Rodell, 1993.
31. Bronfenbrenner, 1988.
32. ZERO TO THREE, 1993, p. 19.
33. Interview with Colin Murray Parkes, May 8, 1992.

CHAPTER 28: Looking Back

1. Sulloway, 1991, p. 30.
2. Bowlby, 1991.
3. Bowlby, 1973, p. 403.
4. Liotti, 1990.
5. According to Ursula Bowlby, John was "fearless rather than brave—he did not have to struggle with fear." Personal communication, March 10, 1992.
6. Bowlby, 1985.
7. Ursula Bowlby, personal communication, February 19, 1992.
8. Holden, quoted by Trowell, 1990, p. 6.
9. Martin, 1991, p. 66.
10. Byng-Hall, 1991, p. 267.
11. Isca Wittenberg, quoted by Trowell, 1990, p. 12.
12. Ursula Bowlby, personal communication, February 19, 1992.
13. Gilmore, 1990.
14. Interview with Bowlby, January 14, 1989.
15. Bowlby, quoted by Dinnage, 1980, p. 60.
16. Rycroft, 1985, pp. 151–152.
17. At a meeting of the American Psychological Association in August 1992, Yale psychologist Sidney Blatt reported that the first question Bowlby asked him when they met was, "Do you consider me a psychoanalyst?" "Ethologist" comes from Gilmore, 1990, in The *Psychoanalytic Quarterly*.
18. Susanna Isaacs Elmhirst, personal communication, June 19, 1992.
19. See, for instance, Silverman, 1991; Osofsky, 1988; Goldberg, 1991.
20. Interviews with Kernberg, February 11, 1989; Pine, February 1, 1989; and Solnit, August 24, 1993.
21. Interview with Eagle, September 21, 1992.
22. See Slade (in preparation, 1997a and 1997b) for a valuable assessment and overview of the many junctures of attachment research and psychoanalytic theory, including the contributions of Fonagy and others.
23. Aaron, 1991, p. 241.
24. Storr, cited in Martin, p. 65.
25. Interview with Storr, July 14, 1993.
26. Rycroft, 1992, p. 80.
27. Rayner, 1991, p. 8. Rayner's paper owed "much of its contents and inspiration" to Juliet Hopkins.
28. Ursula Bowlby, private communications, July 4, 1992; February 7, 1992.
29. Juliet Hopkins, personal communication, July 1993.
30. Ursula Bowlby, personal communication, February 19, 1992.
31. Grossman, 1989, p. 2.
32. Robert Marvin, personal communication, 1993.
33. Bretherton, 1992, p. 762.
34. Ursula Bowlby, personal communication, September 11, 1993.
35. Interview with Waters, January 5–6, 1989.
36. Interview with Ainsworth.
37. Interview with Ainsworth.
38. Interview with Sroufe, December 1988.
39. Interview with Ainsworth.
40. Interview with Ainsworth.
41. Brazelton, personal communication, February 23, 1989.
42. Interview with Sroufe, December 1988.
43. Interview with Eagle, September 21, 1992.
44. Rycroft, 1985.
45. Basch, personal communication, June 1993. See also Basch, 1992.
46. Interview with Lieberman, March 1, 1993. See also Lieberman, 1993.
47. Rycroft also makes this point. Interview, May 8, 1992.
48. Byng-Hall, 1991, p. 267.
49. Interview with Bowlby, January 14, 1989.
50. Bowlby, 1988b, pp. 38.
51. Interview with Ainsworth.
52. Macdonald, 1965, p. 143.

BIBLIOGRAPHY

Abramis, M. (1990). Regulation of mother-infant affective engagement. Unpublished doctoral dissertation, Yeshiva University, New York.

Adler, T. (1991, January). Seeing double? *American Psychological Association Monitor*, pp. 1, 8.

Ainsworth, M. D. S. (1962). The effects of maternal deprivation: A review of findings and controversy in the context of research strategy. *In Deprivation of Maternal Care: A Reassessment of its Effects*. Public Health papers no. 14. Geneva: World Health Organization.

Ainsworth, M. D. S. (1967). *Infancy in Uganda: Infant care and the growth of love*. Baltimore: The Johns Hopkins University Press.

Ainsworth, M. D. S. (1969). Object relations, dependency and attachment: A theoretical review of the infant-mother relationship. *Child Development, 40*, 969–1025.

Ainsworth, M. D. S. (1983). A sketch of a career. In A. N. O'Connoll & N. F. Russo (Eds.), *Models of achievement: Reflections of eminent women in psychology* (pp. 200–219). New York: Columbia University Press.

Ainsworth, M. D. S. (1984). Attachment. In N. S. Endler & J. McV. Hunt (Eds.), *Personality and the behavioral disorders* (Vol. 1, pp. 559–602). New York: Wiley.

Ainsworth, M. D. S. (1985). Attachments across the life span. *Bulletin of the New York Academy of Medicine, 61*, 792–812.

Ainsworth, M. D. S., Blehar, M. C., Waters, E., & Wall, S. (1978). *Patterns of Attachment: A psychological study of the strange situation*. Hillsdale, NJ: Erlbaum.

Ainsworth, M. D. S. & Eichberg, C. (1991). Effects on infant-mother attachment of mother's unresolved loss of an attachment figure, or other traumatic experience. In C. M. Parkes, J. Stevenson-Hinde, & P. Marris (Eds.), *Attachment across the life cycle*. New York: Tavistock/Routledge.

Anisfeld, E., Casper, V., Nozyce, M., & Cunningham, N. (1990). Does infant carrying promote attachment? An experimental study of the effects of increased physical contact on the development of attachment. *Child Development*, 61, 1617–1627.

Arend, R., Gove, F., & Sroufe, L. A. (1979). Continuity of individual adaptation from infancy to kindergarten: A predictive study of ego-resiliency and curiosity in preschoolers. *Child Development*, 50, 950–959.

Aron, L. (1991). John Bowlby, In memoriam. *Psychoanalytic Dialogues*, 1, p. 241.

Arsenian, J. M. (1943). Young children in an insecure situation. *Journal of Abnormal and Social Psychology*, 38, 225–229.

Arvey, R. D., Bouchard, T. J., Segal, N. L., & Abraham, L. M. (1989). Job satisfaction: Environmental and genetic components. *Journal of Applied Psychology*, 74 (2), 187–192.

Babies and day care. (1987, June 7). *The Boston Globe*, pp. A9, A12.

Bakwin, H. (1942). Loneliness in infants. *American Journal of Diseases of Children*, 63, 30–40.

Barglow, P., & Hoffman, M. (1985, May). Mother's effect upon oral phase ego development and attachment. Paper presented at the meeting of the American Psychoanalytic Society, Denver.

Barglow, P., Vaughn, B. E., & Molitor, N. (1987). Effects of maternal absence due to employment on the quality of infant-mother attachment in a low-risk sample. *Child Development*, 58: 945-954.

Barglow, P., Kavesh, L., Contreras, J. (1994). Offspring of working mothers: Peer competence follow-up. Paper presented at the Thirteenth International Congress of the International Association of Child and Adolescent Psychiatry and Allied Professions, July, 1994.

Basch, M. F. (1988). *Understanding psychotherapy: The science behind the art*. New York: Basic.

Basch, M. F. (1992). *Practicing psychotherapy: A casebook*. New York: Basic.

Bates, J., Masling, C., & Frankel, K. (1985). Attachment security, mother-child interaction, and temperament as predictors of behavior problem ratings at age three years. In I. Bretherton and E. Waters (Eds.), *Growing points in attachment theory and research. Monographs of the Society for Research in Child Development*, 50 (Serial No. 209).

Bates, J. E. & Marvinney, D. (1994). Child care history and kindergarten adjustment. *Developmental Psychology*.

Bell, R. (1968). A reinterpretation of the direction of effects in studies of socialization. *Psychological Review*, 75, 81–95.

Bell, R., & Ainsworth, M. D. S. (1972). Infant crying and maternal responsiveness. *Child Development*, 43, 1171–1190.

Belsky, J. (1984). The determinants of parenting: A process model. *Child Development, 55,* 83–96.

Belsky, J. (1986, September). Infant day care: A cause for concern. *ZERO TO THREE,* pp. 1–7.

Belsky, J. (1987, February). Risks remain. *ZERO TO THREE,* pp. 22–24.

Belsky, J. & Cassidy, J. (in press). Attachment: Theory and evidence. In M. Rutter, D. Hay, & S. Baron-Cohen (Eds.), *Developmental principles and clinical issues in psychology and psychiatry.* Oxford: Blackwell.

Belsky, J., & Isabella, R. A. (1988). Maternal, infant, and social-contextual determinants of attachment security. In J. Belsky & T. Nezworski (Eds.), *Clinical implications of attachment.* Hillsdale, NJ: Erlbaum.

Belsky, J., & Rovine, M. (in press). Temperament and attachment in the strange situation: An empirical rapprochement. *Child Development.*

Belsky, J., & Steinberg, L. D. (1978). The effects of day care: A critical review. *Child Development, 49,* 929–949.

Belsky, J., Youngblood, L., & Pensky, E. (1990). Childrearing history, marital quality, and maternal affect: Intergenerational transmission in a low-risk sample. *Development and Psychopathology, 1,* 291–304.

Bender, L., & Yarnell, H. (1941). An observation nursery: A study of 250 children on the psychiatric division of Bellevue Hospital. *American Journal of Psychiatry, 97,* 1158–1174.

Benn, R. K. (1985, April). *Factors associated with security of attachment in dual career families.* Paper presented at the biennial meetings of the Society for Research in Child Development, Toronto.

Bloch, D. (1978). *So the witch won't eat me: Fantasy and the child's fear of infanticide.* New York: Grove.

Bootzin, R., Loftus, E., Zajonc, R., & Hall, E. (1983). *Psychology today: An introduction* (5th ed.). New York: Random House.

Bornstein, M., & Lamb, M. (1992). *Development in infancy: An introduction,* Third Edition. New York: McGraw-Hill, Inc.

Bouchard, T. J., & McGue, M. (1990). Genetic and rearing environmental influences on adult personality: An analysis of adopted twins reared apart. *Journal of Personality, 58* (1), 263–292.

Bouchard, T. J., Jr., Lykken, D. T., McGue, M., Segal, N. L., & Tellegen, A. (1990, October 12). Sources of human psychological differences: The Minnesota study of twins reared apart. *Science, 250,* 223–228.

Bowlby, J. (1940). The influence of early environment in the development of neurosis and neurotic character. *International Journal of Psycho-Analysis, 1,* 154–178.

Bowlby, J. (1944). Forty-four juvenile thieves: Their characters and home-life. *International Journal of Psycho-Analysis, 25,* 19–52, 107–127. Reprinted (1946) as monograph. London: Bailiere, Tindall and Cox.

Bowlby, J. (1951). Maternal care and mental health. Geneva: *World Health Organization Monograph Series* (2).

Bowlby, J. (1958a). *Can I leave my baby?* London: National Association for Mental Health.

Bowlby, J. (1958b). The nature of the child's tie to his mother. *International Journal of Psycho-analysis, 39,* 350–373.

Bowlby, J. (1959). Separation anxiety. *International Journal of Psycho-Analysis, 41,* 89–113.

Bowlby, J. (1960). Grief and mourning in infancy. *The Psychoanalytic Study of the Child, 15,* 3–39.

Bowlby, J. (1967). Foreword. In M. D. S. Ainsworth, *Infancy in Uganda: Infant care and the growth of love.* Baltimore: Johns Hopkins.

Bowlby, J. (1970). *Child care and the growth of love* (2nd ed.). Harmondsworth: Pelican.

Bowlby, J. (1973). *Attachment and loss. Vol. 2: Separation.* New York: Basic.

Bowlby, J. (1979). *The making and breaking of affectional bonds.* New York: Routledge.

Bowlby, J. (1980). *Attachment and loss. Vol. 3: Loss, sadness and depression.* New York: Basic.

Bowlby, J. (1982). *Attachment and loss. Vol. 1: Attachment.* New York: Basic (rev. ed.).

Bowlby, J. (1985). The role of the psychotherapist's personal resources in the treatment situation. Unpublished manuscript.

Bowlby, J. (1987). Early days at the London child guidance clinic and training centre. Unpublished manuscript.

Bowlby, J. (1988a). Developmental psychiatry comes of age. *American Journal of Psychiatry, 145,* 1–10.

Bowlby, J. (1988b). *A secure base: Clinical applications of attachment theory.* London: Routledge.

Bowlby, J. (1991). *Charles Darwin: A new life.* New York: Norton.

Bowlby, J., Figlio, K., & Young, R. (1990). An interview with John Bowlby on the origins and reception of his work. *Free Associations, 21,* 36–64.

Brazelton, T. B. (1983). *Infants and mothers: Differences in development.* New York: Delta. (rev. ed.).

Brazelton, T. B., Koslowski, B., & Main, M. (1974). The origins of reciprocity: The early mother-input interaction. In M. Lewis & L. Rosenblum (Eds.), *The effect of the infant on its caregiver.* New York: Wiley.

Bretherton, I. (1985). Attachment theory: Retrospect and prospect. In I. Bretherton & E. Waters (Eds.), *Growing points in attachment theory and research. Monographs of the Society for Research in Child Development, 50* (Serial No. 209).

Bretherton, I. (1987). New perspectives on attachment relations: Security, communication, and internal working models. In J. Osofsky (Ed.), *Handbook of infant development* (2nd ed.). New York: Wiley.

Bretherton, I. (1991). The roots and growing points of attachment theory. In C. M. Parkes, J. Stevenson-Hinde, & P. Marris (Eds.), *Attachment across the life cycle.* New York: Tavistock/Routledge.

Bretherton, I. (1992). The origins of attachment theory: John Bowlby and Mary Ainsworth. *Developmental Psychology, 28,* 759–775.

Bronfenbrenner, U. (1986, Fall). A generation in jeopardy: America's hidden family policy. *Developmental Psychology Newsletter,* 47–54.

Bruch, H. (1954). Parent education or the illusion of omnipotence. *American Journal of Orthopsychiatry*, 24, 723–732.

Burlingham, D., & Freud, A. (1942). *Young children in wartime London*. London: Allen & Unwin.

Burlingham, D., & Freud, A. (1944). *Infants without families*. London: Allen & Unwin.

Burnham, D. L. (1965). Separation anxiety. In *Archives of General Psychiatry*, 13, 346–358.

Byng-Hall, J. (1991). [Address at John Bowlby Memorial Service]. *Infant Mental Health Journal*, 12, 267–268.

Byrne, S. (1977, May). Nobody home: The erosion of the American family. (A conversation with Urie Bronfenbrenner). *Psychology Today*, pp. 41–48.

Campos, J. J., Barrett, K. C., Lamb, M. E., Goldsmith, H. H., & Stenberg, C. (1983). Socioemotional development. In M. M. Haith & J. J. Campos (Eds.), *Handbook of child psychology: Vol. 2. Infancy and psychobiology* (pp. 783–915). New York: Wiley.

Caper, R. (1988). *Immaterial Facts*. Northvale, NJ: Aronson.

Casler, L. (1961). Maternal deprivation: a critical review of the literature. *Monographs of the Society for Research in Child Development*, 26 (Serial No., 80).

Caspi, A., & Elder, G. H. (in press). Emergent family patterns: The intergenerational construction of problem behavior and relationships. In R. Hinde & J. Stevenson-Hinde (Eds.), *Relations between relationships within families*. Oxford: Oxford University Press.

Cassidy, J. (1988). The self as related to child-mother attachment at six. *Child Development*, 59, 121–134.

Cassidy, J. (1990). Theoretical and methodological considerations in the study of attachment and the self in young children. In M. Greenberg, D. Cicchetti, & E. M. Cummings (Eds.), *Attachment in the preschool years: Theory, research, and intervention*. Chicago: University of Chicago Press.

Cassidy, J., & Berlin, L. J. (1992). The insecure/ambivalent pattern of attachment: Theory and research. Unpublished manuscript.

Chess, S. (1964). Mal de Mère. *American Journal of Orthopsychiatry*, 64, 613–614.

Cassidy, J. and Shaver, P. R., eds., *Handbook of Attachment Theory and Research*. NY: Guilford.

Chess, S. (1987, February). Comments: "Infant day care: A cause for concern." *Zero to Three*, pp. 24–25.

Chess S., & Thomas, A. (1982). Infant bonding: Mystique and reality. *American Journal of Orthopsychiatry*, 52, 213–222.

Chess, S. & Thomas, A. (1987). *Origins and evolution of behavior disorders*. Cambridge, MA: Harvard University Press.

Chess, S., Thomas, A., & Birch, H. (1959). Characteristics of the individual child's behavioral responses to the environment. *American Journal of Orthopsychiatry*, 29, 791–802.

Chess, S., Thomas, A., & Birch, H. G. (1965). *Your child is a person*. New York: Viking Press.

Chira, S. (1994, April 4). Broad study says home-based day care, even if by relatives, often fails children. *New York Times*, p. 20.

Cicchetti, D., & Beeghly, M. (1990). *Children with Down Syndrome: Developmental perspective*. New York: Cambridge University Press.

Clarke, A. M., & Clarke, A. D. B. (Eds.) (1976). *Early experience: Myth and evidence*. New York: Free Press.

Clarke-Stewart, K. A. (1989, February). Infant day care: Maligned or malignant? *American Psychologist*, 44, 266–273.

Collins, G. (1987, November 25). Day care for infants: Debate turns to long-term effects. *The New York Times*.

Crittenden, P. (1988). Relationships at risk. In J. Belsky & T. Nezworski (Eds.), *Clinical implications of attachment*. Hillsdale, NJ: Erlbaum.

Crockenberg, S. (1981). Infant irritability, mother responsiveness, and social support influences on the security of infant-mother attachment. *Child Development*, 7, 169–176.

Crowel, J. A. & Waters, E. (1995). Is the parent-child relationship prototype of later love relationships? Studies of attachment and working models of attachment. Poster symposium presented at the Society for Research in Child Development, Indianapolis, Indiana, March 30-April 2, 1995.

Dinnage, R. (1980, May). Understanding loss: The Bowlby canon. *Psychology Today*, pp. 56–60.

Dollard, J., & Miller, N. E. (1950). *Personality and psychotherapy*. New York: McGraw-Hill.

Dunn, J., & Plomin, R. (1990). *Separate lives: Why siblings are so different*. New York: Basic.

Eagle, M. (1987). *Recent developments in psychoanalysis*. Cambridge: Harvard University Press.

Eagle, M. (1992, August). The relationship between attachment theory and psychoanalysis. Paper presented at the annual convention of the American Psychological Association, Washington, D.C.

Easterbrooks, M. A., & Goldberg, W. A. (1990). Security of toddler-parent attachment: Relation to children's sociopersonality functioning during kindergarten. In M. Greenberg, D. Cicchetti, & E. M. Cummings (Eds.), *Attachment in the preschool years: Theory, research, and intervention*. Chicago: University of Chicago Press.

Egeland, B., & Farber, E. (1984). Infant-mother attachment: Factors related to its development and changes over time. *Child Development*, 55, 753–771.

Egeland, B., Jacobvitz, D., & Sroufe, L. A. (1988). Breaking the cycle of abuse: Relationship predictions. *Child Development*, 59, 1080–1088.

Elicker, J., Englund, M., & Sroufe, L. A. (1992). Predicting peer competence and peer relationships in childhood from early parent-child relationships. In R. Parke & G. Ladd (Eds.), *Family-peer relationships: Modes of linkage*. Hillsdale, NJ: Erlbaum.

Ellenberger, H. (1970). *The Discovery of the Unconscious*. New York: Basic.

Emde, R. (1983). Editor's commentary: The Pinneau-Spitz controversy. In R. N.

Emde (Ed.), *René Spitz: Dialogues from infancy*. New York: International Universities Press.

Erickson, M. F., Sroufe, L. A., & Egeland, B. (1985). The relationship between quality of attachment and behavior problems in preschool in a high risk sample. In I. Bretherton & E. Waters (Eds.), *Growing points in attachment theory and research. Monographs of the Society for Research in Child Development*, 50 (Serial No. 209, Nos. 1–2), 147– 186.

Erikson, E. (1950). *Childhood and Society*. New York: Norton.

Evans, S. (1987, November 7). Psychological risk of day care told. *The Washington Post*.

Fairbairn, W. R. D. (1952). *An object relations theory of the personality*. New York: Basic.

Fonagy, P. Psychoanalytic and empirical approaches to developmental psychopathology: An object relations perspective. Unpublished manuscript.

Fonagy, P., Leigh, T., Kennedy, R., Matoon, G., Steele, H., Target, M., Steele, M., & Higgitt, A. (1992, October). *Attachment, borderline states and the representation of emotions and cognitions in self and other*. Paper presented at Symposium on Developmental Psychopathology, Rochester, New York.

Fonagy, P., Steele, H., & Steele, M. (1991a). Maternal representations of attachment during pregnancy predict the organization of infant-mother attachment at one year of age. *Child Development*, 62, 891–905.

Fonagy, P., Steele, M., Steele, H., Moran, G., & Higgitt, A. (1991b). The capacity for understanding mental states: The reflective self in parent and child and its significance for security of attachment. *Infant Mental Health Journal*, 13, 200–217.

Fonagy, P., Steele, M., Moran, G., Steele, H., & Higgitt, A. (1991c). Measuring the ghost in the nursery: An empirical study of the relation between parents' mental representations of childhood experiences and their infants' security of attachment. Unpublished manuscript.

Fraiberg, S. (1977). *Every child's birthright: In defense of mothering*. NY: Basic.

Fraiberg, S., Adelson, E., & Shapiro, V. (1975). Ghosts in the nursery: A psychoanalytic approach to the problems of impaired infant-mother relationships. *Journal of the American Academy of Child Psychiatry*, 14, 387–421.

Freud, A. (1960). Discussion of John Bowlby's paper. *The Psychoanalytic Study of the Child*, 15, 53–62.

Fromm, E. (1955). *The sane society*. New York: Holt, Rinehart, & Winston.

Furman, E. (1981). Treatment-via-the-parent: A case of bereavement. *Journal of Child Psychotherapy*, 7: 89-102.

Galton, F. (1979). *Hereditary genius: An inquiry into its laws and consequences*. London: Julian Friedmann. (Original work published 1869).

Galvin, R. M. (1992, March/April). The nature of shyness. *Harvard Magazine*, pp. 41–45.

Gewirtz, J. L. (1961). A learning analysis of the effects of normal stimulation, privation and deprivation on the acquisition of social motivation and attachment. In B. M. Foss (Ed.), *Determinants of infant behavior*. London: Methuen; New York: Wiley.

Gilmore, K. (1990). [Review of *A Secure Base*]. *Psychoanalytic Quarterly*, 59, 494–498.

Goldberg, S. (1991). Recent developments in attachment theory. *Canadian Journal of Psychiatry*, 36, 393–400.

Goleman, D. (1991, February 12). Feeling cheerful? Thank brain's left lobe. *The New York Times*, pp. C1, C10.

Goncharov. I. (1954). *Oblomov*. (D. Margarshack, Trans.). Middlesex, U.K.: Penguin. (Original work published 1859)

Goodman, S. (1991, December–1992, January). Presumed innocents. *Modern Maturity*, pp. 25–29.

Gottesman, I., & Shields, J. (1972). *Schizophrenia and genetics: A twin study vantage point*. New York: Academic Press.

Greenberg, J. R., & Mitchell, S. A. (1983). *Object relations in psychoanalytic theory*. Cambridge: Harvard University Press.

Greenspan, E. (1983). *Little winners: Inside the world of the child sports star*. New York: Little, Brown.

Grosskurth, P. (1987). *Melanie Klein: Her World and Her Work*. Cambridge: Harvard University Press.

Grosskurth, P. (1991, September 29). What women wanted. (Review of *Mothers of Psychoanalysis*.) *The New York Times Book Review*.

Grossmann, Karin. (1989, September). Avoidance as a communicative strategy in attachment relationships. Paper presented at the fourth world congress of the World Association of Infant Psychiatry and Allied Disciplines, Lugano, Switzerland.

Grossmann, K., & Grossmann, K. (1991). Attachment quality as an organizer of emotional and behavioral responses in a longitudinal perspective. In C. M. Parkes, J. Stevenson-Hinde, & P. Marris (Eds.), *Attachment across the life cycle*. New York: Tavistock/Routledge.

Grossmann, K., Grossmann, K. E., Spangler, G. Suess, G., & Unzer, J. (1985). Maternal sensitivity and newborns' orientation responses as related to quality of attachment in northern Germany. In I. Bretherton & E. Waters (Eds.), *Growing points in attachment theory and research*. *Monographs of the Society for Research in Child Development*, 50 (Serial No. 209) 233–256.

Haft, W., & Slade, A. (1989). Affect attunement and maternal attachment: A Pilot study. *Infant Mental Health Journal*, 10, 157–172.

Haines-Stiles, G. (Executive producer). (1991). *Childhood*. [Television series.] New York: Thirteen/WNET and The Childhood Project.

Hamilton, V. (1990, Autumn). Reflections on 23 years of learning and friendship with John Bowlby. *The Tavistock Gazette*, 29, 20–23.

Harlow, H. (1958). The nature of love. *The American Psychologist*, 3, 673–685.

Harlow, H. F., & Harlow, M. K. (1966). Learning to love. *American Scientist*, 54, 244–272.

Hartup, W. W. (1963). Dependency and independence. In H. W. Stevenson (Ed.), *Child psychology: The sixty-second yearbook of the National Society for the Study of Education, Part I*. Chicago: University of Chicago Press.

Hazan, C., & Shaver, P. (1987). Romantic love conceptualized as an attachment process. *Journal of Personality and Social Psychology, 52,* 511–524.

Hinde, R. (1991). Obituary: John Bowlby. *Journal of Child Psychology and Psychiatry, 32,* 2, 215–217.

Hopkins, J. (1992). Failure of the holding relationship: some effects of physical rejection on the child's attachment and inner experience. In C.M. Parkes, J. Stevenson-Hinde, & P. Marris (Eds.), *Attachment across the life cycle.* New York: Tavistock/Routledge.

Hughes, J. (1989). *Reshaping the psychoanalytic domain: The work of Melanie Klein, W. R. D. Fairbairn, D. W. Winnicott.* Berkeley and Los Angeles: University of California Press.

Isabella, R. A., & Belsky, J. (1991). Interactional synchrony and the origins of infant-mother attachment: A replication study. *Child Development, 62,* 373–384.

Isabella, R. A., Belsky, J., & von Eye, A. (1989). Origins of mother-infant attachment: An examination of interactional synchrony during the infant's first year. *Developmental Psychology, 25,* 12–21.

Isherwood, C. (1965). *Ramakrishna and his disciples.* New York: Simon and Schuster.

Jackson, D. (1987, July 7). Is day care bad for infants? *Newsday,* Part II, p. 3.

Jackson, D. D. (1980, October). Reunion of identical twins raised apart reveals some astonishing similarities. *Smithsonian,* pp. 48–56.

Jacobson, S. W., & Frye, K. F. (1991). Effect of maternal social support on attachment: Experimental evidence. *Child Development, 62,* 572–582.

Jensen, A. R. (1973). *Educability and group differences.* New York: Basic.

Kagan, J. (1979). Overview: Perspectives on human infancy. In J. Osofsky (Ed.), *Handbook of infant development.* New York: Wiley.

Kagan, J. (1982). *Psychological research on the human infant: An evaluative summary.* New York: W.T. Grant.

Kagan, J. (1984). *The nature of the child.* New York: Basic.

Kagan, J. (1989, August). *The return of temperament in psychological theory.* Paper presented at the 97th annual convention of the American Psychological Association, New Orleans.

Kagan, J., Kearsley, R. B., & Zelazo, P. (1980). *Infancy: Its place in human development.* Cambridge: Harvard University Press.

Kagan, J., & Klein, R. (1973). Cross-cultural perspectives on early development. *American Psychologist, 28,* 947–961.

Kaplan, N. (1987, May). *Internal representations of attachment in six-year-olds.* Paper presented at the biennial meetings of the Society for Research in Child Development, Baltimore.

Karen, R. (1987). *Top dog/Bottom dog.* New York: Donald I. Fine.

Karen, R. (1990, February). Becoming attached. *The Atlantic,* pp. 35–70.

Karen, R. (1992, February). Shame. *The Atlantic,* pp. 40–70.

Kiser, L., Bates, J., Maslin, C., & Bayles, K. (1986). Mother-infant play at six months as a predictor of attachment security at thirteen months. *Journal of the American Academy of Child Psychiatry, 25,* 168–175.

Klein, M. (1975). *The psychoanalysis of children.* New York: Free Press.

Kobak, R. (1987, April). Attachment, affect regulation and defense. Paper presented at the biennial meetings of the Society for Research in *Child Development*.

Kohn, A. (1993, April). Back to nurture. *American Health*, pp. 29–31.

Kohut, H. (1977). *The restoration of the self*. New York: International Universities Press.

Kohut, H. (1980). Summarizing reflections. In A. Goldberg (Ed.), *Advances in self psychology*. New York: International Universities Press.

Konner, M. (1989, January 8). Where should baby sleep? *The New York Times Magazine*, pp. 39–40.

Kraemer, S. (1990). Bowlby speaking. *The Tavistock Gazette*, 29, 16–17.

LaBarba, R. (1981). *Foundations of developmental psychology*. New York: Academic Press.

Lally, J. R. (Executive producer), & Mangione, P. L. (Director). (1979). *Flexible, fearful, feisty: The different temperaments of infants and toddlers* [Video]. Sausalito, CA: Far West Laboratories Center for Child and Family Studies for California State Department of Education.

Lamb, M. E., Thompson, R. A., Gardner, W. P., Charnov, E. L., & Estes, D. (1984). Security of infantile attachment as assessed in the "Strange Situation." *Behavioral and Brain Sciences*, 7, 127–171.

Lasch, C. (1979). *The culture of narcissism*. New York: Norton.

Laslett, P. (1962). The world we have lost. In E. Josephson & M. Josephson (Eds.), *Man alone: Alienation in modern society*. New York: Dell.

Leach P. (1990). *Your baby and child* (rev. ed.). New York: Knopf.

Levy, D. (1937). Primary affect hunger. *American Journal of Psychiatry*, 94, 643–652.

Levy, D. (1943). *Maternal overprotection*. New York: Columbia University Press.

Lewis, H. B. (1987). The role of shame in depression over the life span. In H. B. Lewis (Ed.), *The role of shame in symptom formation*. Hillsdale, NJ: Erlbaum.

Lewis, M., Feiring, C., McGuffog, C., & Jaskir J. (1984). Predicting psychopathology in six-year-olds from early social relations. *Child Development*, 55, 123–136.

Lieberman, A. (1991). Attachment theory and infant-parent psychotherapy: Some conceptual, clinical and research considerations. In D. Cicchetti & S. Toth (Eds.), *Models and integrations: Rochester Symposium on Developmental Psychopathology*. Rochester: University of Rochester Press.

Lieberman, A. F. (1992). Infant-parent psychotherapy with toddlers. *Development and Psychopathology*, 4, 559–574.

Lieberman, A. F. (1993). *The emotional life of the toddler*. New York: Free Press.

Lieberman, A. F., & Pawl, J. H. (1990). Disorders of attachment and secure base behavior in the second year of life: Conceptual issues and clinical intervention. In M. Greenberg, D. Cicchetti, & E. M. Cummings (Eds.), *Attachment in the preschool years: Theory, research, and intervention*. Chicago: University of Chicago Press.

Lieberman, A. F., Weston, D., and Paul, J. H. (1991). Preventive intervention and outcome with anxiously attached dyads. *Child Development*, 62, 199–209.

Liedloff, J. (1977). *The continuum concept: Allowing human nature to work successfully*. Reading, MA: Addison-Wesley.

Liotti, G. (1990, November). John Bowlby: In memoriam. Paper given at conference in honor of John Bowlby, Naples.

Liotti, G. (1992). Disorganized/disoriented attachment in the etiology of dissociative disorders. *Dissociation*, 5, 196–204.

Lopez, T., & Kliman, G. (1979). Memory, reconstruction, and mourning in the analysis of a 4-year-old child: Maternal bereavement in the second year of life. *Psychoanalytic Study of the Child*, 34: 235-371.

Maccoby, E. E., & Martin, J. A. (1983). Socialization in the context of the family. In E. M. Hetherington (Ed.), *Handbook of child psychology: Socialization personality and social development* (Vol. 4). New York: Wiley.

Macdonald, D. (1965). *Against the American grain*. New York: Vintage.

Mackenzie, M. (1990, Autumn). Dr. Marion Mackenzie remembers Dr. John Bowlby. *The Tavistock Gazette*, 29, 13–16.

Mahler, M. S., Pine, F., & Bergman, A. (1975). *The psychological birth of the human infant*. New York: Basic.

Main, M., & Goldwyn, R. (in press). Interview-based adult attachment classifications: Related to infant-mother and infant-father attachment.

Main, M. (1977). Analysis of a peculiar form of behavior seen in some daycare children: Its history and sequelae in children who are home-reared. In R. Webb (Ed.), *Social Development in Daycare*. Baltimore: Johns Hopkins University Press.

Main, M. (1991). Metacognitive knowledge, metacognitive monitoring, and singular (coherent) vs. multiple (incoherent) model of attachment: Findings and directions for future research. In C. M. Parkes, J. Stevenson-Hinde, & P. Marris (Eds.), *Attachment across the life cycle*. New York: Tavistock/Routledge.

Main, M., & Cassidy, J. (1988). Categories of response with the parent at age six: Predicted from infant attachment classifications and stable over a one month period. *Developmental Psychology*, 24, 415–426.

Main, M., & Hesse, E. (1990). Parents' unresolved traumatic experiences are related to infant disorganized attachment status: Is frightened and/or frightening parental behavior the linking mechanism? In M. Greenberg, D. Cicchetti, & E. M. Cummings (Eds.), *Attachment in the preschool years*. Chicago: The University of Chicago Press.

Main, M., Kaplan, N., & Cassidy, J. (1985). Security in infancy, childhood, and adulthood: A move to the level of representation. In I. Bretherton & E. Waters (Eds.), *Growing points in attachment theory and research. Monographs of the Society for Research in Child Development*, 50 (Serial No. 209), 66–104.

Main, M. & Solomon, J. (1990). Procedures for identifying infants as disorganized/disoriented during the Ainsworth Strange Situation. In M. Greenberg, D. Cicchetti, & E. M. Cummings (Eds.), *Attachment in the preschool years: Theory, research, and intervention*. Chicago: University of Chicago Press.

Main, M., & Weston, D. (1981). The quality of the toddler's relationship to mother and to father as related to conflict behavior and readiness to establish new relationships. *Child Development*, 52, 932–940.

Main, M., & Weston, D. (1982). Avoidance of the attachment figure in infancy: Descriptions and interpretations. In C. M. Parkes and J. Stevenson-Hinde (Eds.), *The place of attachment in human behavior* (pp. 31–59). New York: Basic.

Malan, D. (1990). [Contribution to Reminiscences and reflections on John Bowlby]. *The Tavistock Gazette*, 29, 13–16.

Mangelsdorf, S., Gunnar, M., Kestenbaum, R., Lang, S., & Andreas, D. (1990) Infant proneness-to-distress temperament, maternal personality, and mother-infant attachment: Associations and goodness of fit. *Child Development*, 61, 820–831.

Martin, F. E. (1991). John Bowlby, 1907–1991: A tribute and personal appreciation. *Melanie Klein and Object Relations*, 9, 63–69.

Marvin, R. S. (1977). An ethological-cognitive model for the attenuation of mother-child attachment behavior. In T. Alloway, P. Pliner, & L. Krames (Eds.), *Attachment behavior*. New York: Plenum.

Marvin, R. S., & Stewart, R. B. (1991). A family system framework for the study of attachment. In M. Greenberg, D. Cicchetti, & M. Cummings (Eds.), *Attachment beyond the preschool years* (pp. 51–86). Chicago: University of Chicago Press.

Mason, E. (1991). *Where's mummy? The Robertson studies of parent-child separation* [Video]. University Park, PA: Penn State Audio Visual Services. [In references, page numbers refer to transcript.]

Matas, L., Arend, R. A., & Sroufe, L. A. (1978). Continuity and adaptation in the second year: The relationship between quality of attachment and later competence. *Child Development*, 49, 547–556.

Mead, M. (1962). A cultural anthropologists's approach to maternal deprivation. In *Deprivation of maternal care: A reassessment of its effects*, Public Health Papers no. 14, Geneva: World Health Organization.

Miller, A. (1981). *The drama of the gifted child*. New York: Basic.

Miller, A. (1990). *Banished knowledge: Facing childhood injuries*. New York: Doubleday.

Mitchell, E. (1991, September 30). Look who's listening too. *Time*, p. 76.

Miyake, K., Shing-jen, C., Campos, J. J. (1985). Infant temperament, mother's mode of interaction, and attachment in Japan: An interim report. In I. Bretherton & E. Waters (Eds.), *Growing points in attachment theory and research*. *Monographs of the Society for Research in Child Development*, 50 (Serial No. 209), 276–297.

Moore, S., & Freeth, M. (Producers). (1993, April 19). *Medicine at the crossroads*. New York: Thirteen/WNET and BBC-TV.

Morris, D. (1983). Attachment and intimacy. In G. Stricker & M. Fisher (Eds.), *Intimacy*. New York: Plenum.

Morrison, A. (1989). *Shame: The underside of narcissism*. Hillsdale, NJ: Analytic Press.

Mussen, P., Conger, J., & Kagan, J. (1956). *Child development and personality* (4th ed.). New York: Harper & Row.

Neubauer, P. B., & Neubauer, A. (1990). *Nature's thumbprint*. Reading, MA: Addison-Wesley.

Osofsky, J. (1988). Attachment theory and research in the psychoanalytic process. *Psychoanalytic Psychology*, 5, 159–177.

Pastor, D. L. (1981). The quality of mother-infant attachment and its relationship to toddler's initial sociability with peers. *Developmental Psychology*, 17, 323–335.

Phillips, A. (1988). *Winnicott*. London: Fontana.

Phillips, D., McCartney, K., Scarr, S., & Howes, C. (1987, February). Selective review of infant day care research: A cause for concern. *ZERO TO THREE*, pp. 18–25.

Pinneau, S. R. (1955). The infantile disorders of hospitalism and anaclitic depression. *Psychological Bulletin, 52,* 429–452.

Plomin, R. (1987). Developmental behavioral genetics and infancy. In J. D. Osofsky (Ed.), *Handbook of infant development.* New York: Wiley.

Rayner, E. (1991, October). John Bowlby's contribution, a brief summary. Paper read at Bowlby Memorial Service, British Psycho-Analytic Society, London.

Renken, B., Egeland, B., Marvinney, D., Mangelsdorf, S., & Sroufe, L. A. (1989). Early childhood antecedents of aggression and passive-withdrawal in early elementary school. *Journal of Personality, 57,* 257–281.

Ricks, M. (1985). The social transmission of parental behavior: Attachment across generations. In I. Bretherton & E. Waters (Eds.), *Growing points in attachment theory and research. Monographs of the Society for Research in Child Development, 50* (Serial No. 209), 211–227.

Ricks, T. E. (1987, March 3). Day care for infants is challenged by research on psychological risks. *The Wall Street Journal,* p. 35.

Rioch, J. (1988). The transference phenomenon in psychoanalytic therapy. In B. Wolstein (Ed.), *Essential papers on countertransference.* New York: New York University Press. (Reprinted from *Psychiatry,* 1943, 6, 147–156.)

Riviere, J. (1927). (Contribution to Symposium on child analysis). In *International Journal of Psychoanalysis, 8,* 373–377.

Robertson, J. (1953). *A two-year-old goes to hospital* [Film]. University Park, PA: Penn State Audio Visual Services.

Robertson, J. (1962). *Hospitals and children: A parent's-eye view.* New York: Gollancz.

Robertson, J., & Robertson, J. (1967). *Kate, aged two years five months, in foster care for twenty-seven days* [Film]. Young Children in Brief Separation Film Series. University Park, PA: Penn State Audio Visual Services.

Robertson, J., & Robertson, J. (1968). *Jane, aged seventeen months, in foster care for ten days* [Film]. Young Children in Brief Separation Film Series. University Park, PA: Penn State Audio Visual Services.

Robertson, J., & Robertson, J. (1969). *John, aged 17 months, for nine days in a residential nursery* [Film]. Young Children in Brief Separation Film Series. University Park, PA: Penn State Audio Visual Services.

Robertson, J., & Robertson, J. (1971). *Thomas, aged two years four months, in foster care for ten days* [Film]. Young Children in Brief Separation Film Series. University Park, PA: Penn State Audio Visual Services.

Robertson, J., & Robertson, J. (1973). *Lucy, aged twenty-one months, in foster care for nineteen days* [Film]. Young Children in Brief Separation Film Series. University Park, PA: Penn State Audio Visual Services.

Robertson, J., & Robertson, J. (1973). Substitute mothering for the unaccompanied child. *Nursing Times,* November 29. Offprint.

Robertson, J., & Robertson, J. (1989). *Separation and the very young.* London: Free Association Books.

Rodell, S. (1993, July 25). Memo to Hillary: Please have a look at Australia's system [Editorial notebook]. *The New York Times*, p. 16.

Rosen, C. M. (1987, September). The eerie world of reunited twins. *Discover*, pp. 36–46.

Rutter, M. (1981). *Maternal deprivation reassessed*. New York: Penguin.

Rycroft, C. (1985). *Psychoanalysis and beyond*. London: Hogarth.

Rycroft, C. (1992). *Rycroft on analysis and creativity*. New York: New York University Press.

Sagi, A., Lamb, M. E., Lewkowitcz, K. S., Shoham, R., Dvir, R., & Estes, D. (1985). Security of infant-mother, -father, and -metapelet attachments among kibbutz-reared Israeli children. In I. Bretherton & E. Waters (Eds.), *Growing points in attachment theory and research. Monographs of the Society for Research in Child Development*, 50 (Serial No. 209), 257–275.

Sander, L. (1964). Adaptive relationships in early mother-child interaction. *Journal of the American Academy of Child Psychiatry*, 1, 141–166.

Sargent, S., & Stafford, K. (1965). *Basic teachings of the great psychologists*. Garden City, NY: Dolphin.

Sayers, J. (1991). *Mothers of psychoanalysis*. New York: Norton.

Scarf, M. (1976). *Body, mind, behavior*. New York: Dell.

Scarr, S. (1984). *Mother care/Other care*. New York: Basic.

Scarr, S. (April, 1991). *Developmental theories for the 1990s: Development and individual differences*. Paper presented at the biennial meetings of the Society for Research in Child Development, Seattle.

Scarr, S., Phillips, D., & McCartney, K. (1993). Facts, fantasies and the future of child care in the United States. In R. H. Wozniak (Ed.), *Worlds of childhood*. New York: HarperCollins. (Reprinted from Psychological Science, 1990, 1, 26–35.)

Scarr, S. and Weinberg, R. A. (1993). The nature-nurture problem revisited: The Minnesota adoption studies. In R. H. Wozniak (Ed.), *Worlds of childhood*. New York: Harper Collins. pp. 92–105. (Reprinted from I. Sigel & G. Brody (Eds.), *Methods of family research: Biographies of research projects. Volume 1: Normal families*. Hillsdale, NJ: Erlbaum, pp. 121–151.

Schaffer, H. R. & Emerson, P. E. (1964). The development of social attachments in infancy. *Monographs of the Society for Research in Child Development*, 29, (3, Serial No. 94).

Schoenewolf, G. (1990). *Turning points in analytic therapy*. Northvale, NJ: Aronson.

Schore, A. (1994). Affect regulation and the origin of the self: The neurobiology of emotional development. Hillsdale, N.J.: Erlbaum.

Schur, M. (1960). Discussion of John Bowlby's paper. *The Psychoanalytic study of the child*, 15, 63–84.

Segal, H. (1981). *The work of Hanna Segal: A Kleinian approach to clinical practice*. Northvale, NJ: Aronson.

Segal, N. L. (1984, July/August). The nature vs. nurture laboratory. *Twins*, pp. 56–57.

Senn, M. J. E. (1977a). *Interview with John Bowlby*. Unpublished manuscript, National Library of Medicine, Washington, D.C.

Senn, M. J. E. (1977b). *Interview with James Robertson.* Unpublished manuscript, National Library of Medicine, Washington, D.C.

Sennett, R. (1977). *The fall of public man.* New York: Knopf.

Shaver, P. & Hazan, C. (1992). Adult romantic attachment: Theory and evidence. In D. Perlman & W. Jones (Eds.), *Advances in personal relationships.* Bristol, PA: Taylor & Francis.

Silverman, D. K. (1991). Attachment patterns and Freudian theory: An integrative proposal. *Psychoanalytic Psychology,* 8, 169–193.

Slade, A. (1992, September). *Mothers and their mothers: The story unfolds.* Paper presented at the meeting of the World Association of Infant Psychiatry and Allied Disciplines, Chicago.

Slade, A. (1992, October). *Processes of parenting: Remembrance of things past.* Julia Howe Ward Lecture presented at Barnard College, New York.

Slade, A. (1993, March). Affect regulation and defense: Clinical and theoretical considerations. Paper presented at the biennial meetings of the Society for Research in *Child Development,* New Orleans.

Slade, A. (in press, 1997a). Attachment theory and research: Implications for the theory and practice of individual psychotherapy with adults. In Cassidy, J. and Shaver, P. R., eds., *Handbook of Attachment Theory and Research.* NY: Guilford.

Slade, A. (in press, 1997b). Representation, symbolization, and affect regulation in the concomitant treatment of a mother and child: Attachment theory and child psychotherapy. *Psychoanalytic Inquiry.*

Slade, A., & Aber, L. (1987, October). Representational processes in children and adults: Clinical and developmental perspectives. Paper presented at the meeting of the Society of the Institute for Contemporary Psychotherapy, New York City.

Smuts, A. (1977). *Interview with Dr. John Bowlby.* Unpublished manuscript, National Library of Medicine, Washington, D.C.

Sommerville, C. J. (1990). *The rise and fall of childhood.* New York: Vintage.

Spitz, R. (1945). Hospitalism: An inquiry into the genesis of psychiatric conditions in early childhood. *The psychoanalytic study of the child,* 1, 53–74.

Spitz, R. (1947). *Grief: A peril in infancy* [Film]. University Park, PA: Penn State Audio Visual Services.

Spitz, R. (1960). Discussion of Dr. Bowlby's paper. *The Psychoanalytic study of the child,* 15, 85–94.

Sroufe, L. A. (1979). Socioemotional development. In J. Osofsky (Ed.), *Handbook of infant development.* New York: Wiley.

Sroufe, L. A. (1983). Infant-caregiver attachment and patterns of adaptation in preschool: The roots of maladaptation and competence. In M. Perlmutter (Ed.), *Minnesota symposium in child psychology* (Vol. 16, pp. 41–81). Hillsdale, NJ: Erlbaum.

Sroufe, L. A. (1988). A developmental perspective on day care. *Early Childhood Research Quarterly,* 3, 283–291.

Sroufe, L. A. (1989, February 10). Talk at City University of New York, Graduate Center.

Sroufe, L. A., Carlson, E., & Shulman, S. (1993). The development of individuals in relationships: From infancy through adolescence. Unpublished manuscript.

Sroufe, L. A., Cooper, R. G., & DeHart, G. B. (1992). *Child development: Its nature and course* (2nd ed.). New York: McGraw-Hill.

Sroufe, L. A., Egeland, B., & Kreutzer, T. (1990). The fate of early experience following developmental change: Longitudinal approaches to individual adaptation in childhood. *Child Development, 61,* 1363–1373.

Sroufe, L. A., Fox, N. E. Pancake, V. R. (1983). Attachment and dependency in developmental perspective. *Child Development, 54,* 1615–1627.

Sroufe, L. A., & Waters, E. (1977a). Attachment as an organizational construct. *Child Development, 48,* 1184–1189.

Sroufe, L. A. & Waters, E. (1977b). Heart rate as a convergent measure in clinical and developmental research. *Merrill-Palmer Quarterly, 23,* 3–27.

Stern, D. N. (1985). *The interpersonal world of the infant.* New York: Basic.

Suess, G. J., Grossman, K. E., & Sroufe, L. A. (1992). Effects of infant attachment to mother and father on quality of adaptation in preschool: from dyadic to individual organisation of self. *International Journal of Behavioral Development, 15* (1) 43–65.

Sulloway, F. J. (1991, October 1). Darwinian psychobiography. [Review of *Charles Darwin: A new life*]. *The New York Review of Books,* pp. 29–32.

Suomi, S. J., & Harlow, H. F. (1972). Social rehabilitation of isolate-reared monkeys. *Developmental Psychology, 6,* 487–496.

Suomi, S. J., & Harlow, H. F. (1978). Early experience and social development in rhesus monkeys. In M. Lamb (Ed.), *Social and Personality Development.* New York: Holt, Rinehart, & Winston.

Sutherland, J. (1990, Autumn). John Bowlby: Some personal reminiscences. *The Tavistock Gazette, 29,* 13–16.

Tanner, J., & Inhelder, B. (1971). *Discussions on Child Development. Proceedings of the World Health Organization Study Group on the Psychological Development of the Child,* Geneva, 1953–1956. New York: International Universities Press.

Tellegen, A., Lykken, D. T., Bouchard, T. J., Jr., Wilcox, K. J., Segal, N. L., & Rich, S. (1988). Personality similarity in twins reared apart and together. *Journal of Personality and Social Psychology, 54,* 1031–1039.

Thomas, A., Chess, S., & Birch, H. G. (1969). *Temperament and behavior disorders in children.* New York: New York University Press.

Todd, J. (1985, September). Finding my twin brought happiness beyond belief. *Woman,* pp. 40–41.

Torrey, E. F. (1988). *Surviving schizophrenia: A family manual* (rev. ed.). New York: Harper & Row.

Traub, J. (1986, March). Goodbye Dr. Spock: The brave new world of better babies. *Harper's,* pp. 44–47.

Tronick, E., Als, H., Adamson, L., Wise, S., & Brazelton, T. B. (1978). The infant's response to intrapment bewteen contradictory messages in face-to-face interaction. *Journal of Child Psychiatry, 17,* 1–13.

Trowell, J. (1990, Autumn). Dr. John Bowlby. *The Tavistock Gazette, 29,* 13–16.

Troy, M. & Sroufe, L. A. (1987). Victimization among preschoolers: Role of attachment relationship theory. *Journal of American Academy of Child and Adolescent Psychiatry*, 26, 166–172.

Turner, P. J. (1991). Relations between attachment, gender, and behavior with peers in preschool. *Child Development*, 62, 1475–1488.

Vaillant, G. E. (1977). *Adaptation to life*. Boston: Little, Brown.

Vandell, D. L. & Corasaniti, M. A. (1990). Variations in early child care: Do they predict subsequent social, emotional, and cognitive differences? *Early Childhood Research Quarterly*, 5: 555-572.

van den Boom, D. C. (1988). *Neonatal irritability and the development of attachment: Observation and intervention*. Unpublished doctoral dissertation, University of Leiden, Leiden, The Netherlands.

van den Boom, D. C. (in press). The influence of temperament and mothering on attachment and exploration: An experimental manipulation of sensitive responsiveness among lower class mothers with irritable infants. *Child Development*.

Vaughn, B., Bradley, C., Joffe, L., Seifer, R., & Barglow, P. (1987). Maternal characteristics measured prenatally are predictive of ratings of temperamental "difficulty" on the Carey Infant Temperament Questionnaire. *Developmental Psychology*, 23, 152–161.

Vaughn, B., Deane, K., & Waters, E. (1985). The impact of out-of-home care on child-mother attachment quality: Another look at some enduring questions. In I. Bretherton & E. Waters (Eds.), *Growing points in attachment theory and research. Monographs of the Society for Research in Child Development*, 50, (Serial No. 209, Nos. 1–2).

Vaughn, B. E., Lefever, G., Seifer, R., & Barglow, P. (1989). Attachment behavior, attachment security, and temperament during infancy. *Child Development*, 60, 728–737.

Vaughn, B., Gove, F. L., & Egeland, B. (1980). The relationship between out-of-home care and the quality of infant-mother attachment in an economically disadvantaged population. *Child Development*, 49, 483–494.

Wachtel, P. (1977). *Psychoanalysis and behavior therapy*. New York: Basic.

Waller, N. G., Kojetin, B. A., Bouchard, T. J., Jr., Lykken, D. T., & Tellegen, A. (1990). Genetic and environmental influences on religious interests, attitudes, and values: A study of twins reared apart and together. *Psychological Science*, 1, (2), 138–142.

Waters, E. (1978). The stability of individual differences in infant-mother attachment. *Child Development*, 49, 483–494

Waters, E., Wippman, J. & Sroufe, L. A. (1979). Attachment, positive affect, and competence in the peer group: Two studies in construct validation. *Child Development*, 50, 821–829.

Watson, J. B. (1928). *Psychological care of infant and child*. New York: Norton.

Wattenberg, D. (1992, March 2). The parent trap. *Insight*, pp. 6–11, 34–35.

Weiss, R. S. (1975). *Marital separation*. New York: Basic.

Weiss, R. S. (1982). Attachment in adult life. In C. M. Parkes and J. Stevenson-

Hinde (Eds.), *The place of attachment in human behaviour* (pp. 171–184). New York: Basic.

Winnicott, D. W. (1958). *Through paediatrics to psycho-analysis*. New York: Basic.

Winnicott, D. W. (1965). *The maturational processes and the facilitating environment*. New York: International Universities Press.

Wittenberg, I. (1990, Autumn). John Bowlby. *The Tavistock Gazette*, 29, 13–16.

Yarrow, L. J. (1967). The development of focused relationships during infancy. In *Exceptional Infant, 1*, ed. J. Hellmuth. Seattle: Special Child Publications.

Zeanah, C. H., Keener, M. A., Thomas, F., & Viera-Baher, C. C. (1987). Adolescent mothers' perceptions of their infants before and after birth. *American Journal of Orthopsychiatry*, 57, 351–360.

Zeanah, C. H. & Zeanah, P. D. (1989). Intergenerational transmission of maltreatment: Insights from attachment theory and research. *Psychiatry*, 52, 177–196.

ZERO TO THREE/National Center for Clinical Infant Programs. *Heart Start: The Emotional Foundations of School Readiness*. Arlington, VA. [Booklet in two parts.]

ZERO TO THREE, April/May, 1994. [Report on *The Study of Children in Family Child Care and Relative Care: Highlights of Findings* (1994) by Ellen Galinsky, Carollee Howes, Susan Kontos, and Marybeth Shinn.]

INDEX